TROUBLED MEMORY

Troubled Memory

ANNE LEVY, THE HOLOCAUST, AND DAVID DUKE'S LOUISIANA

LAWRENCE N. POWELL

The University of North Carolina Press

Chapel Hill and London

© 2000 The University of North Carolina Press

All rights reserved

Designed by April Leidig-Higgins

Set in Monotype Garamond by Keystone Typesetting, Inc.

Manufactured in the United States of America

The paper in this book meets the guidelines for permanence and durability
of the Committee on Production Guidelines for Book Longevity of the
Council on Library Resources.

Library of Congress Cataloging-in-Publication Data

Powell, Lawrence N.

Troubled memory: Anne Levy, the Holocaust, and

David Duke's Louisiana / Lawrence N. Powell.

p. cm. Includes bibliographical references and index.

ISBN 0-8078-2504-2 (cloth: alk. paper)

1. Levy, Anne. 2. Skorecki family. 3. Jews—Poland—Biography.

4. Holocaust, Jewish—Poland—Biography. 5. Holocaust survivors
—Louisiana—New Orleans—Biography. 6. Duke, David Ernest.

7. Louisiana—Politics and government—1951–. I. Title.

DS135.P63L3996 2000   940.53'18'0922—dc21   99-18568 CIP

04 03 02 01 00   5 4 3 2

Publication of this volume has been aided by generous support from the
following individuals and foundations: Harry J. Blumenthal Jr., The Cahn
Family Foundation, The Robert B. and Shirley K. Haspel Endowment Fund,
Edward D. Levy Jr., Louise L. Levy, The Levy Rosenblum Family Foundation,
The Lucius N. Littauer Foundation, Jean and Saul Mintz, Paul S. Rosenblum,
and The L. J. Skaggs and Mary C. Skaggs Foundation.

Page i: Anne and Lila arm in arm. Anne and Lila found this photo in their
father Mark's wallet after his death in 1991. The picture was probably taken in
1938. Some time after the war Mark wrote his daughters' names on the
photo, for reasons that still puzzle them.

TO DIANA

In remembrance resides the secret of redemption.

BAAL SHEM TOV

CONTENTS

Because of their arrangement of consonants and frequent use of accents, Polish words on the written page look well-nigh unpronounceable to English speakers. But you'll find those appearances deceptive if you keep the following rules in mind:

The *sz* is pronounced as the English *sh*, as in Leshno (Leszno).

The *cz* is pronounced as the English *ch*, as in Chista (Czyste).

The *ł* is pronounced as the English *w*, as in Woodge (Łódź).

The *dz* is pronounced as the English *juh*, as in Zhawashitza (Działoszyce).

The *ż* is pronounced as the English *zhee*, as in Zheelazna (Żelazna).

The *ą* is pronounced as the English *am* or *om*, as in Zambkowska (Ząbkowska).

The *ę* is pronounced as the English *en*, as in Gensha (Gęsia).

The *j* is pronounced as the English *y*, as in Mynster (Mejnster).

I have also followed the Polish rule about feminizing surnames when the action takes place in Poland. Thus, although Ruth was known as Mrs. Skorecki in the United States, in Poland she was known as Mrs. Skorecka.

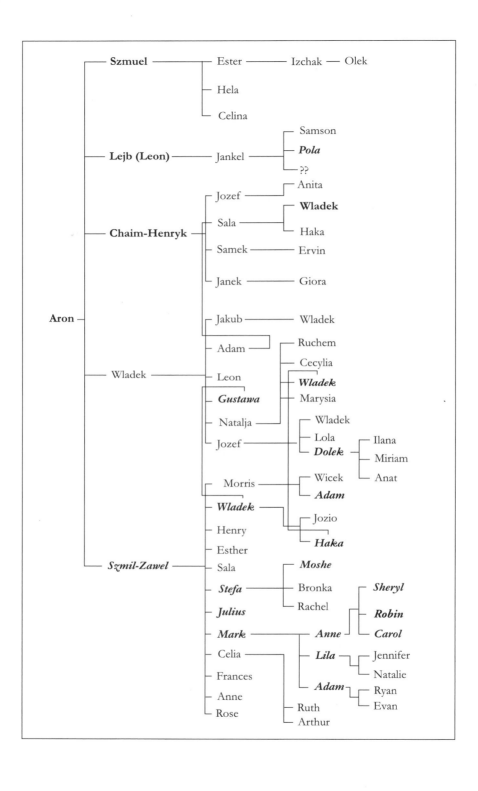

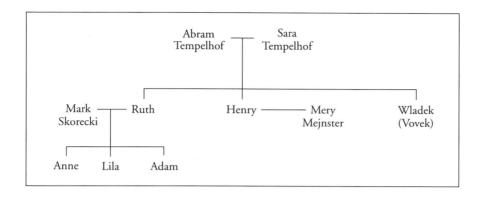

Above: Skorecki-Tempelhof Family Tree (Partial)

Facing page: Skorecki Family Tree (Partial)

TROUBLED MEMORY

THE POLITICAL GETS PERSONAL

During the Great Depression, Governor Huey Long hired some of the best stone carvers and sculptors around to chisel Louisiana imagery into the state capitol. Looming 450 feet above the Mississippi levee in Baton Rouge, the art deco skyscraper fairly drips with historical references. Massive statues of patriots and pioneers guard the portal to the Great Memorial Hall. Inside dozens of historical scenes fill bronze panels on the monumental doors leading to the House and Senate chambers. High up on the walls a frieze depicts Louisiana in war and peace, including a bas-relief of the Kingfish going over plans with the capitol's architects. The most popular visitor's site—a plaque located just off the main hall, behind the elevators—was never part of the original design. Bolted into the Levanto marble wall near three large bullet holes, it marks the spot where Huey and his assassin were gunned down in September 1935.

Traveling exhibits are routinely placed in the Great Memorial Hall, but the forty Holocaust posters ringing the rotunda in early June 1989 set the stage for an improbable clash over the politics of memory. David Duke, the Nazi sympathizer and former Klansman, had just been elected as a Republican to the lower house, and the staff of then governor Charles "Buddy" Roemer thought it was important to remind Louisianians that the destruction of European Jewry was not a matter for debate. For years Duke's mail-order business had been selling such tracts as *The Myth of Six Million*, along with an audio recording of himself discussing the "so-called holocaust." "This stuff's so sloppy . . . the whole thing comes down like a house of cards because it's just bullshit," Duke told an interviewer in 1985, and he went on to characterize the Third Reich's most notorious killing center as an Elysian experience: "You know, they had a soccer field at Auschwitz. They had an orchestra at Auschwitz, and the band was for the prisoner's enjoyment—pleasure."[1] As well known as Duke's views were to the state's Jewish community, most Louisianians were familiar only with his Klan past. About the neo-Nazi beliefs he had harbored since high school, they were completely in the dark.[2]

Nor were they overly familiar with the Third Reich and Hitler's war against the Jews. Fading fast from living memory, the Second World War's darkest chapter had received short shrift in the local schools. To be sure, Louisianians were hardly alone in their ignorance. According to a 1993 Gallup poll, over half of American high school students were unable to explain the meaning of the term "Holocaust."[3] But the historical amnesia was more extensive in the Bayou State, where, as recently as 1992, more than 90 percent of Louisianians lacking a high school diploma admitted knowing little or nothing about the Holocaust and Nazi Germany. If the state's high school dropout rates did not hover at Third World levels, the historical illiteracy might not be cause for concern. But the poorly educated bulk large in the Louisiana electorate, and it was the whites among them who later flocked to Duke during his candidacies for the U.S. Senate and the governorship.[4]

The Simon Wiesenthal Center's branch office in New York had contacted Roemer's staff shortly after Duke's election to offer the state its exhibit *The Courage to Remember*. Placed on easels at five-foot intervals around the hall, the posters traced the history of European anti-Semitism from the Reformation through the Holocaust. They featured two hundred pictures of gaunt concentration camp inmates, starving children, naked women, burning synagogues, and crematoriums. Quotations from Himmler and Hitler, together with anti-Jewish propaganda, were mocked by testimony from victims, survivors, and liberators. The two posters chronicling the Łódź and Warsaw Ghettos in Nazi-occupied Poland showed youngsters being torn away from their parents, and rag-covered women and children lying dead and dying on the cobblestone streets. "It was quite compelling," Roemer's assistant press secretary later remembered. The chiseled and kiln-fired history celebrated by Huey's architects jarred with the tragic memories evoked by the black-and-white imagery of the Wiesenthal exhibit. The posters were a horrific reminder of where racial extremism in modern society can ultimately lead.[5]

Because of Duke's sudden political notoriety, the opening ceremony in the rotunda on Tuesday, June 6, 1989, attracted unusual attention for a traveling exhibit. A Wiesenthal Center representative came down from New York. A forest of microphones towered in one corner of the hall where the governor was slated to talk. Among the approximately two hundred people in the audience were thirty members of the New Americans Social Club, who had come by chartered bus from New Orleans. The club had been incorporated by Holocaust survivors in 1961, just after American Nazi commander George Lincoln Rockwell sent his Virginia-based storm troopers on a "hate ride" from Virginia to picket the local premiere of the movie *Exodus*. Though originating in political controversy, the New Americans had long functioned informally like one of black New Orleans's social and pleasure clubs. The New Americans have jointly celebrated Hanukkah and the Fourth of July, regularly gathering for cards and small talk at one another's homes. For over four decades club members have served as surrogate aunts and uncles for American-born children severed by the Holocaust from generational roots. Weddings, and increasingly funerals, bring them together. Though the active membership has fallen by half, the New Americans still hold monthly meetings and an annual dinner. It was their idea to organize the annual Warsaw Ghetto uprising observance at the Jewish Community Center, one of the nation's longest-running ceremonies of remembrance. But until recently they have steered clear of politics. Duke's February 1989 election to the state legislature from the nearby white, middle-class community of Metairie reawakened dormant fears. Three decades earlier, Rockwell's "hate riders" had numbered less than a dozen. But Duke had managed to move just far enough away from the extremist fringe to persuade over eight thousand voters from Louisiana's wealthiest suburb to let him make law for the state. The New Americans needed little coaxing to take the ninety-minute bus ride north on the interstate for the Wiesenthal exhibit unveiling. David Duke's political breakthrough was serious business, not to mention an affront to memory.[6]

Anne Skorecki Levy was one of the New Americans who went to Baton Rouge for the ceremony. A child survivor of the Holocaust, she and her husband, Stan, run a large antique import business on the edge of New Orleans's fashionable Garden District. He is from Lowell, Massachusetts. She was born in the old textile center of Łódź, Poland. They met and married in the mid-1950s while he was serving in the Air Force in Mississippi. She is all of five feet tall in heels, with a radiant smile and a melodic, lilting voice that harmonizes Polish syntax with the distinctive inflections of Uptown New Orleans. In many ways she and Stan are paired opposites. He tends toward L.L. Bean casual. She dresses to the nines, even when running errands to the corner store. He is self-assured and outspoken, with a sardonic wit. Anne is bashful and diffident, a child of war-inflicted insecurities. When she traveled to Baton Rouge to attend the Wiesenthal opening, it was not to provoke an incident; like the other New Americans, she was there to bear witness.

But then the unexpected happened, prompted by a mysterious, almost unappeasable urge to exorcise nightmares by reliving them in the flesh. The impulse struck just before Governor Roemer rose to speak. The House had just recessed for lunch, and Representative Duke had made several passes through the hall, as if to tell the crowd he was not about to be intimidated. "For some reason," Anne remembers, "I turned to my right and there was

David Duke looking at the exhibit posters. Something overcame me. This man was at the wrong place. This was not the place for him to be. What is his interest in seeing this when he is denying the whole thing?"

His posture upset her, too. Standing ramrod erect at parade rest, Duke was examining the posters as though he were conducting a selection at a railroad siding. "It's nothing anyone else would ever think about," she says. "But as a kid I remember the German soldiers walking around with their hands behind them as they looked over the people in line or on the trucks or on a train. It triggered something in me."

While the crowd focused on the governor, Anne walked quietly over to the freshman lawmaker. The physical contrast between survivor and Nazi apologist was as striking as their ideological differences. Duke's Aryan makeover included not only a new nose and chin but a health club physique for his six-foot-three frame. The petite, dark-haired grandmother had to reach high to touch his shoulder. "What are you doing here? Why are you looking at this?" she asked. Her voice was tremulous. "I thought you said it never happened." Duke ignored her. She tapped him again. "I touched his shoulder two or three times. And, finally, he kind of lost it and became vehement. He barked, 'I didn't say it didn't happen. I said it was exaggerated.'"

Anne lost it too. She raised her voice. By this point her finger was in his face. Her whole frame shook. "What do you mean it's exaggerated? If you think it's exaggerated, I'll be glad to tell you about it!" Duke gazed into the middle distance, no doubt hoping she would go away.

The reporters covering the governor's speech sensed a photo opportunity in the making. The lights and whirring cameras swung from the far corner of the hall where Roemer's podium stood. A murmur swept through the audience. Now that the media was converging on the two antagonists, Duke grew intimidated. He moved away from Anne. She pursued him. He lengthened his stride, bounding past elevator doors paneled with bronze likenesses of thirty-six former governors. She could not move fast enough to keep pace.[7]

When reporters finally cornered Duke in the basement, he was careful to measure his words, conceding the reality of Nazi atrocities but challenging the accuracy of some accounts. For the most part, he repeated what he had told Anne Levy in the rotunda, that the horrors of the Holocaust had been "exaggerated." Duke was merely echoing the propaganda of self-styled "Holocaust revisionists," an international network of far-rightists whose aim is to rehabilitate National Socialism and refurbish anti-Semitic conspiracy myths. Since the late 1970s, deniers have been holding annual conferences at the California-based Institute for Historical Review (IHR).[8] "You ought to go to an IHR convention next year," Duke told an interviewer in 1985.[9] He himself had attended two of its meetings during the 1980s.

But, since his breakthrough into mainstream respectability, Duke was desperate to avoid even a hint of ideological extremism. Thus, standing in the basement, he abruptly cut off further interrogation about his views on World War II. "The Holocaust was not really an issue," he told capitol reporters. "It's not part of my political agenda." He had turned over a new leaf. He was now a born-again "Christian" conservative, whose opposition to "reverse discrimination" and welfare illegitimacy differed little from that of leading Republicans. Whatever he had said or written concerning Nazism and the Klan was musty history, a chapter of "youthful indiscretions" in a book he was determined should remain closed.[10]

But for Anne Levy, whose immigrant success story was self-confirmation of the American dream, Duke's views on the Holocaust *were* the issue. They hinted at darker subthemes in American history—an angry counterpoint of nativist intolerance that, like Europe's ethnic nationalisms, crests during social and economic crises. How could someone who glossed over genocide against ethnic minorities be entrusted to make laws for a melting pot society such as America? Anne was incredulous. In her view Duke's attempt to minimize what he had said and written about the Holocaust had less to do with politics than with democratic decency and civility. The charade defamed her experience as a survivor and a new American, and the anger welling up inside her was both personal and political, bordering on rage.

But Anne Levy's face-off with Duke awakened deep-seated terror as well. It was not simply that Duke's political success represented the survivor's worst nightmare: that it can happen again, "that the moment of horror will recur," to quote psychiatrist Judith L. Herman. Just as distressing was the way Anne's encounter with Louisiana's foremost neo-Nazi had summoned to the surface traumatic memories she had long ago sought to block from consciousness. Torn between terror and rage, she decided to let rage have its way.[11] Hers was a classic illustration of how political commitments are forged: first you get angry, then you find courage.

Shadow campaigns had been Duke's trademark ever since he began running for office in 1975. The charades became more sophisticated—and believable— after he left the Ku Klux Klan in 1980 to found his "white civil rights" organization, the National Association for the Advancement of White People (NAAWP). Thanks to cosmetic surgery, he had acquired the good looks of a television anchorman. His rhetoric began to sound more mainstream, partly because conservative Republicans had made racial codespeak the lingua franca of current politics.[12] As for his Klan past, he often brought it up himself, as if to let audiences know he was a politician who would actually deliver on his campaign threats. But Duke kept his extensive record of Nazi extremism, including a lifelong advocacy of ethnic cleansing and master-race eugenics, hidden in the shadows. Like his views on the Holocaust, they were not winning issues. "If they can call you a Nazi and make it stick," he cautioned a fellow racist in 1986, less than three years before his election to the legislature, "it's going to hurt the ability of people to open their minds to what you're saying."[13]

Duke's masquerade of respectability was more than personal opportunism. It reflected a strategic shift on the part of the wider neofascist movement. By the 1980s far-rightists in both Europe and America were running stealth campaigns similar to Duke's in order to take advantage of the conservative electoral trends of the Reagan-Thatcher era. In the United States the anti-Semitic Liberty Lobby, headed by Willis Carto, a founder of the IHR, even spearheaded the formation of an independent party called the Populists (modeled after Jean-Marie Le Pen's ultra-rightist National Front Party in France). For Carto, third-party politics represented an ongoing effort to channel white supremacist politics back into the conservative mainstream, from which he and other right-wing extremists had been excluded by William Buckley during the 1960s, when American conservatives began the coalition building that eventually placed Ronald Reagan in the White House. Duke had long been close to Carto's Liberty Lobby, so it was hardly surprising when the Populist Party in 1988 chose the Louisianian as its presidential standard-bearer. Six weeks following the general election, after Duke filed as a Republican for the legislative seat he eventually won, the Liberty Lobby gave him access to its mammoth mailing list. Right-wing money and cadres from around the country poured in to aid the Duke campaign.[14] "His race . . . takes on national significance," proclaimed a neo-Nazi writer who visited New Orleans during the campaign.[15]

Duke's legislative victory galvanized the far right because his house seat represented real power, not just another ephemeral primary victory of the kind neofascists had been scoring throughout the 1980s. It meant the movement now had a regular forum for reaching the media and shaping policy debates. That the beachhead had been established in Louisiana, where antielite insurgencies seemed as commonplace as Gulf-borne hurricanes, added to the excitement. Huey P. Long had set the standard during the New Deal, amassing dictatorial powers over Louisiana while building a mass following with real potential for toppling Franklin Roosevelt's presidency. Few right-wing observers expected Duke to replicate the Kingfish's feat, at least not any time soon, but there was a general anticipation that his election would spawn a school of Duke-like candidacies throughout the country, and they pointed to his campaign as a model for similar guerrilla forays against the two-party system's underbelly. Duke himself invited the flattery of imitation when he told a Populist Party gathering in Chicago a few weeks after his election that his Louisiana success "can be repeated in many, many other states in the United States."[16]

Partly because of his decisive defeat in the 1992 Louisiana governor's race, Duke's electoral appeal never crossed state lines. But he was certainly correct to sense that the Sportsman's Paradise offered room to grow. After all, Duke did not get elected in sparsely populated Klan country but in one of those vote-laden, white, middle-class suburbs where state and national elections are now won and lost. Bisected by the Mississippi River, at one time Jefferson Parish had nearly as many illegal casinos as it did dairy farms, until Sun Belt prosperity caused both banks to overflow with shopping malls and tract developments. Metairie (which is on the east bank, immediately abutting the city) paced the explosive suburbanization. The Grand Old Party (GOP) designated it a prime target in the campaign to shatter the Democratic Party's southern base. Campaigns based on race, low taxes, and traditional values forged an alliance between Metairie's bungalow Democrats and the country club Republicans residing in its oak-shaded mansions. In the 1970s Duke's district produced Louisiana's first Republican congressman and governor since Reconstruction. By that time it was already delivering lopsided majorities to GOP presidential candidates. Only George Wallace's 1968 white backlash insurgency, which captured both Jefferson Parish and the state, interrupted the steady march toward Republican dominance. But that had been more than two decades ago, and it was easy to forget how vulnerable this top-down coalition remained to race-coded appeals from the right.

Duke was a Wallace redux. When oil prices collapsed, depressing living standards and causing wholesale disillusionment with the political status quo, Duke deflected economic discontent onto New Orleans's desperately impoverished black underclass. He focused white voter anger over widening inequality on minority set-asides and affirmative action. Because Republicans had field-tested these themes so often in the past, no one should have been shocked when Metairie's white, middle-class majority suddenly deserted the GOP for Duke's backlash alliance against black have-nots. Nor was it surprising, during his U.S. Senate and gubernatorial races, when the reactionary populism fueling his appeal ignited other white suburbs and spread to Louisiana's economically distressed country parishes.[17]

When this blame-thy-neighbor protest broke out in nearby Metairie, however, it terrified Anne Levy. It was not because she felt in any imminent danger personally. Voter anger was seldom directed at Jews; African Americans were the target. As elsewhere in the United States, anti-Jewish feeling in Louisiana had ebbed markedly from the high tide of the 1930s, when such radio demagogues as Father Coughlin had railed openly against Jewish financiers. The real source of Anne's disquiet was the readiness of so many white voters to overlook Duke's anti-Semitism. His actual electoral strength was hard to estimate because white respondents gave pollsters misleading and evasive answers. Unscientific intuition often proved a better guide as to who among one's acquaintances might be swelling Duke's soon-to-be-legendary "hidden vote." His supporters, after all, were the kind of people Anne encountered several times a week. They made deliveries to the Levy storeroom or fixed the air conditioning. They checked out groceries at the supermarket. They sold insurance. Some, as members of the local gentility, purchased nineteenth-century mahogany armoires from Stan's store. "They would never say anything to your face, but for the first time it made me stop and think," Anne says. "I felt uncomfortable."

She also ran across Duke supporters in Metairie, where many of the metropolitan area's biggest malls are located. In fact, her first face-to-face encounter with Duke and the populist frenzy he was capable of unleashing occurred in neighboring Jefferson Parish four months before their publicized standoff in the state capitol. A harbinger of confrontations to come, it took place on the day of the legislative runoff. Anne's eight-year-old granddaughter Jesse was visiting from San Francisco, and on election Saturday she brought her to Metairie's sprawling Lakeside Shopping Center, approaching by way of a six-lane boulevard called Veterans.

Veterans is bisected by a grass-covered "neutral ground." Locals have been using demilitarized zone (DMZ) terminology for their median strips since the early 1800s, when hard-driving American entrepreneurs moved upstream from the Creole French Quarter to build a river port. The middle of Canal Street was the original "neutral ground" between the warring cultures, and the label has stuck. Covering a canal used to discharge torrential downpours, Veterans's midsection is almost as broad as the boulevard itself. That particular election Saturday, however, February 18, 1989, it was anything but neutral. The Duke camp had conquered one of its busiest intersections, taking possession by driving blue-and-white yard signs into the lawn. Pickup trucks with cab-mounted loudspeakers circled the perimeter. Duke was on hand to lead the campaign. Hundreds of friendly onlookers milled around the rally's edge, slowing traffic to a halt. Passing motorists honked approval, many flashing V-for-victory signs to the candidate's legions. The congestion was so bad, Duke did not have to wait for a red light before wading into the clotting traffic. That afternoon he was passing out carnival doubloons stamped with his likeness.

Like the hydraulics of a whirlpool, the traffic flow pulled Anne into the vortex. Before she knew what was happening, Duke had shoved an aluminum coin through the driver's window. It was right in her face. The roar of the crowd surrounded the car. "It happened so suddenly I was startled," Anne says. "I lost my cool and started cursing the man." Then she remembered that her granddaughter was beside her in the front seat. Shaken, she managed to navigate through the hoopla, apologizing to Jesse for the profanity. She wondered why Duke's presence affected her so viscerally. It was as if the memory of the Holocaust was being reexperienced anew, as if the rewind button on a tape recorder was being pressed down against her will. She felt isolated and powerless, which is the essential legacy of traumatic events and their engraved memories. Duke's growing popularity was unraveling a basic trust in a just world that Anne had been trying to rebuild for nearly fifty years.

From his residence across Lake Pontchartrain, near the epicenter of Louisiana Kluxery, Walker Percy understood the electoral dynamics that Anne had found so upsetting. The angry irrationality Duke aroused was not a localized aberration. "If I had anything to say to people outside the state," Percy told the *New York Times*'s Wayne King shortly after the former Klansman's election to the Louisiana legislature, "I'd tell them, 'Don't make the mistake of thinking David Duke is a unique phenomenon confined to Louisiana rednecks and yahoos. He's not. He's not just appealing to the old Klan constituency, he's appealing to the white middle class. And don't think that he or somebody like him won't appeal to the white middle class of Chicago or Queens.' "[18]

Always central to that appeal was Duke's ability to convince would-be supporters of his born-again moderation. The alarming fact to Anne was how easily he was succeeding. Angry about crime, corruption, and the economy, many white Louisianians took his new look at face value. Even conventional politicians winked at his mainstream makeover, preferring to attack his draft record than expose his Nazism. Born of firsthand experience, Anne's foreboding was deep and unshakable. She did not have to consult polls to realize Duke was a sentinel symptom of a deeper malaise. The lessons of history validated her concerns. Hitler had risen to power on the indifference of ordinary Germans to the Führer's political reputation. As a famous study of the Third Reich in a small town explains, local residents "were drawn to anti-Semitism because they were drawn to Nazism, not the other way around."[19] On balance, Duke's menace inhered in his movement's potential to recruit alienated voters with seductive programs of reform and renewal and then to focus anger on target groups—the classic scapegoating syndrome.[20]

"It's bad times," Anne said later, "and when bad times come, somebody has to get blamed. It's a vicious circle. It just repeats itself." Irreversible progress is an illusion.

Anne Levy recovered quickly from her brief election day encounter with Duke, but the effects of their run-in at the Wiesenthal exhibit tended to linger. She was still simmering about Duke's dismissive attitude toward the Holocaust a week following their confrontation in Baton Rouge, when she turned on the car radio while running errands in New Orleans and heard him participating in a "Symposium on Racism" with other local politicians, black and white, and the heads of the NAACP and the Urban League, before a live audience in a downtown hotel. The novelist Lucian Truscott, on assignment from *Esquire* to write a piece on Duke, was in the studio. Duke dominated the show. He bashed drug users in the projects. He blasted away at affirmative action and took savage aim at welfare. Black audience members in line at the mike were unable to get a word in edgewise. "A block of commercials was the only thing that could stop him," Truscott wrote.[21]

Anne was upset when she drove up to the furniture storeroom. Duke's participation in a race relations forum seemed as incongruous as his presence at the Wiesenthal exhibit. "Why is he participating in this? What has he done in his lifetime to bring people together to be able even to participate in a discussion like that?" she wondered. Her husband was standing on the sidewalk out front when she climbed from the car. "Stan, you should be listening to this radio, to what's going on and the discussion taking place," she told him.

"Oh, God, it must be David Duke," Stan said with a trace of annoyance because the subject upset Anne and distracted her around the office. But he was generally supportive of her efforts to confront Duke personally. "If you want to go, go," Stan told her.

"Do you think I should?"

"Damn right, go on."

She reached the studio as the program was winding down. To Duke, Anne looked vaguely familiar, like one of his growing legions of supporters in the white suburbs. He smiled when Anne entered the broadcast area, then pulled up a seat alongside her when the moderator broke for a commercial, saying he wanted to ask a few questions. No doubt he intended to recruit her for one of his phone banks. Anne grimaced, her eyes narrowing. She told Duke she was the woman who had challenged him the week before in Baton Rouge. "You don't remember me, do you, Mr. Duke?" The blood drained from his face, mottling his cheeks with white splotches. Anne said she would like to ask him a few questions too. "Well, that's fine," he answered, fumbling for a phone number in his pocket. "As soon as we finish, I'll be glad to talk to you." But Duke immediately left the room, and when he returned ten minutes later, practically hyperventilating, he was barely able to make one last flourishing speech into the radio mike about our brave boys in Saudi Arabia. Then he grabbed his briefcase and made for the door when she rose to approach him. "As naïve as I am, I thought we were going to sit down in the two chairs outside of the broadcast booth and talk one-on-one," Anne says.

Duke hurried from the building, with Anne pursuing him for the second time in a month. "Mr. Duke! Mr. Duke! How can you say the Holocaust was exaggerated?" They descended the curved staircase. "Wait a minute," she yelled, "if you wanted to talk to me, you better stand like a man and come talk to me. I'm not going to chase you." Her voice rose in pitch. Duke barely paused. "I just don't have any time. I can't," he answered.

Later, over a German beer at a Croatian restaurant in Jefferson Parish, Duke told Truscott that Anne Levy had been sent by the Zionist-Jewish conspiracy. "I was set up.... It's the Jews! You either know about them or you don't! They don't want me to succeed!"[22]

The neofascist journal *Instauration* decried the same malign conspiracy, likening Anne to a "political hit woman." "The Duke phenomenon has been giving some Jews a chance to play Hero for the Day," it editorialized, marshaling as evidence "Ann Levy, the feisty 4'11" veteran of the Warsaw Ghetto, whose shtick is to follow Goliath around crying, 'Mr. Duke! Mr. Duke! Why will you not answer my questions?' "[23]

The discrimination that excludes Jews from men's clubs and Carnival krewes, as the city's Mardi Gras clubs are called, has served as a status ceiling in New Orleans high society since the turn of the century, when non-Jewish parvenus used anti-Semitism to gain access to the social register. Duke's paranoid delusions, however, had a different lineage, harking back to the conspiratorial anti-Semitism of the 1930s when Jews were depicted as a powerful, alien elite culpable for all modernity's woes.[24] As a troubled teenager coming of age during the desegregation crisis, Duke had absorbed fascistic fears of Jews. Now those visceral fears were becoming unmanageable, causing the facade of born-again moderation to crumble, and all because of one diminutive grandmother's passionate convictions—the sum of who she was and what she represented. For Anne Levy, Duke's panic-stricken reaction to demands that he explain his Holocaust views merely confirmed that the man's political change of heart was sheer pretense. It steeled her resolve to expose his hidden agenda. It became the focus of a special survivor's mission.

If Anne Levy's subsequent political activism had a single starting point, it was probably the 1983 American Gathering of Jewish Holocaust Survivors in Washington, D.C. Scheduled to coincide with the fortieth anniversary of the Warsaw Ghetto uprising, the Washington conference was the largest meeting of Holocaust survivors in history, nearly doubling the attendance at the World Gathering in Jerusalem two years before. Nearly fifteen thousand survivors and their relatives crowded into the newly opened Capitol Convention Center. Anne says she first heard about Holocaust denial at the 1983 American Gathering.

Map 1. Poland under German Rule, 1939–1944.
Source: Adapted from Lucjan Dobroszycki, ed., *The Chronicle of the Łódź Ghetto, 1941–1944* (New Haven, Conn.: Yale University Press, 1984).

The three-day reunion in Washington was an instructive lesson in how the search for roots can lead to a quest for meaning. "I'm looking for anyone—cousins, friends, anyone from my town," a Polish concentration camp survivor from Milwaukee told the *New York Times*. Delegates came wearing hand-painted signs advertising for loved ones. One woman wore a custom-printed sweatshirt that pleaded, in bold red letters: "Have you seen my sister, Hena Milich, from Łódź?" Survivors jammed the computer banks to register the names of family members and scroll electronic databases for European friends and relatives. They covered bulletin boards with notes about Polish towns and concentration camps, and clustered near endless rows of tables, each identified by European country, that organizers had cordoned off into a "survivor's village" to facilitate chance reunions.[25]

Anne Levy had also come to the American Gathering on "some remote chance," she wrote two weeks after the event, "someone might recognize my family name."[26] Like many survivors, she was just beginning to confront painful wartime memories. The previous year Dolek Skorecki, her father's first cousin, had shown up unexpectedly from Israel, where he had settled as a pioneer in the early 1930s. Dolek's family had run a typing school in Kielce, Poland, and Dolek, a short, wiry man who exudes natural warmth and loves to paint, was spending his retirement years traveling to Canada and the United States, reconstructing the Skorecki family tree. The branch that had been transplanted to New Orleans originated in Łódź. Anne's mother, Ruth Skorecki, had died ten years earlier of breast cancer, but her father, Mark, a semiretired cabinet-maker in New Orleans, was still living, as were her younger sister, Lila Millen, another New Orleans resident, and brother, Adam, who practices law in Atlanta. Adam had been born after the war in a displaced persons center in the American zone of occupied Germany. What is truly striking about the New Orleans branch of the Skoreckis is that they had lived through the Holocaust as a unit. Rarer still, they are one of the few Polish Jewish families that survived the liquidation of the Warsaw Ghetto *intact*, escaping only days before the Jewish combat organization fired on Nazi soldiers in mid-January 1943—the precursor to the famous uprising that, three months later, resulted in the ghetto's total destruction.

When Anne traveled to the Washington gathering, however, it was with her surrogate family, such people as Shep Zitler and Eva Galler, along with eight or ten other survivors from New Orleans, all members of the New Americans Social Club. "They've always been like the uncles and the aunts that I never knew," Anne says, "so I felt very comfortable." They provided her with a necessary support group. Like other attendees, Anne fed the names of her parents and siblings into the convention's computer terminals, then strolled the hall gazing at name tags. "I was looking to see if anybody would recognize the names, but they didn't."

In the convention center's cavernous hall, near the "survivor's village," conference organizers had set up a small stage with a microphone, where thousands of aging survivors stood patiently in line for the chance to announce, in trembling voice and fractured English, their names and hometowns and occasionally the camps where they had been imprisoned. Sometimes these public self-revelations led to tearful, on-the-spot reunions. But not very often. Anne joined the long line, only to discover on reaching the microphone that she knew too little about her Polish background to provide the audience with helpful clues. In the early 1960s her mother had dictated a memoir concerning the family's unique Holocaust experiences, but Ruth had barely discussed the past with her children, and Anne's father had completely clammed up after the war. It was not until he was well into his eighties that he started reminiscing. When Anne's turn to testify arrived, she felt like she was speaking into a void. "I went up to that podium three times, each time choked with tears, for it was then I realized I didn't know the names of either set of my grandparents or anyone else who perished in that beastly war." Pained by her inability to mourn relatives she barely knew, Anne came away with a heightened awareness of her spiritual kinship with other Holocaust survivors.[27]

She also returned home determined to bear personal witness against Nazi genocide. Partly by design, the moral imperative to remember practically dominated the convention's official proceedings. Conference organizers—many of whom, like Ben and Vladka Meed, were survivors themselves (Vladka was a courier for the Warsaw Ghetto Jewish Fighting Organization)—had been closely involved with the campaign to build the United States Holocaust Memorial Museum on the Washington Mall, and they were therefore deeply concerned with teaching the lessons of the past.[28] President Ronald Reagan helped set the tone in his opening address to the American Gathering: "We who are old enough to remember must make certain those who take our place understand."[29] The thunderous applause greeting his remarks underscored how little nudging survivors needed at the time to shoulder history's didactic burdens. Advancing in age, several were beginning to talk about the war because they knew their passing would silence forever the compelling voices of firsthand testimony, and they feared the Holocaust's enormity might get lost in the bloodless abstractions of academic history. Moreover, unresolved guilt over having passed safely through fires that consumed relatives was likewise prodding survivors who experienced the Holocaust as young adults to begin confronting the past. Heretofore, the dominant mood had been to avoid dwelling on the war. Individual survival seemed largely a result of dumb luck. So what was the point of revisiting traumas that only increased remorse and made one afraid? As they faced death, though, they considered that perhaps their enduring had purpose after all. *Somebody* had to survive to recount the horror. To paraphrase Primo Levi, the philosopher of the death camps, their generation had been given the "awful privilege" to acquaint the world with radical evil.[30]

The public drama of those frustrated reunions in the "survivor's village" had made this much obvious: No one else was going to step out of the historical shadows to testify in their stead. Arbitrary fate had bequeathed the responsibility—and, for some, the guilt—to them alone. Shep Zitler, Anne's surrogate uncle from New Orleans, who was just starting to think about the meaning of his life, put it bluntly: "I survived in order to tell my story. Period."[31] Judging from the volume of personal survivor testimony beginning to flood the book market and oral history archives in the early 1980s, he was scarcely alone in asserting that his tragic family history had greater than purely genealogical meaning.

Besides impending mortality, one other catalyst impelled survivors to step forward with their stories: the increasing audacity of Holocaust deniers. Already propagandizing among high school teachers, by the 1990s "revisionists" would begin buying full-page ads in college newspapers to refute the Holocaust "myth." Denier activism had caused survivor children—the "second generation"—and other social action groups to organize countermovements. "As children of Jewish Holocaust Survivors, we have a special obligation to make sure this doesn't happen again," the thirty-four-year-old chairman of an international network of survivor children told a *Time* magazine reporter covering the American Gathering.[32] In conjunction with survivor groups from Southern California, they were on hand to update the gathering on the "revisionist" activities of the Institute for Historical Review.

What survivors found most troubling, however, was the bold manner in which deniers covered their enterprise with a pseudoscholarly veneer, a tactical adjustment that was helping deniers acquire "the legitimacy of a point of view."[33] Even German conservatives anxious to refurbish a positive sense of German nationalism were starting to take their theories seriously, and they would soon be followed by rabid nationalists in Eastern Europe, who filled the void caused by Soviet empire's collapse with anti-Semitism and other forms of ethnic particularism. By the early 1980s the denial industry had devolved into subdisciplines. Some "revisionists" were specializing in the "fake photography problem." Others debunked Anne Frank's diary, because it was the main vehicle for introducing the young to the Holocaust. A French literary professor named Robert Faurisson—who was convicted in France of deliberate historical distortion—wrote extensively on the "mechanics of gassing" to spread the "good news" that the gas chambers at Auschwitz were a historical fiction. "Revisionism's" pseudoscientific research appeared in the IHR's quarterly, the

Journal of Historical Review, under such titles as "Human Soap"; "Holocaust Pharmacology vs. Scientific Pharmacology"; and "The Problem of Crematoria Hours and Incineration Time," which used algebraic hieroglyphics to prove the Holocaust was a mathematical impossibility.[34] Many survivors were startled to discover how adept deniers had become in the conventions of academic discourse. Those who sampled the literature confessed to feelings of sensory deprivation. They thought they were losing their identity both as survivors and as Jews.[35]

The "revisionist" writer producing the biggest sensation at the American Gathering was Arthur Butz, whose credentials as an electrical engineering professor at Northwestern University in Chicago gave the impression that "revisionism" had seized the academy's most commanding heights. Butz's *The Hoax of the Twentieth Century*, published in 1976 by the anti-Semitic Noontide Press, is practically the Bible of Holocaust denial literature. (Duke's NAAWP News advertised the title for years, calling it "the most important refutation of the Holocaust ever written.") *Hoax* summarizes many of the key arguments of Holocaust revisionism, beginning with the claim that the estimate of six million Jewish deaths is vastly exaggerated and running to the assertion that the gas chambers at Auschwitz were really delousing units. Throughout, Butz is relentlessly conspiratorial about the evidentiary record, dismissing it as the tainted product of postwar "show trials." As for the more than forty thousand linear feet of documents on German genocide captured by the United States alone, Butz says every edict, railroad manifest, and internal memorandum had been planted.[36]

As both a survivor and a member of the "second generation" (by virtue of her parents' survival), Anne Levy was poised to react strongly to the discovery that organized anti-Semites were defaming her experience. But more upsetting than anything was Professor Butz's potential impact on the young. "I was really stunned because here was an educated man who had influence in colleges writing a book saying that it never happened, that it was a hoax," she says. "I got really upset." So upset that she uncharacteristically wrote a letter to *The New Orleans Times-Picayune* shortly after returning home summarizing her new state of mind: "This story must be told and re-told, for in my own lifetime I have heard it said that the Holocaust didn't happen, that it was merely a fabrication of the Jews. Well, when you have witnessed death and starvation and see people comparing concentration camp numbers tattooed on their arms, how could anyone with any sense of compassion believe this never happened?" Moreover, despite its painfulness, she added, the tragic history needed to be continually recounted, "because this should never happen again to any people, be they Jews or anyone else on the face of this planet."[37]

Hers was the patriotism of the assimilated immigrant intensely devoted to America's universalistic creed, but the language of an editorial page scarcely hinted at the intense personal and moral feelings stirring within. Troubled memory was starting to surface unbidden, which is how trauma often asserts its claims on consciousness. Six years later, as her encounters with Duke assumed "the character of an immediate and violent impulse"—which is how Primo Levi depicts the survivor need to inform the "rest" about the story, even make nonsurvivors participate in it—the surge of recollection would drive Anne to embrace a mission of political witnessing.[38] The turn toward politics had all the hallmarks of self-therapy.

Like many survivors, however, Anne Levy's problem was finding the courage to tell her story. It took a long time to share it even with close acquaintances. Her friend Claire Tritt, who with her husband, Abner, publishes New Orleans's only Jewish weekly, never realized Anne was from Poland until the subject inadvertently came up during one of their long, daily morning walks to Uptown New Orleans's moss-curtained Audubon Park. Because of Anne's slight accent, Claire had always assumed her exercise partner had moved to New Orleans from Stan's home state of Massachusetts. "I'm not from New England, I'm from Łódź, Poland," Anne corrected her, and then proceeded to explain how her father, Mark, had been separated from the family early in the war, later found Ruth and the children near starvation in the Warsaw Ghetto, hid the two girls in various nooks and crannies during the wave of deportations that wiped out the world's second largest Jewish community, helped his family escape to the Aryan side, where they passed as non-Jews for the next two years, and finally carried them to the American zone in Germany after the war ended. The Skorecki family did not emigrate to America until 1949, when they sailed directly to New Orleans. "It took about an hour and a half for Anne to tell the story. Another walker was with us that morning, and we were all in tears by the end," Claire said. "People on the street thought something must be wrong with us."[39] Their conversation occurred two years or so after Anne returned from the 1983 American Gathering in Washington.

Sharing her story with friends was easy next to forcing it on David Duke. "It's a really difficult thing she's doing," noted Anne's thirty-three-year-old daughter, Robin, in 1992 of her mother's confrontations with the neo-Nazi. "It's not like she is so articulate and composed. She's barely able to get very direct remarks out. She's a totally emotional package." Although Anne long ago mastered English, her fluency often ebbed away when she was in a Duke-related situation. She would even physically shake. But she never wavered.

After she let anger work for her, the inner turmoil spurred her on. "She just has to get at him and challenge his behavior toward her," Robin says. "It's a very personal thing."[40]

During the three years when Duke's political star was rising in Louisiana, Anne was practically consumed by his public presence. After their encounters in Baton Rouge and at the radio station, she never ceased trying to challenge him. She would drop what she was doing when he appeared on television. The volume had to be turned way up lest she miss a word. Constant busy signals at local radio stations were never a deterrent if Duke happened to be that evening's talk show guest. A couple of times she managed to get through to the switchboard. Always she asked the same insistent question; always Duke ended up soft-pedaling the Holocaust, saying it was not as bad as it was made out to be. Then he would quickly change the subject. Once he asked over the airwaves why she hated him. Before Anne could answer, he switched to the next caller. He refused to take her story seriously, and Anne was incensed. "It's one thing to have academic knowledge about the Holocaust; it's another to have that experience which propels you to wring his neck," Robin explains. "It sort of seems like my mom had no choice." Anne agrees: "I didn't mean to get involved, but something inside made me do it."[41]

If she had personal motives for confronting Duke, her behavior was freighted with political significance. It helped convince Duke's grassroots opponents in Louisiana that the best line of attack was to publicize his extremist beliefs concerning Hitler and the Holocaust. This moral strategy, surprisingly, initially met with widespread opposition. Hardened politicos argued that accusing Duke of harboring Nazi sympathies strained credulity. Better to stick with the road-tested themes of Louisiana mudslinging. Voters would find it easier to believe charges of tax evasion and womanizing. But there was something about Duke's visceral reactions to Anne's public reproaches that underscored the wisdom of attacking his Nazism. Any suggestion that his youthful extremism represented his real attitudes threatened popular support by exposing him as a faker.

Beth Rickey, a Tulane graduate student and Republican state central committeewoman then emerging as one of the former Klansman's most outspoken critics, learned of Anne's capitol confrontation with Duke immediately after it happened. A short while later, Rickey would become part of a small group of activists and academics who came together to form the Louisiana Coalition against Racism and Nazism. Anne's encounter with Duke happened while future founders of the coalition were struggling with basic strategy. The previous month Rickey and friends had purchased several Nazi books from Duke's Metairie bookstore, which doubled as both his home and his legislative office. One title was the notorious *Turner Diaries*, a racist fable of right-wing revolution that inspired the bank robbery and killing spree by a neo-Nazi group called the Order in the early 1980s (including the murder of talk show host Alan Berg) and possibly the bombing of the federal building in Oklahoma City. Lance Hill, a fellow Tulane graduate student and a long-time civil rights activist, had suggested the book-buying idea. But now that Rickey's purchases confirmed suspicions that Duke was still trafficking in Nazi literature, it was unclear how and where the disclosure should be made public. Even anti-Duke lawmakers declined denouncing him on the floor of the legislature, and Rickey failed in her try to persuade the Republican state central committee to censure the new representative from Metairie. The state GOP had just embarked on a disastrous courtship with David Duke, its latest recruit. The setbacks were dispiriting. "I started dragging my feet," Rickey says, "and I was a little afraid of Duke as well. But then I thought if Anne Levy has got the guts to walk up to that man and ask him why he said the Holocaust never happened, I certainly could summon the courage to expose his Nazi book-selling operation." She also wanted to lend moral support. "I wanted to back her up. I wanted to say she has a point. She wasn't paranoid, she wasn't making it up. I thought how I would feel if I had that horrendous experience and no one stood up for me."[42]

The day after Anne confronted Duke in Baton Rouge, Rickey held a press conference in the Great Memorial Hall of the state capitol. Local television picked up the story first. Then the Associated Press sent it nationwide. It was the first major hit against Duke, and it inflicted lasting damage. "Because of the story, Duke was forever tagged with the label 'Nazi book vendor,'" Beth says. "It hurt him, it dogged him, and Anne Levy is indirectly responsible in putting that label on him. She was the catalyst. I don't think the publicity would have had the same moral and political effect had the revelation of his book operation taken place at a different time and place."[43]

Anne Levy's relationship to the countermovement that ultimately defeated Duke was always reciprocal. She needed its moral encouragement. Public truth telling is a form of recovery, especially when combined with social action. Sharing traumatic experiences with others enables victims to reconstruct repressed memory, mourn loss, and master helplessness, which is trauma's essential insult. And, by facilitating reconnection to ordinary life, the public testimony helps survivors restore basic trust in a just world and overcome feelings of isolation. But the talking cure is predicated on the existence of a community willing to bear witness. "Recovery can take place only within the context of relationships," writes Judith Herman. "It cannot occur in isolation."[44]

For Anne Levy, the widening opposition to David Duke furnished the safe context in which to reconstruct her memories. Unexpectedly, she began receiving occasional notes and phone calls from friends applauding her courage.

Then strangers started thanking her for her feistiness. Having been a private individual all her life, she was developing a public persona, and the new identity felt good. "My mother probably would have continued confronting Duke without the positive feedback," Robin believes, "but she would have been torn about whether she was doing the right thing. Little by little all these bits of support provided a framework she could feel secure in."[45]

It was as though the traumatic life events that had shaped Anne Levy were becoming the metaphor through which an emerging moral community was relearning the political lessons of history. And the more David Duke tried to run from a past he wanted to forget, the more Anne felt compelled to confront him with a past she could not forget—and would not let others forget either. Recounting her life story thus became a political mission, and the effect was redemptive.

"Life sometimes throws you strange curves," Anne said in 1992. But the bus trip with other New Orleans survivors to the Simon Wiesenthal exhibit at the Louisiana state capitol was surely the oddest, most unexpected culmination of life experiences. Seeing Duke standing at jack-booted parade rest before ghetto photographs that looked like snapshots in her mind caused disparate pieces of personal history suddenly to fuse together. A lost childhood in Poland, the postwar decompression in Germany and the United States, a recovery from fear for which no twelve-step method had yet been invented, the futile search for roots and the late-in-life realization of her special obligation to remember—these blurred images and poignant moments converged with lightning speed into transparent wholeness. Across the chasm of half a century, a political nightmare that had terrorized a continent and consumed millions seemed to be recurring in her new home, and now, as she waited for the commencement of a ceremony observing that tragedy, the political apotheosis of Holocaust denial in Louisiana stood less than fifty feet away. As Anne said later, something happened: "It was almost like I couldn't help myself."

After that first encounter memories started flooding back. She spoke about her childhood more often, increasingly to public audiences.

Telling her life story required reclaiming a European past that personal memory alone could not recover. It required establishing continuity with Old World family history.[46] Fortunately, there was the memoir that Anne's mother had dictated in 1963, the recollections of friends and other survivors, and a documentary trail in Germany and Poland.

When Anne Levy recalls her prewar Polish past, just about everything is a jumble of names and faces, as if amnesia has played Scrabble with her memory. From time to time her father used to mention his older brothers, Morris, Wladek, and Julius, and his older sister, Stefa. He occasionally referred to Morris's son, Adam, who, close to Mark in age, served with him in the Polish army, probably during World War I, and possibly the Polish-Soviet War of 1920–21 as well. Anne has no visual recall of Morris and Adam, who lived in Warsaw, more than eighty miles away from Łódź, her childhood home. Wladek, on the other hand, and his wife, Gustawa, "a very active, very intelligent woman," according to her nephew, resided only a few blocks down the street from Anne's family, and she saw them often.[1] Their daughter, Haka, big and stout like her mother, with a high forehead and prematurely graying hair, was in and out of Anne's various wartime domiciles. So was Uncle Julius, a dapper dresser who was slightly older than her father and who, unmarried, was living with Wladek and Gustawa when the war broke out. The family surname was unusual for a country where the line between Jews and gentiles was sharp. Skorecki was a Polish, not a Jewish, name.

After her mother died, Anne and her sister, Lila, found yellowing snapshots of Wladek, Gustawa, and Julius in the drawer of Ruth's china cabinet. Mixed in were photographs of Henry Tempelhof, Ruth's younger brother. On the rare occasions Anne's mother talked about Old World relatives, Henry almost always came up. He had been a mechanical engineer in Warsaw and had married a young surgeon named Mery Mejnster just before the war. Anne saw a lot of Henry and Mery after the German invasion.

But the passage of those once familiar names and faces had long ago misted over with time. Today, Anne can say little with absolute confidence about her past, except where and when she was born: Łódź, Poland, on July 2, 1935. Yet even this is far from certain.

The Skorecki family tree is easier to reconstruct than that of the Tempelhofs. The former had so many offshoots. From its taproot in the town of Działoszyce (pronounced Zhow-wah-shitsa), the main trunk branched into nearly one hundred descendants. A few Skoreckis emigrated to America and Palestine in the 1920s and 1930s. A handful, in addition to Anne's family, even managed to survive Hitler's Holocaust.

The Skorecki clan, a family of lumber merchants, descended from five sons born to Aaron and Ruchla Skorecki. "My father always said his family was in the wood business, operating lumberyards and sawmills," Anne says. The oldest of the five sons was Szmil-Zawel, Anne's grandfather. According to his 1934 death certificate on file at the Łódź record office, Szmil-Zawel was born in Działoszyce in 1858.[2] It is hard to go deeper for family roots. As meticulous as the Nazis were about warehousing and cataloguing confiscated Jewish property, saving precious cultural treasures for future museum display, their systematic gutting of synagogues destroyed tons of communal records—inflicting, in Helen Epstein's words, "irreparable damage to one thousand years of Jewish history in barely six."[3] What the Germans overlooked, the Poles of Działoszyce are still pilfering and selling as souvenirs to tourists who pass through.[4]

Nestled in a stream-creased valley in the rolling countryside northeast of Kraków, Działoszyce had been established by Polish nobles almost a thousand years ago as a gamekeeper's village. "Before long," states a 1958 Polish historical pamphlet, "most of the population were Jews engaging in crafts and commerce."[5] The village's transformation into a Jewish shtetl—a Jewish "town"— probably began during the sixteenth century, when noble-owned communities such as Działoszyce emerged as important market centers in the burgeoning grain trade with continental Europe. Before then, Jews fleeing religious persecution in England, France, and Germany had sought sanctuary in Poland's royal cities, where the Crown granted them communal autonomy in order to command their services as tax collectors, bankers, and managers of the mint and the mines. By the fifteenth century, the demographic center of Ashkenazi Jewry had shifted to the Commonwealth of Poland,[6] a territory embracing all of present-day Lithuania and much of Belarus and the Ukraine.[7] By then Polish Jews were also encountering the same anti-Semitic hostility that had originally driven them east. Behind much of the antagonism stood the Catholic Church. But German burghers, who in the thirteenth century were the first to establish towns in Poland, were the Jews' main economic competitors, often instigating anti-Semitic disturbances. The Polish Crown, which was growing weaker by the decade, bowed to pressure that Jews be expelled from royal cities. It was around this time that the Polish *szlachta*, as the "nobility" was called, invited

Jews to relocate to their new market towns. The increasingly powerful szlachta strove to attract not merely new settlers to their expanding domains but also Jewish business skills.[8]

Unlike neighboring Russia and Prussia, then launching absolutist monarchies and centralized bureaucracies, Poland between the sixteenth and eighteenth centuries had fallen under the feudal domination of such great magnate families as the Potockis, Radziwills, and Lubomirskis. On the backs of a newly reenserfed peasantry, they established manorial empires encompassing hundreds of villages. They raised conspicuous consumption to a high art form, dotting the countryside around Warsaw with rococo palaces and formal gardens and steeping themselves in equestrian romance. But to sustain those lavish spending habits they depended on Polish Jews to fill the economic niche between lord and peasant.

Jewish entrepreneurs helped organize the grain trade that flowed down the meandering Vistula River through Warsaw to Dutch traders stationed in the old Hanseatic port city of Danzig (now Gdańsk), Poland's shopwindow to Europe. Jewish traders, long accustomed to crossing linguistic frontiers, peddled the manorial produce far and wide. Jewish tavern keepers played the role of rural moneylender. The magnates appointed Jews to the position of estate manager and steward. Frequently they granted them "leases," called *arendas*, to such valuable income-producing monopolies as the right to distill and sell liquor. By the mid–eighteenth century, more than four-fifths of Poland's rural Jewry were involved in the distilling and distribution of mead, wine, beer, and vodka.[9]

Many Jews also obtained arendas to harvest the ancient oaks and alders in the szlachta's black-green forests, once timber exports started growing in tandem with the burgeoning grain trade. Most of the cutting was done by Polish and Ukrainian woodsmen under Jewish supervision, but Jews themselves often wielded axes. Marked off with red chalk, the felled timber was bundled into rafts and, after the ice melted, floated via canals and such tributaries as the Bug and San Rivers into the Vistula and then into the hands of yet larger Jewish merchants downstream. This historic union between nobleman and Jew quilted Poland with the fields and forests that still define national topography. It is a distinctive landscape that woodsmen like the Skoreckis helped shape.[10]

By the nineteenth century, when it is certain that Skoreckis were residing in Działoszyce, Poland had already been partitioned by powerful neighbors. After 1867 the heavily Jewish area of Galicia, just to the south, was annexed by the Hapsburg Empire. Prussia gained control of Poland's extreme western territories (where Jewish settlement was slight). But Działoszyce, like most of Poland, became part of a Russian-dominated area called Congress Poland.

Under the czars the town's population grew rapidly, nearly tripling (from 1,749 to 6,688) between 1827 and 1893. Jews predominated. They lived around the square or in the Jewish quarter near the shul—the synagogue. They ran Działoszyce's leather tanneries, brick kilns, flour mills, and linseed oil refineries. They managed the gypsum mine and the chicory factory. Nearly all the town's shoemakers, butchers, and tailors were Jewish. So were its coopers, wheel-wrights, harnessmakers, and painters, and this listing hardly exhausts the variety of jobs. Działoszyce was also home to merchants, who outnumbered artisans, and they were Jewish without exception. The bulk were small peddlers who fanned out across the countryside on Monday to buy crops and produce from the local peasantry and returned on Thursday to spend Sabbath with their families. Merchants who owned shops in town dealt in grains, fabrics, and furs; several specialized in goods from Nuremberg. In addition, there were a few "strong-arm young men" who even conducted large-scale smuggling operations across the Austrian border into nearby Galicia.[11]

The town sprang to life during market days, which in Działoszyce fell on Tuesday and Friday. Then the sloping square that spread below the medieval Catholic Church became a hubbub of peasant wagons clattering along cobblestoned streets and ceaseless haggling in Polish and Yiddish in front of stalls brimming with kitchenware. Bargaining was a marketplace ritual. Porters lounged nearby, ever ready to earn tips for making deliveries.[12]

Curiously, none of the sources on nineteenth-century Działoszyce mentions the presence of lumberyards or wood merchants. There were two building supply businesses, however, and possibly one of them was owned by Skoreckis. What is certain is that as late as 1939, Skorecki lumber merchants were combing the countryside for stands of timber to purchase from local peasants and estate owners. "There were several Skorecki families in Działoszyce," says Mendel Riba, who lived there until 1942 and now resides in Tampa, Florida. "One family sold cloth and fabrics. Others were lumber brokers. They were cutting lumber at little towns around Działoszyce, about ten miles away. You never traveled too far in Działoszyce. Everything was close."[13] Judge Moshe Bejski, a Schindler Jew from Działoszyce who served for many years on the Israeli Supreme Court and now heads the Righteous Gentiles Commission of Yad Vashem, remembers that "the Skoreckis belonged to the very, very small group of wealthy people in Działoszyce."[14]

Some Skoreckis may have stayed close to home, but a few family members traveled far afield in search of opportunity. At some time in the nineteenth century, probably after authorities lifted the ban on Jews owning property and maybe even earlier, Anne Levy's ancestors came into possession of timber property in the *kresy*. Veined with drowsy streams, the kresy was an eastern borderland area of marshes and primeval forests, "a place where the devil rests," according to a Polish saying. Now, during the half century preceding the First World War when the Russian and Polish demand for railroad ties and freight wagons grew by leaps and bounds, even these ancient woodlands began to go down.[15] It was probably during this period of intensive lumbering that Anne Levy's branch of the Skorecki family established the sawmill in Horyniec, a small village that lay between Lublin and Lvov, though closer to the latter. Canals and streams linked Horyniec to the San River and thence to the Vistula. By the early twentieth century the hamlet had also become a minor tourist spot. "There was a mineral spa there for curing arthritis," says Eva Galler, a Holocaust survivor who grew up in the nearby town of Oleszyce and today lives in New Orleans. "I went there a couple of times with my mother."[16]

Dolek Skorecki, Mark's cousin who emigrated to Palestine in 1930, has memories of Horyniec too. "The families came there for a summer vacation." Visitors often strolled through the fern-carpeted forest collecting linden tree blossoms for brewing tea. Around fallen trunks drooped mushrooms the size of skillets, and cranberry bogs were plentiful. After one of Poland's soft, replenishing rains, the woodlands exploded with fragrance. "I still remember the smell of the forest and the fresh wood cut by the machines," Dolek says.[17]

It is unclear how the Skoreckis acquired their frontier forest properties. Dolek surmises the mystery is wrapped up in the riddle surrounding the family's non-Jewish name. According to a story he heard as a young boy, the Polish count whose timberlands the Skoreckis had once managed approached the family patriarch about sending a Skorecki to London for training. "Let me have one of your boys," the nobleman allegedly said. "I will send him to England to learn about the lumber industry." At the close of the eighteenth century the Polish nobility had taken as much fancy to forestry experts as they once had to French dancing masters.[18] Dolek believes it was Mark's grandfather, Aron, who was chosen to study abroad. Soon after returning home, the young man became his patron's business partner, traveling throughout eastern and southern Poland looking for timber. But Aron chose to receive his compensation in woodlands, not money—hence the Skoreckis' eastern properties. It is also rumored that the nobleman was named Skorecki—thus their Polish surname. The name was acquired by act of sale. "I was told by my mother that my great-great-grandfather went down to city hall and bought the name," adds a New York–born member of the Skorecki family. This theory is as good as any.[19]

The name change was a stroke of good luck. During the Nazi occupation, the Skorecki surname helped camouflage the family's Jewish identity.

After the Holocaust there was a natural tendency to romanticize the shtetl as a timeless paradigm of Jewish culture. It was as if eulogists believed memory alone could retrieve a vanished world. The tendency is apparent in many of the seven-hundred-plus Yizkor (memorial) books compiled by survivors after the war to commemorate the Jewish towns of Central and Eastern Europe. Działoszyce's own book fits the mold. "Only a few of the younger generation were affected by heterodox or modernist ideas," wrote one contributor. "Daily life was lived to the full in accordance with Jewish tradition, which encompassed everybody."[20] But Jewish towns were not islands in a gentile sea. Outside influences constantly crashed ashore. East European Jews fought an endless struggle to mesh tradition and modernity.[21] Most of the Skoreckis of Działoszyce seem to have been on the side of modernity. Says a family survivor who emigrated to San Francisco from the Soviet Union in 1981, "They were very modern Jews."[22] It was an orientation that would help some of them survive the Holocaust.

The Skoreckis were an Orthodox family, like most Polish Jews; there were only two Reform synagogues in Poland on the eve of the Second World War. Jewish traditionalism was hard to escape in such towns as Działoszyce, where religious festivals endowed the passage of time with reassuring familiarity. Everyday one encountered Jews who lived according to biblical law. Religious commandments—and there were 613 of them—regulated diet and grooming, down to how shoes should be pulled on in the morning. Some prayers had to be murmured at great speed; others recited in singsong while rocking back and forth.[23] Działoszyce boasted an imposing shul, located, like most synagogues in small Polish towns, just off the main square. Nearby stood a *beth hamidrash*, or "place of study." The community had its own heder and Yeshiva—Jewish religious schools. It had a burial society that was "something like a Masonic Order." Hassidism—a mystical, joyous sect founded in the eighteenth century to challenge the intellectual formalism of rabbinical Judaism—had made substantial inroads in Działoszyce. Every so often a Hassidic rebbe came to town to visit his followers.[24]

Traditionalism structured the roles assigned to men and women. Among Jewish men there was no higher calling than religious study, and it was not at all unusual for wives, their heads shaved and covered with a matron's wig, to run the home and keep a market stall while husbands pored over the Torah and the Talmud at the shul from dawn until midnight. Only men learned Hebrew, although women were taught a few rudimentary Hebrew prayers. In fact, Jewish women received hardly any formal education. They spoke mainly Yiddish, which was the native tongue of four-fifths of Poland's Jews on the eve of World War II. (Yiddish is a tenth-century German dialect written in Hebrew and sprinkled with words and folk idioms picked up "on the move" from linguistic cultures far and wide.)[25]

Only three broad commandments applied to women: to light the Sabbath candles, to keep a kosher kitchen, and to maintain family purity. But those three simple obligations kept Jewish mothers occupied nearly year-round with the weekly wash as well as cleaning and cooking in preparation for the next holiday in the religious calendar. The one respite was when they were breast-feeding the newest addition to their growing families, which often numbered as many as fifteen children. For the law of family purity, in addition to requiring that women purify themselves at the ritual bath, or *mikvah*, following menstruation, also restricted permissible sexual activity to days of the month when female ovulation was at its height.[26]

Of Aron Skorecki's five sons, only Szmil-Zawel, Anne Levy's grandfather, was an observant Jew, though he never carried devoutness to the point of abandoning business for the shul. Still, as late as 1934, the year of his death, he appeared regularly in the black caftan, soft hat, and long, white beard of the religious Jew. And he had a lot of children: twelve altogether, or more than twice the number sired by any of his brothers. "Szmil-Zawel was an important person in the family," Dolek says. "He had many daughters and sons." Those dozen offspring, however, had been birthed by two different wives. The youngest child was born when Szmil-Zawel was in his fifties and Natalia, his second wife and Mark's mother, was forty-two.[27]

But none of Szmil-Zawel's children was particularly religious. Nor were his brothers. Most of the Skoreckis of Działoszyce apparently belonged to that emergent Jewish middle-class that began embracing secularism during the last third of the nineteenth century. It is a myth to suppose that the Haskala, the Jewish enlightenment, did not penetrate beyond the large cities of eastern Europe. Modernity reached such provincial towns as Grodno, in Galicia, birthplace of the remarkable artist and writer Bruno Schulz (murdered by the Nazis in 1942), and it infiltrated many shtetls as well. Wladek Skorecki, Szmil-Zawel's younger brother, was one of Działoszyce's early cosmopolitans. He established the town's first nonreligious civil school, and all six of his children, including Anne Levy's Aunt Gustawa, taught there. "All of my father's family were very intelligent," says Dolek, one of Wladek's grandsons. "They knew languages. They knew English and taught English. And Leon, another brother to Wladek, owned all the books of Shakespeare—in English. He had a great library." Wladek's children, learning to play violin, viola, and cello, formed a chamber quartet and performed selections from English operettas. Their cousins took up painting and piano. "My grandfather was a great man," says Dolek. "A lot of the cousins were named after him. That is why there were so many Wladeks in the Skorecki family."[28]

In fact, the Skoreckis of Działoszyce were a family of cousins bound by intermarriage. Gustawa, for example, wed Mark's older brother Wladek, who had been named for an uncle who now became his father-in-law. Their daughter, Haka, married her first cousin, yet another Wladek Skorecki. So it went throughout the entire family tree, the limbs from one branch crossing those of another. Endogamous marriages are often strategies for keeping property in the family. But intermarriage among the Skorecki cousins may have sprouted from shared interests. "Działoszyce is not Kraków, it is not Lvov, it is not Warsaw, it is not even Częstochowa," says Dolek's oldest daughter, Ilana Zuckerman, a sound artist from Jerusalem who is heard regularly on Israeli public radio. "So who can you be involved with?" Unlike in Italy, France, or Germany, Polish Jews rarely married gentiles. And there were no salons in these small towns where the like-minded might find one another across the ethnic divide. "So they wedded each other," she says. "And why not? They were beautiful, intelligent. My father says they were really amusing each other."[29]

Dolek used to tell Ilana strange stories about growing up in a house filled with first cousins. "Only yesterday he said, 'All of a sudden Rocha [his cousin] started to play the piano'—he remembers it like flashes of memory, because he was a child—'and then she was typing with machines, then she was stitching. And then she was marrying some of her cousins. I don't understand it,' he said. It was very charming the way he told me the story."

Ilana continues: "I was longing all my life, even before I was aware and I could put it in words, for the cosmopolitans and the Jewish intellectuals, artists, and scientists who wandered from one culture to the other carrying within themselves the essence of European culture at its best. I found myself, my identity, in the Polish Skoreckis of my mind, of my imagination, because what I had was very little. There is only an uncle and a father and a legend about the family in Poland. Nothing."

Many Skoreckis began to leave Działoszyce in the years just before World War I. By the closing decades of the nineteenth century, overpopulation had deepened the poverty of Polish peasants and the Jewish masses alike, causing shtetls such as Działoszyce to empty their youth into the industrial slums of Łódź and Warsaw. The economic crisis spurred the great transatlantic movement of Russian and Polish Jews to America.[30] One by one, Aron's children and grandchildren joined the migration. Wladek, the schoolmaster, and his brother Haim-Henryk, moved to Kraków, where a few of their children attended the city's lumber academy. Several Skorecki grandchildren relocated to Danzig and Warsaw, becoming lawyers and insurance agents. Two weeks after Dolek's birth his father moved the family to Kielce, where he had been offered the position of magistrate. Soon he established a bank and started a typing school, while his wife opened a wine and liquor store.

Sometime before the turn of the century Szmil-Zawel took his continuously growing family to the textile city of Piotrków, where Anne's father, Mark, was born in 1900. By 1909, when Natalia gave birth to her last child, Rose (who died in 1916), Szmil-Zawel had established his domicile in the booming city of Łódź. City fathers never regarded him as anything other than a "temporary resident," although he lived there for the last three decades of his life.[31]

Until 1820, Łódź was a sleepy agricultural craft center scarcely larger than Działoszyce. But in that year Czarist Russia designated the town an industrial settlement, German capital and engineering skill poured in, and Łódź quickly mushroomed into Poland's second largest city. After 1877, when a new tariff guaranteed Polish mills almost exclusive access to the Russian market, Łódź also became the textile capital of eastern Europe. The population grew at an American tempo, multiplying twentyfold between 1850 and 1900, then doubling again by the eve of World War I. City officials tried to control demographic growth by closely regulating the issuance of residency permits, but such transplants as Szmil-Zawel ignored the restrictions by living off the books. Łódź filled up with a polyglottal population: weavers and spinners from Silesia, Saxony, and Prussia; Polish peasants newly freed from noble estates by the great emancipation of 1867; and Jewish artisans, tradesmen, and workers who, by 1931, made up one-third of the city's six hundred thousand inhabitants.[32]

Artur Rubinstein, the great concert pianist, was born in Łódź during its golden age, and its sounds formed his first auditory memories: gypsy musicians and their trained monkeys who entertained in the apartment courtyards; Russian ice cream vendors and Polish women egg sellers who mingled their chants with the singsong of Jewish used-clothes peddlers. Every morning before daybreak, hundreds of shrieking factory sirens summoned workers to the mills.[33]

Although Germans pioneered Polish textiles, it was Jewish entrepreneurs who transformed the industry into Poland's first big business. Like early Yankee industrialists in New England, Jewish textile barons often started out as merchants and later branched into banking. They excelled at developing the export market and diversifying product lines. Some carried vertical integration to the point of building their own engineering plants so as to fabricate factory machinery difficult to purchase abroad. Enormous fortunes materialized overnight and were put on appropriate display. I. K. Poznański, who employed ten thousand operatives, erected a neo-Baroque palace literally next door to his factory in the center of town.[34]

But great wealth at the top masked stark inequality at the bottom. Although the Jewish community's per capita income exceeded that of Poles, the average Jew hovered near poverty by virtue of living in one of Europe's most overpopulated and least developed countries. Only a minority of Jewish shopkeepers and tradesmen belonged to the middle class. Many Jewish artisans, especially tailors and shoemakers, eked out meager incomes as outworkers stitching, in cramped homes, pieces of final products that they used to produce from start to finish[35]—a loss of craft all too familiar to cobblers of early-nineteenth-century America. Most of the working poor—millhands, deskilled artisans, street peddlers—tended to crowd into either the Bałuty slum or Old Town. Situated in the northern part of the city, Bałuty was one of Łódź's filthiest, most rundown neighborhoods. Its streets were unpaved; sanitation was primitive. According to a 1942 history of the area, the Bałuty slum had "the highest percentage of wooden houses, of decaying houses, of houses in danger of collapsing and begging to be torn down, of houses that had not been repaired in decades, of houses filled with dirt and trash and lacking the slightest comfort."[36]

Yet, for all its extremes of wealth and poverty, the city quivered with nervous energy. "These were neurotic streets, neurotic shops, neurotic people!" the Yiddish writer Sholom Asch noted in one of his most famous novels. Dun-colored skies were smeared with soot. Horse-drawn wagons piled high with yarn and undressed cotton creaked through forests of rail-thin Jews who wore long black coats and swayed in animated conversation. In the evening the streetcars and narrow pavements overflowed with homebound workers trailing the scent of that day's output. "The whole city reeked of machine oil and worsted yarn," Asch wrote.[37] Łódź was a city of whir and buzz. It is not hard to understand why Szmil-Zawel chose to move there. The place was practically a breeder reactor of construction activity.

He settled his family in a Polish neighborhood on the city's south side: at Rzgowska 75 (pronounced Shagovska; Polish street addresses place the number after the street). Rzgowska was a major thoroughfare into town, paved and well kept. An electric streetcar clanged down the center of the street. Entered through a gated tunnel—a porte cochere—the two-story family residence sat sideways to Rzgowska, facing onto an interior courtyard. Szmil-Zawel located his lumberyard in the rear of the property. Across the courtyard and on the other corner of the same block, two of his daughters, Frances and Anna, later established an embroidery shop where they sold flowery table doilies. A few doors away Stefa, another daughter, and her husband, Hersch Silberberg, ran a bakery on the ground floor of a forty-person apartment building. All family paths led to Rzgowska 75, which hummed with activity. There was no doubt who held the upper hand inside the residence: Short and plump in her neat print dresses, her hair drawn back in a bun, Grandmother Natalie, Szmil-Zawel's second wife, was the *balebosteh*, "the master of the house," says Moshe Silberberg, Stefa's son, who today manages an eye clinic at a hospital outside of Tel Aviv. "She was very strict about helping out around the house, but she was a good woman, and very religious, although none of her children were." Large family meals happened regularly, and it was important to be on time. "Give their food to the dog," Szmil-Zawel would tell the hired cook when children or grandchildren came late.[38] In the kitchen sat a wooden tub that the family's Polish maids filled once a week with hot water. "On Saturday nights, when we took our baths, there was always a lot of people in that kitchen," remembers Ruth Gerver, an American granddaughter who visited Łódź with her mother and brother in 1934.[39]

There are no financial documents to go on, but it is clear that Szmil-Zawel belonged to that small Jewish, urban middle class that managed to do well in the face of increasing adversity. At least he was able to pay for his children to attend the Gymnasium, which was beyond the means of most prewar Poles. Non-Jewish businessmen in the neighborhood regarded him as a trusted counselor to whom they could bring their disputes, much as shtetl Jews themselves used to bring communal conflicts to learned elders for arbitration.[40]

By the last year of his life, Szmil-Zawel had wizened into comfortable old age and was spending most of his time at his country dacha raising chickens. "He was a very dignified gentleman who smoked cigarettes incessantly," Ruth Gerver says. "And he was always sending me to the store to buy papierosi, which is what the Poles called cigarettes because they were practically all paper." He died on October 24, 1934, at age seventy-six.[41]

Several years earlier, Szmil-Zawel had already begun dividing the family wood business among his sons. To Morris and Wladek Skorecki, the two oldest boys, he turned over management of the Horyniec operation. Morris eventually moved to Warsaw and expanded his holdings dramatically. "Morris became a very rich man who had all kinds of forests, industrial forests, near the Russian border," says Dolek, Mark's Israeli cousin. During the First World War, curiously, for the area was a battleground, Wladek moved to the Ukraine with Gustawa and Haka to pursue lumber opportunities. Henry, third in succession, relocated to the outskirts of Kiev, eventually becoming a minister of forests. Wladek, or "Big Wladek," as he was known to distinguish him from the family's other Wladeks, was ruined by the Russian Revolution. In the winter of 1920–21 he, Gustawa, and Haka returned to Poland shoeless and in rags. "They had a rough time at the hands of the Bolsheviks," says Dolek. "They came from Kiev wearing sacks." For the next ten years they lived in Kielce, staying for a brief period with Dolek's banker-father. Then, in 1930, Wladek moved his family to Łódź, opening his own lumberyard on the other side of town, at the strategic juncture of major highways leading into the city from the north.[42] It took him little time to get back on his feet. "He was a good businessman, he lived a good life," says his nephew Moshe Silberberg. Gustawa, who was bright and energetic and involved in "all kinds of philanthropic activity," according to Dolek, helped him build his business.[43] As for Szmil-

Zawel's several daughters, they either married, established their own shops, or moved to America.

On the other hand, Szmil-Zawel's youngest sons, Julius and Mark, had a tougher time finding their way. World War I had devastated the Polish economy. The occupying armies of Germany and Russia plundered the country's industrial plant and rolling stock. The Polish textile industry's Russian market vanished after the Bolshevik Revolution. Then the hyperinflation of the early 1920s stymied recovery. No sooner had a modicum of prosperity returned than the Great Depression struck. Unemployment soared to 50 percent among industrial workers. Several of Łódź's large textile firms, teetering on the edge of bankruptcy, were reduced to renting factory floor space to smaller firms.

The hard times spread to the building trades, particularly the lumber industry, which was drawing fire from the newly independent Polish state because of the prevalence of Jewish ownership, and the government in Warsaw sought to push Jews out of the industry so as to make room for Polish entrepreneurs.[44] These were hardly propitious times for entering the lumber business, to say the least. But a place was found for Julius. Shortly after their arrival from Kielce, Julius left his father's house and moved in with Wladek and Gustawa to help manage the northside lumberyard. "He was a logging expert," Anne's mother, Ruth, said. Able to tell the age of trees at a glance, he traveled the forests to select timber for cutting.

Born in 1900, the youngest son of five, Mark was last in line to be brought into the wood business. From time to time he worked for his older brothers, traveling to Horyniec when circumstances required and learning the ins and outs of the trade. He spent two years in trade school as a mechanic and then worked at "wood-making machines."[45] But soon he decided to strike out on his own. Sometime in the 1920s he established a small construction firm and carpentry shop in an apartment courtyard at Piotrkowska 61. Piotrkowska Street was the retail center of Łódź, and Mark's shop was in the heart of downtown. Given his knowledge of wood and machinery, the career choice made sense. He had the gift of craftsmanship. According to Pola Skorecka, a cousin from Działoszyce who survived by passing as an Aryan and today lives in Haifa: "Mark was so capable. He knew everything. He had 'golden hands.'" Mark was adept at building furniture. He did some contracting work at the Poznański Palace. But mostly he built houses, often from the drawing board up. He built a summer home in the country for Stefa and her family: "He was engineer and carpenter," stated Stefa's son Moshe Silberberg. "He made everything. He made the plan. He was the architect. He bought the material. He was an excellent worker." "He was gifted," Dolek adds.[46]

Mark met his future wife at a party. Born in Łódź in 1905, the daughter of a local watchmaker, Ruth Tempelhof was a vivacious, handsome woman with flashing eyes, dark, curly hair, and a smile that could light up a room. She was a smart dresser and, to use her words, "was used to nice things and loved a nice home." Like Mark's family, her parents, Abram and Sara Tempelhof, had emigrated to Łódź early in the century from small towns in southern Poland. Abram Tempelhof's jewelry shop was at Gdańsk 20, where the family lived, a scant three blocks from the Poznański textile factory and palace. "I gathered that her family had been kind of well-to-do people," says Lorena Doerries, an American neighbor with whom she became friendly in postwar New Orleans. But Ruth was idealizing her prewar past in ways survivors sometimes do.[47] According to a financial aid statement submitted in 1936 by his son Henry to the Warsaw Polytechnic University and confirmed by the Łódź Bureau of the Treasury, Abram Tempelhof owned no real estate and was scraping by on sixteen hundred zlotys a year. But Abram, who claimed "bourgeois origins" in papers he filed with city authorities in 1931, and Sara raised their three children—Ruth (the oldest), Henry, and Vovek—to aim higher in life and to appreciate art and music.[48]

Ruth was a real catch for Mark. She had a lot of suitors as a young woman. Mark, five and a half feet tall, with thinning hair and a spare frame, was good looking but not eye-catchingly handsome. "I don't think he was as glamorous as some of her beaus," says Lorena Doerries.[49] "She didn't say that, but that was my impression." But Mark possessed a sly sense of humor. And, according to a fellow displaced person with whom he was in business for a few years in postwar Germany, "He was very decisive. He knew where he was going."[50]

Those qualities impressed Ruth's mother, Sara, too—that and his practical talent for life. "My mother always told me, 'Mark's a good man to marry. He will take care of you through it all.'" As it happened, Sara Tempelhof was prescient.[51] Mark and Ruth were wed on September 1, 1931, by a rabbi, although eight years would elapse before they got around to registering their marriage with civil authorities.

Ruth, like her husband, was nominally Orthodox. She kept a kosher kitchen, without going to the trouble of maintaining separate sets of dishes for milk and meat. She lit Shabbas candles every Friday night. "I know she did it," Anne says. "I saw the menorah there. But she didn't include us in it as parents do today. It was done very quietly and very privately." Suspended between modernity and tradition, as were a lot of urban Jews of her generation, Ruth did not so much break from Orthodoxy as narrow the scope of its influence.[52] Clearly, she was determined to control her reproductive life and not be chained to years of pregnancy and breast-feeding. "My mother always emphasized that she waited four years before settling down with a family," Anne says, "because she wanted to enjoy married life."

Their first years of marriage were fun-filled. Łódź had its share of diversions. "I came from a big city," Ruth said. She and Mark attended concerts and went to nightclubs. She hosted parties and sit-down dinners. She aspired to a good living, hoping one day to have a piano in the parlor, that her children might learn to play. "Ruth wanted to live rich," according to Moshe Silberberg.[53]

Those bourgeois aspirations, however, created strains in the marriage. Mark was better at carpentry than business. Often he would do favors for strangers without charge, or charge them too little. The summer home he built in the country for Stefa and her family he did without pay, because of his closeness to Stefa. "Mark was a helpful person," Silberberg says. "If he had food, you had to have some with him. Ruth used to say, 'Why do you make things for strangers and do nothing for the house?'" She often pressured Mark to earn more money. The strain affected her relationship with the other Skoreckis, who thought she cared for nothing else but money, which was far from the case. The 1930s were straitened times, powerfully focusing attention on matters of livelihood. Yet it is true that Ruth was a social striver, acquisitive, ambitious, and concerned to a fault with appearances. The irony is, during the Holocaust, when survival itself often turned on sensitivity to the perceptions of strangers, Ruth's social ambition would alchemize into a lifesaving skill.

Eventually, Mark started to make headway in his business despite the Great Depression. He hired a full-time helper in his shop. By the mid-1930s he was able to afford to send Ruth to one of Łódź's better hospitals to give birth to their daughters.[54] Nice consumer items began appearing in their home. "I remember they had a radio, which was an oddity for that time," says Ruth Gerver, who visited Mark and Ruth's apartment during her childhood trip to Łódź in 1934.[55] Not long before the war, Mark took his family to the Zakopane ski resort in the Great Tatry Mountains, where Ruth, Anne, and Lila acquired fur coats—a sure sign of status in prewar Poland.

By 1937 Mark moved his family into a comfortable flat in one of Łódź's newest and most fashionable apartment buildings, at Legionów 8 (since renamed Zielona Street) on the corner of Allee Kościuszko. Reminiscent of the late-nineteenth-century rent palaces erected in Vienna's Ringstrasse by the city's triumphant bourgeoisie, the five-story neo-Baroque structure sprawled over an entire city block. "The building where we used to live was the biggest building on the map," Mark said in 1983, with evident pride, during a family reunion at a New Orleans restaurant.[56] On the front of the building huge columns reached between the second and fourth floors, suffocating a tiny royal balcony. A rusticated band of smooth and rough stone girdled the ground floor. Across Legionów Street nestled a small park. On the other side of Allee Kościuszko rose the majestic Kościuszko Synagogue, one of Poland's two Reformed temples. "Rich Jews lived at Zielona [Legionów] 8 before the war," notes the state archivist in Łódź. "Merchants, intelligentsia, because it was the center of the city. Even owners of buildings and factories lived there."[57]

Many of the occupants belonged to the Kościuszko congregation. Their ten-room flats took up the second and third floors, where the landlord, Mieczysław Pinkus, himself a Reformed Jew, also made his residence. A school and a veterans' office occupied the ground floor. But Mark, Ruth, and the children lived on the fourth floor, which had been carved into modest flats for the building's janitorial and maintenance staff. Mark had taken one of the maintenance jobs (presumably in lieu of rent) while continuing to build up his construction business. He may even have been involved in construction of the building, which was probably erected between 1932 and 1937.[58] Although the apartment had only two bedrooms and a kitchen, it was large enough to accommodate a live-in Polish maid named Mary, whom Ruth had hired to help with the children. The new apartment also had the added advantage of being only four blocks from Mark's shop on Piotrkowska Street and from the apartment on Gdańsk of Ruth's parents. Somewhat farther away, at Legionów 55, lived Wladek and Gustawa.

For Anne, the last year before the war was special, "my most tender moments of remembering," as she puts it. Mark had rented a country place in Głowno, thirty miles northeast of Łódź, on the highway to Warsaw, and Ruth and the girls spent three and a half months there each summer. Mark came up every weekend, sometimes bringing with him Ruth's older brother, Henry, and her parents for a visit. Like young children generally, Anne wrung pleasure out of household utensils, filling measuring cups with dry beans and loading them onto the kitchen scale. Surviving photographs from that time show her and Lila digging in the sand with bucket and shovels, broad grins splashed across their faces. In another picture Anne is wearing a sailor's costume. "My parents tried to dress me up like Shirley Temple," she says.

She was a bit of a tomboy as a preschooler, a risk taker. "I remember my mother telling me how Anne used to climb in the doghouse with the dog while I was afraid to go near it," Anne's younger sister Lila says. "She was brave in that way and wasn't as afraid of as many things as I was." "I was a daredevil even then," Anne says.

Back in Łódź, Mark used to take Anne out for strolls to buy balloons or scoops of ice cream from Russian street vendors. The memories of those times have special poignancy. "They were the only moments I remember of a warm and cuddly father," Anne says today. "After that there was no more."

It is obvious in hindsight that Ruth realized some of her social aspirations through Henry Tempelhof, her engineer-brother. When she mentioned him after the war it was always to brag about his university training in Warsaw and his good looks. "She used to tell me he was smart and handsome and had become a professional and was doing well when the war came," says Adam, the son born in a postwar German displaced persons center. "In her mind she wanted me to be like him." Holocaust survivors commonly look on their children as magical replacements for murdered loved ones. But Ruth's psychological projections are all the more understandable because of the physical resemblance between Henry and her son. Adam had his uncle's dark good looks, the same mouth and eyes. Both were roughly the same height. "My mother said her brother was tall," says Lila.[59]

For a Polish Jew, Henry was relatively tall, "between 5′10″ and 5′11″, as I remember, and his younger brother [Vovek] was maybe an inch and a half taller," says Dr. Thaddeus Stabholz, who is semiretired from medical practice in Canton, Ohio, and, like several other Warsaw Ghetto survivors, was well enough acquainted with Henry Tempelhof to mention him in his postwar memoirs.[60] Stabholz had gotten to know Henry and his younger brother during the war, when all three worked at the famous Jewish hospital on Dworska Street in Warsaw. In 1939 the Czyste Hospital was Poland's largest medical facility, and Stabholz's father, a well-known surgeon named Henryk Stabholz, was then in charge of the hospital. During the Nazi occupation and after the hospital was broken up and relocated to the ghetto, Henry became the medical institution's office manager, which meant he was responsible for administering Czyste's physical plant and technical services and certifying official documents. His name appears frequently in hospital records that survived the war. Though eight years his junior, Stabholz saw Henry in social situations from time to time, and they talked whenever their paths crossed at the hospital. "I still have a mental picture of Henry," he says. "One thing I won't forget is his smile. Not really a full smile, but some kind of half smile—a grin. He always wore that grin. I think it was because he was full of humor during a very tragic situation. And when he spoke it was in short, one-sentence expressions. I cannot explain it to you, but if you talked to him, you realized he's somebody." But Anne's uncle was also extremely private. His natural good cheer masked a guarded reserve.[61]

Ruth had reason to take pride in Henry's achievements. In the best of times it was hard enough to meet stiff Polish university entrance requirements. During the interwar period, however, Jews faced special obstacles. The chief hurdle was an unofficial but effective quota called the *numerus clausus* that took effect in 1923. The project of right-wing ultranationalists, the quota aimed at reducing Jewish enrollments to the same proportion that Jews represented in the population at large, which was 10 percent. In 1929, the year Henry matriculated, one-fifth of the overall student body of Polish universities was Jewish; in 1938, when he graduated, the number had fallen to less than 7.5 percent (and 4 percent on Warsaw's campuses, where he was in attendance). On the eve of World War II, Polish anti-Semites were clamoring not merely for lowering Jewish enrollment but also for eliminating Jewish students altogether, and they were growing bolder in their use of violence.[62]

There is no question that anti-Semitism had deep roots in Poland. The deepest sprang from religion, "the supreme divider."[63] The same anti-Semitic folklore that had fueled the expulsion of Jews from western Europe also seeped through Polish Catholicism at every level: Jews were Christ killers who reenacted the crucifixion for fun and sport; they murdered gentile children to use their blood to spice Passover matzo balls; they tortured babies with the barbaric ritual of circumcision; they spread the plague and poisoned wells. Equally defamatory were economic stereotypes stemming from their caste function in the feudal economy. Jewish merchants and petty traders were cunning cheats, and Jewish tavern keepers and moneylenders, Shylocks and connivers. The economic stereotypes bred resentment of Jewish achievement; the religious stereotypes engendered fear of Jewish difference. Together they made episodic pogroms a fact of life. The bloodiest explosion, resulting in tens of thousands of Jewish deaths, occurred during the Cossack-Peasant Uprising of 1648 led by Chmielnicki, which unleashed a century-long frenzy of blood libel accusations.[64] More common were the flare-ups on Easter Sunday and Corpus Christi Day (since, to quote one survivor, "the readiness to beat Jews was proportional to piety"). Market days were likewise attended by frequent tumults, usually after some peasant drank away his profits at a Jewish tavern and cried out, "The Jew has cheated me!"[65]

In fact, so deeply rooted was anti-Semitism in Polish culture that "Zyd"—the word for Jew—was highly charged with negative connotations. It grated on Polish ears, evoking distasteful imagery. Kindly disposed Poles lessened the word's sting by prefacing it with benign adjectives, as in "decent Jew" or "little Jew." To be sure, Jews had their own invidious stereotypes concerning the goyim, and in the countryside Jew and peasant regarded each other with mutual suspicion, fear, envy, but sometimes affection. Still, Polish Jews were a derided people, and "Zyd" possessed about the same idiomatic status that "nigger" does in the American vernacular. Indeed, one sociologist has gone so far as to describe Jews as "the Negroes of Poland." The comparison is a little strained in view of the commercial importance of Polish Jews vis-à-vis the economic marginality of American blacks. A closer analogy is to the free black Creoles of slaveholding New Orleans, who were also relegated to pariah status notwithstanding their craft skill, substantial wealth, educational attainment, and even blood ties to the white elite.[66]

All the same, Poland's traditional anti-Semitism seemed like a low-grade fever next to the delirium that seized the country after 1918, when Poland regained its long-lost independence following the collapse of the three partitioning empires. Now an exclusivist nationalism, often as vehement as the ethnic particularism flaring in areas of the post-Soviet empire, quickly overwhelmed Poland's increasingly feeble traditions of multicultural toleration. The main carrier of the new nativism was an ultra-right-wing movement led by the gifted Roman Dmowski and his National Democratic Party, whose followers were called Endeks (after Endecja, the party's acronym). Dmowski's slogan "Poland for the Poles" rallied the country's growing middle class in the cities, who blamed upwardly mobile Jews such as Henry Tempelhof for Poland's postwar economic slump.

But Polish Jews were not the sole targets of Endek wrath. As a result of the Treaty of Versailles, 30 percent of Poland's newly configured territory was made up of ethnic minorities—Ukrainians, Byelorussians, Jews, and Germans—and their status became a political football when the new successor state was forced to sign a treaty guaranteeing the rights of local minorities. The Ukrainians, the country's largest minority, as well as the Ruthenians, both of whom lived mainly in the kresy, on the eastern frontier, were often on the receiving end of Polish xenophobia, as were German landowners in the former German districts of Posen and the so-called Polish Corridor, which had been carved out of the old reich so as to give Poland access to the sea. Each group responded with its own defensive nationalism. Polish Jews followed suit by gravitating in growing numbers to political Zionism. Yet, Ukrainian, Ruthenian, and Polish nationalists shared one thing that Jews did not: they all viewed the latter as a dangerous foreign element incapable of assimilating into their national culture. Roman Dmowski's Endecja, increasingly reflecting the *völkisch* nationalism brewing in neighboring Germany, attacked Jews as rootless internationalists (never mind that they had been residing in Poland for nearly a thousand years), accusing them of spreading communism *and* capitalism—the twin bedmates of materialism. Jews were everyone's favorite target. They were the principal victims of the rash of pogroms that swept the country in 1918 and 1919.[67] They caught most of the brunt of the economic boycott movement during the 1920s and 1930s. "There was anti-Semitism when I was a boy," remembers Dolek Skorecki. "Poles were displaying signs saying, 'Buy only from your nationality. Don't buy from Jews.'" His mother's liquor store in Kielce, which did a booming business in vodka and wine when Polish peasants got married, was at constant risk.[68]

But as bad as things were on main street, they were even worse in the universities. Just as racial anti-Semitism enjoyed wide support among German and Austrian university students during the interwar years, so did Endecja appeals find great resonance with nationalist youth in Poland's institutions of higher learning. Sixty percent of the gentile students endorsed the Endek program, and they could look to the support of three-fourths of their professors. It was Henry Tempelhof's misfortune to have been a Polish university student at the very time anti-Semitic agitation reached a crescendo.[69]

Graduating from Łódź's technical high school for Jews, Henry Tempelhof matriculated at the Warsaw Polytechnic University in September 1928, just as the campaign to limit Jewish enrollment was shifting into high gear. Housed in a Beaux Arts building famous for its glass-roofed, marbled atrium and founded by one of Poland's leading Jewish railroad builders, Warsaw Polytechnic was the country's preeminent school of engineering.[70] Twenty-year-old Henry enrolled in the university's mechanical engineering division, combining practical coursework in metal pouring with classes in higher mathematics. Three years later he passed his first battery of comprehensive examinations with respectable scores. But then his health began breaking down. He developed a chronic kidney illness. Tumors showed up on his intestines. He blamed his medical problems on the economic pressure that dogged him relentlessly. His watchmaker father, like many small Jewish tradesmen during the Great Depression, was unable to help out financially, forcing Henry to find work as a clerk in the university's Jewish Students Mutual Aid Society. "Because of the rigorous circumstances of existence," Henry wrote in a 1935 petition to the university requesting a temporary tuition waiver, "I became very ill in February of present year and was forced to undergo an operation to remove a growth on the large intestine." It was no ordinary growth. The doctors at Warsaw University's Józef Piłsudski Surgical Clinic had discovered a malignant tumor on the right side of his colon.[71]

Colon cancer is deadly enough when it attacks older men, its prime target: today nearly 60 percent of its victims eventually die from the disease. But it is a particularly ruthless killer of the young because of their vigorous metabolism, which accelerates the carcinoma's metastatic growth. Only twenty-seven years old when doctors diagnosed his condition, Henry most certainly inherited a predisposition toward his disease, and the prognosis was not good despite the fact that right-sided colon cancer has a better recovery rate than cancers occurring elsewhere in the digestive tract. In the 1920s only one in four cases was even operable, and half of these surgery candidates died in the hospital. Of the survivors, 75 percent suffered a prompt recurrence of the disease. Henry's chances of celebrating his thirtieth birthday were probably no better than one in twenty.[72]

Notwithstanding the long odds, doctors at the clinic decided to operate. It was a multistage procedure. Between March and July they performed four operations and then sent Henry to the well-known Jewish sanatorium in nearby Otwock to convalesce. By September 1935, Henry was back in the surgical clinic, where he remained until April 1936. Then he underwent a fifth and, he hoped, final operation. The operations were successful. Surgeons used resection techniques to reroute Henry's digestive tract and close him back up again. His cancer went into remission.[73]

The disease threw Henry's life into turmoil, however. The fourteen-month hospital stay not only interrupted his studies and reduced his income but also added new expenses. "I find myself in critical material circumstances," he told university authorities in November 1936. "My income barely covers my room and board, especially since the state of my health demands [a] very intensive diet." After nearly eight years at the Polytechnic University, he was in worse financial condition than when he began, with no prospect of quick improvement, and he still had three years of classwork ahead of him. He petitioned the university for tuition waivers and permission to defer overdue payments on outstanding student loans.[74]

Mery Mejnster, his soon-to-be wife, had financial problems of her own. How she and Henry met is unclear. They probably knew each other in Łódź: her parents' home, at Gdańsk 31, was only a few doors away from the Tempelhof apartment. Possibly they became better acquainted while Henry was convalescing in the surgery unit at Warsaw University, where Mery was studying to be a surgeon. "It was very, very unusual for a woman then to be a doctor, particularly a surgeon," Dr. Thaddeus Stabholz says. "I only knew of one, and she was a dental surgeon. So Mery was like something special." Tall, with an oval face, dark hair, and hazel eyes, she was only seventeen when she began medical studies in 1929. Having earned straight As in one of Łódź's selective college preparatory schools, and top scores on competitive national exams, she continued making high marks during her first two years at the university.[75] A woman and a Jew needed a stellar academic record to withstand the fierce anti-Semitism then afflicting Polish medicine. The medical faculties were in the forefront of the effort to limit Jewish enrollment. Three years before her matriculation, the anatomy department had declared that Jewish students could handle only Jewish cadavers, lest they profane "consecrated corpses." Because of Orthodox Judaism's strictures against dissection, the Czyste Hospital had difficulty supplying the requisite number of cadavers. "It was a really big problem," remembers Dr. Stabholz, who began medical studies at Warsaw University in 1937. "We had three to four Jewish students to a body, while the ratio was half that for non-Jewish students. So there were fights back and forth." Mery's response was to score "excellent" on her first-year exams, especially in pathology.[76]

But then her finances, like Henry's, gave out. She had never been able to take advantage of Warsaw's lively night life, with its many theaters and nightclubs. Those diversions were available mainly to classmates whose fathers were bankers and physicians.[77] After her second year of medical school, Mery spent most of her free time doing private tutoring to pay the rent and earn a daily meal. "I depend totally on my own resources," she explained in 1932. "I scratch for my living by giving lessons, which this year is very difficult." The university granted her a tuition waiver. The following school term her budget was stretched to the breaking point after her father, a Łódź contractor, abandoned the family and moved to Paris, forcing Mery to take her mother and younger brother into her Warsaw apartment. "To obtain enough tutoring to support three people with whatever work is possible is right now very hard," she wrote the university in 1934, with some understatement. "I find myself in a hopeless situation." The school awarded her a loan of three hundred zlotys (then about sixty dollars).[78]

Meanwhile, according to her transcript, Mery's grades began to suffer. One reason was grade discrimination against Jewish students. "I remember my father mentioning he always asked why everybody always had Cs, nobody had Bs, and him explaining that it was a problem with the professors," notes Stabholz. Stabholz himself never earned higher than a C, which was true of most of his friends. No one complained. "As long as we passed, it was fine."[79]

But the rising tide of anti-Semitic violence on Polish campuses doubtless had something to do with Mery's falling grades as well. From 1931 onward, Jewish students could hardly exit university gates without being physically molested by gentile classmates. Many assailants, their hats cocked to one side, with green ribbons in their lapels to advertise Endek sympathies, went armed with canes and knives. They often belonged to exclusive college fraternities or radical fascist student groups that had splintered off from the Endecja. Soon professional thugs got in on the action by donning student caps and invading lecture halls, brandishing sticks in which narrow grooves had been carved for inserting barely concealed razor blades. One lecturer came late to class to allow the hooligans enough time to clear Jews from the classroom. The assaults reached a zenith at the beginning of the new term. "Autumn manoeuvres," they were called. One of Mery's classmates quit wearing glasses to protect his vision. "I preferred a slight squint in my right eye to broken glass," he wrote.[80]

Dr. Stabholz recalls a bloody incident during an anatomy class when Endek hooligans attacked Jewish students at work in the back of a large lab. One of his classmates, George Szapiro, a large, strapping fellow who is now a neurologist in Warsaw, used a shin bone in self-defense and received a large head wound. A very pretty, blonde-haired, blue-eyed female student was beaten severely. "She was quite bloody," Stabholz says. The agitation never let up. "The Jewish students were on edge all the time," he says. "It was a sort of mental cruelty, if nothing else, and we tried to make a big joke out of it. But it was not a big joke at all. It was a pretty unpleasant memory, very unpleasant."[81]

Although the Endecja never won national power, it did push the political center—occupied by the political allies of Marshal Józef Piłsudski, the father of modern Poland—far to the anti-Semitic right. By 1937, two years after Piłsudski's death, an increasingly weak coalition government had capitulated almost completely to extremist demands, so as to distract attention from its inability to govern. That was the year academic authorities caved in to Endek pressure to create "ghetto benches" on the left side of the lecture halls exclusively for Jewish students. A lot of Jews stood next to the wall in silent protest. "When I studied medicine," Dr. Stabholz says, "we were standing instead of sitting." The defiance often provoked anti-Semites into further acts of violence.[82]

Mery graduated in 1935, two years before the "ghetto bench" policy took effect, but Henry was unable to complete his studies until 1938, and he thus experienced the worst of the anti-Semitic harassment. By now Hitlerian views had achieved mainstream respectability, with a major Catholic publication declaring in February, "Anti-semitism without racism is incomplete." Anti-Semites were now also clamoring for expelling Jewish students, not merely limiting their numbers. And the ruffians who harassed Mery and her classmates and circulated freely among all Warsaw's university campuses were openly advocating "Brownshirt" thuggery. A 1937 student leaflet preached: "Just think: you meet a Jew or a Communist in some dark place. And you set about him! You lay into him, driving the metal into his teeth! Just don't back away, you milksop!"[83]

A debate is currently raging among historians over whether the interwar period in Poland was a prelude to the Holocaust, a time when Jews were pushed to the "edge of destruction," after which the Nazis came along and pushed them over. It is misleading to claim, as some have, that the anti-Semitic excesses of the 1920s and 1930s prefigured the extermination of the 1940s. But there is no denying that the exclusivist nationalism that flourished in Poland on war's eve—among Poles, Ukrainians, Ruthenians, and Byelorussians alike— had lowered gentile resistance to Nazi genocide, making it easier to collaborate in the killing project by placing Jews outside the boundaries of ordinary moral obligation.[84]

The situation that faced such budding Jewish professionals as Henry Tempelhof and Mery Mejnster scarcely improved upon graduation. In 1937 Poland's medical, engineering, and bar associations adopted so-called Aryan paragraphs prohibiting Jewish membership, making it practically impossible for Jews to practice their professions. The rearmament of the 1930s increased demand for engineers—but not for Jewish engineers. Many university-educated Jews either left the country to find employment or slipped into the status of *Luftmenschen*—literally "people of the air," people without prospects and means of support.[85] Mery had a particularly hard time establishing a professional practice. The fact that she shared cramped space with her mother in a fourth-floor walk-up hampered her opening an office in her residence. So she continued tutoring. She occasionally worked as a translator and editor for a medical publication in Warsaw. All the while, she interned without pay in a Warsaw hospital (probably Czyste). In 1937 she petitioned the university for a loan moratorium, given her low earnings of less than 160 zlotys a month. "My income is not sufficient to support two people," she wrote the university (her brother was on his own by now). "I am constantly forced to take out loans." She was not asking the university to forgive her school loan, only to postpone repayment for two years. The university granted her a ten-month delay. Sometime in 1938 or 1939 Mery finally found a position in a surgical unit at Czyste Hospital.[86]

Miraculously, Henry succeeded in opening an engineering office in his Warsaw apartment following graduation. But a short time later medical odds caught up with him. In 1939, four years after the first diagnosis, his cancer returned and he went in for more surgery. This time the doctors performed a colostomy. The procedure, which was then common in America but extremely rare in Poland, entailed closing up the rectum and creating an exterior opening in the abdomen for attaching an external collection bag. Henry's pouch was connected to a part of the colon where the fecal current is liquid and control over bowel movements is difficult to achieve. His bag probably had to be emptied several times a day and the opening irrigated regularly. The technology was fairly primitive. "You could be in an elevator now with ten people wearing a bag and you would never know it," explains a New Orleans surgeon. "But in those days you could pick up the scent of one person a block away. The bags leaked a lot."[87] It is not surprising that colostomy patients tended to become reclusive, embarrassed to go out in public. The sense of reserve beneath Henry's legendary grin had much to do with his medical condition.

So, for that matter, did his entire personality. Then, there were no self-help manuals available to instruct persons with dread diseases how to cope psychologically with their anger, denial, and frustration. It was easy to give in to depression, which inhibited recovery and hastened death. "Every seriously ill person needs to develop a style for his illness," wrote Anatole Broyard, the *New York Times* literary critic who ultimately lost his bout with prostate cancer, "[and] only by insisting on your style can you keep from falling out of love with yourself as the illness attempts to diminish or disfigure you." Norman Cousins, in *Anatomy of an Illness*, recounts how he laughed himself well.[88]

Against lethal odds, Henry seems to have grinned his way back to health. He emerged from the colostomy operation with the same good humor he would wear during the Warsaw Ghetto's darkest days. But few people at the time knew just how much his outlook on life probably stemmed from his medical condition. He kept his health problems to himself. "I never realized he had had a colostomy until the chief of surgery at Czyste, who used to marvel at Henry's nonchalance, told me about it," says Dr. Stabholz. "Henry was not the kind of person who would talk much about himself."[89]

Nor was Mery very self-revealing. Colleagues who worked with her in the Warsaw Ghetto remember her as polite but distant. Sometime in 1938 or 1939, she and Henry Tempelhof were married, and no one seems to have known about it save immediate relatives, although their marital status was reflected in the records of Czyste Hospital.[90] "All the time I thought she was a spinster," says Mark Balin, her fellow surgeon from Czyste days. They also neglected to solemnize their union with civil authorities, but this was not uncommon. "Jews frequently didn't register their marriages and birth dates until their children were five or six, even twelve," noted the deputy manager of the Łódź Public Records Office.[91] Whatever Henry and Mery's ultimate plans, the war soon threw them into disarray.

It was not until May 8, 1939, that Ruth and Mark registered their own marriage as well as the births of Anne and Lila. The timing was not fortuitous. Two weeks earlier, in response to Hitler's demand that Warsaw retrocede the land corridor separating the Reich from the free port of Danzig, Poland had repudiated its 1934 nonaggression pact with Germany and called up reservists. Coming hard upon the Nazi takeover of the rump state of Czechoslovakia, the diplomatic break triggered a war of nerves.[92] "My parents must have had a premonition that Germany was about to attack," Anne explains. Confusion must have reigned at the Łódź bureau the day Mark and Ruth showed up: that is the best explanation for the perplexing affidavits they recorded under their signatures. Not only did they misdate their marriage—1938 instead of 1931— but they listed Anne's and Lila's births as having occurred in 1934 and 1936, exactly a year earlier than the dates Ruth had always insisted were their real birthdays.

The confusion over Anne's and Lila's birthdays was not the only surprise contained in Polish archives. Henry Tempelhof's cancer was a revelation as well. "My mother never mentioned it," Anne says. "She must have known about it because he was hospitalized for such a long time. Maybe she was feeling he went through all of this pain and agony and illness, finished school, became this outstanding human being, and it was all for naught. That's probably what was going through my mom's mind."

As they had in the past, Ruth and the children spent the summer at their country place in Głowno. But war clouds continued to darken the horizon. Among Polish Jews such as the Skoreckis, there was no casual drifting into disaster, as with the vacationers in Aharon Appelfeld's novel *Badenheim 1939*. "We were all the time thinking about war and talking," Ruth said, "making plans in case something happened." By mid-August war seemed imminent. Poland belonged to that half-mythical "German East," where Teutonic knights long ago had sowed the seeds of Germandom and the armies of Hindenburg and Ludendorff had scored Wilhelmine Germany's greatest victories during the Great War. But it was also the sphere where the old reich had suffered its worst territorial losses at the hands of Versailles negotiators, and recovering those ceded territories had been the aim of German foreign policy long before Hitler rose to power.[93]

Just before the invasion, Hitler escalated his territorial demands by insisting on the retrocession of Danzig itself. "The newspapers shriek that the final crisis will come in the next two weeks," wrote a Łódź diarist on August 21.[94] Mark came up to Głowno on Saturday, August 19, just as the Danzig crisis started to boil. The family had to cut its vacation short, he said. The farmer who brought them back and forth from Łódź every summer carried the Skoreckis and their belongings back to the city. It was Tuesday, August 22. The following day, Germany and the Soviet Union announced their signing of a twenty-five-year nonaggression pact. Poland responded by calling up army reservists. Volunteers rushed to dig antiaircraft trenches. There was a run on grocery stores. Back in her Legionów apartment, Ruth immediately began preparing food for the likely emergency. "We were listening to the news and watching," she said.[95]

Her concern was well founded. Home to a large disaffected German minority and the center of Polish industrial might, Łódź was a scant three hours by train from Berlin. The city lay in the path of invasion. "If a war started between Poland and Germany, we would be the first to get it," Ruth said. Little did she imagine how devastating the Nazi onslaught would turn out to be.[96]

Top: Mark Skorecki, Adam Skorecki, and unidentified World War I soldier, ca. 1919–21. Mark is the soldier in the middle. His nephew and close friend Adam, Morris's son, is on the right.

Left: Natalia and Szmil-Zawel Skorecki in the summer of 1934, probably at the couple's country dacha outside Łódź. Szmil-Zawel died a few months after the photo was taken.

Julius Skorecki in the summer of 1934. Always well dressed, Mark's older brother Julius was a seasoned forestry expert, skilled at selecting stands of timber for purchase by the family's lumberyards.

Facing page, top: Anne and Lila with their Polish maid, probably in 1938. This is the maid who, early in the German occupation, helped Ruth transfer some of her belongings into her brother's safekeeping in Warsaw.

Facing page, bottom: Anne and Lila playing in the sand, probably in the summer of 1939, just before the German invasion.

Top: Mery Mejnster's Warsaw University student photo, probably taken in 1929, when she was seventeen years old.

Bottom: Henry Tempelhof's Warsaw Polytechnic University student photo, probably taken in 1928, when he was twenty years old.

Mark and Ruth Skorecki, Abram, Sara, and Henry Tempelhof, with Anne as child. The picture was probably taken in the summer of 1937 at the country place near Głowno that Mark and Ruth had purchased. Mark and Ruth are in the middle; Sara Tempelhof is on the left; Henry and his father Abram, the watchmaker, are on the right.

Three

FROM ŁÓDŹ TO WARSAW

The Second World War began before daybreak on September 1, Mark and Ruth Skorecki's eighth wedding anniversary, when sixty Wehrmacht divisions coming from four directions smashed across the Polish border. Two days later, just after Sunday dinner, incendiary bombs fell on Łódź. The Skoreckis and the other residents of Legionów 8 fled to the cellar. The bombing ceased around two in the morning on September 5. Mark and some of his male neighbors climbed to the street to survey the damage. They brought back disturbing news that personnel in the veterans' office on the ground floor were hurriedly destroying records. "They were afraid," Ruth said of the government officials. "They couldn't keep the promises given to us. Nothing could stop the Germans now." On the fifth day of the invasion, when the Polish government ordered all able-bodied men to the east, where the Polish army would regroup for a counterattack, panic and defeatism seized the city. A mass exodus ensued. Soon all the highways leading from Łódź became thronged with refugees—reservists as well as women, children, and the elderly. Many were on foot, bundles on their backs.[1]

That Wednesday morning, Mark and Ruth, along with their two young daughters, gathered at her parents' apartment on Gdańsk Street to decide what to do. Mark wanted to join the other men who were leaving the city to regroup in the east. Ruth's younger brother Wolf, or Vovek, then sixteen, begged to go with him. Mark said he might travel to Horyniec, southeast of Lublin, to look in on his late brother Morris's lumber mill—but only if conditions were right. After Morris's death no one from the family was at the site to watch over the business. One son had committed suicide. The other son, Adam, who had served with Mark in World War I, was still in Paris. Ruth was unsure how to answer. "I was with two very small children," she said. "But when everyone was going, it was very hard to decide what to tell him." She ended up giving her consent, though she could not have been pleased. She had two young daughters to look after, and bombs were raining down around her.

Mark left her with all their money. "I don't need anything because I am coming back in a few days," he said. Then he kissed everyone goodbye and left with young Wolf. It was September 6. Everyone still believed that Poland's allies, Britain and France, would soon attack and force the invaders to retreat. "A lot of the men left thinking, 'Ah, this war will last a couple of days, and, besides, nobody is going to harm the women and children,'" Anne says. But the war lasted nearly six years, and women were not spared. Nor were children—especially children. They represented a biological future Hitler would eventually try to have canceled. It is sobering how close he came to succeeding.

Not many Jewish men who fled east ever returned. They made up a substantial segment of communal leadership: Jewish members of the Sejm (the Polish parliament), leaders of various Jewish parties, seasoned political activists. They all stayed away, leaving behind a vacuum of weakness and confusion that leaders of the youth-dominated underground were able to fill only with great difficulty.[2]

Wolf returned after only an hour on the road. Choked highways had blocked his path. "You will never believe what I saw on the highways," he said. German dive-bombers and Messerschmidts were strafing columns of refugees. Corpses littered the roadside. The scene was everywhere the same in western Poland. The next day Łódźites heard the boom of approaching artillery. A red glow lit the southern horizon. By Friday, September 8, advance detachments of the Wehrmacht were patrolling on Piotrkowska Street, the main thoroughfare where Mark kept his shop.[3] "Small troops at first and then later the tanks and big troops," Ruth said. All the while, refugees by the thousands were swarming back to the city, but Mark was not among them. Nor did his remains turn up in the improvised morgues filled with bodies retrieved from surrounding fields and highways. Ruth checked them all.

Military resistance elsewhere in Poland crumbled shortly after the Nazi occupation of Łódź. Stories of Polish cavalry charging German Panzers are mostly legend, but some suicidal attacks did occur. On September 17, Soviet forces invaded from the east to claim those parts of Poland handed over to Stalin under the secret protocols of the Molotov-Ribbentrop Non-Aggression Pact. Warsaw continued fighting even after the government evacuated the capital. Every day Polish radio blared Chopin's *Revolutionary Etude*, composed to commemorate the 1830 Polish uprising against Czarist Russia and a powerful symbol of Poland's peculiar strain of messianic nationalism. By September 23, the Nazis had bombed the station into silence. They then reduced the Old Town and Castle district to rubble, the first of a series of demolitions that by war's end would leave virtually all the city in ruins. Caught between Nazi and Soviet troops, the government formally surrendered on September 27. On Thursday, October 5, Hitler was already in Warsaw to review the victory parade.

Jewish leaders were scarcely alone in fleeing German armies. Much of the Poland's governing class had already slipped into Rumania. Later they would escape to France, finally alighting in London, where the Polish government-in-exile would maintain its headquarters for the remainder of the war. The decision to flee was the better part of valor. Nine days before the invasion Hitler had informed his generals that he intended to crush the enemy. "And so for the present," he continued, in one of his more famous speeches, "I have put my ss Death Heads formations in place with the command relentlessly and without compassion to send into death many women and children of Polish origin and language. Only thus can we gain the living space [*Lebensraum*] we need." Those early war aims harked back to the mystical *Drang nach Osten* (Drive to the East) foretold in Hitler's *Mein Kampf*, with its promise to supplant Slavs with German settlers. The first step was to stamp out Polish national consciousness by liquidating the country's elite. Before the occupation was three months old, mobile ss security units called *Einsatzgruppen*, operating in the rear of the army, had executed more than sixteen thousand Poles, many of them members of the clergy and intelligentsia. Five thousand were Jews. The decimation of the Polish elite was but a faint harbinger of what lay ahead. At this stage of the war, the German military objected to the terror campaign, which is why Hitler had tasked the ss with its prosecution. There would come a time when the Wehrmacht not only acquiesced but also played an active part in mass murder.[4]

For several weeks following Mark's departure Ruth and the children stayed in her parents' cramped apartment. She was filled with foreboding about the future. She had difficulty sleeping and worried about her ability to cope in her husband's absence. "The kids kept asking me everyday, 'Where is daddy?' and I had no answer for this question," she said. Buying coal and potatoes for the long winter ahead, Ruth sought sanity in daily routine. She stored the food and fuel in the cellar of her parents' apartment house. It was hard to find fresh bread. Long before the October chill, local inhabitants stood in bakery lines for six hours at a stretch and still came away empty handed. Often Nazi agents pulled Jews from the line. "A poor Jew who doesn't have a servant is condemned to death by hunger," commented one Łódź diarist.[5] Ruth was lucky to have a Polish servant. She still anguished over Mark's absence; it had been more than a month since he had left. She braced herself for the life of a single mother: "I made up my mind that I had to be father and mother for my two girls."

Ruth was not caught off guard by German persecution. Most Polish Jews had closely followed events in the neighboring Third Reich. "We knew very well from the time that Hitler came to power what he would do to other people," Ruth said. Before World War II began, the Nazi regime had rolled back a century-old emancipation, barring German Jews from universities and the professions, seizing their businesses, stripping them of citizenship, consigning them to a racial caste. It was a slow peeling away, as Karl Schleunes has written, of "layers of an assimilation that had been building up since the early nineteenth century."[6] Although interwar Poland had started down the same persecutory road, the anti-Semitic assault had been gradual, in both Germany and Poland, like the imposition of racial segregation in the American South during the late nineteenth and early twentieth centuries. Now, German occupiers struck with a force and concentration that left victims dazed and demoralized. In Łódź alone, before the year was out, the Nazis prohibited Jewish religious ceremonies, froze Jewish bank accounts, and transferred Jewish businesses to a German trusteeship. They disbanded Jewish organizations and institutions, transferring their functions to a puppet body called the Judenrat (Jewish council). They ordered Jews to stay off main streets like Piotrkowska and forbade their using trams and streetcars. They required Jewish adults to perform labor on the public works. Weekly the list of proscriptions grew longer: one day it was a new regulation (*Verordnung*), the next a new public notice (*Bekanntmachung*). Draped with Nazi flags, the streets of Łódź took on an eerie cast.[7]

The compulsory labor order made every Jewish pedestrian the potential prey of casual whim. "They started catching people like dogs in the street," Ruth said of the German roundups. "Old men, young men—high or low, it made no difference—were seized to clean out toilets, houses, streets, and to work in the yards." Some women were ordered to use their underwear to scrub floors and toilets. Invariably the dragnets led to extensive looting and bullying, not to mention outright sadism. One young diarist witnessed two German soldiers tie a Jewish pedestrian's legs to the rear bumper of a taxi cab and then order the driver to speed off. "The unfortunate man's face struck the sharp stones of the pavement, dyeing them red with blood."[8]

What hurt most was the response of some Polish neighbors. Adversity, instead of inspiring solidarity, fostered betrayal more often than not, as the boundaries of moral obligation narrowed to one's own kind. "Plenty of non-Jewish people, people who were working for my husband, people who I would never believe would do this, all turned German," Ruth said.

"I have never been so humiliated in my life as when I looked through the gate to the square and saw the happy, smiling mugs of passersby laughing at our misfortune," a Jewish gymnasium student recorded in his diary. He had been compelled to rake leaves and fill puddles in a German schoolyard.[9]

Ruth herself had a similar experience with the young Pole who had been a helper in Mark's shop on Piotrkowska Street. He had joined the Nazi-sponsored self-defense forces shortly after the invasion. One day he stopped by wearing a black German uniform. "What happened to you?" Ruth asked. "Right now I don't have to work," he said. "I have everything. I get money. They promise me things and I can do what I want." A few days later he returned demanding lumber, threatening to complain to the Gestapo if she refused. Ruth gave in. "I was afraid of him," she said, "and I was hurt, too, when a boy like him did this."

He later had a change of heart, however, after other Poles rebuked him for his collaboration, and he returned a few weeks later to apologize. He was upset because the Germans had refused to release him from the police service. "He felt sorry for himself, not for me," Ruth shrewdly observed.

It was a strange episode, exemplifying in a curious way Polish conduct during the German occupation: very little overt Polish collaboration with the Nazis; numerous instances of Poles who denounced Jews in hiding or openly applauded their destruction; and a surprisingly large number of Poles who took great risks to rescue Jews. Mostly there was self-interested indifference, "purposeful uninvolvement," to use Nechama Tec's apt phrase.[10]

It is always dangerous to make sweeping statements concerning group attitudes, but one is on fairly safe ground about Poland's prewar German inhabitants. In Łódź, where they formed about 10 percent of the population and included both pure Germans and Volksdeutsche (that is, ethnic Germans, or Poles of mixed German ancestry), they were the worst collaborators of all. Under the New Order, Teutonic ancestry definitely had its advantages. And the thirst for vengeance was strong. During the early days of the invasion, Polish authorities had driven tens of thousands of Germans from their homes, dispatching them to jail, internment camp, or to eastern Poland. Meanwhile, roving bands of nationalist thugs sacked German homes and farms. Anywhere between four and five thousand members of Poland's German minority lost their lives in the backlash. Now it was time to settle the score. Łódź's local German community gave the invading Nazis a hero's welcome, bedecking the Grand Hotel on Piotrkowska Street with flowers. They screamed "Heil Hitler" as the German Eighth Army marched into town. Several excited bystanders even jumped onto passing military vehicles.[11]

The psychology of scapegoating works in mysterious ways. As the Nazis battened down on the city's Jews, local Germans turned on Jewish neighbors who had done them no harm. They volunteered to act as spies. Many joined in the street bullying. "It's worse to deal with the local Łódź Germans than a whole regiment from the Reich," observed a Jewish diarist at the time.[12]

Not every prewar German inhabitant embraced the new regime, however.

Ruth mentioned a "certain Schibler," a German textile factory owner who refused to turn against his Jewish friends and neighbors. "The paper said he had a heart attack. He never had a heart attack. We all knew what had happened to him." Here, memory was playing tricks on her, which often happened when she tried to recall the names of public figures and historical events. But Ruth's account of what took place was close enough. The murder victim was actually Robert Geyer, a descendant of the Scheibler family of nineteenth-century textile pioneers, whose "death" was announced by a posted notice on December 24.[13]

Ruth never forgot the day a young ethnic German girl accosted her on the street. Ruth was on the way home. "She started pushing me and spitting on me. I said, 'I am older than you. What are you doing to me?' " "You're a Jew," the girl said, "and I can do whatever I want." "Right now you can see the picture of how they started raising the kids," Ruth said. "A little girl had the power to do this to me."

Meanwhile, one by one Ruth began losing hard-earned markers of bourgeois respectability. Fine possessions meant a lot to this daughter of modest origins. They were yardsticks of status and self-worth, concrete proof that she was somebody, and their loss was felt as psychological diminishment. A mid-November directive that Jews (and Poles too) turn in their radios left her inconsolable.[14] "It was a beautiful thing," she said of the radio Mark had purchased for the family just before the war. "I was heartbroken when the order came out to give it up." A lot of radios had already been seized during the ever-mounting Gestapo raids on Jewish apartment houses, but Ruth dutifully stood in line to hand hers over. "I was afraid like many others," she said. The clerk who filled out the receipt made her feel even smaller. When she told him her maiden name was Tempelhof, the same as the airport in Berlin, he sneered with incredulity. "He wondered how a Jew could have a name like this," Ruth said. "I just looked back and took the piece of paper. I was sure that I would never see our radio again." She was starting to doubt whether she would ever see her old life again.

There were two separate edicts ordering Jews to wear the Star of David—the first a November directive concerning armbands, the second appearing a month later requiring that the star instead be sewn on outer garments—but Ruth remembered only the later branding. The yellow star had to be four inches high and displayed on the right breast and on the back, with the letters "Jude" stitched in the middle of the patch.[15] No one was exempted. "My two girls were two and four and they had to wear the stars also," Ruth said. For four years (or was it three?) she had put off having children, waiting until she and Mark had achieved a modicum of financial security. "Now when I do have children I have to do this," she said. The searing part was having to sew the yellow stars on the expensive fur jackets she and Mark had purchased for their daughters in the mountain resort of Zakopane. It was as though she were defiling an emblem of all the material blessings she had hoped to shower on her children. "When I sewed them on the winter coat I think I was crying [over] . . . what a terrible thing was happening to us and my kids." "That was the first time I realized that I was different," Anne says. The psychological scar cut deep.

By late October, or maybe early November, after weeks of being cramped inside her parents' apartment, Ruth and her daughters moved back to their quarters at Legionów 8. Both apartment buildings had become like penitentiaries owing to the curfew the Nazis had imposed on Łódź's Jewish inhabitants.[16] Every evening at seven the Polish janitors locked the gates, not reopening them until eight the next morning. The nighttime incarceration had the small benefit of creating a new camaraderie among the tenants. "All the neighbors came together then," Ruth said. "This was our pleasure, just to talk with each other, hoping for a miracle." Soon after returning to Legionów 8, however, rumors began circulating that the Nazis were scouting the city for places to house German transplants from the Reich. It was an open secret that they had their eye on the big buildings in the center of town, and Legionów 8 was perhaps the largest apartment building.[17] Already the Germans had shut down the private Jewish school that had occupied a large portion of the Legionów 8 complex. Now it began to appear that they would take over the entire building. Ruth took the precaution of having her maid carry luggage and other personal belongings to Henry and Mery's apartment in Warsaw. "We thought we might end up there," she said.

Sometime in early November, around when the radio order was issued, the residents of Legionów 8 received forewarning that their section of town was probably next in line for ethnic cleansing. A steady stream of Germans had been climbing to the apartment building's roof to take pictures, it was later learned, of the Reform temple on the other side of Kościuszko Boulevard. The Germans were taking many pictures of Jewish institutions at the time. A few days earlier, they had temporarily reopened the city's largest Orthodox shul and ordered communal leaders to hold full service so that a German crew might capture it on film; then they arranged for the filming of a ritual slaughter at a kosher slaughterhouse. (Much of the footage ended up in the Nazi propaganda film *Der Ewige Jude* [The eternal Jew].)[18] The Germans had different plans for the Kościuszko Temple, however. Built by Italian master craftsmen in exact replication of the Königsberg Temple in East Prussia, the synagogue was a massive edifice of turrets and cupolas, a large dome framed by two smaller domes surmounting the roof. "It was a beautiful building both inside and out," Ruth said. On Monday, November 13, they told the Polish janitors to keep their Jewish tenants locked inside the apartment building. Then they built a fence around the temple and trucked in barrels of gasoline. The following night, the city fire department posted guards around nearby buildings. Later that evening, the Germans set fire to the temple.[19] It is hard to tell whether they were trying to celebrate the first anniversary of Kristallnacht in Germany, when members of the SA Brownshirts torched nearly two hundred synagogues and smashed storefront windows (hence the name Night of Broken Glass). Less than a week had passed since that anniversary, so there was likely some connection. Within minutes the temple was engulfed in flames: "The synagogue began to fall down majestically from the steeple," Ruth said. Many of the tenants in Legionów 8 had front-row seats to the arson; several started screaming and crying. Anne's first vivid memory of Nazi times are of the fire: "I remember the adults crying and saying the Germans are burning the temple. That's how I remember the beginning of the war, that's how I recall the beginning of trouble."[20]

On the streets outside, a different mood prevailed. "The Germans were so happy they started giving the Polish kids candy and cookies to celebrate the occasion," Ruth said. It would not be the last time the Nazis seized an opportunity to create discord between Pole and Jew. A few days after the torching of the Kościuszko Temple—as well as the Old Town Synagogue, the city's oldest shul—a Berlin newspaper reported that the fires had been started by Poles in retaliation for Jews having destroyed the Kościuszko Monument in Freedom Square. But that statue of Poland's famous nineteenth-century revolutionary nationalist had been dynamited on November 16 by the Nazis themselves.[21]

The dreaded eviction order was handed down within weeks of the synagogue fires. (Ruth says the notice came at the end of October, but all indications are that it arrived in early December.)[22] It fell to elderly Mr. Mieczysław Pinkus, the landlord and owner, to deliver the bad news. The Gestapo had peremptorily told him that he and his tenants had to vacate the premises on "short notice" and leave everything behind save for a few items of clothing. In other Jewish apartment buildings, "short notice" had been as brief as an afternoon. Given Ruth's rendition of events, the eviction at Legionów 8 probably took place over a day or two. Pinkus tried to talk the German authorities into letting him move into one of the building's smaller apartments. They dismissed his pleas out of hand. The only tenants exempted from the eviction were several Germans, many of whom had been married to Jews until the Nazis summarily dissolved their marriages. To the German former wife of a Jewish neighbor, Ruth transferred a few pieces of furniture that had special meaning. The woman's husband had been evicted just after the Nazis broke up their marriage, but she was one of the few tenants allowed to stay. "She told me not to worry," Ruth said. "She would take care of my things and save them for me." Ruth couldn't help but be worried by the fact that "ss and Gestapo men" had visited the woman several times after her husband had been forced to move out.

Meanwhile, Ruth packed Anne and Lila's clothes and carried them to her parents' apartment, returning to lock up the Legionów flat and hand over the keys to the janitor. Most of her fine possessions—linen, china, silver; in a word, all those heavily invested symbols of bourgeois hopes and aspiration—she left laying out in the open. The Nazis had made it clear that valuable items should be prominently displayed. "I remember my mother had to put her best silver and china on the table and walk out," Anne says. Ruth cried all the way back to her parents' apartment.

As oppressive as the Legionów evictions were, they paled next to the brutality taking place concurrently on Rzgowska Street, where Mark's mother and two sisters still lived. Between December 11 and 17, German police herded nearly every Jewish resident up and down the street into market halls and then packed them into cattle cars destined for the Lublin district of southeastern Poland. The "wild deportations," as they came to be known, were part of a scheme to expel nearly eighty-eight thousand Poles and Jews from western to eastern Poland. For the Jewish contingent the journey was punctuated by calculated humiliations. "All out to the latrines!" yelled a military guard at one of the way stations. There was a stampede to a long wooden plank; old men crowded next to young girls. The Germans took more propaganda photos, shooting some pictures from below to show that Jews defecated together without regard to sex. "I'll never forget that scene," said one of the deportees.[23]

Whether the dragnets on Rzgowska Street affected Mark's two sisters, Frania and Hanna, who owned the doily and knot-tying shop next to his mother's residence, is pure guesswork. But it is probably safe to surmise that they were caught in the roundups. Their names fail to turn up in the various registration forms filled out on Jews who later ended up in the Łódź Ghetto.[24] Nor do any surviving members of the Skorecki clan have any idea what became of them.

We do have hard facts about the fate of Mark's mother, however. In frail health at the time, seventy-two-year-old Natalia Skorecka was hit by a speeding car as she stepped from the pavement in front of her house at Rzgowska 75 shortly after the clearances that evacuated Jews from her street. "The Germans ran her over with an auto," noted Moshe Silberberg, her grandson in Tel Aviv.[25] "They never gave her a signal or anything," said Ruth. The accident scarcely raised an official eyebrow. By this point vehicular homicide had become a recreational pastime among the occupying forces. Back in October, ss vehicles had deliberately plowed into the crowded Astoria Cafe, where Jewish artists and intellectuals used to gather. A hundred people were injured, many of them fatally.[26]

When Ruth arrived at the Rzgowska family residence, Natalia Skorecka was lying inside the house, covered, and close to death. A member of the Gestapo stood nearby. According to records in the Łódź Public Record Office, Natalia died later that afternoon—at four P.M., to be exact, on December 21, 1939.[27] The next day the Skoreckis carried her to the Jewish cemetery in a funeral wagon. Only members of the immediate family were allowed to attend the burial. After the funeral the Germans confiscated the Skorecki property on Rzgowska Street. "I had no parents-in-law left," Ruth said.

Back in her parents' apartment, Ruth became despondent. "Right now everyday was miserable," she said. "I was missing my home, my things. I was not sleeping at night. I was worried in the daytime about what would happen to my children. And everyday they were asking for their father." On December 29 the temperature dropped to seventeen degrees Fahrenheit below zero. The winter would be one of the coldest on record.[28]

Both the deportations of December and the evictions at Legionów 8 were part of a broader Nazi project to redraw the European map, of which the liquidation of the Polish elite was merely the first stage. The rest of the plan envisioned leaching out the multicultural "hodgepodge" of Poland into their constituent elements—Poles, Ukrainians, White Russians, Jews, Gorals, Lemkes, and Kashubs—isolating the "racially valuable elements" and then shoveling the remainder into separate racial homelands, to make room for German resettlement.

A famous top-secret *Schnellbrief* (express letter) issued on September 21, 1939, by SS security chief Reinhard Heydrich to his Einsatzgruppen foreshadowed the plan's vague, early outlines. Heydrich's missive called for concentrating Jews in larger cities, preferably near important rail junctions. His cryptic instructions distinguished "short-term measures" from "ultimate goals." Just what those final plans entailed became clearer after Hitler's October 6 address to the Reichstag enunciating Germany's mission "to establish a new order of ethnographic conditions" in eastern Europe by erecting "clearer dividing lines" and retracting the "splinters of Germandom." The following day the Führer secretly authorized the creation of the SS bureau that was charged with carrying out the mission: the Reichskommissariat für die Festigung deutschen Volkstums (Reich Commission for the Strengthening of Germandom), or RKFDV.

Then came the dismemberment of Poland into new administrative units. Reclaimed for Germandom were Poland's western provinces—Łódź, Poznań, Danzig, and Eastern Upper Silesia—which were incorporated directly into the Reich (Łódź became part of the Wartheland). The remaining portion became a colonial appendage called the Generalgouvernement, administered from Kraków by the emotionally unstable Hans Frank, Hitler's subservient legal adviser.[29] The initial demographic blueprint envisioned three belts of population, running west to east: Reich Germans and Slavs of German descent in the annexed territories; Poles and other Slavs in the Generalgouvernement, which would become a sort of helot colony; and Jews in a reservation centered on the village of Nisko, in the Lublin District, in the southeastern quadrant of Frank's fiefdom. In the newly annexed territories Polish place names gave way to German ones: Oświęcim in Eastern Upper Silesia became Auschwitz; Łódź was rechristened Litzmannstadt, after a World War I German general who had fallen in battle on the city's outskirts. Street names were Germanized, the Polish language suppressed.[30]

Behind this ambitious plan lay a long-standing romance with the "German East" as a sort of paradise lost, a setting where the Volk and its ancient landscapes might be mystically reunited in *Blut und Boden* (blood and soil) harmony, in the tradition of crusading Teutonic knights of medieval yore. "The German East is our nostalgia and our fulfillment," propaganda minister Joseph Goebbels once told German youth.[31] Fixated on securing more Lebensraum, Hitler successfully transformed these irredentist yearnings into a survival-of-the-fittest imperative, placing himself, the man of destiny, at the forefront of the missionary impulse to reestablish the Volk's biological supremacy. In Hitler's mind there would have to be an ultimate reckoning with the Bolshevik-Jewish conspiracy sooner or later. The obsessive and murderous anti-Semitism at the heart of his worldview made such a showdown inevitable.[32] But for the time being even the Führer seems to have assumed that the reckoning would be territorial, that the Final Solution would be emigration rather than extermination, beginning with the uprooting of anonymous Jewish families such as the Skoreckis.[33]

To American readers it may come as a shock that Hitler regarded the "Nordic conquest" of North America as a model for remaking the "German East." In both *Mein Kampf* and his posthumously published *Secret Book*, he faulted previous Teutonic conquerors and pioneers for squandering precious Germanic seed. Pulled by the same economic incentives that had helped draw Jews from western Europe, large waves of German emigration had washed over Slavic lands in the sixteenth and seventeenth centuries.[34] Hitler blamed these earlier colonists for intermarrying with the native population, thereby allowing inferior racial stocks to commandeer German genetic strength for their own national projects. As a result, millions of Volksdeutsche had become isolated in scattered outposts of "Germandom": in the wilds of Volhynia, Bessarabia, the Ukraine, Belarus, the Baltics, and, of course, Poland. Spain had followed the same course to national decay through miscegenation with New

World Amerindians. But the Europeans who colonized North America—"people of the highest racial value"—had avoided this genetic blunder. In Hitler's understanding of American history, European settlers did more than conquer native peoples: they displaced them, shoved them onto reservations, confined them to separate homelands. This sensible racial policy had kept the gene pool pure and inviolate. Hitler thought this demographic project was a good model for Poland and the "restored" east. And, following the invasion of the Soviet Union in the summer of 1941, it became the racial template of Generalplan-Ost, an even more grandiose scheme for the demographic restructuring of Russian territory.[35]

An aloof and essentially lazy leader, Hitler seldom concerned himself with day-to-day governance, preferring to let trusted subordinates improvise policy within a broad framework of the Führer's known wishes. That leadership style permitted such ambitious and loyal subalterns as Heinrich Himmler to seize control of racial policy in the east. One of the most feared men in the Third Reich, the *Reichsführer*-ss did not look true to type. Of medium height and slightly balding, he was emphatically ordinary-looking. A receding chin and puffy cheeks conveyed the impression of a face about to cave in on itself. Pince-nez glasses screened heavy-lidded, hazel eyes, hinting at humorless pedantry. Most high-ranking Nazis feared and disliked Himmler. Whereas his archrival Hermann Göring loved to slap backs and pound tables, the ss chief was taciturn and secretive. He obsessed about astrology, Nordic runes, and the mysteries of the pyramids. During the war with Russia, he amassed a private research collection of skulls of "Jewish-Bolshevik Commissars." He made it mandatory that ss officer candidates prove "Aryan" descent going back to 1750.[36]

But for all his idiosyncrasies, Himmler was a gifted empire builder. From its modest beginnings as Hitler's Praetorian guard (ss stands for *Schutzstaffel*, or "protective squadron") his organization evolved into a veritable state within a state. It seized control of the German police and security forces, constructed a vast concentration camp empire, and established a network of economic holding companies. The ss had its own military branch—the Waffen-ss.[37]

Himmler's success in seizing control of Nazi racial policy stemmed in large measure from his own enthrallment with völkisch mysticism, an enthusiasm that dated back to his student days. If anything, Himmler's plans for Germanizing the east were even more visionary than Hitler's, including a back-to-the-land movement that would reconstitute the German people into a medieval peasantry, defended at strategic points along the eastern marches by a neo-Teutonic knighthood of ss farmer-soldiers. Like all such Nazi projects, Himmler's demographic ambitions depended on getting rid of Jews. In May 1940, as German Panzer divisions were overrunning the Low Countries and France,

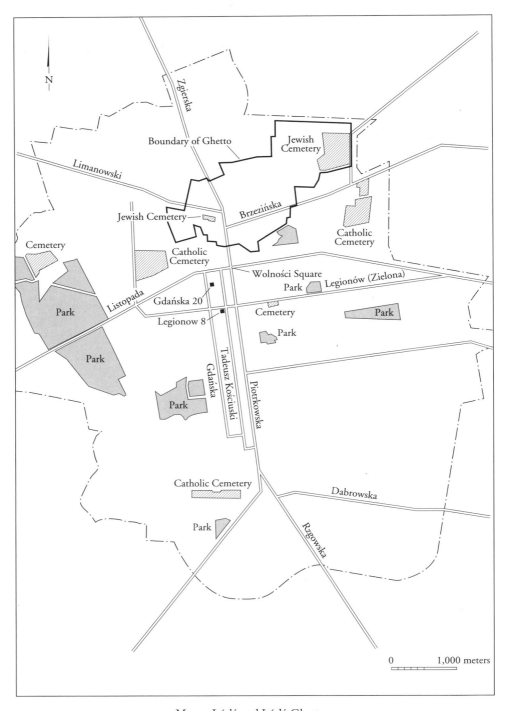

Map 2. Łódź and Łódź Ghetto.
Source: Adapted from Lucjan Dobroszycki, ed., *The Chronicle of the Łódź Ghetto,*
1941–1944 (New Haven, Conn.: Yale University Press, 1984).

Himmler tried to do just that by supporting the German Foreign Office's plan to ship European Jews to the island of Madagascar off the east coast of Africa— a scheme that had originated in 1936 with right-wing Polish nationalists whose own solution to the "Jewish question" was expulsion—and to kidnap "Germanizable" Polish children for eventual adoption by childless ss couples.[38]

Himmler's organization brought Teutonic thoroughness to its population projects. The ss drew up a "national list" that registered the name of every candidate for Germanization. ss Race and Resettlement experts screened Slavs for Aryan features. ss security police vetted their politics, in the interests of "fighting the biological war of population on Germany's frontiers."[39] Vast energy went into the repatriation of Volksdeutsche released by the Soviet Union for relocation to Poland's annexed territories (as well as to East Prussia and other regions of the Old Reich). The population transfers were truly staggering—to make room for the approximately five hundred thousand ethnic Germans "recalled" from Baltic and Slavic outposts, over a million Poles and at least one hundred thousand Jews were driven into the Generalgouvernement.[40]

Demographic restructuring, however, ran into one stumbling block after another. The ss kept setting overly ambitious goals only to scale them back drastically once reality dawned. "Short-range plans" gave way to "intermediate plans," which in turn were quickly shelved. Everything proceeded in fits and starts. Of the half million or so ethnic Germans "evacuated" from Latvia, Lithuania, Volhynia, the Ukraine, and Bessarabia, only about two hundred thousand were eventually resettled in the annexed territories, and fewer still were sent to the Reich as "trial citizens." The remainder languished in observation camps. One problem was the limited availability of homes, farms, and businesses in the incorporated territories. Earmarked for redistribution to Volksdeutsche transplants, most of the choice property confiscated from Poles and Jews were swiftly seized by prewar German residents. In such cities as Łódź, after local Germans and Nazi officials had combed the litter, there was little to choose from. Ruth said that Łódźites in black uniforms and red swastikas, together with their families, had been moved into her old apartment building at Legionów 8. "These were Poles who were given the right to catch people in the street," she said. "To pass this house was like passing a concentration camp." But the new tenants were doubtless local Volksdeutsche who had joined one of the city's self-defense units, the so-called *Selbstschutz*, partly because membership gave one first claim to confiscated property. In Łódź alone over fifteen hundred ethnic Germans enlisted in the Selbstschutz during the first months of Nazi occupation.[41]

The biggest obstacle encountered by the resettlement program, though, was the administrative chaos that characterized Nazi rule. Historians use such terms as "polycratic" to describe the Third Reich's essentially Darwinistic nature. More a movement than a government, the regime was surprisingly un-Prussian. Bureaucracies were piled atop bureaucracies. Governance devolved into a series of "ill co-ordinated special task-forces." Fritz Todt built the auto-bahns. Albert Speer oversaw the cities. Göring managed the "Four-Year Plan" as well as the Luftwaffe. Himmler had the Jewish desk, in addition to control-ling the police and security forces. "It was sort of a willed chaos," explains one historian; an exercise in "self-frustration," says another. The jumbled lines of authority led to chronic jockeying between rival power groups, who were left to fight it out until the brooding Führer felt compelled to intervene. Divided authority suited Hitler's governing style. The totalitarian system of checks and balances ensured that the Führer remained supreme arbiter of all policy dis-putes, while keeping ambitious subordinates on short leashes.[42]

The institutional disorderliness produced more than one bureaucratic mine-field, many of which started exploding once Himmler's ambitions to seize con-trol of the east became clear. The Reichsführer-ss had numerous long-standing enemies in the annexed territories, particularly among the *Gauleiters* (regional leaders), and they now did everything they could to sabotage the resettle-ment program. The stiffest opposition came from Hans Frank. The governor-general, who fancied himself a Renaissance prince, donning the trappings of Jagiellonian splendor, had grand ideas of his own: to transform the General-gouvernement into a model colony by demonstrating the commercial and cul-tural advantages of collaboration, which meant using various ethnic minorities in his territory—the Gorals, Lemkes, and Kashubs, for example—to counter-balance the Poles. But Himmler's determination to use Frank's bailiwick as a dumping ground, while "recalling" local Volksdeutsche to the Reich, sub-verted the governor-general's regal ambitions and worsened the housing and food situation inside the Generalgouvernement. So he dragged his feet at every turn, frequently turning for support to his powerful patron, Göring, whose own agricultural and industrial projects in the annexed territories would retain Polish labor.[43]

In all the bureaucratic infighting over what to do with the Volksdeutsche and the Poles, Nazi policy toward the Jews sometimes got shunted to the sidelines. Indeed, between Frank's and Göring's opposition to wholesale eth-nic cleansing and Himmler's equally vehement insistence on consolidating Germandom, Jewish policy during the war's early phases lurched from stale-mate to afterthought. There would come a time, however, when the admin-istrative chaos and baronial rivalries would work to hasten Jewish destruction.

The Łódź Ghetto came into existence almost by happenstance. Although Nazi ghettoization policy began emerging as early as September 21, 1939, with Reinhard Heydrich's secret memo forecasting the concentration of rural Jews near important rail junctions, Łódź was always a special case.[44] All towns and cities inside the annexed territories fell into a different category, because theoretically they were supposed to be cleared of Jews as expeditiously as possible to make room for the anticipated inflow of ethnic and pure-blooded Germans. Accordingly, on October 30, 1939, Himmler set a February deadline for evacuating Łódź's Jewish community. Hans Frank's entrenched resistance to receiving further deportees, however, rendered the target date unrealistic. In the face of such delays and postponements, Nazi authorities decided to establish a closed ghetto in Łódź, issuing the order on February 8, 1940. The arrangement was supposed to be temporary. Arthur Greiser, the Gauleiter of the Wartheland, viewed ghettoization as a short-term measure to starve Jews out of their remaining possessions. They have "hoarded colossally," he declared, and should be physically segregated "until what they have amassed is given back in exchange for food and then they will be expelled over the border."[45] The Łódź ghetto defied all expectations, enduring until 1944, the last of the great Jewish ghettos to be liquidated by the Nazis, becoming an important war production center, not to mention the antechamber for German Jews destined for Chełmno and Auschwitz.

The Łódź Ghetto's belated establishment gave the city's Jews an opportunity to escape east ahead of deportation, and many did so in the waning weeks of 1939. "A great many Jewish men are leaving the city," wrote the young Jewish diarist Dawid Sierakowiak on November 21. "Trains to Warsaw are terribly overloaded, with everyone heading to Warsaw and Russia!"[46] Vovek, Ruth's younger brother, finally joined the flight, also assuming that Nazi treatment would be less harsh inside the Generalgouvernement. Henry Tempelhof had written his parents to urge that they send his teenage brother to live with him and Mery in Warsaw, and they finally relented. "One day he took off his stars and with a non-Jewish person we let him go to Warsaw," Ruth said. Mark's relatives were also lighting out for the east. Wladek and Gustawa's twenty-two-year-old daughter, Haka, had already fled to Warsaw, while their youngest son was sent to Kielce, where the family had lived until 1931. Julius, Mark's brother, also fled to Warsaw, where he and Haka eventually shared an apartment.

Meanwhile, Mark's sister, Stefa Silberberg, and her family fled Łódź sometime around the turn of the year. Stefa's husband, after escaping from ss detention to Warsaw, made his way to the Ukraine, where she and their two children soon joined him. She was assisted by a German soldier who patronized their bakery and warned them in advance of the impending ghettoization. Ruth never mentioned the Silberberg escape in her oral history. She was angry they had left without telling her, perhaps feeling they should have taken her and the children with them, owing to her inability to travel alone with Anne and Lila.

And she resented their failure to extend more help during Mark's long absence. But, realistically, there was little her in-laws could have done without imperiling their own safety. Nonetheless, Ruth nursed a grudge, and she never let it go.[47]

After a brief sojourn at her parents, Ruth took Anne and Lila and moved in with Wladek and Gustawa at Legionów 55, where there was plenty of room now that their children had fled to the Generalgouvernement. After the Germans had confiscated their lumberyard, Wladek and Gustawa had nothing but time on their hands.

Ruth's new quarters still had the feel of a penitentiary. The janitors at Legionów 55 locked the gate every evening. The Jewish tenants continued to come together after hours to compare notes and share anxieties. But there was a new twist: venturing outdoors even during daylight had become more dangerous than ever after Volksdeutsche from the east had arrived. "The way to the outside led through a double row of Volhynian Germans with sticks," wrote a young Jewish diarist of what it was like to perform forced labor under their supervision, "and they beat us mercilessly with those sticks."[48] This early in the conflict it was still possible to avoid a Nazi impressment gang by having young children in tow, so Wladek and Gustawa started taking Anne and Lila with them while running errands. "When my brother-in-law and his wife went to get food," Ruth said, "they all the time took one of my girls to make sure they wouldn't be taken off to work for the Germans." "This was still a time when being seen with children could help you out of tight jams," Anne notes. "Later on, having small kids was a definite liability."

By early February even stay-at-homes had no guarantee of being left alone. The ss had stepped up their apartment sweeps, ostensibly to ferret out weapons but actually to steal Jewish property. "I remember one day they came to my brother-in-law's house searching all over," Ruth said. "They didn't find guns. They found soap, which was very important at this time to stay clean." Ruth begged them to leave her a few bars for Anne and Lila. The ss men merely stared at her, taking all but two pieces.

Establishment of a closed ghetto was pronounced on February 8. The Nazis had devised a well-thought-out technique for ghettoizing Poland's Jews: operate in the strictest secrecy; issue sudden, precise orders; adhere to a rigid timetable. In Łódź, Nazi authorities mandated that the relocation to the ghetto begin on February 17 and conclude on April 30. People would be moved in batches, street by street, according to a schedule that would be updated every few days. Poles and Volksdeutsche would move out, while Jews moved in. According to Raul Hilberg, the suddenness and the secrecy were necessary "in order to assure the hurried abandonment of a lot of Jewish property, which could then be conveniently confiscated."[49]

The Nazis chose the most dilapidated part of the city as the site of the new ghetto: the Bałuty slum and the neighboring Old Town area (where the nineteenth-century Jewish ghetto had been located). Squalid under ordinary circumstances, the Bałuty section was filthier than usual. Before the war peasants from neighboring villages used to collect the contents of its garbage containers and excrement pits to use as fertilizer. But local farmers had not come at all in 1939, and the pits were overflowing. Rats roamed freely in rancid garbage dumps. Into this rundown neighborhood the Germans proceeded to shove more than 160,000 Jews, some of them refugees from the surrounding countryside. Two and often three families squeezed into apartments seldom larger than a single room. Indoor plumbing was practically nonexistent.

In early May 1940, the Nazis closed the ghetto by surrounding it with barbed wire, decreeing the summary execution of any Jew found outside its boundaries. Residential curfew ran from 7 P.M. until 7 A.M. German Order Police patrolled the perimeter. Łódź was probably the most hermetically sealed ghetto in the Nazi complex—there is only one known instance of a Jewish family escaping to the "Aryan side" of the city and surviving by passing as gentiles, whereas numerous examples exist of such escapes in Warsaw, Kraków, and Lvov. In Łódź the Jews were "cut off as nowhere else."[50]

Exactly when Ruth and her young daughters moved to the ghetto is not entirely clear. It may have been March 15, 1940, the date on both Wladek's and Gustawa's *Anmeldung* (registration) papers on file at the state archives in Łódź.[51] "We all tried to be together and not to lose contact because we didn't know where we would be located," Ruth said. Or the relocation may have taken place on February 29 or March 1, when Nazi administrators, impatient at the slowness with which Łódź's Jews were making the move to Bałuty and Old Town, initiated forced evacuations in the section of town where the Skoreckis and Tempelhof resided.

In any event, the weather had warmed slightly on the day Ruth and the girls made the trek to the ghetto. "The snow was melting and the street was wet and slippery," she said. Gray caravans splashed through the mud all day: the once rich and the always poor, those who were blind, disabled, and ailing ("We feared what might happen to our sick if we left them behind," Ruth said), young mothers nursing babies, older people leaning on sticks, men and women bent double by luggage. They tripped over broken paving stones, dropping their belongings in Bałuty's black, sticky ooze. The ss police monitored the procession. Ruth traveled light, pushing a baby stroller. "The Germans had taken away all of my possessions already," she said. "I had no furniture." Anne and Lila, then only four and two, were worn out by the day-long walk. "They were tired and miserable and crying and hungry," Ruth said, "and I was crying with them because I did not know where I was going or what I was getting into. What would the next order be?"[52]

Ruth and the children initially moved in with her parents, who were sharing a room with a barber. Within two weeks the overcrowding forced her to double up once again with Wladek and Gustawa. Although Ruth's new ghetto apartment was not much larger than that of her parents, it had a kitchen (according to the Anmeldung records), and Ruth entertained hopes of locating a place of her own. The Judenrat—the Łódź ghetto's Jewish governing council—had said it would try to find them one, and Gustawa, who had in the meantime found employment in the Judenrat bureaucracy, was in a position to lend a hand.

Łódź's Judenrat was like most other Jewish councils established by the Germans to handle day-to-day ghetto management. Its members quickly fell victim to historical memory, drawing false analogies to the prewar kehillas that had autonomously governed Jewish communal life in Poland for centuries. It was a fatal assumption. The Jewish councils, in actuality, were little more than puppet governments struggling with the impossible task of serving the needs of desperate constituents while enforcing German dictates. As the Nazis ruthlessly eliminated independent-minded leaders, only Judenrat leaders who evinced "automatic compliance" with Nazi orders lasted for any length of time. It meant deciding who should live and who should die. It meant yielding to that two-thousand-year-old Diaspora instinct of sacrificing a few to save the rest. And no Judenrat leader embraced that ancient fatalism with greater alacrity than the controversial Chaim Rumkowski.[53] The silver-haired, sixty-two-year-old former businessman dispensed with council governance, naming himself elder of the Jews. His picture hung in every office. Public pronouncements referred to him in the superlatives of one-person rule. Rumkowski was the most outspoken proponent of the "rescue-through-work" strategy—the notion that Jewish lives could be saved only by making the ghetto economically useful. He scored a short-term victory by convincing pragmatists in the Nazi administration to transform the ghetto into a vast workshop for supplying uniforms and shoes to the German military. The new arrangement resulted in a slight increase in the ghetto's meager food supply and a prolongation of the ghetto's life.

It also created employment for about ten thousand Jews who worked in the Łódź Judenrat's quasi-feudal bureaucracy, a fact in which Ruth found reason for hope. "Plenty of people worked in this office because they thought they were saving their lives this way," she said. One of them, of course, was the resourceful and highly intelligent Gustawa, who used what little insider influence she possessed to help her husbandless sister-in-law find better lodgings.[54]

Ruth visited the Judenrat everyday "asking them," to quote her, "please, I can't live like this. I needed a place of my own, especially since I had kids."

They finally supplied her with a list of addresses to visit. "Everything was the same. I had to live with strangers." She was terribly depressed about the situation. Anne and Lila continued to ask for their father. Friends had told her so often that Mark had probably fallen on the highway and that she should quit worrying, she had come to believe it herself. She was losing all hope. "I was sure my husband was dead," she said. She was starting to feel trapped.

Mark made contact with his family while Ruth was scouting apartment possibilities. A short, heavy-set stranger approached her on the street. He walked with a slight limp, wearing a slipper on one foot. He was young, and he identified himself as Mr. Zilberberg. He told Ruth her husband had sent him. "What do you mean my husband?" Ruth snapped. "He left in the first of September, and I haven't heard from him. You are telling me stories." She started crying. But the man was persistent. Your husband's name is Mark, he said. Then he pointed to his swollen leg, explaining he had been frostbitten while trying to run away from the Russians and had been hospitalized in Białystok, an old wool-spinning city just inside the Soviet zone of occupation. Mark met him in the hospital, under circumstances that remain unclear. Growing worried when his letters to Legionów 8 went unanswered, he offered Zilberberg money to escort his wife and daughters across the frontier to Białystok. Mark agreed to pay him well, placing the sum they had decided on in escrow with a third party.

Exactly why Mark failed to come in person is a mystery, one of those gray areas that shade the lives of many survivors. Maybe he dreaded the return trip, as did most people who had made it across the River Bug. Or maybe he was afraid an extended absence might cost him a job that paid enough to support his family once they arrived from the west, at the same time offering a modicum of immunity against forced exile to the Soviet Gulags. This last concern was no minor consideration. For the past five months he had been working in a Russian barrel factory, and he must have been aware of the constant danger refugees were under of being deported to Siberia. Hundreds of thousands of them had flooded in from Poland following the 1939 German invasion. But after the Russians had Sovietized the western areas of Byelorussia and the Ukraine, they began deporting the refugees eastward—in February, April, and June 1940 and then in June 1941—in part to ease housing and employment shortages and in part to expel inhabitants of questionable loyalty. The latter were betrayed by a census administered by Narodnyi Komissariat Vnutrennykh Del (NKVD; People's Commissariat of Internal Affairs) auxiliaries, which asked whether the interviewee wished to accept Soviet citizenship or return to Poland after the war. Those who indicated an intention to return home—and most did—were packed into windowless, unheated cattle cars and transported deep inside Russia's frozen wastelands. The first wave stood in subzero weather during the journey of several thousand miles. Casualties were staggering.[55]

Mark himself almost got caught in the Russian net. Before arriving in Białystok he was detained by Soviet authorities near Horyniec, where the lumber mill of his late brother, Morris, was located. He had gone there as he said he would, doubtless traveling through the woods to avoid choked highways, marking his bearings by the moss-covered, north-shaded side of the trees. Only employees were at the mill when he arrived. The Russians would not reach Galicia until after September 17, the day they crossed the frontier to lay claim to Stalin's slice of Poland. Mark had no intention of awaiting their arrival; he was justifiably afraid that the NKVD might arrest him, brother of the town's leading sawmill proprietor. Under Stalinism, one needed to own little property to qualify as a "capitalist."[56]

Mark packed a suitcase soon after arriving in Horyniec and caught a train for Białystok, pretending, as he told his family years later, "like I was going on vacation." Why he chose Białystok is another mystery—perhaps that is simply where the train was heading. In any event, Russian troops stopped the train midway through the journey, hauling everyone to a police station. They marched Mark and the other passengers along a dirt path through a field where a commissar named Sergei—"a little guy but a big shot," according to Mark—interrogated them for hours. Mark's Russian was pretty good, but not good enough to avoid a thorough rifling of his suitcase. The Soviets confiscated both his money (presumably obtained at Morris's sawmill) and his papers. Then they locked him inside a shed for three days and two nights with about thirty men and boys and six women. On the morning of the fourth day a truck drove up, and a man entered the shed announcing that everyone whose name he read had to climb into the rear of the vehicle. When he finished ticking off the names, only Mark, a young girl, and a small boy were left. Everyone else was taken away to a camp.

Commissar Sergei called Mark back inside the shed and told him, "You can go home."

"I can go home? What about my suitcase, and my money and my papers?"

"You can go home," Sergei repeated.

Mark did not press his luck, and he failed to mention what happened to the two children. He walked to the train station, waited forty-eight hours on a hard bench through five or six shift changes by the Russian police, and then squeezed into a tightly packed train heading for Białystok, where local authorities were intensely interested in using refugee labor to revitalize the town's economy.[57] Not long after arriving, therefore, he found employment at the

Russian barrel-making plant, rising quickly to the rank of foreman. In view of all that he had been through and the good position he now occupied, it would have made sense for him to hire a third party to retrieve his family.

When Zilberberg ran into Ruth in the ghetto, he was actually on his second mission to the city. He had arrived there a month earlier, going directly to Legionów 8 but returning immediately to Białystok when he saw the Gestapo loitering in front of the building. Mark told him that was a poor excuse for giving up. "Listen, you have to try it again," he told Zilberberg. "Only this time go into the ghetto where they are putting all the Jews and ask the people at the Judenrat office if they know where my wife is."

After Zilberberg returned to Łódź a second time, the ghetto was still un-sealed, and he was able to enter the restricted zone with little difficulty. He was actually on his way to the Judenrat headquarters when he encountered Ruth on the street, probably recognizing her from photographs Mark had shown him. It took Ruth a little while to recover from the shock of discovering not only that her husband was still alive but also that he had made arrangements for his family to join him in the Soviet sector. She felt faint. Zilberberg said they had to leave soon, which made her feel even more light-headed.

Although Zilberberg insisted the passage to Białystok would be absolutely safe, Ruth was justifiably dubious. True, the Germans were weeks away from encircling the ghetto with concertina wire, but it was still dangerous for fam-ilies to venture beyond the Jewish District. The young single men who slipped out all the time could go on foot, but Ruth and the children had to find a vehicle of some kind and locate a trustworthy gentile. And they had to move quickly, too, before market prices for smuggling Jews from the ghetto went into hyperinflation, as happened after the Bałuty slum was closed off and the trickle of people still able to escape did so by concealing themselves inside coffins and riding out in funeral wagons.[58] Ruth was lucky. "God was good to us," she said, "and we found one [a rescuer]. It was a garbageman, and it was his wagon we hired." They made plans to leave in a week. In the meantime, a dentist and his wife, neighbors of Wladek and Gustawa from Legionów Street, persuaded Ruth to let their eighteen-year-old son come along.

The worst anxiety was separating from her parents as well as her brother- and sister-in-law. "I was absolutely sure I would never see them again." They shared her premonition but told her she had no choice. "You have children and your husband is waiting for you," they said. "You are doing this for your daughters."

Often wrong about dates, Ruth said they left in the middle of February, at five in the morning, but their departure likely occurred in April. At any rate, "it was very cold." She took blankets, the fur coats she had bought for herself and the children in Zakopane, and enough food to see them through the journey. She had some funds. Then she, Anne, and Lila climbed into the rear of the wagon, along with the dentist's son and Zilberberg. "We left with a big scar in our hearts," Ruth said. "We were the garbage this time."

Passage to the Aryan side—as non-Jewish areas of Poland were coming to be called under the new regime—came off without a hitch. The garbageman, who knew the best routes for avoiding Germans, took a shortcut to reach the highway for Głowno, where the Skoreckis used to spend the summer. The border between the Wartheland and the Generalgouvernement lay just beyond the Głowno town limits. The only German they saw came two hours into the trip, and he was a solitary ss man who had temporarily abandoned his motorcycle. He commanded them to halt. Zilberberg told the garbageman, "Drive as fast as [you] can. Don't go straight but zigzag." The Nazi fired his pistol. Ruth hunched over in the wagon, shielding Anne and Lila with her body. Still on foot, the ss man failed to catch up with them. They reached Głowno at ten in the evening and spent the night in a small rundown restaurant where Jews in flight took refuge from time to time. The proprietor charged extortionate prices, but Ruth paid them gladly. "I still had the picture of the ss man running after us," she said.

They stayed in Głowno two days, looking for a Pole willing to drive them the remaining ninety miles to Warsaw. Zilberberg finally hired a baker to transport his party. The Pole insisted that they stay locked in the bakery truck's rear compartment during the entire trip. After drilling holes in the top to let in air, they started early in the morning. Today the road between Łódź and Warsaw is a broad three-lane highway, with generous paved shoulders for slower traffic to slide onto when high-speed drivers barrel down the middle lane. Rows of evenly spaced trees fall away on a flat horizon. Villages cluster together here, separated on both sides of town by roadside Catholic shrines dressed with freshly cut flowers and streamers of pink and blue ribbons. But in 1940 the road was fairly primitive, and horse-drawn peasant wagons slowed the way. The bakery truck was forced to make numerous stops. "I still remember how cold the trip was and how scared we were," Anne says.

On several occasions Nazi soldiers told them to pull over. "Every German voice we heard, our hearts were in our throats," Ruth said. "I was sure it was the end." But the journey was largely uneventful, except for being cramped inside a tight space for more than twelve hours, and they arrived in Warsaw in the evening.

Ruth failed to reach her brother Henry and wife Mery by telephone, so she called Julius instead; he came immediately to take Ruth and the children to the apartment he was sharing with Haka. "We were tired and dirty and miserable," Ruth said. She gave Anne and Lila a bath. Then she tracked down Henry and

Mery Mejnster through the Czyste Hospital on Dworska Street, where Mery now worked. They came over right away. Having lost contact with their families after the Łódź Ghetto was established, they were hungry for news from their hometown.

The family reunion was brief. Eight days after their arrival, Zilberberg whisked them off to Siedlce, a medium-sized city seventy-five miles due east of Warsaw. Siedlce was close to the River Bug, which formed the German-Soviet line of demarcation, but not so close as to be in harm's way. The border was more dangerous than ever, heavily patrolled as it was by Soviet and Nazi soldiers who shot to kill. A barbed wire fence connected to an alarm system of bells alerted border guards whenever intruders ventured into no-man's-land between the lines. "It was better to go through the fields, by Malkinia station," near Treblinka, and to travel in the company of smugglers who knew the habits of the guards, said a Jewish woman doctor who had made the journey.[59] Zilberberg persuaded a local tailor to rent rooms to Ruth for her, the girls, and the dentist's son. The house was "very rustic," Ruth said, by which she meant cramped and dirty. After a few weeks they moved in with a farm family.

Although spring had officially begun, the weather remained cold, and Lila contracted a high fever that refused to subside. Ruth started to panic. They had been hovering near the border for four weeks waiting for a chance to cross. The passage would have to take place at night. But Ruth was not about to carry a feverish young child into the cold evening air. Besides, her money was starting to run out. "I can't take it any more," she told Zilberberg, who tried to calm her nerves.

"I was afraid," she admitted. "The situation every day was worse and worse." Having come this far, Zilberberg was loathe to turn around now. Ruth knew it, too. She decided to give him the slip, catching a ride back to Warsaw with a local farmer. They moved in with Julius and Haka temporarily. Quickly tracking her down, Zilberberg pleaded with Ruth to make the crossing. Be patient, he said. Control your nerves. But he could not budge her. "Tell my husband I don't want to risk my children's lives and try again," she told him. "I'm just going to stay in Warsaw."

Zilberberg and the dentist's son eventually made their way to Białystok, though it is unclear whether Mark's frostbitten courier ever received payment for all his trouble. Mark was extremely upset at the way things had turned out, "surprised," as Ruth admitted, "that I didn't have the nerve or the patience to do this and that I had gone back to Warsaw."

But the anger went both ways. Soon after returning to Warsaw she told Julius that "if Mark wanted to see me he had to try to get me himself, but I could never make it with the girls"—in other words, don't send a proxy. Next time, come yourself.

Whether Ruth communicated her feelings to Mark directly is not recorded. But he seems to have gotten the message. "From the stories my father told in later years," Anne says, "he made up his mind then and there that he would have to come back himself."

But nearly two years would pass before he undertook that journey. In the meantime Ruth discovered she had escaped the sword only to hide in the scabbard.

THE WARSAW GHETTO

There was a substantial inflow of Jewish refugees to Warsaw from western Poland in the winter of 1939–40. Most came on the same vague hope that drew Ruth and her relatives to the city: the Generalgouvernement would be safer than the annexed territories. Everything was relative, of course. Kraków admittedly was vulnerable to the demographic reengineering taking place in the Wartheland and Eastern Silesia, if only because Governor-General Hans Frank had moved his capital there. In May 1940, intent on Germanizing the city, he had even ordered the expulsion of its ancient Jewish community.[1] But surely mass deportation would not take place in Warsaw. How could Germany do without its Jews? Varsovians scoffed. After New York, Warsaw was the second largest Jewish city in the world. And its artisans, manufacturers, and merchants were integral to the general economy. There was no way the Germans could dispense with them.[2]

Yitzhak Zuckerman, a leader of the 1943 Warsaw Ghetto uprising, encountered the delusionary thinking everywhere he turned. "In those days, it meant that, when things were happening in Lublin, people said: 'That won't happen in Warsaw.' When it did happen in Warsaw, they said, 'That happened on Nalewki [Street], but it won't happen on Gesia [Street].' When it did happen on Gesia, they said it happened at number 32, but it won't happen in my house, number 28!"[3]

That Warsaw enjoyed scant immunity was obvious even before Ruth's return from the German-Soviet frontier. The Nazis had already reproduced the anti-Jewish measures they had imposed on Łódź, setting curfews, seizing radios, and banning religious services. Every Jew between the ages of twelve and sixty, including women, was required to perform public labor. Jewish businesses were "Aryanized" and landlords dispossessed. The Germans estab-

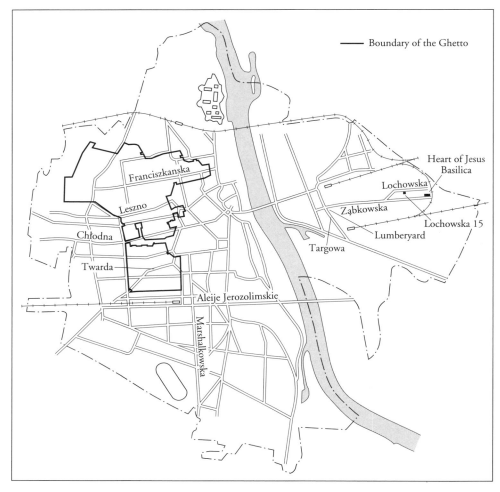

Map 3. Warsaw and Praga, 1939–1945.
Source: Adapted from Antony Polonsky, ed., *A Cup of Tears: A Diary of the Warsaw Ghetto by Abraham Lewin* (Oxford: Basil Blackwell, 1988).

lished a Judenrat headed by a former engineer named Adam Czerniakow. Then came the customary branding: a Star of David armband (in blue and white, not yellow), to be worn by all Jews over twelve. Soon Jews would be excluded from city parks and designated streets and barred from streetcars, except those earmarked "For Jews Only," which quickly became so filthy and overcrowded that passengers found it difficult to breathe.[4] To Ruth it looked all too familiar, and she braced herself for the worst. "It was hard to live because we expected the same as in Łódź," she said.

The most dread fear was a closed ghetto, which the Nazis delayed establishing until late in the year. Yet there were disturbing omens. In March 1940, Nazi health authorities established a *Seuchensperrgebiet*—a "plague-infested area" or "epidemic zone"—in a heavily Jewish neighborhood in the northern district of town, ordering the Warsaw Judenrat to begin erecting a brick wall.

But before a single brick had been laid, a reign of terror was already driving Warsaw's Jews into self-imposed ghettos. In late March the Luftwaffe paid young Polish hooligans to run amok in Jewish neighborhoods while German soldiers snapped pictures of the vandalism. "For three whole days the streets of Warsaw were turned into fields of chaos and disorder," the Jewish teacher Chaim Kaplan wrote in one of the few diaries to have survived the Warsaw Ghetto. Kaplan later witnessed the savage beating of a young Jewish mother by Nazi soldiers, who overturned her baby carriage as she slumped to the pavement.[5]

Ruth rented a place in the predominantly Jewish neighborhood of Muranów, in the very northern district where the Germans had established an "epidemic zone."[6] No doubt a desire to avoid trouble motivated her choice of location. The Germans were less likely to indulge their recreational anti-Semitism in areas where they feared contracting "Jewish" diseases. "Whoever went out on the street went at his own risk," Ruth admitted. But her brother Henry and his wife, Mery, were not happy with her living alone and initially insisted that she and the children move into their small apartment at Dworska 17, to which they had moved after German bombs destroyed their home on Twarda 8. The new flat was near the famed Czyste Hospital where Mery served as the only woman surgeon on the staff.[7] And Henry had become the hospital's office manager, a position of some importance. There was much rebuilding to do: the sprawling medical complex, including Mery's surgical unit, had also been badly damaged during the September air attacks. Henry had his hands full:[8] "He was telling other people what to do," says a retired physician in Ohio who had been a medical student in Warsaw at the time. "Whenever you would see laborers doing work, he was the one directing them."[9]

But Ruth resisted Henry and Mery's entreaties to move in with them. Her brother Vovek, who had found employment at Czyste as a hospital orderly, was also living with Henry and Mery at the time. The apartment was confining, to say the least. How would her brother and sister-in-law make room for three additional people? "It was impossible with two children," she told them.

Henry and Mery saw the logic in her position and helped her find the place she rented in the Muranów District. It was a bedroom in a six-room apartment that she sublet from a couple with a young son. Located at Ogrodowa 30, near Żelazna Street and across from a Jewish orphanage, the five-story building was part of a conglomeration of fifty or so similar apartment complexes. Warsaw was famous for these huge, rectangular tenement blocks, each carved into a maze of interconnecting courtyards through which tenants could sometimes go from street to street simply by moving through the courtyards. During the deportations that commenced in July 1942, these warrenlike labyrinths became veritable death traps. But early in the Nazi occupation the enclosed spaces were still lined with ground-level shops and bakeries, and pulsing with the hubbub of daily life. Aromas of poppy and caraway seeds and bagels fresh from the oven filled the morning air.

The tenement block where Ruth and the girls now rented also housed the State Law Courts, which straddled the block's entire width, serving as an interior corridor between Leszno and Ogrodowa Streets. Ruth's apartment building contained but a single courtyard, which bottlenecked as it backed toward a similar complex entered from Leszno Street. About two hundred tenants resided at Ogrodowa 30—"rich people, mostly," Ruth said, although there were some "poor people," and their numbers would soon mushroom. The couple subletting Ruth her room were likely well-to-do, because their flat, like most high-rent apartments, looked onto the street, where most mornings you could hear the apartment building's janitor hosing down the pavement.

The rent was steep, but Ruth felt lucky to have found the place. "I had hot and cold water, a nice room with beds, clean and comfortable," she said, plus the run of the rest of the house. Another advantage was the proximity of Julius and Haka, who dropped by often to see how she was doing.

She was doing all right, at least for the time being. From the Judenrat, she and her children received monthly ration cards, which failed to provide "enough to live a whole month on," as she herself admitted with considerable understatement. But she was able to supplement these meager foodstuffs with supplies from the "Joint," or the American Joint Distribution Committee, a Jewish relief organization that continued to send supplies to Europe until America's entry into the war. "I went to the office and I gave my name and told them that I had two children and that my husband was in Białystok and that I needed help." She may have had money left over from the cash Mark left with her before heading east, though she never said so. And she could periodically turn to the reserve fund embodied in the personal goods her Polish maid had carried to Warsaw for her earlier in the occupation. "I started selling some of these things to support myself and the kids," Ruth said. Most of all, there was the mail from the Russian-occupied territories. It continued right up to the day Nazi forces invaded the Soviet Union on June 22, 1941, bringing lifesaving infusions of cash and fresh stocks of food from Mark.

"I have to say that my brother wanted to help," Ruth said. So did Julius. She politely declined both offers of assistance, promising to turn to them if she and the girls needed aid. But Ruth would try to put off that day as long as possible. It was not merely because, to use her words, "I didn't want to be a burden to them." Her motives were more complex: "I am a person who when somebody is sorry for me, I do everything to avoid having to ask them for something. In my mind I thought maybe they would think that I was jealous that they had everything. Maybe they would feel bad. So I played the role that I had all I needed." A complicated woman, Ruth Skorecka was an odd mixture of pride, empathy, and status insecurity, a person who placed image management on the same plane with survival techniques, maybe because the two were already beginning to merge. Nonetheless, by subsisting off packages from Mark, occasional support from the "Joint," and the episodic sale of her possessions, Ruth was able to eke out an independent existence.

Very soon she would have reason to feel self-congratulatory about her choice of residence. By the fall of 1940, after Ruth had been living in Warsaw for several months, German authorities finally took steps to establish a ghetto in the former Polish capital. Ruth knew all too well the trauma of sudden eviction. In Łódź it had meant ruination for hundreds of thousands of Jews, including herself and her family. Swirling rumors that a ghetto was in the offing in Warsaw awakened familiar fears. "Right now I had the same feeling that I had in Łódź when they started making a ghetto there," she said.

Other Jews in Warsaw shared her dread. "When we remember what happened to the Łódź ghetto, we are seized by fear," Chaim Kaplan recorded in his diary on September, 26, 1940.[10] Fortunately for Ruth and her daughters, the tenement block that embraced Ogrodowa 30 fell within the boundaries of the soon-to-be-established ghetto.

Like other policies concerning Jews that emanated from the chaotic Nazi bureaucracy, ghetto formation in wartime Poland had a certain seat-of-the-pants quality about it, proceeding according to the whims of local German authorities. For example, there was a noticeable lag time between ghettoization in the Generalgouvernement and the incorporated territories. In Governor-General Hans Frank's area, Warsaw set the pace; every attempt to impose residential segregation on the Jewish community ran into snags. The ss tried to create a ghetto in Warsaw in November 1939, only to see the military veto the project on the grounds that the population transfers would be too disruptive. Early 1940 saw plans to create a closed ghetto in the working-class suburb of Praga across the Vistula River fail as well. The resistance to ghettoization came from not only the Wehrmacht but also Hans Frank, who was no different from other regional Nazi leaders in wanting to see his department emptied of Jews. (He had always been cool toward the idea of setting aside part of the General-gouvernement as a Jewish reservation.) Thus, after learning in the summer of 1940 that Hitler had signed off on the project to resettle European Jewry in

Madagascar, he suspended all planning for a ghetto in Warsaw, even ending construction of the brick wall that the Judenrat had been erecting around the "epidemic zone." In view of the Führer's plan, his own efforts were "practically illusory," he told his assembled court in Kraków.[11]

By September 1940, however, after the Battle of Britain had failed to knock England out of the war, leaving the Royal Navy athwart strategic sea lanes, the Madagascar Plan had also gone by the books. Hence planning for a massive ghetto in Warsaw shifted into high gear. On September 12 Governor-General Frank told his division chiefs that health concerns dictated that Warsaw's Jews could no longer be allowed to "roam around." On October 2, at a rare meeting of eastern party leaders in Hitler's Berlin apartment, Frank boasted of the impending incarceration of Warsaw's Jews inside a walled city. Tacking with the prevailing winds, the head of the Generalgouvernement had become a cheerleader for ghettoization. It would not be the last time that Frank would abruptly change course to suit the shifting Nazi project.[12]

A few warning signs indicated a ghetto was in the offing. In mid-August, Warsaw had been partitioned into three ethnic enclaves, and Jews were systematically evicted from the newly designated German quarter. "Clouds are covering our skies," Kaplan lamented. "Racial segregation is becoming more apparent each day."[13] By late September 1940, "a Ghetto was imminent," said Emmanuel Ringelblum, the Jewish historian and organizer of the Warsaw Ghetto's famous underground archives, Oneg Shabbat.[14] Ruth sensed it too: "They started giving more and more orders and making plans for the ghetto to move the people from their homes."

Yet the ghettoization order still caught most Warsaw Jews by surprise. It was another one of the Nazis' patented sudden strikes aimed at maximizing the confiscation of hurriedly abandoned property. Ghetto authorities in Warsaw even consulted with their counterparts in Łódź before acting. The Nazis sprung the trap on Yom Kippur, blaring the ghettoization decree over public loudspeakers (initiating anti-Semitic measures during Jewish festivals and holidays was also a common Nazi tactic).[15]

According to the initial blueprint, the ghetto would embrace the northern slums of Nalewki and Zamenhof, then slide south through the Muranów District, including the narrow industrial streets just above the main railroad station. Krasinski Park originally fell within the ghetto's boundaries, although not for long. During most of its life span, the so-called Jewish Residential District lacked squares and open areas save for the occasional hillock of rubble from a bombed-out housing block. There were several courtyard gardens, however, many of them formerly attached to Polish coffeehouses, and these became, in the words of diarist Kaplan, "our country places and our summer resorts"—but only for people with means. Most of the gardens charged an entrance fee.[16]

For several weeks after the promulgation of the ghettoization order, the streets of northern Warsaw became bedlam, as 138,000 Jews living outside the designated area traded places with the 113,000 Poles who resided within it. "People were moving in and out the whole time," Ruth said. They carried *Flüchtlingsgepäcks*—"refugee bundles." They moved on a tight schedule, for the Nazis allotted only three weeks for the population transfer to take place.[17] Day after day, wagons groaning with family possessions streamed in and out of the ghetto. Thrown into the melee were thousands of handcarts and ricksha bicycles piled high with household goods. The poor came by foot, bundles slung over their shoulders. Mattresses were strewn over the sidewalks. Sobbing children wailed for panic-stricken parents who dashed to and fro searching for toddlers swept away by the human current.[18] Owing to the tumult and confusion, the Germans had to extend the transfer deadline until November 15. The last of Warsaw's Jews to be relocated were those from the ancient community of Praga, across the river; its fifty thousand members were uprooted in a matter of days.[19]

Even as the transfers were under way, a huge question mark hung over the ghetto's exact boundaries. The Germans were uncharacteristically equivocal. Was Żelazna Street in or out? What about both sides of Sienna? How would the presence of gentile factories and churches inside Jewish neighborhoods affect the ghetto's final shape? "Every street has something that puts it in jeopardy," said Ringelblum. The indeterminacy provoked fierce competition between Poles and Jews to save this block or that street for their own kind, effectively pitting poorer Catholics against a new pariah class of Jewish have-nots. For Jews who had already moved once, usually from larger to smaller apartments, it was a nightmare without seeming end (some families ended up moving as many as seven times). The ghetto's boundaries were not finalized until the close of the transfer period, and even then they were never really final.[20]

On November 16, one day after the resettlement deadline, German authorities ended the suspense about whether the ghetto would be sealed shut. They announced it would be a "closed ghetto" and for emphasis began stringing barbed wired between gaps in the brick wall. The decree "came like a thunderbolt," Ringelblum observed in his diary. Around the perimeter the Nazis established twenty-two gates (later reduced to fifteen) staffed on both sides by Polish and Jewish police and ss police units. By the time the last brick was mortared into place, the ten-foot-high barrier, together with its connecting buildings, ran for almost eleven miles. A clay crust of splintered glass and concertina wire capped the top. Some ghetto inmates called their masonry frontier the "Siegfried Line Extension." Crossing from one side to the other reminded Ringelblum of traversing "a border point between two countries."[21]

From above, the sealed ghetto looked like a giant, misshapen claw hammer that had been nicked and gouged by a thousand competing interests. To accommodate an east-west Polish streetcar line, a wedge sliced through the handle, tapering as it merged with Chłodna Street. Halfway down its shank a corridor abruptly jutted northwesterly along Biała Street, to snatch from the midsection of Ruth's tenement block the huge Law Court complex stretching between Ogrodowa and Leszno Streets. Known as the "Aryan corridor," the wedge effectively separated the large ghetto from the "little ghetto" below Chłodna. After a while a narrow footbridge went up near the intersection of Chłodna and Żelazna Streets. Unless on urgent business, most ghetto dwellers tried to give the wooden overpass wide berth. The ss guards posted there, some of them "old hands" from Łódź, enjoyed forcing Jewish pedestrians to dance and perform calisthenics, roughing up those who lost their balance.[22]

With the closing of the ghetto, one-third of Warsaw's prewar population now occupied less than 3 percent of the city's land mass.[23] It is easy to exaggerate the congested living conditions, and tempting to do so. Many historians have done just that, asserting that population densities inside the ghetto averaged over nine persons to a room (some have inflated the estimate to from fourteen to twenty-one persons per room). The real figure was more like two to three persons per room, which, of course, was crowded enough.[24] And in the refugee centers—the "points," as they were called—the congestion beggared belief. The desperately poor crowded into dance halls and synagogues, apartment courtyards and basement catacombs. They spilled onto sidewalks and pooled in doorways. Maybe as many as one-half of the ghetto population were in this condition. And still the refugees continued to arrive, spurred by Nazi expulsions from the provinces. They came in wagons and on foot, frozen and half dead, with knapsacks on their backs and rags on their feet, their faces creased with fear. "There is no room in the ghetto," lamented Kaplan, "not an empty crack, not an unoccupied hole."[25]

If silver linings had any meaning in the Warsaw Ghetto, there was some consolation in the fact that Ogrodowa 30 fell within the ghetto's shifting borders, which spared Ruth and her daughters the fate of being tossed into the streets. Her solitary room may have felt suffocating at times, but Anne and Lila had free access to the rest of the apartment. Even her rent no longer seemed so steep once ghetto housing costs started to soar owing to the overcrowding. Most important, her relatives were still nearby to offer moral support. "My husband's brother Julius came to me to say that we would work this out somehow," Ruth said. "The same by my brother and his wife. They said not to be afraid because we would be together. But it was very hard to listen to people because you could never tell. Maybe they would disappear someday themselves, and I would lose contact."

It had happened before: blood might be thicker than water, but even family ties could dissolve when survival was at stake. The sealing of the ghetto reawakened Ruth's fears of desertion and abandonment, intensifying a single mother's anxiety for the care of her daughters. An old question returned with renewed intensity: "What was I to do with my two children?"

One thing to do was to maintain hygienic standards, for living conditions in the ghetto resulted in the spread of infectious disease. Ruth strove for cleanliness, trying her best, as she put it, "to keep the children clean, in a clean, nice room." But observing good hygiene was no easy task. Even soap was scarce. The gluey bars passing for soap in the ghetto disintegrated when exposed to water. "It makes one dirty instead of clean," a teenage girl recorded in her ghetto diary.[26] And so Ruth's anxiety deepened: "Of course, sometimes I cried all night thinking what might possibly happen to us at some future date."

Several kinds of epidemics wracked the ghettos, from tuberculosis to typhoid. But typhus fever, which was not the leading disease killer (tuberculosis probably was), inspired the most dread.[27] Caused by the microorganism *Rickettsia* and spread by body lice (both the clothing and head varieties), the disease begins with flulike symptoms: a rapid rise in temperature, often to 103 or 104 degrees Fahrenheit; chills and achy joints; severe headache. On the fourth or fifth day a rash appears on the shoulders and torso, quickly spreading to the limbs, hence its alternative name, "spotted fever." Early on the disease is hard to distinguish from malaria and measles; one signal difference is the absence of a facial rash. In its epidemic stage, "spotted fever" can be unforgiving. Such epidemics have probably decided more campaigns than all the great captains of war combined. "The epidemics get the blame for defeat, the generals the credit for victory. It ought to be the other way around," wrote Hans Zinsser, typhus's principal biographer.[28]

Typhus fever's heyday was between the sixteenth and eighteenth centuries. By the twentieth century, medical science had vanquished the disease everywhere in the modern world except in isolated regions of eastern Europe. Scientists had established that overcrowding and poor hygiene were the leading culprits in typhus's transmission, and they had discovered an effective serum. German medical researchers were in the forefront of these epidemiological breakthroughs, which makes the creation of the Warsaw Ghetto all the more perplexing.[29] For in Warsaw and throughout the Generalgouvernement, it was German doctors and public health officials who were decisive in the creation of a sealed ghetto, effectively producing, in the words of historian Christopher Browning, "a self-fulfilling prophecy."

The public health rationale for the ghetto was that typhus would kill more Germans than disease-resistant Jews, who therefore had to be strictly quarantined. Some historians have discerned in these arguments an exterminationist conspiracy to wage germ warfare against the Jewish population. Although anti-Semitic malevolence was clearly present, the quarantine policy was actually more reflective of racism's coercive power to warp even scientific discourse. The public health director of the Generalgouvernement had once authored a scholarly paper on "ethnic identity and spotted fever." If the idea was medieval, so was the solution: a medieval ghetto.[30]

The ghetto's first major outbreak of typhus began in April and ran through October 1941. It likely originated in the overcrowded "points," where the destitute huddled together day after day in the same lice-ridden clothing, because it was the only way to stay warm, given the coal shortage.[31] Conditions were just as bad in the congested cellars of the tenement blocks, including Ogrodowa 30. "Poor people had been laying down sick with fever and hunger for days, just keeping up with a little water," Ruth said.

With the coming of warmer weather, the epidemic erupted from the basements and refugee centers. It was impossible to navigate the packed streets without brushing up against the clothing of typhus carriers. "The lice are omnipresent," complained Ringelblum. "They literally fly through the air." It was especially bad in the narrow Karmelicka Street. But even on such broad avenues as Leszno, where young mothers often parked their carriages to sun their infants, the human multitude swirled through the street.[32]

A lice comb was essential. "They used to sell them on the streets," says Dr. Thaddeus Stabholz. "The comb was made of black plastic and the teeth were very close together. It was for head lice."[33] Ruth obtained a comb when she found lice in Anne's and Lila's hair. "My mother used the comb and some kind of bad smelling liquid," Anne says. "I had thick curly hair, and the comb had to go close to the scalp. Between the smell and the pain, I can't forget it."

And thus, with the onset of spring, typhus raged out of control, increasing in severity during the summer and peaking in early fall. Over fifteen thousand cases were officially reported, but the actual figure may have been five times greater, and typhus probably touched every family in the ghetto.[34] The reason for the underreporting is that the cure was worse than the disease. "Woe to the tenants of a courtyard where a case of infectious disease has occurred," lamented Kaplan.[35]

For one, it could result in every occupant in the building being sent to quarantine stations, where crowding approached that in the "points" and sanitary conditions were deplorable. For another, it could bring down a building blockade by disinfection squads, who saturated apartments with sulfur and sulfur dioxide and plundered all the belongings. It could also mean standing outside in line for hours on end, waiting to be processed at one of the ghetto's four steam baths, where careless, sometimes malicious attendants ruined everyone's clothes by mixing everything together and trampling them in the mud. It is said that one's chances of recovering from the fever were far superior to surviving the delousing.[36]

The worst calamity was contracting typhus itself, since that could mean institutionalization in one of the ghetto's hospitals, either Czyste or the Berson-Bauman Children's Clinic. Not many typhus victims were ever hospitalized, even at the height of the epidemic; in the Warsaw Ghetto, hospitals were places to be avoided. The director of Czyste offered one reason: "The hospital has ceased to be a hospital; it is not even a poor-house."[37] Dr. Izrael Milajkowski, director of the Judenrat health department, offered another: the hospitals had become "places of execution," he told the underground archivist Emmanuel Ringelblum.[38]

Czyste Hospital was not moved to the ghetto until early 1941, although its one-thousand-person staff had been resettled there during the October population transfers. Ruth was vague about where Henry and Mery (and presumably younger brother Vovek) were now living. It seems to have been somewhere on Leszno or Elektoralna Streets, close to the eastern wall. As office manager, Henry had to have shouldered a heavy share of the responsibility for the move; in addition to supervising the hospital's clerical and custodial staff, he controlled the hospital's ambulances and horse-drawn wagons. A former acquaintance, Dr. Thaddeus Stabholz, said the vehicles could not be used "without his knowledge."[39]

The move itself was traumatic. Everything bolted down had to be left behind, the Germans said, which meant abandoning such up-to-date equipment as X-ray machines. And instead of consolidating Czyste's various units in one location, as was originally planned, the Nazis decided to disperse them throughout the ghetto. Thus, the departments of infectious diseases and pathology were put at Stawki 6–8, on the ghetto's northern rim. The central administrative offices went to Elektoralna 12, and obstetrics and gynecology, to Tłomackie 5. And surgery units where Mery practiced were stuffed inside a building formerly occupied by the Polish State Tobacco Monopoly at Leszno

1, across from the famous Tłomackie Synagogue.[40] Henry and Mery were broken up about the move, Ruth said. "They didn't know how they could put all the facilities in such a small place as was provided for them. But what could they do? They started thinking of how to take with them the most important equipment."

Henry, Mery, and the Czyste staff smuggled in as much contraband equipment as possible, concealing it in patients' beds and inside the vehicles Henry controlled. "It was like a caravan," remembers one young Jewish doctor. "Horse-drawn wagons filled with patients, furniture, supplies, books, food, and equipment paraded to the ghetto wall where the ss questioned—and often confiscated—every item."[41] The end result was a hospital in name only, "a complex, patched together, inefficient, and overstrained entity," as the historian of Jewish medicine in the ghetto has written. Because of a bed shortage, cots were jury-rigged from pieces of scrap metal and castaway pipes. Patients lay in hallways or shared the same dirty, soggy mattresses, swapping infections. There was an acute drug shortage. Operations were sometimes by candlelight because the hospital could not pay its electric bills.[42]

Henry had his hands full helping to keep the hospital afloat. Almost by default, he had become Czyste's chief liaison to the Judenrat, partly owing to a stoic temperament molded by his ongoing struggle with colon cancer. "He never complained," Henry's own surgeon once marveled to Stabholz. Henry's liaison function cemented a close relationship with Nahum Remba, a Yiddish-speaking Zionist who had worked in the ghetto's education bureau before becoming secretary of the Judenrat personnel department. Tall and robust, Remba had a reputation as a gay blade and an idler. "One could meet him in all the offices, gossiping and joking," wrote a former Jewish policeman.[43] But between the fun-loving secretary and the engineer with the perpetual half grin, there was a natural affinity and a genuine liking. The friendship served each man well. "Remba talked to Henry whenever he needed something." And the reverse obtained too: "Because of Remba, Tempelhof could do quite a few things for the hospital. It is a long story."[44]

But Henry's contribution to the hospital's well-being could be only meliorative. The Germans had returned Jewish medicine to the dark ages, and they were indifferent to the hygienic fate of even small children. The Berson-Bauman Children's Hospital on Sienna was "a real hell," a Jewish nurse said in March 1941. "Children, sick with measles, lie in twos and threes to a bed, all with the rash, all red and purple, with running, tearful eyes, shaved little heads, with scabs and sores densely covered with lice." And over everything hung the stench of excrement and pus because two-year-olds too weak to move simply defecated where they lay.[45]

By the summer of 1941, as the typhus epidemic worsened, every ward in both hospitals except surgery had become an infectious disease unit. They were the last places one would want to send sick children.

For a frightening moment it appeared as though both Lila and Anne might end up in the children's hospital. Lila had taken ill shortly after Ruth and the children had temporarily moved out of Ogrodowa 30 to a rented room in a neighbor's apartment. Ruth said the relocation was prompted by a "typhoid epidemic." Typhoid, an acute form of dysentery, also plagued the ghetto, but that particular malady had nearly died out by the time of Ruth's arrival in Warsaw. The epidemic that drove her from Ogrodowa 30 was most certainly typhus. A case of "spotted fever" had been reported in the cellar, probably in late spring or early summer. In June alone 280 apartment buildings were closed due to outbreaks of typhus.[46] The conditions for its rapid spread were right: scant soap, congested living quarters. "When you live in a room with a number of families without food or heating, everybody can see how people weren't thinking about staying clean," Ruth said.

All the tenants in Ruth's building understandably took alarm over the typhus case in the basement. If the authorities caught wind of it, they would blockade the entire building, sending everyone to the steam baths. The tenants of Ogrodowa 30 tried to subvert the disinfectant routine by hiring a private doctor to treat the typhus victim. Handling the case privately was a common stratagem among residents able to foot the bill. But the Judenrat health authorities must have discovered the case, because the victim eventually ended up in the hospital. (It is not recorded if he survived the stay.) That Ogrodowa 30 would now undergo quarantine was certain. To avoid that fate and the inevitable visit to the delousing center, Ruth approached an unnamed friend in a neighboring building, asking if she could stay in her apartment with Anne and Lila until the quarantine was over. Ruth offered to pay rent. "I didn't want to go to the public baths," she said. The friend said yes.

But shortly after moving in, Lila came down with a fever. It was a "high fever" at that, and Ruth was panic-stricken. She was afraid to mention her daughter's illness to her temporary hosts for fear of being asked to leave. "As soon as they would find this out they would tell me to go, because at this time everybody was afraid of the sickness," she said. Yet Ruth could not call a pediatrician either, "because the girl would be put in the hospital with all the children with typhus." So she phoned Mery, asking her to stop by but to come in street clothes, not her white uniform, lest other tenants take fright. Mery dropped in but was unable to offer expert advice. "I don't know what to tell you," she said. "I'm not a baby doctor, but I think this is measles. Give her aspirin and put her to bed or at least manage to keep her warm. There is nothing else to do." The diagnosis turned out to be correct. Red spots appeared on Lila's face in a few days.

But the prescription of plenty of bed rest was not practical: it would set off the same alarm bells as a doctor's house call. So Ruth put on a performance, the first of several she would learn to stage over the next several years. Dressing four-year-old Lila in warm clothes, she sat with her in her arms in a chair all day long, day after day. When the woman with whom she was staying asked why she remained indoors, Ruth simply replied that she did not care go outside. It must have been a convincing performance, her answers coming with unaffected nonchalance, for her friend dropped the subject—or at least she never indicated to Ruth she suspected anything was amiss. Sometimes it was simply wiser to leave things unstated.

Mery stopped by everyday in mufti, bringing advice from pediatrician friends and no doubt aspirin too. At night, to shield her oldest daughter from the contagion, Ruth slept between Anne and Lila. In the morning she rose before everybody else, quickly dressed her feverish child, and was sitting in the armchair by the time the apartment was astir. Lila's fever broke on the eighth day, just as the quarantine lifted at Ogrodowa 30 so that Ruth and her girls could return to their own apartment.

Though drenched in disinfectant, their bedroom had apparently been spared looting, and Ruth and the girls had escaped the quarantine. But, as it happened, they had not evaded the steam treatment. Because their names did not appear on the list of tenants who had undergone delousing, the janitor told them the only alternative to visiting the public baths was severe punishment. Their experience at the disinfectant unit was not as bad as it might have been. They were not shorn. Their only serious tribulation was to be sprayed with "a special kind of disinfectant soap," as Ruth put it, and harassment by the Nazi staff. "The German nurses gave us a lot of trouble."

There is a curious sidebar to Lila's near-miss encounter with the children's hospital: Ruth never mentioned that Anne also came down with a serious illness, arguably worse than her sister's. All Anne remembers is that "they put suction cups on my skin. There was a fire used to heat these glass cups which they put on my back for a while. The cups sucked in the skin, and when they took them off there were blue welts. It was very painful. I don't know what it was about."

Dr. Stabholz has a pretty good idea what was taking place: "The suction cups were called 'banki.' They were used for pneumonia. They put fire on them and then placed them on the skin for 15 or 20 minutes. All that it did was draw the blood to the surface, creating purple hematoma. It helped some, because the little blood that went out of the lungs let one breathe easier. That was the only reason for it. It didn't cure, just helped a little bit, if any, to breathe." "Mrs. Levy has a good memory," he adds.[47]

Pneumonia was frequently a side effect of typhus, at least during its course in the Warsaw Ghetto. Thus it may have been that Anne, not Lila, who came closest to being sent to the children's hospital. For unknown reasons, Ruth never mentioned the incident. It is though it had dropped completely out of her memory, or was shoved out. "My mother focused more on Lila's frailties," Anne says. "I guess it is because she and my father always considered me a tomboy, the daughter who was more willing to take chances."

Ghetto inhabitants who came down with typhus were much more likely to die from hunger than from the disease itself. The chief reason that Czyste Hospital had become a medical death row was lack of food. "The patients die from hunger in the hospital, because they get nothing to eat but a little soup and some other minor nourishment," Ringelblum recorded in his diary in August 1941.[48]

Under Nazi rule Catholic Poles were not well fed either: a mere 699 calories a day (compared with 2,613 calories for Germans), according to a 1941 Polish source. But German authorities placed Warsaw's Jews literally on a starvation diet: 184 calories per day, or less than 10 percent of the recommended daily allowance. The first head of the Transferstelle (Transfer Authority), the Nazi agency that regulated economic activity in the ghetto, including the food supply, was supremely blasé about the nutritional effects of German food policy. "The rapid dying out of the Jews is for us a matter of total indifference," he once proclaimed.[49]

The withering away would have been rapid indeed but for smuggling. Judenrat head Adam Czerniakow estimated that four-fifths of the ghetto's food supply came from contraband. Nazi-imposed scarcity caused food prices to soar by 2,700 percent, giving rise to a new class of economic risk takers. They ranged from daredevil children in tattered windbreakers who wriggled through cracks in the wall and rain culverts, to teenage gangs who shimmied down drainpipes and blended in with funeral processions to the Jewish cemetery, where they scaled trees and dropped into the adjoining Lutheran graveyard. So much smuggling took place in the State Law Courts that it became known as "the bourse."[50]

The bulk of the contraband entering the ghetto, however, was organized by rings of prewar criminals with the wherewithal to pay bribes. They became a new elite, consuming their profits at expensive restaurants and coffeehouses. "I remember on Leszno Street there was a nightclub," Ruth said with astonishment. At the apex was a Jewish Gestapo the Germans had established to combat "profiteering." Nicknamed the "Thirteen," after its address on Leszno 13, the organization used its ambulance mainly to convey illicit goods. (The Germans liquidated the Thirteen in July 1941.) Two higher-ups in the organization, Kohn and Heller, eventually took the operation private, spinning off a streetcar line dubbed "Uncle Kohn's Cabin" because of its filthy, crowded condition—the tram that smuggling built.[51]

The black market brought in plenty of food, "from honey cakes to the choicest wines," wrote diarist Kaplan.[52] But much of it was barely edible: dirty turnips and last year's carrots, black bread that tasted like sawdust, and tiny fish so rotten they were nicknamed "stinkies." A popular meat delicacy was rectum sausage, which was hard to get. Later on, a marmalade substitute derived from coagulated horse blood came on the market.[53]

Availability of foodstuffs was one thing; affording them was another. Contraband also flowed out of the ghetto in the form of canned fish and clocks, even chocolate and cigarettes, but fewer than a third of the ghetto's inhabitants derived sustenance from the smuggled exports. Everyone else worked for starvation wages or was unemployed. The once ubiquitous Jewish draymen, their horses transferred to Polish competitors, eked out an existence by harnessing themselves to their own wagons. A few hundred young men earned pocket change from bicycle-driven rickshas, the ghetto's only taxi service. The Judenrat's six or seven thousand employees, including hospital personnel, received below-poverty salaries, and these were never paid on time. The rest of the ghetto population simply went without work. Lawyers, businesspeople, artisans, and unskilled laborers—all were idle.[54]

The combination of mass hunger and unemployment led to a sell-off of Jewish property, which was one of the intended results of the starvation policy in the first place. The propertied middle class sold jewelry and silverware. The less affluent hawked clothing and linen. People even recycled gold caps and inlays. The bargains attracted swarms of Christians, like market days of yore. "The whole length of Gęsia street has become a gigantic bazaar," Ringelblum exclaimed.[55]

But not for the bottom half of the ghetto population, who had little or no money. "These were people who just had nothing," Ruth explained, and could not afford even rancid produce. They subsisted at the Judenrat's community kitchens, where once a day hot, watery soup laced with oats and an occasional cabbage leaf was ladled into their bowls. Its nutritional value was practically nil.[56]

Another source of nourishment available to the poor was crucial: the community kitchens run by various house, courtyard, and tenement committees. Practically every apartment building in the ghetto operated one. The courtyard committees belonged to an umbrella Jewish self-help organization known by the acronym ZTOS, which received funding from the "Joint" and the General-gouvernement and therefore operated independently of, and often in competition with, the Judenrat. Affiliates of ZTOS ran their own nurseries, hostels, Yiddish schools, and public health clinics. But the backbone of Jewish self-help were the house and tenement committees—"cells of limited self-government," as the historian Yisrael Gutman calls them. By September 1940, two thousand building councils had come into existence, many of them managed by women.[57] The committees met every evening to discuss common problems. "We would get together with our neighbors in the building and talk about the terrible situation we were in," Ruth said. She and her neighbors did more than talk, however. They organized lending libraries and courtyard nurseries; they staged concerts and dramatic presentations. Soon the courtyards, cluttered with broken furniture and drying laundry, metamorphosed into centers of intense local patriotism where every boy over ten had a public duty to perform, and every adult, a subcommittee to join. "We had to find some means of restoring cohesion, of calming fears, of teaching people to help each other," wrote a member of the Jewish Bund who had been involved in setting up the committees.[58]

The most important work remained poor relief, for every courtyard felt a responsibility to feed the destitute who lived in the cellars. So-called spoon committees collected money and spoonfuls of flour and gruel that every tenant was expected to contribute, and "a sort of vox populi" enforced collective compassion.[59]

Ruth got involved with poor relief work at Ogrodowa 30 early on, and not because of moral coercion. She needed a job to supplement her monthly income. The money Mark mailed regularly from Białystok was not enough to survive on, and her rainy day fund of personal possessions was quickly dwindling in the ongoing sell-off. But she was afraid to leave Anne and Lila alone and seldom did except when she brought the girls to a nearby self-help nursery, where they received hot meals.[60] So when her courtyard formed "a little joint treasury or community fund to help out those who needed help" and asked if she would like to have the job doing the weekly collections, she said yes. Although the salary was modest, it covered the rent, and the work was home-based. "This was very fortunate for me at this time because of my children," she said. After they came home from the nursery, she locked them in the bedroom as she made her collections. This way, she explained, "I was able to watch them and feed them and keep an eye on them."

Soon the house committee at Ogrodowa 30 decided to start pooling food for the people in the cellar, some of whom, Ruth said, "were so sick that they could no longer move from the beds." Ruth came up with the idea of having

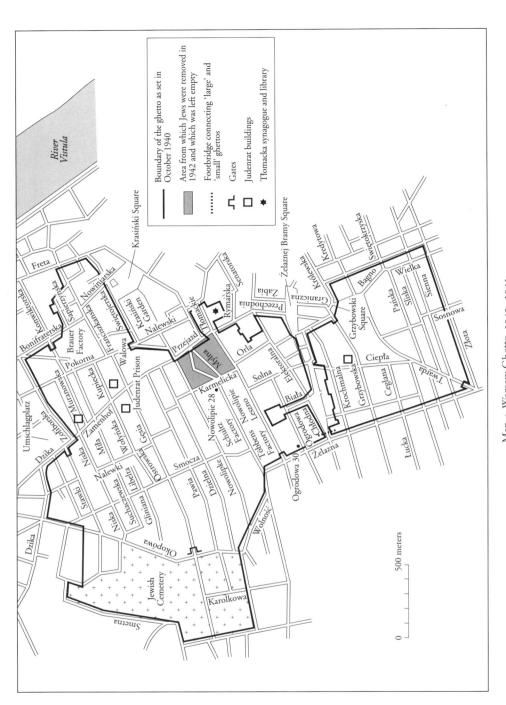

Map 4. Warsaw Ghetto, 1940–1943.

Source: Adapted from Antony Polonsky, ed., *A Cup of Tears: A Diary of the Warsaw Ghetto* by *Abraham Lewin* (Oxford: Basil Blackwell, 1988).

the building's tenants set aside a small portion of each day's hot meal. Most of her neighbors could afford the sacrifice. "The rich people even at this time were living fairly normal lives, some still had maids," Ruth said. The house committee agreed and asked her if she would be willing to collect the food too. She said of course, because she was already collecting money for the courtyard fund.

So, every afternoon Ruth went from apartment to apartment with one big pot. "Whatever someone cooked went into this pot," she said. "Sometimes this was all mixed up—one person made chicken soup, the other had sauerkraut, the other had vegetable soup. The conglomeration made me feel almost sick to look at." But the soupy blend of fifty different meals looked like heaven-sent manna to the bedridden, feverish people in the cellar. Their faces lit up when they came to the pickup point every afternoon with their crockery. "It was as though they were getting ready to eat a superbly cooked meal in a first-class restaurant."

Ruth raced from apartment to apartment, running up and down five flights of stairs. "Believe you me, it was a very hard job," she said. "I was very exhausted, and I was not feeling too good, because in this time there were epidemics going around." Nonetheless, she was more than happy to make the sacrifice. An awful premonition drove her on: "I made a picture of myself when my children and I would be in the same situation that these people were in."

As bad as things were in the cellars, they were far worse on the streets, where homeless people beyond number begged for food and money. There were child choral groups, ranging in age from four to ten. There were choirs with cantors, bands with instrumental and vocal soloists, bassos who sang arias all day long. Some beggars struck theatrical poses. Others formed partnerships, one man fainting while the other pled for food. "This is not ordinary panhandling, it is artistry," exclaimed Kaplan. But all too quickly the theater turned surreal. The poor swelled with starvation edema, their skin turning a velvety yellow.[61] "We started to see people in terrible condition," Ruth said.

Beggars turned aggressive. They pounded on apartment doors. Stationing themselves near food stalls and community kitchens, they tore bread from customers' hands, stuffing it in their mouths and covering it with spittle so that its owners would not want it back.[62] Ruth said it happened to her one Saturday when she went to Anne and Lila's nursery to fetch bread for their lunch. A tall man in rags with a swollen foot standing near the kitchen doorway pounced on her as she left the building. "Before I even knew what was going on he took away my portion of bread," she said. "I started fighting with him. I tried to take back my bread, but he was so quick. Like a starving tiger, he devoured the

Map 5. Street Grid, Selected Areas of Warsaw Ghetto

THE WARSAW GHETTO

bread." She returned to the nursery in tears, but there were no extra rations. Fortunately, a woman on the staff offered to split her bread ration with Ruth. "I went home lucky," Ruth said.

Not everyone did. A teenage girl on the way to the doctor with a glass jar containing her sick mother's feces was beaten severely by a snatcher who wolfed down the stool sample before realizing his mistake.[63]

The worst sight was the child beggars, whose numbers increased dramatically in the summer and fall of 1941. They usually waited until after the 9 P.M. curfew to appear in public; then they stood in the middle of the street crying out for bread. It was an awful sound, their shrill, insistent cries, impossible to hush if your apartment faced the street, as Ruth's did. One ghetto diarist in 1941 recorded this impression of child starvation: "The streets resound with the futile screams of children dying of hunger. They whine, beg, sing, lament and tremble in the cold, without underwear, without clothes, without shoes, covered only by rags and bags which are tied by strings to the meager skeletons. Children swollen from hunger, deformed, semiconscious; children who are perfectly adult, somber and tired of living at age five. They are like hoary old men and know only one thing: 'I am freezing, I am hungry,' so quickly have they grasped the fundamentals of life. . . . Ten percent of the young generation have perished already. Every day and every night hundreds of children literally die on the pavement and there is not prospect of ending this tragedy."[64]

Of course, the ghetto hospitals were in no position to relieve the acute malnutrition. Hospitals lacked food not only for patients but for the staff as well. The ghetto's beleaguered physicians still had their minds, however, notwithstanding Nazi efforts to "prohibit the Jews from thinking,"[65] and they focused their intellectual energies on organizing an underground medical school and conducting a clandestine hunger disease study, the most thorough and far-reaching of its kind. It was one way to protest the medical medievalism that the Nazis had imposed on the ghetto. Published after the war, the study tracked physiological changes wrought by starvation—the edema, diarrhea, weakened immune system, and changes in blood pressure. Some findings resulted from exacting forensic work in the hospital's pathology department. Some came from firsthand observation of their own withering away, because, as Dr. Stabholz explains, "even those who wrote the book about hunger were really hungry."[66] And much material was drawn from everyday observations in the refugee centers and on the hospital wards, because practically every patient showed some effects of starvation.[67]

Human samples lay not merely in the hospitals but literally on the sidewalks. "Everyday we found hundreds of people dying in the street from hunger and sickness," Ruth said. Their eye sockets were deeply cratered, their skin scaled with scabs. Mothers sprawling in doorways nudged their lifeless children, thinking they were merely asleep. Naked corpses covered with newspapers were pinned in place by brick and bomb rubble. Frequently the cadavers had been dumped by relatives eager to evade burial costs and avoid having to surrender the deceased's ration card. A beggar would swiftly appear out of nowhere and strip them of their clothes.[68]

Ruth tried to shield Anne and Lila from these macabre scenes, locking them inside the apartment. "They didn't understand what was going on, and I couldn't explain to them how terrible the situation was," she said. But the grim reality was everywhere, and all Anne had to do was sneak a peak from the window to lose her innocence. "That was the worst part of all," Anne says. "You could just see people laying on the ground dying from malnutrition. Old, young, all kinds of people. Men, women, children. The sad part was nobody had any clothing. It was cold, winter. And somebody would die and the next person would come and take their clothes off—whatever they had on—and cover them with newspaper, because whatever this poor soul had, they needed it."

Beginning in April 1941 and running through December, along a trajectory that paralleled that season's typhus epidemic, mortality rates climbed rapidly. At the end of April the official weekly mortality rate averaged from 150 to 500 a week; by midsummer it had soared to above 1,200. And from then on until May 1942, the monthly death toll never fell below four thousand and often exceeded five thousand. Overall, an estimated ninety-eight thousand Warsaw Jews—nearly one-quarter of the inhabitants—died in the ghetto, mostly from hunger and exhaustion. It is impossible to know for sure, because the cause of death could just as easily have been typhus, tuberculosis, or pneumonia, which are masked and to some extent caused by starvation.[69] In any event, the deaths were numerous enough to overwhelm the ghetto's primitive funeral industry. "Pinkiert, the King of the Dead, keeps opening new branches of his funeral parlor," Ringelblum wryly observed.[70] It was "a wholesale business," said Kaplan. Pinkiert's black-clad workers piled corpses into handcarts and horse-drawn wagons, stuffing several bodies in a single coffin. They buried them in mass graves, naked, side by side, separated by a board and shrouded in paper that was recycled for the next crop. The funerals were so commonplace no-body paid them any mind after a while, except the occasional madman who ran after every hearse yelling, "Did the departed leave his bread card?"[71] "There is a marked, remarkable indifference to death, which no longer impresses," Ringelblum rued in August 1941. "One walks past corpses with indifference." By October he was lamenting the ebbing away of human sympathy: "People have grown as hard and unfeeling as stone."[72]

By now the compassion fatigue had begun to sap the social solidarity of the courtyards. Arguments and quarrels broke out. Tenants balked at contributing toward the care of starving refugees. "Here are 5 zloty and let me alone," they would say peremptorily. Starvation began to corrode the bonds of parenthood. "The abandonment of children . . . has become a mass phenomenon," Ringelblum wrote in his diary in March 1941.[73]

Yet it was the maternal instinct that kept Ruth going. "I never let myself give up or relent because all the time I told myself when I give up and fall apart, then my children are lost too." And people all around her were indeed starting to give up. "Plenty [of] people took their own lives," she said. "They couldn't stand things anymore—to live with the fear of danger from moment to moment."

Through the first half of 1941 things were at least bearable for Ruth and her daughters. Her job paid the rent. Packages with food that Mark had purchased on the Białystok black market arrived regularly. The only drawback was retrieving them from the ghetto's solitary post office, which was usually a madhouse. "You have never seen a country fair until you have seen the Jewish post office at work," exclaimed Kaplan. "It is utter confusion." People stood in line for hours only to discover that their packages had been pilfered of their contents. All of Mark's parcels seem to have arrived safely, however. "I received plenty of packages, and everybody was happy for me," Ruth said. "And with the packages from my husband I got enough to keep up."[74]

But deep down, Ruth was scared. Enclosed in every package were letters from Mark urging her to "try hard" and promising that he would do "everything that he could to come together." The pep talk scarcely banished her fears: "I was all the time afraid of the morrow, the next week or next month," she admitted.

"So went the story week after week and month after month," she said. At least until June 22, 1941, when Nazi forces invaded Soviet territory. After that things began to unravel, as Ruth and her two young daughters commenced a downward slide toward starvation.

Ruth had a terrible time with wartime dates. Beginning with 1940 she consistently got them wrong. She said, for example, that Nazi Germany attacked the Soviet Union on June 22, 1940, which is a year too early. Names and addresses, whether in Łódź or Warsaw, never gave her the same trouble; her recall of places she had lived twenty years previously was keen. But she kept losing track of Holocaust chronology, and the memory lapse is hard to explain. Survivors do experience difficulty connecting their pre- and postwar lives across the caesura of the Holocaust. For them, the war period often becomes frozen in time, defying integration into an ongoing life story with beginning, middle, and end—a classic symptom of traumatic memory. But Ruth's shaky sense of chronology probably derived from the puzzling discrepancy in her daughters' birthdates, both of whom were likely born a year earlier than Ruth, intent on restoring twelve months to their stolen childhood, had always insisted was the case. And thus, as she tried to reconstruct from postwar memory the onset of the Holocaust, it is entirely possible that she made the event-filled period of 1940 consume most of 1941, forcing that year to encroach on 1942, and so on, until war's end obliged a balancing of the calendar. The point needs to be made if only because her postwar narrative is marred at critical junctures by these curious misplacements of historical time.

A date she did not forget, however, was June 23. That was when the last package arrived from Mark in Białystok. "After this I lost contact with him," she said, "and right now started my tragedy. What was I to do?" There was some forewarning of the tough times ahead. Shortly before losing touch, Mark, anticipating hostilities between Hitler and Stalin, stepped up the shipment of care packages because, as Ruth said, "he was sure we might lose contact again once this war broke out." A lot of Jews sojourning in the Soviet sector must have had the same premonition, for June was a peak month in the delivery of parcels to the ghetto. And then the mail from the east suddenly ceased.[75] Ruth stockpiled as much of Mark's shipments as she could, but they did not add up to much of a food bank. "By very careful apportionment I figured that this would not last me more than two months," she said.

The real challenge lay in making Anne and Lila understand the importance of rationing their food, of making one meal do the work of three or four. Anne was just about to celebrate her sixth (or seventh) birthday and Lila was four (or five) when the war between Germany and Russia broke out. "How do you tell two children that you can't give them food now, but we must wait until tomorrow?" Ruth asked. "It was very hard, and the kids don't understand." She anguished over sending her daughters to bed hungry every night.

Meanwhile, the war news was not good. The Germans had dubbed their 1941 operation "Barbarossa," after the myth-shrouded medieval emperor on whom nineteenth-century German nationalists used to center their völkisch rituals. The Nazi attack on the Soviet Union replicated the stunning Blitzkrieg victories in Poland and France. Within a week the Wehrmacht had captured Lithuania and Latvia. By the end of September, it had forced the surrender of Kiev, the capital of the Ukraine, taking 650,000 Russian soldiers as prisoners of war. By early December, armies were on the outskirts of Moscow, bombarding the Soviet capital. Only an early and severe winter caused the German war machine to stall, allowing Soviet forces to launch the first of several massive counteroffensives. But the scope of Hitler's lightning-quick conquest was still monumental, and the mood in the ghetto instantly darkened. "The latest news has left even the most hopeful among us dejected," Kaplan confessed. "It seems this war will go on forever."[76]

Białystok fell in a matter of days, isolating Mark behind German lines, and Ruth's old fear of abandonment returned with a vengeance. This time her barely concealed resentment of Mark's long absence broke through the surface. After all, her husband had been away from the family for nearly two years. About his resourcefulness there was no question. His capacity for hard work was never in doubt. But what about his courage? Was his oft-repeated pledge to reunite with his family worth the stationery on which it was written? Ruth was beginning to have her doubts: "I was sure that I would never see him again. I was sure that he would run away from the Germans as he had done in Łódź," she said.

So she surrendered hope of ever reuniting with her husband; her brother and sister-in-law, and even Julius and Haka, gave up on Mark too. Once again, as happened in Łódź when she became despondent, she grew resigned to a life of single motherhood. Henceforward, she would be "playing the role of mother, father, and supporter."

She was also losing hope for her parents back in Łódź, whom she had not heard from in over a year. She and her brothers toyed with the idea of paying to have the elder Tempelhofs brought to Warsaw. The "Thirteen" specialized in smuggling Jews across frontiers, and many of them were exiles from Łódź and thus knew their way around the city. "Of course," as Ruth conceded, "making a trip like this was a big danger and required a good deal of money." In fact it took a lot more money than Ruth or her brothers could possibly afford— anywhere from fifteen hundred to three thousand zlotys per person.[77] When they learned the going price, Ruth and her brothers abandoned the rescue project. "This was impossible to think of at this time," she said.

By now even Ruth's once prosperous neighbors were starting to feel hungry. The food situation in the autumn of 1941 grew desperate when German authorities, after months of official laxness, suddenly decided to crack down on smuggling so as to prevent bootleggers from spreading typhus beyond the walls. In mid-November, posters announced that Jews found outside the ghetto without a pass would receive the death penalty. In November, the Nazis executed eight young smugglers, six of them women; in December they executed fifteen more. Meanwhile, child smugglers became target practice for Nazi guards, who amused themselves by shooting the children perched on the wall "as if they were sparrows."[78]

The ghetto food supply collapsed, triggering a new round of hyperinflation. Now the most treasured family heirlooms went on the sales block. Moreover, even the kind of people who resided at Ogrodowa 30—"respectable, formerly well-to-do people who never had to worry about matters of food," Kaplan said—began queuing up in front of the community kitchens, rubbing elbows with the desperately poor waiting beside them for a bowl of soup.[79]

The new reality invaded Ruth's courtyard. She encountered it on her daily rounds. "At this time, things got bad," she said. "People had less and less. When I went on my tours to collect money, people would steal from me the things I had gotten from my husband." She never raised a commotion: "I just didn't have the heart to do anything about it." The truth is, she probably suspected her landlord, whom—oddly—she never once mentioned by name, fearing eviction should she level an accusation. Her anxieties deepened. Her food stocks were depleted: "I was thinking, How long would these supplies last me, and then what?"

As always, her fears focused on the children: "Of course everybody wants to live, but most important were my two girls. They didn't understand what was going on, and I couldn't explain it to them," she said.

While Ruth was off making her collections one day, Anne found a jar of jam her mother had stowed on top of a cabinet. "It was really well hidden, but I knew it was there," Anne says. She ate it all. "I don't even remember sharing it with Lila. My mother was really angry. I had eaten everybody's food. I got a spanking for it. I haven't enjoyed jam since then." Ruth never mentioned the incident, probably out of a sense of shame. "I guess she felt guilty for not being able to feed us," Anne continues. "She was at wit's end, and this was the worst thing I could have done. When you get angry about your child eating something to kill the hunger, you have to feel pretty miserable."

As terrible as Ruth felt, one thing she never did: venture from the apartment without a fresh face. The fact is, rouge and a crisply ironed dress had become a strategy for fighting back defeatism. "I am a person who doesn't like to show on the outside what I am feeling on the inside," she said. "So I all the time was with a smile on my face, polite to the people, keeping myself dressed and clean, with the last lipstick that I had on my lips." Many smartly dressed women such as Ruth showed up on ghetto streets even as the breadlines lengthened. Diarists decried their conspicuous display, viewing it (along with the escapades of wild youth and all-night cabarets) as another instance of the moral decay overtaking the ghetto. "On Sienna Street, where the Jewish aristocracy lives," Ringelblum wrote in disgust, "fashion is in full swing again." Modish women wore "French blazers" and full-length skirts, small, round hats, and high heels made of cork. When the weather warmed, silk dresses splashed with large flowers became the rage.[80] The high fashion, however, was not always hedonistic escapism. Like camp inmates who bathed in dirty water to assert their dignity, good grooming was a way of withholding consent, a way "to remain alive, [and] not begin to die," noted Primo Levi.[81] In a paradoxical kind of way, that is what Ruth's vanity had also turned into: an instrument of moral survival.

Invariably she became unglued after returning to the apartment from a hard day's work. Locked in the bedroom, Anne and Lila had not eaten all day. Ruth fed them whatever food she was able to scrounge. Then, after washing her girls, she sent them to bed in famishing hunger. Always they asked why they could not have more; always she answered that they had to wait until tomorrow, had to conserve food. After they fell asleep, she fell apart. "I started to cry my eyes out," she said. "I couldn't sleep at night. I knew very well what might happen to us."

But the following morning, she would put on fresh makeup, a clean dress, and go out again. Nobody ever suspected her real state of mind. The clothing concealed the person. "Of course wherever I went to collect the money everybody was sorry for me because I was by myself with two children," Ruth admitted. "But at the same time they had a good deal of respect for me for keeping up like I was." Pride in appearance helped her keep going.

Just when she thought things could not possibly get worse, they suddenly did. As part of the program to contain typhus by curbing smuggling, the Nazis decided to eliminate buildings with both Aryan and Jewish entrances, moving the wall into the center of the street. They decided to constrict the ghetto's boundaries by liquidating the little ghetto below Chłodna Street. The Judenrat talked them out of that drastic step, but the Germans continued to nibble around the edges, shrinking the ghetto a block here, a street there.[82] One area targeted for resettlement was a knob that jutted westward from Ogrodowa Street. Ghetto maps indicate that Ogrodowa 30 fell just shy of the evacuation zone. Nonetheless, Ruth's five-story apartment building abutted property that the German entrepreneur Walter C. Többens had recently incorporated into his growing industrial empire, which probably explains why, in the fall of 1941, Ruth and her neighbors were told to expect eviction any day—and on five-days' notice, if past experience was any guide. Fortunately for Ruth, the evacuation deadline for her Ogrodowa neighborhood kept being postponed, but for only a short time. In early November the Nazis began building a wall down the middle of Żelazna Street, close to Ruth's apartment. With food running low and her cash reserves practically depleted, Ruth now faced the real possibility of moving with her children into the same typhus-infested cellars whose inhabitants she was helping to feed.[83]

By now, Anne and Lila were developing distended bellies. They grew thinner and more listless, and their complexions turned sallow. Whether they developed the "bloody diarrhoea of starvation" is unclear.[84] But they were obviously sliding rapidly toward death. If Ruth had decided to swallow her pride and seek assistance from relatives, she apparently had second thoughts. "Julius tried to help me a little," she said, "but everybody was living from what they had saved up." She did not want to add to their burden.

She herself was close to the breaking point. "In my mind I had just one thought," Ruth recalled. "I have to die because I did not have much strength or energy left. And I was losing this."

In retrospect it is easy to understand Ruth's skepticism about Mark's ever rejoining his family. A lot of young men who had fled to the Soviet sector early in the war never came back. Moreover, many families failed to make it back. Mark's older sister, Stefa, and the rest of the Silberbergs were deported from Kiev to a coal mine in Siberia; later, like other Polish Jews trapped inside Russia after the outbreak of war between Russia and Germany, they were allowed to travel to Kazakhistan, where General Władysław Anders was assembling a Polish army under Soviet control.[85] Mark came close to sharing his sister's fate. Only his amazing gift for making himself economically indispensable seems to have saved him, not once but several times.

At the barrel factory where he had worked since arriving in Białystok, for example, he quickly became a foreman. The bosses in these hurriedly thrown-together plants often selected shop supervisor positions by staging fabrication contests. At one wartime plant where Mark worked, they made snowshoes; whoever molded the wood and weaved the cane the quickest would be named foreman, the bosses told the workers. Mark always won such contests easily, for his hands were nimble and his understanding of wood and machinery was flawless. "Daddy could do anything when it came to making something or fixing something," noted Adam many years later.[86] Both the skill and the foreman's position shielded Mark from deportation. Several times the commissars rounded up everyone but their Jewish foreman from off the shop floor and transported them to the east. But Mark was one employee they could not afford to lose. Who would train the next batch of workers? On one occasion he was mistakenly carried off with the rest of the work crew and placed on a train for Siberia. They rode for a day, and then the transport stopped to let the workers stretch their legs and relieve themselves. Just then a truck came speeding up. A man climbed down, made for the milling workers, and read off five names, one of whose was Mark's. The truck then drove him and the others back to Białystok.

In his last letter, enclosed in the package that arrived from Białystok on June 23, he wrote that the Russians had wanted to evacuate him to Moscow but that he had refused. He wished to stay close to his family, he told his superiors. "He told me he was not going anyplace and that he was staying right there," Ruth added. A few days later, as German troops bore down on Białystok, he asked his Russian bosses for permission to go to Warsaw, but they insisted that he accompany them to Moscow instead. He wriggled free of that arm-twisting by simply staying put when his superiors fled. But now he faced a much graver danger. The units of Army Group Center that roared into Białystok on the morning of June 27 were swiftly spreading a Nazi net that caught more than 2.5 million Jews, along with hundreds of thousands Soviet prisoners of war.[87]

For the fifty thousand Jews of Białystok, one-fifth of whom, like Mark, were refugees from Poland, June 27 became known as Red Friday. Following in the Wehrmacht's wake were *Kommando* units of Einsatzgruppe B, one of four ss mobile killing teams operating in the immediate rear of the invading army, for by now the Wehrmacht had completely swallowed whatever reservations it had once entertained about ss terror tactics. The killing unit assigned to Białystok was Order Police Battalion 309. A few days before the invasion, the commanding officer informed his company commanders that they had been granted license to shoot all Jews and "Bolsheviks" on the spot. The Białystok *Aktion* (action) began as an old-fashioned pogrom—beatings, beard burnings, random shootings—and then swiftly escalated into mass murder. Armed with automatic pistols and hand grenades, at eight in the morning members of the police battalion started chasing Jews through the narrow, winding streets of the old Jewish Quarter, driving them into the marketplace and toward the Great Synagogue. "I bet you in the whole United States, you don't got a shul like this," Mark said years later. "It was a circle like the Superdome. It went around and around. You could go all in and out, and in the middle was the bima"—the bar in front of the pulpit. Meanwhile, at the marketplace, German troops had marched Jews to a park, stood them against a wall, and shot them in waves until nightfall. But several hundred of those who had been stampeded toward the Great Synagogue were shoved inside. Dousing the entryways with gasoline, the Germans threw a grenade into the shul. The blaze quickly spread to adjacent buildings. Anyone trying to escape was shot down. Mark saw it all. "The Germans drive in over there," he said. "There were 600 people. They nail all the doors and blow it up, and I was standing outside. I was outside." The following day thirty wagons hauled more than two thousand corpses to a mass grave.[88]

More than an isolated incident, the Order Police killings in Białystok were the opening salvos of the Final Solution, the first blood spilled in a new anti-Jewish offensive whose explicit objective had shifted from emigration to genocide. It is hard to know exactly when the shift had occurred, for no Führer order has ever been found; given the bureaucratic chaos characterizing the Nazi state, as well as Hitler's odd decision-making style, it is doubtful one ever will. Since the 1980s, the gaps in the evidence have led to a spirited, sometimes angry debate between interpretive historical camps known as "intentionalists" and "functionalists." Essentially it is an argument over the role of individuals and ideology in history, versus that of impersonal forces and institutions. Intentionalists focus on Hitler and the continuity of his ideological obsession with Jews, implying if not asserting that mass murder had been Hitler's objective all along, perhaps as early as the 1920s. The functionalists, stressing bureaucratic structures and policymaking, depict the Holocaust as emerging piecemeal from the chaos of war: improvised rather than planned, coming from the bottom up instead of the top down, with Hitler barely in sight. Like most historiographical debates, this one has largely reached consensus by splitting the difference, a compromise supported by the preponderance of the evidence. Historians today generally agree that the Final Solution resulted from the interaction between the Darwinistic nature of the Nazi bureaucracy and Hitler's murderous anti-Semitism, with the Führer very much at the center of things.[89]

The Nazi decision to use murder to solve the "Jewish Problem" was no doubt reached during the planning phases of Operation Barbarossa. By then, Hitler's ceaseless radicalism, his self-image as a man of world-historical destiny, his vision of Russia as the "Garden of Eden" of future Germanic settlement, his conviction that there must be some ultimate reckoning between Germany and "Jewish Bolshevism," his fear that time worked against him in any two-front war, and, finally, his mounting frustration over repeated failures of the demographic reengineering project—all were causing the Führer to think about Lebensraum and the Jewish Question in a radically new way. The stone wall over emigration was a terrible disappointment. The Madagascar plan had proven a nonstarter. The Lublin reservation project came to grief over badly botched transportation arrangements—and the resistance of Hans Frank to Jewish settlement in his jurisdiction. And now expansion into Russia meant a vast new number of Jews under Nazi control, at a time when Jews in both the incorporated territories and the Generalgouvernement were already beginning to back up.[90] Thus, sometime during this period, the Führer apparently decided to slaughter Russian Jews captured by his armies and to turn the invasion of the Soviet Union into a veritable *Vernichtungskrieg*, a "war of destruction." Then, soon after reaching this decision, he expanded the annihilation project to include *all* European Jews. But he does not appear to have issued a Führer order. "Everything that can be discussed should *never* be put in writing, never!" he told Nazi party leaders in 1937.[91] How he made his new intentions known is pure guesswork. It was probably in a conversation with Heinrich Himmler, who could have been the one to have suggested the genocidal option to Hitler in the first place, thus to steal a march on his rivals for favor in the Führer's eyes. For that was how policy was frequently made in the Third Reich. "Incredible as it may seem," writes Michael Marrus, who has summarized the scholarly debates over the Final Solution with exemplary clarity, "an 'order' to send millions of people to their deaths may have been no more than a 'nod' from Hitler to one of his lieutenants."[92]

Once the annihilation decision started spreading outward from Berlin, it is stunning to realize how rapidly functionaries throughout the Nazi bureaucracy sought to align themselves with the new policy. The German doctors who ran the public health department in the Generalgouvernement were in the forefront of the self-coordination. It was not a major adjustment. After all, their decision to seal Jewish "plague carriers" inside such ghettos as Warsaw, by bringing on the very pestilence the quarantine was supposed to curb, had effectively legitimized the Hitlerian worldview that Jews were vermin. Acquiescing in extermination was, psychologically, an easy next step. Indeed, at the very moment Governor-General Frank had decreed the death penalty for all unauthorized Jews discovered outside the ghetto, the head of his public health department was telling a meeting of Nazi doctors, "We sentence the Jews in the ghetto to death by hunger or we shoot them." His remarks elicited "applause, clapping." Everyone understood that shooting was the new method of execution.[93]

Fanning out in four directions, the ss Einsatzgruppen included detachments of Order Police, as well as cadres of security police from the Reichssichersheithauptamt (RSHA), the headquarters of the combined ss Security Force. Eventually, the ss recruited anti-Semitic elements from among the ethnic Germans, Ukrainians, and Baltic peoples in their zone of occupation, sending them for training to a special camp near Lublin called Trawniki. Plied with vodka before going into action, the Trawniki units proved the most ardent killers of all. Many of the Germans who made up the Einsatzgruppen were ordinary men, mostly in their thirties, and a disproportionate number hailed from Austria. A surprising number of them were university trained. There were many lawyers, as well as professional opera singers, pastors, and Ph.D.'s and M.D.'s. The doctors instructed shooters how to execute neck shots so as keep their tunics from being splattered with the brains of victims: The usual routine was to force Jews to stand and sometimes lie, sardinelike, in antitank ditches and open pits. Then they sprayed them with machine gun and rifle fire. Twenty thousand Jews were murdered in Ponary Forest outside Vilna. Thirty thousand perished in a huge ravine at Babi Yar, near Kiev. The slaughter gave rise to a kind of "execution tourism," as off-duty German soldiers, Leicas slung from their shoulders, snapped photos of the open-air shootings. By the time operations had ceased in 1942, the Einsatzgruppen had murdered as many as 1.3 million Jews; the death toll for 1941 alone reached five hundred thousand. All through the summer ss police units, fresh from Kraków, swept back and forth through the Białystok District slaughtering stray Jews.[94]

Not every Jew in Białystok was murdered immediately. At the beginning of August 1941, several thousand were crowded into a ghetto and managed to survive until the deportations of August 1943. That the Białystok Ghetto lasted as long as it did says something about the interest of the local German civil authorities in exploiting Jewish skill and labor, as well as something about the determination of the de facto leader of the Judenrat, an engineer named Ephraim Barash, to take a page from the book written by his counterpart in Łódź, Chaim Rumkowski. Thus, after compiling a registry of skilled workers, the Białystok Judenrat pursued the same "rescue-through-work" strategy as was used in Mark's hometown, establishing a plethora of workshops and factories, some of which were owned by Germans, others by the Judenrat, and still others by Jews themselves. The industrial plants supplied the Wehrmacht with saddles, uniforms, and shoes.

Mark had no trouble finding employment as a foreman in one of the German-run plants, although doing what was never clear, except that it was not fabricating wheelbarrows—perhaps it was making snowshoes. He started saving money. Relative to other ghetto residents, he was in a good position. As had happened under the Russians, Mark's exceptional skill kept him off the evacuation lists that the Judenrat were forced to draw up occasionally. "They tried to keep people who were good workers like him," Ruth said. Little doubt exists that Mark, had he so desired, could have remained in Białystok until the liquidation of the ghetto two years later.[95] But he was growing anxious about his family. He had not been in contact with them since the invasion. It was late fall. The weather had turned cold. Sometime in late November 1941, he decided to make for Warsaw.

The journey would not be easy. "All the highways and all the gates from the ghetto were watched by the ss men and Gestapo," Ruth said. He told his German supervisor about his plans to return to Warsaw and reunite with his family. "Forget it," the man said. "You know the minute that you get out of the ghetto, they will kill you like a dog." Mark had to have known about the ongoing Einsatzgruppen sweeps: by this time practically everybody inside the Białystok Ghetto did.[96] All the same, he had made up his mind to go. He was afraid to travel alone, though, so he asked a young worker under him to come along and the young man agreed. Exiting the gate was easier than he had anticipated. When Mark told the ss guard where they were going, he waved them through. Someone will kill you later, he said. But Mark said he didn't care. "I'm taking a chance, anyway," he replied. "After all, what was life in the ghetto? I will die if I stay. Maybe I will make it." Then he and his young companion walked out.

They threw away their Star of David armbands, donned the clothes of country people, and began walking. They hitched several rides. "Mark walked and rode with a number of people," Ruth said. They did not have the highways to themselves, however. Several hundred Jews who had fled east early in the war were beginning to trickle back to Warsaw around the same time, bringing confirmation of the awful rumors of Einsatzgruppen activity in former Soviet territory.[97] Though less than 120 miles separated the two cities, the trip from Białystok to Warsaw took Mark and his companion about a week. After arriving he stood outside one of the ghetto gates, observing labor gangs leaving the ghetto under guard. Then he approached one of the ss soldiers standing at the gate and said he wanted to go in. Mark was still dressed like a peasant, and the guard mistook him for a non-Jew. He may even have been carrying false identity papers. The guard apparently asked Mark why he wanted to go in: "This place is only for Jews. And when you go in, you will never come out." "I'm going in," Mark said. "I just want to see somebody."

The guard waved him and his young friend through the gate. Ruth said it was a wintry Saturday morning in December, probably the fourth, possibly the eleventh. Dates aside, it was, as Ruth put it, "a day I never can forget." She was getting ready to make breakfast for the children. Her supplies were practically exhausted. Anne and Lila were in terrible condition. She herself was at wit's end. "My children grew thinner and thinner," she said. "My nerves were taut and tense with expectation of what might come next." She heard a knock on the door. She was in her own room at the time. The people with whom she was living answered the door. They were taken aback when a strange man asked for Ruth. "They were afraid who this might be," Ruth said.

Ruth came into the hallway and saw her husband. Anne remembers what happened next: her mother fainted. "Believe you me," Ruth said later, "I didn't know whether this was true or just a dream, but one thing I do know, this was a miracle."

But for Mark the homecoming was a jolting revelation. He hardly recognized his children: Anne and Lila looked like untouchables. Ruth was equally unrecognizable. The separation had lasted over two years, and as Ruth explained, "At the time he had left us, [we] were in a different condition."

Anne recognized her father immediately, but four-year-old Lila thought he was a stranger and took fright whenever he came near. "In the beginning it was really a tragedy for my husband," Ruth said, "because it was hard to take this coolness of his daughter."

All Ruth's neighbors came to the apartment when they learned of Mark's return, amazed that anyone would traverse the Nazi killing fields to come to the ghetto. Ruth called Henry and Mery with the news. She telephoned Julius and Haka. "When we all came together, it was a reunion that is hard to describe," she said.

The celebration was short-lived. His young daughters had to be nursed back to health. Mark told his wife not to worry. "I saved all the money that they paid me," he said. He went to a section of the wall where smuggling still occurred, buying coal and wood to heat the room, as well as food.

Mery Mejnster must have given him advice about how to nurse starving people back to health. As Anne remembers, "He cut up little squares of bread and butter and fed them to us one piece at a time, knowing that if we ate too much at one time, it would make us sick." Gradually their strength returned. Little by little Lila began to get close to her father, imitating Anne's example. "She started to call him 'daddy,'" Ruth said.

"What made this man come back nobody knows but him," Anne says. "I guess it was his commitment to family, to my mother, to his children. Why else did he come back? He could have made a life for himself and been like a majority of the other men. When he began telling his stories about the hazards he had to go through to make his way back, it was clear it took a lot of courage."

"These are the things you remember," she adds. Ruth remembered them too. Mark's return no doubt soothed long-standing resentments. "This was really a miracle," she noted, "because had he not come, we would be lost and going like the rest of the Jewish people."

For Ruth there were other benefits to having Mark back. "It was easier to manage with my husband now and not have the burden of the responsibility by myself," she said. Mark looked forward to the new responsibility. "I rest a little and then I will start looking for a job," he told his wife.

five

SCHULTZ'S SHOP

A workaholic, Mark wasted little time looking for a job. The one that caught his eye was the janitorial position that had recently become available at Ogrodowa 30 and 32. Earlier that summer Nazi authorities had ordered Polish janitors still living in the ghetto to move out, and the decree triggered a fierce competition among prospective replacements. Though the concierge positions paid nominal salaries, they came with attractive perquisites. The chief one was a free place to live. "All the janitors had apartments," Ruth said, "so we thought we could have the apartment and the job." The other perk was off the books: the power to charge fees for opening house gates during curfew hours, which enabled janitors to levy tribute on the smuggling trade. Mark wanted the janitor's position "not so much for the money but for the security," Ruth said. But many aspirants wanted these jobs for both money and security. The courtyard committees that did the hiring were besieged with applications from "former big shots"—merchants, physicians, engineers, even landlords—and "a great number of lawyers." Only one in a hundred were successful, however, and they were more adept at charging access fees than keeping the building clean, judging from tenant complaints about garbage accumulating in the courtyards. For the janitorial position at Ogrodowa 30 Mark had but a single competitor, plus the added advantage of a wife blessed with the gift of friendly persuasion. "All our neighbors were helping us in trying to get this job," Ruth said, which was doubtless due to her tireless campaigning. But she and Mark were up against an equally determined aspirant, and one who apparently enjoyed insider connections. Camping out at the front gate, "after two or three nights the other man started fighting with us and trying to put pressure on us," Ruth said. "So we just gave up the job."[1]

Concierge positions had another thing in their favor. Janitors received work cards that exempted them from compulsory labor. As was true in Łódź, ever since the invasion able-bodied Jewish men out on the streets during daylight hours had run the risk of being shanghaied by labor press gangs. The roundups became routine when Nazi labor quotas fell short of voluntary compliance. Poles were also dragooned for forced labor; many were sent to work on German farms and factories and to build the autobahns. Jews were rounded up to replace Polish labor and to perform backbreaking labor on public works. Large numbers were shipped for extended periods to German labor camps scattered throughout the Generalgouvernement, often to work on frontier fortifications close to the pre-1941 Soviet border.

The Jewish Police force (the so-called Jüdische Ordnungsdienst), staffed largely by well-to-do young men, had a major role in conducting the roundups and earned the lasting enmity of the ghetto population. Identifiable by their dark blue police caps and military belts, they pulled Jewish men off the streets and dragged them from streetcars. "It was a real orgy," Emmanuel Ringelblum wrote of one such action in April 1941. Whether conscripts were sent to work camps or mustered into one of labor battalions that left the ghetto and returned daily, the work was hard and dangerous, which is why the quotas were seldom filled voluntarily. "Plenty people going out to work never came back," Ruth said. "Some were killed who were sick at work." Nazi guards provoked fights between conscripted workers. They tormented observant Jews, ripping off their beards and making them stand against the wall with phylacteries strapped to their foreheads so that they could perform target practice. One gloveless Jewish worker forced to spend a day unloading blocks of ice in subfreezing temperatures had to have his hands amputated.[2]

"My husband didn't want to go out to work like this," Ruth said with some understatement. There was the added fear of another long separation. "From the time when we had separated in 1939, we promised each other that we wouldn't do this again."

Fortunately, a different kind of employment possibility had materialized just before Mark's arrival from Białystok. "We heard that the Germans were making a factory in the ghetto which made all sorts of things—clothes, shoes with wooden soles—and my husband got together with some of the neighbors and talked this over," Ruth said. In actuality, beginning in the summer of 1941, not one but sixteen German "shops," plus an assortment of Jewish-run industrial enterprises often affiliated to the German shops, arose in the ghetto, and all were privately owned and operated (unlike in Łódź, where the Judenrat managed most of that ghetto's numerous industrial workshops). The first growth spurt occurred in the spring of 1942, when the eastern front ground down toward stalemate and military procurement officials (the Rüstungs-Inspektoraten) accelerated the shift of war production to central Poland to escape Allied bombing. There was grim irony in the emergence of ghetto-based industry at such a late date, inasmuch as central authorities in Berlin had already decided to annihilate the Jewish population, including skilled workers. But, for the time being, the creation of German "shops" in the Warsaw Ghetto gave highly skilled workers such as Mark Skorecki crucial breathing room.[3]

The German enterprise that interested Mark was Schultz's Shop, also known as Big Schultz's to distinguish it from a smaller German firm in the ghetto known as Little Schultz's, which specialized in knitted wear. The proprietor, Fritz Emil Schultz, a jowly, bulbous-nosed fur merchant and manufacturer from Danzig engaged in supplying winter clothing for the German army, moved his operations to the ghetto in September 1941. To offset the loss of western markets, several old, patrician trading firms from such great port cities as Hamburg, Bremen, and Danzig eventually found their way to the ghetto after securing trading monopolies in the occupied east.[4] The most notorious was Walter C. Többens, the Hamburg merchant later convicted of war crimes, whose military apparel empire was destined to become the largest industrial enterprise in the Warsaw Ghetto.[5] But a close second in size was Big Schultz's, or F. E. Schultz & Co. GmbH.

Schultz opened his plant at Nowolipie 44/46, a pair of adjoining buildings whose courtyards before the war had been the site of a Jewish-owned leather manufacturing plant. Along the eastern border and across the back rose five-story apartment dwellings. Thanks to friendly relations with the Viennese banker who ran the Transferstelle (the German agency in charge of the ghetto's economic life), the Danzig fur merchant also gained possession of the plant and machinery once owned by his prewar Jewish suppliers, who conveniently stayed on to help manage their old properties. Although nearly every courtyard had its quota of shoemakers and tailors, Nowolipie had not been a factory area.[6] So Schultz made do by shoehorning his rapidly growing enterprise into the courtyard's nooks and crannies and detached interior buildings, eventually spilling over into random sites elsewhere in the ghetto. Pedestrians strolling past Nowolipie 44/46 would have had a hard time guessing what lay beyond the locked gate: a warren of tailor shops, weaving and cutting rooms, shoe and boot departments, a sock-knitting division, a machine shop, an electrical works department, a chemistry lab, a lumber yard, plus an assortment of washing, drying, pressing, and storage rooms. The only telltale signs of industrial life were the plumes of smoke drifting out of the courtyard and the caravans of trucks and horse-drawn wagons that periodically formed in the street to haul away mattresses, boots, fur-lined hats, and overcoats destined for German soldiers on the eastern front.[7]

Mark got a job in the division of Schultz's Shop that fabricated wooden soles, which became commonplace as leather shortages mounted.[8] Located in the rear of the complex, next to the lumberyard, the wooden sole department (Holzsohlenfabrikation) was small in comparison with Schultz's other divisions; when Mark began work in late December 1941, the total payroll could not have exceeded twenty employees.[9] Stuffed with lathes, saws, and sanding machines, the cramped, wood-cluttered workshop resembled a queer-looking dungeon. Work benches were closely spaced, and long, crisscrossing belts connected the machinery to wheels and pulleys high up on the wall. Row after row of wooden soles climbed toward the ceiling in pigeon-toed formation, like battlements in an M. C. Escher print.[10]

Like other German shops, Schultz's initially had difficulty attracting workers because of the low wages (barely enough per day to buy half a loaf of bread) and long workday (from 6 A.M. to 6 P.M., according to the postwar deposition of a Jewish worker in Schultz's knitting shop).[11] But Mark liked the fact that the factory fed its workers daily (Ruth mistakenly said three times a day) and let them take home the food.[12] To improve productivity, all German proprietors, including Schultz's, even increased daily rations to the level of Judenrat employees—or double the ghetto average. To a father still nursing his young daughters back from near starvation, a guarantee of basic nutrition was a major consideration.

On balance, it seemed an opportunity worth pursuing. And the more he turned matters over in his mind, the more sure he became that even this bleak situation had possibilities. He would make himself useful; he would become indispensable. He had done it before; he could do it now. It was not that large a challenge. As Ruth explained, "My husband was very interested in this factory, because he was thinking that with his general ability, he could perhaps find a secure place for his family." Mark quickly proved his mettle. In no time at all, he was promoted to foreman of the wooden sole department.

The promotion came none too soon. Just a few weeks after Mark signed on at Schultz's, ghetto authorities finally issued eviction notices to tenants at Ogrodowa 30, making all the energy expended earlier on the janitor's position seem glaringly beside the point. The order to evacuate came just as the Skoreckis were pondering, in common with the rest of the ghetto, how they were going to stay warm. On Christmas Eve, a week or two before the evacuation order,[13] an ss Police decree issued under Himmler's signature ordered Warsaw's Jews to turn over their furs within three days, so that they could be redistributed to troops on the Russian front. "It matters not whether a coat is luxurious or a peddler's old sheepskin," Chaim Kaplan lamented in his diary. "All fur collars, cuffs, boots, even scarfs, must be delivered in tribute."[14] Ruth did not mind parting with the fur coat she had purchased before the war during a vacation at the winter resort of Zakopane. "I didn't particularly feel like wearing it at this time anyway," she said. Only six and a half and already starting to show signs of emotional precocity, Anne also understood the necessity of relinquishing her fur jacket. But for Lila the fur coat order was a "tragedy," Ruth recalled. "She didn't want to give up her little coat." In fact, as if to compensate for the disintegration of ordinary symbols of childhood, she had come to regard her jacket as an imaginary friend; "she was afraid for her little fur coat," Ruth said. The night before the deadline, Mark and Ruth hid Lila's jacket, telling her the next morning that someone had stolen it while they were asleep. Lila was inconsolable. She cried for several days. "What can you explain to a four-year-old kid? What can you tell her?" Ruth said. "We were just lying to her, and that was that. She had to believe it." The next day, before reporting for work, Mark dropped off his wife's and daughters' fur coats at the Judenrat office on Gryzbowska Street. Not long afterward the thermometer dipped to minus four degrees and stayed there.[15]

Now, with temperatures hovering below zero, "the Germans"—to quote Ruth—"started pushing us out from the apartments." Mark approached his Polish supervisor, a native of Danzig (now Gdańsk) named Stelmaszek and told him he needed to find a place as soon as possible for himself and his family to live. If it could be arranged, he wanted lodgings close to the factory in order to keep an eye on Ruth and the girls. Stelmaszek had obviously grown fond of Mark and was able to lend a hand. Part of the agreement that had brought Schultz & Company to the ghetto was the understanding that German authorities would make apartment space available to the workforce. Some places had just fallen vacant, Stelmaszek told Mark, and one apartment was across the street from Schultz's. Ruth never specified the address. A prewar planning map indicates that it was probably Nowolipie 43 or 47, two apartment buildings controlled by Schultz's that were directly across from the porte cochere leading to the factory courtyard.[16]

"The new apartment was not large, and it was not comfortable," Ruth said. It had only four rooms and two beds, and the kitchen faucet ran cold. "Hot water we had to heat ourselves." By this time Ruth was down to a few pots and plates, the rest of her kitchenware having been sold off to buy smuggled flour and potatoes. Yet the sparse furnishings were less irksome than the severe overcrowding. At Ogrodowa 30, she and the girls had been forced to share space with only one family. At Nowolipie 43, owing to the shrinkage in the ghetto housing stock, she and her family had to make room for seven other people: a childless couple, together with a forty-year-old jeweler by the name of Rubens and his wife and five-year-old son. In addition, Julius and Haka moved in with them as well. Mark and Ruth and Anne and Lila shared one of the two beds; everyone else slept on the floor. "It was a hard life," Ruth said, "because I was never used to living with others." But the alternative could have been much worse. Several of her Ogrodowa neighbors may have ended up in one of apartments on Nowolipie Street that Poles had vandalized prior to their eviction. The previous occupants had removed windowpanes, locks, frames, even entire floors, leaving only the exposed crossbeams. "Simply a complete demolition," Emmanuel Ringelblum wrote in his journal.[17]

Foremen such as Mark had some voice in who would be hired. Many Skorecki neighbors from Ogrodowa Street expressed interested in finding employment at Schultz's Shop, especially after the eviction order, and Mark promised to do what he could for them. "We all the time tried to help our neighbors and to do favors to others," Ruth said. Mark approached Stelmaszek about hiring his friends and neighbors. He was able to find jobs for Julius and Haka, as well as for some of his Ogrodowa neighbors. Ruth said finding work for everybody was not easy, but at this early stage it was not impossible either. From December 1941 to July 1942, the payroll at Schultz's Shop climbed from 806 to 4,775, after which it soared to nearly 14,000, contracting just as suddenly to 8,000.[18] When that happened a once inestimable privilege threatened to turn into a terrible responsibility. For then someone would have to help the German management to decide who should stay and who should go, which in the summer of 1942 was tantamount to choosing who should live and who should die.

The Skoreckis were probably still settling into their new flat at Nowolipie 43 when the "Final Solution conference" met in a villa in the Berlin suburb of Am Grossen Wannsee on January 20, 1942. The meeting had been called by Reinhard Heydrich, Himmler's ambitious head of the powerful Reichsicherheitshauptamt (RSHA), or Reich Security Main Office, to coordinate planning for the extermination project Hitler had approved that summer or fall. In contrast to his boss, who resembled a ferret ("If I looked like him, I would not speak of race at all," a high-ranking Nazi once said of Reichsführer-ss Himmler),[19] the tall Heydrich was central casting's version of the blonde Nordic, and he was widely rumored to be Hitler's personal choice as a successor. Yet there was a trace of effeminacy in both his pear-shaped physique and high-pitched voice, and his personal habits belied the heroic ss image.

Before joining the Nazi Party, Heydrich had been cashiered from the German navy for sexual indiscretions with the daughter of a Bremen businessman. There were also unsubstantiated rumors of drunken binges in Berlin brothels arranged by one of his adjutants. But he was a strict disciplinarian, a born intriguer, and a take-no-prisoners bureaucratic infighter. Though leery of his subordinate's overweening ambition, Himmler knew how to put Heydrich's ruthless determination to effective use. Heydrich played a key role in the liquidation of Himmler's archrival Ernst Röhm during the 1934 SA (*Sturmabteilung*, or storm troops) purge known as the Night of the Long Knives. He helped his superior consolidate ss power over the German police and security forces—the linchpins of totalitarianism. In late September 1939, Heydrich became head of the newly created RSHA.[20]

Now, during the fateful summer of 1941, as ss special action teams answerable to him stepped up their killing pace and Hitler signaled his interest in the complete annihilation of European Jewry, Heydrich grabbed control of the unfolding destruction process by securing Hermann Göring's signature to a three-sentence directive. Dated July 31, 1941, the brief document authorized Himmler's deputy to arrange for "the complete solution of the Jewish question in the German sphere of influence in Europe," designating Heydrich plenipotentiary of the Final Solution. It was a highly significant directive. For if Himmler controlled the police and security apparatus, Reich Marshall Göring, as head of the Four-Year Plan, Hitler's 1936 blueprint for rearmament and geopolitical expansion, dominated the economy and the state, and his authorization effectively ceded authority over Jewish affairs to the ss alone. The directive effectively ended the obstructionism of Hans Frank. It cut through the Gordian knot of overlapping jurisdictions. So far as Jewish policy was concerned, it placed the regime's civil and military machinery completely at the disposal of Himmler and Heydrich.[21]

Under Heydrich, planning and coordination of the kind necessary for killing many people quickly proceeded on a fast track. Deportation trains began rolling eastward even before Nazi leaders had perfected the machinery of mass murder.[22] Shaken by an open-air shooting staged at his request in Minsk in August 1941, Himmler ruled out use of gunfire to commit mass murder for fear ss troops would find that genocidal methodology emotionally stressful. That fall and winter saw a flurry of experiments with alternative killing methods. ss leaders in Minsk field-tested explosives, tossing hand grenades into ditches and blowing up a bunker filled with patients from a psychiatric hospital. The explosions failed to kill everyone, however, and the cleanup afterward (body parts were found hanging from trees) was messy. Then a mobile gas van was rigged up for use by Einsatzkommandos in the east, and by December 1941, a similar vehicle, operating out of Chełmno, in the Wartheland, began gassing Jews trucked in from the Łódź Ghetto. Earlier that fall camp officials in Auschwitz also experimented with prussic acid (known by its brand name, Zyklon-B) by gassing to death several hundred Russian prisoners of war (POWs). But it would be more than a year before this killing factory reached peak efficiency. And it would not be until mid-March 1942 before permanent gassing installations were ready in the Generalgouvernement.[23]

In the meantime, the machinery of mass murder was beginning to break down, and Obergruppenführer-ss Heydrich, "who liked to act first and hold conferences afterward," felt compelled to call a conference. Many problems required untangling, ranging from intermarriage to Jews in war-related industry, and there was an overall need to improve bureaucratic coordination. Originally scheduled for December 9, 1941, but postponed at the last minute, perhaps owing to America's entry into the war, the Wannsee Conference opened at noon on Tuesday, January 20, 1942, took about eighty-five minutes to complete, and concluded with a luncheon.[24]

Twelve subalterns from state, police, and party hierarchies attended the meeting, including a heretofore obscure *Sturmbannführer* (major) from the Jewish desk at Gestapo headquarters named Adolf Eichmann, who kept the minutes. Heydrich, the thirteenth participant, was in the chair and did most of the talking. He reviewed the checkered history of emigration. He said the new Jewish policy would entail "evacuation of the Jews to the East," embracing 11 million people altogether, including Jews in England. Organized into labor columns, most of the evacuees would "fall away through natural decline," while the survivors of this "natural selection" process, representing the hardiest specimens of Jewry, would be "treated accordingly"—by which he clearly meant mass murder, since "treatment" was the euphemism Einsatzgruppen commanders used in official communiqués to report murder tallies from the field.[25]

By now bureaucratic circumlocutions were becoming habitual as Hitler's war against the Jews increasingly devolved into a matter of administrative routine—of routing memos and requisition requests and resource allocations among turf-protective agencies. Language was drained of moral and emotive content. Final Solution functionaries communicated in Nazi newspeak. Jews were never killed; they were "treated" or "sent farther east." They were not earmarked for extermination but "selected" or given "special treatment." Deportations were "migrations" or "evacuations." Brutal roundups were "actions." Jews were "resettled in the east." They were "wandering" and then somehow "disappeared." Says Raul Hilberg, the dean of American Holocaust historians: "These terms were not the product of naïveté; they were convenient tools of psychological repression."[26]

But around the conference table that Tuesday afternoon, according to testimony Eichmann gave at his 1961 trial in Jerusalem, the talk was direct and unfettered. There, in the parquet-floored meeting room, where Pans and fauns frolicked in bas-relief on the high ceiling and tall windows provided a view through leafless beech limbs onto the frozen lake, the deputy ministers and higher police chiefs spoke bluntly, "not in the language I had used in the minutes. . . . The talk was of killing, elimination and annihilation."[27]

To salvage as much German "blood" as possible, hold down the number of "interventions" on behalf of individual Jews, and reassure ordinary Germans that only Polish Jews were being deported, conference attendees spent a lot of the scheduled time nitpicking the fate of German "half-breeds" (*Mischlinge*, or Jews of mixed ancestry) and Jews who had married "Aryans." They devoted several minutes to the disposition of Jews who were elderly and disabled, who were highly decorated World War I veterans, and who were "prominent" persons. They discussed at length arrangements for deporting "foreign Jews." Some Mischlinge would be permitted to stay on in Germany if they volunteered to be sterilized, whereas others would be evacuated to the "east." The remainder would be sent, along with elderly Jews and Jewish war heroes, to an "old-age ghetto," which was subsequently established in the Czech town of Theresienstadt, the show ghetto that became an antechamber to Auschwitz.[28]

In stark contrast, attendees spent little time on an agenda item of vital concern to such Jewish families as the Skoreckis: an exemption for Jewish war production workers, at least until suitable substitutes could be found. At the meeting, Göring's representative pointedly had Heydrich reaffirm his promise not to deport Jews who worked in the arms industry. Though the Wannsee deferment merely ratified previous understandings between the ss and war industry officials, it came at a time when Jewish skilled labor was in greater demand than ever. In early December a surprise counterattack by Soviet forces outside Moscow nearly turned into a German rout. Then came America's entry into the war and the prospects of a second front. Anxious to knock Russia out of the conflict before turning to his western flank, Hitler rebuilt his army with German war workers at the same time that he stepped up war production, drawing replacements from conscripted Poles.

The shipping of Poles to the Reich aggravated labor shortages in the Generalgouvernement, however, rendering Jewish war workers even more indispensable in the eyes of the Wehrmacht and various armaments officials. Himmler begrudged making any exemptions. Economic considerations should play no part in deciding which Jews lived or died, he said. And he harbored deep suspicions of tailor and shoe shops, such as Schultz's in Warsaw, which to his mind were trying to protect their Jewish workers by masquerading as arms plants. But, things being what they were, Himmler had to go along with exemptions for Jewish workers even in questionable establishments like Schultz's. The Wehrmacht had contracted with that firm and others in the Warsaw Ghetto for winter uniforms for its eastern armies.[29]

Himmler may have held such skilled Jews as Mark Skorecki in low esteem, but Mark's German and Polish employers clearly did not, and events would demonstrate their readiness to do whatever they could to shield him from deportation. For their new foreman, it quickly became obvious, not only was good with wood and machinery but also was quick on his feet. "I think he liked to invent things," Anne's future husband explained, who observed him in his antique furniture workshop after the war, "and he would be able to put A with

B and make C, and make it work." His father-in-law had a pronounced competitive streak as well. "Oh, you don't know what you're talking about," he would say during arguments about some technical aspect of cabinetmaking. "Let me show you." And then he would improvise a special tool out of scraps from appliances lying around the shop.[30]

It was as though all the genius of east European Jewish artisanry had flowed into Mark's hands. And Schultz's management realized as much after German procurement officials placed an order for wooden buttons. The owner called Stelmaszek, Mark's supervisor, to the head office about the requisition, because the all-wood products were fabricated in his department. Could Stelmaszek devise a program for manufacturing buttons of various sizes, Schultz asked? The supervisor could not, but he thought that one of his Jewish workers might be able to. "Skorecki," Stelmaszek told his new foreman, "maybe with this you win something, so try to think of how to set up machines to handle this."

The offer placed Mark in a dilemma, a "tragic paradox," to use Ringelblum's observation concerning the plight of Jewish workers in the German shops. To survive, Mark had to help save the very military force that would eventually try to destroy him.[31] But the choice was clear. "Mark wanted to save our lives," Ruth said. "And so he started to build a machine." The first one was a small machine. Stelmaszek brought some of its samples to the head office and returned with the news, "We can make another department—a button department." Mark constructed a few more machines, then he built a machine that drilled holes in the buttons. The payroll in the wooden sole department increased; two shifts were set up, day and night. The work was done mostly by women, whom Mark trained. If Stelmaszek had not appreciated beforehand the rare find he had made in Mark Skorecki, he did now. "The supervisor said that he was very glad he had found a man like Skorecki who can do so many things," Ruth said, and the Pole would use the Wannsee exemption to protect his Jewish foreman from the ss as long as he could. From Stelmaszek's perspective, here was a Jew who was indispensable, indeed.

But he could not protect him indefinitely. For within the anarchic, competitive, bureaucratic structure of the Third Reich, where semiautonomous satraps won advancement in Hitler's eyes by outdoing one another in expressions of anti-Semitic zeal, the killing process had a radicalizing effect. Hans Frank, who had overseen the creation of German factories in the Warsaw Ghetto and had marveled in a November 1941 speech at the craftsmanship of Polish Jews, abruptly shifted course when his listening posts in Berlin told him that genocide was the new Jewish policy. On December 16, 1941, the governor-general called together senior members of his administration in Kraków: "Gentlemen, I must ask you to arm yourself against all feelings of sympathy. We have to annihilate the Jews wherever we find them and wherever it is at all possible."[32] It was clear evidence that mass murder would prevail in any contest between economic calculation and ideology, and that the industrial deferment granted to skilled Jews such as Mark could be terminated without notice.

After most of the delegates had left the Wannsee villa, Eichmann joined Heydrich and Gestapo head Heinrich Müller around the marble fireplace in the main hall. From both ends of the room Corinthian columns rose to a vaulted ceiling. Heydrich was smoking and drinking cognac when Eichmann entered. Unaware of Heydrich's habits, the Jewish affairs expert had never seen his boss use tobacco or alcohol. Heydrich was in good spirits. The conference had gone off without a hitch. Frank had been bested, and the Foreign Office silenced. The RSHA chief insisted that Eichmann and Müller join him in a series of toasts. "We all had drinks then," Eichmann later remembered to a German journalist who had tracked him down in Argentina before his capture by Israeli agents. "We sang songs. After a while we got up on the chairs and drank a toast, then on the table and then round and round—on the chairs and on the table again. Heydrich taught it to us. It was an old North German custom. . . . [W]e sat around peacefully after our Wannsee Conference, not just talking shop but giving ourselves a rest after so many taxing hours."[33]

Shortly after the Berlin meeting Heydrich returned to Prague and a new position that had been added to his portfolio—acting *Reichsprotektor* of Bohemia and Moravia, in the rump territory of Nazi-controlled Czechoslovakia. He had received the appointment in September 1941. With Hitler's New Order seemingly fast approaching, Heydrich wanted a territorial principality he could call his own. Moving his family into an estate outside Prague that had been confiscated from a Jewish banker, he established his headquarters in the Hradcany Castle overlooking the Vltava River. He destroyed the Czech underground with a reign of terror, also commencing a secret program to expel all Czechs except those suitable for "Germanization" and to colonize Bohemia and Moravia with a race of "Nazi warrior peasants," along ss lines, beginning with the resettlement of ethnic Germans from the east. That fall the Czech government-in-exile targeted Heydrich for assassination. The attack took place on May 27, 1942, as Heydrich was being driven from his country estate to the castle in an open roadster. The acting Reichsprotektor had ignored requests from Hitler and Himmler that he travel with an escort. He felt the presence of armed guards would communicate weakness to the underlying Czech population, whom he held in contempt. As his car slowed for a long hairpin turn in its descent toward the city, two resistance fighters, one Czech, the other Slovak, who had been parachuted into the country by the Royal Air Force (RAF), attacked his vehicle.

The primary assassin's semiautomatic weapon jammed. Instead of speeding off, Heydrich, sitting in the front seat, jumped up with his pistol and ordered his driver to hit the brakes. Just then the other resistance fighter stepped from the shadows and lobbed a bomb at the roadster, striking the rear wheel, hurling pieces of shrapnel through the vehicle. Heydrich staggered from the car and began exchanging pistol shots with his first assailant. Then he collapsed on the pavement. The bomb had driven pieces of horsehair and upholstery wire into his spleen. After being operated on Heydrich lingered on for a few more days, quoting sentimental doggerel just before slipping into a coma. He died on the morning of June 4.[34]

Heydrich's state funeral in Berlin was the most elaborate ever staged by the Third Reich. Black bunting hung everywhere. Flags flew at half-mast. Himmler delivered a long funeral eulogy, followed by Hitler. The Führer spoke but few words; he was still stunned by the death of his protégé. "Heydrich, he was the man with a heart of iron," he muttered as he patted the cheeks of Heydrich's young sons. Hitler ordered that the ss leader's death be avenged in some appropriate way. Three thousand Jews were transported from Heydrich's "old people's" ghetto at Theresienstadt to Auschwitz. But by now, massacring Jews had become commonplace, so the Nazis also destroyed two Czech villages. The most well known was Lidice. On June 9, the evening of Heydrich's funeral, ss security police rounded up the town's population, separating the adult males (who were shot on the spot), transporting the children to Chełmno (where they were gassed, except for eight with blue eyes and blonde hair who were adopted by German families), and sending the women to Ravensbrück concentration camp, from which few returned. And then, for good measure, they burned the town's buildings to the ground and dynamited the rubble. Heydrich's killers committed suicide during an ss effort to flush them from the catacombs of a Prague church. The Nazis displayed their heads on spikes. As a lasting memorial to the fallen ss hero, the Germans renamed the Nazi extermination project then in full swing in the Generalgouvernement. Henceforth it was to be known as Aktion Reinhard: Operation Reinhard.[35]

State secretary Josef Bühler, Hans Frank's delegate to the Wannsee Conference, informed attendees that he wanted the evacuations to commence immediately in the Generalgouvernement. But the Final Solution called for moving from west to east, beginning with the Reich-Protektorat, then shifting to incorporated areas such as the Wartheland. Chełmno, the first death camp, which was initially located in a former castle, began operating on December 8, 1941, when wave after wave of Jews, some recently arrived from Germany but the greater portion from the Łódź Ghetto, were stuffed into a gas van furnished by the RSHA's automotive department in Berlin and driven to the forest. The killing center was established at the urgent behest of Arthur Greiser, the Wartheland Gauleiter who had been wrangling with Hans Frank over the latter's refusal to accept Jewish deportees from Łódź and Poznań. But killing operations would not begin in the Generalgouvernement until March 17, 1942, when the fixed-gassing installation at Bełżec, a scant twenty-seven miles from Horyniec, the site of the Skorecki family's prewar lumber mill, became operational, followed in April by the onset of gassings at Sobibór on the River Bug. Even then the killings began not in the western sections of the Generalgouvernement, but in the eastern ghettos of Lublin and Lvov.[36]

Rumors of the Chełmno gassings caused scarcely a ripple in the Warsaw Ghetto, but news of the evacuation of Lublin, an old spiritual center of Polish Jewry, "a city of scholars and writers," was a different story. Some thirty thousand individuals, nearly three-quarters of the Jewish population, disappeared without a trace, said informants who had eluded deportation.[37] The location of Aktion Reinhard headquarters, Lublin was the first ghetto liquidated in the Generalgouvernement. Himmler had named an old crony, the Lublin District's higher SS and police chief Odilo Globocnik, to direct the mass murder operations in the Generalgouvernement. Of Slovenian descent and Austrian upbringing, the hotheaded Globocnik, or Globus, as he was called by intimates, was a disreputable character even within party circles. In 1933 he fled to Germany after murdering a Viennese jeweler; six years later, following the *Anschluss*, he was forced to resign as Gauleiter of Vienna because of charges of currency speculation. Himmler rescued Globocnik's career by appointing him SS and police leader of Lublin in November 1939, and the Austrian repaid his patron with slavish devotion. Himmler tasked him with the hands-on job of carrying out the Final Solution because the two men were equally captivated by the prospect of recovering the "German East."

With the onset of the war between Russia and Germany, Himmler's SS confected its most grandiose scheme yet for repopulating Poland, Belarus, Transnistra, and the Ukraine—a plan called Generalplan-Ost (Master Plan-East)—and in the summer of 1941 Globocnik, claiming to have discovered traces of ancient German settlement in his bailiwick, proposed that the Lublin District be used to anchor the new demographic engineering project, beginning with the settlement of SS garrisons of Nazi warrior-peasants. In July, as SS Einsatzgruppen were conducting sweeps through newly conquered Soviet-occupied territory, Himmler accepted the proposal during a visit to Globocnik's headquarters. SS economic enterprises, along with a slew of young planners and architects, were transferred to Lublin. Construction commenced on a new concentration camp at Majdanek (which subsequently became a death center as well). And shortly thereafter, either in the late summer or early fall of

1941, Himmler appointed the Lublin ss police chief to head the soon-to-be-renamed Aktion Reinhard. To expedite the Germanization program, the thick-necked, square-jawed Globocnik placed Lublin's ghetto at the top of the deportation list. Reports of the Lublin evacuations in March and April 1942 sent shockwaves of fear throughout the Warsaw Ghetto. "We tremble at the mention of Lublin," Chaim Kaplan recorded in his diary.[38]

But then those deeply etched delusions—that Warsaw enjoyed charmed immunity—could come to the fore. The Judenrat abetted the wishful thinking. Engineer Czerniakow, the council president, dismissed firsthand reports from two survivors of the Lublin Ghetto as exaggerated. Older Zionist leaders scoffed at them as well. "You Revisionists were always hotheads," one told youth leaders who pleaded that the time had arrived for Warsaw's Jews to prepare for armed resistance. "It's impossible to wipe out a population of half a million souls. The Germans will not dare to exterminate the largest Jewish community in Europe. They will still have to reckon with world public opinion. And finally, there is the assurance of the Governor-General Frank, that Warsaw, Radom, and Cracow will remain." It was the historic Jewish reflex, born of millennia of persecution: Hold tight, this too shall pass. And stand ready to sacrifice a portion of the community if thereby you can save the rest.[39]

From March through July 1942, the ghetto's moods wavered between optimism and despair, with optimism usually gaining the upper hand. "We were always a nation bound by hope," Kaplan recorded in his diary, "and so we shall remain." Pet theories on the war's progress, down to forecasts of the exact day and hour of German defeat, were the topic of conversation. Spirits soared when America entered the war. Reinhard Heydrich's assassination stirred hopes of early salvation. Jews argued and debated military news with Talmudic intensity, weighing every victory and defeat in the balance.[40] Hardly immune from the euphoric expectations, the Skoreckis grasped at straws of optimism. "Maybe in the meantime somebody would deliver us," Ruth said. "Maybe the Germans would be defeated, and we would be free."

But the ghetto mood could just as suddenly turn gray, like the leaden skies that cloaked Warsaw during most of that cold, sodden spring. News from North Africa of Rommel's victory over the British triggered despair. The continuing silence of the West concerning the plight of Europe's Jews deepened the despondence. And then there were the mounting reports of ghetto liquidations elsewhere in the Generalgouvernement: in Zamość and Kraków, Tarnów and Włodawa. What did it all mean? And what was one to make of Hitler's recent anniversary speeches gloating over his prophesies concerning the fate of international Jewry? On January 30, 1939, in a famous address to the Reichstag, the Führer had predicted the "annihilation of the Jewish race in Europe" should another world war break out. For all of its characteristic bombast, the prewar speech was probably a call for expulsion. But now, with reports seeping in almost weekly of the disappearance of yet another Jewish community, Hitler's January 30, 1942, anniversary speech took on darker shadings. It was at such moments that doubts surfaced about Warsaw's presumed privileged status. "Are you any better than the people of Lublin?" Kaplan asked Warsaw's Jews. "Will they leave Warsaw alone and be content with smaller massacres and pogroms?" another ghetto diarist, Abraham Lewin, wondered. "It gives me a feeling of deep unease to ask such questions: what makes us better than the Jews of Wilno or Kraków?"[41]

The mood swings grew more frequent following the Night of Blood on Sabbath eve, April 18, 1942. Accompanied by Jewish policemen, the Gestapo rang the doorbells of scores of residents, courteously inviting persons named on their sixty-person list to step into the courtyard, where they were executed under the glare of powerful flashlights. Though not every targeted victim was at home, fifty-two Jews were killed that evening, including several concierges who dawdled answering the bell. The hit squads left a few bodies at the gate, ordering victims' families to clean up the blood. A stunned community tried to make sense of the violence, so terrifying in its randomness. The Jewish underground was convinced the nighttime raid was directed at them and their publications, which had spread like wildfire. It is one of the lesser ironies of the Warsaw Ghetto that German authorities ignored Jewish political activity while savagely suppressing the Polish intelligentsia as part of its campaign to eradicate Slavic national consciousness.

Yisrael Gutman has discovered nearly fifty underground newspapers in the ghetto from every position on the ideological spectrum. In their soup kitchen meeting halls and through the columns of their mimeographed bulletins, right-wing Zionists and left-wing Bundists carried on a slash-and-cut dialogue. "We had even begun to debate and insult one another, as in the good old prewar days," Emmanuel Ringelblum observed. "We imagined that anything went."[42] It is true that the ss does seem to have targeted members of the underground, a fact that Judenrat president Czerniakow seized on to insist, with scant success, that the political parties cease their clandestine publications. But the midnight executions also lacked a clear pattern, and it threw the community into panic and near hysteria. What did the victims have in common?[43]

Not everyone gave way to panic. Henry Tempelhof was relatively unruffled. Dr. Thaddeus Stabholz, then a student in the underground medical school, ran into him a few days after the Night of Blood. Henry's reaction was, " 'Well, it's the war.' He didn't try to joke about it. 'Well, if that's all it would be, if only fifty Jews would be killed, fine.' But, you know, everybody else was saying, 'My God, fifty Jews were killed in one night! How could that happen?' " Henry had the rare ability to make people smile, to lift their spirits. "He was always full of humor during a very tragic situation," Stabholz says. "People felt better after talking to him."[44]

But even Henry must have been slightly unnerved by the increasing tempo of random killings in the ghetto. The raids usually took place on Friday evenings, Sabbath eve, but the schedule was haphazard and the victims unrelated, as before. "The worst part of this ugly kind of death is that you don't know the reason for it," Kaplan wrote in his diary.[45] The best explanation is that it was a deliberate ploy to terrify and terrorize the population, to sap their powers of organized resistance by killing potential leaders.[46] The murders kept everyone on edge, including Ruth. On May 29 the barber at Nowolipie 50, cater-corner to the Skoreckis' apartment, was found murdered. A week later a man and a woman were gunned down by German officers near Nowolipie 22 at the corner of Karmelicka Street. Three days after that, loud shots and beaming searchlights woke residents living near the corner of Nowolipie and Żelazna Streets, at the other end of the long tenement block. The number of victims the next morning was estimated at between eighteen and sixty. There had been random violence in the ghetto before, but nothing like this. "Every day we saw people running from ss men to hide and wait until they passed," Ruth said. "Every day had its atrocities and tragedies."[47]

But then stubborn Jewish optimism kicked in. False communiqués from the front vanquished entire German armies. History texts were ransacked for reassuring parallels. Ghetto inhabitants enjoyed reading about 1918, the year Kaiser Germany surrendered. They pored over chronicles of Napoleon's invasion of Russia, reveling in his defeat by the weather. But the resort to history was a flight from reality. There were no precedents for what was taking place, said the trained historian and underground archivist Ringelblum. In the past the Jewish children, earmarked for Christian conversion, were almost always saved. The disturbing reports of the slaughter of the young trickling in from recently liquidated ghettos indicated a new chapter was being written in Jewish history. But, except for the underground, most everyone else in the ghetto was too exhausted to think straight. "The Jews' nerves are ragged," Kaplan wrote in his diary. "Thus we are shunted from hope to fear, from despair to consolation and back again."[48] "An unremitting insecurity, a never-ending fear, is the most terrible aspect of all our tragic and bitter experiences," Lewin recorded in his journal.[49] It was hardly a frame of mind for rationally weighing risks when real disaster befell the ghetto.

Some ghetto inhabitants did heed the warning signs by converging on the "shops." Encouraged by signals from German authorities, Judenrat officials in every ghetto eventually began preaching a "rescue-through-work" strategy. In Warsaw they found many takers. Steadily the payroll at such places as Többens's and Schultz's began to climb. By March 1942, the number of employees at Schultz's approached eighteen hundred; by June it had reached thirty-five hundred.[50] "At this time plenty of our neighbors were trying to get jobs there," Ruth said. Typically, Mark promised to do what he could. His friendship with Stelmaszek, had deepened. They often closeted themselves in the office, pretending to talk business when, according to Ruth, "they were discussing the situation and what was going on." Mark's intercessions must have had some effect. The workforce of the wooden sole division, which probably numbered fewer than twenty when Mark hired on in December, soared to ninety-one by mid-July.[51]

There was a surreal interlude as the Warsaw Ghetto neared its final days. In early May 1942, just as the weather warmed and ghetto youths climbed to the rooftops to sunbathe and catch the scent of linden trees on the other side of the wall, German film crews wearing Luftwaffe uniforms invaded the walled-up quarter. One day they snatched smartly dressed women off the street to set the scene at fashionable ghetto coffeehouses and cafés. There were reports of young men and women being forced to perform simulated sex acts in ritual bathhouses while motion picture cameras rolled. There were the usual staged scenes of German soldiers rescuing Jewish youth from Jewish and Polish police brutality. "This was all for propaganda," Ruth said disgustedly, "to show the world that they were treating everybody well."

It was around this time that big Schultz's managers probably arranged to have photographs taken of the various departments and bureaus in their growing enterprise. The film crews shot pictures of the wooden sole department, the lumberyard, and the tailor and furrier shops. They snapped photos of the storerooms, the vegetable gardens, and the winter potato beds, as well as the dispensary and head office. About the only scenes omitted from the photo album were the squalid living quarters where Schultz's Jewish workers were forced to live, often ten to a room.[52]

By mid-July the Warsaw Ghetto was awash in rumors, and the mood was changing daily. On Saturday, July 18, near hysteria greeted reports that forty freight cars had pulled up along the four railroad sidings at the *Umschlagplatz*, the dirt-covered loading area bordered by Stawki, Niska, and Zamenhofa Streets, just beyond the northern wall, where the Transferstelle processed ghetto exports and imports. The panic continued the following day, fueled by reports that Jews in growing number were being removed from the Gęsia Street prison and summarily executed. Calm returned on Monday, but panic stormed back the next day. This time the hysteria had a rational basis. On July 21 the Germans had closed several refugee centers and rounded up the homeless. More alarming was the order evicting the infectious disease ward and pathology department from Stawki 6–8, the former schoolhouse and customs building abutting the Umschlagplatz. Most of Czyste's scattered departments were told to consolidate at Leszno 1, where Mery Mejnster's surgical ward was located. Of the hospital's 760 patients, most were discharged or ran away. The remainder shuffled in slippers to new quarters or rode in rickshas.[53]

Since January, Adam Czerniakow, the Judenrat president, had been plagued by queasy premonitions of the ghetto's imminent demise. In late April, when Germans asked his office for ten maps and a head count by apartment building, he wondered, "Is a decision in the offing?"[54] By July 20, the rumors were so thick that he sought official clarification. Several Gestapo officers whom he approached pled ignorance. One derided the rumors as "utter nonsense." Heinz Auerswald, the German lawyer whom Governor-General Frank had appointed ghetto commissioner in May 1941, with orders to turn it into a productive entity, told Czerniakow that any rumors crossing his desk be passed along to the Higher ss police leader. The Judenrat president was somewhat assuaged by vague assurances that Jewish orphans then being held in a detention center would be transferred to reformatories. After all, he had been dealing with these German officials almost on a daily basis for months, sometimes years. Surely, they would not deliberately mislead him. The engineer told his subordinates to quash the rumors winging through the ghetto.[55]

Auerswald not only misled Czerniakow but also "actually made a fool of him on the very eve of the impending tragedy."[56] A few days earlier, a company of the Lublin-based Einsatz Reinhard battalion, which helped with larger ghetto-clearing operations, had set up a *Befehlstelle* (command post) at 103 Żelazna Street. On July 19, Himmler, after touring Sobibór and Auschwitz and learning that Treblinka, the last of the Aktion Reinhard camps, was ready for operation, issued a secret order from Odilo Globocnik's headquarters in Lublin declaring that the Generalgouvernement must be emptied of Jews by the end of the year to achieve "the necessary ethnic division of races and peoples for the New Order in Europe" and to promote "the security and the cleanliness of the German Reich and its sphere of interest."[57]

Both Himmler and Globocnik wanted to move fast lest delay invite intervention from civilian and military officials on behalf of certain categories of Jews. The Reichsführer-ss had brought Hans Frank to heel by exposing the corruption in his administration, including the governor-general's diversion of confiscated furs for personal use. In June Frank signed an order transferring all authority over Jewish affairs in the Generalgouvernement to the ss. Far from offering immunity, Warsaw's size and historical importance as Europe's largest Jewish community practically guaranteed its destruction. When its ghetto disappeared, it would mean that a long stride toward the Final Solution had been taken.[58]

Adam Czerniakow's illusions came crashing down at 10 A.M. on July 22, when cars carrying members of the resettlement staff pulled in front of the

Judenrat offices on Grzybowska Street and ss Sturmbannführer (captain) Hermann Höfle marched into the chairman's office.[59] Just outside the wall, ss Ukrainian auxiliaries, detachments of Latvian soldiers, and special units of the Polish "Blue" police girdled the perimeter at twenty-five-yard intervals. The Ukrainians were members of the Einsatz Reinhard company that had arrived the week before; the Latvian soldiers had been brought in from Riga. Both units numbered about two hundred soldiers apiece. Though a lowly captain, Höfle, an "old fighter" from the days of Hitler's disastrous 1923 Munich beer hall putsch, had been assigned by Globocnik operational responsibility for coordinating death camp deportations.[60] Höfle was all business when he entered Czerniakow's office. The phones had already been disconnected. The Judenrat head recorded in his diary what happened next: "We were told that all the Jews irrespective of sex and age, with certain exceptions, will be deported to the East. By 4 P.M. today a contingent of 6,000 people must be provided. And this (at a minimum) will be the daily quota."[61] It was the eve of Tishah-b'Ab, a traditional fasting period for mourning the destruction of the Second Temple in A.D. 70 and the 1492 expulsion of 150,000 Jews from Spain. The tragedy about to unfold, the liquidation of the Warsaw Ghetto—"the largest slaughter of a single community, Jewish or non-Jewish, in the Second World War," according to the historian Martin Gilbert[62]—dwarfed even the Inquisition. And it was much more compressed in time: from July 22 to September 12, including a few minor intermissions, 250,000 Warsaw Jews at a minimum were driven to the Umschlagplatz and loaded into freight cars.[63] Only later did the actual destination become known: a death camp that had recently been constructed seventy miles to the northeast, near the junction at Malkinia, on the Warsaw-Białystok line.

Höfle told the aging engineer that his wife would be shot if the deportations were impeded. Other officials of the Judenrat were already being held hostage. Czerniakow nonetheless refused to sign the expulsion order. The next day, after learning from his wife, an educator active in the field of child care, that the orphanages were in grave danger, feelings of hopelessness overwhelmed him. That evening at 7 P.M. while alone in his office, he asked the maid to bring him a glass of water. He was white as a sheet and his hand was trembling. "Thank you," were his last words. Then he swallowed one of the cyanide pills he kept locked away in a tiny bottle in his desk drawer. When the maid reentered his office after repeated ringings of his phone, she found him dead in his armchair. He had left two notes on his desk. The one to his wife begged her forgiveness. The other asked his Judenrat associates not to view his death as an act of cowardice. "I am powerless, my heart trembles in sorrow and compassion," it read. "I can no longer bear all this. My act will show everyone the right thing to do."[64]

Czerniakow's death marked the passing of an older generation of accommodationist leadership. The youthful ghetto underground, men such as Emmanuel Ringelblum and Marek Edelman to whom the torch of leadership was about to pass, castigated Czerniakow as a weak man for failing to urge resistance upon his imperiled community.[65] Two decades later, when she revisited those years in an emotionally wrenching effort to pin down painful wartime memories, Ruth judged the Judenrat head in personal rather than political terms. Confusing him with Chaim Rumkowski, elder of the Łódź Ghetto, all she could recall through receding memory was that the president of the Warsaw Judenrat had somehow tried to save the children, including her own: "He tried as hard as he could to work for the Jewish people. He was a very honest man and a family man with children of his own. And he understood what a terrible situation the Jews were in." Her judgment fairly summarizes the scholarly consensus on Czerniakow, which holds that the engineer took his own life rather than be an accessory to mass murder.[66]

Silence filled the empty streets in the tense hours before 4 P.M., when the resettlement orders were pasted on ghetto walls and the sides of major buildings. Suddenly, a tide of people washed over the pavement. "The street became a human sea," Vladka Meed recalled six years later, "as people milled about in front of the German posters, straining to read between the lines, to fathom the meaning behind the words." At such times ghetto inhabitants usually whispered; now they wrangled and conjectured aloud. Two questions were on everyone's mind: " 'Where are we going? How many will be deported?' The posters offered no clue." The cryptic notice did state that deportees would be allowed to bring along fifteen kilograms (or thirty-three pounds) of luggage; money, gold, and other valuables; and sufficient food to last three days.[67] Those misleading signals were enough to stimulate the ghetto's incurable optimism.

But most eyes were drawn instantly to the exemption clauses. The deportation order would not affect members of the Judenrat, including hospital workers at Czyste and Berson-Bauman, which meant that Henry, Mery, and young Vovek Tempelhof were safe for the time being. And it would not apply to workers in the German "shops," or to members of their immediate family, which meant that Mark, Ruth, and Anne and Lila, now seven and five years of age, respectively, enjoyed temporary immunity, as did Julius and Haka, also Schultz's employees. But the clause that caused the biggest stir was the promise of an exemption for "all Jews capable of work who so far have not been included in the work process." When coupled with the fact that the first ghetto residents to be deported were panhandlers and refugees from the "points," the vague statement fostered the illusion that only seventy thousand unproductive members of the community would be evacuated and that the remainder, some three hundred thousand or so individuals, who signed on with a German "shop" would be able to shield themselves and their family members from deportation.[68]

In hindsight, it is obvious that the exemptions were merely the opening salvos in a divide-and-rule (Yisrael Gutman aptly calls it "divide and kill") campaign that continuously sifted an exhausted community into the reprieved and the condemned, then dividing the remnant again and again and again. First, the homeless were pitted against the productive; then the exempt against the nonexempt. Soon workers were arrayed against family members, skilled workers against unskilled workers, essential shops against nonessential shops. And so it went, wrote Ringelblum as he surveyed the wreckage, with circles "continually contracting" and the Germans "continually deceiving, declaring that the resettlement operation was over, in order to prevent a revolt."[69]

Hindsight also reveals that the Nazis were not about to permit three hundred thousand Jews to remain behind as work Jews. Nowhere close to that number would be granted exemptions. In negotiations with armament officials anxious to minimize the loss of skilled Jewish labor, Himmler had driven a hard bargain. The exemptions would cover only thirty-five thousand Jewish "armament" plant workers and their families, he said, or about one-tenth of the ghetto's total population. This remnant was to be reconstituted into an ss-managed labor camp within the interstices of the old ghetto.[70]

But few ghetto inhabitants were aware of these prior arrangements, and thus for them finding work immediately became the sole topic of conversation. There was a mad scramble to obtain an *Ausweis*, a "work permit," with its talismanic lettering, "Not subject to resettlement." Each morning after the curfew expired, the shops were engulfed with applicants from both ends of the social spectrum, cursing and screaming, trying to elbow their way to the front. Once prosperous businessmen and professionals, with secondhand sewing machines purchased for kings' ransoms tucked under their arms, jammed the employment bureaus. Fashionable café women clamored to be hired as seamstresses. The elderly shaved their heads to conceal graying hair.

The extraordinary outpouring of job seekers stimulated the establishment of a host of joint enterprises between Germans and Jews, to make brushes and mattresses, stitch headkerchiefs, and do printmaking. A cottage industry of small Jewish shops, many no larger than two people in an apartment kitchen, sprang up. "Gradually, all the larger dwellings and cellars were converted to industrial use," said one ghetto memoir writer. There was a black market in forged work permits, which were scalped on the streets like tickets to a championship sporting event. But above all else, ghetto residents bent their energies toward finding work in large German shops such as Schultz's and Többens's.

People with means even offered bribes in the thousands of zlotys for the privilege of being hired. The payroll of the big German shops shot up, often way beyond capacity. From a high of 4,775 in July, the workforce at Schultz's leapt to 13,850 in August, and the payroll at Többens's grew commensurably. In the wooden sole department where Mark Skorecki was foreman, the number of employees more than doubled in a matter of weeks: from ninety-one to two hundred, and Mark, who was constantly being besieged by friends and neighbors, no doubt did his part in driving up the numbers.[71]

The popularity of Schultz's and Többens's as places of employment stemmed from the belief that they were safer sanctuaries than the Johnny-come-lately enterprises. The perception was not illusory. As these things went—and admittedly they never went far in the ghetto—Schultz's *was* able to offer greater immunity to its workers by virtue of the close relationship between upper management and the local armaments bureaucracy.[72] If the Wehrmacht could not shield every Jewish worker deemed essential to the war effort, at least its procurement staff could notify German employers when a roundup was scheduled, and they in turn could send word down the chain of command that laborers should bring their families to the relative safety of the shop floor.

Holocaust survivors universally testify that sheer luck is what saved their lives, and a good part of Mark's good fortune has to do with his relationship with Stelmaszek, who promoted him, helped find jobs for friends and relatives, and located the apartment at Nowolipie 43, where Mark moved his family after their eviction from Ogrodowa 30. Ruth never divulged many details about Stelmaszek other than to mention that the Danzig native was "part Polish and part German," which is to say he was a Volksdeutscher, although, because of his fluency in German, the Nazis mistook him for a *Reichsdeutscher*, a "full-blooded German."

Two survivor testimonies given in Łódź in 1948 and now on file at the Jewish Historical Institute in Warsaw make reference to a "Stanislaw Stelmaszka, headmaster of carpenters/joiners," and the spelling and supervisory roles are close enough to the person discussed by Ruth as to encourage the inference that the two were probably the same man. After all, the only carpentry performed at Schultz's was in the wooden sole department and its contiguous lumberyard. But then one is brought face to face with a huge discrepancy in Ruth's perceptions of Stelmaszek and the postwar judgments of the Łódź deponents regarding headmaster Stelmaszka. According to one of them, this particular supervisor "tormented Jews working in the woodworking shop and he caused many accidents. One Jewish worker was shot by him."[73]

Whether the two supervisors were one and the same is impossible to determine concretely. The historical record on such cases is filled with seeming contradictions—of anti-Semitic Poles who rescued Jews, of ss men who treated Jews kindly, even of sadists who suddenly discovered benevolence. It is hard to impale the Holocaust on a moralistic syllogism. Whatever Stelmaszek's treatment of other Jews in the woodworking division, he viewed Mark in a special light. After the July 22 resettlement order, he put Ruth on the payroll, in effect providing the Skoreckis with a kind of double immunity, and then he let her stay at home with the children. "All we had to do was punch the clock," she said. But nothing rivaled in importance Stelmaszek's access to privileged information. "The supervisor got all the news all the time," Ruth said. And in the privacy of the office, where the two men often closeted themselves, he relayed the information to Mark whenever circumstances warranted.

That early-warning system helped the Skoreckis and other Jewish factory workers circumvent SS techniques for emptying the ghettos, which emphasized surprise, speed, terror, and deception—principles that had been perfected during the Lublin deportations back in March. In the beginning of the Warsaw liquidation, however, the Einsatz Reinhard units brought in by Sturmbannführer Höfle and the local Gestapo remained in the background, each day drawing up a schedule of streets and apartment buildings slated for evacuation and conducting spot checks. In other ghettos the task of preparing deportation lists usually fell to the local Judenrat. But in Warsaw, following Czerniakow's suicide, the Jewish council became a cipher, and such limited power as it possessed shifted to the two-thousand-man Jüdische Ordnungsdienst, the Jewish Police, which carried out the initial roundups.[74]

Disproportionately manned by lawyers, the Jewish Police had never been popular with ghetto inhabitants. Often the policemen took bribes. Some treated ordinary Jews with disdain. "An honest and good Jew never took this type of job," Ruth said, "but plenty of crooked people volunteered to take the uniform and these Jews did terrible things to their own people because they were sure nothing would happen to them." There were a few idealists in the ranks: some Jewish policemen believed they could act as a buffer between the ghetto and the Nazis. But that pretense was shattered by the onset of the deportations, and thereafter it is hard to defend them with the excuse that they had no choice. "Of course they had no choice—from the moment they decided to be policemen," said Yitzhak Zuckerman, a leader of the ghetto revolt whose greatest regret was not having executed several Jewish policemen early on.[75]

The Jewish Police began by emptying the jails and the refugee centers and by rounding up everyone off the sidewalks who failed to present a work permit. They formed the day's catch into rectangles in the middle of street and marched or carried them by horse and wagon to the Umschlagplatz. There was pandemonium. From just beyond the perimeter of the rectangle, Jews scanned the tightly packed crowd, looking for relatives. But it was dangerous to get too close. Indeed, it was dangerous to be outside at all, and when one ventured outdoors it was wiser to run rather than walk. Because they had daily quotas to meet, the police, sometimes aided by Judenrat employees with white armbands, were seldom punctilious about whom they nabbed. A young mother still in her bathrobe and slippers stumbled into a street blockade while hurrying to buy morning milk for her infant. Her papers were back in the apartment with her baby, she said. The Jewish Police refused to let her retrieve the Ausweis. When she resisted four of them smashed her to the pavement. They beat her, pitching her into the back of a wagon as she screamed in "a half-crazed voice somewhere between a sob of utter human despair and the howl of an animal."[76]

Vladka Meed witnessed one of these surprise street dragnets a few blocks from the Skoreckis' apartment. The police had thrown up a roadblock at a busy intersection to check the papers of pedestrians. Meed had a work permit, so she was waved through the checkpoint. Her attention was grabbed by a middle-aged woman's unavailing scream for help. "A few moments later," she writes, "two little girls, sisters about 10 and 12 years old, weeping steadily, were hoisted into the same wagon. They made no protest, uttered no cries, but submitted passively, hand in hand, their eyes roving, perhaps seeking their mother. Seated in the wagon, they huddled close to one another, crying silently. Even the policeman on the wagon was moved. He fumbled in his pockets for something, then stroked their foreheads." After the wagon filled up and sped off for the Umschlagplatz, bystanders gathered up hastily scribbled goodbye notes to family members that the deportees had tossed onto the pavement.[77]

"Men have become beasts," Chaim Kaplan recorded in his diary on the liquidation's fifth day. "It is the Jewish Police who are cruelest toward the condemned." Ruth agreed: "Sometimes they were worse than the Germans." Before the first week was over, eight members of the Jüdische Ordnungsdienst took their own lives.[78]

By then, the local Gestapo and Höfle's Einsatz Reinhard unit had taken direct charge of the deportations, and the blockades now proceeded methodically, courtyard by courtyard. They followed a set pattern. They always commenced with Jewish policemen invading a courtyard, sometimes as early as five in the morning but usually around six. They blew their whistles and shouted, "Alle Juden 'raus" (all Jews out). Some tenants tried to hide. Others escaped via secret courtyard passageways or clambered across roofs and over fences. Caught by surprise, most families hurriedly packed travel bundles. What to take? What to leave behind? Overpowering fear paralyzed clear thinking. Hands and feet seemed to move in slow motion. After ten or fifteen minutes the tenants assembled in the courtyard. Then ss Ukrainian and Lithuanian auxiliaries, following procedures worked out in Lublin, rushed up the stairwells and stormed each apartment in search of hideaways. There were sounds of windows shattering and axes smashing doors. Shots rang out. Loud wailing pierced the air. "The children, in particular, rend the heavens with their cries," Kaplan said. After examining each person's papers, everyone lacking valid work permits was marched to the caravan of trucks and wagons waiting on the cobblestoned street outside to carry them away. Then the mixed units would move on to the next courtyard and repeat the entire operation. Except for rare nighttime Aktions, the blockades were usually over by noon.[79]

The Skoreckis had front-row seats to the devastation—or at least Ruth and Haka did, along with the other woman who had moved in with them. Their apartment at Nowolipie 43 fronted the street, and from the outset much of the action focused on Nowolipie between Karmelicka and Smocza Streets. On Thursday, July 23, the police blockaded buildings near the corner of Karmelicka, dragging away young and old alike. "Mothers and children wander around like lost sheep: where is my child?" Two days later the apartment buildings at Nowolipie 10–12 were surrounded. On Tuesday, July 28, the Germans expelled everyone from Nowolipie 29, leaving their furniture heaped in the courtyard. A week later they expelled everyone from Nowolipie 45 immediately adjacent to the Skoreckis' place, sending them to the Umschlagplatz. Midday scenes near the corner of Nowolipie and Smocza Streets reminded ghetto diarist Lewin of "a hunt for wild animals in the forest."[80] That is how Ruth remembered the Nowolipie evacuations: "All the time when we looked out the window, we saw plenty of ss men running up and down the streets with guns in their hands or whips. When they found somebody in the street not working they either killed them or took them away." Many of the people executed on the spot were old and infirm, who were sometimes carried to the Gęsia Street cemetery and shot there. Ruth and Haka took a big risk observing the carnage from their apartment. The ss soldiers often fired at spectators peering from their windows, once killing a grandmother with a single shot.[81]

At the end of July the Nazis expanded their blockades to entire tenement blocks. And, again, much of the activity took place on Nowolipie Street, chiefly in the vicinity of Schultz's. Now the evacuations were part of a plan to house Jewish workers near the German factories by concentrating them in adjoining apartment buildings. The Nowolipie resettlement action, described afterward by Ringelblum as the "slaughter at Schultz's," was a bloody operation. All day Friday and Saturday, ss and Jewish Police units, assisted by Ukrainians, evicted every Nowolipie apartment resident between Karmelicka and Smocza Streets, in order to make room for Schultz's workforce. At least five thousand tenants were expelled (some estimates run as high as ten thousand), and over three hundred people murdered. "The turmoil and the terror is appalling," wrote Lewin, who witnessed much of the slaughter from his vantage point near

Karmelicka Street. Mothers cried out for their children, who were seized off the streets.[82]

It is doubtful whether Ruth personally witnessed this particular blockade, for by this stage of the liquidation Mark, who received advance warning by Stelmaszek whenever a selection was scheduled for the Nowolipie neighborhood, was most assuredly bringing his family to the factory for added security. Many Jewish workers in the German shops were doing the same. As the liquidation entered the second week, it was common knowledge that German authorities, pressed to meet daily quotas and prodded all the while by Himmler and Globocnik to get the Aktion over with, had begun to disregard the exemption papers of worker dependents caught in the dragnets—a practice that would become the norm in a matter of days. Even off-duty Jewish policemen were occasionally hauled away to the Umschlagplatz despite having valid papers, prompting some members of the police force to seek employment as guards in the German shops (over the protest of the workers already there). If the safest place to be during a blockade was a German shop, the Skoreckis were lucky indeed that their own sanctuary was in one of the safest factories.[83]

But not even such large German shops as Schultz's were truly safe, because, beginning in late July, ss units periodically invaded the German plants to cull out the "illegals" who were crowding the shop floors nearly to suffocation. There was not much for the stowaways to do except "sit around in dread of German blockades," according to Lewin, "and . . . hide themselves in all kinds of dark corners."[84] Ruth possessed a genuine Ausweis, thanks to Stelmaszek, so she was relatively safe while inside the factory. But Anne and Lila were at risk, notwithstanding their putative exemption as dependents, and Mark possessed too much flinty realism to entrust his young daughters to the obvious hiding places amid the machinery and piles of wood, fur, and fabric. Instead, he built a special compartment under the storeroom floor inside his workshop, next to the stacks of wooden soles that reached to the ceiling. A routine was quickly established. Whenever Stelmaszek tipped him off that the ss were planning to blockade their Nowolipie neighborhood, including the factory itself, Mark ran across the street and brought Ruth and the girls to the shop. As soon as they entered the wooden sole department, Anne and Lila slid into the crawl space under the floorboards. There were no frantic commands, no barked orders from Ruth and her husband telling their daughters to do this and not do that. Yelling was unnecessary. "Just be quiet," is all Anne remembers her parents saying. "It was never an explanation," she says, "just you had better do it, or the Germans will find you."[85] Then Mark loosely covered over the saw-cut edges on the floor with piles of wooden soles.

Although Ruth possessed valid work papers, it was important that she look busy. "I had to stay and do something," she said. And because the Germans were looking for featherbedding, and not merely forged documents, it was essential that the staged routine appear convincing. "So I pretended like I was a worker putting the wooden soles on the shelves," she added. She stationed herself close to Anne and Lila's hiding place. That way she would be able to comfort them from time to time with hushed words and to check on whether they were getting enough air. Breathing was difficult inside the cubbyhole. The compartment was scarcely larger than a shallow grave, and wood shavings and sawdust were everywhere, filling the air with minute particles. The heat was oppressive too. During the first two days of the liquidation a light, cooling drizzle had blanketed the ghetto, slickening the cobbled streets, but thereafter, until the deportations ended in mid-September, a ledge of high pressure covered central Poland, and the days grew hotter and more humid. It normally took the ss about three hours to complete a sweep of Schultz's, and Anne and Lila had to remain motionless all the while. Any restless shifting about to adjust clothing or scratch an itch could attract attention. Sneezes and coughs were verboten. And sobbing was something you simply learned to stifle.

These were always anxious moments in any shop, that terrifying instant when German and Ukrainian soldiers appeared at the entrance. Women hurriedly applied makeup and brushed their hair, mothers ran to hide their children.

"Are all the workers here?" a German voice demanded of the supervisor.

"Is no one hiding?" an officer barked next.

"No, Herr Offizier," was the reply.

And then security forces swarmed the premises, prying into closets, peering under tables and machines, overturning piles of cloth, looking for stowaways. Workers remained riveted on their tasks. No one dared look up from his or her bench. Meanwhile, the supervisor circled the shop floor hissing, "Keep working! Keep working!"[86]

Nerves remained taut long after the ss had departed. But terror-stricken parents needed extra time to recover from the experience. "It is hard to describe the feeling of my husband and myself when we had to do this," Ruth said of one of these shop raids after they put Anne and Lila in their hiding places. "And we did this plenty of times."

Only after the ss units had exited the factory and left the Nowolipie area would Mark dash across the street to make sure that the coast was clear. And only then would Ruth and the girls return to their apartment at Nowolipie 43. The homecoming could be grisly. The head of the Judenrat housing bureau was staggered by the aftermath of one shop incursion: "One day while climbing the stairs, I had to wade in blood almost above my ankles," he wrote shortly after his escape from the ghetto. "I shall never forget seeing a tuft of hair and piece of brain glued to the wall of the staircase." Ruth and the children never witnessed scenes so gruesome, but they commonly found sick people murdered in their beds. And the truly frightening thing was, as Ruth put it, "we started getting used to this terrible exercise."[87]

Mark himself nearly caught an ss bullet following an Aktion in the shops. It was probably around August 4, the day the resettlement forces evacuated the tenants at Nowolipie 45, next door to where the Skoreckis lived. This time the advance warning came late. When Mark ran to fetch his family, Ruth had to run out so quickly she left the afternoon's meal cooking on the stove. The girls were hastened into their usual hiding place under the storeroom floorboards. Ruth shifted swiftly into her sole-stacking routine. Then Ukrainians, "mean and rough with guns in their hands," as Ruth remembered, entered the area. No group of Nazi collaborators were more feared than the Ukrainian nationalists whom the ss had recruited, usually on the basis of extreme anti-Semitism, to serve as death camp guards and help with ghetto-clearing operations. The Ukrainians brought in by Sturmbannführer Höfle to assist in emptying the Warsaw Ghetto had a bad name even among the ss police because of their heavy drinking and brutality. "These were very rough men, with no heart at all," Ruth said. "It made no difference to them if they had to kill someone." Which is why the Nazis, after plying them with vodka, ordinarily assigned their Ukrainian auxiliaries the grisly work of shooting women and children: it eased the psychological burden.[88] Mark, believing it was safe to return to the apartment for a spot check, walked in on a Ukrainian soldier just as he was destroying the food still simmering on the stove. The Ukrainian had a gun in one had, and an axe in the other. "Mark was really lucky at this moment that the Ukrainian didn't kill him," Ruth said. The soldier failed to see Mark. He heard him race down the stairs, though. He chased after him, running into the street. Mark barely got away, shaken to the core by the close brush with death. "When he returned to the factory his face was as white as paper," Ruth said.

It was probably that day or the next that real tragedy struck the Skorecki apartment. During the deportations Ruth even lost track of days, as did most people who looked back on that period from the vantage point of decades. "That whole period is like one long night or one huge shadow which enfolded everything and I can't remember anything in sequence," wrote the pediatrician Adina Blady Szwajger. "There are only images that run into each other—I know that's how things happend [sic] but what and when?"[89]

But what Ruth does vividly recall is that during one of the blockades, ss guards carried away the wife and five-year-old son of the jeweler Rubens who had followed the Skoreckis from Ogrodowa Street to Nowolipie 43. Rubens probably worked at Schultz's, although Ruth never said so one way or another, so he likely possessed a valid Ausweis. The former jeweler tried to persuade the Nazis to take him too. For some reason they refused, Ruth said. She surmised it was because of perverse malice. "Their sadism was so great that they got a great pleasure of seeing people suffering like this," she explained. But the story does not quite add up. The resettlement units, anxious to meet their daily quotas, normally jumped at the chance to load volunteers in lorries bound for the Umschlagplatz. "When a child was caught, the father would willingly join him for deportation," wrote a former Jewish policeman. "Hundred of families went to the Umschlag [sic] because of the children," Ringelblum said. But many fathers and husbands, like Calel Perechodnik, a Jewish policeman in the nearby resort town of Otwock, declined to join their wives and children on the trains, and they were later consumed with remorse and self-reproach. Twenty-seven-year-old Perechodnik swallowed cyanide pills a year after his family had been deported.[90] The jeweler Rubens waited only a few days after losing his own family to commit suicide. "After this he took his life," Ruth said. "We found him dead. This happened to many other people too."

Suicides were numerous in the ghetto during the deportations, 155 in August alone according to a report by the Nazi governor of the Warsaw District.[91] In fact, many just gave up. The crying and screaming began to abate after the first week. People climbed into the wagons submissively. They turned themselves in at the Umschlagplatz. Some ghetto inhabitants had been lured there by the offer of three kilograms of bread and a jar of marmalade promised by German authorities to anyone who volunteered for resettlement. Starved and exhausted from dashing between courtyards to evade deportation, as many as twenty thousand people accepted the offer during the few days the policy was in effect. The Nazi ploy reawakened that incurable Jewish optimism. It aroused the all-too-human inability to accept one's own mortality, feeding ghetto delusions that Warsaw would be spared the fate of Jewish communities elsewhere in Poland. Why would they feed us if they mean to kill us? The trains are going to carry us to Smolensk where we will dig trenches. And what about the postcards some ghetto inhabitants had recently received from relatives saying they were fine?[92]

By August 1, the tenth day of the deportations, nearly sixty-five thousand residents of the Warsaw Ghetto had been shipped to Treblinka, followed a week later by another fifty-three thousand deportees. The ghetto's once busy streets resembled a graveyard. "It is as if the earth had opened and swallowed up all its crowds and noises, its secrets and vices, and the entire tribe of ants that scurried through its streets from dawn until curfew," wrote Kaplan on July 29. Five days later, after smuggling out his diary to a Polish friend, Kaplan himself disappeared. It is believed that he and his wife perished at Treblinka.[93]

Many of deportees rounded up during the first week in August came from the southern part of the walled quarter, the so-called little ghetto below

Chłodna Street, one of the first areas of the ghetto to be completely evacuated, save for the outpost of one of Walter C. Többens's industrial shops.[94]

Szwajger, the young doctor at the Berson-Bauman Children's Hospital, watched the deportees streaming out of the "little ghetto." Just beyond the wall she saw a Polish woman in a flowered housecoat watering plants on her balcony while a living funeral passed by only feet away: "They kept going past, they kept going past, with prams and all sorts of strange objects, hats and coats and pots or bowls, and they still kept going past."[95] It was only week two of the liquidation, and there was still more than a month to go before the Great Deportations would end.

THE VEGETABLE BIN

Sometime before August 13, while the liquidation was in its third week, the Skoreckis moved to a new apartment at Nowolipie 28. The Nazis had encircled the tenement blocks on both sides of Nowolipie from Karmelicka to Smocza Street with wooden fences that ran close to the curb, assigning Többens's the odd-numbered and Schultz's the even-numbered side of the street. The two firms were told to consolidate their operations, laborers included, in the apartment buildings encompassed by their "blocks," though Többens's retained a small shop area in the now liquidated "little ghetto." The ss threw up guard gates around the perimeter to regulate access to the shop areas.

The middle of Nowolipie soon resembled the River Styx. Workers were not allowed to cross the cobbled thoroughfare to visit friends in the neighboring factory. Emmanuel Ringelblum, the underground archivist, called the enclosed blocks "special ghettos," with their "own bakeries, drug stores, grocery stores, shoe stores, barbers, even synagogues—separate towns, even to the point of local patriotism—when it came to fundraising." But a somewhat different image lingered in Ruth's mind. "We were like in a cage with no hope of coming out," she said.[1]

Much turmoil accompanied the relocation of workers to their new quarters. "Fights flared up over housing allotments," remembers Vladka Meed, who later became a courier for the Jewish underground. And there was a mad scramble to seize the furniture and household goods abandoned by previous tenants recently hustled off to the Umschlagplatz. But foremanship still had its privileges, "one of which," Ruth said, "was getting a better apartment." And so the Skoreckis were assigned a street-front flat on the third floor of the five-story building at Nowolipie 28, the next-door neighbor to the old Judenrat kitchen before its liquidation on August 1. One of Schultz's seamstress shops was located in the courtyard at this address. Mark arranged for Julius and Haka to move in with them, "so that we could be together no matter what might happen," Ruth said. And the Skoreckis also made room for a young couple with a daughter roughly the same age as Anne and Lila; the father was one of Mark's helpers. The new place was larger—six rooms instead of four. But it was still cramped, and there was hardly any room to move around. As Lila remembers, "It was a very small apartment, with a couple of closets and a few pieces of furniture, some of which were built by my father so that he would know exactly what was in them and how they were constructed."[2]

No sooner had Jewish workers like the Skoreckis settled into their new quarters than their tenement cages turned into traps. From August 15 through September 6, Hermann Höfle's Einsatz Reinhard security force and the Gestapo placed the German shops under almost continuous siege in an effort to weed out the "illegals" and those who were unfit for work, thus reducing the ghetto labor force to the thirty-five-thousand-person quota Himmler had set on the eve of the deportations. On August 16, the Nazis issued a proclamation canceling all family exemptions. Panic spread through the shops. "Everybody had to go to work, women and old people included," Ruth said.[3]

For a short period thereafter Stelmaszek continued to wink at Ruth's phantom relationship with Schultz's, letting her punch the time clock and then return to the apartment each morning to watch Anne and Lila. But the preferential treatment soon caused resentment among other shopworkers, and Stelmaszek became uneasy. "Mr. Skorecki, I can't do it anymore," he told Mark one day. "People come to me and ask, 'Why is it that Mr. Skorecki's wife stays home and doesn't work?' " He told Mark that Ruth had to start coming to the factory every morning like the rest of the labor force, that she had to be seen working. But for the Skoreckis the question then arose, what were they to do with their two girls? For over a week now, the ss had been deporting dependents from even large shops such as Többens's. Exemptions for family members had become worthless. "It looks like there is a policy to liquidate women and children," the ghetto diarist Abraham Lewin wrote on August 11, after the Germans had hauled away forty screaming children from Többens's day care center.[4] Ruth knew with a mother's certitude what had to done: "I told Mark, 'I'm not going without the children.' "

Thus beginning in mid-August, every weekday morning at 6 A.M. Anne and Lila accompanied their parents to the wooden sole department, returning home at six in the evening, except on Saturdays, when the workday ended at noon. Many couples who still had children also started bringing them to the factory area every morning. For much of the workday the Skorecki sisters played imaginary games with the wooden soles in the storeroom, in the rear of the shop. "We didn't have toys," Lila says.

"If I close my eyes I can remember that place," Anne adds. "It was a small area, just where the soles were." There must have been times when the two girls ventured into the shop area. One picture appearing in the Schultz's photo album contains a ghostly image of a young child watching bandsaw operators turn blocks of wood into shoe bottoms. Midday the factory kitchen carried a huge soup kettle to the rear courtyard, where workers in the main factory at Nowolipie 44–46 lined up to fill their bowls and receive slices of bread. They ate in their respective departments. Initially, Anne and Lila accompanied their parents to the soup line. "Everybody knew we were there," Anne says, "and they made room for us to get our food first." But that practice ended quickly. Once Schultz's workers had been consolidated in one place, the tempo of ss raids picked up considerably.

This time the raids were different. No longer spot checks of individual departments as workers hunched over their benches and machines, they were "selections," because now the ss was intent on removing not merely "illegals" but any worker who could not pass an appearance test. Workers were ordered to assemble outside, usually in rows of five. Ruth said the formations occurred in the street, and some no doubt did. But other sources suggest the selections were ordinarily in the front and rear courtyards at Nowolipie 44–46. Jewish parents faced a new set of choices: should they leave their young children alone in their hiding places inside the factory, or stay with them to provide moral support, shush the crying, allay the trembling? Or should they bring them outside to the formations? The third option was surprisingly popular. "Most of the people took their kids in the streets and tried to hide them in the ranks," Ruth said. Doing so was a grave risk, but some parents had no choice. Many young children were too frightened to be left alone in some dark corner, and their hiding places were too small to accommodate an adult.

There was no question that Mark and Ruth would leave their daughters behind. When a selection was announced, they hurried them into the hidden floor compartment inside the storeroom, covering the trapdoor loosely with wooden soles so that air could get in. "Just be quiet," they said, as they customarily did, before leaving to join the other workers outside. The routine was always the same. The heat was oppressive. People stood in ranks for hours. The Germans inspected hair and hands, pulling people out of line whose palms were soft. They removed the elderly. One survivor of these selections, Sophia Leviathan, whose husband was a bookkeeper in the main office where she herself worked for a spell before moving on to the seamstress department, remembered workers being told to go to the left or the right. "This one word, right or left, decided life or death. Left meant you might live longer; right, that you were bound for death."[5] Ruth did not remember the Germans proceeding so formally in this particular setting; they simply yanked people out of line, she said. "We never knew who would be chosen next. When they saw an older person, they told him to step out into a special rank. People who were weak were called to the side. So were those who looked pale and weak, regardless of age. Sometimes even when they didn't like the faces of the Jews, the ss men called them aside." It made no difference whether they were skilled specialists, said Lewin: anyone who was lame or appeared sickly got pulled from the ranks.[6]

And many children were taken. The ss had little trouble spotting stowaways in the formations. They were the tiny workers garbed in adult clothes, the telltale bulge in the fold of a mother's dress.

Meanwhile, Ukrainian soldiers and their German leaders combed the yard and workshop in search of "illegals." You always knew when they had made a discovery: a scream burst from a woodpile or flew from an open door or window. Inside the factory, tension was high. Safety turned on how quiet you were. Having a parent close by could make a difference. Sophia Leviathan, cuddling her young child, hid on the cellar steps next to a revolving piece of machinery, as condensation from a piece of tubing dripped regularly on her head. The child fell asleep in her arms. "It made one tired, awfully tired."[7] She escaped detection. But a lot of parents who hid with their children in the factory were not so lucky. Nor were scores of children who had been left inside alone. "Most of the kids were very spoiled," Ruth said, with more than a trace of disapproval, "and it was very hard to hide those who didn't want to listen when they were told to sit and be quiet. Thank God, our two girls were very quiet and listened to whatever we asked them." For hours Anne and Lila lay in their subterranean compartment, in ink-black darkness and dust, not moving, not even whispering. It must have helped to have had each other.

"After a day like this, hundreds of people were taken out of the factory and carried away to God only knew where," Ruth said. Sometimes the number of victims was larger than that.[8] "Today [Thursday, August 13]," Lewin recorded in his diary, "about 3,600 people were removed from Többens' buildings, mainly women and children." On the Sabbath, two days later, the Nazis carried away another large batch of people from the shops. On Monday they swept through German factories yet again, the third time in five days.[9] "The orders, inspections, selections came so soon after the other that we had no time to think," Ruth said. "We had only one thing in mind and that was to save our lives. We prayed to God to give us help and to give my children the strength to bear up under all these atrocities."

There was a lull from August 18 to 20 when the Einsatz Reinhard unit traveled to the nearby resort and sanatorium town of Otwock to liquidate its ten-thousand-person ghetto. When they returned the "selections" resumed with renewed fury, because now there were fewer people to pull off the streets and each Jewish policeman had been told to deliver seven persons a day or else turn in his own family. "Yesterday," Lewin wrote on August 23, "the Germans rounded up mainly women and children with rampant viciousness and savagery."[10]

Evenings offered little respite. After a moonlit Soviet air raid on August 20 (several workers at Schultz's were killed during the attack), ss troops came regularly to the factory to enforce the nighttime blackout, firing at windows where light peeked out. "Sometimes we heard them running up the stairs. We felt sorry for the people that they were running to," Ruth said.[11]

There was a big selection at Schultz's Shop on August 25, under a blazing sun. In three hours, twelve hundred of the two thousand people assembled in the courtyards at Nowolipie 44–46 were taken to the Umschlagplatz. Those allowed to remain filed past a table to have their work permits revalidated and stamped. The German shop owners were becoming alarmed. Their patrons in the Nazi hierarchy, the Wehrmacht, and officials of the armaments agencies had even less influence than they themselves with the ss officials in charge of the liquidation. Some high-ranking military officers, concerned that the selections were endangering production quotas for winter uniforms, were even forced to wait in the hall at the Żelazna Street Befehlstelle before presenting their remonstrances. On August 26, Fritz Schultz and Walter C. Többens concluded an agreement with the ss to stabilize their workforce at eight thousand workers apiece, far and away the largest allotment granted to any of the shops. Despite the agreement, the selections continued. On September 2, the ss once again placed both German factories under heavy siege. "From Schultz's alone they took out several thousand workers," Lewin wrote in his diary.[12]

It is a sentimental myth to suppose shared adversity gives rise to spontaneous solidarity. Too often Nazi persecution undermined group feeling, raising survival hopes among tomorrow's victims so as to secure their acquiescence in the destruction of today's prey. The tightening noose inevitably produced dissension among classes of victims. The penultimate fratricide occurred in the camps, where the law of the Lager said (to quote Primo Levi), "eat your own bread, and if you can, that of your neighbor," and where interpersonal relations frequently degenerated into Darwinian struggles for survival.[13] In ghetto factories the atomization seldom descended to that level, but the discord was hard to miss. Fearing that factory overcrowding endangered the legitimately employed, workers and clerks lashed out at Jews seeking sanctuary in the shops. There was class conflict. "The workers turn on the intellectuals," Lewin wrote in his diary on August 7. "A shocking experience." Lewin also noted discontent over children hiding in the shops: "No good would come of it.

Everyone was worried." This was the mood in Vladka Meed's shop after the ss nabbed an older worker and a mother and her child during one of its periodic raids.[14] Resentful envy even boiled up at parents who had thus far succeeded in shielding their children. "When I saw all the time that there were less and less children and that people started being jealous, I didn't blame them," Ruth said.

But a deeper feeling lay behind that resentment. Ruth was never explicit, but it is visible between the lines and appears in much of the literature: several Jewish foremen in the German shops were unpopular because they were the ones often forced to help choose who would be downsized in the interest of ss economy. "Jewish [work] directors helped catch the illegals," Ringelblum wrote in his diary after the liquidation. In its November 1942 report to the Polish government-in-exile in London, the ghetto underground complained about Jewish shop foremen who helped draw up "selection" lists. That fall the nascent Jewish combat organization, after shooting the head of the Jewish Police, even "carried out several more assaults against a few Jewish foremen who caused most of the suffering on the part of Jewish slave-labourers," wrote Marek Edelman, today the only surviving commander of the organization.[15]

It is hard to be precise about what transpired inside Schultz's, for the evidence is sketchy at best. Sophia Leviathan's 1945 testimony is the most detailed information extant on how the selections were carried out at Nowolipie 44–46. At the August 25 selection, she writes, while the courtyards filled with workers, and Schultz himself, big and broad like a "terror-inspiring giant," stood in the door between the two courtyards, a Jewish employee (*ein jüdischer Angestellter*) from the head office went through the ranks separating essential from nonessential workers. But how would someone from the office know who to remove unless shop supervisors told him in advance? And how would the supervisors know which workers were dispensable unless they consulted Jewish foremen? Maybe there was not consultation but rather a crude form of coercion. According to Leviathan, during a later selection Jewish department heads (*jüdischen Abteilungsleiter*) were told that they themselves would go to the trains should any worker preselected for deportation turn up absent.[16] In either case, it is a grassroots illustration of the ss divide-and-kill policy in action.

What role if any Mark Skorecki played in deciding the fate of workers in the wooden sole department will never be known. Ruth is mum on the subject. She is curiously elliptical about where the deported workers ended up, although everybody in the ghetto knew by then that it was the killing center at Treblinka. At one point she indicates that they were sent to a "concentration camp," at another that they were "carried away to God only knew where." After the war Mark never discussed the subject, except to mention to Dolek Skorecki, his Kielce-born Israeli cousin, that he, Mark, was the only one in the shop who knew what he was doing and for that reason the other workers "tried to do everything to save him," because if he were not there to run the operation, "they would be sent to the death camps. And so they tried to help him and his family also—the two daughters."[17]

There is no question that Mark saved lives before the "selections." He helped find jobs at Schultz's for friends and neighbors. He taught the inexperienced how to work with wood and handle machinery. He improvised a process for fabricating wooden buttons, thereby creating more jobs and prolonging employment. But then came the great contraction. The personnel cuts mandated on August 26 by the ss surpassed 40 percent of the factory workforce as of August 1942. Assuming they were distributed equally across all Schultz's divisions, the wooden sole department alone would have had to terminate eight-four of its two hundred workers.

The Einsatzkommandos were unconcerned over how the cuts were made. They wanted to fill their quotas. But Stelmaszek cared; his job depended on meeting production goals. And experienced laborers cared, which is why there are so many reports of shopworkers who turned against new hires and "intellectuals" for taking up space. It is easy to imagine the pressure Mark felt from above and below: from a supervisor, on the one hand, who wanted to minimize the adverse impact on productivity, and from skilled workers, on the other, who were all too humanly willing to sacrifice the unproductive, that they themselves might live. It happened in the death camps, too, when a falloff in train arrivals raised fears among Jewish work gangs that they themselves were due for extermination. Richard Glazar, one of few survivors of Treblinka, relates what happened when a camp officer walked into his barrack wearing a wide grin and told prisoners, after a considerable lull in camp activity, " 'As of tomorrow . . . transports will be rolling in again.' And do you know what we did? We shouted, 'Hurrah, hurrah.' It seems impossible now. Every time I think of it I die a small death; but it's the truth. That is what we did; that is where we had got to. . . . [I]t meant life—you see, don't you—safety and life."[18]

If there came a time when the devil wanted his due, it probably happened during one of Mark's many closed-door office meetings with Stelmaszek, when he passed along to his valued foreman the news that the head office wanted so many workers cut from the wooden sole department and who did Mark think should be let go? Maybe he told Mark that his participating in the winnowing process was the quid pro quo for Stelmaszek tipping him off whenever a selection was imminent, for allowing Ruth temporarily to stay home with the children, and for permitting Mark to construct a hiding place in the storeroom. Maybe nothing needed to be said but was simply understood. If this was the Faustian bargain Anne's father had to accept to save his family, it is merely another illustration of the choiceless choices for which the Holocaust is infamous. As Primo Levi has observed, "Survival without renunciation of any part of one's own moral world—apart from powerful and direct interventions by fortune—was conceded only to very few superior individuals, made of the stuff of martyrs and saints."[19] "In my mind," says Adam Skorecki, "my father is a true hero in the sense that he did what it took to save his family and to live at a particular point in time. For him that was all there was. There was nothing after that."[20]

But even if Mark had been spared the terrible responsibility of deciding who should stay and who should go, some workers in his department, especially those less than pleased with how the "selections" turned out, no doubt suspected that he had exercised a voice. Their Jewish foreman certainly met often enough in private with the Volksdeutscher supervisor, and at a time when workers were being removed right and left. Foremen in other German factories were helping management to make cuts. Stelmaszek evidently had less than a stellar reputation with some Jewish employees who testified after the war. In the minds of workers embittered by the loss of a close friend or relative, these admittedly circumstantial facts must have added up to an open-and-shut case against even a foreman who had earlier helped find them lifesaving employment. And, plainly, nothing Mark might have said or done could have allayed those resentful suspicions. No wonder that he decided sometime late in August to find an alternative hiding place for his daughters. "We were afraid to keep them in the factory," Ruth said, "but still I had to go to work, I couldn't go home with them." What were she and Mark to do?

There was always the furniture in the apartment at Nowolipie 28. Mark had built or modified most of it, particularly the kitchen storage bin. Vegetable boxes were then common in Poland. The boxes were not bought in stores. People built their own, usually out of pine, placing potatoes and vegetables on the top and keeping coal in the bottom. The bins opened from the top because people liked to sit on them. As Ruth explained, "Mark made a compartment in the bottom of this box and we decided that this would be the hiding place for our two girls."

Mark probably enlarged the bin, for the run-of-the-mill varieties, measuring about three feet by two feet and as long as they were high, surely were too small to accommodate even such diminutive children as Anne and Lila. Anne's memory is of a box the size of an English coffer of the kind she and Stan sell today in their New Orleans antique store—"about 45 inches long and three-and-half-feet tall." But Mark could not have made the bin too much larger than normal. "That would invite suspicion," says Teresa Prekerowa, a Polish historian of Jewish wartime rescue who herself participated in rescue work. " 'Oh, what do you have inside? It's so big,' they would ask."[21]

What occupied the interior of the Skorecki vegetable bin were two benches that Mark had built against each end wall. The seats faced each other and were slightly tilted so as to give his daughters more head room. He left space for a small potty, though Ruth is silent on this point, only mentioning that he put a blanket inside the hidden compartment. "They had to have had a little potty inside," Prekerowa says, a point that gibes with Anne's own memory. The upper part of the chest Mark filled with trash because vegetables were in short supply, and any potatoes left in the box the Ukrainians would steal anyway. "If you lifted the top all you would see were rags and messy stuff, just junk," Anne says. "But it had a false bottom that you entered from the back, and this is where we would spend the day."

On this latter point, however, Anne and her mother disagree. As Ruth explained the routine: "We told the kids when they heard footsteps on the stairs that they must run and hide in this box. It was a terrible thing for us to have to teach children to hide like this, but we had no other alternative." In other words, while she and Mark were working, Anne and Lila had free run of the apartment, subject to certain rules. Ruth said she laid down strict orders that her daughters not look out the window because "this was a front apartment facing the street, and someone might possibly see them and take them away and I would not know what had happened to them." There was also an equal danger that soldiers might shoot them from the street below. But rules against childhood curiosity were hard to enforce. And, as Ruth herself admitted: "Sometimes kids are kids, and they looked through the window, and believe you me, they saw terrible things. They saw more blood running in the gutters of the ghetto at such a young age than a person in a hundred years would see in his whole lifetime."

It contradicts everything we know about Mark and Ruth—about their foresight and planning, their anticipation of contingencies, their superabundance of caution—to suppose that they would have left their young daughters unconcealed in that apartment for even fifteen minutes. For, after all, "kids are kids," as Ruth said. Moreover, two small children would not have been able to crawl into the rear entrance on their own and then muscle the rather stout box flush against the wall, so that its false bottom would not be visible to the casual eye. "It was very heavy," Prekerowa says of the typical vegetable bin. "Maybe with two of us pushing we could move it," Lila speculates. "I don't know." Maybe, but probably not.

The more likely scenario—and this is how Anne remembers events—is that each morning before work, her father dragged the vegetable bin away from the wall, put a blanket on the miniature seats, and gave Lila and her some bread and water. Characteristically, Mark and Ruth said little before leaving. "All we were told is, 'You stay here and we'll be back,'" Lila says. "But in actuality they didn't know if they were going to come back, either." Then her father pushed the pine box back against the wall.

And from that point onward, from six in the morning until six at night, Monday through Friday, and half a day on Saturday, the two sisters had to sit silently in the bottom of the kitchen storage bin. There was no mother's voice to whisper soothing reassurances every so often as shoe soles were shifted to improve air flow. And it was cramped, to say the least. "If they were inside, they had no room to move," Mrs. Prekerowa says. "They couldn't stand up. Impossible." Occasionally a shaft of light lay aslant the compartment, silhouetting motes of coal dust.

Lila and Anne remember little of what went on inside. Lila recalls long silences. "While we were in there," she once told radio journalist Plater Robinson, "we couldn't make any noise, we couldn't cry, we were just trained to keep quiet, because it was the only way we could survive."[22] Anne also has difficulty remembering whether she and her sister spoke. "We must have said something to each other but I draw a blank. About other things I can close my eyes and I'm back there. But I just don't remember what happened when we were together in that cabinet. It's like somebody put a curtain down and I just really can't feel it."

The memories that stayed with the Skorecki sisters of their time together in the vegetable bin are primarily aural. "There was no mistaking the sound of German boots on the cobblestoned streets or on the stairwell," Anne says. "They knock on the door louder," Lila adds. "In fact, they don't knock, they pound. You can just tell it's somebody who's coming to hurt you."[23] The bin would jiggle as the security forces lifted the lid and rifled the contents. And then Anne and Lila's hearts, now racing, would leap to their throats until they thought they might choke on fear.

"What I don't understand, even now that I'm a mother and grandmother, is how my sister and I sat there quietly," Anne says. "I can't even keep my own grandchildren quiet." Ruth attributed her daughters' gift of solitude to nurture. "I trained them this way," she often said, and there is something to the explanation. "We were brought up in the European way," Lila says.

Anne elaborates: "It was always that children were seen and not heard, and if you were among adults you didn't butt into conversations. In fact, the difference between an American and a Polish upbringing was like night and day. There was no input. Whatever your parents said, you had to do. You had to toe the line. And my sister and I were so used to listening to what my parents said, that it became a habit and a hard habit to break—I guess because for so long life itself depended on our obedience."

But Ruth was asking her daughters to do more than merely follow orders. She was demanding that they leapfrog adolescence and jump directly to adulthood, which is a psychological capability that has less to do with nurture than with nature. Restless and whimpering children were not "spoiled." They simply lacked innate survival instincts. "You grow up real fast when you're seeing death on the streets and you're afraid and your parents are always hiding you," Anne says. "I guess it's because of self-preservation that you do those things."

Anne and Lila were scarcely alone in their hothouse maturation. Testifying at Adolf Eichmann's 1961 trial in Jerusalem, Dr. Aharon Peretz, who survived the Kovno Ghetto in Lithuania, was amazed at how "children three or four years old understood the entire tragedy. . . . How they clammed up when it was necessary. How they knew how to hide. We ourselves did not believe that small children, when we wanted to give them a shot of sedatives and the kid would say, 'Doctor, this is not necessary. I will not scream.' We were always amazed at the adult attitude of these children." Adina Blady Szwajger, the young pediatrician at the Berson-Bauman Children's Hospital in the Warsaw Ghetto, was equally struck by the young tubercular children who had less fear of death than she herself. "Doctor, . . . don't be frightened. We're not in despair," they said, to comfort her. Ministering to older children posed a special challenge to ghetto doctors, "because they were, after all, older and wiser than we by a whole century of suffering and by the deaths of those nearest to them."[24]

But Peretz and Szwajger could hardly have been describing the generality of Jewish youngsters alive when the war began. Less than 1 percent of Jewish children in Poland during the Holocaust survived, and in the Warsaw Ghetto the percentage was even smaller.[25] Mastering silence and solitude, vanquishing fear and trepidation, apparently require gifts that only the rarest of children possess.

Anne no doubt had more of whatever it was that survival required, whereas Lila clung to her mother, became deathly ill, and stayed attached to small possessions. Anne was the risk taker. "My sister is braver than me," Lila admits. "She would do and try things more easily than I would. That's even true today." Anne was a tomboy, a born daredevil, the four-year-old who climbed into the doghouse at her grandparents' country place to play with the big German shepherd dog, while her parents took alarm that the dog would attack her. It was as though her fear of dark enclosures had been vanquished long before she was ever told to crawl under the floor or into the back of the vegetable bin.

"I had to go for a medical test the other day, a CAT [computerized axial tomography] scan," Anne said in 1993. "Have you ever had a CAT scan? It's a weird feeling because it's like a tunnel that goes over you. I just kept my eyes closed. But a lot of people panic because it is very close quarters and you just have to lay there. But I was there, and I was okay. In fact, while I was inside the CAT scan, I thought to myself, 'why should I be afraid of this tunnel? I've sat in the darkness before.' It didn't bother me. And I think that's why I was probably willing to go inside the kitchen chest. I had done that before." Lila would probably have panicked during a CAT scan, Anne surmises. Her younger sister hates crowds and tight spaces. "Give me room. That's what I say," Lila declared in 1993.

Yet it required Anne and Lila's combined courage to endure the dark spaces they cohabited during their last days in the Warsaw Ghetto. "If either one of us was left alone in our various hiding places," Lila believes, "I don't think we could have made it. I really don't. One of us would have let out a sob. One of us would have said something or done something that would have given it away." But simply knowing she could touch her sister, hear her breathe, feel her closeness, was quiet reassurance even if words were never exchanged. Lila continues: "It was harder probably on my parents than on us because at least we had each other. When we had to hide, we hid together."

As sisters, they are very different people. They do not share the same interests, and their temperaments are poles apart. Were they thrown together today, it is hard to imagine them becoming close friends. But few sisters are as close as Anne Levy and Lila Millen. They talk on the phone at least once a day. "I guess it's because of our shared experiences that we are as close as we are," Anne says. "Lila is Lila, and I am me, and we accept each other." It is an intimate bond that was forged in a crucible where their combined reserves of fortitude helped the other to survive.

The fear left a hard residue, though. It numbed some ghetto inhabitants, tormented others. Abraham Lewin captured the mood well: "Not one of us is sure to survive, especially women and children, who are left living with the threat of destruction every day, every minute. The knowledge of this so preys on their nerves that many nearly go insane."[26] Ruth more or less said the same thing twenty years later: "Every minute of every day we were afraid of what might happen to us," she said. The fear, always relentless, was about to become worse.

Despite the countless times it has appeared in the Holocaust literature, details about the Umschlagplatz remain vague. Was it encircled by a fence or a wall? How many gates and sentry posts were there? How many buildings? Did they have three or five stories? Were warehouses and huts located there as well? Was the vast assembly area paved or covered with dirt and trampled grass? Survivor accounts conflict wildly, doubtless because the fortunate few able to escape the staging area were too focused on survival to conduct a mental inventory of the Umschlagplatz's characteristics.[27]

On one thing all accounts agree: the Archives Building where the Czyste infectious disease ward had been located until the eve of the deportations was now serving as a holding pen for human cargo. The three-story building lay just inside the Umschlagplatz. Even during the liquidation's opening phases, the Jewish Police and local ss units, assisted by Waffen-ss troops and Trawniki auxiliaries, had rounded up more deportees than the daily freight trains could accommodate, so the surplus people were locked inside the building, as reserves. "Sometimes there are several thousand people waiting a day or two to be transported because of a shortage of railroad cars," Kaplan wrote in his diary shortly before he vanished. Inside, the water had been turned off, and the toilets had backed up. Mud and feces covered the floors. The smell of urine and fear filled the air.[28]

There is also widespread agreement concerning the presence of a first aid clinic at the Umschlagplatz, though accounts differ over whether it was located inside the archives or in a detached shed. It came into existence when the Germans transferred the Berson-Bauman Children's Hospital to the Umschlagplatz, and then, according to Marek Edelman, "opened an emergency aid station there—a malicious gesture toward those sentenced to death."[29] If the Germans had conceived the aid station to reinforce the illusion that the trains were destined for work camps in the east, a few key members of the Judenrat and the hospital staff turned the illusion against the Germans by converting the tiny clinic into an underground railroad of rescue and escape.

Until then, few people had managed to flee the Umschlagplatz on their own. Those with means sometimes succeeded in bribing their way to temporary freedom, but that was not invariably the case. Ruth mentioned a "millionaire" employed at Schultz's who offered as ransom every penny he still possessed to free an eighteen-year-old son seized during one "selection." "We were sure that the old man would go crazy," she said. He even managed to secure a personal interview with Schultz himself, who said there was nothing he could do. From time to time representatives from Schultz's and Többens's were able to rescue a few skilled specialists indiscriminately pulled from the shops by the ss, but even this became difficult as the liquidation dragged on.[30] Most of the rescue activity at the Umschlagplatz, however, occurred through the first aid clinic, and it focused on public figures. The idea of saving a favored few was controversial among ghetto intellectuals. The issue had arisen earlier during debates over how to dole out inadequate relief supplies. "One is left with the tragic dilemma," Ringelblum wrote of one of these debates. "Are we to dole out spoonfuls to everyone, the result being that no one will survive? Or are we to give full measure to a few—with only a handful having enough to survive?" And how should one reconcile this picking and choosing with the notion that every Jewish life was precious? Such debates were usually resolved with an agreement to let each organized Jewish group select the individuals they wished to save.[31]

That is pretty much how things were done at the clinic. Members of the Judenrat and the hospital staff selected for rescue individuals they thought might be of potential value to a reconstituted Jewish community. For its part, the youth-dominated underground bent most of its energies during the deportations trying to rescue members who had been caught in the Nazi net. Young Edelman said he stood at the Stawki Street gate every day for six weeks identifying people to save. The hands-on rescue work was carried out by the hospital staff—nurses, doctors, medical students, and office personnel—who changed shifts twice a day. They wore white hospital jackets and carried work permits that allowed them to move about freely. They pulled rescue candidates inside the clinic, gave them white coats and nurses headkerchiefs, and then drove them out in an ambulance. Coffins were used too. Later, when the Germans started inspecting the ambulance, the clinic staff began breaking the legs of people they were trying to smuggle out—without benefit of anesthesia. "They would wedge a leg up against a wooden block and then smash it with another block," Edelman said in 1977.[32]

No one worked harder at the clinic than Henry Tempelhof's friend Nahum Remba, the secretary of the Judenrat who used to joke and cut up during his rounds of the various offices maintained by the Jewish Council. By this stage most Judenrat members had forfeited whatever credibility they still had with the ghetto population. When the ss informed them on July 22 that they would have to participate in resettling unproductive Jews in the east, "Not a single councilman stopped to consider . . . whether the Jewish Council should undertake to carry out the order at all," Edelman wrote. But the secretary of the council objected: "Gentleman, before you pass to the technical means of executing the order, stop and think—should it be done?"[33] The only person who heeded the warning was Remba himself. By all accounts he worked tirelessly at the Umschlagplatz to rescue Judenrat employees and other public figures, including the famous children's book author and educator Janusz Korczak (a nom de plume; his real name was Henryk Goldszmit).[34] On August 6, Korczak arrived at the Stawki Street staging area leading a column of 192 children from his orphanage. They carried blankets and walked hand in hand between files of Nazi soldiers. At the prompting of a teacher, they sang a marching song: "Though the storm howls around us, let us keep our heads high." Korczak, "a stooped, aging man," cradled a five-year-old child in each arm. The scene burned itself in the memories of everyone who glimpsed it from behind closed curtains. Korczak had passed up several earlier opportunities to escape the ghetto. He always believed his place was with the children. His last chance came at the Umschlagplatz when Remba offered to smuggle him to freedom. Korczak turned that offer down as well. "This was no march to the train, but rather a mute protest against this murderous regime," Remba wrote later of witnessing Korczak and his orphans board the Treblinka-bound freight cars.[35]

If Remba threw himself into rescue work at the Umschlagplatz, so did his friend Henry Tempelhof, according to Dr. Thaddeus Stabholz. "The [Umschlagplatz] clinic was the creation of Remba, Tempelhof, and a couple of doctors and nurses, so it was not Tempelhof's child," he says. "But once the idea of creating a clinic [crystallized], he worked quite hard on it. Quite hard. I cannot tell if he was there every single day, but from what I heard, he was over there quite a bit."[36] After fifty years, it is impossible to substantiate Stabholz's memory fully, but much suggestive circumstantial evidence exists. As office manager, Henry had authority over a lot of Czyste's physical property, including the ambulance that was used to carry people from the Umschlagplatz. And, because of his struggle with colon cancer, he possessed the insouciance, the "grace under pressure," to quote Hemingway's definition of courage, that rescue work at the *Umschlagplatz* doubtless entailed. But, most of all, there is Ruth's own 1963 recollection of her brother and Mery visiting her and Mark inside Schultz's tenement block while the liquidation was at full throttle. Henry and Mery were now working at Stawki Street, they told them. The hospital was in a "three-story" building, "not far away from where the trains were waiting for the people who had been selected." Henry and Mery always arrived at Schultz's Shop "in an ambulance and pretended that they were coming in for a patient." Then Ruth added this revealing fact: "My brother had to come in a white coat."

In the late summer of 1942 there was only one reason anyone from Czyste Hospital would work at Stawki Street, wear a white coat, and drive an ambulance: to rescue people from the Umschlagplatz. It was too dangerous to be there otherwise. By mid-August Jewish policemen, desperate to meet their seven-head-per-day quota, were seizing even doctors, whose white coats fetched good money on the black market.[37] Henry seems not to have mentioned his rescue activity to his older sister, probably because he never felt comfortable blowing his own horn. For all of his grinning good humor, deep down he was a laconic person. "It's very amazing," Dr. Stabholz says, "because you were one small step away from hell, one tiny step to being deported to Treblinka. His courage was exemplary. Both he and Remba were very outstanding individuals."[38]

Although Mery also put in volunteer hours at the Umschlagplatz clinic, she had even less free time than her harried husband. During the deportations all three surgery units at Leszno 1 were staggered by a rising tide of gunshot victims—6,687 all told, according to statistics compiled by the Judenrat.[39] Operations continued around the clock, physicians and nurses literally swimming in blood. One of Mery Mejnster's colleagues, another woman surgeon, penned this account:

> They were supplying us with loads of work.... They brought wounded to the hospital constantly. The most common wounds were in the head and

abdomen, and in second place were arms and legs. Shots, mostly from close range with dum dum bullets, created atrocious wounds. I remember a young woman around 20 years old, whom I had seen already in bed on the hospital floor, covers drawn over her head in deep shock. She seemed to be sleeping quietly. When it came her turn to be operated on I removed her cover. In the middle of her abdomen was a wound the size of a dessert plate with the edges torn in shreds, and with the stomach, liver, and part of the intestine hanging out. The wound described above was the entry of the bullet. The exit was in the vicinity of the left lumbar loin, about the size of a human head. How could we operate there? The older doctors agreed with my opinion. When she regained consciousness she had horrible pain. All we could do was give her morphine, with no limit. Within 24 hours came death, the deliverer. We were getting 60 or 70 of this kind of patient daily. . . . The operating room was busy non stop. Instruments were sterilized constantly, and on the table were long lines of victims. . . . In the air was the strong smell of fresh blood. Carts with new victims replaced those already operated on. Sweat ran down our faces and underwear stuck to the hot wet, torsos of operating surgeons. . . . The action was still in progress. A person turns into a robot. Cuts, sews, and—most important—tries not to think about it at all.[40]

To crown it all, on August 15 the ss ordered that the Trauma Division at Leszno 1 reduce the number of patients in recovery from 600 to 150, telling the house surgeons to conduct the "selection" themselves. Instead, the chiefs of surgery made the choices during evening rounds.[41]

How Mery stood the excruciating strain can only be surmised, for, like her husband, she was a private person. But another colleague, a young medical student at the time, remembers her bearing up remarkably well. "She was always on time and always working hard," he says. "She would come the first to see the patients and leave the last. A really wonderful person. She wasn't very pretty but very hard working . . . and she was very polite. But in the meantime she kept a distance with anybody else."[42] In the midst of it all, Mery managed to find time to do rescue work at the Umschlagplatz clinic, probably because the lifesaving vocation for which she had been trained no longer seemed to have much point.

The reports Henry and Mery brought to Ruth and Mark from the Umschlagplatz were not very edifying. The Tempelhofs described horrific scenes of family separations. "Some tried to run away from the train, but they were killed on the spot," they told Ruth and Mark. "It was a terrible picture."

Much of the shooting was hardly random. Just before the departure of the daily transport, Ukrainian and Lithuanian guards fired wildly into the human cargo milling around the loading area to stampede them into the open boxcars. They charged the crowd, using rifle butts to mash people inside the wagons before pulling the doors shut. Ordinarily the trains left between four and five o'clock in the afternoon, usually towing sixty cars. All the wagons were grossly overcrowded: 120 to 150 people in spaces meant to hold no more than 70; eye-stinging chlorine was sprinkled all over the floor. "It was one big toilet," said a deportee who managed to escape. The transports were also woefully behind schedule. The *Ostbahn* (eastern railroad) officials with whom the ss had negotiated the diversion of rolling stock calculated that the trip should take only four hours. Actually it took three times as long, and the cars were not unloaded until the next morning. Things were beginning to back up at Treblinka.[43]

Located ninety miles away near the River Bug, in a secluded, pinewood forest fringed by pilasters of white birch, Treblinka was the last of the three Aktion Reinhard death camps to become operational (it commenced gassing on July 23, with the first transports from the Warsaw Ghetto). But it led them all in sheer lethality: upward of nine hundred thousand Jews, as well as a few thousand Gypsies, died there between July 1942 and October 1943.[44] All of the Aktion Reinhard facilities—Belżec, Sobibór, and Treblinka—followed more or less the same pattern. Laid out as compact rectangles, usually six hundred by four hundred meters, the killing centers were subdivided into two camps and girdled by two barbed wired fences, the inner one of which was inter-woven with pine and juniper branches to heighten the seclusion. The "lower camp" embraced the reception and sorting areas, as well as the living quarters of the ss staff and Ukrainian and Lithuanian guards; it was where the storage sheds were located and where trains pulled up every morning around 9:30 A.M.

The smaller "upper camp" encompassed the gas chambers and the burial pits. At Treblinka a thirteen-foot-high "tube" of juniper-laced barbed wire curved for one hundred meters between the reception area and the massive brick building housing the three gas chambers. Near the entrance to the "tube," which the Germans derisively nicknamed *Himmelstrasse* (road to heaven), and near the woman's undressing station was a sign that read, "This way to the showers."[45]

The entire killing system, from physical design to murder methodology, was the handiwork not of the ss but of members of a top secret euthanasia pro-gram called T4, as it was administered out of Hitler's personal chancellery at Tiergartenstrasse 4 in Berlin. Aimed at cleansing the gene pool of defective elements—euphemistically called "life unworthy of life"—the euthanasia pro-gram is clear proof that Nazi genocide had other antecedents beside crude anti-Semitism.

Also driving the killing project was a biomedical vision of proper racial hygiene. During the first two years of the war, over seventy thousand Germans with mental disorders and physical disabilities were gassed to death in six separate euthanasia centers scattered across Germany and Austria, figures that do not include the hundreds of German and Polish Jewish patients in psychiatric hospitals killed during the same period and the five thousand children with disabilities who were murdered by other means. In August 1941 loud protests from Catholic and Protestant clergy forced Hitler to issue a stop order, which did not stop the euthanasia so much as shift the killing methods from gas to lethal injection and starvation. But the stop order did free up some T4 personnel for redeployment to the Generalgouvernement.[46] That fall ninety-two members of the euthanasia program were reassigned to Odilo Globocnik's soon-to-be-renamed Aktion Reinhard headquarters, all of them eventually becoming involved in running its three death camps.

The highest ranking and most important of the T4 transfers was an Austrian Nazi named Christian Wirth, who adapted the euthanasia program to the mass-production killing demands of the Final Solution. An overlap in killing technology existed between the German euthanasia centers and the Polish death camps, from ersatz shower rooms lined with white tiles to the administering of carbon monoxide. The key differences were that the T4 installations used expensive bottled gas and cremated the human remains. During experiments at Bełżec, the prototype camp, Wirth concluded that 250-horsepower armored car diesel engines were a more economical source of carbon monoxide and that burial worked better than burning. At Treblinka a jury-rigged trolley system carried the victims from the back of the gas chambers to chlorinated earthen pits that "undulated like waves" owing to the intermittent explosions of fermenting bodies in the hot summer sun. The individual pits were about the size of an Olympic swimming pool.[47]

"Treblinka was a primitive but efficient production line of death," a former German camp guard told documentary filmmaker Claude Lanzmann.[48] And during its first month of operation the system worked fairly well. Trains pulled up along a short spur running from the main line at Malkinia; a long whistle from the midmorning train alerted Ukrainian and Lithuanian guards to assume their posts. A smaller locomotive pushed twenty cars at a time through a branch-woven gate to the three-hundred-meter unloading dock at the front of the camp.

Wirth had also devised the processing routine used in all three Aktion Reinhard camps, which pivoted on deception and speed. A large sign proclaimed in Polish and German that Treblinka was a transit camp, and to avoid epidemics, new arrivals needed to bathe and undergo disinfection before being sent on to a work camp in the "east." They were told to turn in their valuables to a cashier in exchange for a receipt. The men entered an undressing barracks on the right and received strings to tie their shoes together. Women and children went into the barracks on the left. They shed their clothes at five different stations. The women's heads were shaved in the "beauty salon," and the hair was later threaded onto bobbins, converted into industrial felt, and, after being combed and cut, manufactured into slippers for submarine crews (human hair repels water) and felt stockings for the *Reichsbahn* (government railroad). Everything was done quickly. "The victims should be rushed, made to run," Wirth concluded, "so that they had no time to look around, to reflect, or to understand what was going on." Naked men, in batches of three hundred, were always the first to be funneled through the leaf-shrouded tube. They were often lashed. "Faster, faster," the guards yelled, "the water's getting cold, and others have to use the showers, too." Nearby a three-person Jewish band played loudly to drown out the metallic gargle of the tank engines.[49]

Although asphyxiation from carbon monoxide happens quickly because of the affinity that hemoglobin has for that gas over oxygen, it took about twenty-five minutes before a chamberful of victims had been completely suffocated. Because of the crowding and clinging, the corpses had been fused together into "a single block of flesh."[50]

Meanwhile, the elderly and infirm, the wounded, indeed anyone, young or old, who might otherwise slow down the production line, were taken to the other side of the sorting yard where a fake first aid station called the *Lazarett* concealed a vast, continuously burning pit. There they were shot in the nape of the neck with a 9 mm pistol and rolled down the sandy embankment.[51]

The processing of a sixty-car transport containing five to six thousand Jews—from unloading and undressing to gassing and burial—lasted on average between two and three hours. The killers had normally finished by lunch, which usually consisted of meat and potatoes and such fresh vegetables as cauliflower. Then they took a half-hour nap. Ordinarily the procedure would not resume until around 9:30 the next morning. "The pace in Treblinka is truly breathtaking," its first commandant, a T4 physician, wrote his wife on July 30, after the first week of operation. The tempo was indeed awesome. By August 28, over three hundred thousand Jews, chiefly from the Warsaw District, had perished in the Aktion Reinhard system's foremost death center.[52]

But just at that moment Treblinka broke down. Himmler's July 19, 1942, order directing that the Generalgouvernement be emptied of all but essential work Jews by year's end had overstressed the entire Aktion Reinhard system. Bottlenecks developed within the railroad grid feeding the three death camps.[53] The Nazis had divided the Generalgouvernement into five districts, and, for purposes of extermination, assigned Bełzec the districts of Kraków, Lublin, and Lvov, and Treblinka those of Warsaw and Radom. Perched at the apex of a death triangle that stretched along the River Bug, Sobibór was supposed to receive the overflow from the other two camps. But when the rail lines to Sobibór went out of commission, all overflow was diverted to Treblinka. By mid-August, daily transports had jumped from six to twelve thousand victims. The tank engines feeding gas to the chambers kept breaking down. Trolleys leading to the burial pits derailed. Bodies began piling up. A steam shovel was brought in from a nearby work camp qua stone quarry (also called Treblinka) to excavate more burial pits. But still the corpses accumulated.[54]

Meanwhile, trains from Warsaw and elsewhere within the death center's feeder region remained parked outside the secluded camp for days on end, under a broiling sun. Children tried to slake their thirst by licking the sweat from their mothers' breasts. The death tolls inside the boxcars soared. The stench of bodies partially consumed by chlorine was overwhelming when the boxcars were finally emptied at the unloading dock. Now even the reception area started overflowing with bodies that quickly bloated in the August heat. "All around, just earth, sky, and corpses!" exclaimed one survivor.[55] The sight of decaying bodies destroyed any illusion that Treblinka was a transit camp. Panic spread among new arrivals. From surrounding towers Ukrainian and Lithuanian guards shot Jews on the spot.

Finally, on August 28, the brass at Aktion Reinhard headquarters in Lublin, livid at the bedlam at Treblinka, suspended further operations until normality could be restored. Wirth himself, who by then oversaw the three camps, came to Treblinka personally to supervise the cleanup. He cashiered the commandant, replacing him with Franz Stangl from Sobibór. To serve as Stangl's assistant, from Belżec Wirth brought in the preternaturally handsome Kurt Franz, whom the camp's work Jews nicknamed "Lalka" (the doll).[56] Both were veterans of the T4 program. Stangl was staggered by the carnage he saw upon arriving at Treblinka. "It was Dante's Inferno," he told the journalist Gita Sereny in 1971 from his Düsseldorf prison cell, burying his face in his hands.[57]

The cleanup took about a week. Night and day they burned bodies. They dug more pits. Though the transports resumed on September 3, the improvements continued apace. After the murder of an SS-Oberscharführer (technical sergeant) by one of the work Jews, Wirth, who remained onsite for several more weeks issuing "detailed instructions," reorganized the *Sonderkommando* (special detachment) labor gang system. Heretofore able-bodied Jews were selected from each morning's transport to help with the processing, then murdered at the end of the day; now work Jews were kept alive for the duration or until misconduct or poor health dictated that they be replaced.

The division of labor became more refined: there were special kommando squads for unloading the boxcars and for sorting and packing the belongings (more than one thousand cars left Treblinka stuffed with plunder). Separate gangs cleaned the tube and the gas chambers. One crew carried the bodies, this time by means of leather straps attached to their arms instead of the unwieldy trolley system. Another squad buried the corpses (always head to foot), covering them with a thin layer of sand and chlorine. "Dentists" removed gold fillings. Stangl spurred construction of two new gassing buildings, effectively doubling capacity, and lowered the ceiling so as to ensure the asphyxiation of small children. Before the new year he and Kurt Franz had workers convert the unloading dock into a faux train station, replete with false doors and fake windows and signs that read "Ticket Counter," "Waiting Room," and "To the Białystok Train." There was even a dummy clock whose painted-on hands never left 3:00 P.M.[58]

Stangl also launched a beautification program at Treblinka. Potted plants were placed on the five broad steps leading up to the gas building's entrance; a Star of David was hung over the gabled door. Draping the door was a dark synagogue curtain bearing the Hebrew words: "This is the Gateway to God. Righteous men will pass through." During a lull in the transports, Kurt Franz had a camp "street" constructed. It had benches and flower gardens and was lined with white gravel. Old barracks were reconstructed into a replica of a Teutonic village. He had workers build a zoo.[59] Franz's motives are unknown. But Stangl's own busywork formed part of his coping mechanism: it was how he "compartmentalized" his thinking, smothered scruples in deadening routine, and tightly focused his moral outrage on such minor infractions as "cheating" and petty theft rather than monumental crimes like genocide. He also found relief in drink. Most of all, Stangl rationalized that his victims were not people. "They were cargo."[60]

After Wirth's reorganization and Stangl's "reforms," Treblinka became a murder factory, swallowing up victims with an industrialized rapacity second only to Auschwitz. It had fewer survivors than its better-known counterpart. Of the hundreds of thousands who arrived through its camouflaged gate almost every day during the camp's sixteen-month existence, only forty lived to tell about it. Not one was a child.

Once every so often a Jewish youngster got momentarily overlooked in the pandemonium of processing a transport. The survivor Samuel Willenberg relates the fate of one of them, a rag-draped girl around Anne Levy's age who was left standing on the platform after the rest of her Warsaw transport had been herded into the reception area. Clasping a half-eaten loaf of bread, she chewed nervously on the edges of a brightly colored babushka that covered her head. Fear flooded her large, doelike eyes. A pair of red high heels, doubtless given to her out of pity by someone in the ghetto, encased her tiny feet. Just then the bow-legged ss-Scharführer (sergeant) whom Treblinka's work Jews called the Angel of Death because he had charge of the Lazarett approached through a gate that led to the sorting yard. With a stick, he gently prodded the young girl into the sorting yard. Her red heels sank into the sand. Strewn everywhere were suitcases and valises plastered with international stickers. Hills of clothing lay across the open plain. "The entire yard gives the impression of a market," a member of the Jewish sorting team said later.[61] The small girl must have had the same initial reaction.

She wandered among the suitcases as though browsing an open-air bazaar. From one valise she pulled out a rainbow variety of kerchiefs and flung them in the air. By now, all work in the yard had stopped. The sorters were frozen in place. Then the little girl withdrew a pair of spectacles from another suitcase and stiffened with fear. They were children's eyeglasses. She threw them into the sand. The intuition of where she was and what lay ahead flooded over her. The Angel of Death resumed pushing toward the Lazarett and the Red Cross flag that fluttered outside. He nudged her inside. A few minutes later a shot rang out. Then, "silence, utter silence everywhere." The ss-Scharführer strode back to the yard, reholstering his pistol and slapping invisible dust from his palms. As if on cue the sorting yard suddenly exploded with cracking whips and angry curses. The Jewish *Kapos* (prisoners in charge of work parties) screamed, "Work, you bastards! *Schnell! Schnell!*" "The noise, we knew, was not meant for us," Willenberg wrote. "It was the only possible way of protesting at what we had just witnessed. Thus we paid the little girl from Warsaw our last respects."[62]

On September 5, two days after Treblinka resumed operations following its week-long shutdown and three days after heavy blockades had removed thousands from Schultz's and Többens's, the Einsatz Reinhard unit ordered the Warsaw Ghetto's remaining 120,000 or so inhabitants to pack enough food and clothing to last two days and report to the ghetto's north end for one final comprehensive "selection." The Germans had converted a several-block area bounded by Gęsia, Zamenhofa, Lubeckiego, and Stawki Streets into a huge human sorting yard. The workers at Schultz's would be temporarily housed on Miła Street, the north end's main east-west concourse. The ss resettlement staff termed the Aktion an *Einkesselung*. The word means "encirclement" in German, but survivors, noticing its close similarity to the Yiddish term for "kettle," or *kesl*, seized on the cauldron metaphor to express the seething fear that convulsed the sorting area for almost a week. By the time the Aktion had finished on September 12, 1942, forty-six thousand additional Jews had been transported to Treblinka.[63]

Schultz's workers only learned of the kesl order when Jewish police stormed the factory tenement block between 3:00 and 6:00 A.M. Sunday, banging on doors, yelling at startled occupants to be ready to leave by ten o'clock that morning. Don't lock the apartments, they were told. No one was exempted from the order to congregate in the roped-off containment zone. "Husbands, wives, old people, young people. We all had to go to Miła Street," Ruth said. Anyone found outside that area after the midmorning deadline would be killed on the spot.[64]

One purpose of the Aktion was to flush out "illegals" and "wildcats." The other objective was to slash the ghetto population—down to the thirty-five-thousand-person maximum set by the ss. "Every factory, every shop, every social institution—including the Jewish police—received a quota from the Nazi authorities," wrote one underground leader. Moreover, the directors of these organizations were handed the responsibility of choosing which of their members they wished to save, along with a specified number of life tokens to distribute to the chosen ones. Some of the talismans were metallic tags, but most were merely numbered slips of paper. The eight-thousand-person quota Schultz had negotiated with the ss two weeks earlier was allowed to stand.[65]

Whether Mark received the same advanced warning as he had during earlier selections is hard to tell. Ruth never mentioned police pounding on the apartment door, though she surely would have remembered it. But, according to her, she and Mark learned of the kesl order in the most perfunctory kind of way: "One day, the ss men came to the factory and told the owner Mr. Schultz to tell all the supervisors of all the departments to tell the people," and so on. What Ruth does remember is the terrifying unavoidability of it all. "At this time no one could help us," she said, "because all the foremen and everybody had to go. If a foreman would try to hide, his absence would be noticed first of all."

So Ruth and her husband fixed a shoulder pack, filling it with a few things, "including children's clothing and a little bread." If there were alternatives to bringing their girls along, they did not immediately leap to mind. The only thing certain at this stage was the impracticability of leaving them inside the vegetable bin for days on end. Their surviving that solitary ordeal and remaining silent indefinitely was hard to imagine. Ruth and Mark gave way to seeming inevitability.

"We were ready to go," she said.

Suddenly, Mark had second thoughts. He had extra time on his hands because the contingent in which he and his family would travel to Miła Street was not slated to leave until late in the afternoon. Maybe something Stelmaszek had told him earlier sparked misgivings. Or perhaps Mark simply remembered the stories Henry Tempelhof and Mery Mejnster had related about scenes they witnessed at the Umschlagplatz—the family separations, the children being torn from parents, the shootings, the slaughter. Whatever the source of his reservations, he was never the type to be paralyzed by indecision. At the last moment Mark told his wife: "I don't want to take the two girls. I'm afraid that they will never come back."

Anne's father was always on the lookout for new places to hide his family, and during his spare hours he stumbled on a possibility in their own apartment building. It was a subcellar that ran beneath Nowolipie 28 and an adjoining building, and it had been used as a leather tannery before the ghetto's creation. Narrow windows near the ceiling gazed level with the street. Mark decided to stow his daughters in the abandoned tannery while he and Ruth were at the kesl. He worried about leaving them alone for such a long time. One of their neighbors was nearly seventy. He had a five-year-old grandson who was deaf and could not speak. "We were sure that he and the young boy would never come back if they went [to Miła Street]," Ruth said. So, Mark asked the elderly man if he was willing to stay behind in the subcellar with all three kids. According to Ruth: "He said OK. He had nothing to lose."

Mark must have hastily brought mattresses to the cellar; at least Anne remembers their being there. He gave the grandfather a loaf of bread and a teakettle of water. Then he closed off the stairs leading to the subbasement and camouflaged the opening with trash and debris. "And at five o'clock we went off," he said, forty years later.[66]

"I can't explain our feeling having to leave two small children," Ruth said, "not knowing whether we would come back, not knowing whether the Germans, while searching the houses, would find them, which of course would be the end of their lives." She added, "We were just praying to God to keep the kids in His hands."

From 10:00 A.M. through dusk, the ghetto that Sunday looked as though its surface had been set in motion. Workers who departed from Schultz's "block" left at staggered times, first forming into customary rows of five. The distance to Miła Street was about one mile, and the heat was stifling. They filed through the Nowolipie gate, made a left on Karmelicka, then a right on Nowolipki, then left again on Zamenhofa, ending with a final left-hand turn onto Miła Street. Two football fields away the Stawki Street gate opened onto the Umschlagplatz. Many children were in the ranks: "Most of the people took the children with them," Ruth said. They carried them in their arms or pushed them in strollers. The older ones walked next to their parents.[67] Lining the perimeter were whip-wielding ss men armed with guns. "Not one of us knew what the Germans might do to us," Ruth said. "We were herded like cattle."

During the mile-long trek, Ruth was overwhelmed with anxiety. "We always expected the unexpected," she said, which in this context could mean only that she and Mark expected the worst. Thus they reminded friends "to remember that we had left two children in the second cellar" should they fail to survive the "big selection."

The Skoreckis filed into a five-story building on Miła Street, sharing an apartment with three other families, one of whom may have been the parents of the boy who stayed behind in the subbasement with Anne and Lila. Julius and Haka were probably staying somewhere nearby, though Ruth is silent on this point. The kesl was unbelievably crowded. In the Miła Street apartment building where Sophie Leviathan stayed, people colonized the stairwells and overflowed the courtyard. The sidewalk resembled a vast urban encampment.[68]

It was hard to sleep at night because of the scourge of fleas and the unending gunfire. Everyone's nerves were shattered. Hope and despair traded places almost on an hourly basis. One minute ghetto diarist Abraham Lewin was sure he was headed to the Umschlagplatz, the next he was overjoyed at news that his shop supervisor was on his way to bring him and fellow workers back to the shop. When he failed to show up after a few hours, the emotional pendulum swung widely in the opposite direction. "Once again our resolve is weakened," Lewin wrote, "and we fall into deep despair that is many times worse." Lewin started yielding to fatalism. He fantasized what it would be like to die. "I thought: the whole thing will only last 10–15 minutes, the execution, that is, and it will all be over."[69]

A craving for food helped keep one's mind off death. "Even in such terrible hours as these a hungry person wants to still the hunger," Lewin said. And by the third day of the "selection," the hunger had become famishing. Many parents had packed only a single loaf of bread, hoping to leave room in their knapsacks to hide small children.[70] Quarrels broke out over food; thefts mounted. Lewin witnessed five tiny children lying on a mattress in the street crying almost nonstop for two days, screaming, "Mummy, mummy, I want to eat!" Only a few people offered them food, one a middle-aged man who broke down in tears. Why feed them if they were going to die anyway? was the common rationalization. "There is no feeling of common fate, of mutual aid," Lewin lamented. "People wander around aimlessly like shadows."[71]

A sizable number of the aimless strays were forsaken children. "Hardly anyone bothered about the children, who wandered about, neglected among the masses of humanity," writes Vladka Meed. Until now they had been everyday sights at the Umschlagplatz, where the pediatrician Szwajger regularly gathered young children who had been abandoned by their mothers. "Maybe the mothers had wanted to save the children from death, or maybe only themselves? Fear of death is something that can't be described. You have to live through it to understand," she wrote.[72]

Inside the cauldron, however, the desertions became pandemic whenever a particular shop or group was told it had to undergo a "selection" and show its "life tickets." Getting one of those life preservers after they had been handed out to the chosen few was almost impossible. But the mere fact that a slim chance did exist powerfully focused one's concentration. "Everything else was suddenly of no importance," Edelman writes. "Some fought for the piece of paper loudly, shrilly attempting to prove their right to live. Others, tearfully resigned, meekly awaited their fate."[73] There were no tickets for children; they were doomed, seen as albatrosses around the neck, maybe even life sentences for anyone accompanying them. Many eight- and ten-year-old youngsters, instinctively grasping their awful reality, ran away in order to improve their parents' survival chances. "How wise and understanding they were, those little ones, trying to persuade their mothers to go on without them, insisting that they, the children, would somehow manage to escape on their own," Meed writes.[74]

Many parents stayed with their children. Many chose to accompany them to the Umschlagplatz, or tried to. But parental abandonment was common too. One author of the November 1942 report on the liquidation of the Warsaw Ghetto, sent by the underground to the London-based Polish government-in-exile, told about the wifeless father of two children, a six-year-old girl and a newborn baby, who was "offered the chance of life, but without his children. He left them in the middle of the street and walked through the gate. The little girl's cry of 'Daddy!' had to be heard to be believed. I shall never forget it."[75]

"Comrade Bernard," one mother told the Bundist underground leader Bernard Goldstein during an encounter on Miła Street, "after all, one *can* have another child." She stared at him, waiting for a response. Goldstein was speechless, though he knew what she was contemplating. "To walk up to the selection with her daughter at her side was certain death for her and the child. Otherwise, perhaps only the child." Her sobbing husband, pounding his head with his fists, cried out that he was going with his daughter.[76] Yet, the overpowering fear of death, as Szwajger said, did make people do unimaginable things. As Ruth put it, "At times like this, the happiest parents were those who had no children."

If Ruth sounded enigmatic, it was because she understood all too well the unbearable strain that parents in the ghetto lived with day in and day out. There must have been moments during her stay in the cauldron when she too wished for emotional release. "My husband and myself and the parents of the little deaf boy were sick with worry," she said, "because we didn't know what was happening to our children." Mark even started regretting that he had left them behind.

"I can't express my feeling," Ruth said. "I wasn't worried about much else but my two little girls. I sure that I would never see them. I was sick. I couldn't eat or drink the whole time. My throat was closed up with fear." Then came release: "After two days, the Germans through a loudspeaker told us that we could go back, but we had to come into the street and form ranks."

The "selections" on Miła Street proceeded shop by shop, group by group.

The workers at Schultz's were fortunate that their sojourn in the kesl lasted only three days. What is puzzling about Ruth's rendition of events during the "big selection" is the omission of references to "life tickets." She and Mark must have obtained them, along with Julius and Haka and the parents of the deaf boy who was in hiding with his grandfather, Anne, and Lila. The tokens were distributed at the shop level, in some instances just before the group's departure for the containment zone.

The shopworkers at Schultz's received theirs in the Miła Street buildings where they were being temporarily housed the night before the "selection." Leviathan left this account: "A Jewish employee of the firm sits down below in the doorway to the concierge's living quarters. He has been instructed by Schultz to issue eight hundred numbers and to hand over the names of eight hundred workers entered on a list. Children as a matter of course receive no numbers. He writes and writes. Today the possession of a number decides life and death. Again worry arises for the children. What is to become of the children? Morning comes. We have to line up on the street in alphabetical order. He who has received no numbers, stays back."[77]

But Ruth never mentioned passing through the preselection line. She could not have forgotten it: those sorts of moments do not easily vanish from memory. Because of Mark's position, perhaps she had received her talisman ahead of time. Or maybe Mark himself had been forced to take a hand in drawing up the list; it would not have been a responsibility he relished, nor one that he would care to talk about later or have his wife dredge up. "No one, perhaps, can imagine the torment of those whose task was to sift the lists and decide who was to be sacrificed," Goldstein wrote shortly after the war.[78] But someone had to do the sifting, and the pressure to do so came from not only the Germans but also the workers. When the head doctor at the children's hospital expressed reluctance to hand out the "life tickets," Szwajger told her she must or no one would survive. "Everybody said she had to do it," Szwajger wrote, "but it was vile because, after all, none of us would like to decide who is to live and who is to die, yet we demanded it of her."[79]

Whatever transpired among workers in the wooden sole department before loudspeakers blared out the command to form ranks in the street can never be known. What is certain, though, is that when the selection order finally did shatter the morning calm of the third day, panic overtook the Miła Street building where Mark and Ruth were staying. Lack of a life ticket was tantamount to capital punishment. But even those fortunate enough to have received a number remained vulnerable. During "selections" the ss randomly pulled registered workers from the ranks for no better reason than physical appearance. By now everyone knew the drill by heart. Women hastened to apply rouge and lipstick and iron out wrinkles in their dresses. Men put shoe polish in their hair to hide the gray; they shaved with whatever implement lay at hand. Everyone wanted to look hale, healthy, and well-rested.[80] It would have been like Ruth to join the other women in putting on her best face. Good grooming was not only who she was but had become a habit of survival as well. Meanwhile, parents who had brought their children to the kesl bustled about seeking to protect them. The older children they dressed to look like young adults. The younger children presented a special challenge. "Among our group were doctors who had drugs to give to the kids to put them asleep to keep them from crying out," Ruth said. *Schlaffmittel* (soporifics) was the term Leviathan used for them.[81] Supplies were limited, and some families who failed to obtain sleeping drugs committed suicide en masse. "People who read this perhaps won't believe that this can be true," Ruth said. "But this is exactly what happened, because I went through it myself, as did many others."

Parents who received drugs, however, heavily sedated their youngest children. The smallest children they placed inside their backpacks or in the bottom of their strollers. burying them under a mountain of clothes. Then everyone filed out into the street, in the usual ranks of five. The wait outside could last up to eight hours.

Every selection more or less conformed to a set pattern. ss soldiers barked out, "go to the left, go to the right," clubbing and shooting anyone offering the slightest resistance. Those sent to the left were led to the Umschlagplatz. The sifting could be frenzied. A young German officer, lashing out with his fists, shouted hysterically, "Because of you, accursed, damned, leprous Jews I have already lost three years of my life, . . . you dog." Diarist Lewin said entire families were slaughtered. The old rules of engagement seem to have been held in abeyance. Instead of providing immunity, rouge and lipstick now had the opposite effect. "The best-looking and most elegant women perished," Lewin said.[82]

As for young children whose sleeping drugs wore off while the selection was taking place, they hardly had a chance. Alexander Donat's powerful postwar memoir immortalized what happened when a baby's cry burst from the knapsack of one man. "The ss officer froze and a thousand men and women held their breaths," he wrote. Then a Ukrainian guard rushed over and plunged his bayonet into the backpack until it was soaked in blood. All the while the ss officer overseeing the selection cursed the ashen-faced father, pummeling him with his riding crop. Seconds later the Ukrainian shot him dead. Thereafter the Einsatzkommandos probed every pack and bundle with their bayonets.[83]

According to Lewin, a selection's severity varied by shop. "With some groups the inspection is not so severe," he wrote. "Other groups on the other hand have enormous losses." Everything seemed to depend on chance. But much turned as well on the presence of German shop owners. Throughout the selection on September 8 representatives from the German shops were on hand to protect their labor force to the extent they still could. Walter C. Többens and Fritz E. Schultz even showed up personally.[84] The winnowing that Ruth and Mark underwent that Tuesday probably fell toward the mild end of the spectrum. It was terrifying enough.

Ruth and Mark spoke of what happened on Miła Street. According to Ruth:

Of course, the ss were all over—in one hand with their whips and in the other, their guns. They screamed for us to be quiet, for us to stay in ranks, for us not to talk to each other. Then they started selecting people. They started looking for kids. They checked the strollers, to see that kids weren't being hid. Some people had no strollers, and all they could do was take their kids in their arms. These were the first who lost their kids. The kids were put to one side, as were the sick and the old. Many of the children started screaming, calling for their parents. . . . Plenty of the parents wanted to go with their kids. But the sadism of the ss was great. It gave them pleasure to break up Jewish families. I still can't understand as I think back on it today [1963] how they could do these things. These men had wives and children of their own—sick ones and old ones who were dear to them. Couldn't they picture what it would be like for them to have to go through something like this themselves? But the ss were like wild tigers, without feeling and heart. They started selecting people, separating husbands from wives, and vice versa, and I remember my fear that maybe the same thing would happen to Mark or me. What would happen to us then? And what would happen to our children? An ss man then came by our group and told us to stay in ranks. We saw the coldness and hardness in his eyes as he gave the order to all of us after the selection. He told us we could go back to the big ghetto.

Twenty years after his wife dictated her story, Mark supplied a few additional details: "When we went over there to make the selections, the officer was standing there with a gun. They pulled people out. They pulled you out and lay you down. . . . Three go, two go, one go—they take out hundreds of people. Then they come to us. Momma makes a bad start. She started too early. Maybe she's nervous, but she start too early."[85]

It was due to worry, Ruth said.

I was thinking so much of my children in the cellar that when he said everybody could go, I stepped out before he told us to start walking. I saw a terrible face looking at me. He raised his hand with the gun. In the other hand he had a whip. I was between my husband and my brother-in-law, Julius. My husband's niece Haka was in the front of us. I thought to myself that I was finished. My brain was not working at all at this moment. I didn't know whether I was alive or dead already. I just saw a mean, hard, cold face looking at me. I was sure that in a second I would be dead. "Oh my God!" I had nothing to lose. I just looked straight in his eyes, as though to ask him what did I do wrong and what did he want from me? Then a miracle happened. He lowered the gun and let me go. When we started walking tears came to my eyes and my relatives' eyes also. Nobody walking with me could believe that the ss man didn't put me to the side with all the others who had been selected.

"Somehow you gotta have luck too," her husband said years later of that "elusive entity" responsible for saving so many Jewish lives, "because they let her through."[86]

The walk back to Nowolipie Street had its own perils. Looting by the ss and the Polish "Blue" police had strewn ghetto streets with the rubble of domestic life. Smashed furniture, kitchenware, and banks of clothing littered every block, and the pavement looked as though it had been dusted by a midsummer snowstorm of torn bedding.[87] The ss continued to yank from the moving columns people who appeared weak or who walked too slowly. The wife of a neighbor—a German Mischling who was unaware of his Jewish ancestry until Nazi genealogists traced it back three generations—was pulled aside when she fell off the pace. "He was broken and tears came to his eyes," Ruth said. He asked to go with her, but the Nazis said no.

"There were hundreds of tragedies like this," she continued. "I don't know how many took place to the rear of us. I just saw those in front of me." They heightened the anxiety of a mother already worried sick for the safety of daughters left in hiding. She could think of nothing else. "Walking home I was just praying to God that I would find my children alive and that nothing had happened to them. The mile was like a thousand miles," she said.

Her heart sank, though, when she and Mark arrived at Nowolipie Street in the afternoon of September 8. ss guards were at the gate leading to the Schultz's tenement block. "We saw terrible pictures," Ruth said. There were no dead bodies; they had been carted off. But blood was everywhere. It was pooled in the streets. It stippled the sides of the buildings. It was from victims discovered hiding in the apartments and in attics and cellars. A terrible image seized Ruth. "Maybe this blood was from our kids," she thought. "I was close to a nervous breakdown."

Their apartment had been ransacked. "I saw all the doors and drawers open. The bed was messed up." Whether the vegetable bin had been rifled, she never said. But doubtless its contents had been picked over thoroughly as well. While Ruth waited in the apartment, Mark ran to the subcellar. "Thank God, this time again a miracle happened to us," she said. "We found the girls, the little deaf boy, and the old man safe." Mark later said that he had found eighteen additional people hiding inside the abandoned leather tannery.

Ruth was shading the truth, as she often did when feeling guilty about traumatic events affecting her daughters. The miracle in the basement was partial at best. Anne and Lila's almost three days of subterranean hiding were tension packed. Through the window near the ceiling they could see Nazi soldiers and their German shepherd dogs milling around on the pavement outside. The Nazis used many dogs during the liquidation, about twenty-four hundred of them according to one estimate.[88] They barked and sniffed at the window. "That was scary," Anne said, "because you could see them and hear them talking. The Germans knew their dogs were smelling something, but they never found us." The neighbor boy who was deaf also sensed the terror that flooded the room— perhaps the fear on faces, the stiffening of his grandfather's frame—for he started screaming; as Anne remembers, he started "making loud, strange noises." To keep the five-year-old quiet, the older man cupped his hand over his grandson's mouth. The boy must have struggled, for his grandfather held on tighter. He felt responsibility for not just a grandson but also the daughters of a neighbor who had tried to save them all. How long he kept his grandson's mouth covered is unclear, but it was long enough to cause suffocation. The boy was dead when Mark broke into the subbasement. "I see it now," he said four decades later. "He held his mouth and his breath and he killed him. And we were there."[89]

Ruth never mentioned, of course, the reaction of her neighbors to their son's asphyxiation at the hands of his own grandfather, because she never could bring herself to admit to strangers, and maybe not even to herself, that the boy had actually died. It is an example of how survivor guilt can throw up roadblocks to the return of memory.

Many survivors of the "big selection" had great difficulty dredging up that time and place. For doctors employed at the Umschlagplatz the whole purpose of medicine had become a nightmare of euthanasia. "To offer one's cyanide is now the precious, the most irreplaceable thing," Marek Edelman wrote. "It brings a quiet, peaceful death, it saves from the horror of the cars."[90] When he penned those lines in 1945, he was describing the Stawki Street mercy killings administered in early September 1942 by his unnamed friend, the pediatrician Adina Blady Szwajger. At the request of fellow hospital workers, she injected morphine into the alabaster arms of sick, aging parents. She saved enough for the young children. One young girl named Marysia, suffering from tuberculosis of the lymph glands, had begged Szwajger not to desert her. She and the other children on the ward had already been orphaned. "Doctor, we all know that we haven't got mammas or papas any more and that we're not going to live through it either. But will you stay with us to the end?" "Yes, Marysia, I'll stay with you to the end," Szwajger said.

It was around the time that the head doctors were handing out life tickets to the hospital staff but before Szwajger knew whether she would be among the chosen few. The doctor in charge bet on youth, so she received a ticket, which she pinned on her uniform. Then German and Lithuanian soldiers burst into the hospital. Together with another doctor she took the morphine upstairs, and they fetched spoons. "And just as, during those two years of real work in the hospital, I have bent down over the little beds, so now I poured this last medicine into those tiny mouths." Downstairs she could hear screaming as the ss pulled the sick from their beds and drove them toward the cattle cars. Szwajger waited until 1988 to write about those events. Nothing she did during the last two years of the war as an underground courier could cancel out the day she gave the children morphine. "And that's why I was always different from everybody else," she wrote. "Nobody ever understood this. Everybody thought I'd forgotten about everything and didn't care any more. I'd hardly see anybody who came to visit. I didn't want to."[91]

There were other child casualties among Schultz's worker families who went to the kesl. Several small children who had been drugged into silence and then buried under clothing and bedding never woke up. They had suffocated by the time their parents were able to excavate them from the bottom of their prams and strollers. "After this we had much less people and of course a lot less children," Ruth said laconically.

To be as exact as the numbers permit, after the "big selection" a ghetto of 350,000 had shriveled to a mere 55,000 inhabitants, almost half of whom were "wildcats" in hiding. Eight thousand Jews are believed to have escaped to the Aryan side. Another 10,000 or so were murdered during the course of the forty-six-day liquidation. The best estimate available indicates that a minimum of 265,000 Jews from Warsaw perished in Treblinka.[92]

The age structure of the remnant community had been radically skewed. According to a census completed at the end of November 1942, over three-fourths of the survivors fell between the ages of twenty and forty-nine, and they were disproportionately male. The elderly had almost completely vanished. So had the children. Less than 1 percent of the population nine years and younger when the deportations began was still alive six weeks later. Only 243 of them were girls of Anne's and Lila's ages.[93]

"A child was a rarity, to be guarded jealously from even as much as a stranger's glance on the streets," wrote Alexander Donat. "We are the tiny remnants of the greatest Jewish community in the world," Lewin lamented as the big selection was reaching a terrible culmination.[94]

The last selection of the summer occurred on September 21—Yom Kippur, the Day of Atonement—when several hundred members of the Jewish Police, together with their families, were deported to Treblinka. The Germans had lured them with the pretense of awarding them medals. It is said that during the train ride the policemen tossed their green caps through the barbed-wire apertures in the cattle cars. The Jewish Sonderkommandos working in the reception area recognized them anyway and hustled the men onto the gravel path that curved toward the gas chambers.

"When the rumor of that tragedy reached me," Yitzhak Zuckerman, a leader of the ghetto uprising, wrote later, "I didn't shed a tear. That was the perverse 'reward' they got from their German benefactors."[95]

seven

ESCAPE

Most victims of the Holocaust perished between March 1942 and February 1943: "At the core of the Holocaust was a short, intense wave of mass murder," writes the historian Christopher Browning. The crest came during a ninety-day period commencing in August 1942, when more than 400,000 Jews, mainly from the Generalgouvernement, were gassed at Bełżec, Sobibór, and Treblinka. September saw the asphyxiation of another 259,000 victims, followed in October by 295,000 more. Altogether, of the 1.5 million Jews consumed by Aktion Reinhard, more than 70 percent perished in those three months alone, and this figure does not include the death toll from Auschwitz and Chełmno for the same period or mortality rates from open-air shootings throughout the occupied east.[1] Trains remorselessly continued to pull in from Kielce and Radom, from Piotrków and Pińczów, and from Warsaw, for even after the great liquidation, the prewar capital still confined the largest number of potential victims.

Działoszyce, the Skoreckis' ancestral shtetl, was liquidated in September 1942. It had been occupied by the Nazis within days of the 1939 invasion, when motorized units rumbled through the town. Anti-Jewish measures ensued in rapid-fire succession: the Germans established a Judenrat and a Jewish police force; they confiscated Jewish businesses, severing the historic connection between Jewish tradesmen and Polish peasants; they imposed a curfew and restricted travel; they required forced labor from all males above fourteen years of age, sending them regularly to Kraków to build canals, dig ditches, and fortify embankments along the River Vistula. Casual indignities such as beard shearing became routine. Smuggling flourished. It was the Warsaw Ghetto experience writ small.

Działoszyce derived one advantage from its postage-stamp size: the Germans did not bother to establish a permanent police station in the town or create a closed ghetto. But that advantage contained a seed of disadvantage. The shtetl became a magnet for refugees from nearby communities damaged by Luftwaffe bombs. Some came from as far away as Łódź. Another influx followed the March 1941 closing of the Kraków Ghetto. The town's Jewish population soon ballooned to over ten thousand. The community, which had lived hand to mouth during the interwar period, dealt with the overcrowding and food shortages as best it could. Kinfolk made room for relatives. The Judenrat, which was staffed largely by the prewar communal leadership and caught the usual ire from the ghetto population for implementing Nazi orders, tried to serve the collective welfare. The synagogue was fitted out with ledges for sleeping and became home to nearly a thousand refugees. The beth hamidrash (the house of study) was converted into a communal kitchen that served fifteen hundred meals a day. When dysentery, typhoid, and typhus ravaged Działoszyce in 1941, the town's minuscule medical community managed to contain the epidemics before district authorities in nearby Miechów could find out and impose a draconian quarantine.[2]

Despite the absence of barbed wire, the town's Jews were still cut off from the outside world and thus unprepared when the end came. Rumors started trickling in during the summer of 1942 about whole Jewish communities being deported to unknown destinations. Toward the end of August the atmosphere grew thick with foreboding. The apprehension, however, was vague, unfocused. "Nobody in our town could even imagine such a thing as the death camps," writes the eminent Israeli jurist Dr. Moshe Bejski, who testified at the 1961 trial of Adolf Eichmann in Jerusalem.[3] A Schindler Jew, Bejski had grown up in Działoszyce. On Tuesday, September 1, ss forces struck suddenly, as they always did, abruptly cordoning off the town. The following day or possibly the day after, as firsthand accounts differ, the Nazis ordered Działoszyce's Jews to assemble in the market square at specified times according to street address and to bring a small bundle filled with work clothes. There was the usual recreational barbarism. Jews were ordered to perform calisthenics and then shot while standing with arms outstretched above their heads. Steadily the square filled with people. Later in the day horse-drawn wagons driven by Polish peasants arrived in the market square. A selection began. The Nazis pulled aside twelve hundred to two thousand older people and women and loaded some of them onto the wagons. The remaining Jews were marched to the train station, shoved onto open trucks, and driven to a large meadow on the outskirts of Miechów twenty miles to the west. Meanwhile the peasant wagons carrying the community's older people and women clattered toward the Jewish cemetery. In the distance columns of Jews then making their way to the train station heard the rattle of machine gun fire. Survivors later learned that the wagon occupants had been buried in three mass graves in the cemetery east of town.[4]

At Miechów an estimated twenty thousand Jews from six towns were funneled onto a large open field. At noon the next day the Nazis told the men to form ranks of five and march with upraised hands before a German officer, who directed them with his finger to the right or to the left. The entire selection took about two hours. Two thousand young men deemed suitable for heavy labor were loaded into open rail wagons. The remainder were stuffed into the train's enclosed boxcars. The locomotive stopped on the outskirts of Kraków to offload the young men culled for work assignments at the Prokocim labor camp. Then the train proceeded on to Bełżec, the first of the Aktion Reinhard camps to become operational.[5] The killing center was less than thirteen miles as the crow flies from the Skorecki lumber mill at Horyniec. According to extant records, the Miechów convoy, including the bulk of Działoszyce's remaining Jewish population, arrived at Bełżec on September 7. Its human cargo was probably gassed the following morning.[6]

There was a subsequent roundup in Działoszyce of several hundred Jews who had managed to elude the first liquidation and snuck back to the shtetl. They fell into the Nazi net during another surprise German cordon in early November 1942. Several were shot inside their hiding places. Most of the rest, according to a postwar report, "were all exterminated two months later, and, buried in a common grave in the valley behind the Jewish cemetery." Only a handful escaped through the snow-covered Christian cemetery, hiding in peasant barns or local mills until it was safe to travel.[7]

As for the two thousand Działoszyceans marked for slave labor, their story intersects with a narrative made familiar to millions through Steven Spielberg's film *Schindler's List*. In December 1942, about twelve hundred of them were transferred to the notorious Płaszów stone quarry commanded by the rifle-toting Amon Göth. There they worked for various German firms, including Oskar Schindler's Emalia works. In May 1944 they underwent the infamous selection that saw hundreds of women and children shipped to Auschwitz. In October 1944, as the Russian army was nearing Płaszów, several hundred Działoszyceans were hastily transferred to Gross-Rosen, a concentration camp inside the Reich and, following a brief stay, forwarded on to Oskar Schindler's pseudo-ammunitions factory in Brinnlitz, Czechoslovakia, then part of the Protectorate of Bohemia and Moravia. Amounting to less than 5 percent of Działoszyce's prewar Jewish community, these Schindler Juden represented the bulk of its postwar survivors. "That is the end of community which had lived a full Jewish life for hundreds of years," writes Dr. Bejski.[8]

There is another wartime drama with which the Działoszyce story intersects, this one involving the sensitive subject of Jewish honor: resistance during the Holocaust. It is tempting to include a wide range of oppositional activity under that rubric, from shooting a gun to maintaining a stiff upper lip, to rebut the slanderous accusation that Jews went like "sheep to slaughter." But overstretching the term's meaning is hardly necessary, for much Jewish *armed* resistance did take place during the Holocaust, notwithstanding the formidable obstacles: the Nazi collective reprisals; the unavailability of weapons; the dim prospects of success; and most of all the absence of civilian support owing to the pervasiveness of Polish anti-Semitism, especially inside the Home Army (Armia Krajowa, or AK, the military arm of the London-based government-in-exile). All the same, in the Generalgouvernement alone there were three ghetto rebellions (the Warsaw Ghetto uprising chief among them) and four attempted rebellions. There were uprisings in six different concentration camps and death centers, including Sobibór and Treblinka. There were seventeen communities that contributed partisans to the armed groups that operated in Polish forests. Indeed, during 1942 and 1943 half the partisans in Poland were Jews.[9] Some of them were from Działoszyce. Later called Zygmunt, their small partisan band operated in the Pińczów and Miechów areas attacking Nazi patrols and German economic targets, steering clear all the while of the Home Army, which had killed three Jews in Działoszyce alone. The Jewish partisans of Działoszyce held out for two and half years before a force of German gendarmes armed with light artillery overwhelmed them.[10]

All in all, by the autumn of 1942, when historic shtetls such as Działoszyce were going under, it was clear that Jewish armed combat was an idea whose time had come. Or at least such was the view of dedicated, young Jewish revolutionaries who were enamored of heroic ideals and prepared to die for a lofty cause. But for family men like Mark Skorecki, escape was always the number one priority. And his was the attitude of most Polish Jews who slipped the Nazi noose and stayed inside the Generalgouvernement. Overwhelmingly they became involved not in armed resistance but day-to-day survival on the "Aryan side," either passing as Polish Christians or physically hiding in bunkers and false rooms.

Most of the time, the alternatives of resistance or escape coexisted harmoniously. But during the Warsaw Ghetto's final days, from the Great Deportations in the summer of 1942 through the uprising in the spring of 1943, the two strategies often clashed and sometimes openly conflicted, pitting young fighters against such workers as Anne Levy's father, for whom family survival remained paramount.

Though more than fifty years have passed since the historic Warsaw Ghetto uprising, it is still easy to evoke the mood that drove Jewish youth leaders toward open revolt. Their emotions were raw, close to the surface: a combustible mixture of anger, shame, vengeance, and frustration. Six days into the Great Deportations they embraced the idea of armed resistance. It happened during a July 28, 1942, gathering in a ghetto apartment on Dzielna Street. "At that meeting," wrote Yitzhak Zuckerman, also known by his underground name "Antek," and at twenty-eight the movement's graybeard, "we decided to establish the 'Jewish Fighting Organization [Żydowska Organizacja Bojowka, or ZOB].' Just us, all by ourselves, and without the parties."[11]

The parties he was referring to were various Jewish political movements, of which there had been no dearth during the interwar period. The two decades preceding the Nazi invasion had witnessed the remarkable efflorescence of political and associational life among Polish Jewry: two great religious parties; a plethora of Zionist subparties running the spectrum from right to left; and several left-leaning political groupings, chief among them the socialist Bund. Each party had its own press (130 publications appeared during the interwar period alone). Each sponsored youth movements, pioneer groups, and sporting and exercise clubs to attract young recruits. Politics pulsed through shtetls as small as Działoszyce, where Zionist tickets garnered majorities,[12] but the nerve center was always Warsaw. The main argument was over Jewish identity, which Jewish political parties debated with Talmudic intensity. Heirs to the universalist yearnings of the Enlightenment, the Bundists contended that Jewish identity should be civic and open to cross-ethnic, class-based alliances; the Zionist groupings, who were set on preserving a separate Jewish identity either in Poland or in Palestine, emphasized cultural autonomy. The passion with which positions were held frustrated wartime efforts to forge a popular front of armed resistance.[13]

The real stumbling block to military action, however, was the caution and misapplied realism of older party leaders. Most of them were family men, and they "spoke, thought, and concerned [themselves] about surviving the war," noted Ringelblum.[14] Their arguments were well rehearsed for why military resistance should be postponed if not rejected altogether: the time was unpropitious, the Jewish community was too weak, this too shall pass. On July 22, 1942, the very day the trains started leaving for Treblinka, at a meeting called by the pioneer youth leaders of the left-leaning Zionist movement (who provided the initial impetus behind the Jewish Fighting Organization), there was a sharp confrontation between revolutionary youth and the leaders of all the parties in the ghetto. Zuckerman urged that an attack be mounted against the Germans at the gates, to sound the alarm. The older men vetoed the idea. The clinching argument came from a historian and erstwhile member of the Polish parliament, who predicted that only eighty thousand ghetto inhabitants would be deported and that the Aktion would be over in a week or two. With him it was a matter of historical responsibility: "He said that there are periods of resignation in the lives of Jews as well as periods of self-defense. In his opinion, this wasn't a period of self-defense. We were weak and we had no choice but to accept the sentence." The meeting went on for hours. Already furious over the caution of their elders, the pioneer youth leaders were made even angrier by news the following day that Judenrat head Adam Czerniakow had committed suicide, making his death a private affair instead of issuing a warning to the community. And so it was that Zuckerman and his young comrades, in anger and frustration, four days later formed the Jewish Fighting Organization—the zob—all by themselves, "without the parties."[15]

During the deportations, the zob was a combat organization in name only, militarily so weak it could do little more than set fire to a few warehouses and botch an attempt on the life of the Jewish Police commander assigned to the Umschlagplatz. Most of their energies during this trying period went toward protecting remnants of their movement from deportation, often by rescuing fellow activists through the Umschlagplatz first aid clinic where Henry Tempelhof and Mery Mejnster worked from time to time. A serious blow befell the zob when several key members, along with a cache of hard-to-obtain weapons, fell into Nazi hands on the eve of the "big selection" in the "cauldron."[16] The liquidation's aftermath left a bitter residue of guilt and shame. We should have launched a killing spree against Jewish policemen, Zuckerman said; "for us, that was our great failure and disgrace."[17]

On September 13, 1942, the last night of the Great Deportation, the zob leadership called another strategy meeting in one of the ghetto apartments. This time only the youth leaders were present. The mood was extremely glum. "We were ashamed to look into each other's eyes," one later wrote.[18] They were downcast at the Polish response: Polish women in morning housecoats who scarcely looked up from watering the flowers on their second-story balconies as Jewish neighbors just beyond the wall were driven to the Umschlagplatz, and a government-in-exile that did little more than issue rhetorical appeals on behalf of the country's Jews. They were despondent that the Allies remained silent in the face of mounting reports of the destruction of Jewish communities.[19] A turning point in Jewish history had arrived, they believed, and they felt the weight of that history heavy on their shoulders. "We were all one family in these fateful hours," Zuckerman said, "a group of activists burdened by Jewish fate with an unparalleled responsibility." It should occasion no surprise that the plan of action favored by the overwhelming majority gathered that evening sprang from heartbreak rather than reason. It was to use the organization's meager stock of gasoline to attack the gates. Between them the young fighters were down to one rusty pistol and a couple of sticks and iron bars. Zuckerman, who had favored such an attack at the outset of the deportations, now objected that such an action was tantamount to collective suicide. A head taller than his comrades, with a shock of wavy hair and movie star good looks, down to a leather overcoat of the kind favored by the Gestapo, Antek cut an imposing figure among the young fighters. The attack would have no resonance and influence, he argued; the timing was wrong. And for what purpose? "So this little group would die an honorable death?!" All evening hurtful recriminations flew back and forth. Finally, in the predawn hours the group came around to Zuckerman's point of view, and the meeting concluded with the resolution to meet with force the next major Nazi Aktion in the ghetto.[20]

The ZOB spent most of the fall and winter of 1942–43 rebuilding its shattered organization. A top priority was creating a united Jewish front. Such an organization was necessary to win political legitimacy in the eyes of the Polish underground, who controlled the flow of money and munitions. Thus with the acquiescence of the older generation of party leaders, they established a Jewish National Committee. Then, to overcome the reluctance of Jewish Bundists who were philosophically opposed to any all-Jewish activity, they set up a parallel Jewish Coordinating Committee. The latter arrangement made it possible for young Bundists such as Marek Edelman and Vladka Meed to join the ZOB.[21] Regarding themselves as a "national" movement, they made contact with young activists in Białystok, Będzin, and Kraków. Meanwhile, other young Zionist leaders such as Mordechai Anielewicz—"about twenty-five, of medium height, with a narrow, pale, pointed face and a pleasant appearance," according to Ringelblum—began returning to the ghetto. Soon Anielewicz would become the overall commander of the Jewish Fighting Organization.[22]

The reconstituted ZOB spent much time raising funds, an essential task. The London-based Polish government-in-exile and the American Joint Distribution Committee channeled funds through the Polish underground, although not before AK operatives heavily discounted the hard currency. The Judenrat anted up too, and substantial amounts were brought in by "exes"— expropriations from rich Jews. The ZOB used the money primarily to purchase weapons, which were scarce and expensive (after Stalingrad, some returning Wehrmacht soldiers gladly sold their arms on their way home to the Reich). Pistols fetched the highest prices because of ease of concealment. By January the ZOB had less than twenty revolvers on hand. "Altogether we asked [the Polish Home Army] for a few score, and they didn't give them to us. That was their crime," Zuckerman said.[23]

Learning to use the weapons was as difficult as their procurement, because live target practice inside the ghetto risked disclosure. So the young fighters practiced quick-draw exercises, each shooter marking where the imaginary bullets had hopefully landed. They learned the art of making Molotov cocktails, which they confected out of lightbulbs, removing filaments and filling the insides with sulfuric acid; bottles were scarce in the ghetto, and it was important to ensure that the glass containers smashed on impact.[24]

In the meantime, the ZOB took steps to establish control of the ghetto by taming (and sometimes absorbing) the "wildcat" gangs of young Jewish toughs that had sprung up after the deportations to exploit the ghetto's unsettled conditions and to fight the Germans. They moved against the Jewish Police and collaborationist elements within the Judenrat. They became more proficient at assassination. In late October ZOB operatives gunned down the new head of the Jewish Police, boldly announcing the death sentence on posters placarded throughout the ghetto. A month later they executed the head of the Judenrat's economic department for his zealous cooperation with German authorities.[25]

To deal with the omnipresent threat of traitors and informers, the Jewish Fighting Organization kept its numbers small, forming tight-knit combat cells based on prewar movement affiliation, for, as Zuckerman explained, "strangers can't operate together; there has to be some 'glue' between them." The cells were called "fives," after the number of members in each unit.[26] There is debate about the Jewish Fighting Organization's overall membership, which probably numbered no more than six hundred members, and even that total is open to challenge. Close friends from before the war, the young ghetto fighters forged even more powerful bonds in their underground cells. "The fighting unit was just like a kibbutz," writes Simha Rotem, who is better known by his underground name, "Kazik": "we slept together, ate together, trained together, and performed operations with the same comrades." Love affairs flourished.[27]

But another motive impelled young members of the ZOB to withdraw into companionate groups of fellow warriors: a considered decision to cut family ties lest the values of rescue and survival weaken resolve. They understood perfectly well how family feeling had inclined the older generation of party leaders against military action, and they were determined to prevent the same sentiments from weakening their own resolve. That rationale also prompted them to rule out the construction of bunkers, because, as Zuckerman explained, "we were afraid that if we had a bunker someone would panic during the fighting and retreat to the bunkers. We made mistakes consciously and deliberately because it never occurred to us that any of us would remain alive after the April Uprising."[28]

And that was the linchpin assumption of the entire armed resistance strategy—the conviction that the ghetto remnant was already doomed, that the only choice remaining was the manner of dying. "The idea of death had become integrated into our outlook," wrote Meed. "We knew that all roads led toward it." "The truth was," explained Zivia Lubetkin, the Zionist comrade and future wife of Zuckerman, "we all desired a different death, a death which would bring vengeance upon the enemy and restore the honor of our people."[29] In any event, every ZOB fighter expected to die. Thus when the other youth leaders deferred to Zuckerman's logic during that stormy September 13 meeting, agreeing to rebuild their crippled organization before firing a shot, they were not so much rejecting collective suicide as postponing its occurrence.

The Warsaw Ghetto revolt, in other words, was really about Jewish honor and the construction of historical memory. Marek Edelman, recalling those heroic times from the wistful distance of about thirty years, captures that aspect with a sardonic touch: "We were convinced that it was necessary to die publicly, under the world's eyes. . . . After all, humanity had agreed that dying with arms was more beautiful than without arms. Therefore we followed this consensus."[30]

There was something quintessentially Polish about all this, a spirit akin to the messianic romanticism of Polish nationalism itself, with its apotheosis of heroic sacrifice and death with honor. In fact, the ZOB's understandable obsession with answering the taunts and libels of scornful Polish anti-Semites, especially within the AK, is hard to miss. "They didn't trust us," Zuckerman said. "They said: 'The Jews won't defend themselves.' They insulted us and said sneeringly that the Jews went like 'sheep to slaughter.' But when we asked for weapons they said they didn't believe the Jews would defend themselves." "We wanted to prove to ourselves and to all Jews and to the Poles and to the Germans as well, that we would not be led like lambs to slaughter," adds Lubetkin.[31]

So ZOB members would fight and die with dignity. Their weapons would pierce the world's silence. They would rescue Jewish honor. But all the while they would also be making choices never fully recognized at the time and only dimly acknowledged later on. They would be eliminating escape and rescue as viable options, on the theory that their only choice was between honorable and dishonorable death. They didn't rule out saving children or even the artistic and intellectual notables in the Jewish community whom the party leaders favored saving. "But," as Ringelblum wrote of Anielewicz and his comrades, they "would not lend a hand to this."[32] They would use their meager resources instead to buy weapons.

During the Solidarity struggles in the 1970s, in a famous interview with the Polish journalist Hanna Krall, Edelman guessed that pistols in the ghetto cost between three thousand and fifteen thousand zlotys on the black market, or about the cost of maintaining as many as three Jews on the Aryan side for a month. "If you were then faced with a choice—one revolver or a single person's life for a month . . ." Before Krall could finish her question, Edelman cut her off: "We weren't ever faced with that kind of choice. Perhaps it's better that we weren't."[33]

But the truth is, the Jewish fighters did face such choices, and Edelman, at some level of consciousness, seems to have sensed as much. One reads it between the lines, mainly in the diminution of the moral certitude that had impelled him as a young revolutionary to take up arms. Over and over again he downplays the grandeur of the uprising, elevating a young woman's determination to join her mother in the cattle cars to the same moral plane with his own decision to stay and fight, as though her ethic of caring was commensurable with the heroism of the uprising itself (which in a sense it was). He calls attention to another young woman whose mother committed suicide in order that her daughter might receive the life ticket that she, the mother, had received during the big selection in September 1942. The self-sacrifice seems meaningless in retrospect, because the daughter obtained a mere three months' reprieve. "That was a lot," Edelman insists, "because she managed to get to know love during those three months."

These after-the-fact reflections have all the wearied irony of a survivor-cardiologist who has spent most of his adult life in medicine "shielding the flame" from God's occasional moments of inattention, extending his patient's life sentence by a few years until God finally snuffed it out. But that tone is far removed from the heroic rhetoric the young fighters used in a manifesto sent to the Poles during the first days of the ghetto uprising: "Long live the fraternity of blood and weapons in a fighting Poland!"[34]

What pulled Mark Skorecki was the ordinary virtue of caring, not the heroic virtue of self-sacrifice. He was in his early forties, he had a family, and his priorities reflected his character and where he found himself at this fateful juncture of history: a father, husband, brother, and uncle whose commitments were first and foremost concrete rather than abstract, specific to real individuals rather than generalized to noble ideals. There was no way this intensely practical grandson of Działoszyce was going to glorify honorable death if a chance remained to save his family. Let the young rebels in the ZOB rescue Jewish honor. He was going to rescue Jewish people within his universe of obligation. Ever since his return from Białystok that universe had come to include not merely a wife and two young daughters but his older brother Julius and their niece Haka, both of whom, through Mark's intercessions, had found work at Big Schultz's and thus safety from the past summer's selections. And quite possibly Mark also felt some responsibility toward his in-laws, Henry Tempelhof and Mery Mejnster, and maybe even his helpers in the wooden sole division. If so, it was an awfully heavy burden for one man to carry.[35]

Notwithstanding ZOB objections, the ghetto remnant after September was consumed with the idea of building hideouts in the wreckage of their now devastated community. A stark mood change had overtaken the forty to sixty thousand Jews who had survived the liquidation. There was numbness, anger, and vengeance. There was guilt and shame. There was a sense of terrible personal loss, as the ghetto swelled with broken men bereft of families and reason for living. But one attitude seemed universal: clear-eyed recognition that Treblinka meant death and that German intentions were untrustworthy.[36] During the summer deportations ghetto residents had also rushed to build hiding places, but those makeshift shelters bore slight resemblance to those constructed in the autumn of 1942.

The new lairs were built for more or less permanent occupancy, for the simple reason many survivors calculated they could outlive the Nazis by burrowing deep inside the ghetto until war's end—whenever that might be. The new hideouts, therefore, were elaborate; many were winterized, even outfitted with toilets, running water, and electricity. Jewish craftsmen and engineers had a hand in the construction of many of these hiding places, converting cellars, attics, and alcoves into living quarters capable of accommodating dozens, sometimes hundreds, of people. Hinged stoves opened onto passageways that led to hidden attics or basement bunkers. Where the water had been shut off, the stowaways simply set nearby buildings ablaze to force the municipal fire department to turn the water back on. "There is altogether too much talk about hideouts—more talk than action," complained Ringelblum, whose sympathies and ties were to the young leadership of the nascent Jewish Fighting Organization.[37]

But ZOB disapproval scarcely deterred the frenetic search for long-term shelter. Says the historian Lucy Dawidowicz, "The ghetto soon became an enormous underground network of honeycombs connected by hundreds of invisible arteries, its inhabitants able to move about a square block without going outdoors."[38]

Most of the bunker-building activity took place within the interstices of the central ghetto, which had become a veritable no-man's land in the aftermath of the liquidation. Underground denizens soon nicknamed the area "Mexico," on account of the freebooting plunder committed by wildcat gangs of young survivors. Hundreds of houses and apartments stood abandoned, the air filled with the stench of unburied corpses. In the evening window sashes banged in the wind, remembered Zuckerman, "and every word echoed—a real 'ghost town.'"[39] During daylight hours hardly anyone could be seen on the streets save for Jewish work gangs moving under armed guard between assignments, because in mid-October the Nazis promised to shoot on sight anyone caught traversing that area without a pass. They made good on those threats too: 360 ghetto inhabitants were gunned down in October alone. A German named Klostermayer would ride through the ghetto with friends in a ricksha using wayward Jews for target practice.[40] One silver lining in all this was the collapse of prices for bedding and linen, which could be had for the asking because it was lying around everywhere. Heating costs had plummeted as well. To obtain fuel inhabitants simply chopped up furniture or dismantled wooden buildings. But the street peddlers were gone, and black market activity literally went underground.[41]

The official ghetto now consisted of "island factories," to use one Bundist's characterization of the ghetto's new landscape, each of the islands surrounded by fences, guard-controlled gates, and "the heavy silence of death."[42] Occupying the northwest quadrant were the brushmakers' shops, located just over the wall from the oak- and birch-shaded Krasinski Park where Poles still picnicked during warm weather and the peals of children's laughter mingled with the tinkling of the merry-go-round. Walter C. Többens maintained a sizable factory in the erstwhile little ghetto to the south, roughly where Twarda crossed Prosta Street. The largest complex was Többens-Schultz, where the Skoreckis were confined. Three smaller German shops were also encompassed within this fenced-off area, squeezed together with their larger counterparts between Nowolipki and Leszno Streets to the north and south and Żelazna and Karmelicka Streets to the east and west.

But the old Jewish quarter had ceased to be a ghetto in any meaningful sense, becoming instead a collection of *Konzentrationslager*, or KZS (concentration camps)—or "a mass labor camp," to quote Israeli historian Yisrael Gutman. The transformation was in keeping with Himmler's long-range plans. In his ongoing struggle with the Wehrmacht and armaments czars for the control of Jewish labor, including a late September meeting mediated by Hitler himself between Himmler and manpower chief Albert Speer, the Reichsführer-SS had effectively wrung the concession that ghetto production would henceforth fall under SS purview. Now military procurement authorities were required to route their requisitions through Himmler's bureaucracy. Now work Jews were to be completely segregated "in order to facilitate their removal from the production line in due course." And now, because prisoner salaries were unheard of in the Nazi camp system, shopworkers were deprived of even their heretofore meager wages, which Himmler confiscated by requiring German shop owners to pay the SS a daily head tax for every Jew employed. In lieu of wages the workers received coupons that were redeemable for "permissible goods." The new dispensation amounted to a kind of slave rental system.[43]

Inside the island factories proper, especially the sprawling Többens-Schultz complex, the mood ranged from anger and gloom to fear and trembling. Bad to begin with, the overcrowding became infinitely worse after the summer's liquidations. Some apartments were without light and gas; most were downright filthy, largely owing to the disproportionate deportation of women and children. Many of the male survivors, such as the diarist Lewin, were filled with grief over family loss. "It is not easy to make peace with the thought and with the images that accompany it," he wrote of the deportation of his wife of twenty-two years. "How was this gentle and delicate women killed?"[44] There was open anger over the loss of wages and the stretching of the workweek to include Sundays. On the shop floors discipline became more stringent, and tardy workers were dispatched to outside labor camps. In his diary Ringelblum recorded both acts of sabotage and instances of betrayal, for the extreme circumstances called forth extreme reactions. "Everybody has to work for nothing," he wrote. "People live by informing."[45] Every now and then the pall would momentarily lift. During the September 1942 High Holidays, Fritz Schultz, having been approached by a workers delegation, secured permission from German authorities to allow his laborers to observe Yom Kippur in the courtyard of the main plant area. "Next day we got our visitors," Ruth said, referring sarcastically to the periodic ss sweeps through the factories. In mid-October, when Schultz's received orders and raw material sufficient to last until April, "there was universal rejoicing," according to Ringelblum. "People drank toasts, threw parties, and the like." But the elation quickly vanished. Ruth's "visitors" returned, as they always did. "The Damocles sword of extermination hangs constantly over the heads of the Warsaw Jews," Ringelblum lamented.[46]

The constant raids by ss security forces and their Ukrainian and Baltic auxiliaries were part of an ongoing effort to winnow out illegals and hold the Jewish labor force to the agreed quotas. A big raid in all the shops occurred in mid-September, not long after the big selection in the kesl. More sweeps took place in October following yet another high-level conference between the Wehrmacht and the ss regarding Jewish war workers. In early November they struck again, hauling away from several shops anywhere from six hundred to one thousand Jews, mainly women and children.[47] "No one knows what all this means," Lewin recorded in his diary. Every night he tossed and turned, tormented by Dostoyevskian nightmares and reassured not in the least by news reports trickling in from the outside world of Hitler's obsessive reiteration of prophetic threats made before the war in a now famous speech to the

Reichstag, the oration delivered on January 30, 1939, in which Hitler warned "international Jewish financiers" that another war would result in "the annihilation of the Jewish race in Europe!"[48] By the fall of 1942 Hitler was in a gloating mood. "People always laughed about me as a prophet," the Führer said in his address on November 8, 1942. "Of those who laughed then, innumerable numbers no longer laugh today, and those who still laugh now will perhaps no longer laugh a short time from now."[49]

"Hitler's latest speech weighs on us heavily," Lewin wrote a week after its delivery. "In these words there was an explicit threat of extermination for the few surviving Jews."[50] And always there were the incessant shop raids. "Every day we expected these visitors with new surprises," Ruth said. "And these surprises made us more and more nervous."

They also intensified the latent conflict between young ZOB rebels and veteran workers, who blamed the former for endangering shop safety after the SS discovery of a weapons cache in one of the shops brought on a fresh round of raids.[51] That internecine conflict was probably the source of the deepening animosity between the ZOB and several Jewish shop foremen, as well. For in the same October 30 placard announcing the assassination of Jewish Police chief Jacob Lejkin, the rebels also announced the conviction of "the managers of the shops and members of the *Werkschutz* [Jewish factory police], due to their cruel treatment of the workers and the 'illegal' Jewish population," then declaring, *"Retaliatory measures will be adopted in all their severity."* Those threats were followed up with several assaults against a few Jewish foremen.[52]

Mark Skorecki was likely not among the targeted foremen, even assuming he was forced on occasion to be party to who would stay and who would go. Nor did the ZOB ever have a large presence inside Big Schultz's, though there were a few cells inside the larger Többens-Schultz complex.[53] Whatever the ZOB might have thought of Mark Skorecki, if they thought about him at all, did not concern him. Uppermost in his mind, as it was in the thoughts of nearly everyone else in the desolated ghetto, was arranging a secure hiding place for his family. Even Stelmaszek was beginning to doubt his ability to extend indefinite protection to his indispensable Jewish foreman and increasingly vulnerable family. "Every time it gets worse and worse," he told Mark, referring to the ongoing raids. "You have to start thinking of something in case they make you go out again or start searching for people. Make a hiding place wherever you can."

That was easier said than done, for constructing hideouts and bunkers in the shops was always more difficult because of the closer German scrutiny.[54] Fortunately for Mark, he was freed of the burden of building something new. He merely had to improve something previously discovered: the secret leather tannery in the subbasement of his building. Extending beyond the foundations of their own apartment building, the second cellar was large enough to accommodate huge numbers of people, yet secure enough to keep them safely concealed. So, after Stelmaszek warned him to look for a new hiding place, Mark began bringing his wife and children to the abandoned tannery whenever another selection was in offing. "We were afraid to stay in the top part of the building," Ruth said, "so all the time when our supervisor let us know to expect something, we ran to the cellar." And not only Ruth and her young daughters, but all the women and children still inside the blocks also fled to that subbasement, bringing with them the increasingly scarce infirm and elderly. There they stayed for days at a time. Luckily, enough scrap wood was lying around to provide heating fuel against the bitter cold of the approaching Polish winter. Although Ruth is spare with details, the Skoreckis' new underground hideout must have been rigged by Mark and the other men for longterm occupancy. Because before long only the men started showing up for work at Big Schultz's, leaving the women and children to spend the day in the cellar. Ringelblum seems to have known about the sanctuary. "In another place," he wrote in his diary, "they used a secret tannery, specially built into a cellar, for a hide-out."[55]

Whenever Ruth had to accompany her husband to the shop, she and Mark would leave Anne and Lila by themselves for the day in the subcellar with the other stowaways. They were lucky to have two obedient children. Ghetto hideouts were constantly being exposed by young children who panicked or whimpered when ss troops with leashed dogs were in the vicinity. Ringelblum mentioned one such incident in an apartment building on Nowolipie Street when Ukrainians, partying next door, heard a child cry out on the other side of a false wall where twenty-six Jews were hiding. The ss auxiliaries chopped it down, shot six of the illegals on the spot, and shipped the rest to the Umschlagplatz.[56] But Anne and Lila, having passed through what Ringelblum called "a stern schooling for life," knew how to keep quiet, and thus there was little chance, as sometimes happened with Jewish children who proved ungovernable, that the older hideaways in the second cellar would bar their admittance.[57]

During the fall Mark was transferred to the night shift. He chose to bring Ruth and the children with him every evening, bedding down the girls in the false floor of the shop's storeroom beneath mounds of wooden soles. Stelmaszek, who did not work at night, gave his trusted assistant the keys to his office. Eventually, he gave him permission to cut out a cubbyhole in the floor area beneath the desk. Lined with a blanket, the crawl space was large enough to accommodate all four Skoreckis. Most of the time they received advance warning from the front of the factory whenever the ss made a surprise visit. Hurriedly Mark would stow his wife and daughters inside the desk-covered compartment. Then he would lock the office door and squeeze in beside them. One evening, while Ruth and the kids were sleeping on the office floor instead of in their floor compartment, in order to stretch out and get more sleep, the SS burst in on them before Mark could bustle his family inside their hidden bedroom. "The Germans were running with flashlights all over the factory," Ruth said. The kids scampered under the desk, but Ruth had barely enough time to pull the blanket over her. Mark locked the office door. Then he went out to palaver with the soldiers. This was the supervisor's office, he told them, and he did not have a key to open it. The SS shined their flashlights through the door's glass pane, conelike beams playing on the office walls. Mark must have been amazingly cool under pressure. The SS never thought to search him or jimmy the office door. "God was good to us," Ruth said. "The Germans never saw me laying on the floor underneath a blanket. They left the factory and took, as always, a number of people with them." Such close calls caused her and the girls to remain in the tannery as often as possible.

It was in November 1942 that the Skoreckis began thinking seriously about escaping from the ghetto. Autumn frosts hinted at the approaching severity of the Polish winter—and the winter of 1942 proved to be one of the coldest on record. Once plentiful heating material grew scarce as furniture and wooden buildings vanished up the chimneys of countless ghetto stoves. Stelmaszek himself was becoming more and more concerned about the Skoreckis' long-term chances for survival. The information he picked up on the radio and from other sources and dutifully passed on to Mark was deeply troubling. "The Germans are trying to destroy all the Jewish people," he told his foreman behind closed doors. "And this was not only in Warsaw, but all over the oc-cupied place where the ghettos were made for the Jews"—confirmation, in effect, of the stream of never-ending reports trickling in from other sources concerning the disappearance of ancient Jewish communities across Poland. "We were very fortunate to have a person like this to help us," Ruth said. "Through his information, we tried to help others too."

The cumulative impact of Stelmaszek's tidings undercut the premise that had sent so many Jews flocking toward the shops at the onset of the Great Deportations. It was now obvious that survival through work offered scant immunity from extermination and that the Skoreckis should do everything possible to flee to the Aryan side. Growing glum about the future, many Jews were reaching similar conclusions. "How long shall we remain in the ghetto?" Ringelblum asked himself that autumn. "How long shall we live? How long shall we survive?" In November a commotion broke out at Nowolipie 52, just up the street from the Skorecki apartment at Nowolipie 28, when groups of Jews posted there began to escape. "The workers have scattered in all directions," Lewin recorded in his diary. "They are afraid that they will be rounded up and sent somewhere from which there is no return."[58]

Starting in earnest during the Great Deportation, the flight from the ghetto gathered mounting momentum that fall and winter. Precise figures are impossible to come by. Some historians place the total as high as forty-two thousand. More plausible estimates, pegged to the number of Jews believed to have been in hiding in Aryan Warsaw, range between fifteen and twenty-four thousand.[59] What can be said with greater certainty is that few of the escapees were poor, and only a tiny percentage belonged to the working class. Overwhelmingly they came from the intelligentsia: medicine, law, education, engineering, journalism, trade, and industry, which are the careers that gave one money, gentile connections, and the assimilationist appearance and language skills necessary for survival on the Aryan side. Poor Jews from ultra-Orthodox and exclusively Yiddishkeit backgrounds faced tremendous disadvantages.[60] It is hard to pigeonhole the Skoreckis. They clearly were not members of the intelligentsia as conventionally understood. But they were secular Jews, possessed a Polish name, spoke fluent Polish, and, thanks to Ruth's social striving, understood the code and cues of the bourgeois lifestyle. The Skoreckis even had money, plus a couple of gentile contacts in Warsaw.

Part of the money the Skoreckis had managed to save in the predeportation period. But Mark, probably because of his foreman status, continued drawing a salary from Big Schultz's even after the ss had confiscated the wages of most shopworkers, and he and Ruth began saving as much of it as they could manage. It was around this time that they tried to make contact with a former priest and his wife then living in Aryan Warsaw. The wife's father had helped manage the lumberyard owned by Wladek Skorecki back in Łódź. Ruth never mentioned the couple's name, though she did say she knew their address. It is always possible she was trying to conceal a disappointment all too familiar to many ghettoized Jews who contacted gentile friends for help. Old Polish acquaintances frequently pulled back, offering a multitude of excuses. Their neighbors were untrustworthy; a Volksdeutscher with ties to the Gestapo lived next door; the wife's sister would object; their presence would attract too many suspicious visitors. But, as Ringelblum said, "The only real reason was fear, fear of the Germans, fear of punishment for hiding Jews."[61] What passed between the Skoreckis and the gentile couple when they finally made contact in the late fall of 1942 is pure guesswork. All we know for sure is that the Polish couple would prove helpful to the Skoreckis later.

Mark and Ruth possessed cultural and economic advantages enjoyed by few other workers at Schultz's, but none was more important than the active assistance of Mark's immediate superior. "Mr. Stelmaszek started thinking with us as to how we could get out," Ruth said. Most Polish managers in German shops were notorious as extortionists and hard taskmasters. "A noble individual was rarely to be found among these gangsters," Ringelblum said. But Stelmaszek was different. Or maybe he just embodied the old Polish maxim that "every Pole, even the greatest anti-Semite, had his own Jew of whom he was fond," and Mark Skorecki happened to have been Stelmaszek's personal favorite at a time when paternalism could mean the difference between life and death. Like much of this story, the truth is shrouded in mystery.[62]

But despite their advantages, arranging an escape was far from easy. "It took us a long time to figure a way to get out, because this was very dangerous," Ruth said, adding, though hardly as an afterthought, that "it took money also."

Then a piece of good luck came their way in December 1942, largely owing to Mark and Ruth's singular success in safeguarding their two young children from the Nazis. A Polish military veteran who had been wounded early in the war and who used to visit Big Schultz's in connection with his job in a German factory outside the ghetto learned of the Skoreckis' plight from Stelmaszek. During one visit to the wooden sole department the Polish military veteran told Mark and Ruth about Jewish children who had already been placed in the safekeeping of nuns. On a return visit a short while later, apparently following preliminary inquiries with contacts on the "Aryan side" and possibly after having received assurances that the Skorecki girls spoke good Polish and knew how to behave, he offered to help smuggle Anne and Lila out of the ghetto.[63] "He told us that he would be glad to see if he could put the children in a convent for us," Ruth said. Were the Skoreckis interested? That initial feeler would result in the eventual escape of the entire family.

Few if any subjects in recent history are more contentious than Polish-Jewish relations during the Holocaust. Mutual suspicion and recrimination loom over the topic. On one side there is suppressed guilt and righteous indignation, on the other fear and hatred. Most of the time Poles and Jews, neighbors for nearly a millennium, talk past one another in "a tragic dialogue of the deaf," although there are recent signs of a cooling off, even an opening up of common ground.[64] Poland was the setting of Nazi genocide, and that irreducible fact has scarred Jewish survivors and Catholic Poles alike. Many of the former, their perceptions colored by memories of prewar anti-Semitism and postwar pogroms, reproach Poles for seeming indifference to the Nazi destruction of ancient Jewish communities. The London-based government-in-exile, they say, wrung their hands instead of urging Catholic Poles to aid imperiled Jews. Within occupied Poland the official underground acted as though the Jewish tragedy was of secondary concern at best, reflecting thereby the triumph of exclusivist nationalism in Polish politics. Yes, the argument goes, there were kindhearted Poles who succored and saved Jewish compatriots. But the altruism of the few pales beside the betrayals of denouncers and blackmailers, the collaboration of the Polish Blue police, and the back-stabbing—literally—of anti-Semites within the AK. To all this the Poles have a typical response: the Jews got what was coming to them; the Poles did everything they could under the circumstances; the Poles were victims, too, which was true, for early in the German occupation the two populations received almost "separate but equal" persecution. The debate, which frequently resembles a competitive struggle over the primacy of suffering, is not always very edifying.[65]

Mutual suspicion even clouds Polish and Jewish perceptions of the institution that was likely behind the convent proposal the Skoreckis received that December. The organization was called the Konrad Żegota Committee, or simply Żegota, which was a cryptonym for the Council for Aid to Jews.[66] Sprouting from a leaflet published in August by a well-known Catholic woman novelist protesting the world's silence about the destruction of the Jews, Żegota had evolved by early December into a full-fledged component of the Polish "underground state." Until the Warsaw Uprising of 1944 (not to be confused with the Warsaw Ghetto Uprising in April and May 1943), much of the Polish resistance involved the establishment of shadow institutions to counteract Nazi efforts to atomize Polish society. Żegota was a reflection of this Polish determination to retain vestiges of national life. The multitiered organization included both Jewish and Polish members. Eventually it expanded into a vast network of cells ministering to the needs of hidden Jews. Various departments of Żegota specialized in finding housing and clothing, forging documents, and organizing medical care for Jews on the "Aryan side." There was a Children's Section dedicated to the rescue and care of Jewish children. Most of Żegota's activities were confined to Warsaw and surrounding communities, although it did have branches in Lublin and Kraków, among other places. Funding arrived regularly via couriers parachuted into Poland from the government-in-exile in London and from Jewish philanthropy in Great Britain and the United States. There is no question that Żegota performed courageously in the face of daunting challenge.[67]

But like everything else touching on the Holocaust, Poles and Jews are unable to agree about the scope of Żegota's good works. Some Polish officials claim that the organization saved between forty and fifty thousand Jews throughout Poland; many survivors say the number was much less. Some Poles underscore the generous level of funding provided by the government-in-exile; many Jews begin and end with Ringelblum's curt assessment that

Żegota's activity was "limited by lack of funds and lack of help from the government."[68] And there is also disagreement about the convent proposal Mark and Ruth were asked to consider.

The project seems to have originated with the head of Żegota's Children's Section (Irene Sendlerowa), who had long been involved in placing Jewish children in Catholic convents and orphanages. The numbers were not negligible: an estimated two-thirds of the seventy-four female religious communities located in the Generalgouvernement may have sheltered as many twenty-five hundred Jewish children during the course of the war. Several of the religious orders were based in Warsaw. (Those inside the Wartheland had been closed down.) Most of this rescue work happened on an ad hoc basis: Jewish foundlings made their way to a convent on their own, or Jewish parents brought their children to the Mother Superior, asking that they be looked after until war's end. Just as often some Polish intermediary, usually a priest who had known the parents from before the war, arranged the placement. Catholic institutions were good places to hide youngsters. "Orphanages and churches were the safest asylums for Jewish children," said Meed, who later became a courier on the Aryan side. "The nuns generally could be relied on not to report the Jewish children even when they learned that they were Jewish."[69] "In fact," according to Nechama Tec, a leading authority on rescue activity in wartime Poland, "most youngsters who survived by passing stayed in convents, monasteries, and orphanages."[70] Many of them were young girls of Anne's and Lila's ages.

By December 1942, the demand for hiding places in Catholic convents had apparently reached the point where Żegota's Children's Department had to systematize what had heretofore been an improvised activity. According to Ringelblum, who is the best source on the matter, controversy erupted as soon as the ghetto learned of the proposal to transfer Jewish children to convents and Catholic orphanages. Many Jewish intellectuals decried it as a Catholic scheme to steal Jewish souls by converting the young, as the church had done during previous crises in Jewish life. There were accusations that profit was at its root—six to seven hundred zlotys per child per month. Some said it was merely a whitewash effort to salvage the church's tarnished reputation abroad given its inaction in the face of Nazi crimes against Jews in Poland. The debate devolved into a choice between martyrdom and Marranoism: passing as Christians in the manner of Sephardic Jews during the Inquisition. "We must follow the example of our fathers and accept martyrdom in His name. We have no right to give our blessing to the conversion of our children," argued Orthodox leaders and "certain national groups." At a time of widespread slaughter, others answered, "the soul of each and every Jew is precious, and we must take pains to try to preserve it."[71] The argument went back and forth. Unable to reach consensus, the underground leaders finally resolved to leave the matter up to individual choice: "Jewish parents were left to decide for themselves," Ringelblum said.[72]

And that is precisely how the convent proposal came down to the Skoreckis—as a proposition, proffered by a wounded Polish veteran with undoubted ties to Żegota, to be accepted or rejected by them alone.[73] Given their deepening worries about the ever-growing peril facing Anne and Lila, for Mark and Ruth the choice was clear-cut. As Ruth explained, "This was a hard decision to make because we always tried to be together, but we didn't believe we could keep on saving their lives, so we were glad to try to do this." They were ready to break up the family. For many Jewish families still in the ghetto, voluntary separation was becoming the commonplace strategy. "Jewish families rarely crossed to the Aryan side together," wrote Ringelblum in his history of Polish-Jewish relations written while he was hiding in a bunker on the "Aryan side." "First the children went, while the parents stayed on in the Ghetto in order to mobilize the necessary funds for staying on the Aryan side, as they did not have the money to fix up the whole family." Lacking funds, many parents were never able to escape.[74] But even those who did manage to cross to the other side still chose to leave their children with Catholic families or institutions. By now it was almost conventional wisdom that Jewish families who stayed together greatly lessened their chances for survival. "Everyone who recognized the obvious," wrote former concentration camp inmate and child psychologist Bruno Bettelheim, "knew that the hardest way to go underground was to do it as a family; to hide out together made detection by the ss most likely; and when detected, everybody was doomed. By hiding singly, even when one got caught, the others had a chance to survive." Bettelheim was criticizing the 1950s sentimentalization of the Anne Frank story, faulting her father Otto Frank for his decision to keep the family together. That was not a mistake many Jewish families inside the Warsaw Ghetto were prone to make, which is why so many of them were willing to leave their youngsters with Catholic families or institutions, even knowing full well that it might result in their never seeing them again. But this was a gamble Jewish parents knew they had to take, and it was a risk Mark and Ruth believed they had to accept.[75] "So we told the Polish military man that when it is possible we would like to try to get our kids out and have them sent to the convent," Ruth said. "And so we were waiting about how we could get the kids out . . . to bring them to the nuns and let them raise them and take care of them."

In the meantime, there was a slew of arrangements to take care of. The operation would cost money, how much Ruth never specified other than to mention that the Polish veteran "had been told by Mark that we would of course pay him for this." There was the matter of escape. How would the two girls be taken out of the ghetto? Leaving with one of the work gangs, the most common method of escape, was out of the question. Being escorted through the sewers by Polish sanitation workers, another popular alternative, was even less of an option. Those subterranean passages were dangerous even for adults. About two meters high, Warsaw's central sewer coursed with a mighty flow of sewage, branching off at several points into narrow side channels that could be navigated only on one's stomach through excrement and foul stench. The only other alternative was to go through the gates, which meant bribing one of the guards. But who could say whether the guards would stay bribed? As Meed explained, "While one might bribe the German sentinel, one could never be certain that he might not decide to shoot his victim after all."[76] But the ever reliable Stelmaszek proved helpful here too. Living outside the ghetto, Mark's supervisor passed through the gates every morning and evening. He became familiar with the shift changes and the personality of the guards. "By the gates there were mean guards and at other times those who were not so bad," Ruth said. "Stelmaszek talked with these men and learned more about them. He tried to get to know some of them, to try to do something." Finally he found a guard with a price. Then he found a means of conveying the girls through the gate. It was the chauffeur for a high-ranking ss official who came to Schultz's every couple of days to check up on things. The driver agreed to transport Anne and Lila out of the ghetto. "Maybe we could put the kids in the trunk of this car, cover them with blankets and put them to sleep with drugs and get them out while the ss man was on an inspection," Stelmaszek said. It was the best possible way to escape: in the company of a German *Begleiter* (escort). "This constituted an extraordinary blessing," Ringelblum said of the activities of these German rescuers.[77]

"Everything was prepared," Ruth said, "and we were just waiting for the right moment." And then the convent arrangement suddenly fell through, without much explanation. Ruth said the Polish veteran simply told them during one of his visits that "it was too late to give the kids up to the nuns, there were too many kids there already." True, the convent project never moved beyond the talking stage, but there is no evidence of a slackening flow of Jewish children into Catholic institutions. On the contrary, this was exactly when the volume began to increase. It is hard to avoid the conclusion that the arrangement came apart because Ruth had never been keen on it in the first place and had begun having second thoughts almost as soon as she had agreed to hand her children over. Such feelings were hardly surprising. "The mothers who entrusted their children to us were close to tears," wrote Meed, adding that "some mothers could not bring themselves to part with their children." Parents feared that their children might be lost to Catholicism, turned out in the streets when the money ran out, or kidnapped and held for ransom by Polish thugs. These things were known to have happened.[78]

Meed and one of her companions tried hard to convince one mother to let them carry her young son beyond the wall. "I can't do it," she told them. "My son has no one but me now. I guard him like the apple of my eye. Together we have endured all this misery and misfortune. Without me, he would perish." Meed was at a loss for words. Her companion, more composed, used calm reason. The ghetto was about to explode in combat. Her son would be safer on the Aryan side. He would be able to survive there. "Manya [the mother] heard him out in silence, the battle between emotion and reason mirrored in her pale, drawn face." She refused to budge. Both mother and son perished in the ghetto uprising.[79]

Thus when Ruth said that parting with her children was "a hard decision," she likely meant it was much harder than even she was willing to admit to herself let alone admit to strangers later on. And therefore, as the moment of separation drew close, she commenced spinning a skein of excuses for why she needed more time, why conditions were not yet ripe, why the day after tomorrow would work better than today or the next day. "I can see why she would have had all these hesitations," Anne says. "She made a long trip to Bialystok only to say bring me back to Warsaw shortly after arriving. It was too much for her then. It was probably too much for her now. And after seeing what had happened to so many children inside the ghetto, she couldn't just give up her own children to destiny. She was afraid. Afraid whether we would survive, and afraid whether we would survive as Jews if we did survive."

Or maybe Ruth's hesitation reflected a self-awareness too painful to acknowledge of the tenuousness of her own survival, of how much her own life chances were now tied up with those of her children. Anne is insightful here as well: "I think my mother's mental health was at stake. On the outside, if you looked at this woman, she was stoic. But on the inside, she was dying over the choices she had to make. I doubt whether she could have gone through with the decision to send my sister and me to a convent. Eventually she would have fallen apart. It was as though she needed the responsibility of our care in order to survive."

And that is one of the fundamental truths of the Holocaust: that survival required not merely luck, skill, money, and connections but also relationships and human solidarity. "Everybody had to have somebody to act for, somebody to be the center of his life," Edelman once told Hanna Krall, as explanation for why a comrade was probably doomed when his girlfriend was taken to the infamous Pawiak Prison in Warsaw. "He has no reason to live any more. Now he will get killed."[80] The phenomenon was all too familiar in the camps, where isolated prisoners were the first to abandon hope and metamorphose into those "musselmen" who shuffle through camp memoirs like living ghosts parading toward the abyss. "It was important not to be separated from one's group," the French resistance fighter and Auschwitz survivor Charlotte Delbo once wrote. "Each one of us had experienced fully the fact that an isolated individual is defenseless, that you cannot survive without the others . . . who hold you up, or carry you when you can no longer walk, those who help you hold fast when you're at the end of your rope."[81] But the reverse was true as well, as Terrence Des Pres has brilliantly phrased it: "The survivor's experience is that the need *to* help is as basic as the need *for* help. . . ."[82]

So, it is hard to envision Ruth Skorecka surviving apart from her young children. She was high-strung, taut, nervous. She seemed always on the verge of coming unraveled. But the care of Anne and Lila powerfully concentrated her attention, leaving little room for the self-pity of which she was capable, of which any human being would have been capable in similar circumstances. Anne and Lila were ballast that kept her from capsizing. Ruth almost went under during her abortive trip to Białystok. She came close to drowning during the imposed famine in the Warsaw Ghetto. How she would have fared had she handed her two girls over to the Catholic sisters is not even a close call. The grieving and anxiety probably would have been her undoing.

And that is why the miraculous survival of the Skoreckis from Łódź was always a matter of mutuality. It is a half-truth to say that Ruth saved her daughters, because Anne and Lila also saved their mother by virtue of their possumlike ability to curl up in silence when detection and death drew near. And they indirectly saved their father as well from the defeatism that had overtaken several of the wifeless men in gloomy shops such as Schultz's following the Great Deportation. Theirs could easily have been his fate. He was already in his forties. Most of his life must have seemed behind him by now. Without a wife and children to protect and defend, what future lay before him? Why even bother to go on living?

And then, just as suddenly as the convent arrangement fell through, another escape possibility opened up. Doubtless because of Ruth's procrastination, the Polish military man had in the meantime worked out an alternative arrangement in the working-class suburb of Praga on the other side of the Vistula. "Mr. Skorecki," he told Mark one day, sometime in late December or early January, "I have a place. I know two ladies, a mother and a daughter, who are willing to take in someone, of course with a good Polish accent, fluent enough that they would not be recognized as Jewish." "This woman and her daughter were very nice people," he continued, "and they could give up one room and help someone who was in need and who wanted to get out of the ghetto."

The two women, mother and daughter, were named Katarzyna and Anastazja Piotrowska, respectively, although the daughter usually went by the diminutive Natalia. The Polish military man had known the Piotrowskas from before the war, when he had run a shop on Praga's Ząbkowska Street close to where the Piotrowskas had lived. A son, Czestow Piotrowski, also a military veteran and a mechanic by trade, had died in 1940 of stomach and back ailments. The death sent the father into decline. Recently retired from his job at the Vodka distillery plant on Ząbkowska Street, Adam Piotrowska had died in March 1942. Now without significant breadwinners, the Piotrowska women could use the extra income that boarders might bring in.[83]

Mark spent little time mulling over the offer. "Mark told him not to tell this to anyone," Ruth said. "He told him that he would like to have this place." His wife and daughters would have to go out first, and he would follow them after a decent interval. "I'm a foreman in this department, and when people see that I am gone, there would be a panic and my wife and two children would not be able to get out afterward." For Mark Skorecki, privilege at Big Schultz's continued to have its perils.

One of the first things Mark and Ruth did following their meeting with the Polish military veteran was to consult that evening in their apartment at Nowolipie 28 with Julius and Haka. "We locked ourselves up in our rooms," Ruth said. They told Mark's brother and niece of the Piotrowska offer. Ruth and the children would leave first, Mark would come later. There was room for Julius and Haka. Did they want to come along? Their initial reaction was cool. "They were afraid and weren't too excited with the idea, because they thought nobody could come out from the ghetto," Ruth said. Maybe they would stay put, maybe something would work out. By this point, Mark had lost all illusions, assessing every situation in the light of cold reason. "Little by little they are taking us away or killing us," he told Julius and Haka. "We are 99 percent sure of death if we stay here. We have nothing to lose by trying to get out of the ghetto." It was a point Mark's brother and niece found hard to dispute.

A short time later, on a Saturday afternoon in early January—probably the day after New Year's—Ruth's brother Henry and his wife, Mery, made another one of their clandestine visits to the apartment at Nowolipie 28. They came by ambulance again, this time with Ruth and Henry's younger brother, Vovek. The short trip from the Czyste Hospital's new location on Gęsia Street was more dangerous than ever. A week earlier a doctor and his wife, along with a few other Jews, were killed while traveling from the hospital to the Többens-Schultz area to visit relatives.[84] Mark and Ruth told her brothers and Mery about their escape plans and asked if they cared to join them. There was room for them too. Henry and Mery declined, and so, apparently, did Vovek. "We don't have children," they said. "We can do this in the last minute when things become very bad." They never offered more reasons for procrastination, or if they did Ruth failed to mention them. But feelings of Hippocratic obligation likely held them in place. That attitude still pervaded the embattled Jewish medical community in the ghetto even after that summer's devastating deportations. Szwajger explained the feeling forty-five years later: "We had our duty as human beings and . . . we were there to help. That is why this medicine was 'superhuman' and why, although it is all like one great wound, it is the most beautiful thing of all."[85] That Saturday Ruth and her brothers and sister-in-law parted with dread and apprehension: "I never knew what would happen to us, let alone what might happen to them. Or who among us would be lucky enough to stay alive."

Ruth and the girls were supposed to leave on Thursday, January 7, 1943. She had already stuffed their belongings inside a naval duffel bag and sent it by way of the Polish veteran to the friend who was a former priest and his wife for temporary safekeeping. The military man told the couple that the Skoreckis would be leaving the ghetto soon. "Of course, they were very glad," Ruth said. But Ruth rather quickly seems to have found new reasons for staying put. She was worried over whether her would-be hosts fully understood the grave risks they were running by agreeing to take in the Skoreckis. By now the Nazis had made compassion a capital crime. On October 28, 1942, the high commander of the ss and the police for the General Government had decreed the death penalty for any Pole who "consciously provides a refuge for a Jew, that is, whoever houses, feeds, or otherwise conceals a Jew outside of the residential area." For good measure, he also threatened camp internment for all civilians who failed to snitch on good Samaritan neighbors. The announcement was posted everywhere, on ghetto walls and all over the Aryan side.[86]

Anxiety in the ghetto usually ran high on Mondays, since the Germans typically launched their deportation raids on the first day of the week. On January 4, three days before Ruth and the girls were slated to escape, apprehensions soared owing to reports that Ukrainian troops had arrived in Warsaw. "We have again been attacked by a sense of uneasiness and startling fear," Lewin wrote.[87] The Polish veteran also dropped by the wooden sole shop that Monday to report all was in readiness. Ruth told him of her moral misgivings. Did the Piotrowska women know what they were getting into? "I don't want to lie to the Piotrowska women," Ruth said. "I want them to know that we are Jews, because when the Germans find out that they were keeping Jewish people in their home, we would all be killed together. We never want to do anything that would hurt other people just to get a good for ourselves." He reassured her that the mother and daughter knew exactly what they were getting into. "I told them the truth," he said, "and they have accepted it."

Then the new getaway plan hit a snag because of a last-minute change in the gate assignment for the Thursday morning shift, forcing a change in schedule. Two days later the escape had to be scuttled yet a second time because of a surprise German tour of the plant. "So we had to think of other arrangements," Ruth said. Meanwhile, the ss chauffeur, still assuming that Anne and Lila were to be carried to a convent, asked what the holdup was. In a few days he would be coming to the factory with his ss boss. When would the girls be ready? Soon, Stelmaszek told him. Soon. The Polish military man was starting to worry. "He came again and asked what had happened," Ruth said. "He was afraid maybe something had happened to us. We told him that it was impossible to go out on the day that was planned—they would try it again."

It was no ordinary surprise inspection visit that had caused the latest change in plans. Himmler himself, who had long taken a special interest in Warsaw, had thrown the entire ghetto into an uproar on January 9 during an unannounced visit to the former Polish capital. He wanted to see for himself whether his July orders had been carried out that Warsaw—indeed, the entire Generalgouvernement—be emptied of all but war-essential Jews by the end of the year. His ongoing quarrel with the Wehrmacht and the armaments procurement chiefs had reached the boiling point. Himmler was convinced that his rivals were colluding with local German industrialists to perpetuate a rump ghetto, both to line their own pockets and to avoid service on the eastern front, and that some local ss officials were part of the arrangement. That Saturday Himmler roared through nearly deserted ghetto streets, two armored cars to his front and rear. They sped past Abraham Lewin. "It may be that the head-butcher actually drove by, in order to see with his own eyes the fruits of his 'work,' the destruction of the greatest Jewish community in Europe. He was no doubt happy with the results," Lewin wrote in one of the last entries of his diary.[88] But Himmler was distinctly unhappy at what he discovered, expressing his displeasure two days later in a letter to the Higher ss Police chief for the Generalgouvernement. The ghetto's Jewish population stood at forty thousand (which was probably thirty thousand shy of the real total but still well in excess of allowable limits). The German shops, producing mostly clothing, leather goods, and wood products, were "fictitious armament plants" run by Jewish foremen and guarded by Werkschutz. The whole thing was a sham, a far cry from the tightly run labor camps that had mushroomed all over Poland. Worse, the German plant owners, especially such large operators as Fritz Schultz and Walter C. Többens, the latter of whom drew Himmler's special wrath, were nothing better than war profiteers who deserved to be conscripted and sent to the Russian front forthwith. The Reichsführer-ss laid down a new deadline: liquidate the entire ghetto by February 15, beginning with the immediate transfer of sixteen thousand work Jews to a concentration camp and the deportation of eight thousand illegal Jews, presumably to Treblinka. Within a few weeks the ss spelled out where these camps would be: Trawniki and Poniatów, in the Lublin District.[89]

Even Mark's supervisor, whose closeness to the Schultz management put him in touch with late-breaking rumors, seemed shaken by Himmler's visit. "Mr. Stelmaszek told us that he himself was thinking of leaving," Ruth said, "because the Germans were supposed to take the whole factory and them someplace. Maybe they would send him too. He didn't want to go along for the affair."

It was not until the following Wednesday, January 13, 1943, that the pieces had fallen into place for a successful breakout—or at least most of the pieces. Although the right guards were on duty, the chauffeur was not available, so Mark found an alternative means of conveyance: "a garbage truck, a smelly garbage truck," as Anne describes it. It was a shrewd choice, actually. Trash collectors had long been involved in smuggling contraband in and out of the ghetto, and some of the sanitation workers were kindhearted. During the Hanukkah Festival in December 1941 three garbagemen had snuck in toys and food, including a pine tree they cut down as a personal gift, to the children in Janusz Korczak's ill-fated ghetto orphanage.[90] Now trash collectors would be carrying gifts out of the ghetto: a nervous mother and two frightened children. The time of departure had been set for between nine and ten in the morning, when the garbage truck was scheduled to make its regular collection at Schultz's and would pick up Ruth and the girls in front of Nowolipie 28.

Not surprisingly, Ruth had another attack of nerves, this time brought on by self-doubts as to whether she could pull off a convincing impersonation of an Aryan. Contemporary history had branded Jewishness onto her soul. "How could I pretend that I wasn't a Jew, when I was so conscious of the fact already?" she said, admitting, "I was afraid of everyone, every face."

Where Ruth agonized, Mark acted—and decisively. "Mark didn't want to put up with all my fears," Ruth said. "He just told me that I must go and that nothing would happen to me. 'After a few days, I will be with you,' he said. There was no alternative. I had to think of the kids and make up my mind to do this for them." And then when the truck arrived, he pushed her into it before she could change her mind. Everything was hurried, even the goodbyes, "so that," as Ruth said, "I wouldn't have time to think. He knew that if I thought a little longer I would never go. I was afraid."

Then, just to make sure she did not change her mind and order the garbage truck to bring her back, as she had done while waiting to cross the River Bug, the German Jew whose slow-moving wife had been yanked from line during the march back from the kesl climbed into the truck's cab, posing as a garbage helper. Mark had persuaded him to accompany his family to the other side to see that they got out safely and keep Ruth from trying to return. The wagon passed through the gate, Ruth and the children crouching in the garbage, because their presence in the cab would have attracted too much attention.

"The guards were there, but they let us go because of the bribe," Ruth said. In the no-man's land between the big and little ghettos, they saw ss men running around looking for runaways. The truck came to an abandoned building partially destroyed by bombs. Ruth and the girls and the German climbed down and went inside. Ruth gave him her blue Star of David armband, and he kissed the kids and told them goodbye.

She and her young daughters started walking down the street. Ruth was in a daze. "At this time, I didn't know what I was doing," she admitted. When they last met, the Polish military man handed her written instructions: take this number streetcar, get off at such and such a stop, go to this building, climb to the fourth floor. And he offered her one final piece of advice: "Don't be afraid. Just act normal like nothing was happening, until you get to the place where the woman and her daughter live." The address was Lochowska 15, on a six-block street that branched off from Ząbkowska Street about one mile east of the Vistula River.

But moral support left her fears unvanquished. First, she lacked a forged identity card (*Kennkarte*), and this when Ruth was sure that her Jewish identity was evident. "When I came out from the ghetto, in my mind and with my imagination I was thinking that everybody knew who I was," she said, "and I was sure that thousands and thousands of eyes were focused upon me. Maybe any moment someone would come up to me and say, 'Listen, you are a Jew. What are you doing here?' I was just praying to God to take me and my children in His care and save me from mean people."

Thousands of eyes may not have been gazing at her, but it is easy to understand why Ruth was worried about the stares of strangers. Aryan Warsaw was crawling with blackmailers and hooligans who specialized in shaking down Jews in flight and in hiding. The extortionists were given a Polonized Yiddish name: *szmalzcowniks*, from the Yiddish (and German) word *Schmalz*, meaning "grease" or "lard." Most szmalzcowniks were teenage thugs who often worked in gangs. They lingered where Jews came into contact with the Aryan side: near the gates, along the route to a work post, at the train station, in public squares. They roamed the parks, even haunted cafés, restaurants, and hotels formerly frequented by Jews. They used code words to signal confreres when prey wandered near. Jews were "cats" who slinked through city streets, and szmalzcowniks would meow when they thought one was in range. They were adept at recognizing Jews in disguise too, much more so than were the Germans. Sometimes it was the way hidden Jews walked or dressed that tipped off the blackmailers. Sometimes it was the way they talked: their Polish was too polished, evidence of university training, or it was inflected by Yiddish. The heavy breath of garlic gave Jews away, as did the scent of garbage and sewage on one's clothing, indicating recent escape. Jewish men and boys were always at much greater risk because of circumcision: szmalzcowniks enjoyed forcing male suspects to drop their trousers, and the only way to pass the inspection was to have undergone an expensive and painful skin graft procedure or to have on your possession a medical certificate of "phimosis" attesting that the circumcision was medically necessary. Wriggling free from szmalzcowniks cost bribe money, and usually more than one payment to more than one szmalzcownik. The Jewish underground was furious with Polish counterparts for failing to take vigorous action against the szmalzcowniks. Żegota begged the government-in-exile to suppress the blackmailers, but the Polish underground did nothing more than issue warnings, and the szmalzcowniks continued to have free run of the streets. There were so many that the Germans quickly learned that the fastest way to secure pedestrian assistance in nabbing fleeing suspects, Jew or gentile, was to yell, "Catch that Jew!"[91]

As she made her way to the streetcar stop, Ruth's nervousness was altogether understandable. The area near the boundaries of the old ghetto was infested with more szmalzcowniks than any other part of the city. Ruth and the girls quickly boarded the streetcar when it arrived. They rode several blocks before Ruth asked the conductor when they would reach the street where she was to get off. He told her they were heading in the wrong direction. They needed the streetcar with a different number. "I was confused," Ruth admitted. She hurriedly climbed down at the next stop, Anne's hand firmly in her grip. The important thing was to act normal. But then, as the tram clanged off toward the next stop, she looked down and realized Lila was still on board. "This was a terrible moment for me," Ruth said. "I was sure this was the end of my little girl."

She sprinted after the tram, hoping to catch it by the time it reached the next stop. Ruth never mentioned Anne's whereabouts. Only seven-and-a-half, she was too small to keep up with her mother. Ruth must have told her to wait at the tram stop while she ran after her sister. The moment had to have been filled with terror: Anne, the only Skorecki who was recognizably Jewish standing unguarded in a part of town where szmalzcowniks were known to congregate. Ruth was lucky. "The conductor was a nice fellow," she said, "he saw what had happened, he stopped the streetcar and let down my little girl. So thank God I had them both." Or maybe the conductor was more than nice. Maybe he realized, from the panic of Ruth's face, the scent on her clothes, and her unfamiliarity with city streets, that she and her children had just fled the ghetto and needed help. It was such small gestures, casual defiances of Nazi edicts and swimming against the szmalzcownik tide, that Jews on the Aryan side depended on every day to avoid detection.[92]

Her nerves jangled, afraid more than ever that "someone might read on my face that I was a Jew," Ruth managed to regain her composure. She studied the written instructions, boarded the correct streetcar. They crossed the Vistula, probably over the famed Poniatowski Bridge that Marshal Piłsudski had dramatically walked across in 1926 to take control of the government. At the intersection of Targowa and Ząbkowska, the tram headed east down the middle of Ząbkowska's one-hundred-foot-wide cobblestoned street, past a newly constructed lumberyard and the marketplace, as well as the neo-Gothic facade of the vodka distillery where Pani Piotrowska's late husband used to work. This is north Praga, the old and once heavily Jewish part of town. The buildings are mostly dark brick, crumbling and faded today. Window balconies jut out from the upper floors; storefronts line the street level. Ruth and the girls disembarked at Lochowska Street, about a half mile before Ząbkowska dead-ends at the imposing Basilica Serca Jezusowego (Basilica of the Heart of Jesus), one of the city's largest Catholic congregations. They veered north and then slanted toward the east again, walking a half mile or so down Lochowska's stone-studded surface, past the jagged picket fence guarding a fallow truck garden. Snow was on the ground. Four stories tall with a hip roof, Lochowska 15 is a block-long apartment building of adjoining courtyards. Today the neighborhood is ringed with Soviet-style high-rise towers. But during the war a building just like the one containing the Piotrowska apartment stood across the street, just beyond a small triangular park. Built in 1936 and covered in stucco, Lochowska 15 looks less weathered than many of the apartment buildings along Ząbkowska Street.[93]

The Skoreckis entered the building through a wooden gate which resembled a stable door and which opened through a narrow masonry tunnel onto a tiny courtyard, where a small Catholic shrine, framed between two windows latticed with lead, was slotted into the far wall. Ruth and the girls turned left inside the tunnel, passing the concierge's flat and entering the dimly lit stairwell. The Piotrowska apartment was number 12, on the top floor. Seven flights of stone steps switchbacked every eighth step like a canyon trail. There was an iron railing to hold on to. Facing the street and with a small balcony, the Piotrowska apartment shared an entranceway and a bathroom with apartment number 10, which looked onto the courtyard. During the streetcar trip across the city, the walk up Lochowska Street, and now the ascent of fifty-six stairs, Ruth was tense with fear. "I was asking myself where I was going and what kind of face I am going to see. I didn't know what kind people I would find. I was just afraid with whom I was to meet at this minute. But I couldn't help myself. I had to go on with this."

Dusk had settled over the day by the time she knocked on the door. It was around 5:00 P.M., and almost seven hours had passed since they had fled the ghetto. Young Natalia Piotrowska opened the door. She must have been taken aback by Anne. The girl was recognizably Jewish. But Natalia reacted not in the least, a smile quickly stretching across her face. Just shy of her twenty-seventh birthday, at four feet ten inches, she was even shorter than Ruth.[94] She spoke in Polish: "Mrs. Skorecki, I have been waiting for you. What happened? You were supposed to come last week." She brought them inside, closed the door, began taking care of Anne and Lila, removing their coats. Supper was already waiting for them. "This was a great easing off for me," Ruth said. "Both ladies were very friendly. The smile on their faces warmed me and gave me new strength to start my new life."

Natalia and her mother, Katarzyna, told Ruth to freshen up. They washed Anne and Lila, fed them and put them to bed—"a beautiful, clean bed." They made Ruth eat. After supper the Polish military man arrived to see if the Skoreckis had arrived safely. He stayed for two hours. "They all tried to cheer me up, and to make me relax and get rid of some of my fears," Ruth said. She asked him to contact Mark to let him know they were safe. He promised to do so. The German shops were about the only remaining locations inside the ghetto that still had telephones. Using them required mastery of "the art of apparently banal conversation," to use Ringelblum's characterization.[95] By now Stelmaszek and the Polish veteran were no doubt highly practiced in the language of codespeak.

Day after day they waited inside the Piotrowska's apartment for Mark to join them, sitting quietly whenever the Polish women received visitors in the kitchen. "At this time we had no papers or documents in order to pass among the rest of the people safely," Ruth said. In the evening the Polish veteran dropped by to look in on the Skoreckis and to reassure Ruth that Mark would arrive soon. But he was vague as to details, and the news he brought from the ghetto was far from reassuring: "things in the ghetto continued to get worse and worse," the Pole reported.

Mark and Ruth's parting had been so rushed Mark never told his wife how and when he intended to leave the ghetto. "He just pushed me into it all before I could think," she said. Actually, Mark had no escape plan at the time other than a generalized readiness to seize the first opportunity that cropped up. One did arise after the ss chauffeur dropped off his superior at Schultz's for an inspection. Mark then arranged to have the driver carry him through the gate the next time he brought the ss official to the ghetto, in the meantime handing the chauffeur his possessions for safekeeping (and probably for collateral). The chauffeur returned a few days later. The ss official told the driver he could have off until it was time to pick him up. The chauffeur retrieved Mark at the factory. They drove through the gate unchallenged, Mark behaving as if he were just another Jew being carried to some daily work assignment on the

Aryan side, which occurred frequently. The driver dropped him off a few blocks from the Piotrowska apartment. Mark paid him, receiving his possessions in return. Eight days had passed since Ruth and the kids had escaped, and Ruth said it had felt like eight weeks. The reunion was joyful.

Mark brought bad news, however. Since Ruth and the girls' escape from the ghetto, there had been "another big selection," he told them. "Everybody was afraid that the Germans were getting ready to liquidate the whole place and send them to a concentration camp." The fears were solidly grounded. At 7:30 A.M. on Monday, January 18—"the unsuspecting Monday," as one ghetto eyewitness remembered—a mixed force of Letts, Lithuanians, Poles, and Germans swept through the central ghetto in an effort to remove the eight thousand illegal Jews Himmler had complained of nine days earlier. The resettlement Aktion was the initiative of Warsaw's ss police commander, who was anxious to get back in his chief's good graces. But this time the Germans were in for a surprise. Except for the approximately three thousand Jews caught off guard by the earliness of the hour and marched to the Umschlagplatz, most inhabitants in the central ghetto fled to their hideouts when news spread that an Aktion was under way, refusing to come down to the courtyard when the ss troops and Jewish Police yelled *raus* (get out, come out). They were no longer taken in by pious reassurances that valid work permits would be honored and that the eastern resettlement was for work alone.[96]

The biggest surprise for the Germans was armed resistance. It erupted as Nazi forces were escorting hundreds of Jews to the trains, including members of the combat unit led by ZOB commander Mordechai Anielewicz. The young fighters had been caught in their house on Miła Street, near the Umschlagplatz, and the Germans, not realizing they had captured a unit of the ZOB, gave them a few minutes to get dressed. It was just enough time for the unit's members to stuff weapons inside their clothing. At the corner of Zamenhof and Niska Streets, the Stawki Street gate visible in the distance, the fighters burst from the edge of the marching column and hurled grenades at the soldiers. Several Germans fell, along with most of the Jewish fighters, except for a handful under Anielewicz, who retreated to a house on Niska Street. The rest of the column dispersed. Then the fighting shifted to a nearby building on Zamenhof, where a Jewish combat unit commanded by Zuckerman repaired to the top floor to wait for the Germans and be close to their escape route across the snow-covered rooftops of the blocks. They heard the German boots pounding up the stairs. One of Zuckerman's fighters was sitting in the front room reading a book by the Yiddish writer Sholem Aleichem when the soldiers burst into the flat. It never occurred to the Germans to order hands up. The ZOB member put aside his book and shot them in the back when they entered the next room. Other fighters threw grenades after the fleeing

Germans. There was shouting and whistling in the street. "Regular Prussian shouts, but mixed with pain," Zuckerman said. More armed resistance erupted elsewhere in the ghetto. The idea was contagious, this killing of Germans, and the fighters grew bolder by the hour. Zuckerman's men did not bother to shoot one Nazi soldier who later climbed to the top of their building: "They simply grabbed him and threw him off the roof from the fourth or fifth floor," he said.[97] Thereafter the Germans were leery of entering the blocks.

It was a spontaneous uprising, an unplanned reaction to a German planned surprise. As Zuckerman later admitted: "If there had been time, if there had been signs of the impending *Aktsia*, if we had gotten information one day before, I would have called a meeting of the [Jewish] Coordinating Committee, and they probably would have started arguing. Somebody would have said it was only 21,000 or 20,000 Jews and, if we didn't let them go, we would jeopardize the whole ghetto; and so we had to consider and see how things developed, and so forth. They would have warned us that we were assuming an historic responsibility for a fast annihilation and, as a result, there would have been opinions and arguments. But when everything happened suddenly, all possibility of considerations and arguments vanished."[98] And, he might have added, so did the accommodationist theme in Jewish history.

The Többens-Schultz central factory complex escaped the January Aktion relatively unscathed. On the third day, January 20, two SS companies brought in from Lublin surrounded the German shops between Leszno and Nowolipki Streets and began combing the premises for illegals. Caught by surprise, the ZOB had only one armed member in the shop area, who managed to shoot at an SS officer and still escape.[99] The Germans yanked about 400 Jews out of Big Schultz's and a few days later pulled out 170 more, shipping them to Treblinka. Twenty-three of the workers selected at the shop had worked in the wooden sole department. Mark had escaped on January 21, the second day of the SS blockade of the Schultz-Többen's area.[100]

One ghetto institution that did not escape unharmed was the Jewish hospital, now made up of remnants from Czyste and the Berson-Bauman Children's Hospital. Since the Great Deportations, the ghetto's medical service had been concentrated in cramped quarters at Gęsia 6–8. Despite shortages of every kind, including staff, who lived on Franciszkanka Street, the hospital remained a beehive of activity following the summer's liquidations, "with people coming and going constantly," as a Bundist member of the underground remembered, and packed knapsacks and bundles lying everywhere as both staff and patients stood "ready to move at a moment's notice."[101] All the same, the hospital was caught by surprise on the Aktion's first day. A comparative handful of the staff and patients managed to squeeze into prearranged hiding places before the Nazis burst into the premises. But the rest perished. On January 18 four hundred patients were driven to the Umschlagplatz; those too sick to move were simply murdered on the spot—"killed in bed, shot in bed," Mark told Ruth. Many were infants, because the staff had gambled—erroneously—that the Nazis would not murder babies. A grisly scene greeted the survivors when they emerged from their hideouts. Corpses lay on and under the beds, on the floor. The surviving medical staff now either fled to the Aryan side, as did Szwajger, becoming couriers for the underground and Żegota, or tried to salvage a functional hospital from the wreckage. "Surgery quickly became active again," remembered one survivor. But it is doubtful whether Mery Mejnster was still on the staff.[102]

It is hard to pinpoint the date of her murder. The authoritative *Martyrdom of Jewish Physicians in Poland* states simply, "She perished in the ghetto (1941 or 1942)."[103] Dr. Thaddeus Stabholz places her death during the Great Deportation. "There was a problem when Henry Tempelhof was working at the Umschlagplatz; his wife, I believe, was caught in the evening And the Jews who were caught in the evening did not go to the Umschlagplatz; they went straight into cattle cars, and he could not do anything when he came home and his wife was gone."[104] But Ruth distinctly remembers meeting with Henry and Mery in January 1943, shortly before she and the girls fled the ghetto, so Mery must have perished after 1942. The best guess is that she was among the 150 Jewish physicians who were captured during the January 18 Aktion at the Gęsia Street hospital and sent to Treblinka.[105]

After Mery's disappearance, the famous Tempelhof grin disappeared too. "Henry got really sad," Dr. Stabholz says. "He didn't smile any longer, and I didn't see him too much because it was a very dangerous period."[106] They would encounter each other a few months later in a boxcar headed for Majdanek.

Warsaw Ghetto starving street children with their mother. (© Willy Georg, "Symptoms of starvation included not only emaciation, but often swollen limbs," in *In the Warsaw Ghetto: Summer 1941* [New York: Aperture, 1993])

Young newsstand boy. (© Willy Georg, "A boy selling newspapers," in *In the Warsaw Ghetto: Summer 1941* [New York: Aperture, 1993])

Wooden Sole Shop scenes: These photos were probably shot in the spring of 1942, and possibly very early in the liquidation, when older men and women and children crowded into the ghetto's German factories to seek the safety of work but just before the ss began its systematic sweeps to clear out "illegals." (From "Album der Firma Shultz"; © Stiftung Neue Synagoge Berlin–Centrum Judaicum)

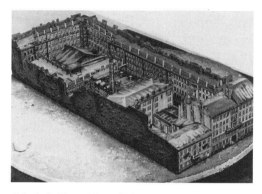

Schultz's Shop, Nowolipie 44–46.

Schleifmaschinen (sanding machines). Mark probably set up the machines and organized the production in this and the other departments shown in these photos.

Schweifenabteilung (band saw department). Note the young child standing behind the stack of wood on the lefthand side of the picture. Stelmaszek's office (the Polish supervisor) was probably behind the glass door at the far end of the room.

Holzsohlenlager (wooden sole storeroom). Mark and Ruth used to hide Anne and Lila under a floorboard in this room during the increasingly frequent surprise ss sweeps of the German shops.

Above: Henry Tempelhof, probably in 1939 or 1940, around the time he became the office manager of Czyste Hospital, Warsaw's Jewish hospital.

Facing page: Mery Mejnster's "Fragebogen" (questionnaire): All Polish and Jewish medical personnel were required by the Nazis to fill out one of these forms. Mery's was found in the main Medical Library at Warsaw University.

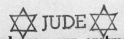

Personalausweis Nr. *6497*
ausgestellt

A ½

Fragebogen zur erstmaligen Meldung der Heilberufe.

Kwestionariusz dla pierwszego zgłoszenia zawodów leczniczych.

Heilberufe im Sinne dieser Meldung sind: Ärzte, Apotheker, Zahnärzte, Dentisten mit Berechtigung die selbständige
Kwestionariusz obejmuje następujące zawody lecznicze: Lekarzy, aptekarzy, dentystów, uprawnionych techników dentystycznych, nieuprawnionych techników dentystycznych,
Praxis auszuüben, Zahntechniker ohne Berechtigung die selbständige Praxis auszuüben, Feldschere, Hebammen,
felczerów, położnych, pielęgniarzy, pielęgniarki, masażystów, masażystki, pomocników ambulatoryjnych, laborantki, desynfektorów.
Krankenpfleger, Krankenpflegerinnen, Krankenschwestern, Masseure und Masseusen, Sprechstundenhilfen, Laborantinnen, Desinfektoren.

Die Fragebogen müssen gewissenhaft und sorgfältig ausgefüllt und deutlich geschrieben werden. Vor der Aus-
Kwestionariusz winien być wypełniony czytelnie i zgodnie z prawdą. Przed wypełnieniem należy odczytać wszystkie pytania.
füllung sind zunächst sämtliche Fragen zu lesen.

Gesundheitskammer des Distrikts: **Warszawa**
Izba Zdrowia Dystryktu:

Kreishauptmannschaft: **Warszawa**
Starostwo Okręgowe:

Kreis: **Warszawa**
Powiat:

Art des Heilberufes: **lekarz**
Rodzaj zawodu leczniczego:

1. Familienname (bei Frauen auch Geburtsname): **Mejnster nazwisko męża: Tempelhof**
   Nazwisko (u kobiet zamężnych, nazwisko panieńskie):

2. Vorname (Rufnamen unterstreichen): **Mery**
   Imię (główne imię podkreślić)

3. Ständiger Wohnort und Wohnung: **Warszawa, Dworska 17**
   Stałe miejsce zamieszkania (ul. nr domu i mieszk.):

4. Praxisstelle bezw. Arbeitsstätte:
   Miejsce wykonywania zawodu:

   a) bei selbständigen Heilberufen Praxisstelle: **Ambulatorium Czerniakowska 74**
   przy zawodach samodzielnych miejsce wykonyw. praktyki:

   b) bei angestellten Heilberufen Arbeitsstätte (Arbeitgeber, Krankenhaus, Klinik usw.):
   przy zawodach niesamodzielnych miejsce pracy (pracodawca. szpital i t. p.):

   Szpital na Czystem

5. Heitmatanschrift: **Warszawa**
   Miejsce przynależności:

6. Tag, Monat und Jahr der Geburt: **6.3.1912.**
   Dzień, miesiąc i rok urodzenia:

   Geburtsort: **Łódź**   Kreis: **Łódź**
   Miejsce urodzenia: Powiat:

7. Sind Sie ledig, verh., verwitwet, geschieden? **zamężna**
   Stan (wolny, żonaty, owdowiały, ewentualnie rozwiedziony):

   Der Ehefrau a) Mädchenname: b) Geburtsdatum:
   Żona a) Nazwisko panieńskie: b) data urodzenia:

8. Zahl und Geburtsjahr der Kinder (die Verstorbenen in Klammern): **Niema**
   Ilość i wiek dzieci (zmarłe wymienić w nawiasie):

   1.   2.   3.

9. Religiöses Bekenntnis: —
   Wyznanie religijne:

10. Staatsangehörigkeit am 1. 9. 1939: **polska**
    Przynależność państwowa w dniu 1. 9. 1939:

Right: Lochowska 15, the apartment building in Praga where the Piotrowskas lived and where the Skoreckis stayed for ten months after their January 1943 escape from the ghetto.

Bottom: Natalia Piotrowska Gorecka at table next to the armoire where Anne hid when company came.

Ruth Skorecka's photograph from forged "Aryan" papers. It wasn't until I studied the back of this photo and saw the barely legible name "Stanisława Skorecka" that I realized this was Ruth's official "Aryan" photograph. Her stern visage should have tipped me off, however.

eight

Mark fled the ghetto with the understanding that Julius and Haka would follow him out a short while later. Also slated to escape around the same time was a young, childless couple Mark had promised to help. The husband had worked with Mark at Schultz's and lived on the fourth floor at Nowolipie 28. "Mark had told him before he left that he was leaving and that he would try to make a place for him in the same place where we got located," Ruth said. About a week or two later the Polish military man arranged their escape, and a short time after that he helped Haka get out as well.

Julius never made it out. He was supposed to move in with the former priest and his wife, but he returned to his apartment just before he was due to escape, saying he needed to retrieve a forgotten item. He walked into a surprise ss selection. Ruth said the Germans sent him to a concentration camp (probably the Trawniki ss labor camp in the Lublin District where Fritz Schultz's operation was beginning to be reassembled by the ss). "This was a bad stroke of fate," Ruth said, for "if he had not gone to his apartment he would have gotten out." Or Julius may have felt more comfortable with the dangers he already knew and was looking for an excuse to stay behind. That attitude was not unusual inside the ghetto, even after the January 18 Aktion. The Skoreckis never heard from Julius again.

There were two ways of hiding on the Aryan side: you could stay "under the surface" by living around the clock in underground bunkers, false rooms, or hidden attics, as Anne Frank's family in Amsterdam had tried to do. Many ghetto escapees, such as the historian Emmanuel Ringelblum and his family, made this fatal choice.[1] Or you could live "on the surface" by concealing your Jewish identity and adopting a Christian one. The Skoreckis chose to stay aboveground by passing as Polish Catholics, and so did Haka and the young couple. But this decision necessitated obtaining false legal documents, which were absolutely essential in an environment where spot checks and forced roundups were almost daily events. The foundation of a new identity began with baptismal certificates, birth certificates, and marriage certificates; then came Polish identity cards, German identity cards, and registration cards; finally, various permits regarding basic needs were required—food ration cards, work permits, residency permits. Haka and the young couple had secured Aryan papers before their escape, but they were poor forgeries and had to be replaced. Mark and Ruth, on the other hand, like most Jews who fled the ghetto at the last minute, had no papers whatsoever, especially the important Germany identity cards known as Kennkarten, replete with photographs, fingerprints, and the official Generalgouvernement stamp. "Right now we were just looking for a person who could do this," Ruth said—that is, who could prepare fake papers. Until that happened, all seven Jewish fugitives had to stay indoors, "sitting and waiting," as Ruth described it, falling completely silent in the next room whenever the Piotrowskas received company in the kitchen.

Fortunately, Aryan Warsaw was awash in black market documents, deriving either from blank forms stolen from the various municipal bureaucracies or from counterfeit mills. Most of the political parties ran such operations, as did the Home Army, which had several forgery cells, even supplying Żegota with false documents until that rescue group established its own "legalization bureau." The Skoreckis gained access to this counterfeit network through a building administrator with underground connections. "He had been recommended to us," Ruth said, "and he did this for other people also." Building administrators, who oversaw several apartment buildings, were key intermediaries between the municipal housing authority and the resident concierges and porters found in every Warsaw multifamily dwelling. They issued residency permits, which they recorded in their own registries before filing them with the city housing bureau. Tenants who changed addresses had to present their previous residency permit to the concierge, who in turn filed it with the building administrator to whom he reported, and so on. From this one paper link it was possible to generate a whole chain of forged documents. The building administrator contacted by the Skoreckis possessed a rare advantage: several left bank apartment buildings in his charge had lain vacant since being bombed out during the 1939 invasion. "He told us that he could make us papers as though we were living in one of these houses which had been destroyed," Ruth said. "Nobody could check on this, since he had the books in his hands himself." But it would take at least another two weeks to prepare the papers, which meant more enforced idleness inside an apartment scarcely large enough for two occupants.[2]

They could live with the cabin fever for another fourteen days, however, since none of the fugitives intended to stay with their hosts indefinitely. The young couple had made plans to leave as soon as their Aryan papers were ready. So had Haka. Even Mark and Ruth meant to move out once their documents were at hand—and not merely from the Lochowska 15 apartment but from Warsaw itself. Their last name was a problem: Skorecki was too well known in Warsaw because of Morris's successful lumber business. It would be easy enough to connect Mark with Morris, plus there was always the chance some trader might recall having seen the younger brother during a buying trip to the Horyniec mill. True, Mark and Ruth could change their surname, which many Jewish fugitives living "on the surface" eventually did. But the Skorecki family name was, as Ruth explained, "a good Polish name, so we decided to keep it." And then there were Anne and Lila to consider. It was not easy teaching children a new name. Who knew when they might stammer out their real one in an unguarded moment. Even the most self-controlled Jewish children could become "giveaways," blurting out remembered sights from parts of town everyone knew were Jewish, thereby betraying entire families, along with gentile protectors. Innocent slips of the tongue, like uttering some Yiddish phrase, happened all the time, usually with lethal consequences.[3] Though remarkably well disciplined, Anne and Lila, only seven and five, were still children. So, weighing the risks on both sides of the question, Ruth and Mark elected to stay with the Skorecki surname, changing only their own forenames because "Ruth" obviously connoted Jewishness in prewar Poland. (She never divulged in her memoir what her wartime pseudonym was, but the name on the back of a wartime photograph suggests it was Stanisława.) And then, just to be on the safe side, Mark and his young helper decided to seek employment in another city as soon as their Aryan papers were ready. Besides, as Mark said, "we cannot stay like this indefinitely. We have to look for work."

They had heard factory jobs were available in the vicinity of Lvov, a former outpost of the Austro-Hungarian empire and a center of textile production. Mark was familiar with the area. On the edge of the Russian steppes, the old Galician capital was close to Horyniec. But Mark wanted to stay out of Lvov proper, where a large ghetto was still in place and the ss was a looming presence.[4] He and his young helper traveled by train, moving from one small city to the next, checking in with the local *Arbeitsamt* (employment office) to present papers showing evidence of former employment. They finally located a factory willing to sign them on and then wait while they returned to Warsaw for their families. The entire trip to and from Lvov took five days. "They tried to do everything quickly," Ruth said, "and not stay long in any given place"— especially train stations, where heavy war traffic caused long waits and szmalzcowniks and Gestapo agents lurked behind every kiosk. Remembers one survivor from Lvov: "These [depots] became a hunting ground for professional blackmailers. . . . Many didn't make it past the railroad station."[5]

Mark and his companion almost became trapped in a rail station on their return journey. Like a lot of travelers in wartime Poland who were in a hurry or wished to avoid spot checks by Nazi authorities, they paid a porter to stand in line and buy their tickets for them. But the ploy attracted attention rather than diverted it. Just as they were about to entrain, two ss men pulled Mark and his friend aside and brought them to an interrogation room. They checked their papers, asked a lot of questions, and then isolated them in separate rooms. "Luckily Mark and the man gave the same answer," Ruth said. But one of the officers was still suspicious; in fact, Mark overheard him tell the other agent he thought the two travelers were Jewish. Surprisingly, the security police never acted on their suspicions, never forced Mark and his young friend, say, to drop their pants. Maybe it was because Mark and his friend possessed employment papers and Kennkarten that could pass close scrutiny. "Maybe this helped," Ruth surmised.

Maybe so. But another factor may have been at work, one that Ruth had puzzled over before: a peculiar human quality that could cause even ss guards to look the other way when Jews smuggled food into the ghetto. "Some of these men had heart and understanding," she said. More than once these unexpected expressions of Nazi compassion made Ruth wonder about the psychological makeup of the perpetrators. Of their anti-Semitism she had no doubt; hatred of Jews was a given, like the certainty of dawn and dusk. But prejudice never summed in her mind to a sufficient explanation for the sadism she had witnessed so often in the recent past. It perplexed her. "These were people who had families and children too," she said. "How could they do these terrible things to other people? We couldn't figure this out." Ruth had her suspicions, though. A shrewd judge of character, she noticed that the atrocities usually happened when Germans acted as a group, not as individuals. Ringelblum was baffled by the same behavior: "It's characteristic that when alone individual Germans behave humanely."[6] But where the ghetto archivist talked of Germans, Ruth spoke of males. As she described the group dynamic, "Separate, these ss men had some heart, but together they were afraid for each other."

It was a keen observation, for male peer pressure—in this instance, the masculine fear of being thought a coward in the eyes of other men—was often the impulse prompting ordinary men to slaughter women, children, and the elderly in countless shtetls such as Działoszyce, and to do so face-to-face instead of from bomb sights two miles above. The historian Christopher Browning, who has studied the mass murder sprees of one German police battalion, traces the homicidal transformation of its ordinary members to "the pressure for conformity—the basic identification of men in uniform with their comrades and the strong urge not to separate themselves from the group by stepping out."[7] Indeed, the ss high command, to fortify Nazi hardness, made constant appeals to patriotism and the iron virtues. Himmler himself did so famously in a speech delivered in October 1943 to ss commanders gathered in Poznań, Poland: "Says every party member, 'Sure, it's in our program, elimination of the Jews, annihilation—we'll take care of it.' And then they all come trudging, 80 million worthy Germans, and each has his one decent Jew. Sure, the others are swine, but this one is an A-1 Jew. Of all those who talk this way, not one has seen it happen, not one has been through it. Most of you know what it means to see a hundred corpses lie side by side, or five hundred, or a thousand. To have stuck this out and—excepting cases of human weakness—to have kept our integrity, that is what made us hard. In our history, this is an unwritten and never-to-be-written page of glory."[8]

Except this time, in Lvov at least, peer pressure lacked critical mass, as well as an instigating leader, and so everyday decency won out over the cult of male toughness. The ss men released Mark and his companion. The sympathetic officer even warned Mark, "Listen, I let you go, but you watch yourself on the way to your family." "This was a miracle," Ruth exclaimed, as she often did whenever the family defied impossible odds.

Shaken by the experience, Mark and his young friend resolved to stay put after reaching Warsaw. "They didn't want to do this again," they told their wives. "They said they wanted to look for something right in Warsaw." As well known as his brother's name may have been around town, the risk of detection seemed much smaller than the perils of traveling by train with young children, one of whom looked Jewish, through rail stations overrun by szmalzcowniks and ss security police.

But then, not long after Mark had returned from Lvov and had decided to remain in Warsaw and with the Piotrowskas, he and Ruth were forcefully reminded of just how dangerous Aryan Warsaw could be. Problems had arisen with their new residency papers. Now that they had decided to become subtenants of the Piotrowskas, they had to make their residency official by registering their papers with the Lochowska 15 building administrator, who happened to be a woman. Natalia Piotrowska, who seems to have known her well, told the Skoreckis she would bring their residency permits personally to the administrator, bypassing the concierge. The transaction took place without a hitch. "She took the papers from Natalia and told her that she would fix everything up the next day in the office," Ruth said of the building administrator. "Meanwhile, we were sitting in our room."

The following day, disaster nearly struck. The building administrator came back from the housing bureau with disturbing news. "One of us had to come down to the main office," she told the Skoreckis. "She didn't know why." Nor did Ruth and Mark know. Panic swept through the tiny apartment. Everybody was now at risk—Haka, the young couple, the Piotrowska women. Had the concierge voiced suspicions to the administrator? "At this time the important person in our building was the janitor," Ruth said. In fact, resident janitors were the most important figures in every multifamily building in the city. Deserved or not, house porters had reputations as police informers. "You had to stay away from the concierges, but that wasn't easy," wrote the ZOB operative known as Kazik.[9]

Nor was it easy for the Skoreckis and the other shut-ins at Lochowska 15. The house janitor was an older man named Matyslak Szczepan who cleaned the premises twice a week and, during the war, was responsible for locking the gate at night and unlocking it in the morning.[10] His first-floor apartment just off the porte cochere allowed him to keep an eye on the comings and goings of tenants, visitors, and strangers. He must have been slightly curious about the lack of traffic in and out of the Piotrowska flat. "He never saw us going out from the apartment very much," Ruth said, "so maybe he and the people with whom residences were certified and to whom administrators had to go, had gotten together." There was no way of telling, and the uncertainty was nerve-wracking. "We were sure we would be discovered as Jews and that something would be done to us. We thought that this would be the end. . . . At this time, we were all afraid of our shadows," Ruth confessed.

Ruth had to represent the Skoreckis the next day at the housing bureau. "Mark couldn't go because it was too dangerous for him," she said, alluding to her husband's circumcision. But the unasked question on everybody's mind was whether Ruth was equal to the emotional challenge. Temperamentally high-strung, she was jumpier than usual because of recent events. She placed a call to the building administrator who had falsified their residency papers. He tried to reassure her: "Just go and don't show your fear." The Piotrowska women tried calming her as well. "The two ladies said not to be afraid. The greatest danger would be not to go." But her hosts must have secretly doubted Ruth's ability to ad-lib her way out of a tight spot, because twenty-six-year-old Natalia Piotrowska said she would accompany Ruth the next day when the building administrator brought her to the housing bureau.

Ruth could not sleep that night. The trip downtown the next morning with her two escorts had the icy feeling of a death march. "I was 100 per cent sure that I would never come back from over there," she said. "In my heart and in my mind I had just one thing: DEATH."

When they arrived, hundreds of people were milling inside the Address Department of the Record Office in City Hall. Ruth dreaded entering: "I could think of only one thing. Someone was going to come up to me and kill me."

Her fears were not hysterical. It was an open secret that the living bureau, as the housing office was also known, was crawling with Nazi informers. "Hardly a day went by without the Gestapo dropping in to search for the addresses of some political 'criminals' or others," said one Pole involved in rescue work.[11]

She waited for what seemed like an eternity after the Piotrowskas' building administrator took the apartment registry to the clerk and pointed out Ruth as the person he had asked to see. The clerk told the administrator to have a seat. He ordered Ruth to stand in line until he had finished with the people in front of her.

What now ensued Ruth recalled with the vividness of a day-old memory: "I waited, but I didn't know whether I was dead or alive. I was afraid of what he might ask me and the answers I would give. I was thinking that maybe I would never see my family again. When everybody had left, and I was alone with him, and he took my slip (which showed where I had been living before) and I came to him, he asked me, 'Are you Mrs. Skorecki?' He said, 'Tell me the whole truth. How much did you pay for this piece of paper?'

"At this minute my fear was great. I was sure I would never make it. But God is good. He put words in my mouth. The clerk maybe saw the fear in my face, too. He said, 'Listen, I don't want to hurt you. I don't want to hurt anybody, especially you, because I see you have children. But tell me the truth. How much did you pay for this?' "So, I just looked at his face and I said to him: 'I can see you never can hurt anybody but I really don't understand what you are talking about.' But I wasn't sure if it was my voice I was hearing or somebody was talking for me."

Just then another person came to the window requiring attention, and the clerk told Ruth to wait while he took care of the matter. After finishing, he took up her papers again and said, "See, in this minute I can do something mean to you."

But he did not. Maybe his request that one of the Skoreckis come personally to the bureau was merely his way of reassuring himself that his underground confederate was not handing out forged papers to Jews who could not pass as gentiles. In any event, he stamped her housing certificate, entered it in his record books, and returned her false Aryan papers. For Ruth it was an epiphany: "I understood in this moment that he knew what the situation was, and I just told him, 'Thank you very much, and God Bless you.' "

Ruth was hardly out of the woods yet. Now it was the building administrator's turn to test her suspicions. The length of time Ruth had spent with the clerk seemed odd. Why did he keep her so long? she asked. Ruth blurted out an answer that did little to allay the woman's doubts. "I said to her, 'he just called me to find out how the other administrator at the other building is doing now. It was stupid.' " It must have struck the Lochowska administrator the same way, because no sooner were they out the door than she asked Ruth and Natalia to accompany her to an old synagogue recently converted into a secondhand furniture store. At the time Ruth's mind was "a hundred miles away," as she put it, still thanking God for having guided her past dangerous shoals. Now she was being called on for the second time in the same day to stage another performance, and to do so without time for rehearsal. She was anxious to get home to her family, knowing they were probably sick with worry. "But I couldn't tell the woman that somebody was waiting for me in fear," Ruth said. "I had to go with them. This was a terrible thing when you have to do something like this."

Ruth was in a fog as they strolled to the synagogue. "They were talking to me and laughing, but I really didn't have my mind on what they were saying because my mind was on my children and husband," she said. Ruth never mentioned what the laughter was about, but anti-Semitic humor was likely part of it. It was not uncommon for rescuers to advertise their anti-Semitism in order not to appear as "Jew lovers," and Natalia just then had every motive for wanting to throw the administrator off the trail.[12] For Ruth the bargain hunting inside the old synagogue brought to the surface churning emotions of anger and grievance, yet she dared not betray her inner state. "This was a holy place for me," Ruth said. "The furniture was the best and came from all of the beautiful homes of the Jewish people. And when I saw what the Germans did, I was crying inside from not being able to say anything to anyone." For two hours the three women browsed through Jewish bric-a-brac. There was more laughter, more lighthearted banter, but Ruth maintained her composure. "Walking around with them and looking at the furniture, not one time did tears come to my eyes," she said. "Finally the administrator went home, and I with the young lady went to our home, too." How convinced the building administrator was by Ruth's performance is anyone's guess. Ruth was still learning the art of dissembling, and she had been walking on eggshells the entire day. Perhaps the administrator, like the clerk, simply chose to suppress her suspicions. It is impossible to tell for sure.

The walk home seemed to go on for miles, past the market on Ząbkowska Street and the vodka distillery where Natalia's father used to work, down the cobblestoned lane beneath tree branches just beginning to bud following a hard winter. "I can't explain the faces in the room when I came home to my family," Ruth said. Immediately she took Mark to the side to explain what had happened. From her rendition of events he was certain that the housing bureau clerk was a blackmailer and that soon he or one of his confederates would come calling for money. The only thing distinguishing blackmailers from szmalzcowniks is that the former worked the flats instead of the streets, using official tips and close surveillance to track down Jews in their hiding places, and then demanding exorbitant sums as the price of silence. "If the *schmalzowniks* [*sic*] are wasps that sting their victims," Ringelblum wrote from his underground bunker on the Aryan side, "the blackmailers are vultures that devour them."[13] Ruth called the building administrator who had supplied their forged documents. He came directly to the Piotrowska flat to reassure them personally. A smile was spread across his face. "Don't worry," he told her. "Nobody will come to you, and nobody will ask you for anything. I know the housing bureau clerk very well." He was being truthful. The clerk, Ruth later discovered, knew all about the forgery ring and seemed to be part of the operation.

The verbal reassurance assuaged her worries only slightly, however. "This was easy for him to say, but we were living with fear in our hearts," Ruth said. Every evening in bed the Skoreckis tossed and turned, tensing up when they heard footsteps on the stairs or a car door slam. "Many nights we spent sleepless waiting for somebody to come get us," Ruth said. Now that Haka and the young couple had moved out, the apartment was much less crowded, but the tension had abated hardly at all.

The problem with passing was that one never knew whom to trust. A stranger's smile might be a sign of danger, not civility. Surprise encounters with old acquaintances were occasions for averting gazes, not shaking hands and slapping backs. A meowing at your back might signal the presence of a szmalzcownik alerting a confederate that he had found another Jew to shake down. Every muffled conversation drifting in from the sidewalk after curfew, every sudden rap on the door, could set hearts racing. It was essential to be wary not merely of concierges but also of suspicious neighbors who sniffed out Jews in every new subtenant. Buying groceries was a strategic operation akin to fencing stolen property, best done in phases lest sudden changes in a family's consumption habits invite unwanted questions; likewise with gas and electric usage, which was closely monitored by municipal account executives. The dread of "denunciation"—that is, being denounced as a crypto-Jew—never let up. The whole atmosphere was permeated by doubt and suspicion.

Even trips to the market were seldom spontaneous, especially after January 1943, when the Germans intensified their spot checks so as to fill forced labor quotas for the Reich. Rather, they were command performances, practiced repeatedly in one's mind until charlatanry became second nature and then, just to be safe, rehearsed a few more times. Myriad details had to be considered. Were the dark roots showing in your platinum makeover? Was your Polish sufficiently free of Yiddish singsong to obviate posing as a "deaf-mute and donning the sign *Taubstumm*? Was your fictional family pedigree—parents' names, mother's maiden name, names of siblings—burned into memory? How solid was your grasp of Catholic ritual and custom? What did the priest do after confession? (He taps on the confessional.) What was your name day, and who was your patron saint? You had to be prepared to answer such questions at the drop of a hat. And all the while, as you struggled to keep the lies straight, you had to appear natural, unrehearsed, and, most of all, unafraid. Any furtive glancing around, any nervous fidgeting, could attract the attention of the szmalcowniks or the ss.[14]

The hardest task facing Jews en passant was eye control. Getting the dialect down was easy by comparison. You could always embroider your alibi, master the proper gait and swagger, polish the segue from fake jollity to grim visage, depending on mood and circumstance. You might know church customs, including the novenas, backward and forward. You might, in other words, be the perfect Catholic Pole in every respect and still be betrayed by "sad Jewish eyes," dark pools of fright too deep for concealment. There is no doubt Ruth had those eyes, and they may have saved her life at the housing bureau or the synagogue by arousing the compassion of ordinary Poles. But for most Jews living "on the surface," those melancholy eyes were "a special danger sign." Wrote the zob courier Vladka Meed: " 'Your eyes give you away,' our Gentile friends would tell us. 'Make them look livelier, merrier. You won't attract so much attention then.' But our eyes kept constantly watching, searching the shadows ahead, glancing quickly behind, seeing our own misfortune and foreseeing even worse to come. Haunted by fear of betrayal, our eyes betrayed us; and this knowledge only increased our fear."[15]

The unremitting watchfulness exhausted people. Wearing a mask you could never remove was trying. One zob operative on the Aryan side preferred the physical hardships of partisan life in the wintry forests to the emotional tribulations of passing in the city. "I was often gripped by a strong desire to confess," he said of his days in Aryan Warsaw. Meed, another Jew who passed, often snuck back into the ghetto for emotional relief. At least there she could be herself. In fact, the constant worry of being denounced by neighbors, shaken down by szmalcowniks, or nabbed by the police or ss caused a fair number of Jews to return to the ghetto permanently. Others volunteered for forced labor in Germany (where disguising one's Jewish identity was ironically easier). A few even traveled to the new ss work camps being set up by Fritz Schultz and Walter C. Többens in the Lublin District. One Jew abandoned his guise and surrendered at Treblinka.[16]

The Nazis knew how to exploit the psychological fatigue. One of their more brazen deceits for coaxing fugitives from hiding was the offer of safe passage to Switzerland (among other places) for any Jews able to afford a visa. In the spring and summer of 1943 wall placards and radio bulletins directed interested parties to report to the Hotel Polski on Długa Street across the Vistula, in downtown Warsaw. Three thousand Jews, many of them well-to-do, were inveigled into swallowing the bait, usually because of the same fatal optimism that had caused "selectees" to tramp to the Umschlagplatz for free bread and jam. Several were also driven by a loss of hope. Adina Blady Szwajger's first husband went to the Hotel Polski because "he did not want to go on, he didn't even want to live." There were many like him. Mark heard about the visas-for-sale scheme from the Polish military man who had helped the Skoreckis flee the ghetto, and Mark became momentarily intrigued. But he pulled back immediately when he learned that the Jewish Police were involved (actually it was the Warsaw Gestapo who concocted the scheme). "Mark said that he was not going, because he knew this was just a trick. It was the same old story. A promise of something just to lure us to a concentration camp or something terrible," Ruth said. According to her, the episode ended in the drink. "The Germans just threw them in the water," she said—a widespread myth at the time.[17] The truth was scarcely better. During a September 1943 raid on Hotel Polski, the Nazis shot three hundred Jews and took the rest to the notorious Pawiak Prison in Warsaw, whence they were deported to transit camps in France or to Bergen-Belsen. All but seventy-seven survivors eventually disappeared into Auschwitz.[18]

If the Skoreckis could not relocate to the Lvov region, let alone finagle visas to Switzerland, it meant Mark had no choice but to look for work in Warsaw. Their supply of funds was obviously limited, but just as crucial was the necessity of appearing gainfully employed. "At this time it was very dangerous not to go to work and just to sit in the house," Ruth said. And if unable to find employment, at the very minimum Jews trying to survive "on the surface" had to leave their apartments every morning, returning in the evening as would other breadwinners, meanwhile spending the day constantly on the move, avoiding such danger spots as public parks and trams. Mark's young helper found a job soon after vacating the Piotrowska apartment, as had Haka, who found work as a live-in housekeeper for a childless couple in business for themselves. "She was happy that she found something," Ruth said—and for good reason. For Haka it was the perfect job, providing food, shelter, and a good "cover." "Such positions with Polish or German families were much sought after," noted Meed.[19]

Mark never applied to the Arbeitsamt, probably because it risked his being referred to a job site far distant from the apartment and he wanted to remain within a short hike from home in case of an emergency. So he walked the streets every morning in search of work. There was an almost jaunty self-confidence about his quest. Natalia Piotrowska thinks it was because of his Polish exterior: "He spoke fluent Polish," she says, and he looked and dressed Polish too. Plus his surname was Polish, though this was of some concern because of the familiarity of his brother's name around Warsaw. "All the time we took chances, hoping that nothing would happen to us," Ruth said. In truth, her husband's risk taking stemmed from faith in his "golden hands." It was as though he knew he would rise quickly in almost any line of work once he got a foot in the door. Finally Mark found employment as a manual laborer in a factory that fabricated barracks and horse stables for the Germans, possibly for use in labor and concentration camps. Ruth never identified the plant or its location, except to mention that one of the owners was named Smolenski. The factory, it seems clear from city planning maps, was situated on Białystok Street, on the site of a present-day school, and its lumber yard, which occupied a fenced-in open space between two low-rise apartment blocks, stretched from Białystok Street to the parallel-running Ząbkowska Street.[20]

The people in the head office asked Mark what kind of work he was seeking, and he answered simply and truthfully that "he could do a lot of things and was willing even to do odd jobs, like carrying wood, just to make a few zlotys." So they said, fine, come back tomorrow prepared to work. And they paid him three zlotys a day, the sum he had received when he had started at Schulz's eighteen months earlier, assigning him the backbreaking job of hauling lumber around the plant. He cared less about the meager salary and demanding labor than the fact he now had a job where he would be seen coming and going each morning and evening like the other men in the building. Every day at dusk he returned to the apartment slumped over with fatigue. "He never worked like this, carrying lumber on his back," Ruth said. Occasionally he brought home sacks of scrap lumber to use for cooking. At noon Ruth carried him his lunch, and they would sit and talk quietly in the corner while Mark finished his meal. Then she would return to the apartment, remaining indoors almost always, consumed with worry that someone at Mark's new job might recognize the Skorecki surname and link him to his deceased Jewish brother. And then it would be Ruth and the children's turn to be led away to the trains, or maybe shot on the spot. "It was a very hard life," she said. "We never had one real moment of peace, because all the time we thought at any minute somebody would find out about us."

Before long Mark started pulling in more money, as he surely suspected he might. It was a thrice-told tale of how to make yourself indispensable to the bosses. Discovering their walk-in employee was a diamond in the rough and "not just an ordinary lumber carrier, he knew machines," the owners promoted him to foreman and raised his pay. They discovered he could handle men on the shop floor, whom he taught how to operate the equipment and do a better job so that they too might earn more money. Everyone liked and trusted him. Mark suspected that some of the workers he befriended were "Aryanized" Jews like himself, but he kept his suspicions to himself. Meanwhile, the bosses increasingly came to rely on Mark's judgment. They started calling him into the office to talk over business matters. Learning he had an excellent feel for wood, they asked him to be on hand whenever lumber salesmen dropped by the plant to take bulk orders. Ruth was rather terse in describing her husband's growing responsibility at the barracks and stable factory: "he was important to the business." In fact, he was becoming indispensable.

Being called to the office, however, had its drawbacks. For one, it made it hard for Mark to avoid discussions of war and politics. Frequently the talk turned to the eastern front and how the war was going there. Mark kept his own counsel for fear of saying something that might arouse suspicion, although too much taciturnity also raised questions. Already he was beginning to retreat into those deep silences for which he would become famous after the war. And he was becoming a past master at mincing words: "When they asked him what he thought about different things happening in Warsaw, and on politics," Ruth said, "he would say that he was of the same mind as they were."

But engaging in political small talk was much easier than controlling inner anxieties, which became almost impossible to mask during the Warsaw Ghetto's final days, when the skies above the old Jewish quarter billowed with smoke and the western horizon glowed red with insurrection.

The Jewish Fighting Organization (the zob) received scant forewarning of the ghetto's imminent liquidation when the Germans, at six in the evening on April 18, two days before Passover, surrounded the wall with Ukrainian and Lithuanian auxiliaries and beefed up the guards at the gates. For three months the Nazis had been using psychological ploys to lure Jewish shopworkers into voluntary compliance with a scheme to relocate them and their machinery to the ss labor camps at Trawniki and Poniatów in the Lublin District. But the zob had thwarted the resettlement project at every turn, and by mid-April, Heinrich Himmler, his patience now completely exhausted, ordered the high police chief for the Generalgouvernement, Friedrich-William Krüger, to liquidate the remaining ghetto forthwith. Following the January 18 fiasco, neither Krüger nor Himmler had much confidence in the ability of Warsaw's ss commander and police chief, Dr. Ferdinand von Sammern, to carry out their instructions. And therefore, as a backup, they dispatched to Warsaw an ss *Brigadeführer* (major-general) by the name of Jürgen Stroop, a former police officer then stationed in Lvov. Decorated for service with the Waffen-ss on the eastern front, Stroop had compiled an impressive record suppressing Poles and Ukrainian partisans. One historian ranks him among "the vilest, most repulsive thugs in the entire ss."[21]

One reason the Nazis delayed the ghetto's liquidation for three months was old-fashioned greed. By now the ss's economic division, known as the Wirtschafts-Verwaltungshauptamt (Economic-Administrative Main Office), or WVHA, and led by the Mussolini look-alike Oswald Pohl, had extended its tentacles throughout the Polish economy. To disguise ss control before the war, the WVHA had set up various holding companies to secure dominant positions in the German furniture-making and building materials industry. Now it was using the same methods to extend mastery over key sectors of Polish industry. To ensure an ample supply of cheap labor, in March 1942 Pohl persuaded Himmler to transfer the ss's burgeoning system of concentration and labor camps from Heydrich's RSHA to the WVHA. In March 1943, Pohl and other ss business tycoons, smelling profit in the German shops staffed by Jewish workers inside the Warsaw Ghetto, set up a new holding company, ss-Ostindustrie GmbH, or Osti, for short. It was to become sole proprietor of the multifarious enterprises now owned and operated by Walter C. Többens and Fritz Schultz, among others, after their plants and labor force were transferred to Trawniki and Poniatów.

The WVHA's intrusion into Jewish affairs triggered a long-running feud with the police and security forces inside the RSHA, who feared Pohl's economic ambitions would gum up the machinery of mass murder. "Eastern Industries! I only have to hear the word 'industry' to be nauseated," went one complaint. But there were other ss police officials, including the head of Aktion Reinhard himself, Odilo Globocnik, whose cupidity was aroused by Pohl's economic vision. Globocnik became Osti's director, contracting with Walter C. Többens to handle the transfer and manage the plants. And Többens, still smarting from Himmler's insistence that he face prosecution for war profiteering, did not balk at the terms. For the ghetto this ss detour into economic self-aggrandizement meant a short reprieve, inasmuch as such important men as Globocnik now had a personal stake in seeing that the transfer of the ghetto's capital and labor occurred with a minimum of disruption and loss—and over a three-month schedule if need be.[22]

There was another reason the ss moved slowly: fear of Jewish military reaction. The January 18 outbreak had clearly stunned the ss, confounding anti-Semitic stereotypes. Jews were not supposed to fight. Where did they get bombs, even primitive ones? How many "bandits" were there? It is obvious in retrospect that they overestimated the true strength of the Jewish fighting force, because the Germans terminated military actions after only a few days. Militarily, it was a major blunder. At the time, the ZOB possessed few weapons, ten at most, depending on who is doing the counting, and its organizational strength was feeble. "Had the Germans known the truth," one Jewish fighter, Tuvia Borzykowski, later wrote, "they would probably have continued the raids, Jewish resistance would have been nipped in the bud as a minor, insignificant episode. By interrupting the extermination action on the 21st of January the Germans allowed us to better organize and arm ourselves."[23]

The ZOB used its three-month reprieve to good effect. Baptism under fire had transformed callow youth into seasoned fighters. "A change occurred in us," Yitzhak Zuckerman wrote. "The past months had made us mature and sober."[24] The number of fighting units grew to twenty-two, each one organized, as before, according to party and movement affiliation. Disagreement exists about the total number of fighters on the eve of the April uprising; four hundred is probably a safe estimate. But it remained a youth movement despite expansion, a cohort of twenty-somethings who lived off jam and saccharine-sweetened tea, so as to husband their funds.[25] Every island in the ghetto archipelago save the small factory on Prosta Street in the erstwhile "little ghetto" contained ZOB units. The ZOB evolved a more complex division of labor, and it established a department of finance to collect "exes"—expropriations—and a department of enforcement to persuade evaders to pay up. It maintained two jails, one in the Schultz's shop area, to confine recalcitrants or their close family members until ZOB demands were met. The ZOB grew bolder. It pulled off bank heists and broke out forty workers imprisoned in the jail at Schultz's. It administered beatings with sticks to "wildcat" groups involved in extorting money from wealthy Jews. Executions of Jewish Police captains, as well as prominent men in the community who collaborated with the Gestapo, continued apace, although the ZOB tried to keep these to a minimum. "We weren't bloodthirsty," Zuckerman wrote; "we didn't want to turn killing into an everyday thing, because you could easily get used to it."[26]

Such self-restraint was typical of the ZOB, which attached paramount importance to maintaining a high moral level among its fighters. In fact, the preservation of moral self-discipline may have been the ZOB's supreme accomplishment, for everywhere else in the ghetto, remorseless Darwinism was selecting out the traits of unfettered individualism, extinguishing even family feeling.[27] Zivia Lubetkin, Yitzhak Zuckerman's lifelong companion, attributes the ZOB's ethical standards to its one-for-all ideals:

We were able to endure the life in the ghetto because we knew that we were a collective, a movement. Each of us knew that he wasn't alone. Every other Jew faced his fate alone, one man before the overpowering, invincible enemy. From the very first moment until the bitter end, we stood together, as a collective, as a movement. The feeling that there was a movement, a community of people who cared about each other, who shared ideas in common, made it possible for each of us to do what we did. The greatest tragedy was that the Jews did not know what to do.

From the very first days of demoralization in the ghetto until the final days of destruction and death, they did not know what to do. We knew. Our movement values showed us the goals and how to achieve them. This was the source of our strength to live.[28]

Meanwhile, they stayed focused on building up their supply of arms. Some flowed in from the AK, which "saluted" the ZOB by delivering fifty pistols to the ghetto (the Polish courier pinched one as a souvenir), and sharing the recipe for Molotov cocktails. With its mounting revenues the ZOB purchased more weapons on the black market, often from disillusioned Wehrmacht soldiers returning home from the Russian front. It was a motley assortment they amassed: bullets of varying calibers; weapons made in England, Poland, Germany, Belgian, and Russia; but very few rifles.[29] The Jewish Fighting Organization knew it needed as much time as possible—time to acquire more weapons, to recruit more fighters, to coordinate military action with the Polish underground, and to dig tunnel mines. They excavated two tunnel mines, one at the Nalewki Street gate, the other at the entrance to the Többens-Schultz complex, and packed each tunnel with explosives, rigging up electrical detonators, one of which drew its power from Schultz's multifarious shops.[30]

Meanwhile, the ZOB absorbed the twofold lessons of January 18. First, each fighting group had to be prepared to act independently, without central direction, because the next Aktion, when it happened, would likely come as a surprise and result in the cutting off of communications between areas and units. Second, the outnumbered and poorly armed ZOB fighters should engage German forces only at close quarters, inside the courtyards and from balconies and rooftops, to maximize the effect of their pistols and grenades and offset Nazi military superiority. The close-quarter strategy, in turn, necessitated preparing lines of retreat between battle positions inside the apartment blocks. Thus the ZOB knocked holes in attic walls, constructing hidden passageways. Within weeks, most of the ghetto archipelago was interlaced by an attic-level communication grid. "At first we used to get lost," wrote Borzykowski, "but in time we got to know the labyrinth, and the passages became veritable streets, taking the place of the real ones."[31]

As the ZOB paved "highways in the clouds," the ghetto's civilians burrowed deeper underground. After the January 18 Aktion, an already lively interest in constructing bunkers became a veritable mania. By day, especially in the central ghetto, Jews scavenged the rubble for wood, brick, and other building material. By night the area rang with the pounding of hammers. The bunkers grew larger, more elaborate. They were dug deeper and provided with several entrances, to avoid entrapment by the Germans. It was not merely a new realism about German intentions that drove the building activity forward but also a more stubborn optimism in the ghetto's ability to outlast the Germans. The Nazis had just taken a terrible drubbing at Stalingrad, which renewed desperate Jewish faith that German defeat was imminent.[32]

Managing the ghetto's mood was always a major challenge for the ZOB, however, and its success at doing so is not always self-evident.[33] After January 18 the ZOB had supplanted the Judenrat leadership in almost everyone's eyes. But whether the civilian population was fully in agreement with the strategy of resisting German relocation efforts is another question. The Jewish Fighting Organization continued to grapple with the dilemma (to quote Yisrael Gutman) of "whether it had the right to deny Jews an opportunity to extend their lives for a few more months or the duty to persuade them not to leave and to prevent others from leaving the ghetto."[34] More often than not, it discouraged escape. Above all else, it sought to thwart the transfer of shopworkers to SS camps in the Lublin District. The ZOB's greatest success was winning over the noncombatants who lived and worked outside the Többens-Schultz complex. Only twenty workers out of four thousand in the Brushmakers Shop area showed up voluntarily at the Umschlagplatz at the appointed time. There was scant compliance at Hallman's woodworking shop, as well, where ZOB units set fire to machinery the day before the scheduled departure. The incident provoked Többens to issue a proclamation describing himself as the Jewish workers' best friend and pledging idyllic conditions at Trawniki and Poniatów. "Tebbens [sic] promised the Jews pie in the sky," Borzykowski wrote. As commissar in overall charge of the transfer operation, Többens requested a face-to-face meeting with the ZOB command staff, even sending beforehand a few Jewish foremen who had already been transferred to the Lublin camps to persuade shopworkers to cooperate with the resettlement. The Jewish Fighting Organization responded to the olive branch by executing one overzealous Jewish foreman and chasing off the others. They tore down Többens's wall proclamations and destroyed his printing press. All that Többens's diplomatic feelers accomplished was to legitimate the ZOB as the new rulers of the ghetto. "The fact that the German official saw fit to argue in public with the J.F.O. [that is, the Jewish Fighting Organization] greatly increased our prestige in the eyes of the population," Borzykowski wrote.[35]

Inside the sprawling Többens-Schultz complex, however, where most of the Jewish workers slated for relocation to the SS camps at Trawniki and Poniatów were concentrated, the struggle for the hearts and minds of the workers met with mixed results. From time to time the Skoreckis picked up bits of news about the Nazi effort to transfer the Schultz operation to "a farm-like concentration camp near Lublin," Ruth said. "Some said they were not going. They expected death there at Lublin, so they said they were staying in the ghetto." But other Schultz employees did step forward voluntarily: 292 of

Schultz's workers left on transports on February 16, 1943; another 662 departed on March 17; then 448 additional workers boarded the trains on April 15, four days before the uprising.[36] And these numbers do not include the volunteers from Többens's shops.

Többens and Schultz enjoyed a modicum of success in winning over the elite Jews—"people close to management of the plants, favored skilled workers and volunteers"—in short, the category to which Mark himself had once belonged.[37] "What else is there to do?" asked a former Warsaw advertising agency executive who said he was volunteering to go to Poniatów. "They'll deport us from Warsaw in any case. Don't have any illusions about that. We have only two choices: escape to the Aryan side, or Poniatowa. Personally, I prefer the latter to continual blackmail and living like a rat in a hole." He dismissed the warning that Poniatów was a trap. The zob were "a bunch of romantic kids." In Többens he trusted. "I know him personally and I think he's telling the truth. Oh, he's no better than Brand [Carl Brandt, the Gestapo chief], but he's making too much money from exploiting the Jews to be eager to get rid of us. He'd stop at nothing to keep his shops going and he's got more influence than you think. All those ss murderers are his partners, or in his pay, from top to bottom." But in actuality, it was the other way around, and Többens, who was now in the pay of the ss, was hardly in a position to make guarantees of any kind—as events would prove soon enough.[38]

By mid-April, even the most pessimistic ghetto inhabitants were sure that the Nazis would postpone taking action until after Passover. The false confidence caused an eerie mood of normality to steal over the morally exhausted populace. People baked matzos. They changed dishes, brewed wine, did spring cleaning. "One could smell and see in the courtyards the approaching festivities—as if nothing had changed from the old days," Borzykowski wrote. Then the Germans struck, suddenly, as was their wont. With Többens's voluntary resettlement program laying in shambles and most German shops still filled with work Jews, despite the piecemeal compliance inside the Többens-Schultz complex, Himmler had run out of patience. The relocation project had dragged on too long. The deadlines for effecting the transfer were long past. It was time for decisive action.[39]

Because it was so unexpected, the 6:00 P.M. encirclement on April 18 struck terror into the ghetto population. Civilians hastily stuffed their rucksacks with linens, foodstuffs, and clothing. The zob fighters stood at the ready. "The moon was full, the night was unusually bright," remembered one Jewish fighter.[40] Between one and two in the morning, as the command staff of the Jewish Fighting Organization assembled for a *kumsitz*, a "get-together," word arrived by telephone that the Aktion would begin at 6:00 A.M. Except in the Többens-Schultz shop area, where subterranean shelters were scant, most ghetto residents now went underground. Here and there a mother with a screaming baby dashed confusedly between hideouts, trying to find space. Inside the shelters inhabitants squeezed together on wooden shelves. "Everyone sensed that he would be entering the underground bunkers with little hope of soon seeing the light of day," wrote Lubetkin. By 5:00 A.M. hardly anyone remained aboveground apart from five hundred or so ZOB fighters and a 250-person force of the Jewish Military Union (ZZW, the right-wing revisionists who insisted on complete autonomy). The ZZW forces were mostly stationed around Muranowska Square near the Brushmakers Shop area, though a few units were also located in the Többens-Schultz complex.

When the command was given, the ZOB fighters unpacked their revolvers, retrieving from storage its pipe bombs and Molotov cocktails (estimated to number two thousand). Each partisan received ten to fifteen rounds of ammunition and four or five homemade hand grenades. Selected units were given rifles and two submachine guns. Then the fighters climbed the stairwells, assuming positions on balconies and behind curtained windows. Some clambered up to the rooftops. And a few were stationed inside strategic courtyards. "A tremor of joy mixed with a shudder of fear passed through all of us," wrote Lubetkin.[41] Then a ghostly silence descended over the ghetto.

The peace was shattered at 6:00 A.M. when a mixed force of Wehrmacht troops, Waffen-SS soldiers, SS Order and Security Police, Polish Police, and a Trawniki battalion made up of Ukrainian and Baltic SS auxiliaries simultaneously penetrated the central ghetto at the gates opening onto Nalewki Street and the intersection of Gęsia and Zamenhofa Streets. Well-armed, they numbered in the hundreds—a lorried infantry accompanied by tanks and armored personnel carriers. Heralded by a car mounted with a powerful loudspeaker, the invading troops were jaunty. They swaggered. They sang marching songs. It was a glorious spring morning. A blazing sun hung in a cloudless sky, flooding the ghetto's dark corners with brilliant light.[42]

The storm broke first in the vicinity of the Nalewki Street gate, just after one of the German columns reached the corner of Gęsia Street. From their balconies and rooftop perches, three ZOB combat units rained down grenades and Molotov cocktails, opening fire from three directions. The German forces dissolved into disorganized retreat, leaving behind dead and wounded, as Jewish fighters rushed into the street firing their weapons Regrouping, the Nazis quickly returned to the ghetto, this time hugging the walls, and again were repulsed. Around 2:00 P.M., after a three-hour intermission, they returned for a third try, this time under the cover of the Luftwaffe, which bombed ZOB-controlled buildings. The day's action ended when fire forced the Jewish fighters to flee through the attics to their next battle position.[43]

The sharpest fighting of the first day, however, took place at Muranowska Square and at the intersection of Zamenhofa and Miła Streets. At the former location, revisionist (zzw) units had smuggled in a machine gun through a tunnel they had dug to the Aryan side. Now they deployed the automatic weapon to mount what Brigadeführer Jürgen Stroop, soon to be in overall command of Nazi forces in the ghetto, described as "very strong resistance."[44] From four in the afternoon until eight at night, zzw fighters completely stymied the German advance. They set a tank on fire. Atop one building they unfurled a blue-and-white flag and the Polish national flag. Meanwhile, German forces had more than they could handle at the Miła-Zamenhofa intersection. Waiting until a Nazi column preceded by a human wall of Jewish policemen had reached its midpoint below a zob-occupied balcony, Jewish fighters let loose with a sudden shower of grenades and Molotov cocktails. Then a four-sided crossfire commenced, punctuated by zob submachine gun fire. Nazi forces disintegrated into pandemonium. German dead and wounded lay everywhere. Cried out one astonished Nazi, "Juden haben Waffen! Juden haben Waffen!" (The Jews have weapons!).[45] Just then a Molotov cocktail hit another Nazi squarely on his helmet. "He ran screaming, his uniform in flames," Borzykowski said.[46] As in the Nalewki Street engagement, the Nazis withdrew in disarray, returning a short while later with two tanks, but the armored vehicles fared as badly as had the infantrymen. Both were set ablaze by pipe bombs and Molotov cocktails, and the bigger vehicle of the two, now completely engulfed in flames, lumbered off toward the Umschlagplatz. Eventually, the larger, more accurate weaponry of the German forces, outdistancing the zob's handguns, compelled the Jewish fighters to abandon their battle posts. There was only so much that stealth and surprise could accomplish against heavier battalions. But they had accomplished much.[47]

It is impossible to give a precise body count for the two belligerents. Casualties among the zob were assuredly light, although the Revisionist forces in Muranowska Square sustained heavier losses. Stroop's report says the Nazi casualties on the first day were also minimal—one dead, 24 wounded, a transparently bogus estimate.[48] Whatever the true figure, the blow to ss pride and prestige was far greater. Both Friedrich Krüger, the ss Higher Police Chief for the Generalgouvernement, and Heinrich Himmler were enraged at the day's events. Krüger cursed and shouted over the telephone. He said that it was "a stain on the ss' good name, caused by 'this intelligent doctor of philosophy from the Tyrol' [von Sammern] and that the 'stupid fellow' should be put in jail." Himmler was not ready to place von Sammern behind bars, if only because there were quite a few Austrian doctors of philosophy in the ss. None-theless, he did order von Sammern's immediate dismissal, replacing him, on the afternoon of the first day, with Stroop. Placed at Stroop's disposal were almost five thousand seasoned troops, a squadron of Luftwaffe bombers and fighter planes, and an untold quantity of submachine guns, light machine guns, heavy machine guns, rifles, antitank guns, mortars, howitzers, flamethrowers, plus more ammunition than he could ever possibly use. Now the liquidation of the Warsaw Ghetto would commence in earnest.[49]

The no-nonsense Stroop, however, quickly ran into trouble on April 20, his first full day of command and, ironically, Hitler's fifty-fourth birthday. He had made his main objective the evacuation of the Brushmakers area in the ghetto's northeastern quadrant. But things went badly when Stroop's attack column, at two in the afternoon, became bunched at the factory gate, just above the mine tunnel the zob had excavated weeks earlier, and stood waiting as the guard approached to let them in. At that moment one of the zob commanders in the area powered up the electrical detonator. It was "a tremendous explosion!" remembered Simha Rotem, "complete chaos."[50] Severed limbs and chunks of cobblestone flew into the air. Bodies were crushed, fences crumbled. As the Germans fled in panic not once but twice, Jewish fighters let loose with grenades, Molotov cocktails, and pistol fire. An hour later two or three Nazi officers wearing white strips in their lapels appeared on the scene requesting a fifteen-minute truce, but the partisans, shooting one German, drove them off. Stroop's forces achieved quicker results in Muranowska Square, where by day's end revisionist fighters, incurring heavy casualties, were finally routed by concentrated firepower. What remained of the crippled unit slipped away through the zzw tunnel to the Aryan side only later to be betrayed and ambushed in a nearby forest.

It took Stroop another day to quash armed resistance in the Brushmakers area, and his methods foreshadowed what lay ahead for the rest of the ghetto. Frustrated that so few work Jews had complied with the evacuation order, Stroop decided that evening, as he wrote in his daily report, "to evacuate the block by force or to blow it up."[51] Eventually, he chose to blow it up. On Wednesday, April 21, the third day of the uprising, forces pounded away at the compound with Howitzer cannons positioned just beyond the ghetto wall. Then they set the entire area ablaze with Luftwaffe bombs and flamethrowers. Hundreds of Jews suffocated to death. Marek Edelman, the Bundist activist who had helped rescue Jews at the Umschlagplatz first aid station during the Great Deportations, was overall commander of this sector, and it was all he could do to lead his five units through the choking black smoke and collapsing walls to unite with the main zob force in the central ghetto. The fierce heat turned shattered glass into gummy liquid. Shoe soles bonded to the glutinous pavement. Edelman's men, their faces covered with wet cloths, finally made it through a six-foot gap in the wall after shooting out the lamp in a German searchlight, eventually descending to a bunker beneath Franciszkanska 22.[52] It was a serendipitous conjunction of Skorecki family history and a world historical event. For ever since September 1942, or just following the Great Deportation, the building above Edelman's new command post had been the residence of the brothers Tempelhof (and Mery Mejnster too, until her death in January 1943). Franciszkanska 22 was the principal abode of other hospital personnel as well, administrators and nurses. "Possibly twenty people, thirty people, I don't remember the number," says Henry Tempelhof's friend Dr. Thaddeus Stabholz. "And Henry was living with the hospital personnel at Franciszkanska 22." It is a safe guess that the remaining Czyste staff were already in that bunker by the time Edelman and his men arrived.[53]

Although Stroop badly wanted to inflict the same scorched-earth tactics on the Többens-Schultz complex, political considerations initially dictated moderation. That policy went by the boards at the conclusion of the second day, after Molotov cocktails and pipe bombs set fire to a tank moving through the area.[54] Stroop informed managers in the Többens-Schultz area that he intended to evacuate all shop personnel starting at six o'clock the following morning. He was not going to be gingerly about it, either—plant machinery or no plant machinery. "If a voluntary departure proves impossible," he wrote in his daily report, "I will also purge this part of the Ghetto by force." This was precisely what Többens and Schultz had feared. The two German proprietors now circulated among their workers urging compliance; Schultz even addressed a mass assembly in the factory courtyard where Mark and Ruth once stood in ranks five deep for ss selections. Their pleas appear to have had some effect, for fifty-two hundred Jews came forward the next day for resettlement, were marched under armed guard to the Umschlagplatz, and transferred to the Lublin camps.[55]

Odilo Globocnik made one last attempt to protect the Többens's and Schultz's fixed plant and machinery; as Globocnik was a director of Osti, these represented his assets as well. At the onset of the invasion of the shops, the Aktion Reinhard chief rushed to Warsaw from his Lublin headquarters to stay Stroop's hand. His arrival on the scene triggered a dispute that was arbitrated by Himmler himself, in favor of Stroop. On April 22, the Reichsführer-ss cabled back the message that "the combing of the Warsaw Ghetto must be carried out thoroughly, with a hard heart, without mercy. It is best to proceed rigorously. The incidents in Warsaw prove how dangerous these Jews are."[56]

To say that Stroop now acted with "a hard heart, without mercy," is putting it mildly. What he proceeded to do was convert the Többens-Schultz complex into a vast crematorium. Pockets of armed resistance, mounted by zob and revisionist units alike, he burned out with an arsonist's glee. Over the next ten days fierce combat turned Nowolipie and Leszno Streets into a wheel of fire, with partisans setting warehouses and machinery ablaze to prevent their transfer while Stroop's men torched remaining buildings and bunkers, including the abandoned leather tannery where Ruth and the children had once taken refuge. Some of the fiercest fighting of the entire uprising occurred in the Többens-Schultz area on April 27, after Többens and two deputy directors, one of them Jewish, at 11:00 A.M. warned worker holdouts to come forward. When no one heeded the warning, most of the factory complex went up in flames, including rows of sewing machines, belts and pulleys, mounds of shoes, and piles of pelts.[57] By April 30 the inferno had spread to the lumberyard next to the wooden sole shop. "Everything all around us is covered in smoke and ashes from the burning buildings," Fritz Schultz recorded in his diary a short time later.[58]

By May 2, what remained of Fritz Schultz's operations had been reconstituted at the ss camp at Trawniki. His factory force had dwindled to slightly more than fifty-six hundred workers, none of them apparently from the wooden sole division. The shop that Mark helped to run fails to appear in the Schultz factory organizational chart at Trawniki, nor does Stelmaszek show up in the extant records. Mark and Ruth never learned what became of him. Whatever his reputation might have been among other Jews in his division, the Skoreckis owed him their lives, and they always acknowledged the debt.[59]

By the third or fourth day of the Aktion, Stroop had also given up on conquering the central ghetto by conventional means and turned to the same military arson he had used to destroy the Többens-Schultz complex. He called in Stuka dive-bombers, which dumped tons of incendiary explosives on the mammoth apartment blocks. He ordered howitzers to blast away at free-standing walls. He had sappers blow up the entrance to every cellar, while flamethrowers licked gateyard corridors with tongues of fire. ss troops shot Jews as they ran, blinded by flame and smoke, from burning buildings or leaped from rooftops and upper-story windows. The Germans joked about performing target practice on Jewish "paratroopers."[60]

Stroop's burn-them-out policy not only caught the Jewish Fighting Organization off guard but also shattered the heroic vision underpinning its strategy. "We had dreamt of hand-to-hand combat, a final battle," wrote Lubetkin—a cathartic Armageddon, a fight to the death, in which the Jewish warriors would be defeated but not before shedding rivers of German blood. Now their best-laid plans had been confounded, and they felt adrift.[61] By destroying the attic passageways connecting the zob's various combat positions, Stroop's resort to systematic arson forced the Jewish fighters to go underground. All day long they remained in subterranean bunkers, venturing out only after dusk, usually with rags around their shoes to muffle the sound, occasionally bumping into German scouting parties in the dark. "Living in continuous night, we lost count of days, weeks, months," wrote Borzykowski. "We hardly knew whether it was night or day."[62]

Every one of those bunkers had been built by Jewish civilians. Stroop had not anticipated encountering so many underground shelters—his final report, for example, dated May 24, 1943, mentioned having destroyed 631 bunkers[63]— and their ubiquity clinched his decision to reach for the matchbook. ss arson now rendered conditions inside those basement havens unbearable. Bunker walls and ceilings radiated ovenlike heat, exuding "the mildew of decades." Some people were literally cooked alive, their broiled bodies crusted over with the ash that carpeted the basement floor following a conflagration. Once a building over a bunker started burning, the best hope was to hold out until nightfall, when the Germans habitually left the ghetto and it became possible to venture forth in search of new shelter.[64]

But new hiding places became increasingly hard to find as more and more of the ghetto went up in flames. Not a few bunkerless refugees took to the sewers. "I will never forget what I saw when I first descended into the sewer," wrote Borzykowski just after the war. "Masses of refugees were huddling in the filth and the stink, in pipes so low and narrow that only one person could pass at a time, walking in a low crouch. They lay on the ground in excrement and other filth, pressed to each other. Some of the elderly people and children had fainted, with no one paying any attention. The stream of sewage washed away the bodies of the dead, making room for the living. The wounded lay there bleeding, their blood mixing with the sewage." Besides being filthy, the environment was also unstable. From time to time, Stroop ordered creosote poured into the sewers and the passageways blocked. He had the channels flooded, literally flushing people through the pipes. The huddle of refugees Borzykowski had encountered had completely vanished when he returned a few hours later. "I saw only wet rags, shoes and a pair of glasses."[65]

Most noncombatants evicted by the flames, however, sought sanctuary in a steadily diminishing supply of bunkers, which rapidly filled to overflowing. Sanitary conditions worsened from bad to deplorable. Oxygen became so scarce it was nearly impossible to light a candle. People literally sat with their mouths open, gulping air. Food stocks dwindled, then disappeared. The wailing of children begging for food provoked the fury of bone-weary adults who feared the whimpering would attract enemy attention and betray the entire bunker—which often happened. Mild by comparison were conditions in the old refugee shelters—the "points"—in the preliquidation ghetto. It was as though each and every bunker had been stuffed with emaciated people of the kind who used to haunt the entranceways of Judenrat ration stores and snatch bread from recipients as they exited. "The stifling heat was unbearable," wrote one ZOB fighter; "people behaved like complete lunatics, ready to steal food from one another at gunpoint."[66]

The ZOB's finest moment may have been as much moral as martial. There is something superhuman about the Jewish Fighting Organization's success in maintaining discipline amid chaos. Tuvia Borzykowski described the pandemonium that overtook a bunker where he and other ZOB fighters were staying when smoke burst into the chamber. The exits became clogged with people. "In that darkness, amidst clouds of suffocating smoke," Borzykowski wrote, "the fighters started to bring some order and first rescue the non-combatants. Some of our comrades went outside to clear the passage so that the people could come out. Inside we untangled the bodies, and one by one, in a chain, the people left. The last to go were the fighters." By now it was early evening and the inhabitants of Borzykowski's bunker and other burned-out shelters had taken refuge in the cratered rubble of nearby courtyards. The ZOB units in the area formed them into rows of three and led them, convoy-fashion, to a larger series of courtyards at Miła 9, where other now homeless civilians were cowering in the charred ruins. Just before they marched away, a ten-year-old girl emerged from a passageway connecting two courtyards, pleading in a thin, childish voice to save her mother, who was on fire, trapped inside the bunker. The girl was also badly burned and in terrible pain. Several fighters rushed into the passageway, but fiery debris had already fallen on the women. The young daughter became hysterical, refusing to believe her mother was gone. "We had to take her by force," Borzykowski said.[67]

But these occasions of moral triumph, by calling to mind a responsibility the ZOB was unable to discharge fully, elicited feelings of guilt. Zivia Lubetkin was also on the scene at Miła 9, whose three capacious courtyards reminded her of a human anthill. She and her comrades felt powerless. "The crowded, cowering masses of Jews huddled around us waiting for a word of hope from the fighters' lips. We were bewildered and lost. What should we say to them? What could we say to ourselves? How terrible was this feeling of helplessness! How grave the responsibility we felt as the last desperate Hebrew warriors!" In truth, all that she and the other ZOB leaders could do was order their own fighters to find new shelters and tell the crowd of noncombatants to do the same. "We instructed the people to find temporary refuge within the ghetto," Lubetkin continued, "but they wouldn't leave us. They attached themselves to our fighting units and followed them." Finally, the civilians scattered, some into bunkers, others through the manholes and into the sewers.[68]

After about ten days of the uprising, the ZOB leadership concluded it was time to flee the ghetto, thus they sent to the Aryan side two representatives, one the boyishly handsome Rotem, or Kazik.[69] They were told to make contact with Zuckerman, who had left the ghetto on April 13, six days before the uprising erupted, to replace the ZOB's representative to the Polish underground state. Zuckerman was on a mission to arrange not merely further arms shipments from the AK but joint operations as well. But soon after reaching the Aryan side, Zuckerman discovered to his dismay that the AK had never been serious about coordinating military activity with Jewish partisans, hoping instead to stave off a military confrontation until Germany and the Soviet Union had bled themselves to death. "History paid them back," he said, looking ahead to the cataclysmic Warsaw Uprising of 1944. By the time Kazik had reached the Aryan side, Zuckerman was more than ready to redirect his energies toward arranging the escape of the ZOB remnant trapped inside the burning ghetto. But making those arrangements would take time.[70]

Indeed, as the uprising entered its third week, the plight of the ZOB grew more desperate by the hour. The Germans had started using dogs and sound-detecting devices to ferret out undiscovered bunkers. They bribed deliriously hungry captured Jews with loaves of bread into betraying other hideouts. There was an unvarying routine for emptying a bunker: first the Germans shouted, "*Alles heraus!*" then they pumped in a cloud of poison gas. The ZOB leadership, still under the overall command of Mordechai Anielewicz, fled from one burned shelter to another, finally alighting, in early May, in an immense bunker at Miła 18.

Stretching for a couple of city blocks and containing every sort of amenity, from hot and cold running water to electricity, Miła 18 was indubitably the most elaborate bunker in the entire ghetto. A system of addresses had been devised, some of them darkly sardonic (one room was called Treblinka; two others, Trawniki and Poniatów), to help people find their way through its maze. Ruling with an iron fist over its denizens of thieves, prostitutes, and pimps was a thick-necked, potbellied character named Shmuel Asher. Jocularly known as "King of the Underworld," the hard-swearing Asher dictated when they would eat and where and when they would sleep. But to the ZOB units he was a convivial host, welcoming Anielewicz and others with open arms, which did not always happen in bunkers already filled to the brim. Before long Miła 18 became as badly congested as the other shelters. The water supply ran low. Exhausted from hunger, people fouled themselves where they lay. The young Jewish fighters themselves succumbed to lassitude, spending whole days lying on beds of rags, recounting war stories for the umpteenth time, finding inner peace recalling jobs well done, on occasion losing themselves in heated ideological arguments, as in days of yore, over the merits of Hebrew versus Yiddish, Zionism versus Communism. And then Asher would come running over cautioning them to lower their voices lest they bring disaster down on the entire bunker.[71]

Through it all, Mordechai Anielewicz tried to lift the spirits of his fighters. At first his own mood was upbeat, even ecstatic. On April 23, while the ZOB was still able to conduct tactical operations, Anielewicz had written Zuckerman his famous last letter, penned in Hebrew and delivered by Pinkert's mortuary men via the cemetery. "Things have surpassed our boldest dreams," he wrote buoyantly. True, conditions inside the bunkers were becoming intolerable; the oxygen was low. And the pistols they had taken such pains to procure had proved worthless. We practically don't use them, he wrote. "We need grenades, rifles, machine guns, and explosives." Despite the adversity he was ebullient: "The main thing is the dream of my life has come true. I've lived to see a Jewish defense in the ghetto in all its glory and greatness."[72] But a week later, after he and the ZOB command staff had shifted their headquarters to Miła 18, his spirits began to wane. Anielewicz was one of those leaders who possessed, as Lubetkin remembered, a "deep feeling of personal responsibility." And thus, at least once a day, he would try to make personal contact with every one of his fighters inside the sprawling bunker, picking his way over prostrate bodies, using his elbows to disentangle himself from one knot of people as he moved to make contact with another. Yet, toward the end, when his staff sought further instructions, he too lacked answers, for there were none.[73]

On Friday, May 7, at about three in the afternoon, they heard the Germans banging on the ground above Miła 18. Plaster fell from the ceiling. For three hours the pounding persisted. Mothers covered their children's heads with blankets to muffle the crying. After the Germans left, the ZOB command staff concluded that the time had arrived to evacuate their forces, and they dispatched two squads to the Aryan side, one under Borzykowski via the Smocza Street sewer, the other under Lubetkin, who was sent to the bunker at Franciszkanska 22, where Marek Edelman was posted with the surviving fighters from the Brushmakers area. Lubetkin reached Edelman's headquarters safely, but the Borzykowski group stumbled into a German night patrol, and were forced to spend the entire next day in a burned-out bunker, fending off swarms of rats, gray and yellow, some the size of cats, who ripped off bits of decaying flesh from the decomposing corpses inside.[74]

Neither the Borzykowski nor the Lubetkin group, now accompanied by Edelman, was able to return to Miła 18 until about 11:00 P.M. the following day, but they arrived too late. The scene was as quiet as a graveyard. They discovered a few fighters wandering in the rubble, dazed from poison gas. The Germans had arrived around noon that day, as the fighters were lying on their cots, they told their comrades. While the civilians obeyed SS orders to vacate the bunker, the ZOB units stayed inside, convinced they could stick it out until nightfall, when the Germans would leave and they could surface and search for new quarters. But Stroop's men pumped poison gas into the bunker. Aniele- wicz told his fighters to put wet cloths on their faces. Just then, Aryeh Wilner, whom Zuckerman had replaced as representative to the Polish underground, yelled out, "Let us kill ourselves first rather than surrender to the Germans alive!" One fighter pulled out his revolver and shot his mother and then him- self. Then the bunker erupted in pistol fire. Only a handful of fighters able to crawl near the exits and breathe in fresh air managed to survive. The rest all perished, entombed beneath impenetrable debris left by Nazi dynamite.[75]

The ZOB surviving groups picked their way back to Edelman's command bunker at Franciszkanska 22, whose great advantage was that it afforded direct access to the sewers. Anticipating a dawn attack, the Jewish fighters decided to send Borzykowski and ten or twelve healthy men to the Aryan side through the sewers, to arrange an escape for the rest. Now occurred one of those miraculous episodes that crop up regularly in survivor stories, if only because survival in Nazi-occupied Poland was miraculous by definition. Just when the Borzykowski group feared it had gotten lost, they saw a light approach in the distance. The brighter it got, the surer they felt it was a German patrol. They had been walking for hours, sometimes on all fours, finding their way blocked now and then by a dead body, fighting all the while wave after wave of liquid sludge. The light turned out to be from Kazik's flashlight. He was accom- panied by two Polish sewer workers who had been hired to guide him to the ghetto on the false promise that buried gold might be their ultimate reward. Kazik was actually on his way back from the ghetto when he ran into the Borzykowski group. He too had visited the eerie stillness of Miła 18, which made him feel, as he later wrote, like "the last Jew in the Warsaw Ghetto."[76]

They decided to divide into two groups. The group led by Kazik forged ahead to the Prosta Street manhole, where Kazik ascended to the Aryan side and left to arrange transportation for the rest of the fighters. The other group returned to the Franciszkanska 22 bunker to retrieve the surviving remnant. Abandoning the bunker at Franciszkanska 22 was wrenching. They had prom- ised ZOB fighters stationed in a bunker on Nalewki Street that they would link up the following day at dawn. But they felt they could not wait that long. The Germans would surely attack their bunker before then. They were also trou- bled in mind about the civilian inhabitants of Franciszkanska 22, whose des- perate need continued to assail the Jewish fighters with awful reminders of their own helplessness as leaders. Some of those helpless noncombatants quite likely were the brothers Henry and Vovek Tempelhof, together with other hospital personnel from Czyste.[77]

As the ZOB fighters made ready to leave, the question of what to do with these civilians pressed to the fore. Months earlier they had elected to place the salvation of Jewish honor above the rescue of Jewish people, a choice they believed imposed by History. But their strategic decision involved moral trade-offs, and the compensatory price tag continued to haunt them until the moment when they dropped down into the sewer and felt the cold slime splash around their ankles. As Lubetkin remembered: "An argument breaks out at the entrance of the bunker. People are following us. There are many of them, civilians, old people and children. It is clear to us and to them that this avenue of escape will mean their certain death. They don't insist on joining us. After speaking with the leader of the bunker we agree that we will take some of his young men." An older man then jumped down into the channel and refuses to go back. The fighters agreed to let him come along. The rest of the civilians, including the brothers Tempelhof, remained behind. With his medical condition Henry would have had difficulty dragging his colostomy bag through the city's waste channels, but Vovek, still young and vigorous, could have made it. Apparently he chose to stay with his older brother. Those kinds of decisions were made all the time—relatives choosing to accompany parents or siblings to the Umschlagplatz and almost certain death, rather than flee or fight. It makes the entire issue of valor—the juxtaposition of armed resistance and "sheep-to-slaughter" submission to death—seem off-key, indeed, off the point altogether.[78]

It was morning by the time the Franciszkanska group of eighty reached the Prosta Street manhole, bone-tired from having crawled for two hours through what Lubetkin called "a narrow, filthy hole," dragging and carrying their wounded. Immediate relief was not in sight, however. Kazik was still trying to arrange ground transportation, so they squatted and sat in the raw sewage. Overhead, beams of light slicing through the perforated manhole cover were shuttered out by pedestrian shoes or passing autos, like the flickering sepia of a silent film. They heard the hurried footsteps of people heading to work, the playing and shouting of children, the bustle of the everyday world. Meanwhile, two fighters returned to Franciszkanska 22 in hopes of retrieving their comrades on Nalewki Street, but the Germans had already blocked the passageways. Then further disappointment struck when word reached them through the manhole that Kazik had still not arranged transportation and they would have to stay where they were indefinitely. They slumped down in the sewage, their bodies closely pressed together. Someone lowered down hot, watery soup and bread through the manhole, but it barely slaked their thirst and hunger. In desperation one of the half-poisoned survivors of Miła 18 drank the sewage slime. Meanwhile, to find space to stretch out, one group of fighters broke away to look for room in a connecting pipe.[79]

At around 10:00 A.M. on May 10, after languishing in the sewer for thirty hours, Kazik finally arrived with one of two trucks he had hired on the pretext that they were to pick up and deliver wooden soles of the kind Mark Skorecki once fabricated. Forty or so of the fighters quickly scampered out of the manhole and into the truck. Polish civilians looked on in horror. "We were some sight: lumps of filth with emaciated faces out of which stared dead eyes," said Borzykowski.[80] The truck sped away, however, before the fighters who had sought more legroom in a side channel could reach the manhole opening, and the other truck never appeared. The first vehicle crossed the Vistula River, traveling in a roundabout way to evade German checkpoints, eventually reaching the Lomianki Forest. It was a beautiful spring day, just like the morning the uprising began. The trees were fragrant. Birds chirped everywhere. The refugees from the sewer were greeted by a contingent of ZOB fighters from the Többens-Schultz complex who had escaped at the end of April via a tunnel at Ogrodowa 27, across the street from where Ruth and the girls had been living when Mark had returned from Białystok seventeen months earlier. The Többens-Schultz fighters baked bread for their exhausted comrades. Just then the Miła 18 survivor who had quenched his thirst with raw sewage collapsed. "He died right there in front of us," Lubetkin wrote.[81]

The fighters who remained behind in the sewer eventually lost patience and climbed up to the street, taking refuge in a nearby building. They were betrayed to the Nazis by a Polish collaborator and gunned down in an ambush. A few weeks later several ZOB fighters who had left the Lomianki Forest and returned to Warsaw died in a fire ignited by a match someone had casually thrown on the ground inside an abandoned celluloid factory in Praga, where they had set up quarters.[82]

At 8:15 on the evening of May 16, in a show of Nazi triumphalism, Brigadeführer Stroop dynamited the Tłomackie Synagogue on the eastern edge of the now ruined ghetto, declaring, "The Jewish Quarter Of Warsaw Is No More!"[83] The death notice was premature. Pockets of Jewish resistance remained in the wreckage until September 1943, when the Nazis brought in Polish laborers and Greek and Czech Jews to salvage the rubble. During one lunch break a group of Polish laborers were startled at the sight of bearded men emerging from the ruins begging for food, for weapons, and for help to reach the Aryan side. The help never arrived. "They were the last of the Warsaw Ghetto freedom fighters."[84] The Nazis then proceeded to level what remained of the old Jewish Quarter, leaving behind "a broad field of rubble three stories deep."[85]

Three decades after the uprising, Edelman told the Polish journalist Hanna Krall: "In the Ghetto we made the decision for forty thousand people. . . . We decided that they would not voluntarily collaborate in their own deaths."[86] Edelman and his young ZOB comrades, however, had made another decision for the noncombatants, this one tacit rather than explicit: to give primary focus, both before and during the uprising, to the rescue of Jewish honor rather than individual Jews, on the altogether defensible grounds that most were going to perish anyway. History has crowned the young rebels with appropriate laurels, for humankind understandably needs to honor heroes willing to die for their beliefs, to be reassured that some ideals are worth dying for.

Notwithstanding the retrospective accolades, all fully justified, because the young rebels virtually reinvented modern Jewish identity and changed history, a few veterans of the ghetto uprising remained troubled by guilt. For everyone else the war had ended in victory, with a sense of relief, accomplishment, and fulfillment. But for such zob veterans as Edelman it was "a lost war, and all the time I was haunted by a feeling that I still had something to do, somewhere to go, that somebody was still counting on me and I had to go rescue him." It is difficult not to see in Edelman's desire to engage in rescue a tacit admission that he and his zob colleagues just possibly could have done more to save Jewish lives before the uprising. True, they could not have saved many, and those they did rescue in all probability could have looked forward only to a few months' reprieve, not permanent salvation. But more could have been saved had the young fighters deployed their material and moral resources in a different way. Such a judgment is no criticism of their wartime valor, but it is a reminder that heroism, like many human actions, entails moral trade-offs, and that virtue is seldom unalloyed.

Edelman seems to have assuaged at least part of his guilt by becoming a cardiologist. "As a doctor," he explained wryly, "I could continue to be responsible for the life of at least one person—so I became a doctor."

Mark and Ruth never betrayed any trace of resentment toward the ghetto fighters. Like every other Jew then struggling to make it on the Aryan side, Anne's parents followed the uprising with rapt attention. Every evening on the radio they listened to Stroop's "official"—and inflated—reports of Jewish "bandits" killed or captured during the day's engagements. They watched smoke and ash plume up from the ghetto. There were days when westerly winds blanketed Praga with a drizzle of singed pages from Jewish prayer books. Poles living near the ghetto wall told the Skoreckis of seeing young men and women with guns in their hands remaining atop burning buildings instead of leaping to dubious safety. "They fought for weeks," Ruth said. "Of course, this was not easy, because the Jewish people had only a little ammunition and the Germans had tanks and munitions." The outcome was never in doubt. She knew that. Everyone did. But the unequal struggle being waged by Jewish fighters against a superior foe filled Ruth with awe and admiration.

Through it all, however, one question recurred with morbid insistence: the fate of her relatives inside the burning ghetto. "Every day I didn't know what had happened to my brother and his wife and to my younger brother," she said. "They had promised in the last minute to escape from the ghetto, and I believed that they would keep the promise. I hoped everything would work out okay." In truth, her stomach was tied in knots.

Ruth had no way of knowing that Mery Mejnster had probably perished before the April uprising, most likely during the Aktion carried out by the Germans against the hospital three months earlier. Nor would she discover until a few years following the war what had befallen her brothers, Henry and Vovek Tempelhof. Miraculously, both had managed to survive the uprising, for during the day of May 9—the same day the ZOB fighters had left the Franciszkanska 22 bunker—the two of them turned up among several hundred Jewish captives corralled by the Nazis at an assembly point on Nalewki Street. Most of the bunkers in the Franciszkanska, Gęsia, and Nalewki Street area had been flushed out around the same time, and the survivors were temporarily detained on Nalewki Street before their removal to the Umschlagplatz. Henry's close friend and collaborator in the first aid clinic rescue operation, Nahum Remba, was at the Nalewki assembly point, as was Jósef Stein, director of the hospital, and Dr. Thaddeus Stabholz, another friend. Stabholz, Remba, and Stein had been in a bunker at Gęsia 3 or 5, which was connected by a tunnel to the hospital across the street at Gęsia 6. Stabholz himself, along with five others, had once tried to reach the sewers from their Gęsia bunker, even engaging in a hand grenade attack on a German patrol car before returning to their bunker a short while later. Their shelter was destroyed by the Nazis on May 8. "I remember it indirectly," Stabholz says, "because the night before I listened to the radio. It was when the Americans forced the Germans to surrender at Tunis and Bizerta in North Africa."[87]

Stabholz had seen little of the brothers Tempelhof following the January 18 Aktion. Henry was not much involved in hospital affairs after that, spending most of the time at his quarters at Franciszkanska 22. During the three months before the uprising, the hospital operated on a shoestring, and Henry simply had little to do. "There was no food, no heat at the hospital, so it was extremely difficult," Stabholz says. "We knew we had a very short time ahead of us." On May 9, at the Nalewki Street assembly point, there was a reunion of sorts among the hospital personnel from the various bunkers. "We sort of bunched together, just in case, to be in the same boxcar"—on the faint hope they might be able to jump from the train. As they apprehended would be the case, the entire group of four or five hundred prisoners were marched to the Umschlagplatz, and then the hospital contingent was shoved into a small room on the second floor of a school building the Nazis were using to hold Jewish deportees. About fifty people were already inside; some had been there for as long as five days without food or water. Dried blood, rags, and newspapers covered the floor. There was barely room to sit down. Stabholz and his companions from the hospital, including Director Stein and Nahum Remba, together with their wives and the brothers Tempelhof, made space by drawing up their legs.[88]

Now followed thirty-six hours of anti-Semitic recreation that can only be described as depraved. The Nazis conducted savage body searches, beating to a pulp anyone who opened his mouth. They gang-raped young women, often shooting them on the spot afterward. With his fiancée forced to look on, Stabholz himself was made to kneel in a corner of the room the prisoners had set aside as their latrine, then an ss officer fired shots around his head. That evening, after shouldering a large chest in front of the door leading into the room, ss guards hurled smoking stink bombs through the window, training a searchlight on the opening so as to take aim at Jews who tried to jump to the ground. Seven prisoners were killed by rifle fire, several others badly wounded by ricocheting bullets. The reek of decomposition and defecation hung over the room, and people were literally dying from thirst. Midmorning of the second day of confinement, just after the exhausted prisoners had fallen asleep, club-wielding thugs burst into the room yelling, "Out! Out!" Stabholz and the Tempelhofs were funneled through a gauntlet of head and body blows and stuffed, along with nearly 150 others, into a waiting boxcar meant for less than one-third that number. People stood on tiptoe to get air. The smell of lime rising from the floor was overpowering and burned the lungs; the heat was unbearable. When the train clattered away at noon, then switched onto a different track a short distance from the Umschlagplatz, the human cargo realized the destination was Treblinka. Several passengers were crushed to death en route, blood hemorrhaging from their noses and mouths. "People are dying in awkward positions," Stabholz wrote in 1947.[89]

At Treblinka's receiving platform most of the passengers and all of the women, including Stabholz's fiancée, were rushed into the changing yard and then hustled through the tree-latticed tube leading to the gas chambers. But about two hundred of the men were pulled aside as they reached the gate. Stabholz was one of them; so were Nahum Remba and Henry and Vovek Tempelhof. The selectees were loaded back onto the train after the freight cars were emptied of corpses and swept clean of trash and excrement, and the rail transport soon headed back to Warsaw. There was room to sit down this time, even opportunity to slake their terrible thirst during the train's short idle in the city, where they bribed a Ukrainian guard for a pail and a half of water with a wad of zlotys, rolled inside a rubber tube, that a fellow deportee had been able to conceal inside his rectum. Then the train headed southeast toward Lublin and likely internment at Majdanek. For everyone else the physical misery inside the boxcar had slackened by degrees. But not for Henry Tempelhof. Now his preexisting condition, which had doubtless been the secret to his remarkable stoicism, began to drain even his wells of fortitude. As Stabholz describes the scene in his 1947 memoir: "I am in the same car with Natek [Nahum Remba], Pinek, and the brothers Tempelhof. The older Tempelhof, an engineer and office manager in the hospital, suffers terribly. He has cancer of the rectum and has had a colostomy. He is supposed to irrigate the bag once a day. Now he is rotting alive."[90] The image of Henry tinkering with his colostomy bag remains with Stabholz even today. It is a memory of smell as well as vision. "I remember Henry was really suffering," Stabholz says. "It was a big stench. Even he himself could not stand it. I remember this thing very well."[91]

The "excremental assault," to use Terence Des Pres's inimitable phrase, had finally worn down Henry's inner defenses, and he became morose after it became clear the train was destined for Majdanek. He surrendered to a defeatism unlike any he had ever displayed in the past. "The older Tempelhof says it would have been better to die in the gas chamber in Treblinka," Stabholz wrote in his memoir. "There, all is over in a few minutes. Who knows what is in store for us now?"[92]

But Henry and his brother, mirabile dictu, endured this awful trial too. And then, when the transport halted in a small ss camp on the outskirts of Majdanek, they survived yet one more selection: a foot race across an open square during which those who were lame were weeded out. Miraculously, Henry's legs did not betray him. Then a column of men, including the Tempelhofs, Stabholz, and Remba, were marched for a quarter of an hour along a dusty road beneath the blazing sun to Majdanek. The camp, also called Lublin-Majdanek, lay along the Lublin-Zamość-Chełm highway adjacent to the city of Lublin and was, like Auschwitz, a mixed facility—part concentration camp, part forced labor camp, and part killing center, with three gas chambers and a large crematorium. But the men from Henry and Vovek's transport were earmarked for forced labor, and so they were assigned to one of the men's "fields," or "camps." There were five "fields" altogether (actually six, but one of them was never occupied), and they abutted one another in a long row: one camp was for women, one was for the hospital, and the other three were for various categories of male prisoners. Stabholz went to camp 4, Remba and the brothers Tempelhof to camp 3, the worst compounds of the lot. Shortly after their arrival, however, Remba became a *Blockschreiber* (or *Blockälter*), one of the prisoners responsible for disseminating ss orders, and Henry and Vovek were picked to be his *Stubendiensts* (assistants). The perception is widespread that Nazi camp officials chose Jewish helpers for their sadism and selfishness, a claim more mythic than anything else. Certainly the generalization would not apply to Remba and the brothers Tempelhof. For they quickly resumed old habits of mutuality. Through the barbed wire separating camps 3 and 4, Henry, Vovek, and Remba were soon slipping portions of lifesaving bread to one of Stabholz's starving friends. Their altruism had been fire-tested before when they used the cover of a first aid clinic during the Great Deportation to rescue Jews at the Umschlagplatz. Henry Tempelhof and Nahum Remba were obviously not the type of men to surrender easily to the survival-of-the-fittest ethos prevalent in the Nazi camp system, no matter what kind of short-term privileges they may have received.[93]

Yet, if Henry and Vovek Tempelhof had weathered tempests hardly imaginable, their future remained as clouded as ever.

Though Ruth at the time knew nothing of her brothers' whereabouts, let alone their ordeals, she had to have been very worried. After all, as she herself admitted, "the ghetto was destroyed," which likely meant everyone in it. But it was not merely the apprehension that kept her on edge but also the stress of having to keep everything bottled up inside. As she explained: "We had to play the role that we had nothing to do with all this in order to save the lives of our children. We had to endure everything with a big wound in our heart." But that was easier said than done when the people all around were expressing hurtful opinions. The Skoreckis happen to have been fortunate to have worked and lived among Poles who were moved by the ghetto's fiery demise. "The people with whom I was living and the non-Jewish people were heartbroken too," Ruth said, "because this was all so unbelievable." Ruth's experience with Polish opinion was probably typical. Although the evidence is mixed, it seems clear, to use Zuckerman's apt characterization, that "the Polish street in those days was pro-Jewish." Even Ringelblum, who took a different view, and was often openly conflicted on the question of Polish-Jewish relations, the subject of his final book, admitted that Polish interest in the uprising was intense.[94] Yet, within that rapt interest swirled currents of open contempt and eddies of outward indifference that tested the self-control of every Jew who tried to survive "on the surface."

"I didn't hear any expression of sympathy from the Poles about what was happening to the Jews of the city," wrote Simha Rotem. "Some of them even seemed happy about the 'purification' of Warsaw's Jews."[95] "The bugs are burning," exclaimed some gentile onlookers of Jürgen Stroop's scorched-earth strategy, according to Ringelblum's sampling of Polish opinion. "Joy over Warsaw's being cleansed of Jews was spoiled only by fear of the morrow, the fear that after liquidating the Jews the Germans would take the Poles in hand."[96]

And just as dispiriting as the open contempt was the indifference, which telegraphed perhaps more emphatically than transparent hatefulness the clear message that Jews fell outside the Polish "universe of moral obligation." "That is just for the Jews," a youthful Pole remarked grinningly as he rode the carousel in Krasinski Park soon after the burning of the Brushmakers's Shops, and then "returned for a second ride on the swing."[97] The tinkling from the carousel haunted the Jewish fighters. "We could see a merry-go-round, we could hear music," Edelman told Krall, "and we were terribly afraid that this music would drown us out and that those people would never notice a thing: us, the struggle, the dead."[98]

Perhaps the anti-Semitism was all the more raw because of Easter's near convergence with Passover in that fateful spring of 1943. For Poles the Christian festival of crucifixion and rebirth had traditionally fueled the inflammatory blood libel of Jews as killers of Christ, and this Easter seems to have stirred those embers more than ever among rabid anti-Semites. The Jewish-Polish writer Adolf Rudnicki captured that spirit in his book *Easter*:

> As soon as the words were heard: 'You may go, the mass is finished, halleluiah, halleluiah!' the congregations hurried from the overcrowded churches, their souls still aglow, all vernal, with freshly cut flowers in their hands, towards the walls to watch the spectacle. To watch Warsaw's Paschal [Passover?] spectacle. . . . As long as there was daylight they hung out under the walls. They gazed, they talked, they regretted. They regretted the goods, the properties, the legendary Jewish gold, but, above all, the flats and houses, 'the finest houses in the city.' They said: 'Could not King Hitler have solved this question in some other way?' . . . Behind the walls the people were dying convinced that human bestiality had reached its limits. And, indeed, what more could there be: But we, who were on the spot, saw how tiny, how insignificant is human conscience. The explosions shook the earth and the streets but not the people.[99]

Mark and Ruth Skorecki heard more than their share of overt anti-Semitism, certainly enough to test their moral endurance too. The worst expressions seemed to come from gentiles who had been entrusted with the heirlooms and personal property of Jewish neighbors. "It was a terrible thing to go through, listening sometimes to the discussions of the people, because plenty people who had Jewish friends from before the war and with whom some of these Jewish people had left their possessions upon entering the ghetto, were glad to have these possessions," Ruth said, adding for good measure, "Plenty of people were like this."[100] But the Skoreckis were fighting for their lives and those of their children. There was no alternative but to grit their teeth and lock away their feelings from gentile eyes. Fear, anger, grief—emotions hard to conceal because they penetrate so deeply, taking on the character of involuntary reflexes—had to be covered over with the same outward indifference displayed by Polish anti-Semites themselves. But that was the emotional price one paid every waking hour for survival on the Aryan side, especially "on the surface."

THE LUMBERYARD	

The fact that Easter holiday fell just as Jürgen Stroop commenced burning down the ghetto only added to the emotional heaviness weighing on the Skoreckis. For in Catholic Poland, Easter was a season for being up and about, and the Skoreckis had to follow suit to show the neighbors, especially the ever suspicious janitor, Mr. Szczepan, that they were "like everybody else." They had to go to Good Friday Mass with the Piotrowskas. On Holy Saturday, when the Catholic Churches in Poland are garlanded with flowers and children accompanied by their parents bring dyed eggs and food to be blessed, the Skoreckis had to do the same. So Mark walked with Lila the mile to and from the vast Heart of Jesus Basilica at the end of Ząbkowska, where the priest sprinkled with holy water her cloth-covered plate of food—"so that the janitor would see that we were just like everybody else."

There was one Easter custom Ruth had to ad-lib herself: the tradition of exchanging Easter cards with friends and relatives. All her life she was alertly attuned to social amenities, a striver ambitious for status and desperately anxious to be liked. It meant being pleasant in public. It meant accruing the outward markers of acceptance. So she came up with the idea of sending postcards to herself. Mark and the Piotrowskas bought about ten cards, and the four of them filled in and addressed the lot, making out "as though these cards came from friends in Warsaw." A few days later Mr. Szczepan brought them to the door along with cards for the Piotrowskas, to receive the customary gratuity janitors expected for hand-delivering mail. "So I gave him a tip like everybody else," she said, throwing in for good measure a well-timed grace note: "I said to him I didn't expect so many cards."[1]

Natalia and her mother were impressed by Ruth's guile and exquisite timing. "They would never have thought of something like this," they told Ruth. "This was good for all of us, because danger to me was danger to them." This recognition was arrived at eventually by all righteous gentiles that both rescuers and the rescued were tethered to the same danger and that henceforth they would have to perform their charlatanry in nearly perfect harmony.[2]

There was still Easter dinner to endure. The Piotrowskas had invited friends and relatives, together with the Polish military man who had arranged the Skoreckis' escape from the ghetto. It was apparently a family tradition whose cancellation would have invited suspicion. Mark and Ruth had to sit through the late afternoon meal with pasted-on smiles of amiability, struggling against showing distraction, acting nonplussed when one of the guests referred (as surely one of them must have) to the smoke pluming up across the river, and feeling all the while terribly empty inside. They turned in a convincing performance despite their inner turmoil. "The friends sitting at the table didn't know with whom they had the pleasure of sharing the eggs and the egg nog," Ruth said in wry triumph. Even the Polish military man complimented them "for doing so well in our role." It was as if with each charade Mark and Ruth were committing to sensory memory another false face, a new surrogate personality to be called in from the wings whenever cued by the danger du jour. On all such occasions, particularly during that holiday occasion, Ruth locked in on one thought: "God help me, keep me in your hands, and watch over us." That religiosity would deepen over the next few years.

Too young to comprehend the historical tragedy unfolding around them, Anne and Lila never faced the challenge of constantly having to reinvent themselves day after day, as did their parents. But they had their own emotional challenges to overcome. One was a severe case of cabin fever, because, as Ruth admitted, "the kids were still locked up in the apartment." Nor was it a very big apartment. One entered it through a narrow kitchen past a wood-burning stove veiled by a lace curtain. The Piotrowskas slept here, next to the front window at the far end, their bed concealed by another curtain. The living room was scarcely larger than the kitchen. There was a built-in fireplace, plus a sofa and a dining room table. On the wall hung crosses and pictures of Jesus and family photos, including a fogged-over marriage picture of Mrs. Piotrowska and her late husband of the kind one might find in immigrant households around the turn of the century. Tall glass doors opened onto an iron-railinged balcony that jutted out two feet toward the street, running parallel to other balconies on the building's facade. And looming up over the sofa and table and chairs was the apartment's most distinctive furnishing: a massive mahogany armoire that stood stolidly against the wall next to the fireplace. Several feet deep and about as wide as it was tall (and it was seven feet tall), it had three doors, the middle and widest of which was glazed over with a tall mirror. "We bought the armoire during the war," Natalia Piotrowska says, which was when the Nazis made a lot of confiscated Jewish furniture available at cheap rates to the local population. She never volunteered where she and her mother had purchased the expensive-looking piece of furniture.[3]

In any event, these two spaces, the oblong kitchen and the cramped living room, defined the boundaries of the Skorecki sisters' existence for nearly eleven months. They could hear children playing on the grassy triangular square in front of the building and in the courtyard inside, but they were never allowed to join in the play. "They didn't understand why I never let them go down, and I couldn't explain it to them," Ruth said. When the weather was nice Ruth opened the balcony doors to let in light and fresh air.

Of the two sisters, Lila, the blond-haired and fair-complected one, was given slightly more breathing room. Ruth took her to church and occasionally on shopping trips. From time to time Natalia even took her for walks in the park, after remonstrating with Ruth that it was not good to keep a young child inside all the time. The first stroll nearly resulted in disaster. As was her wont, Ruth overdressed Lila. "You shouldn't send her out in such nice clothes, because everybody notices her more," Natalia said. "We should take her only in plain clothes, so that she wouldn't be different from other kids." Ruth never made that mistake again.

At least Lila was paroled from the apartment from time to time. Anne never ventured outdoors because of her dark curly hair and olive complexion. "My sister is lighter than me," Anne says, "so she didn't have to stay inside. I looked Jewish so I had to remain indoors."

Once Ruth and the Piotrowskas tried to change Anne's appearance by dyeing her hair. "They took bark from some tree and boiled it in real, real hot water. And they tried to dye my hair with that awful hot water on my head. But it just didn't work," Anne says. In fact, the only thing it accomplished was to accentuate the red in Anne's hair, which in blonde-haired Poland at the time was the equivalent of advertising one's Jewishness, for in prewar Poland mainly Jews had red hair.[4] So Anne stayed inside, except for late summer evenings when Ruth tied a babushka around her eldest daughter's head and held her on her lap on the front balcony to give her a little fresh air and relieve the claustrophobia.

Moreover, Anne stayed inside the mahogany armoire when strangers came to the apartment. "If anybody knocked on the door, I would go into the wardrobe where you would hang your coats," she says. "I really didn't exist," she laughs. She must have been in the armoire throughout the Easter dinner. No wonder Ruth was relieved when the company finally left.

There is a chapter in a book of survivor and rescuer testimony that conveys a sense of what young Anne's existence must have looked like to anyone who might have accidentally pulled open the glass door to the Piotrowska armoire.

It is an account by a young woman escapee from the ghetto of her visit to the apartment of a Polish rescuer. Many guests were present.

> When everybody was talking, our host gave me a sign, unnoticed by the others, to follow him into the next room. I noticed a huge wardrobe in the corner of the large room. My host led me to it. On one side it was slightly moved away from the wall. I looked behind the wardrobe and could hardly keep from crying out in surprise. I saw a small Jewish boy, dark-haired, about six years old. His brilliant dark eyes were almost all that I could see in the dark. That sight was something that shocked me terribly.
> I learned after from his mother, and from the owner of the flat, that when somebody strange was in the house the host's children took care of the little boy. They gave him his food behind the wardrobe, the night pot and everything he needed. They did this very cautiously so as not to arouse the suspicions of the neighbours or anyone dropping in.[5]

Change the gender, add a few gentile children, and the kid in the closet could have been young Anne Skorecka. There were many such prepubescent shut-ins throughout Aryan Warsaw at the time.[6]

While Anne was hiding in the armoire and the ghetto was vanishing in smoke, Hermann Höfle, the ss Sturmbannführer from Lublin who, on the morning of July 22, 1942, had stormed into the office of Judenrat head Adam Czerniakow ordering him to sign the Warsaw resettlement decree, helped clarify a conundrum that never ceased to puzzle Ruth. It was whether the Nazis in the ghetto ever felt guilty about their callousness, because surely they had loved ones themselves and could empathize with Jewish grief over family loss and separation. In the spring of 1943, after returning to Lublin, Höfle's newborn twins died of diphtheria. The ss officer broke down at the cemetery. "That is the punishment of heaven for all my misdeeds!" he shouted.[7]

Raul Hilberg, the dean of Holocaust historians, relates that tale along with its obvious moral: "It is perhaps not accidental that the Germans, who were particularly brutal in their treatment of Jewish children, were now most afraid for their own." That is indubitably true, but it remained the case that Polish Jewish children, such few as still survived, remained by far the most imperiled and that the threat came from the barrel of a Lüger as well as from childhood diseases.

One day in August 1943, as Ruth was leaving to bring Mark his lunch, Mr. Szczepan followed her through the porte cochere to the street in front of the building. To cool the living room in the late-summer heat, Ruth had started leaving the balcony doors opened during the day, and neighbors across the way in Lochowska 18 (the building is no longer standing) had noticed strange children playing in the Piotrowskas' living room. "Mrs. Skorecki, I want to ask you something," Mr. Szczepan said. "Across the street from your apartment, on the same floor, people come to me and ask if the people in your apartment are Jewish. Why are you always in the apartment? Why don't the children play with others?"

Ruth stood frozen with fear. "When he said this to me, I was sure that this was the last minute of my life," she said. Residing in Lochowska 18 at the time was a young woman who was known to fraternize with the Germans. "No one in the neighborhood knew the company she was keeping until she was dropped off one day by a big German car. Maybe she made love to them," Natalia Piotrowska surmises.[8] Maybe so, and maybe it was this young woman who commented to the janitor. In the end, though, it hardly mattered whether the suspicion was voiced by a collaborator or by an ordinary resident. Once launched in a Polish neighborhood, the rumor that a newcomer might be Jewish had the insurmountable advantage of a head start, and contingency plans had to be set in motion quickly.

Ruth's immediate challenge, however, was convincing the janitor right then and there that his informants across the street were gravely mistaken. Every Jew living "on the surface" of Aryan Warsaw sooner or later faced this challenge, if not from ordinary Poles then from szmalcowniks and blackmailers, and these challenges arose time after time. They called for quick thinking. "Very well, let's go," Vladka Meed said indignantly to szmalcowniks who accosted her in downtown Warsaw and demanded a three-thousand-zloty ransom. "You will be called to account for casting suspicion on me and for your attempts to blackmail me." They let her go. A Jewish woman who disguised her features behind dark mourning clothes used to approach strangers she caught staring at her intently on the tram and ask them for the time. Simha Rotem, who led his ZOB comrades to the Aryan side on May 9, accepted these challenges with a kind of unzipped chutzpah. When his landlady once accused him of being a Jew, Kazik said he'd prove to her that he was not; she said go ahead, prove it. "I unbuckled my belt, unbuttoned my fly, and pulled down my pants; when I was down to my underwear, she turned around and walked out. This was the kind of 'existential problem' you came across on a normal day; it was not unique at all."[9]

Ruth had to act just as quickly. She could scarcely afford the near paralysis that had gripped her at the housing bureau earlier in the spring. At first she feigned amazement. Then she reacted with stage-polished indignation. "I don't understand how people can say this," she huffed. "You see Mark every morning and evening coming and going to work. Right now I am going to him with lunch. How can these people say things like this?" She started yelling at him. Gone was the doe-eyed vulnerability she had displayed to the housing bureau clerk. There was nothing plaintive about her voice and manner now. It was the offensive defense, the scene in the middle of the street. The playacted fury probably saved the Skoreckis' lives and that of the Piotrowskas as well. Ruth had never revealed this side of her personality before, and precisely where in her psyche the alter ego had been hiding is not entirely clear. Perhaps it was in the zone of often unstated ambivalence about their origins that assimilating minorities sometimes feel—not so much self-hatred as resentment of traditionalists for clinging to ethnic habits that embarrass social strivers who seek acceptance by the majority culture, followed by guilt for feeling embarrassed in the first place. Wherever Ruth's alter ego came from, it emerged without rehearsal. Ruth simply became an anti-Semite on the spot—and so convincingly that Mr. Szczepan apologized profusely, saying he knew she was not Jewish; her papers had checked out; the housing bureau had given her a clean bill of health; she had received Easter cards and all that; but he had to raise the matter with her because "the people across the street think something is wrong."

It was a rather amazing transformation,[10] and Ruth emerged from the encounter covered with guilt. "This was a hard thing to do," she said, "to play a role like this when so many different thoughts and emotions were going through me." By going the anti-Semite one better, she was repudiating not only her own culture but also, in some respects, her very being at a time when the world of Polish Jewry was rapidly vanishing.

There was scarcely time to dwell on these thoughts as she hurried to Mark's factory. The walk seemed like miles, she said. All she could think about was the immediate peril facing her family and the Piotrowskas. "This was a dangerous thing when somebody started thinking that we were Jews," she said. Mark was terrified when Ruth brought him the news. They sat in the corner of the factory talking quietly. Later that evening when Haka dropped by while running market errands for the childless couple with whom she resided as live-in maid, they shared their predicament with her, but she could offer little else but solace. "At this time nobody could help each other, everybody had to work his own problems out for himself," Ruth said.

They temporized informing the Piotrowskas of Ruth's encounter with the janitor. There was always the danger that the two women might ask them to move out immediately, leaving them homeless and dangerously exposed. Such evictions happened all the time. Jewish hiding places on the Aryan side were constantly "burning," as the slang phrase for the discovery of Jewish flats and hideaways would have it. And thus Jews were continually changing places of abode, in some cases as often as twenty-five times, owing to blown covers, snooping janitors, or suspicious neighbors. Something always seemed to go wrong. True, the Skoreckis were different. They were not imprudent; they were clever and resourceful, and Mark brought in extra income, which also eased the burden. Still, to the Piotrowskas the Skoreckis represented potential danger, and no rescuer wished to end up like the Polish family in Łódź who were publicly hanged during the war for harboring Jews.[11] In addition to these concerns were the strains of cabin fever, which under Nazi occupation frequently worsened into "barbed wire illness" (Stacheldrahtkrankheit), with its symptoms of heightened anxiety and embittered quarreling. "The flare-ups always began with the little things, like clothes in the bathroom," remembers Teresa Prekerowa, who sheltered several Jews during the war. It could lead to dueling stereotypes. You're dirty, the Pole would tell the Jew. You're dumb, the Jew would respond. "It was often that Jews told Poles, 'We are more intelligent than you,' and it made the Poles crazy," says Prekerowa. "It was a very difficult situation."[12] In an apartment as small as that of the Piotrowskas, with two shut-in children who no matter how well behaved must have gotten underfoot from time to time, the temptation to seize an excuse for politely asking their guests to move on must have been alluring in the extreme, and the Skoreckis were too shrewd not to have sensed that enticement.[13]

In a word, Mark and Ruth had good reason to worry about how the janitor incident would affect their hosts. Would the Piotrowskas ask them to leave? There was no way of knowing in advance, and they surely must have agonized over what to do, weighing parental duty to their children against moral obligation to newfound friends. In the end the Skoreckis did what conscience dictated. "Of course, we told the ladies about the incident with the janitor because we didn't want to lie to them," Ruth said. What the Piotrowskas said when they heard the news, Ruth never revealed. But their final decision comes through loud and clear. The Skoreckis were to remain at Lochowska 15 for the time being. Whether the calculus of self-interest had influenced the Polish women's decision is pure guesswork. But it is just as likely that the Piotrowskas were gradually growing habituated to altruism as they found themselves drawn deeper into rescue activity. Or maybe both considerations were mixed together, if only because human motivations are like compounds that cannot easily be leached into constituent elements.[14]

All the same, things had changed forever at Lochowska 15. As Ruth explained the new realities, "We would have to move, but not right away but later, because to do so immediately would be suspicious."

Thus now began an elaborate charade to deflect suspicion, a pantomime of normality, an extraordinary effort to appear ordinary. Ruth started shopping more often. She took Lila down to the play area in the courtyard and for walks.

"They had to see us going to work, to shop, etc.," she said. "We tried to keep up our face," she added. Mark was himself a pretty good chameleon, and cunning as well. The next evening, on his way home from work, he invited the janitor to visit the factory and help himself to the scrap lumber lying around the yard. And when the janitor did drop by the factory Mark told him to come again any time he needed wood for cooking and heating. In a sense he was simply showing off, for by now Mark was a foreman with a lot of authority and status around the factory. But, at the same time, the ruse reflected a shrewd understanding of the economy of gossip and envy: "We did this so that the janitor could tell the people about Mark and his position," Ruth explained. "So that people would ask themselves: how could a Jew work in an official place like this?" The ploy worked, or at least Ruth believed it did: "It took some of the suspicion away from the people."

Meanwhile, she began preparing the ground for the inevitable move from Lochowska 15, casually letting everyone around the neighborhood know that she and Mark were looking for a larger place to live, "in order to make the people think we weren't running." They had two criteria: Mark wanted to reside within walking distance of the factory, and Ruth wanted to live beyond the snooping purview of immediate neighbors. It was not an easy bill to fill. They looked for months.

Through it all, dark-featured Anne continued her exile inside the apartment. The fear never let up. "We were still afraid," Ruth said, "and we heard so many terrible things happening to Jewish people who were discovered." Yet in early November 1943, just as the Skoreckis were about to find a new place to live, old friends from Schultz's and the brothers Tempelhof were also facing horrendous events in the Lublin District.

Back in October 1942, while struggling with the Wehrmacht and the German armaments czars for control of Jewish labor, Himmler had predicted that even these work Jews would one day disappear "according to the Führer's wishes." But no one could have foreseen this happening as suddenly as it did, particularly so soon after the relocation of plant and personnel from the Warsaw ghetto to the ss work camps at Poniatów and Trawniki. The ss had invested much time and trouble in effecting the transfer. Some higher-ups in the organization had a vested interest in seeing these reconstituted enterprises yield a profit. But then occurred an abrupt change in short-term direction, captured in the terse language of a German arms inspector's report, which stated that on November 2 and 3, 1943, both the Schultz and the Többens factories suffered "an unexpected and complete withdrawal" of their Jewish labor. The Aktion was given the code name Erntefest, or "Harvest Festival."[15]

For eight months Himmler's obsessive need to hide the evidence of Nazi mass murder had been preparing the ground for this new killing spree. Starting in March 1943 the Reichsführer-ss intensified his effort to exhume the burial pits in such primitive killing centers as Chełmno, Bełżec, Sobibór, and Treblinka and to incinerate and rebury the human remains. At Treblinka the Nazis brought in an excavator, built roasting racks consisting of railroad rails laid atop concrete pillars, used petrol-doused brushwood to fire the corpse-laden grill (later adding fat women because they burned faster), and then crushed the residual bones with round sticks. The fact that Auschwitz was now operating at peak capacity and that Jewish raw material in Treblinka's supply basin had been depleted was one motive for the mopping-up operation. But German military reverses on the Russian front were probably the paramount motive in Himmler's eyes. For the ss chief reacted angrily when he learned in March that Aktion Reinhard head Odilo Globocnik had disregarded orders to commence the body-burning operation, preferring to bury bronze tablets with the corpses "stating that it was we who had the courage to carry out this gigantic task." And Himmler's obsession grew even more compulsive following the outbreak of ghetto uprisings in Warsaw, Vilna, and Białystok. The ss brought in a second excavator. From April through July 1943 the outdoor cremation at Treblinka went on day and night. To the thousand or so Jewish Sonderkommandos who carried the corpses to the roaster and then hauled away and reburied the bone chips and ashes, it was clear that the end was near for the them too. Train arrivals delivering fresh victims had slackened since May. The rows of clothing and shoes in the sorting yard had eventually disappeared. Stripped of their delusions that work might bring salvation, the Jewish workers at Treblinka staged an armed revolt and breakout on the hot afternoon of August 1 or 2 (details vary in the memory of surviving eyewitnesses), while the camp commander was roaring drunk. All but one hundred prisoners were eventually recaptured and killed.

In mid-October a more extensive revolt and breakout occurred at Sobibór, including the axe-murders of most of the ss staff, and it sent shock waves throughout the Generalgouvernement. Hans Frank convened a special conference in Kraków to assess the security situation in the Lublin-area camps. If one thousand work Jews at Sobibór could wreak such havoc, what damage might forty-five thousand work Jews collected at Majdanek, Poniatów, and Trawniki cause? The Frank conference commissioned a special report. But Himmler, anxious to contain the contagion of Jewish rebellion and conscious of the approaching Russian front, was not about to wait on a report. He decided to act immediately as well as comprehensively. Recent events had shown that piecemeal liquidation of the camps ran the risk of triggering a chain reaction of camp rebellions. Himmler would therefore kill that Jewish remnant all at once. It was, to quote historian Christopher Browning, "the single largest German killing operation against Jews in the entire war." Such was the background to the "Harvest Festival."[16]

Shrouded in secrecy, the Aktion was planned out as a military operation. Police units and ss forces, including elements of the Waffen-ss, collected in the Lublin District from throughout the Generalgouvernement. In late October Jewish work details from Majdanek, Poniatów, and Trawniki dug trenches, some of them zig-zag to foster the illusion they were part of air-raid defenses, on the outskirts of the three camps. On the evening of November 2 there was a crowded staff meeting of the commanders of the police and ss units and camp commandants. The actual shooting began somewhere between six and seven the next morning following roll call, when Jewish prisoners were pulled aside, ordered to strip and heap their clothes in a pile, then marched to the killing field with their hands behind their head and told to file into the trenches and lay face down. Sitting on the edge of the burial pits were members of the ss security police, or sd. Each was armed with a submachine gun, and behind them stood other sd members ready to reload guns passed back to them by the triggermen. As one batch of Jewish victims was slaughtered, the next group was ordered to lay atop the corpses of the preceding group. The shooting lasted the entire day, with loudspeakers blaring music at full blast in a vain attempt to drown out the screaming and staccato gunfire. "The whole business was the most gruesome I had ever seen in my life," one perpetrator later testified. At Trawniki, where workers from Big Schultz's were now concentrated, the November 3 death toll ranges between six and ten thousand. At Poniatów, which was liquidated the following day, the body count reached fourteen thousand, most of them workers from the Többens clothing enterprise—so much for Többens's promise of safety and good treatment.[17]

Very few Jewish workers and their families survived Harvest Festival. One woman from Többens who did escape described how the workers and their families in early November were gathered in the camp hall, then separated by sex, whereupon the Germans marched them to the woods and forced them to strip and hand over their money and jewelry. Miraculously, she still had a young daughter. She explains what happened next:

> We undressed quickly and, our arms uplifted, we went in the direction of the ditches we had dug ourselves. The graves which were two metres deep were full of naked bodies. My neighbour from the hut with her fourteen-year-old, fair-haired and innocent-looking daughter seemed to be looking for a comfortable place. While they were approaching the place an ss man charged his rifle and told them: "Don't hurry." Nevertheless we lay down quickly, in order to avoid looking at the dead. My little

daughter was quaking with fear, and asked me to cover her eyes. I embraced her head; my left hand I put on her eyes while in my right I held her hands. In this way we lay down, our faces turned downwards.

Shots were fired; I felt a sharp pain in my hand, and the bullet pierced the skull of my daughter. Another shot was heard very close nearby. I was utterly shaken, turned giddy and lost consciousness. I heard the groaning of a woman nearby, but it came to an end after a few seconds. . . .

Time passed very slowly. When darkness fell the Ukrainians came back once more and covered the grave with spruce foliage. I was terribly frightened. I thought that they might burn the bodies. I wanted to shout that I was still alive, but the words stuck in my throat. When I perceived that they were going off I allowed myself to raise my head. I glanced at my daughter. Her face was usually oval, but now it was round and as pale as a sheet. With my lips I touched her back and hair, and her little hand slipped out of my hand. I looked at my own left arm, which ached very much and I saw two holes and blood trickling from them.

With three other naked woman she managed to crawl from beneath the foliage covering the ditch and escape into the forest, later buying clothing with money secreted on her body.[18]

The largest death toll occurred at Majdanek, where an estimated 16,500 to 18,000 prisoners, some of them brought in from nearby subcamps, were machine-gunned to death on November 3. By this time Dr. Thaddeus Stabholz had been transferred to Auschwitz, which ironically saved his life. Earlier at Majdanek, when an ulcer developed on his leg because of abrasions caused by wooden shoes, Stabholz had been selected to be sent to the gas chamber. But through a Pole he managed to get word of his plight to Henry Tempelhof, who then notified a mutual physician friend. "They swapped me with a body of a dead prisoner and got me out." Then Stabholz was sent to the camp hospital and, shortly after recuperation and release, transferred to Auschwitz. "I owe Henry my life," he says.[19]

The brothers Tempelhof, along with Henry's good friend Nahum Remba, presumably perished on November 3, 1943. Like the rest, their bodies were cremated in the ditch where they died. For weeks a "bestial stench" hung over the Lublin District caused by the reek of burning flesh.[20]

There was a half-built office attached to a warehouse in the rear of the lumberyard supplying the stable and barracks factory where Mark worked. A seven-foot-high wooden fence with two gates encircled the yard, just beyond which, on the same lot, stood a feed store. Constructed from blocks of straw and mud, the office was little more than a hovel. It lacked flooring and had only one door and a single window. There was no porch, and snow often drifted under the door. Most big-city families, even in war-ravaged Warsaw, would never have chosen to live in such rude quarters unless they had something to hide, and Mark, who was now being paid higher wages and enjoyed measurable status around the area, could certainly have afforded better accommodations for his family. One locational advantage was the absence of nosy neighbors down the hall, but that did not mean they were completely out of sight. Abutting the yard was a three-story, low-rise apartment building, cut up into interior courtyards, with a crumbling brick facade and wooden balconies. These had been Jewish courtyards until the creation of the closed ghetto in November 1940. Now the apartment building was occupied by Poles from the left bank who had been relocated here because their own homes had fallen inside the newly designated Jewish quarter. "We traded places with the Jews," said one old-time resident who had lived on Nowolipki Street before the war.[21] More menacing was the five-story apartment building across the street, with its ground-level bars and tobacco shops. It too had probably been a largely Jewish building, if only because this section of north Praga had until very recently been mainly Jewish. The high-rise had a mansard roof, and windows in its top two or three floors overlooked the lumberyard.

If the lumberyard was hedged all around by Poles who had just come into a windfall of expropriated Jewish property and therefore had selfish reasons to think ill of the people with whom they had swapped places, Mark still felt impelled to ask one of the bosses for permission to billet his family in the office shack. He decided to approach Mr. Smolenski, but doing so was a huge risk. As Ruth herself admitted, "this was very dangerous for Mark because the boss might get suspicious, and we didn't know what kind of person our boss was. Was he for or against the Germans?" As it happened, Smolenski was a Polish military veteran with ties to the Home Army, and he was decidedly hostile to the Germans. But, like many members of the AK, he felt scant solidarity with the Jews qua Jews: among North Praga Jews before the war, he had been regarded as a notorious anti-Semite. A fellow survivor whom the Skoreckis got to know in postwar New Orleans grew up on Ząbkowska Street not far from the lumberyard, and he remembers Smolenski standing inside his courtyard gate on Saturday mornings throwing buckets of water on Jews as they passed by on their way to synagogue. "I said to the Skoreckis, 'How could you have worked for him? He was a very mean man.'"[22]

The answer was simple: "We had no choice," according to Ruth. Up until now they had been having slight success finding a residence that met their stringent requirements of job proximity and neighborhood privacy. Time was starting to run out. They could not postpone the move indefinitely, especially because Ruth had already spread the word around Lochowska Street that they were looking for larger quarters.

So, Mark made his request of Mr. Smolenski, confecting what he believed was a plausible rationale for wanting to move into the shack.[23] Entering the plant office one late autumn day, he told his boss, "Listen, I have to move from the place I'm staying now because some relatives of the people with whom we're living were coming, and I have to give up the room, and you know that I don't want to have to rent an apartment far away from work. I was looking around here in the neighborhood, and I wonder if it is possible to take the office shack and fix this up and move in with my family. At the same time my wife would be there the whole day, and she could keep an eye on the lumberyard."

Smolenski was more than slightly incredulous. Was Mark sure he wanted to move his family into this shack? There was no toilet, and water would have to be fetched from an outside spigot. Mark said he still wanted the place. He would be close to his family, he reiterated. Smolenski said he would have to talk it over with his partner. Two days and several anxious prayers later, the Skoreckis learned Smolenski's decision: It was okay to move in. Give him a little time to get it fixed up, Smolenski told Mark. Mark thanked him but said he could not wait. He would do the fixing up himself after hours and on weekends. His haste to move in must have aroused further suspicions.

In any event, on the very same day that Smolenski gave his consent, Mark moved Ruth and his daughters into the unfinished office. Around the Lochowska Street neighborhood, when word got out they were relocating to a shack in the lumberyard instead of a bigger apartment, Ruth covered the first lie with a new one about how Mark had been asked to double up as watchman at the lumberyard, forcing a change in moving plans. Now the Skoreckis had two lies to synchronize: one to Smolenski about having to make room for the Piotrowskas' relatives, and another to Lochowska Street neighbors about Mark's being asked to add security guard duties to his other responsibilities around the plant, which sounded plausible except that it entailed moving his family into an unfinished shack. If Mark was such an important person around the barracks and stable factory, why would he have to live in a hovel? Catching the Skoreckis in a contradiction would obviously take little effort on the part of anyone willing to invest the time, and Mark and Ruth necessarily had to stay on their toes simply to keep their stories straight, depending on whom they wished to deceive. But this is what life on the Aryan side was like for Jews attempting to make it "on the surface": entanglement in a snowballing skein of knotted fibs and self-evident lies, often leading to exposure, imprisonment, and death. And what was truly ironic about this survival-driven need to lie was a hangover of guilt for lying in the first place. Ruth worried constantly that she might internalize character traits she scorned under normal circumstances.[24]

According to Ruth, the family moved into their new home a month before Christmas, but the relocation more likely took place in early November. They bought two beds. The Piotrowskas lent them a few pots and cooked their first meal. Someone else lent them an armoire in which to hang their clothes, and curiously, unlike the other items mentioned in her memoir, Ruth described this piece of furniture exactly: it was a "cedar wardrobe." The armoire was not large enough to contain all their belongings, so additional clothing was hung on the wall, then covered with sheets. Shortly after moving in Mark bought a wood stove and rigged up a vent and pipes. Every day after the five o'clock whistle, and on weekends as well, he made home improvements, often working with Ruth until late in the evening. Ruth never said whether her husband laid down a wooden floor or framed the door and window, but judging from his meticulous craft standards, he likely did. To insulate the shack from the skin-piercing drafts of the Polish winter, on the inside walls he nailed black tarpaper of the kind then used in stables, and Ruth painted the paper white to make the shack less dark and gloomy. She partitioned off the kitchen with heavy material wired to the ceiling. To make up for the lack of indoor plumbing she kept two buckets next to the stove, one filled with clean water and the other with dirty water. For the next ten months this rude warehouse office was to be the Skoreckis' home. "Even so, this was to us a beautiful palace," Ruth said, "because no one was watching me as some of our neighbors had done at the apartment house."

That was not entirely true. From the five-story building on the other side of Ząbkowska Street tenants were still able to look down into the lumberyard, which actually made it more important that Mark and Ruth maintain the appearances of domesticity. Leaving the girls locked up inside the office shack, Ruth began visiting the big public market across the street where every Thursday and Friday morning peasants from the country would bring in chickens, butter, cheese, and eggs. "It was a very, very big yard," remembers Solomon Radasky. "A few hundred feet, may four or five hundred feet long, and about two or three hundred feet wide, maybe more."[25] Ruth strolled among the stands, squeezing the produce, exchanging pleasantries with vendors and fellow shoppers, and hoping all the while that the ss would not ask to see her identity papers. These daily shopping trips were fraught with danger. Toward the end of 1943, as a result of continuing military reversals on the eastern front and the increasing tempo of resistance activity inside Poland, especially among Jews, the Germans intensified their crackdown on the subjugated population. The ss and Polish police started blockading entire sections of the city, spot-checking for Kennkarten and other papers, often shooting on the spot Jews and "unregistered enemies." The deepening repression spurred the creation of several so-called defense committees to safeguard Polish homes from "misfortune"—a euphemism for Jews. "It is becoming more and more imminently dangerous to live illegally without a hide-out," the ghetto historian and archivist Emmanuel Ringelblum wrote from his hideout on the Aryan side. But even hideouts were no longer safe. Excavated under a Polish garden, Ringelblum's "melina" was blown in March 1944, when he, his wife, and their thirteen-year-old son were hauled away to the infamous Pawiak Prison and murdered.[26]

The most dangerous places to be in these parlous times, however, were public markets of the kind Ruth frequented every day. These venues attracted prey and predator alike, and increasingly more of the latter as the Nazis stepped up their security checks. Hardly a day passed that the ss did not run a dragnet through the open-air stands at the Ząbkowska Street market, searching for illegal Jews as well as Polish politicians and military personnel. Ruth was constantly treading into this danger because it was necessary to offset the other continual danger in the Skoreckis' lives: the danger of arousing "the suspiciousness of people noticing that we lived here in this kind of place." She never went into the bustling public market without fear in her heart and a prayer on her lips, begging God to "save me from the ss, make them blind to me," to use her words. "I was afraid that the minute they came to me that they would see right away who I was." The police and ss never did ask her for her papers. She was convinced it was because He had indeed heard her prayers. "God was good to us. He all the time was watching," she said.

Ruth's unusual circumstances forced her to do another thing Jews living on the surface seldom attempted: seek out new friends from among the local population. It was generally understood that Aryanized Jews were better off remaining wary of strangers and confining personal contacts to Poles whose reliability was beyond question. Yet, given the conspicuous isolation of the Skoreckis' existence inside the lumberyard, excessive caution and circumspection carried risks of their own.[27] Why were they staying inside all the time unless they had something to hide? Why didn't they socialize with the neighbors? Ruth desperately wanted to keep such questions out of circulation. Thus to prevent neighborhood gossip, on her return from the market Ruth made a practice of stopping by the neighborhood drygoods store where she bought her elastic and thread. She became friendly with the owners, too, commiserating with them about the fate of Polish relatives who had been arrested and taken away, shaking her head in horror and disbelief over "what the Germans were doing to all of us, Jews and non-Jews," without ever once letting on that she herself was Jewish. Ruth had a gift for empathy—a friendly ear, a warm smile, a soft shoulder. And she was becoming adept at fending off suspicions even before they found voice. She and her family were living as watchguards in the neighborhood shack until they could find a larger and nicer place to live nearby, she volunteered. It was a convincing lie. The only problem was, the fib failed to jibe with tales previously spun for the benefit of Smolenski and their Lochowska Street neighbors, which meant she now had to juggle three sets of lies while keeping straight in her own mind which lie she had told to whom. Nonetheless, Ruth went through this pantomime day in and day out, increasing the danger on one front in order to mitigate it on others, and for the same reason: "I had to keep up with the non-Jews."

Keeping up with the gentiles also meant being conspicuous about celebrating Christmas, which came around within weeks of their relocation to the office shack. Because their front yard was visible to two or three floors of neighbors in the high-rise building across Ząbkowska Street, there was no way the Skoreckis could observe the Yuletide in private. According to Ruth, Natalia Piotrowska, who had been stopping by regularly to help her spruce up the rude office shack and lift her spirits, came up with the idea of bringing the holidays to the lumberyard. But it may have been Ruth who suggested the idea. Natalia's mother, Katarzyna, had died of dysentery in November, shortly after the Skoreckis had moved out. It was the third major family loss in three years: first Natalia had lost her older brother in January 1940, then her father two years later, and now her mother, who was only sixty-four years old at the time of death.[28] With the most important family celebration on the Christian calendar fast approaching, Natalia must have felt terribly alone and stricken with grief. Only eleven years her senior, Ruth immediately reached out to Natalia, like a surrogate big sister or a young aunt. "When the mother was dead, I told the daughter that during the holidays I would celebrate and she would come to my house," Ruth explained. "She deserved this because she had been with me whenever I needed her. The whole time from the beginning she never let me down." The two women were starting to bond through a common bereavement stronger even than the shared foxhole mentality that had originally brought them together. A short time later, Natalia came up with what arguably had been Ruth's idea all along.

"We will all come to you, and you make a Christmas tree," Natalia suggested to Ruth. "We will bring our gifts and put them under your tree. And before Midnight Mass on Christmas Eve we'll come to your house, and the next day you will cook all the things we eat on Christmas—there is a whole course. Then we will all come to eat at your house on Christmas Day." Natalia had thought things through down to the smallest detail.

On Christmas Eve Natalia helped Ruth decorate the tree and brought presents from her Lochowska 15 apartment to place under it. Before Midnight

Mass, thirteen of her neighborhood friends and relatives, plus the military man, stopped by on their way to church. The next morning Natalia and a few others arrived early to unwrap presents. Later in the day the other guests from the night before showed up for the traditional Christmas Day meal, and afterward everyone spilled out into the yard. They drank heartily. They sang Christmas carols—"the lady [Natalia] started teaching the kids to sing them." They stayed until the evening. The planning had been flawless. Everything came off without a hitch. "For the people living in the neighborhood, they saw we had guests for Christmas dinner," Ruth said. "With this we passed like everybody else."

But the make-believe Christmas was scarcely a time for the Skoreckis to let down their hair. Only two of the fifteen guests—Natalia and the Polish military man—were supposed to know that the Skoreckis were Jewish. During those two days of merriment every word had to be measured, every smile chiseled on with artisanal care. Impromptu fun was risky business. Mirth was calculated; relaxation, just plain hard work. "It was hard to be the hostess, hard to play this role, hard not to show on our faces what we were thinking in our hearts," Ruth said. And when the guests finally left, she added, with a huge sigh of relief, "We just said thank God that no one had discovered us for what we really were."

Ruth never said so directly, but the Piotrowskas were devout Catholics. Natalia, for her part, went to church every Sunday, and more frequently in May and June because of the special celebrations, prayers, and observances that clustered around that time of year. Sometimes she went in the evening too. The Heart of Jesus Basilica was about one mile away, not too long a walk if you were serious about your religion.[29] Soon, with Lila usually in tow, Ruth started tagging along. Partly it was for protective coloration—"to show the people around that I wasn't different from them," as she put it. And when she entered and sat down inside the Basilica, "I did everything that everybody else did. I never made a false move to make someone superstitious." Whether this included also attending confession Ruth failed to say. But it is evident she participated in the rest of the liturgy. She and Lila memorized the catechism and the Catholic prayers. Clutching her prayer book, Ruth sang hymns, crossed herself, and knelt when the rest of the congregation was cued to give thanks. At the time Ruth attended Heart of Jesus, the Order of Silesians, famed for their ministry to young people, had been brought to the church to work with the young toughs and juvenile delinquents who still populate this part of Praga, known to locals as *Szmulki*, Polish slang for a place where crime is rampant, where it is unsafe to venture. "This is a unique church," says its current pastor, Father Jan Gniedziejko.[30]

Heart of Jesus is also vast, perhaps the largest church in Warsaw. Built between 1907 and 1923, with construction funds provided by the aristocratic Radziwill family, the structure was modeled after St. Peter's Basilica in Rome, down to and including twenty-four granite columns brought in from the Holy See. The interior, except for twelve Corinthian columns made of polished marble running down each side of the nave and the massive chandeliers hanging between each of them, is sparsely furnished, as befits a working-class congregation. Even today there are no pews and benches, only folding wooden seats closely packed, separated by four-inch-wide prayer rails. Paintings of the disciples and Jesus in various stages of crucifixion fill panels along each wall, both above and between the confessional booths. And to the left of the altar is a portrait of a black Madonna and child, like its famous original in Częstochowa. High overhead near the dome of the apse is a bas-relief of a many-branched silver candelabra that blazes forth from its gold-encrusted background whenever the late afternoon sun slants through the stained glass windows of the basilica's northwestern wall.

At first, keeping mind and soul together during the hour-long services must have taxed Ruth's composure. Some prayers can go on for at least five minutes, doubtless causing such religious impostors as Ruth more than once to mumble the words while praying that no one nearby noticed her discomfort. And what did she do during the communion part of the service, when parishioners step into the aisle and kneel to receive the Host and wine from the priest as the altar boy cups a napkin under each communicant's chin? Not everyone takes communion at each service, and Ruth probably stayed put as often as she could. But it is hardly likely she was able to evade this sacrament for the entire year she frequented services at the basilica. Even in a parish of twenty-five thousand she would have been familiar to regulars because of her gregariousness if nothing else, which though an ally in recent close calls was an enemy of the anonymity she now must have craved. As was the case with many other Aryanized Jews forced to don the camouflage of Catholicism, Sundays and other Catholic religious holidays were usually the worst time of the week or, to use Meed's words, "a particularly excruciating ordeal." All Jews could do was sit and listen to the murmured prayers of nearby votaries while visualizing murdered parents in their Jewish prayer shawls lighting sabbath candles.[31] Ruth herself attended Catholic services with the same double consciousness— doing as the Romans did yet knowing all the while, as she put it, that "in my heart, of course, I was a Jew." One can easily imagine Ruth mentally transfiguring the silver candelabra high above the altar into a Jewish menorah and then breathing more easily after the priest wiped clean the sacramental chalices, a telltale sign that Mass was drawing to a close.

Yet for Ruth the playacting at Catholicism was no empty ritual as it was for most Jews trying to make it "on the surface." In fact, after a while she began to enjoy going to Heart of Jesus, so much so that Lila, who had never been exposed to Judaism before the war, eventually crossed the line between pantomime and reality and became a Catholic girl, largely, one suspects, because of her mother's devout example. "My sister really took to the religion," Anne says. "It became her real faith." Not that Ruth ever crossed that line herself, but she did take church attendance more seriously than most Jews who mimed Catholicism merely for survival's sake, in the process developing a sort of natural, instinctive ecumenism. "I explain it this way," she philosophized later in life: "Whether you are a Jew praying in a church or a Catholic praying in a synagogue, when you are honest and praying to God, it is no difference where you pray. I was happy to come into a holy place like a church, in the first place to show people around that I wasn't different from them, and in the second place because I had no holy place to go. So, I held the prayer book and prayed to God to save us from those who might hurt us."

But the more deeply Ruth immersed herself in Catholicism, the more fervently she attempted to reconnect with Judaism. This was a new departure, for she had never been particularly religious before the war. "I was not strictly an Orthodox Jew," she said. Moreover, a new openness to religion was also unusual among survivors, since the more common reaction to wartime tribulations was a loss of faith, not renewed piety. After all, what kind of God would allow innocent babies to be slaughtered?[32] You really did need the patience of Job to accept God's ineffable ways. But Ruth went against the grain, never once questioning the divine order of things. Instead she became a modern-day Marrano, like the crypto-Jews in post-Inquisition Spain who practiced Judaism secretly while outwardly embracing Christianity. "I was in the role of two religions," Ruth said, "doing what the Catholics did and doing what I was supposed to do as a Jew."

Or at least she tried to do what religious Jews were supposed to do respecting Jewish law, but following those commandments to the letter was largely impossible in wartime Poland. Ruth resorted to improvisation, praying directly to God for special dispensations normally granted by rabbinic courts and Talmudic scholars. During the 1943 Jewish New Year (Rosh Hashanah), while the Skoreckis were still living with the Piotrowskas at Lochowska 15, Ruth, to use her words, "prayed to God and told him that I couldn't observe the Holiday like I was supposed to." On Yom Kippur, the Jewish calendar's most sacrosanct day, she fed the children but refrained, along with Mark, from eating the entire day. "I felt better for having fasted. I had done something I was supposed to do and which was part of me," she said.

She remembered vaguely that the Torah was read at Monday and Thursday services, but according to Orthodoxy only men were supposed to read the

Torah.[33] So Ruth improvised by fasting on those two mornings. "I never in my life did this before, but in this time I was sure, I don't know now why, that this had to help me," she said. Maybe so, but Ruth was taking a chance by fasting so regularly. People were in the habit of dropping by unexpectedly to see the Piotrowskas and were usually offered a midmorning snack for hospitality's sake. Often the question came up why Ruth never joined in. "I told them I had an upset stomach and I couldn't hold anything down," she said. She hated to fib, violating as it did norms of personal probity that had governed her conduct before the war. "It was very hard to have to come out with lies like this," she said, "but God was my witness that I was not a real liar, but just to save four lives." Yet more lies in addition to those she had already told imperiled the very lives she was trying to save. There were only so many times you could have indigestion before people started to wonder why.

Ruth began taking even greater risks after the family relocated to the relative anonymity of the office shack. The principal risk was attempting to keep a kosher kitchen. The practice seemed to defy all reason and common sense, considering the circumstances. Certainly it was impracticable. But Ruth persisted because observing kashruth was one of women's central duties under Jewish law, and it was, she believed, the very least she could do. Thus, whenever meat was available she soaked it for a half an hour in one of the buckets she kept next to the stove, then immersed it in salt for another sixty minutes. Entering her kitchen understandably required top-secret clearance. The curtains were always tightly drawn. "Maybe this was foolish to do this," she confessed. "Somebody might see us." Mark thought it was more than foolish: he said it was downright reckless. But Ruth was headstrong and held her ground against Mark. "The whole time I was playing the role of a non-Jew I did this," she said of her improvisational kitchen Judaism.

Ruth even tried to fulfill the commandment that Jewish woman light candles on Sabbath eve, which was almost as chancy as trying to keep kosher. She knew it was a big risk. "This was dangerous. There was a night watchman," she said. Ruth rationalized the gamble by saying it was not "a big candle." Instead, on Friday evenings she lit small candles and placed them on the stove and around the kitchen, but always in irregular order, not side by side as custom required, so as to be as inconspicuous as possible. Ruth was facile with quick explanations. "When somebody came in and asked why do you have candles," Anne explains, "my mother said, 'Well, the lights went out. We don't have any electricity.'" Ruth's religious risk taking, however, drove Mark to distraction.

He had every reason to be concerned. The night watchman was no ordinary Pole. He was Ukrainian, and Ukrainians were notorious for virulent anti-Semitism—and their meanness too, according to Ruth. Not all of them fit this mold, and numerous stories exist of Ukrainians who rescued and helped Jews during the Nazi occupation. But Ukrainian history was famous for having cultured a hatred of Jews, and the night watchman enjoyed scant immunity.[34] "We were very afraid of him, from having listened to him talk about the Jews," Ruth confessed. The Skoreckis never felt relaxed in his presence. Frequently he stopped by the shack on his evening rounds to get a cup of coffee, and whenever he was in the yard Ruth made Anne and Lila say their bedtime prayers loud enough for him to hear. "Sometimes he told us that the kids said the prayers so beautifully it was just a pleasure to listen to them," Ruth said. The prayers seem to have dispelled any suspicions the night watchman might be harboring about the Skoreckis. But Mark's irritation at her compulsive extemporizing of Jewish religious custom burned stronger than ever. What might she do next? Keeping a kosher kitchen and lighting Sabbath candles while Jew haters roamed the yard was like sticking your head in the lion's mouth. Ruth was not to be deterred, however. "I was so deeply sure that this was helping me that I wouldn't listen to him," she said of Mark's admonitions.

And herein lay the basis of her obsessive need to seek anchorage in Jewish traditionalism, "like somebody drowning in the water trying to catch whatever he could to save him," as she once put it. For over and above any wish she may have felt to atone for becoming a make-believe Catholic was an even more primal need to assert control over larger-than-life forces. "I believed something had to have saved us," she often remarked of her deepening involvement in the spiritual. And the only coherent thread she could discern in recent events was the miraculous. This metaphysical outlook was shared by several Jewish survivors who tried to "live on the surface" or hide out in attics and bunkers. If people in wartime Poland prayed a lot, it was because, as Adina Blady Szwajger has written, "the supernatural had somehow become closer" and perhaps more necessary.[35] Except for Ruth, the supernatural had become almost palpable.

For one, she felt enormously lucky. Many refugees from the ghetto had to stay locked up all the time. Several who ventured out in public lost their lives simply "because of their language, face, or personality," Ruth said. But the Skoreckis, or at least most of them, were not forced to live like hermits. Ruth could walk the streets, although nervously. Lila could attend church and find childhood solace in organized religion. Mark had a job—and, after the turn of the year, a good-paying one at that. "In this hard life, we were lucky to be together, to have Mark working, and to be able to go to the market," she said.

But Ruth also felt pangs of guilt about the good fortune because it involved more than one individual, which was rarer. "I knew very well that we were the only whole family that ever got out of the ghetto," she said, and then conceded in the same breath, "It was very dangerous to be together with the whole family." Of course, what Ruth failed to add is that the danger probably stemmed from her decision to keep the Skoreckis intact against all better judgment and good advice. There is little doubt that the "Aryan side" dangers faced continually by the family would have diminished appreciably had Ruth consented to send the girls to a convent, especially Anne, the child who had to be physically hidden by parents obliged only to hide their Jewishness.

Thus the more Ruth inventoried her good fortune and wrestled with guilt, the more convinced she became that something other than blind luck was guiding the Skorecki destiny. Indeed, from December 1941 on, the Skoreckis seemed, from Ruth's perspective, to have been blessed with a kind of divine immunity. And so she intended to do everything possible to keep the miracles on schedule, down to and including improvising obedience to Jewish law despite the entailment of yet further risks. "You think that when you do this," she said, "you believe with all your mind and heart that this will help you."

Ruth never took the supernatural for granted. In her mind, miracles did not simply happen; they had to be coaxed and acknowledged. And she continued coaxing them for the rest of her life. "My mother had her own way of talking to God," Anne says. "With her it was very private. She tried not to let anyone see her, but I know she did it."

Thus, if Ruth practiced Judaism by stealth, it was a way, in her words, both "to thank God for being so good to us" and to gain power over events that seemed opaque to human reason. Or was the good fortune that had befallen the Skoreckis since arriving on the Aryan side the result of miracles or mundane altruism, sometimes heroic, but mostly not? In Nazi-occupied Poland even charity was fraught with ambiguity. Nothing was as it seemed.

"You Poles are a strange people," an ss official once told an informer. "Nowhere in the world is there another nation which has so many heroes and so many denouncers."[36] The Nazi's bafflement is shared by most students of Polish conduct during the Second World War. The country defies facile generalizations. For example, in any comparison of national responses to the Holocaust, Poland, along with its Baltic neighbors, is practically off the scale when it comes to Jewish victimization, and for good reason: over 90 percent of the country's prewar Jewish population perished at the hands of the Germans and their native collaborators. Every known precondition of genocide seems to have been present in wartime Poland. Its dismembered territory fell squarely within the ss command zone, where overwhelming force and terror left scant room for dissent and evasion. Polish anti-Semitism, a deeply embedded cultural tradition, had achieved stunning political fulfillment just before the war. Indeed, on the eve of the Holocaust few Polish gentiles were willing to acknowledge that their Jewish compatriots fell within the national "universe of obligation—that circle of persons to whom obligations are owed, to whom the rules apply, and whose injuries call for the expiation by the community," to use Helen Fein's often-quoted definition of "common ground."[37]

Finally, there was the ethical failure of the church, everywhere the custodian of the collective conscience by virtue of its monopoly on moral sanctions. In Bulgaria steadfast opposition from the leader of the Orthodox faith succeeded in staying the hand of a native bureaucracy otherwise inclined to collaborate with the Final Solution. In wartime Poland, by contrast, the Catholic Church acquiesced in the persecution of the Jews. The Papacy has to shoulder a large share of the blame. Apart from issuing timid statements concerning the wrongness of racial distinctions, never once did the Pope denounce Nazi mass murder as a cardinal sin. In 1936, the primate of Poland, Cardinal August Hlond, whose brother had once headed Heart of Jesus, said it was immoral to hate yet endorsed the "moral" struggle against Jewish atheism, communism, and pornography and condoned boycotts of Jewish businesses. The cardinal's moral equivocation set the tone during the Nazi occupation. The hierarchy never made a move to squelch a rabble-rousing Warsaw priest who filled the columns of the fascist press with anti-Semitic propaganda.[38]

Yet Poland also stands out for its Good Samaritanism—or at least individual Poles stand out. No other country approximates its honor roll of "righteous gentiles," the title bestowed by the Yad Vashem Holocaust Martyrs and Heroes Remembrance Authority in Jerusalem on non-Jewish rescuers.[39] Since 1963, spurred by the Eichmann trial, the state of Israel has approached this matter with utmost seriousness. Achieving coveted "righteous gentile" status is exceedingly difficult. Candidates must be nominated by those they helped rescue, and their cases fully documented. A commission headed for many years by Judge Moshe Bejski, formerly of Działoszyce, then vets their credentials. Ordinary acts of kindness are insufficient. Rescuers had to have acted for humanitarian motives alone. They must have risked their lives. And they cannot have received remuneration, although rent and food payments are permissible. Candidates who meet these stringent qualifications are flown to Israel and honored at a solemn tree-planting ceremony along Yad Vashem's Avenue of the Righteous. There they are presented with a medal bearing the Talmudic inscription, "Whoever saves a single soul, it is as if he had saved the whole world." Some even receive pensions.[40] As of 1997 slightly more than thirteen thousand medals have been awarded by Yad Vashem, and Poles have received 35 percent of the total—in fact, nearly three-quarters of the medals conferred on all Eastern and East-Central European nationalities, which is an astonishing statistic considering that Poland was the sole country in Europe where death had been decreed for anyone caught helping Jews.[41] It is not easy to reconcile Poland's disproportionate share of "righteous gentiles" with its doleful record on Jewish victimization. But then again, historical experience usually defies social science formulas. "Generalizations break apart on the stubborn particularity of each country," two historians of the Holocaust in France remind us.[42]

Moreover, ample reason exists to believe that the official "righteous gentile" figure grossly understates the true number, especially in Poland, where some estimates run as high as 360,000. The actual figure will never be known. It is not simply because so many of the rescued and their saviors are dying (if they had not perished already during the war). The other obstacle is the unwillingness of rescuers, particularly Poles, to acknowledge their heroism, and Natalia Piotrowska is one of them. When asked in 1993 how she felt about having helped save four Jewish lives, she answered bluntly: "If I had known they were Jewish, I wouldn't have helped them. I wouldn't have taken that risk. No one would have taken that risk." She stuck to that story during a subsequent visit, adding that she did not appreciate a stranger from America, with Polish translator in tow, interrogating her about wartime activities while a young neighbor sat in the living room. "I don't want people to know my business," she said.[43]

Plainly, Natalia Piotrowska knew who the Skoreckis were and had known from the outset. "She had to have known," says Anne firmly. "I mean, what did she think I was doing in the armoire all those hours? Why did everyone make such a fuss about dying my hair?"

Natalia was not alone in wishing to guard her anonymity. Right after the war many Polish rescuers were afraid to own up to being Good Samaritans for fear of provoking native anti-Semites. Jew hatred was stronger than ever immediately following the Final Solution, largely, one suspects, because the mass redistribution of Jewish property by the Germans had given so many Poles a material stake in the disappearance of the country's Jews. "I'm afraid," a peasant woman involved in wartime Jewish rescue told a documentary filmmaker in 1992 who wanted to publicize her heroism. "What if someone breaks into my house to look for gold under the floor?"[44] Considering the area of Praga where Natalia had lived all her life, one can easily imagine her sharing those apprehensions even in the 1990s. But in her case, a more compelling motive than physical fear was probably in play: guilt and embarrassment at disclosing the truth to friends and relatives still living from the war years. It is abundantly clear that Natalia had enlisted them without their consent in elaborate charades to camouflage the Jewish identity of the Piotrowskas' wartime tenants. The Easter dinners at Lochowska 15, the conspicuous Christmas celebration in the lumberyard, the countless instances of impromptu tea and crumpets in the kitchen when guests unexpectedly dropped in—all these episodes literally imperiled everyone. True, because theoretically the guests did not know who the Skoreckis were, Natalia's cousins and acquaintances could claim deniability. But this was splitting hairs. After all, who during the Nazi reign of terror was prepared to entrust her personal safety to Gestapo respect for legal niceties? Following the war these considerations must have confronted Natalia with a painful choice. Should she tell friends and relatives about the risks she exposed them to during the occupation? Could she possibly explain her conduct? Instead of trying to do so, for half a century she kept everything a secret and resisted intrusions into her past.[45]

But here is where the story grows more intriguing, for it is hard to imagine Natalia's friends and neighbors not suspecting something was amiss. Why would anyone consent to celebrate Christmas with casual acquaintances billeted inside a drafty, poorly heated shack isolated in a bleak lumberyard in the dead of Polish winter? Didn't anyone find it strange? Probably her friends and relatives did. During the war, extreme circumspection was far from uncommon. Most neighbors, it turns out, knew all along that Jews were being kept by such and such a couple but simply chose to keep their suspicions to themselves until after the liberation, if they brought up the subject even then. There was one rule of thumb during the occupation and for many years thereafter: the less one knew, the better. "The overwhelming principle was to say and know as little as possible," write two social psychologists who have studied "righteous gentiles."[46] Natalia and her friends and neighbors concurred: "During the war it was better not to talk too much with neighbors," she says. "Everybody was a little bit afraid of talking too much because it could be dangerous. And this is why we didn't know too much about each other."[47]

There is another piece of evidence to consider, albeit circumstantial. Almost without exception Jewish rescue occurred within networks. Minimally, it required ten rescuers to save one Jew. Hanna Krall, who conducted the famous 1977 interview with Marek Edelman, said forty Poles participated in her rescue. "Every Jew on the Aryan side needs a friend or rather friends . . . to surround him with a sympathetic atmosphere, take care of him and put their hearts into fixing up his unending, daily trouble," wrote Ringelblum of the Polish network who cared for him and his family. Several of these rescue operations were complex organizations, such as Żegota in Poland; Landelijker Organisatie voor Hulp aan Onderdinkers (National Organization for Assistance to Divers [the name given to hidden Jews in Holland]), or LO, in Holland; Comité d'Inter-Mouvements Aupres des Evacués, or CIMADE, in France, and the remarkable Huguenot congregation of Pastor Andre Trocmé in Le Chambon-sur-Lignon in the south of France. But most underground railroads were informal and ad hoc, carefully woven webs of associates whose involvement started out gradually and then, before they realized what was happening, metamorphosed into major commitments. Social psychologists call it the "foot-in-the-door" effect, the dynamic process of one favor leading to another in an escalating hierarchy of good deeds until, say, a loutish womanizer such as Oskar Schindler finds the sole act of heroism of which he was capable and is transfigured into Oskar Schindler the nonpareil rescuer. Altruism was evolutionary.[48]

The challenge of starting a rescue network, however, was knowing whom to trust. Which friends and relatives were reliable, who was discreet? Routine intimacies had to be reevaluated, well-worn social conventions sifted through for clues as to who combined the right mixture of empathy and discretion. It is hard to imagine Natalia asking incautious and indifferent friends to join an activity whose security could so easily be compromised. Whomever she recruited, therefore, they probably were already intuitive enough to figure out they were being asked to help camouflage a Jewish family living on the brink of disaster. If Natalia failed to divulge her real motives, it was for fear of burdening them with a knowledge both parties knew they were better off not having. The only wonder is the failure of Natalia and friends to clear the air after the war, to ask each other what they knew and when they knew it. But maybe fifty years of communist totalitarianism made it hard to discard habits of secrecy.[49]

In any event, something out of the ordinary was taking place in this neighborhood. Not long after the Skoreckis left Lochowska 15 to take up quarters in the lumberyard, the Polish girl who consorted with the Nazis and may have tipped off the janitor about seeing a strange Jewish girl in the next building moved out of the area as well.[50] Did neighbors drop hints that a change of scenery would be beneficial? And what are we to make of the fact that the pastor at Heart of Jesus Basilica, Father Michal Kubacki, with the assistance of the Catholic lay order Caritas, housed and hid two Jewish children, arranging for the issuance of false baptismal certificates? He was "noble and just and decent," testified one of the rescued Jews after the war. Or consider the woman supervisor of the order who suspected the ethnic origins of one of her Jewish wards but was "as silent as a rock."[51] Did Father Kubacki suspect that other members of his congregation were also ersatz Catholics trying to conceal their Jewish identity, like the nervous, dark-haired, sad-eyed Ruth Skorecka with the little blond-haired girl? The moral texture of everyday life in Nazi-occupied Poland seemed like it belonged to another planet. "You can't imagine it," says Teresa Prekerowa. "You can't understand every implication."[52]

If Natalia Piotrowska's altruism is puzzling, so is the behavior of Mark's boss, Mr. Smolenski, the anti-Semite. All along Mark and Ruth were worried he might discover their Jewish identity and hand them over to the Gestapo. It turns out their worries were ill-founded. Smolenski had discovered Mark's Jewish identity early on—and in the way Mark and Ruth feared he might all along. A lumber dealer trying to make a sale at the stable and barracks plant recognized Mark's surname when Smolenski called him into the office for a consultation. "Listen, do you know who you have in this place?" the salesman asked Smolenski after Mark returned to the factory floor. Through dealings with Morris Skorecki's sawmill before the war, the salesman had gotten to know Mark's brother, and he figured out that the Skorecki who had just left the office was related to the Jewish lumber dealer. Smolenski was unfazed. "It makes no difference to me," he said. "Skorecki is a good worker, and he has done plenty for our place of business. We never had work being done so well before." And then he issued a veiled threat: "You better keep this to yourself and don't say anything to anyone." Mark never learned of this encounter until a year later, after the Russians had liberated Warsaw. In the meantime, he noticed that his boss had stopped calling him into the office when salesmen made their rounds.

Soon there was another indication that the relationship between Smolenski and the Skoreckis had moved onto another plane: the friendliness of one of Mark's Polish coworkers, an older man, who used to give him copies of the bulletins smuggled in from the London-based Polish government-in-exile. The paper kept them up-to-date about the political and military situation in the east, reporting on Jews who had escaped from the ghetto and were receiving help from friendly Poles. Its columns even listed the dates of Jewish holidays. The bulletin made the Skoreckis aware of the underground's existence in a way they never had been previously. "Of course, we never tried to come in contact with these people," Ruth said, "because we didn't know who was in the underground." Before long the Pole, who they later learned belonged to the Polish underground, started stopping by the Skoreckis' shack every Sunday after Mass to drop off the London bulletin. Usually he was drunk because he liked vodka, and he often brought candy for the children, giving them each a few zlotys to buy things with. "He loved our two children," Ruth said, "but I don't know why he was so nice to us." It was probably because Smolenski, who also had ties to the Polish underground, told him to make his presence known around the Skorecki shack, in order that neighborhood szmalzcowniks might know that the family in the lumberyard enjoyed Home Army immunity. The Polish "Secret State," now that the tide of battle was turning against the Germans and the Russian front was getting closer, was starting to command ever greater respect from the underlying population.[53]

Pan Smolenski, the anti-Semite, was probably moved by the old Polish reflex, "He's my Jew; leave him alone"—an instinct akin to the racial paternalism of white elites in the American South. But more complex motives were likely at play too, just as with the case of Natalia Piotrowska. What impelled these two rescuers to take the risks they did and to continue to take them, each evolving a "rescuer self"?[54] There is a burgeoning literature on the sociology and psychology of "righteous gentiles," but the sociological literature is frankly inconclusive. Rescuers do not cluster on one or two rungs of the social ladder. They derive in almost equal proportions from the working class and the middle class, the peasantry and the intelligentsia, the educated and the unlettered. Nor are they conspicuously religious or unusually politically active.[55] There have been attempts to identify them as social marginals, people who marched to a different drummer and were impervious to the good opinion of friends and neighbors. But, apart from a psychological ability to act independently of social norms, there is little evidence showing that rescuers were anything but organically embedded in the communities in which they lived.[56] Efforts to categorize them by gender—to correlate the altruistic impulse with the empathetically different voice of women who have been nurtured to value relationships over cold, rule-driven logic—have also been unsuccessful.[57]

The only universal factor that leaps out is that rescuers almost always acted impulsively, without forethought or a rational weighing of the risks involved. Or, as the child of parents rescued by the remarkable Huguenots in the French mountain village of Le Chambon once pithily remarked, "People who agonize don't act; people who act don't agonize."[58] Their involvement began gradually, usually with someone asking them to lend a hand, followed by their answering, "yes, of course, naturally." Today they profess embarrassment when anyone suggests theirs was an act of heroism. By their lights they were merely doing the right thing, indeed doing what they had always done. Helping others, even strangers in need, came naturally. It is what they were accustomed to doing before the war and what they returned to doing, rather nonchalantly, after it, because the moral life is something that is led continuously, not every now and then. One does not switch it off and on between moral crises. Woven deeply into the piecemeal habits of daily living, Good Samaritanism is simply who "righteous gentiles" were as a matter of course: namely, ordinary people of ordinary decency. Thus, when the moment of moral choice arrived, they acted naturally, which is to say, impulsively, because, as Iris Murdoch has argued in *The Sovereignty of Good*, "at crucial moments of choice most of the business of choosing is already over."[59]

"To be a rescuer was a question of character and conviction," says Teresa Prekerowa, who herself helped rescued Jewish families during the Nazi occupation. Her small apartment in Warsaw is furnished with the embellishments of civilized taste. Books are piled up on antique furniture. An oriental rug lies on the floor. On the wall hangs an Impressionist oil painting of a Warsaw courtyard. She has given a lot of thought to the moral conundrum of rescue, and to her it is not much of an enigma at all. "It was their duty, not a question of grace. It was a duty, a simple duty."[60] Simha Rotem put it somewhat differently when describing a Polish policeman who assisted the remnant of the Jewish Fighting Organization after they reached the Aryan side: "He was a human being—and that wasn't a simple thing in those days."[61]

During those dangerous times Natalia Piotrowska and Mr. Smolenski plainly met that threshold of humanity. In fact, the circumstantial evidence is overwhelming that Natalia and her mother, at least, became rescuers in the classic way: they were asked to keep one rent-paying Jewish family for a limited period of time but ended up sheltering three additional Jews and then allowing the original family to stay indefinitely, becoming more and more complicitous in their tenants' charade of camouflage and concealment. These were hardly the acts of persons unaccustomed to habit-forming good deeds. But there is no way of ever knowing what moved the reticent Natalia, her feet now swollen by gout, to take the risks she did. Nor will we ever fathom how she was predisposed toward altruism. It would have been revealing to have conducted an in-depth interview regarding her moral code, her motives, her upbringing. Did her mother and father spare the rod and rely more on moral reasoning— parenting styles associated with the inculcation of altruism in children? Did they lead by moral example, demonstrating in their concern for strangers and people not like themselves—such as the Jews of prewar Praga—that difference was to be respected, that all people should be treated with dignity? It is a good guess that she did learn these lessons from her parents, or at least her mother. But there is no way of ever knowing for sure.[62]

Ruth Skorecka never forgot what Natalia and her mother had done for her family. She and Natalia stayed in touch by letter for many years following the war, even after they moved to New Orleans, a bonding that was not at all unusual of many relationships between rescuers and the Jews they assisted.[63] "She all the time helped us out," Ruth said. Her testimony is probably all we will ever know about the ethical enigma surrounding the Piotrowskas of Praga.

Not long after moving his family to the lumberyard Mark received close to irrefutable evidence that Mr. Smolenski knew the Skoreckis were Jewish. Snow had been drifting under the door of the office shack, and Mark wanted to carpenter something together to keep out the elements. A few weeks before Christmas he asked Smolenski's permission to build a porch. Smolenski's response was a revelation: "Mr. Skorecki, I tell you something. Don't do anything. Let this go as it is. You never lived like this before, and I'm sure that when the war ends, you will never live like this either. You and your family just try to manage for the time being. Don't build anything. Just leave things as they are." Mark was speechless, almost uncomprehending, and he tried to act nonplussed. But, as Ruth explained, "in his heart and in his mind at this minute he understood that Mr. Smolenski knew who we really were, and Mark didn't know what to tell him." Smolenski quickly changed the subject, however, when he saw the confusion spreading over his foreman's face.

"I am 100 percent sure that Mr. Smolenski knows who we are," Mark told Ruth that evening. Ruth was equally shocked. "He didn't do anything harmful to us," she said. "He gave Mark a job, gave him raises, made him a foreman. I couldn't believe it all."

Mark felt he had to express his appreciation in some way. A verbal thanks might have imperiled Smolenski by compromising his deniability, so Mark chose to make his acknowledgments in a way he always felt most comfortable doing: He would build a Christmas toy for Mr. Smolenski's partially paralyzed young son. He had already made dolls out of cloth and sawdust for Anne and Lila. But he wanted the gift for his boss's son to stand out. "I have to make for this kid something that nobody has, which couldn't be bought with money," he told Ruth. So, he began building a wooden car. He equipped it with foot pedals. He worked on it nonstop in his spare time—after work and on Saturdays and Sundays—to have it ready by the holidays. He painted it red, added a door, and traced the boy's name on the body. He finished it the day before Christmas Eve, and then gave it to one of the delivery drivers as he was leaving the yard, instructing him that the package was to be dropped off at Smolenski's home. Mark had wrapped the gift to keep the driver from knowing its contents. "We didn't want to show that we were doing something special," Ruth explained.

Smolenski's wife was dumbfounded when she removed the wrapping and discovered a wooden car bearing the handpainted name of her son. She immediately called her husband at the office, so certain was she that the gift had come from him. "She had never seen anything like the car in her life," she told him over the phone. But Smolenski did not know who had sent the gift, and he would not until he arrived home that evening and called the delivery driver. He was profoundly moved when he learned that Mark had sent it, so much so that the following day—Christmas Eve—he had one of the workers at the factory bring Mark an envelope containing a three-thousand-zloty bonus. He had the bonus sent directly to the lumberyard shack, which was unusual. "Mr. Smolenski wanted to show everyone how he respected Mark by sending the bonus to us at our house," Ruth explained. But he may also have intended to remind the neighbors in the overlooking high-rises that this family in the lumberyard lived under the umbrella of his special protection.

The following day, on Christmas, late in the afternoon after Natalia and the other guests had left, Smolenski brought his wife and small son to the lumberyard to thank Mark personally. "Everybody who was over for dinner had eyes only for the little car," Smolenski told his foreman, "and they all said that they had never seen anything like this. The boy of course was more happy with this gift than with any of the others he had received. This was something special to him."

Mark and Ruth were overwhelmed not only by the courtesy call but the substantial bonus. They never expected such a huge sum. At his current rate of salary it would have taken Mark quite some time to accumulate that amount. All the Skoreckis ever wanted was a safe place to hang their identity until the climate improved. As Ruth put it, "The biggest gift which could be given to us at this time [or to any Jew trying to pass in wartime Warsaw] was knowing who we were and letting us alone. . . . This was something we were thankful for day in and day out—to have a place like this and to be treated like human beings, like everybody else in the place."

The elation and relief at feeling human again, however, soon taught Mark the treachery of relaxation. He let go at the holiday office party that year, not in words but by drinking. "Polish people drink plenty," Ruth said. "It was considered a display of masculinity to consume a large quantity of alcohol without getting drunk," added a Pole who lived in Warsaw during the Skoreckis' sojourn in the capital. But Mark was not used to drinking, and he could not hold his liquor.[64] Two stiff glasses of vodka later and he was, to quote Ruth, "a little tipsy." Actually, he was drunk or, as he put it, "finished." On his way home he took the foolish risk of buying a loaf of black-market bread from a street corner dealer. ss soldiers saw him and ordered him to halt. He started running with the bread in his hand. He was not afraid, however; the liquor had made him lightheaded. He was laughing. He managed to slip into the lumberyard without detection. He was still laughing—"a good deal," as Ruth remembered—when he entered the office shack. Smelling liquor on his breath, she asked him what had happened and tried to put him to bed. "I was afraid of what he might do when like this, and I saw the fear on the faces of the two little girls."

Anne and Lila were terrified. They had been taught to be wary of strangers, and now their father—the person single-handedly responsible for rescuing them from starvation and deportation and bringing them to safety on the Aryan side—had suddenly turned into a stranger himself. "He wasn't my father," Anne says. "He took on a whole different personality that I didn't understand. It wasn't him. He was giddy and laughing and saying things that weren't him. I never forgot it, because he wasn't this giddy person. He never did that."

Ruth finally got him into bed, and he awoke the next morning hungover with guilt. What if he had said something the previous evening to imperil his family? Mark was worried sick. Worse was his daughters' icy attitude toward him, reminiscent of Lila's remoteness following his arrival from Białystok two years earlier. For several days following the incident Anne and Lila—now eight and six—refused to go near him. "It took them a while to realize that their daddy was the same one they had before," Ruth said. It was the last time Mark lost control until he reached his late eighties.

It was rare for the Skoreckis to venture beyond the lumberyard for anything save essential business. "We were trying not to come out too often with the kids," Ruth said. "We were staying inside most of the time." Even when gentile friends invited them over to celebrate the New Year, they begged off with the excuse that they had to stay home with the children. The truth was, as Ruth explained, "we had no patience for this." They did send New Year's greeting cards to friends in Praga and entertained them when they stopped by on New Year's Day, bringing their own liquor. Like her husband, Ruth was unused to drinking, "but at this time I couldn't afford to be different." She imbibed moderately, however.

Once in a while they made visits to Natalia. On Shrovetide, the day before Ash Wednesday, they slept over at Lochowska 15, fasting with her the next day. On Easter 1944, their second one on the Aryan side, Natalia came to the lumberyard with a neighbor and a Piotrowska cousin. They brought along home-brewed vodka to have with the Easter dinner Ruth had prepared. Earlier that morning Mark had brought Lila to the basilica to have her plate of colored eggs blessed by the priest. This Easter was easier than the last one; at least, Ruth was spared the charade of mailing herself Easter cards like she had done the year before. But the festivities were still a chore. All public functions were; it was hard to appear carefree when your insides were tied in knots. "Thank God, the Easter holidays were over, too," Ruth exclaimed in visible relief after the company had left and she and Mark could relax into comfortable anonymity inside the wooden fence.

To Anne and Lila the lumberyard must have seemed like emancipation after the solitary confinement of the Piotrowskas' Lochowska Street apartment. No longer did they have to stay locked indoors without end. Once a week, when workers and delivery men were not in the yard, which was usually on Sundays, Ruth let the girls play among the stacks of lumber—always under her watchful eye, of course. "That was when the lumberyard was closed and nobody would come in," Anne says. "It was the only time we were really free to walk around." Like everything the Skoreckis did, however, Anne and Lila's recreation was also part of a larger strategy of balancing privacy with public routine. Ruth was constantly trying to imagine what the neighbors might be thinking, and nothing she did was without ulterior motive. Even spontaneity was calculated. In the spring, when the weather warmed in the afternoon, Ruth took chairs outside "to show that people were coming to me." But acting normally with her daughters was problematic. The real perplexity was what to do with Anne. There was no way Ruth could conceal from neighbors that two children lived in the lumberyard, if only because the lavatory was outside. It was one thing to keep the oldest behind the fence all the time; it was another never to let her leave the shack. That would raise suspicions. "I was afraid of the people across from the place where I was living," Ruth said of the residents in the five-story apartment building overlooking the lumberyard. "They might begin to wonder why the kids never came out to play." So, she let Anne play in the yard from time to time. From a distance perhaps it would be difficult to tell she was Jewish.

But onlookers might be able to tell from afar that the bigger of the two girls was probably old enough to attend school, and this worry drove Ruth to customary supplication. "I prayed to God that no one from this building would come out with the suspicious idea seeing that the kids didn't go to school and that they all the time played only in the lumberyard," she said. It was taxing, this life on the Aryan side, this constant necessity of inventing and reinventing a new false front. Every solution seemed to create another problem. There was never surcease.

The matter of Anne's and Lila's education, however, was for Ruth more than a problem of strategy and tactics. It touched on the future and Ruth's fervent hope that her daughters might attend college, even become professionals like her brother Henry Tempelhof and his surgeon wife. Lila had barely reached the age when kids begin formal schooling, but Anne was already two or three years behind her peers. Ruth felt terrible about sacrificing Anne's education to her safety, but there was no other alternative. "Everybody can understand sending them to school was impossible," Ruth said. As a stopgap measure, however, she began a program of home schooling for Anne and Lila. Natalia gave her a few elementary schoolbooks, which she supplemented with books on loan from the library. "Every day I worked a little with Anne. I gave her homework," Ruth said. "I remember my mother having a pencil and a book trying to teach us the Polish alphabet," adds Anne. The mother-and-daughter tutoring went on for months.

"It wasn't easy to try to teach, because my mind was occupied with other things," Ruth said. But these private lessons in the lumberyard did help divert her thoughts from day-to-day survival and focus them on the future. "All the time I was thinking that maybe if they lived through all this, the war would end and they could get a regular education, and we would all get out of this terrible nightmare," she said. A surfeit of optimism may have ill-equipped victims for dealing with Nazi trickery, but it was hard to nourish the will to live without believing tomorrow would bring a better day, if not for oneself, then at least for one's children.

One aspect of life on the Aryan side bothered Ruth to the end of her days, likely making those one-on-one sessions with Anne all the more special. It was that she had to favor one child over another. Reading the memoir Ruth dictated after the war to a former seminarian who lived across the street, one would never get the impression she treated Anne and Lila differently. The topic of her daughters almost always appears in the plural tense. She did things with both girls, never with one alone. She took them to church together, sent them in tandem with their cloth-covered plates for the Holy Saturday sprinkling, draped them alike with rosaries and crosses on chains. When visitors called, Anne and Lila both curtsied for company and then returned to their playing. They strolled together in the park. They seemed to have been joined at the hip. But actually, Anne had to stay under wraps most of the time because of her darker complexion. It was Lila who was granted temporary parole, not her older sister, except for Sundays in the lumberyard. It was Anne who had to squeeze inside the cedar armoire the Skoreckis were loaned when they moved to the lumberyard. Anne must have been hunkered down inside the cedar wardrobe when Natalia brought her friends to Mark and Ruth's place to help the Skoreckis publicly celebrate Christmas. Anne cannot remember; that entire period is foggy in her mind. But it is hard to imagine her forgetting such an occasion in light of her often joyless, hidden childhood, so Mark and Ruth must have been keeping her out of sight during the Yule festivities.

Ruth was not merely disingenuous with her interlocutor and the reader but with Anne herself. She was not always truthful with her oldest daughter about what the rest of the family was doing while she remained locked inside the Lochowska Street apartment or the office shack. Well into adulthood Anne still believed that her father and younger sister only circled the church when they carried the Easter plate to the priest for his blessing, because that was the story she had always been told. "They never really went into the church," Anne says. "They went around the church. They made believe they celebrated Easter." But it is clear from Ruth's memoir and the physical characteristics of Heart of Jesus, which abuts a field and is not easy to circumnavigate, that they went into the basilica, not around it, and that the deception involved not just the priest but an older daughter who would have felt unwanted at being left out of even make-believe family excursions. And why didn't Ruth, who actually looked forward to attending Mass, not accompany Lila to the Basilica? Why was the agnostic Mark the escort? The only explanation is that someone had to stay home with Anne, and Ruth figured it might as well be her, to let the mother console the shut-in sibling about the fact that Lila alone was permitted out in public. Discriminatory parenting, even if born of dire necessity, was clearly gnawing at Ruth's conscience.

Only one place in her dictated memoir did Ruth ever flirt with full disclosure. It is where she described Anne's home schooling. Without skipping a beat she launched directly into a curious discussion about a woman she met while visiting her friend who was formerly a priest and his wife. The couple had helped with the Skoreckis' escape from the ghetto by taking in the bagged belongings Ruth had sent out of the ghetto in January 1943, and they were supposed to have taken in Mark's brother Julius until he stumbled into an SS dragnet. Ruth called on the couple from time to time. One day they introduced her to another visitor in the apartment. They said she was Jewish just like herself, adding that she had also fled the ghetto with two daughters. She seemed out of place in a large city such as Warsaw, especially since she was trying to pass as a peasant woman. A long, full skirt and distinctive blouse hung loosely from her body. A shawl draped her head. Instead of allowing the wearer to blend in, the garments attracted attention. But one thing was clear: you could never confuse the woman in the peasant costume with the well-groomed Ruth Skorecka, who always dressed well, if only to conceal her inner feelings. The other striking feature about the woman was that she had two daughters who resembled Anne and Lila in everything but age.

As Ruth told the story:

Before the war these two girls had started in universities, but right now when they went out from the ghetto, they rented an apartment with a family as I had done. The same administrator who had prepared our papers made their papers also. One of the daughters went out from time to time, say to a library, etc. The other daughter was all the time locked up. . . . When people left the apartment, she came out. But when company came or when they expected someone to come, she was locked up. They were just trying to think what they could do.

The mother played the role of a country woman. She always had a basket on her arm. When she needed a book, she went to the library, and when she came to the library, she said she needed the book for her boss's daughter. She was playing the role of a maid. The book was actually for her own daughter who was kept locked up.

The girl who was locked up was of a dark complexion whereas the one who was going out from time to time was of a lighter complexion.

Still fitted out in country raiment, the Jewish peasant woman occasionally stopped by the lumberyard "because," as Ruth explained, "she had no one to talk with." Ruth always welcomed her company. "She was going through the same thing as we were," Ruth said. "And I was glad from time to time to talk over our troubles with somebody whom I could trust." And then, just as suddenly as this digression began, Ruth changed topics one more time, mentioning in the very next sentence that "my niece Haka from time to time came to see us."

The coincidences are hard to credit: two daughters close in age but strikingly different in complexion; the normal life of the fair-complected sister juxtaposed against the stowaway existence of her darker sibling; the preoccupation with education, especially college training; the hint of home schooling made possible by library book loans; the peasant woman presenting herself as a maid when she checked out books; and now the abrupt appearance of Haka, who herself was passing as a maid and who was probably the person who was checking out books for Anne. But the real giveaway was Ruth's specification of the hiding place. Ruth did not merely say that the peasant woman's dark complected daughter hid in a closet, another room, or the attic. She said, "The other daughter was all the time locked up in a *cedar [ward]robe* [emphasis added]"—the sole piece of furniture that Ruth had described concretely.

Anne immediately recognized the dissemblance taking place. "That's me," she said when reminded of her mother's peasant woman tale. "I'm the girl in the cedar wardrobe."

If the fictional subterfuge of the peasant woman story allowed Ruth to assuage guilt for her discriminatory parenting, a deeply felt need to compensate for Anne and Lila's stolen childhood seems to have led her to contrive another lie that would mire her in guilt for the rest of her life: the true age of her daughters. There is little doubt Ruth was shading the truth about Anne's and Lila's dates of birth, not withstanding her postwar insistence that she had waited four years from the date of her marriage in 1931 to have children. She probably postponed motherhood only three years. In her memoir, for example, Ruth notes how unnamed visitors began to inquire why Ruth was not preparing Anne for her First Holy Communion. In Catholic culture it is an important rite of passage signifying that children have reached the age of moral judgment and, now knowing right from wrong, may join the rest of the congregation in the sacrament. First Communion is usually solemnized when the child reaches ten years of age. The year before, Catholic children begin receiving instruction in the catechism. For the confirmation itself girls wear white dresses and garland their hair with flowers; boys, black suits with a white carnation in the lapel and, in Poland, a white ribbon tied in a bow around the left arm. Parents beam with pride. It is a very big event in Poland, commemorated by Communion photographs that hang over the beds of most Catholic children. One Jewish boy trying to pass as an Aryan had to obtain a doctored picture to protect his false identity.[65] Ruth became extremely nervous when questioned about Anne's First Communion. She crossed the street when she saw nosy neighbors approaching. She came up with all kinds of excuses when she could not avoid neighbors. And when she had run out of excuses, she would simply say she would get around to Anne's religious training next week or the week after that. The subject was ticklish "because," as Ruth let slip in her narrative, "if I took her to communion I would have to go to the priest and tell him what was going on and who I was." It was an admission, of course, that Anne had not been attending Mass at all. More than that, it was tacit acknowledgment that Anne was a year older than Ruth had insisted she was after the war. If Anne were only eight, as Ruth kept saying she was, the issue would never have arisen. Catechism instruction does not typically begin until age nine.

For Ruth the lies kept piling up until she felt she would choke from guilt. Objectively, there was no reason she should have felt that way. Ordinary ethical categories had scant relevance in Nazi-occupied Poland, where the moral order had completely collapsed and Western civilization came close to shedding its skin. But, as did other Holocaust survivors, Ruth still believed the decalogue of everyday life ought to apply, and she could be hard on herself when the demands of survival forced her to break its simple rules. The constant effort required to keep one's moral self-image intact may have been the hardest challenge faced by survivors. Most means-end dilemmas entail one big decision, and one either looks back or moves ahead. But Jews passing on the surface in Aryan Warsaw wrestled with the dilemma everyday, and they seldom enjoyed the luxury of putting unavoidably disagreeable decisions behind them. The need to lie and dissemble and then seek self-justification seemed unending.

In some ways living as an interloper within range of normal domesticity rendered everyday deceits all the more intolerable. "Plenty times when I was standing in my door or looking through the window," Ruth said, "I saw housewives cleaning and I felt jealous. I wish I didn't have to live like this. I said to myself, 'God, please hurry up the time when I return to a normal life and won't have to lie and can keep house as others.'" But one lie she had committed herself to for life: the age of her daughters.

Mark's niece Haka soon discovered that the live-in maid job she had once counted herself fortunate to have landed was not so enviable after all. One reason Haka stopped by the lumberyard on her way to or from the public market or the library was to complain to Ruth about the abusive behavior of her employer. "Her boss was a drunk," Ruth said. "When he drank too much he bothered and pestered his wife. Haka was not happy to have to go through all this." The man probably abused Haka as well, although the subject of sexual harassment was too delicate for someone of Ruth's Victorian temperament to broach in a memoir. Although miserable in her job, Haka nonetheless appreciated it for keeping her alive. Then good fortune struck. A male cousin, another Wladek, had been working under false papers for a big German contractor who was building installations in Gdańsk for the German authorities. Balding, with an Errol Flynn mustache and an engaging smile, this Wladek was dashing and debonair, a real man of the world. One day his employer started getting friendly with him and said, "Look, you don't have to hide yourself. I know that you are a Jew, but I want to help you. If you know somebody that you are looking for, I will help you." Wladek said, as a matter of fact, there was somebody— "my first cousin, a girl. I want to see where she is." The employer gave Wladek a license to travel to Warsaw to recruit labor for a construction project he then had under way.

Wladek traveled in a German uniform and began searching the streets. Perhaps he had some kind of lead, possibly from the former priest and his wife who had moved to Warsaw from Łódź. In any event, he visited Natalia Piotrowska at least once.[66] Then, while strolling the streets of Warsaw, he caught a glimpse of Haka. "She had a special kind of movement when she walked," remembers Dolek Skorecki, their cousin from Kielce. "And he saw from far away somebody going like that [gestures], and he said this must be this cousin, Haka."[67]

So, he started following her. Haka took fright. "She thought that some soldier was going after her, and she was afraid," Dolek says. "She went into all kinds of shops." Soon she came to the realization that her pursuer was her cousin Wladek. Shortly after that encounter Haka quit her job and returned with her cousin to Gdańsk, where she became a maid in his boss's household for the duration of the war.[68]

For Mark, Ruth, and the children still back in Praga, war's end was finally getting closer.

HOMECOMING

A major reason for staying inside the lumberyard as much as possible was physical security. The subject of safety was always in the air, and the topic of conversation invariably arrived at the question, How would it all end? Would they escape with their lives? "In this time, everybody was afraid for their lives," Ruth said. "A man who had been in the military or in politics was especially in danger."

Conditions in Warsaw went from bad to terrible after Governor-General Hans Frank issued his October 2, 1943, decree "On the Prevention of Offenses against the German Work of Reconstruction in the General-Government." The proclamation set up Summary Security Police Courts that handed down mandatory and immediate death sentences for actions as trivial as "the un-licensed slaughter of livestock." The real intent was to play off the Polish population against the underground by driving home the point that the re-prisals would continue until the Resistance ceased attacking German person-nel and military installations—a clear instance of the Nazi practice of "collec-tive responsibility." Now the street sweeps grew vicious, indiscriminate, and much more frequent. In addition to the regular police squads, the Germans deployed units of the Wehrmacht, the Luftwaffe, and the Hitlerjugend (Hitler Youth). Poles found on the street with suspicious papers were loaded into police lorries and hauled away to the notorious Pawiak Prison. They were not so much detainees as hostages, for within days many lost their lives in so-called street executions: mass killings on city streets that were first cleared of pedes-trians and shoppers and cordoned off to traffic. Announced from street corner loudspeakers, the executions happened all over Warsaw, several of them in Praga. Between October 15, 1943, and February 15, 1944, the official death toll in Warsaw alone was 1,640 persons, which was probably only one-third of the true figure. The reign of terror failed to break the bond between Polish civilians and the "Secret State." As soon as the Germans carried off the corpses and washed away the blood, covering indelible spots with sand, knots of civilians would gather at the murder scene to place flowers and candles. In response, the Germans increasingly resorted to using the ruined streets of the old ghetto as the place of execution.[1]

In their never-ending search for illegals, Jews, and underground operatives, the ss frequently barricaded the streets bordering the big lot where the lumberyard was located. During one dragnet, while Mark was at work, Ruth heard machine gun fire. Deathly frightened that the Nazis might enter the yard, she peeped through a hole in the fence. "They were chasing a man who they were sure was a Jew," she said, "and he tried to come to the feed store on the lot, and they shot him." He was actually a Catholic with proper papers. "The Germans made plenty mistakes like this, and everyday we had new surprises." During his Christmas binge, Mark was indeed lucky to have made it back inside the lumberyard without being detected.

In July 1944 the reign of terror reached new fury as the German military position came apart in the east. During a five-week period of continuous combat the previous summer, including the great tank battle at Kursk, the Soviet juggernaut had pushed the Germans back 150 miles along a 650-mile front. Unnerved by the setback, Hitler uncharacteristically ordered the construction of an "East Wall" behind which to defend the German conquests of 1941–42, like the "West Wall" along the Rhine. But the wall never reached beyond the environs of Leningrad, and the German high command was caught completely off guard when the Russians resumed the offensive on June 22, 1944, three years to the day after the commencement of Operation Barbarossa. This was Stalin's payback for the invasion of 1941.

Indeed, the Soviet summer offensive of 1944 was a sort of Blitzkrieg in reverse, "1941 the other way around!" to quote Alexander Werth. The Nazis were overmatched in every category: planes, assault guns, artillery, mortars, and tanks, especially the versatile T-34s, now pouring out of Russian factories in volumes unimagined. Along the Byelorussian front, where the main assault would land, Russian forces outnumbered the German Army Group Center by a factor of two to one. There was also no way of rushing in reinforcements from the west, where Allied forces had already broken out of their Normandy beachheads and were driving toward the Rhine. The Führer's options were dwindling.[2]

Heralded by one of those massive artillery barrages that were signature openings of historic Russian offensives, Soviet armies plunged forward along four fronts stretching from the Baltic to Kiev, sweeping around both sides of the forty-thousand-square-mile Pripet Marshes, the "Wehrmacht Hole," as the Germans came to call it. Meanwhile, Nazi forces, in conformance with Hitler's orders, tried to hold the line at all costs and treat occupied cities as "fixed fortifications," at the same time as they were repeatedly flanked and enveloped. In the Minsk pocket alone the Russians captured more than one hundred thousand German soldiers, marching the remnant through the streets of Moscow a short time later. During the offensive's first twelve days, Soviet forces destroyed twenty-five German divisions, scarcely pausing as they smashed their way west, often outrunning their supplies. Within a month they had pushed back the German lines 200 miles, then driving forward another 150 miles with even greater alacrity. Vilna fell on July 13, and Białystok, two weeks later. The fastest moving force—the one that would bring quickest relief to Warsaw—was the First Byelorussian Front under Field Marshal Konstantin Rokossovsky. Crossing into Poland on July 18, he captured Lublin on July 23. Two days later his forces established a bridgehead across the Vistula thirty-five miles south of Warsaw. Shortly afterward, the Second Tank Army, which had been detached from Rokossovky's command in anticipation of hooking up with Russian army groups approaching Warsaw from the north and east, had penetrated within seven miles of Praga.[3]

On the streets of Warsaw there was no mistaking the collapse of German fortunes. That July, bedraggled Wehrmacht soldiers crossing the Vistula from the east, their eyes lowered and uniforms splotched with mud, walked alongside horse-drawn wagons piled high with the detritus of war. Quietly Nazi officialdom began evacuating the city. Once high-and-mighty Volksdeutsche started fleeing to the Fatherland. Toward the end of the month Nazi authorities broadcast from loudspeakers and wall placards orders that one hundred thousand civilians were to report for labor on military fortifications around the city. But most of all, in a panicky effort to staunch the mounting outbreaks of sabotage behind their lines, Nazi security forces intensified the repression. "The reign of terror threw the entire Polish population into a panic," wrote Vladka Meed. "Even worse was the dread among the Jews in hiding in Gentile homes."[4]

The apprehension was all the greater because of Russian bombs. Beginning on July 29 the skies over Warsaw became cobwebbed with the contrails of the Red Air Force. Bombs fell everywhere, soon joined by Soviet artillery shells. "The bombing held a twofold danger for us—the danger of being hit and the danger of being disclosed," wrote one Jew who was then hiding on the Aryan side.[5] For the Skoreckis this double bind was particularly harrowing.

"People started running again to the cellars," Ruth said of those July days. But the porchless guard shack where she and her family lived barely had a floor let alone a basement. "I was just in the street," Ruth said laconically. Worse, it was in a yard attached to a German war plant. "When the bombing started at night we were in the lumberyard," Anne says, "and I remember walking with my father and hearing these terrible noises. The bombs just kept dropping but they missed us." The deafening sounds were hard to forget.

At first, the Skoreckis took shelter at the same feed store where Ruth had witnessed the gunning down of the Catholic man in flight from the ss. The women proprietor had invited them to stay with her during the air raids. But because it was on the same lot, the feed store was nearly as vulnerable as the office shack, and it had the added danger of being in a zone of stepped-up ss activity. Then, good fortune came their way. "Someone told us to come and sit in the cellar of the big building across from our place during bombings," Ruth said. Who it was that extended the invitation Ruth never mentioned, but she and Mark were appreciative, to say the least. Warsaw nights were becoming engulfed with the roar of exploding munitions. Thus after receiving the invitation, whenever they heard Russian planes droning in the distance, the Skoreckis scampered into the basement of the five-story apartment building across the street, nestling in for the night next to its upstairs occupants. "We went with blankets and pillows and slept on the floor," Ruth said.

What she encountered in the cellar came as a revelation. Though busy with their own affairs, "these people," to quote Ruth, "were nice to us and to our children. All the people in the cellar knew that we were the watchman for the lumberyard. We were all friends at this time." The debut of the dark-complected child who never set foot outside the yard and seldom saw the light of day caused nary a ripple. The building's occupants apparently already knew about Anne and, having assimilated the odd behavior, had long ago made up their minds about the right course of action.

Or perhaps, like the rest of Warsaw at the time, they were simply preoccupied by the approach of the Warsaw Uprising, which began on August 1. The atmosphere during the waning days of July was thick with expectation, leavened, of course, by fear of German reprisals. "It won't be long now . . . perhaps tomorrow. . . . Just let the signal come," knots of people would whisper whenever they gathered to heed the thundering of distant guns. "The streets look different," wrote Simha Rotem, now performing rescue work on the Aryan side for the Jewish underground. "You didn't see housewives carrying shopping bags or officials rushing to work; and you could feel something in the air, a tension steeped in exaltation."[6]

From inside their makeshift air raid shelter the Skoreckis enjoyed a front-row seat on the approaching drama. The cellar was a beehive of activity. People of all ages were constantly coming and going, and they had guns, for which there was a reason. As it happened, the building was, in Ruth's words, "one of the headquarters of the underground." Judging from the heavy foot traffic through the basement, it may very well have been a Home Army munitions storehouse as well: two of the AK's four secret arms caches were in Praga.[7] "One night they tried to send out the whole group," Ruth said. Without being told, she knew they were leaving to fight the Germans. The underground bulletins to which she had been privy had been hinting for weeks that a citywide uprising against the Nazi occupiers was a looming possibility.

The sixty-three-day Warsaw Uprising of 1944 commenced when factory sirens started wailing at 5:00 P.M. on August 1, one day after Soviet tanks had reached the outskirts of Praga.[8] The decision to revolt had been considered for months. To spare civilians needless suffering, the government-in-exile based in London had excluded large cities such as Warsaw from its anti-Nazi sabotage campaign in eastern Poland. But by 1944 it was manifest that Stalin meant to control the country's political future. At the 1943 Big Three Conference at Teheran, he had secured Roosevelt's and Churchill's agreement to the westward shift of Poland's frontiers. Nor was it easy to ignore his determination to eliminate Poland's prewar leadership. Elements of the prewar elite had already ended up in mass graves in Katyn Forest outside Moscow, where Germans in April 1943 announced they had uncovered the remains of thousands of Polish officers missing since their 1940 imprisonment by Soviet authorities.[9] For the sake of national independence, Polish officials therefore concluded, in the words of German historian Hans Roos, that Soviet troops "ought to be welcomed as guests in an already liberated capital, not as conquerors." "The national sense of honor and dignity," no less than political independence, was at stake, announced one member of the Polish underground. The government-in-exile and its military and political agents in Warsaw saw no other recourse but to authorize the Warsaw Uprising. Still, insurrection was a huge gamble. No one from the Polish "Secret State" tried to coordinate the uprising with the Soviet military. There was the naïve expectation that the Russians would simply come to their aid if the revolt ran into trouble. But what if the Soviets could not or would not intervene?[10]

At first things went well for the insurgents. The entire city, including Praga, erupted spontaneously—"just like the Jewish people fighting in the ghetto," Ruth said. Civilians poured into the streets to improvise barricades from torn-up slabs of paving stone. The forty-thousand-person-strong AK, together with its allies from the Communist left, the much smaller People's Army (Armia Ludowa, or AL), though outgunned, enjoyed the element of surprise. Rather quickly they captured several German facilities and won supremacy over most sections of the city, including Old Town, whose narrow winding streets and timbered buildings bordered the Vistula. But the Home Army failed to seize such key installations as the airport or gain control of the Kierbedz Bridge. The Germans had little trouble regaining entry to suppress the insurrection in Praga. After five days they began systematically counterattacking AK positions in Warsaw. It was a savage assault, a wholesale reprisal against a people whom Nazi racial theory ranked only slightly above the Jews. Enraged at the treachery all around him—the uprising of the Maquis in southern France in June and the Slovaks in July, not to mention the abortive attempt on his life by renegade officers inside his own headquarters—Hitler decreed, "Warsaw will be wiped out," and then he turned the job over not to the Wehrmacht but to Reichsführer-ss Heinrich Himmler.[11] As had happened during the Warsaw Ghetto revolt the previous year, the Germans, lacking stomach for house-to-house fighting, pummeled the city with artillery. Every forty to fifty minutes German Stukas carrying one-thousand-pound incendiary bombs flew so low over the city that the black crosses under their wings were visible to fighters positioned on the rooftops. The ss forces sent in by Himmler were composed of German criminals and Russian deserters. The worst was the Kaminski Brigade, whose lawlessness was so brutal even the Nazis had to execute its Cossack leader. ss troops massacred civilians by the thousands. They raped elderly cancer patients and systematically pillaged every neighborhood in their path. Smoke braiding up from blazing buildings blocked out the sun. Charred bodies, rotting in the street, filled the air with the stench of death. Hastily dug graves pocked Warsaw's parks and back lots.

The fiercest fighting took place in Old Town, which may have been bombed more than any comparable area during the entire war. As their position eroded the insurgents took to the sewers, just as the ghetto fighters had done the year before. Many became delirious and sick off the fumes rising from the sludge. With well-tested methods, the Germans pumped gas and poured fire down the manholes, throwing in grenades whenever they heard movement below. They booby-trapped tunnel roofs with pinless hand grenades that blew to bits unsuspecting people whose heads scraped the metal. "There were full-scale battles below," writes one historian of the uprising, "as men fought hand-to-hand and drowned each other in excrement." Old Town fell on September 2, 1944, a month after the insurrection started.[12]

Meanwhile, the Russians were in no position to come to the aid of the insurgents, and events would soon prove they were in no mood to do so either. It is one of the most acrimonious chapters in the history of Polish-Russian relations. "Sooner or later the truth about the handful of power-seeking criminals who launched the Warsaw adventure will be out," Stalin said disgustedly of the Polish leaders for their failure to consult Soviet commanders. "Let's be serious," Marshal Rokossovsky told an American journalist who interviewed him at his Lublin headquarters while the uprising raged. "An armed insurrection in a place like Warsaw could only have succeeded if it had been carefully co-ordinated with the Red Army." The Polish commanders, he continued, were "like the clown in the circus who pops up at the wrong moment and only gets rolled up in the carpet. . . . If it were only a piece of clowning it wouldn't matter, but the political stunt is going to cost Poland thousands of lives. It is an appalling tragedy, and they are now trying to put the blame on us."[13]

The Russians had good reason for failing to intervene. Early in August, German panzer divisions counterattacked and destroyed the Soviet tank army outside Praga, and thereafter Rokossovsky's forces concentrated their energies at the Magnuszew bridgehead thirty-five miles south of the city. But Stalin also evinced scant interest in the fate of the uprising. Not until the insurrection had nearly been crushed did he allow Allied planes to use airfields behind Russian lines to deliver badly needed supplies to the insurgents. And during a lull in the fighting between Soviet and Nazi armies, while Warsaw was collapsing into rubble and cinder, one Home Army commander reported observing "sun-bathing by both sides of their front lines, although the distance between their positions is only 300 metres."[14]

Praga escaped the wholesale death and destruction occurring on the other side of the Vistula, but conditions in this working-class suburb were far from rosy. "Right now it was dangerous for all of us to go into the streets," Ruth said, "because the orders from Himmler and the other big shots became worse and worse." The Germans invaded churches to monitor sermons. They arrested and executed people on the slightest pretext. They destroyed buildings. "The Germans were," to use Ruth's language, "mad and filled with hate . . . and plenty people were killed just like the way we kill a roach. It went on every single day. Sitting in the cellars, everybody was thinking of how to get out of this alive. Everybody was afraid and mixed up."

Paradoxically, the pervasive gloom eased Ruth and Mark's psychological burden. For a year and a half they had been forced to dissemble the relentless anxiety that had been their constant companion, and now they could, in an odd sort of way, feel relaxed about their nervousness because disquietude had become the norm. "For us it was easier. Everybody was now in the same situation," Ruth explained.

For Jews residing on the left bank of the Vistula, near the uprising's center, the circumstances were much more dire. Ghetto fighters from the ZOB were often in the thick of the combat, sometimes fighting shoulder to shoulder with the AK against a common foe. It was a strange and exhilarating feeling but also more than a little dangerous. Jews who joined the Home Army were frequently sent on the most dangerous missions. A few were shot in the back. Most ZOB veterans chose to fight with the Communist underground. Inside Jewish bunkers, conditions approached the nadir reached during the ghetto revolt. One group of twenty Jews was forced to hide out in a bomb-damaged cellar that had been hastily converted into a cemetery. Vladka Meed, in her capacity as a courier for the ZOB, visited the site after one heavy bombardment. "It was a scene of horrible carnage," she recalled. "Handkerchiefs covering their noses and mouths, Jews were picking up pieces of human flesh from the ground. The stench was nearly intolerable. A German hand grenade had struck several of the graves, disinterring and disintegrating the recently buried corpses. Nevertheless, the Jews preferred to stay in this gruesome sanctuary with its suffocating atmosphere and rebury the bits of human flesh, rather than cope with the hostile Gentile hoodlums outside."[15]

Toward the end of August, when renewed shelling and aerial activity signaled the resumption of the Russia offensive against Praga,[16] Mark decided that the Skorecki family had to make preparations to leave. He dug a big hole behind their shack in the lumberyard, stuffed the family's clothes and valuables in a suitcase, wrapping the valise plus assorted loose belongings in tar paper, and buried the bundle in the ground. Then he stacked lumber on top of the freshly turned dirt. The decisive moment for Mark had come when the Germans ordered all able-bodied Poles to report for work, possibly inside the Reich, and set a deadline. "I will leave from here," he told Ruth. "I'm not going with the Germans." By virtue of their membership in the Polish reserve, Smolenski and his partner were equally alarmed. Smolenski told Mark he was evacuating his wife and disabled son to the resort town of Otwock, twenty miles southeast of the city. Mark said he intended to head for the country. But which way to go? Street corner amplifiers blared out two choices. "The loudspeakers scream the whole day, the whole night: 'Go to the South. Go to the North. Go to the Russians. Go to the Germans.' I decided to go to the Russians," Mark recalled almost forty years later, which means he probably went due east.[17] An exact destination was hazy in his mind. "We of course didn't know where to go," Ruth admitted.

Before departing they went to see Natalia Piotrowska at Lochowska 15 to learn her intentions. "She was going to stay in Warsaw because she had no children or husband," she told Mark and Ruth. That evening while everyone in the cellar was getting ready to bed down for the night, an engineer and his wife asked the Skoreckis about their plans for the next day. The deadline for reporting to German work details was set for that time. The Skoreckis had gotten to know the couple during their nightly sojourns inside the cellar. The couple had a teenaged son and were nice to Anne and Lila. Mark told them he intended to leave for the country. "They said we are going with you," which suited the Skoreckis just fine.

The next morning they locked up the shack, put Lila in a stroller, put knapsacks on their backs ("with a little food, bread mostly"), and started for the country. "It wasn't an easy walk," Ruth said. "It was hard to take kids along on this type of thing." Lila was crying. All the while they were on the lookout for Germans. "Luckily we didn't run into any," Ruth said. She derived sly pleasure from knowing the other couple never suspected the Skoreckis' true identity. "The engineer was in the Polish Reserves. But they were walking with Jews. In this minute we were all in the same boat." Still, the situation was difficult.

It seemed like the hike went on forever. "We walked, we walked, we walked, we walked, we walked, and we walked," Mark said late in life.[18] Ruth said the two families trekked about seven or eight miles into the country before Mark had to rest against a farmer's fence alongside the road. "It was hot, and my Dad got sick," Anne says. He told Ruth he was burning up with fever and was unable to go any farther. The farm was on the edge of a village, and there were, perhaps, twenty or thirty people milling around. "We couldn't let him stay on the highway," Ruth said. "The Germans might spot him." There was nothing left to do but ask the farmer for permission to spend the night in his barn. Ruth and her companions told the peasant they had a sick man on their hands and young children. The ailing man would probably feel better in the morning. Then they could look for another place. "The farmer said okay, I let you in." He was hungry for news from Warsaw.

The farmer and his wife fed the kids and gave Ruth and the engineer and his family something to eat as well. There was no medicine on hand for Mark. And he expected none. "Mark told us not to do anything, just to leave him alone. He just wanted to sleep."

He felt no better the next morning. In fact, it took him several days to re-cover. Ruth told the engineer and his wife, "Listen, if you want to go some-where else, go ahead." There were safer places to be than a combat zone. She would wait here until Mark got better. The Polish couple said no: "We are stay-ing together with you. Where you go, we go also." The farmer and his wife were just as friendly, telling their city guests they could stay as long as Mark was feeling ill. For Anne and Lila the stay at the farmhouse was like being on sum-mer vacation for the first time since early childhood. The two sisters and the teenaged boy started playing with the farmer's many children. If anyone de-tected Jewish origins in Anne's dark features, they kept their suspicions private. Meanwhile Ruth and the engineer's wife helped out around the house, offering to pay the peasant couple for the milk, eggs, and other food they consumed.

"Little by little Mark started feeling better," Ruth said, "and we started thinking of going somewhere else to look for a place to stay." But the farmer and his wife said, "Why do you have to go somewhere else? You can stay here." The first day Mark felt well enough to be up and about the farmer discovered he had a magician in his house. Mark accompanied the farmer to the field. He always liked paying his own way, in service if not in money, making himself useful. Besides, he had skills the peasant needed: much of the farm machinery was broken down and in disrepair. "First thing in the morning," Mark said, "I see he walks out and wants to repair a machine. I went out and showed him how to fix the machine." And then he turned his attention to his host's other machinery problems. Mark's reticence vanished when it came to inanimate objects. He was quietly self-assured, taking charge without anyone's fully realizing he was now in control. "We're going to do this, and we're going to do this, and we're going to do this," he told the farmer. And they did just that, mending every plow and harvester on the premise, and when they finished overhauling the farm machinery, Mark helped the farmer bring in his harvest, even lending a hand, along with the engineer, in baking the country bread. The farmer insisted on paying him for his services, but Mark would not hear of it. He did take the farmer up on one offer. The barn had filled up with other fugitives fleeing the war zone, and the first night after Mark repaired a piece of machinery, the farmer told him, "Now, you and your kids and your wife are going to sleep in the attic, over my house, and you're gonna eat in my house." There were no stairs to the attic, only a ladder. Equipped with blankets furnished by the farmer, every night the Skoreckis and the engineer and his family climbed into the attic. It was rough and crude. The floor was hard, the roof leaked. But complaint was the furthest thing from the Skoreckis' minds. "It was the best accommodation you can get," Mark said. They were happy to be away from the war-ravaged city.[19]

Ruth said they stayed in the country two or three weeks, but the sojourn was probably more like a month. "Of course, the farmer didn't know he had the pleasure of being the host to a Jewish family," Ruth said. "We went to church on Sunday, we started fixing our Sunday meal for dinner, and in the evenings we prayed like the other couples." There was no way to exclude Anne from the religious charade, and she had to mumble and copycat her way through the service and prayers as best she could. The routine was soon broken up, however. The sound of booming guns started coming closer and closer, as did German troops and their Ukrainian Hiwis. They encamped in nearby fields and forests and lined the highways. They made their headquarters in the area. They even entered the farmer's house looking for guns. Mark understood the babble of different tongues—Russian, Ukrainian, German, and Polish—but he kept his linguistic fluency to himself, not merely to allow him to eavesdrop on conversations not meant for civilian ears but also to disguise a multilingualism that only Jews possessed at this time in this corner of the world. All the while, Mark continued working in the fields, like a hired hand. "And all the time," Ruth added, "we tried not to let them know we were going up into the attic." It might have invited suspicion.

Though bombs and artillery shells never struck the village near where they were staying, they soon started falling over the general vicinity. "Plenty of times we saw flames from places which had been bombed," Ruth said. It was around the second or third week of their country sojourn, and Mark told the farmer it was time to build a bunker. It had to be done by stealth. Rounding up local villagers, at 4:00 A.M. one morning they went to the field and began digging a hideout. They must have worked fast and efficiently to escape detection. The underground bunker was large—about fifty feet long and twelve feet wide, with benches gouged into the earthen walls and entrances placed at both ends. As fast as they worked, it still took the men three days to excavate the bunker and cover it with logs and mud. Inside they put blankets, mainly for the children. "When things were bad we went in and when things were silent we came out," Ruth said. Mark was pleased with himself for having performed a protector's role that by now had become second nature. "In case planes come, we gonna have a home here," he told his helpers. "And I was supervisor in building the protection."[20]

One night German soldiers came to the farmhouse asking if anyone inside understood German. The farmer gestured toward Mark, saying he thought he understood a few words and phrases of the language. The soldiers told Mark, "Listen, tell the farmer that everybody has to go with us. The Russians are very close, and tomorrow maybe too late to get out." "OK," Mark said in the misleadingly meek tone his voice assumed when a situation struck him as particularly absurd. Then he told everybody—the farmer and the engineer's families, and through them, the villagers—that they needed to pack up food and, after dark, slip quietly into the bunker. "One by one we went in," Ruth said. The men locked up the house, then covered up the dugout, hunkering down for an extended stay.

They remained underground for two days. "From time to time we heard the ground shaking from a bomb being dropped far away," Ruth said, "and we all prayed to God to save us from the bombs." On the second night things fell oddly silent. "We didn't hear a thing—voices, bombs, nothing—QUIET," she said for emphasis. After a while Mark told the group, "Listen, one of us has to go out and see what is going on around us and why it is so quiet." Then he volunteered to check himself. Everyone had become disoriented by the long confinement. Mark thought it was still dark when he emerged to the morning light. Neither Germans nor Ukrainians were anywhere to be seen. Their horses were gone. The military vehicles had departed. He ran back to the dugout with the news. "Something has happened; the German is going." The farm folk and their city guests scampered to the surface, shaking off dirt and anxiety. They found the house untouched. The Germans had apparently concluded that the farmer's family had left as they had been instructed to do. Ruth fed the kids. "Everybody can understand our feelings at this moment," she said.

It was premature to feel completely relieved, however. Although the Germans had left, the general area still fell inside a war zone. One night shortly after abandoning the bunker, Mark was awakened by bombardment. "I stayed by the window and just looked out," he said. "It was four o'clock, three o'clock in the morning, and dark outside, . . . and I look out and see something moving—in lines, in lines—moving! And I was not sure. But here comes the Russians. They were all on foot. And they came in."[21]

They must have arrived sometime following the Soviet capture of Praga on September 14 after four days of heavy fighting, because the Russians who came to the farmhouse were on a mopping-up operation and were scouting for any Germans still lurking in the area. Mark and Ruth told the soldiers they were Polish. But a senior officer soon entered the dwelling and told them, according to Ruth, "that we were all free and that we didn't have to be afraid of anything. The Jews didn't have to fear any more either. Everybody is free now," he continued, "and you can do what you want to do from here on out." Apparently Jewish himself, the officer asked Mark and Ruth point-blank: "Are you Jewish?"

"I looked at Mark and he looked at me," Ruth said. They said nothing in reply but went off by themselves to the side. "It was very hard in this time to tell the people with whom we were staying that we were Jews," Ruth said, and Mark had no intention of doing so now. He told his wife they were returning to Praga. "We are not waiting for anything. We aren't waiting one minute. We are just taking the kids and our things and we are going back." His mind was set. He had endured too much to risk betrayal or worse at the hands of Polish anti-Semites. Things must have been said around the farmhouse and inside the bunker to have placed him on full alert.

The farmer was baffled by Mark's sense of urgency. "Why are you so hungry to leave?" he asked. "You were so many weeks with us. Stay and enjoy this with us." Mark and Ruth respectfully declined. They had left their valuables in Warsaw, they told him, and needed to return to check on their safety. "Of course, we thanked him with all our hearts," Ruth said, "but they were thankful to us and Mark because due to him they didn't have to run but could hide right by the house. They didn't lose anything by not following the Germans' orders to leave." From Mark's perspective the accounts had been settled.

Loading up their backpacks, they started back for the city that very morning, without the company of the engineer and his family, who apparently had decided it was too risky to return just yet. Russian soldiers had advised against returning because the Germans had mined the roads leading into Warsaw. On the way back they saw craters along the highway and heard explosions in the distance. "It was very dangerous in this time to go back," Ruth admitted. But Mark was adamant. They pressed ahead. It took the entire day to reach Praga. The walk formed another chapter in a book of accumulating miracles. "Like all the time before," Ruth marveled later, "God was with us now too, and we were happy about coming out of the grasp of the Germans. We couldn't think of anything else but to go back."

But back to what? Urban anonymity, or perhaps to better-known dangers? But maybe that was all they wanted at the time. City life at least provided some cover. The routine was familiar, the lines well rehearsed, as was the anxiety. Now that everyone around them felt relaxed, the Skoreckis were left alone once again with never-ending fears and the exhausting fatigue of keeping them disguised. "For us, every moment was too much already," Ruth said of their Aryan masquerade. Liberation for the Poles may have meant resuming quasi-normal lives, but for disguised Jews such as the Skoreckis, it signaled a return to the stage and the pressures of performing. At least in Warsaw the routine was familiar and would not have to be continually improvised.

And that was the problem with passing in wartime Poland: you never knew when it was comfortable—or even safe—to resume casual normality. The feeling of being different, apart, and frightened never dissipated. It was as though constant exposure to anti-Semitism had scarred its victims with an inferiority complex that might never heal. An assumed Aryan identity might save a life, but its cost was an eavesdropping familiarity with the pervasiveness of Polish contempt for Jews, like a sixth sense about what people were saying behind your back. Disguised on a peasant's farm, they may have heard the worst.

They went directly to Natalia Piotrowska's apartment at Lochowska 15 when they arrived in Praga that evening, grabbing a bite to eat. "Thank God, everything was all right with her," Ruth said. "And she was very happy to see us and happy that we had saved our lives." The news about other acquaintances was less cheerful. "Plenty of her friends and plenty of the men had been taken away by the Germans"—presumably to do forced labor in the Reich. The Skoreckis stayed only long enough to eat dinner. Mark was anxious to return to the office shack, to check up on things in the lumberyard and the factory. He and Ruth had heard that abandoned businesses were being indiscriminately rifled by local inhabitants.

The walk back along Ząbkowska Street confirmed their worst fears. The looting was rampant. "We saw hundreds of people carrying off different things because hundreds of business places were unoccupied," Ruth said. The anarchy had already invaded the lumberyard, where everything not nailed down seemed to be disappearing. Wood was vanishing by the cord, and this on the eve of the harsh winter months ahead. "The whole neighborhood was carrying out material," Ruth said. The only thing spared by the mob was the buried suitcase and other Skorecki family items.

Just then, Mark took a big chance, given the fact that in prewar Poland looting and pogroms often went hand in hand and that his identity was probably under some suspicion in the neighborhood. He forthwith ordered everybody to return what they had taken. "I'm in charge of this place right now," he said. "This belongs to Mr. Smolenski and his partner, and he gave me the authority to take care of his property." And, miraculously, the looters not only desisted, but some even returned what they had already plundered.

Leaving Ruth and the girls in the shack, Mark locked up the lumberyard and ran over to the factory. "There the picture was the same," Ruth said. "People were taking whatever they could. So Mark told them the same. The owners are not here, but I have the power to take care of the factory, too." "We were happy that we had come in time, because in this time plenty of places like this were cleaned out," Ruth noted. "Nothing was left."

It was another risky gesture, though. Neither Mark nor Ruth had the slightest inkling of how the owners were faring. From Smolenski they had heard nothing at all; presumably he was still in the summer resort of Otwock with his family. When he or his partner might return to Praga was an open question. The roads were still heavily mined making travel extremely dangerous.

But Mark was proud he took the risk. It was the right thing to do, he felt. "In our mind we were thinking of what we could do for our bosses," Ruth explained. "We were grateful for all the things that they had done for us. They knew who we were. We felt like we were paying back a bill which money could never pay back. Because of these men four lives, which are worth millions of dollars, were saved. We were happy that we had the opportunity to show them appreciation for what they had done for us." That was typical of the Skoreckis: honor even unspoken moral contracts, and settle all ethical accounts in full. Lying might be unavoidable, but that was scarcely an excuse for not balancing moral ledgers when the chance arose.

Fortunately, the Skoreckis did not have to move back into the office shack. Mark had found an empty six-room apartment—"a real apartment," Ruth exulted—in the four-story building next to the lumberyard. It was on the ground floor. After moving in, Mark locked up the factory and the lumberyard and hunkered down until conditions improved.

Although Praga itself had been liberated, daily existence remained perilous. In mid-September, shortly after capturing Praga, several Soviet-affiliated Polish infantry regiments established small bridgeheads on the left bank of the Vistula, but they were quickly pinned down by German tank and artillery fire, and Marshal Rokossovsky, who never believed his forces were in condition to capture Warsaw, withdrew the units after only a few days.[22] For the rest of the month and periodically throughout the fall of 1944 Soviet forces used the working-class suburb as a staging area to attack Warsaw. It increased the precariousness of everyday life. "Plenty of people who went out never came back," Ruth said. "Many a bomb took the life from these people." Mark ventured out of doors only to get food, and every time he did so Ruth and the children worried he would never return. In the meantime, the family spent long hours under the stairs in the basement. "Many times we had to go in the cellar to protect ourselves from the bombing," she added. During bombing lulls, German loudspeakers urged Pragan civilians to sabotage property and cross the Vistula. The Russians blasted similar amplified appeals to the other side of the river. "Of course, none of us were paying attention," Ruth said. "We knew what the score was already."

But it was not merely the bursting shells that kept noncombatants on edge; Soviet intentions were another cause for worry. "Lots of people were afraid of the Russians," Ruth said. "They didn't know what to expect from them." The immediate concern was the heavy-handedness with which the Soviets quartered their troops. For weeks on end Russian soldiers bivouacked in backyards, while officers became uninvited guests in civilian apartments. To avert that possibility, the Skoreckis asked the woman whose feed store occupied the same lot with the lumberyard to move in with them. They had room to spare. The strategy was not foolproof. "From time to time we had to let in some Russian to spend the night, too," Ruth said. "We had to do this. They would come in anyway and we might get in trouble."

Then, in November 1944, Mark's boss returned suddenly to check up on his factory and apartment. His family was still in Otwock. He had lost contact with his partner. Smolenski was surprised to find his property still intact. From his country refuge fifteen miles away it was easy to hear the artillery shelling in Praga and pick up news of the wanton pillage and looting. When neighbors told him the Skoreckis had moved to a nearby apartment building, Smolenski went directly to their place. "I can't explain the happy moment when he came back," Ruth said. The three of them spent that evening swapping stories about their experiences since fleeing the city. And then he spent every night thereafter with the Skoreckis, boarding in their apartment notwithstanding the fact that he had relatives in Praga. It was a time for divulging secrets. One evening after supper, while sharing a few drinks alone in the apartment, Smolenski told Mark and Ruth the whole story: about the salesman who had recognized Mark's surname in the office one afternoon; about the time he had refused Mark's request to build a porch; and about the other intimations he had received that the Skoreckis were actually Jewish. It was an odd sort of confession because practically in the same breath he admitted, to use his own words, "I was not too crazy about Jewish people, but you and your family are the likes of whom I have never met in my life."

"I'm glad I could do something for you too," Mark said, in reply, explaining why he had prevented the mob from looting him, "because you saved four lives. We were in your hands the whole time. Whenever you wanted, you could have let the Germans know who we were." So far as Mark and Ruth were concerned, that was the central point, not Smolenski's obvious anti-Semitism. That Smolenski could easily have turned over the Skoreckis to Nazi authorities but never did was a mitzvah—a "good deed"—the Skoreckis never forgot. Nor were they unmindful that he had kept them on his property even when others had broadcast their suspicions, thus rendering him an active abettor, not an unwitting accomplice, in the eyes of the ss. That too was an act of human solidarity for which they remained forever thankful.

On January 17, 1945, just as Soviet forces were about to encircle the capital, the Germans evacuated Warsaw. It was the opening salvo of an invasion that would ultimately unleash more men, machines, and fighting fury than had any military campaign in human history. The juggernaut was relentless. Two days after the Russians took Warsaw, they captured the old textile center of Łódź, the Skorecki homestead. By early February their armies were on the banks of the Oder River poised for a final thrust against Berlin itself.

What the Russians found on Warsaw's left bank was a heap of rubble devoid of all visible human habitation. After quashing the uprising, the Nazis sent three-quarters of a million civilians to forced labor camps both in Poland and the Third Reich. Then German demolition squads, fulfilling Hitler's wrathful orders that Warsaw be "razed without trace," dynamited the city's still-standing buildings. The medieval Old Town was reduced to rubble. Libraries and museums vanished completely. Where five bridges had once crossed the Vistula, "at the war's end only twisted steel girders jutted from the water at odd angles," reported an American emissary who visited the city a year and a half later and found refugees still burrowing in holes in the ground. The final body count was equally stupendous: nearly fifty thousand military casualties on both sides, and upward of two hundred thousand civilian victims. Untold numbers, many of them Jews who had been hiding underground since the ghetto's destruction eighteen months earlier, were buried alive beneath the fire-blackened mass. In a few short months Warsaw had literally become one of the world's largest graveyards.[23]

But that scarcely deterred refugees from streaming back to the city after the Russian takeover. Sprinkled among the returnees were a few Jews. "Of course, not many," Ruth conceded. But, miraculously, one was a Skorecki—Morris Skorecki's youngest son, Adam, who had served as a guide to a Soviet general. One day he showed up unexpectedly in the uniform of a Polish officer. "And that night he also comes in with two cases of vodka and we had a big party over there," Mark later recalled. "A liberation party!"[24]

There was not a whole lot to celebrate, however. Most of the Jewish survivors were single parents or unmarried young adults. "Sometimes the wife was with the Germans and the husband was with the Russians," Ruth explained. "With kids nobody took chances like we had, keeping the whole family together." The major exception were the nearly 140,000 Polish Jews who had fled to the Soviet Union shortly after the 1939 invasion. But even after their repatriation in the spring and summer of 1946, it was exceedingly rare to encounter, in the words of one American journalist, "the miracle of whole Jewish families."[25] "As far as the age structure is concerned," writes Lucjan Dobroszycki, himself a survivor, "this population forms a demographic pyramid whose top was lopped off and whose base was pared down: there were relatively few older people and children, for they most of all had been denied the right to live."[26]

Surrounded by young daughters, Mark and Ruth must have struck the surviving remnant of Polish Jewry as the beneficiaries of charmed immunity.

Except for the current of returning refugees, Pragan days blended into one another. Business was stagnant. Nobody knew where they stood with the Russians, who were continuing their roundup of Polish officers, politicians, priests, and any others who, to quote Ruth, "they thought could be dangerous to them." Adam Skorecki dropped out of sight, and Mark and Ruth do not appear to have heard from him again during the postwar period.

Not long after Soviet armies reached the Oder, clearing Poland of German forces, the Skoreckis decided to go back to Łódź. The unexpected appearance of Mark's cousin had heightened their curiosity about the fate of other family members. "We thought maybe some of our relatives would turn up," Ruth said, "and that we could have our apartment back where we had lived before the war and had left everything." Their decision to return to Łódź upset Smolenski, though. He begged Mark to stay, even offering to bring him into the business. He promised to give his foreman anything he asked for. Mark politely declined, advising him to sell his business and move to England or the United States "because later on this would never be his." He had another reason for turning down the offer. Despite the liberation, the Skoreckis continued to live as non-Jews, even celebrating Christmas again so as to avoid divulging their real identities. "We told him that we didn't want to let people know who we were now," Ruth said, "because we wanted to go back to our city and again be the same as before." Smolenski refused to take no for an answer, although no was the only answer he would ever receive.

It was decided Ruth would return to Łódź first, while Mark stayed behind with the children in Praga. Much later in life, when he was eighty-three, Mark said he was the one who traveled back home to find lodging for his family.[27] But in light of Ruth's fear of separation, it was assuredly Mark who stayed behind because adult men traveling alone were more likely than single women to face arrest and forced labor impressment. In any event, Anne does not recall his being away from the family during this period. "It would have made such an impact that I would have remembered it," she said.

Ruth made the journey in early February 1945, stopping first at their old apartment building at Legionów 8 in downtown Łódź. The Russians had already taken possession of the premises, converting most of the apartments into offices for the provisional Polish government. The family's belongings had completely vanished, along with the gentile neighbor who had offered to hold in safekeeping a few of her more precious possessions. Gone as well was the janitor in charge from before the war. The concierge from the building across the street recognized Ruth as she was leaving. They knew each other from before the war, and he invited her to stay in his apartment until she located a place for the family to live. There was the usual trading of war stories. Ruth told him about "living on the other side of the fence," as she characterized the Skoreckis' Aryan phase, but said nothing about their thirty-two month confinement in the Warsaw Ghetto. Those searing memories were too painful to revisit just yet. The reunion with the concierge had a bittersweet quality, reminding her of how far she had slid down the social scale, yet making her thankful for any chance to reconnect with the prewar past. "Maybe in my life I had never stayed in a janitor's house," she mused, "but in this time it was for me like finding a relative."

That was uppermost in her mind—learning the fate of her Łódź relations—and the first thing the next morning she went directly to what she referred to as "the Jewish federation" to check the registries for Skorecki and Tempelhof names and to register the names of her own family. The "federation" was actually a branch of the Central Committee of Jews in Poland, which had been established in Lublin in November 1944, with financial support from various Jewish organizations around the world, such as the American Jewish Committee and the Joint Distribution Committee. Except for a parallel organization of Orthodox Jews called the Religious Congregation, the Central Committee represented a broad cross section of every ideological shade of Polish Jewry. In his capacity as the highest-ranking member of the ZOB, Yitzhak Zuckerman had a seat on the committee. Much of the organization's activity involved conducting registrations at such locations as Praga and Łódź, to help returning refugees trace missing family members. The work went on day after day for months on end. One of the busiest branch offices was in Łódź, which saw a heavy volume of traffic in February, when Ruth reported to its bureau. Nearly 4,400 survivors registered that month, but hardly any of them were from the Łódź Ghetto, and no Skoreckis or Tempelhofs appeared on the lists. In fact, by the end of 1945 only 877 of the entire registration were survivors of the Łódź Ghetto.[28]

The people working at the Łódź office of the Central Committee knew Ruth from before the war, and they asked her the question they routinely put to all survivors. Was she by herself? The answer had always been the same: Yes, no one survived but me. This time it was different. No, Ruth said, "I have my husband and my two girls." The reaction stunned her, clouding the moral meaning of the risks she and Mark had taken to keep family intact: "They started looking at me as though I were crazy. They asked me what was I saying. 'You see how many people are in this office? Not one of us has his whole family like you. We are just by ourselves.' They thought that many people were sort of crazy at this time, and they looked at me with sorrow and pity. They couldn't understand how my story could have come about. They were sure I was making it all up. Tears came to my eyes. I didn't say anything. I just asked them to put my name down in the register. Maybe somebody would ask if I were alive."[29]

The incredulity on the faces of the clerks burned like a solar afterimage when she exited the office. She stood on the street outside going over in her mind the fact that even her own people doubted her veracity. Here she was finally telling the truth for the first time in years, and the immediate response was that she was lying. "I really was hurt," Ruth said, "because of all the terrible things I had gone through. They couldn't believe that I had survived when so many others hadn't."

She understood the reasons for their reaction. She has seen something similar among grieving parents in Schultz's Shop who resented the Skoreckis' success at safeguarding their daughters from the relentless ss dragnets. Now, as then, Ruth tried to see matters through their eyes: "I felt that people who didn't believe my story were jealous of me for having gotten through all this mess. But I didn't hold it against them because had I been in their shoes, I would have felt the same way."

There was still the matter of finding a place to live, which was not easy to do. She visited a bureau that assigned available housing to refugees. They told her she had to wait. After five days of staying at the janitor's apartment, a furnished flat turned up at Legionów 5, across the street and a few doors down from where the Skoreckis had been living when the war broke out. "Of course, I was very happy that I was so lucky in finding such a nice apartment," Ruth said. Thanking the janitor, she hurried back to Praga with the good news, and the family packed their things, said goodbye to everybody, and left immediately. Smolenski redoubled his entreaties that Mark stay with him. He offered his foreman a partnership. Mark demurred once again. "For the time being I am going back to Łódź," he told his former boss. "For how long I don't know."

Mark was impressed with the apartment his wife had located. Almost forty years later he could still remember its opulent appointments. The flat had been occupied by "a German big shot," he later recalled in his fractured English. "Everything in a house that you cannot find in the United States except in a millionaire's home, this was all there. A piano, silver, china, everything you can think of! And all of it grabbed from the people. . . . And I went to the government. 'Here is the key,' they said. 'Move in.' And I went and moved my family in."[30]

One of Ruth's first tasks after returning to Łódź was to bring Anne and Lila to the Łódź branch office of the Central Committee to let the registry clerks see for themselves that she had not been lying or deranged. The visit dispelled all doubts. In fact, it elicited praise. "The people made a big fuss over us because there weren't that many children," Anne recalls. "Knowing my mother, she must have felt gratified that all the hard work and struggle had been validated. And she surely liked the fact that for a change she was finally able to be honest instead of engaging in this make-believe existence with its constant lies. That fact alone must have lifted a heavy burden from her conscience."

But then she had to start coming to terms with survivor guilt. She soon discovered the fate of her parents: "I found out that they had died in 1942," Ruth said. "In June my father and one month later my mother." To be exact, according to extant ghetto records, the dates of death for her parents were June 12, 1942, for Abram Tempelhof and July 11, 1942, for Sara, who died of tuberculosis, a common side effect of extreme hunger.[31]

Nearly as traumatic as learning the fate of her parents was witnessing the condition of most survivors. Often the first to return were the Jews who had hidden in the woods, sewers, and attics, many of them hollow-cheeked, broken, and alone. "Plenty of people came back from hiding places in which they had stayed for months, never seeing the light of day, and with little food, and when they went out the light blinded them," Ruth said. Next came the camp survivors, who by far made up the largest contingent (nearly half the total in 1945, before the heavier Soviet repatriation of 1946), and they were the worst off. The majority were extremely ill: "physical and mental wrecks," according to one official report. Spectral figures, many had lost their teeth. Their hair was dry and close-cropped, their feet badly swollen, their skin diaphanous. Death's proximity seemed to stare from cavernous eyes. Ruth believed the camp survivors she came across were on the verge of death at the time of liberation, and she was uncannily close to the truth. One-third of the sixty thousand camp inmates liberated by the Allies in 1945 died within two weeks.[32] Yet it was not the poor physical condition of the less fortunate survivors that stirred Ruth but their aloneness. "Everybody was by himself, without their families. No relatives, nothing," she said, adding for extra emphasis, "THESE WERE HITLER'S LEFTOVERS."

It is a natural human impulse to compare degrees of suffering. Even today Poles and Jews quarrel over the primacy of suffering at the hands of the Nazis. Ruth never made those comparisons, doubtless regarding them as illegitimate. She seems to have adopted the attitude that each person's distress was unique and at the same time linked to all human suffering. "To tell the truth," she said with understated insight, "we were all invalids and all had our sicknesses." But she did feel fortunate to have survived with her immediate family intact and to have received an apartment with all the conveniences. She had made a promise to herself: "Whoever I knew who needed help, I would be ready to help in whatever way I could."

How Mark supported himself after returning to Łódź is not entirely clear. Much later in life he mentioned doing maintenance work for their new apartment building and also operating a shop of some kind near the family flat. Doing what, he never said, but it was not in the building trades.[33] "We no longer had our construction business," Ruth said. Finding work at the family lumber business was out of the question. Soon after returning to Łódź, Mark went to his brother Wladek's lumberyard, but the Pole who had managed it before the war (the father-in-law of the former priest who had helped the Skoreckis escape the Warsaw Ghetto) told him everything was gone. He ran into the owner of Legionów 8, Mieczysław Pinkus—"a millionaire; a Jewish guy but assimilated," according to Mark—who had, like the Skoreckis, suddenly reappeared with his wife and only daughter after a several years' absence. "Where is everything?" Mark asked. His former landlord remembered only that their belongings had been stored in the attic. After that they disappeared, he said. And so had much of the material foundation of the Skoreckis' prewar way of life.[34]

A lot of unexpected visitors dropped in at the Skoreckis' new apartment on Legionów Street. During Passover—the first Jewish holidays the Skoreckis had openly observed since the war began—Mark encountered a Jewish friend who had owned one of Łódź's largest machine tool factories before the 1939 invasion. There was always a special poignancy right after the war about meeting up with even casual former acquaintances and comparing survival notes. The factory owner had spent the war in England serving in the government-in-exile, assisting the Polish underground's efforts to distribute money to people in hiding throughout Europe. "We didn't know too much about all this," Ruth said, because the Skoreckis had received little if any outside financial aid during their sojourn on the Aryan side.

Shortly after VE Day, on May 8, 1945—when noise-making and marching bands took over the streets, as Ruth recalled—the son of Mark's barber appeared at the door. The young man could not have been much older than twenty. His parents had died during the war, and the young man, who had been carried off to fight with the Russians, returned home in the uniform of a Soviet officer. With him was an attractive young woman he intended to marry. He apparently stopped by the Skoreckis to seek their assistance with the nuptials. Although Mark was forty-five and Ruth six months shy of forty, they had become de facto community elders by virtue of the catastrophic decimation of old and young alike. Ruth always relished the role of social chairperson, and this was her first postwar opportunity for taking charge. She did it up right. "Of course he would like to have a Jewish wedding," she explained, "so I arranged it." She pulled off the minor miracle of finding a rabbi who had gone into hiding during the war—where, she never knew, but he had to have been one of the rare few missed by the Nazis. After a simple service, the wedding party descended on the Skorecki apartment. Because the gaiety contrasted so dramatically with the gloomy furtiveness of the war period, Anne remembers the laughter that filled the living room as though it were yesterday. Two photographs survive from the occasion. In one, the pensive groom and his laughing bride sit wedged between Mark and Ruth on the sofa. In the other, surrounding the newlyweds, are a dozen men and women, all in their twenties or early thirties. They are laughing and smiling, including Ruth, the clearly proud hostess. Standing in the bottom center of the photograph in front of the bride are Anne and Lila. The young woman's hands are resting on each girl's shoulder, not only to make them feel part of the occasion but, perhaps subconsciously, to use them as stand-ins for all the nieces and nephews who would have been part of the festivities but for the Holocaust. The camera caught Lila just as an unselfconscious grin leaked across her face, but Anne's expression is harder to decipher. Slightly ajar to show clenched teeth, her mouth is frozen somewhere between a smile and utter bafflement, as though unable to make up her mind whether it was safe to unbuckle the straitjacket that had so long restrained the emotions of a stolen childhood. The bridegroom's vacant face is equally hard to read; he seems distracted, lost in thought. And on Mark's visage is the stolid grin of an ID photo. There is no doubt that joy filled the apartment that day, but it was scarcely unalloyed.

By now Mark and Ruth had learned the fate of most of their relatives, with the exception of Henry and Vovek Tempelhof. Haka had returned from Gdańsk to check up on her parents. The last official trace of Wladek and Gustawa Skorecki was a Łódź Ghetto registration form dated March 20, 1942, indicating a change of address. According to the caretaker at the family lumberyard, they subsequently disappeared into the maw of the ss camp system. Somewhat more likely is their probable asphyxiation in the gas vans at

Chełmno in June 1944.[35] In either case, to quote Ruth, "Haka's parents were dead."

Occasionally there was good news, some of it inexplicably omitted from Ruth's postwar memoir. Among the trickle of visitors who showed up at the Skoreckis' apartment from time to time were members of Mark's family, such as Pola Skorecka, one of his Działoszycean cousins. She had been in the Łódź Ghetto, in the camps at Auschwitz, and, at the time of her liberation, in a labor camp in Czechoslovakia. Upon being freed she traveled to Kraków to look for her family and inquire after her brother. "No one survived. I was alone," she said. Then she ran into a cousin on the street and asked, " 'Where are the Skoreckis?' 'They are in Łódź,' he answered. So I traveled to Łódź, went to the Jewish Community office and said, 'I am a Skorecki. I am looking for someone from the Skorecki family.' " They directed her to Mark and Ruth. "Ah, Pola," Ruth exclaimed in joy. "I was the first Skorecki she had found," Pola said— other than Haka, whom Ruth had been in touch with off and on for most of the war anyway.[36]

Ruth was less happy to see Stefa Silberberg and her family, though, which probably explains why she elided their homecoming from memory. Before the invasion their relationship had been cordial. Stefa had been Mark's favorite sister. They had been very close. "Before the war we had good contact," remembers Moshe, Stefa's son. "Very good. Ruth was a good aunt. We came to play with the kids, the young kids, my sister and I." Stefa's family had returned to Łódź in May 1945, via Kazakhstan and Byelorussia. But the postwar reunion with Ruth was anything but warm. "She [Ruth] was a little annoyed with us. Why? She said we had not helped her family. We fled and didn't stay, and she was all alone."[37] Ruth never forgave them for what she viewed as abandonment, nor was she ever able to put it out of her mind, even though they represented the only family she still had. Many survivors held grudges forever, and Ruth Skorecka was true to type.

Despite the occasional surprise reunions, Łódź was, for Ruth and Mark, a morbidly fragmented community. Not even the shards of smashed families were visible in the wartime rubble and debris. Ruth badly wanted to put a tombstone over her parents' graves. Jewish custom dictated that one be erected a year and a day after the date of death, and more than enough time had elapsed in the case of Abram and Sara Tempelhof. Ruth leafed through volumes of burial registries at the cemetery office in an effort to locate their plots, but to no avail. "The Germans had messed up all the cemeteries," she said, "and there was nothing that I could do. I was very hurt." Vladka Meed experienced the same pain after the war when she searched out her father's burial plot amid the toppled tombstones and rifled graves in the Gęsia Street cemetery abutting the gutted Warsaw Ghetto. Desecrated skulls lay everywhere. "Nothing. Nothing was left me of my past, of my life in the ghetto, not even my father's grave," she wrote.[38]

If the past had been obliterated, whether a future in Poland could be built was also unclear. Because it was the country's principal commercial and industrial center, Łódź had been spared the wanton destruction inflicted on the capital. To be sure, the Germans had burned out the ghetto. They had even built bonfires with the contents of the city's major libraries, looting as well the National Museum of its art treasures. But the city proper was left intact, many apartments had been made available by the German evacuation, and soon it would attract twenty thousand Jews, making Łódź the largest and most culturally important Jewish community in postwar Poland.[39] The Skoreckis tried hard to return to normal life. Although regular schools were still closed, Ruth continued teaching the girls at home. And she even arranged for Anne and Lila to take piano lessons from a cousin who had fled to wartime France with her engineer husband and two young sons and was now trying to make ends meet by teaching music. But as hard as Mark and Ruth tried to pick up the pieces of their former life in Łódź, it was a huge strain. There were too many bad memories, too many reminders of lost friends and dead relatives, too much uncertainty. A looming uncertainty was the postwar resurgence of anti-Semitism.

Ruth usually approached the subject of Polish anti-Semitism gingerly, for fear of giving offense. Yet it is clear that it was on her mind at the time. Across Poland survivors often returned home to ugly assertions that Hitler's sole mistake was that "he didn't kill all the Jews."[40] Many Jews had accepted an appointment in the Soviet-sponsored Provisional Government based in Lublin, in part because persecution at the hands of the Poles had left them with few alternatives. But identification with a hated regime only revived ancient canards about the Bolshevik-Jewish conspiracy. Hard-wired into Polish folk consciousness, even the old Christ-killer, blood-libel anti-Semitism revived in all its virulence. Not until late in 1946 did the Jesuit church in a village near Łódź yield to protests and remove from the altar a glass-enclosed coffin of a mummified infant and a sixteenth-century painting depicting Jewish ritualistic murder of a Christian child.[41]

Meanwhile, pogroms spread across Poland. The government's own statistics reported 351 Jewish murders between November 1944 and October 1945—doubtless an undercount. Kraków, where Governor-General Hans Frank had made his headquarters, experienced anti-Jewish riots in August 1945; Sosnowiec and Lublin saw similar outbreaks later in the fall. Działoszyce did not escape the anti-Jewish violence either. A few of its Jewish inhabitants returned after liberation to look for kinsfolk. They had been in the Płaszów labor camp. Some doubtless had been saved by Oskar Schindler. But his altruism was unable to save them now. Writes Judge Moshe Beijski: "So two or three dozen Jews arrived in Działoszyce, naked and barefoot and lacking for everything. But the Poles were not prepared to accept even that handful. They had made up their minds that once the town was without Jews it must remain so. One day they murdered Samuel Piekarz, Ben-Zion Chernocha and Yorista. Those murders served as a warning to the others, who fled that selfsame night. Since then no Jewish foot has trodden the streets of Działoszyce."[42]

The worst outbreak of anti-Semitic violence occurred in Kielce, 120 miles south of Warsaw, in July 1946, after a Christian boy reported being kidnapped and held prisoner by Jews in a local cellar, where he claimed to have witnessed the ritual murder of fifteen other Christian children. A mob of five thousand, including a socialist factory director, surrounded the Jewish Community Center, shouting, "The Germans did not kill you, but we will." They thereupon slaughtered forty-one Jews, mutilating genitals, crushing bones, tearing off limbs. Polish militiamen and local officials participated in the massacre. The Catholic bishop, whose seat was in Kielce, refused to intervene. A short time later the boy whose fantastic tale had unleashed the violence confessed to having been coached by a Home Army anti-Semite. Terror-stricken Jews throughout Poland responded to the Kielce explosion by building stockadelike structures and laying plans to flee Poland.[43]

It was all so mystifying and frightful. Some of the irrational violence stemmed from rational self-interest: the reluctance of many Poles to relinquish confiscated Jewish businesses acquired from the Nazis. The new Polish owners were bitterly resentful about having to part with wartime windfalls. But some of the violence may have welled up from deeper springs of psychic numbing due to having witnessed such horrid crimes—a numbing that, in the words of Michael Steinlauf, "is characteristically accompanied by anger, rage, and violence through which the survivor attempts to regain some sense of vitality."[44]

And just as worrisome as resurgent anti-Semitism was the Russian clampdown on the private economy. Every Jew Mark and Ruth met after returning to Łódź had lost a business or a factory. First it was the Germans who seized their enterprises; now it was the Russians. There may have been some consolation in knowing that Polish anti-Semites enjoyed only temporary possession of confiscated Jewish property, but the feeling soon gave way to fear of a more comprehensive seizure of property. One Jewish friend was even afraid to admit that he had once owned a seized factory. "It was very hard to be in business," Ruth said. "We didn't even try to start one."

All the while the Russians were becoming more invasive of personal liberties. "There was no privacy at all," Ruth complained. "They started giving us trouble everyday looking for vodka and telling us that they had to stay with us."

As it happened, their fancy apartment came with strings attached. "The Russians didn't have enough places to stay," Anne says, "and they wanted to stay in nice places. So an order came out that in that particular building, my family had to house and feed them if they wanted to spend the night there. Whatever they wanted in the way of food and quarters, we had to provide it."

Memories of the first time Soviet soldiers came to their apartment door remained with Mark forty years later: "One night there was a knock on the door. It's all dark. 'Open up,' they shouted. 'Who are you?' I said. 'The Army. Soldiers. Russians.' But I don't want to let them in," Mark said. "And I don't let them in." Unable to sleep at night, he claimed he kept them at bay for a week.[45] But, according to Anne, her father eventually had to unbolt the door. The Soviet soldiers took over her parents' bed. Ruth was ordered to serve meals with the best china and silver. One morning Mark awoke after the Soviets had left and found his watch and boots missing. The thefts made a lasting impression. "I don't know what the history of the watch was, whether he had always had it from before the war," Anne says. "But I know that after that he never wore jewelry. He never had a watch, he never wanted to wear a watch, and he never explained why."[46]

The Russian crackdown gave rise to diffuse feelings of déjà vu. "We saw plenty of people in our city who started wearing Russian uniforms," Ruth said. "Plenty of people joined the NKVD, too, which was like the Gestapo." The fear of talking openly and freely recurred. Ruth grew leery once again about leaving the girls alone to go shopping. "We didn't know what could happen to us," she confessed. "Again we were in a predicament. Should we run or stay in Łódź?"

One thing they ruled out was a return to Warsaw. It was not for lack of effort on Smolenski's part. Mark's former supervisor followed the Skoreckis to Łódź two weeks after they had left Praga, and he made several more visits after that. Their feelings of gratitude were as strong as ever. "We made our home his home," Ruth said. "We tried to do whatever we could for him." Smolenski had journeyed to Łódź not to make a social visit but to change Mark's mind about joining his firm in Warsaw. The Skoreckis gave him the same answer that they had in Praga, now elaborating in ways they would have felt uncomfortable doing while still in Warsaw. As Ruth described the conversation: "We told him that we were very sorry. We liked all the people who had done so much for us in the bad times of Hitler's regime and we respected them very much, but we couldn't go back to live a double life and to tell all our friends in Warsaw who we were. Our friends had sometimes said bad things about Jewish people, and we didn't want to hurt their feelings by letting them know that we were Jewish and that we had been hurt by some of the things they had said. We explained to Mr. Smolenski that it would be hard for us to do it again, to go back to the bad memories. So we told him that we would just stay like we were here, where we didn't have to pretend and could be ourselves."

Smolenski had doubtless wounded their feelings by granting them special immunity from his generalized dislike of Jews, but Mark and Ruth never told him so directly to his face. Two decades later she still found it difficult to sort through conflicted feelings, to sift resentment from gratitude and filter out the hurt from the warm memories. One thing she knew for sure: Returning to Warsaw would reawaken the old ambivalence, the convoluted emotions, the painful memories of living a lie. It might even mean changing friends or hiding their identity, and they were tired of lies, deceit, and disguises. Again and again Smolenski returned to Łódź. "Of course, all the time we made him feel at home," Ruth said. But he could never make them budge from their original refusal.

Recrudescent anti-Semitism, combined with Soviet oppression, pushed the Skoreckis toward leaving Poland altogether. The Russian theft of Mark's watch and boots was a bellwether: "I think that was the last straw," Anne says. To deter further encroachments by restless enlisted men, Mark and Ruth bought temporary peace by taking in a Polish lieutenant and nailing his officer's name-plate to the door. But the general insecurity was getting worse and worse. "When the Russians came it was like history was repeating itself," Anne says. Mark decided it was time to get out. At first Ruth, giving way to inertia, told her husband she was willing to tolerate the intrusions. "I was tired of running from place to place," she said. But Mark had other ideas. Having lived in Russian-occupied Białystok for two years, he was familiar with the Soviet modus operandi. "No, we've got to go out from here," he told his wife.

Ruth does not seem to have put up much of a fight. There was little to hold them in this historic textile center: their families had been swept away, their possessions were gone, and their roots had been torn up and set ablaze. "We had nothing to stay for here," she said, "and there was no future for our kids either." The last consideration was probably decisive. What had kept Ruth going through the selections, close calls, anti-Semitic banter, faked Catholicism, and—always—the fatiguing, relentless fear of detection and death was her determination to save her daughters' lives. She had preserved two children in the face of incredible odds. Now she needed to think about their future. "After all that our children had gone through," Ruth concluded, after second thoughts, "Mark was right. We had to get out."

The war had been over five months now, and few family members had come back. People could still move around with relative freedom. But who knew how long that would last? The repression would take a turn for the worse in November following the promulgation of a decree against "dangerous crimes with regard to the reconstruction of the state."[47] "If we waited, we might never come out," Mark and Ruth reasoned. Toward November, they resolved to go to the American zone in Germany, under cover of false papers identifying them as German Jews. Their ultimate destination was the United States, where two of Mark's sisters had emigrated in the 1920s.

They planned their escape with eleven other adults. Joining the party was the wife of the former priest who had befriended them in Warsaw. Her husband had since abandoned her. She told the Skoreckis she wanted to go wherever they went—an interesting role reversal between rescuer and victim. A Jewish friend who had lost his factory also asked to tag along. "He had nothing now," Ruth explained. Mark's niece Haka joined the group, along with her cousin Wladek who had rescued her off the streets of Warsaw. Pola was supposed to join them as well but got detained in Kraków, where she was told to wait for a wire announcing the departure date. "I waited and waited but the telegram never came," Pola says. "They left without me."[48]

Their departure heralded a mass outflow of Polish Jews to the American and British zones of occupied Germany and to the Jewish homeland in Palestine. It would be the commencement of real freedom but not the unshackling from troubled memory. The loosening of those chains would take a lifetime.

The group needed new identity cards before they could travel. "We had to have papers showing we were German Jews," Ruth said. Fortunately, such papers were easy to come by. If postwar Poland had a growth industry, it was counterfeiting documents with red seals calculated to impress unsophisticated Russian soldiers. Smuggling was another booming business. Europe at the time was webbed with underground railroads operated by guides who ferried refugees to the American and British zones of occupation for a fee. Safety was the major consideration. Lawlessness was rampant right after the war, and the anti-Semitism then being encouraged by Polish nationalists to discredit the new Communist regime in Lublin made every Jew a target of violence. "Even if only to get across the territory of Poland, the Jew first of all had to remain alive," wrote Yitzhak Zuckerman. Equally perilous was the Czechoslovakian border, which American journalist I. F. Stone called one of "the most dangerous frontiers in Eastern Europe." Polish border guards were notorious for shooting first and asking questions later. Finding an experienced "operator" to navigate you past these dangers was almost a life-and-death necessity, and Haka managed to find one. Shortly afterward the party of thirteen adults and two children made ready to leave.[1]

They departed Łódź sometime in October 1945, heading southwest for the Silesian city of Wrocław (formerly Breslau), where they spent a few days before traveling to an unnamed city closer to the Czech border. There were surprisingly few run-ins with the Polish population. The Soviets were another matter. "The whole time we were checked by the Russians to see if we had vodka or money," Ruth said. In all likelihood the Skoreckis and their companions crossed at Trutnov or Nachod, two Czech border towns favored by the Jewish underground. By month's end they were in Prague. According to the

Map 6. Europe, 1993

tracing bureau records of the International Red Cross, Mark registered with the Council of Jewish Community for Bohemia and Moravia, located in the Czech capital, on October 31.[2] The Skorecki party then spent eight more days in Czechoslovakia, eating saltless food at Soviet-run public kitchens and checking up, in Ruth's words, "on how the next border line was."

Prague was an ideal vantage point for assessing frontier conditions, since it was a hub in the underground network called Brichah ("flight" in Hebrew) that shuttled an estimated 250,000 Holocaust survivors out of Eastern Europe between 1945 and 1948. A joint venture of such Jewish resistance fighters as Zuckerman and the Haganah, the Israeli underground, Brichah funneled survivors into the American zones of Germany and Austria as a way of bringing pressure on Britain to open up Palestine. During the brief period that U.S. troops occupied western Czechoslovakia (George Patton's Third Army stayed in Pilsen from May 1945 until June) many American personnel were involved in the Czech leg of the rescue operation—such as Rabbi Eugene Lipman, an American army chaplain who became involved with the survivor community among whom the Skoreckis lived from 1945 to 1949. Lipman worked closely with Red Cross personnel bringing trainloads of Jewish refugees from Prague to Pilsen. Midnight runs by U.S. Army trucks relayed refugees between underground stations spaced forty to fifty miles apart. "The rescue was in little pieces because the actions were in little pieces," explained Rabbi Lipman. "The chief reason is, they weren't legal." By the time the Skoreckis arrived in Prague, however, American troops had already withdrawn from Czechoslovakia, and thus the Skorecki party would have to reach Germany on its own.[3] Prague was still a good place for receiving helpful advice about where to attempt a crossing. Someone told the group to go to a small town in the country and to travel at night. It was probably Broumov, near the famous Bohemian spa of Marienbad.

It is around ninety highway miles from Prague to Marienbad, and the Skorecki party traveled the distance on foot. "We moved mostly at night, walking in the fields and forests," Anne says. They had a lot of company. Hitler had uprooted an entire continent in his quest to Germanize the east and obtain slave labor, and the Third Reich's sudden collapse seems to have set it in motion. Over 14 million refugees filled the roads during the first summer of peace.[4] And just as that population tide receded, millions of German expellees, displaced by the Potsdam Agreement, washed westward from the Sudetenland, Silesia, and East Prussia. People traveled singly. They moved in vagabond packs. One family even crossed Europe on a camel liberated from a German zoo.[5] "Everything was really wild," says Roman Kriegstein, a handsome twenty-two-year-old concentration camp survivor who would shortly become Mark's business partner in Germany. Like the Skoreckis, Kriegstein was also in transit at the time, traveling with his mother and sister from Poland to the tiny Bavarian town of Tirschenreuth, where a survivor relative had ended up following the surrender. "Everything was crazy. People were wandering in all directions. Thousands were going from here to there, from there to here. I mean it was unbelievable."[6] In the dangerous confusion Wladek Skorecki, Haka's Kielce cousin and wartime companion, became separated from the party when he wandered off to buy a beer at a nearby tavern. The group had to proceed without him.

The Skorecki party reached the German frontier in late November. The Czech village of Broumov near Marienbad is but a short hike through the woods to the German hamlet of Mähring, where an American military outpost had been located to monitor border activity. The Skoreckis waited until nightfall to attempt a crossing. Then they hid in a farmer's barn. Local villagers, however, had complained that refugees had illegally crossed into Germany. Thus early the next morning American troops, under orders to seal the border in order to hold down the burgeoning refugee population, pushed the Skorecki party back into Czechoslovakia. The soldiers roused the group so abruptly they almost lost all their belongings. "Everybody started grabbing their things and we went out," Ruth said.

The Czech border with Germany was no less hazardous than its frontier with Poland. The area where the Skoreckis were huddling had become a gateway for German expellees from the Sudetenland. Hundreds of thousands of them were pooling up along the border, and the refugee throngs attracted predators. "Roving bands of Germans and displaced persons [are preying] on refugees coming across the border without proper papers through forests and thick woods," the American Military Government commander in the district reported during the winter of 1945–46. As a sideline to their burglary rings, knife-wielding border ruffians stole refugee luggage. Polish smugglers armed with submachine guns barreled through the Mähring outpost in hijacked British military vehicles. The unsettled conditions made the Czech border police edgy. Around the time the Skorecki party had reached the border, Czech gendarmes shot two women and a young man as they attempted to sneak into Czechoslovakia, killing one woman and hospitalizing her two companions.[7] Meanwhile, the Skorecki party of fifteen had ballooned to seventy-five. "We didn't know who a lot of them were," Ruth said. One was a Polish priest who, in an ironic reversal of role-playing, was passing as a Jew to increase his chances of getting into the American zone. Sleeping in the thickly wooded Bohemian forest, the begrimed refugees were growing cold and tired.

"After four days, a general came," Ruth said. Whether he was a real general or merely some beribboned captain is unclear. Whatever the rank, astonishing reports that Jewish youngsters were living on the border were sufficient reasons to attract the American officer to the frontier. Anxious though they might be to keep the refugee population from mushrooming out of control, the U.S. Army was also keen on avoiding further bad publicity. In September 1945 an envoy sent by Earl G. Harrison to investigate treatment of Jewish survivors had issued a stinging report. General George Patton, who made no secret of the fact he regarded Jews as "lower than animals," caused an uproar when one of his armored divisions injured several members of a Brichah convoy seeking entry to the American zone. Around the time the American officer visited the Skoreckis' forest hideout, U.S. forces were trying to undo the political damage by opening the border to Jewish refugees.[8]

The American officer was not fooled by their forged papers. He told them to be on the level. "We told him the truth," Ruth said, "because it was terrible to have to think of having to go back to Poland." He promised to return the next day with transportation for the entire group. The next evening, in the middle of the night, an army truck pulled up to their Czech encampment. "All of a sudden they said, 'Get on this truck right now,'" Anne recalls. It was a typical olive-drab, two-and-a-half-ton army truck, minus the canvas top.

"Then they hustled us on board. That's how freedom really began: with an order."

Initially, the soldiers allowed only the women to climb in the back, promising to return for the men. A history of separations flashed through Mark's mind. "Mark had left me for a few days one time," Ruth said, "and the few days turned out to be a long time." Mark insisted on accompanying his family, and the soldiers finally let him clamber onto the back of the open-air truck. The vehicle raced along the winding, hilly roads at breakneck speed. "The man was driving so fast I thought we would all fall out," Ruth recalled, "but none of us said a thing. We were all dirty, too, because we had been living like pigs." After a few hours of bouncing around in the chill autumn night, they arrived in the small town of Tirschenreuth, population five thousand. Set in the rolling hills of the Upper Palatinate and bordered on the east by miles of interconnecting ponds, Tirschenreuth was the governmental seat for the Landkreis—the equivalent of a rural county in the United States. The town had its own U.S. Military Government Detachment, one of hundreds of such local units that administered the German occupation. Also stationed in Tirschenreuth was United Nations Relief and Rehabilitation Agency (UNRRA) Team 168, a multinational squad of medical personnel and welfare workers responsible for refugee care. The roofless army truck deposited its refugee passengers in front of its headquarters.

Tirschenreuth in 1945 presented strange sights to Polish Jews fleeing Poland after the Holocaust. American troops were playing pitch and catch with a baseball in front of the UNRRA center when the Skoreckis arrived. They were extremely nice to Anne and Lila, showering them with chocolate and sticks of gum. "We didn't know what chewing gum was," Anne says. "They had to give us a user's manual. 'Chew, don't swallow,' they said."

After they jumped from the truck, a leather-jacketed young man rode up on a motorcycle, brimming with a self-assurance that seemed as odd as his attire. Things were great in the American zone, he told the weary passengers. You do not have to fear anything again. "Look at my shoes, my clothes, my motorcycle. It's wonderful here," he repeated. The Skoreckis were speechless. "None of us opened our mouth," Ruth said, "we were just listening and not talking." The young cyclist grew impatient. "You mean none of you in this whole truck will talk?" he demanded. "You can speak Polish, German, Yiddish, or whatever you like." But the Skorecki family, along with the other fresh arrivals, held their tongue. "We were all afraid," Ruth explained. For six years terror had dominated their lives, and the fear was not about to disappear by the mere act of crossing territorial boundaries. Frontiers of the soul first had to be traversed.

When the rest of the men arrived, everyone was taken to a big meal spread out on white linen tables. It was a festive occasion, "a celebration." Jewish refugees who had been arriving in Tirschenreuth since the surrender turned out in force. There were about 150 of them—mainly young, Polish, and unmarried. "It was very unusual for us to see a family with children," says Erna Rubinstein, a Polish Jew who was then working as secretary and interpreter for the local UNRRA team and today splits her time between Syracuse, New York, and Boca Raton, Florida.[9] As Ruth described the scene, "plenty of people from the city were waiting because they had found out about us. There was only one family here—Mark and mine." The emotionally shattered survivors needed a family nucleus around which to rebuild the broken pieces of Jewish community life, and the Skoreckis had seemingly dropped out of the sky to play that role.

It was a stroke of luck that brought the Skoreckis to this remote section of northeastern Bavaria. For one, it meant not having to stay in an enclosed displaced persons (DP's) camp, where most postwar refugees ended up after liberation. Administered by UNRRA, hundreds of these camps were sprinkled throughout occupied Europe. The initial policy was to lump DP's together according to country of origin, which meant many survivors were initially forced to live side by side with Polish and Baltic nationals who had served as SS camp guards and were now refusing repatriation for fear of prosecution. "As matters now stand, we appear to be treating the Jews as the Nazis treated them except we do not exterminate them," declared Harrison in the blistering report he submitted to President Truman in September 1945. Conditions never got this bad in Tirschenreuth's eight DP facilities, however. But even its widely scattered camps, which were often little more than converted factories and Lagers, were plagued by the usual overcrowding and social demoralization. The largest was at Flossenbürg, a stone quarry-cum-concentration camp that had furnished paving stones for Hitler's autobahns. After the war it was run for a short spell by a dictatorial Dutch sea captain who once stopped a camp soccer match because he disagreed with a referee's call. "This camp suffers from the psychological hazards of its past," one UNRRA field supervisor observed at the time.[10]

By the time the Skoreckis crossed the border, there had been a major shakeup in American policy toward Jewish refugees. Stung by the Harrison Report, General Dwight Eisenhower directed that survivors be reassigned to private billets and segregated camps, ordering an increase in their daily rations to twenty-five hundred calories (twice that of German civilians).[11] Much of the caloric increase came in the form of peanut butter, which they had never seen before. "We didn't know that you had to spread it on bread," says Mary Ferber, a Polish survivor who had ended up in Tirschenreuth after the war. "So we put it in a cup and put sugar on top of it and ate it by the cupful. We overate."[12] Many Jews who trickled into Tirschenreuth were lodged in the Bayerischer Hof Hotel, the town's largest inn (it has since burned down). Situated on the Marktplatz, the two-story structure peered through a broken canopy of linden trees at the Rathaus—the local government building—diagonally across the square. Today the square is lined with benches. Every house window is lipped with flower boxes that blaze with geraniums when the weather turns warm. The streets are scrubbed clean. According to UNRRA records, the Bayerischer Hof housed around 130 survivors. They usually took their meals together in the hotel's communal dining room.[13] Mark, Ruth, and the girls were initially assigned a large guest room on the second floor, but they were soon moved to a two-room suite overlooking the Marktplatz. A fireplace warmed the living room. After years of close confinement, the hotel had the feel of an unexplored Victorian mansion. "This is where our childhood began," Anne says. "What was left of it."

While much childhood remained—the teen years—there was much catching up to do as well. Anne's and Lila's self-esteem had been shattered. And, because violence had dominated their early years, they had lost basic trust in the adult world as a just and safe place. With Anne and Lila the distrust came out in a fear of strangers. Pola, Mark's younger cousin, noticed it immediately when she was reunited with the family in postwar Łódź. "They were fearful. They were afraid," she says, in her high-pitched voice. "Both girls were, but especially Lila."

It doubtless helped that the Skorecki sisters could retrieve some of their lost childhood within a survivor community that itself was coping with trauma and loss. Most of Tirschenreuth's postwar Jews came out of the camps or emerged from hidden forest bunkers and dank cellars. Several survived end-of-war death marches, when Nazi leaders hurriedly relocated camp inmates from the east to remote Lagers inside the Reich. They felt terribly helpless and alone— clinical manifestations later diagnosed as post-traumatic stress disorder.[14] A woman doctor captured the feeling in a postwar memoir: "How was I able to survive in Auschwitz? My principle is: I come first, second, and third. Then nothing, then again I; and then all the others."[15]

The traumatic events of war and genocide not only engendered feelings of profound isolation but also became deeply engraved in memory, like wounds that refused to heal. "The psychological problems were much more difficult than the other problems," says Rubinstein, who, together with three younger sisters and two other women, lived through Auschwitz and Płaszów and then survived a forced march into Czechoslovakia. Nervous anxiety plagued many survivors. They suffered from various psychosomatic illnesses. They experienced flashbacks and recurring nightmares. They felt emotionally numb. "Everything was for me dead," says Dora Appel, a Jewish DP in Tirschenreuth who had lost her entire family.[16] And the question haunting every survivor was how to forget the past, how to block out painful memories.

A few survivors believed they could exorcise the offending memory by taking vengeance on Germans. Such talk occurred frequently just after the war, pledges to poison the wells and rivers of Germany, but Jewish humanism thwarted the impulse toward collective revenge. Rubinstein remembers one young man in the early postwar period who tried to turn a machine gun on fleeing Nazis only to discover the therapeutic impossibility of getting even. "He thought he had the hatred and could kill someone, but instead he killed himself."[17]

The best therapy for recovering from traumatic memory, we now know, is to talk about it. But just after liberation the overwhelming majority of survivors wanted to forget. It was partly due to the peculiar qualities of memory, especially memory of a traumatic event, which is not a neatly packaged series of recollections filed away in some storage cubicle of the mind, later retrieved on demand, like accessing computer files on a hard drive. In fact, the trauma is not "remembered" in the commonsense meaning of the term but reconstructed, re-created, indeed relived, and often in its original emotional intensity. Primo Levi captured this side of trauma in his last book, *The Drowned and the Saved*: "The memory of a trauma suffered or inflicted is itself traumatic because recalling it is painful or at least disturbing."[18] For this reason it is always better to confront painful memories within the context of caring relationships. Victims of violence and terror need an audience—friends, relatives, even a political movement—that is willing to bear witness to their suffering. The empathetic environment does two things: it helps restore basic trust in community, and it allows survivors to refashion traumatic memories into ongoing life stories. But Germany in the immediate postwar period was hardly a caring context. The environment was neither safe nor therapeutic. Even those charged with helping the victims of Nazi persecution were at sea. "It seems altogether incredible today that when the first plans for the rehabilitation of Europe's surviving Jews were outlined, the psychiatric aspect of the problem was overlooked entirely," wrote one postwar psychiatrist. "Everyone engaged in directing the relief work thought solely in terms of material assistance." Little wonder that most survivors in such DP centers as Tirschenreuth tried desperately to suppress memory.[19]

Roman Kriegstein recalls that period as one of willed forgetfulness: "Right after the war, none of the survivors were talking about the past. We didn't want to think about it. Sure, a lot of people needed therapy, like the young men who went to war in Vietnam and came back with all kinds of mental problems.

Today when people go through traumas like this, there are psychiatrists and psychologists. We had nobody. Those things were unknown at the time. We lived mostly for today and tomorrow, not for yesterday."[20]

One thing survivors did with little prompting was to come together. If the essential insult of trauma is to disempower and isolate individuals, the instinctive response of Polish Jews who had been thrown together in postwar Tirschenreuth was to re-create a sense of community. They had little in common save shared persecution. "You had religious people, you had Zionist people, you had businesspeople, you had workers," said Henry Wahrman, a young survivor who came to Tirschenreuth with his younger brother from the nearby Flossenbürg concentration camp.[21] In late 1945 the town's survivors organized the Committee of Liberated Jews in the Landkreise Tirschenreuth, Kemnath, and Neustadt, an offshoot of the Central Committee of Liberated Jews formed in Munich earlier that summer. Later on, the committee elected Mark its president. At forty-six, he was practically an elder statesman. He spoke flawless Polish, which made him seem worldly next to Yiddish-speaking survivors. And, though quiet, he had a sly wit and an easygoing, friendly personality. "Mr. Skorecki was much more relaxed than most of the survivors," noted Erna Rubinstein. "I think having children had a lot to do with it."[22]

Rather quickly, members of the Jewish committee of Tirschenreuth seized control of the survivors' collective life. They rented a room a few doors from the Rathaus and turned it into a synagogue, storing the Torah in a closet and using a small wooden table as a pulpit. American army chaplains such as Rabbi Lipman, who had gotten to know Rubinstein and her sisters in Czechoslovakia and looked in on them from time to time, assisted with the services when passing through town. The Tirschenreuth committee organized a lending library. It staged dramas and recitals. One play even confronted the immediate past: " 'Six Years in a Bunker' described the fate of a Jewish family during the terrible time of Nazism," reported the community's cultural chairman to the Munich Central Committee.[23] There were soccer teams and Ping-Pong clubs ("In Tirschenreuth I used to play a lot of Ping-Pong," recalls one survivor).[24] Although the "Joint" (the American Joint Jewish Distribution Committee) contributed funds through Tirschenreuth's UNRRA team, survivors frequently organized buffet dinners to raise money for special projects. They traveled as a group to movie theaters in neighboring towns. On Saturday evenings the hotel dining room became a dance floor, with Anne and Lila often sitting at the top of the stairs watching the grown-ups come and go. "The community kind of meshed, and we stuck to our own," Anne says. "We were close and getting closer," adds Kriegstein.[25]

Those first years of freedom were spent not simply rebuilding community but also recovering lost family, and the two activities were linked psychologically. Both the International Red Cross and UNRRA, as well as the World Jewish Congress, operated tracing services. Survivors crisscrossed Germany visiting DP camps in search of relatives, bringing lists of names for people to examine, scanning crowds for faces from the past. The tracing services took down dates and places of birth, prewar addresses, wartime locations. They asked for names and addresses of relatives living abroad. "Cecylia Skorecka sends greetings to Mozes Frenkiel in Auschwitz and Abram [Dolek] Skorecki in Palestine," ran a typical survivor message, this one from one of Dolek's Działoszyce cousins who had emigrated to Sweden right after the war.[26] Dolek, then an insurance company accountant in Haifa, often acted as a go-between for the dispersed remnants of his once large Polish family. He helped reunite the Skoreckis in Tirschenreuth with Wladek, who had become separated from the group during the trek from Prague to Germany. "At that time we got letters from Haka at one place and then Wladek at another place," he recalled. "Then we made contact with them." A few months later Wladek found his way to Tirschenreuth.[27]

The most emotionally wrenching quests were for loved ones swallowed up by the war. Fantasies of being reunited with missing parents and spouses had buoyed many survivors during dark spells, and they found it hard to let go of that comforting thought, even in the face of facts to the contrary. For the longest time Ruth was unable to admit that her brothers Henry and Vovek and Mery Mejnster, Henry's wife, might never reappear. "All the time I was sure from some place like plenty of other people they might come back," she said. And there were just enough startling reunions after the war to keep fragile hopes like hers alive.

By the second year of freedom, however, most survivors accepted the reality that absent spouses and relatives had probably perished. And so they started marrying or remarrying. They were generally in their twenties and happy to be alive. Erna Rubinstein wed a Jewish doctor she met at the UNRRA hospital in Tirschenreuth—by miraculous coincidence, the son of a woman prisoner she had known at Camp Płaszów. A short time later her younger sister Celia married Roman Kriegstein, the first wedding held in Tirschenreuth's makeshift synagogue. A rash of survivor weddings took place in 1946 and 1947. Genuine love usually cemented the unions. But a few Jewish DP's married to overcome grief and restore lost family, and the therapy was not always successful. "I didn't feel any love," one Tirschenreuth survivor says of her postwar marriage. She wanted to have children but felt dead inside. "I can't take it," she told a physician from whom she sought counseling. "My husband wants to come to me . . . it was terrible. You are supposed to be happy, you are supposed to enjoy, and I saw before my eyes something else always." She eventually did bear a son in Tirschenreuth. Many of her friends had children too, including Celia Kriegstein, who bore twin sons in 1948. The newborns signified rebirth of the community, and local survivors took pains to make it public. "At 1100 hours we were the guest at the naming of the first Jewish baby born in Tirschenreuth since the end of the war," reported the local military government officer on August 24, 1946. The tiny Jewish community was beginning to sink roots in time and place.[28]

No matter how busy they were raising families and rebuilding community institutions, Tirschenreuth's survivors always found time for Anne and Lila. "They were two nice girls," says Dora Appel. The Skorecki girls represented younger brothers and sisters lost in the war, symbols of a generation almost entirely consumed in the Holocaust. "We all were looking at them like something from heaven," says Janiá Sudkiewicz, who originally came from Poznań, near the German border.[29] The survivor community showered them with gifts and attention. "A pat on the head, sweets, whatever they had—they really made a fuss over us," Anne says. It was a nice environment for unstructured play. In the spring of 1946 they were joined by two other Jewish girls roughly the same age—Helenka and Danusia Rubinstein—who had spent much of the war with their mother foraging in the woods after their money had run out and after the Polish peasants who had been hiding them were denounced by collaborators and their homes set on fire. They arrived in Tirschenreuth with a distant relative, just ahead of the postwar resurgence of Polish anti-Semitism. "My mother herself was involved in an ambush by the Poles after the war, and she was almost killed," says Danusia Rubinstein, now Dr. Dorothy Kunstadt, a Manhattan cardiologist. In Tirschenreuth their mother was mostly confined to a sanatorium. Helenka and Danusia moved into the Bayerischer Hof Hotel with the couple that had led them out of Poland.[30]

In the spring and summer Anne and Lila and their new playmates liked to congregate near the benches lining the Marktplatz, a favorite gathering place for adult survivors. They perched on the groundfloor window sills of the hotel. They attended a Zionist summer camp. Anne liked to garden and developed a little plot of land down the hill from the hotel. Some of the adults would take the girls on picnic hikes to the ponds just outside town. Anne liked to tag behind Mrs. Rubinstein's teenage sister. "I remember her pigtails," Rose Rosenberg said of Anne in 1994. "She was always around me. But I already felt above her because she was younger."[31]

The girls had the run of the Bayerischer Hof Hotel, which always seemed to bare new mysteries. Danusia, who was Lila's close friend, stumbled into an attic full of German books. "I taught myself to read. I spent a lot of time doing that," she says. "And I spent a lot of time sort of day dreaming."[32]

Anne made pleasurable discoveries as well. "One time I got into the attic and found all kinds of toys: small miniature furniture, dolls, books, just things children normally play with," she says. "I felt a little guilty taking over some-body else's things. But, then again, not having had anything else, I didn't feel that bad about it."

Their parents worked hard to integrate them into normal life. Mark bought the girls department store dolls to replace the sand-filled ones he had made for them in Praga. Anxious to make up for lost time, Ruth enrolled Anne and Lila in a Polish-language school organized by UNRRA and supplied with U.S. Army paper and pencils; surprisingly, considering the gap in their formal education, they were on par with other classmates. ("My mother did a good job teaching us the basics," Anne says.) Before long, Ruth had arranged for them to take private English lessons from a Czech instructor who visited the hotel three times a week. Music training came next, accelerating a childhood on the verge of becoming overhurried. "In Europe most children played an instrument," Lila says, "and my mother wanted us to play one, too. She wanted us to have a feeling of belonging," as well as middle-class respectability. When Ruth dis-covered that Professor Adam Dolzycki, the former conductor of the Warsaw Opera House Orchestra, had slipped into one of Tirschenreuth's DP camps, she approached him about accepting Anne and Lila as piano students, and he agreed. In between organizing a DP orchestra, he gave lessons to several local children, DP and German alike.[33] Tight-lipped and humorless, his long, wavy hair parted down the middle, Dolzycki played the role of European professor to the hilt. "He was a stern taskmaster," Anne says. If she missed a key, he slammed the piano. Do it my way or else, he would erupt. Both sisters did well, but Anne became a dedicated student. She was always practicing on the piano in the hotel dining room, and the hard work paid off. There were frequent recitals, usually held on Sunday afternoons in the hotel or in the central hall of the Rathaus. The concerts drew large crowds, including the mayor and other local dignitaries. Anne's performances of Chopin, Mendelssohn, and Clementi invariably stood out. One year she took first prize at the student piano compe-tition, which was reported by the local paper. The close-knit survivor commu-nity took special pride in her accomplishments. "Here she had just come from real hell on earth, yet she played beautifully," says Rubinstein. She was very good, they all said.[34]

She was just beginning her teens. After years of hiding, the attention was nice. There were innocent flirtations too. A young German boy used to stand on the pavement in front of the hotel window where Anne liked to gaze out onto the Marktplatz. "This young boy would look up at me and I would look down at him," she says. "He would come every once in a while, maybe every other day. Then he asked me if I would go for a walk with him. And I went. [Laughs] But we just walked around the corner. If my parents would have known that, they would have killed me." Most of all, it felt good to be open about her cultural identity. "I had been afraid to let the word 'Jew' pass my teeth when we were in Praga," Anne says, "even while in hiding."

But Lila fled when survivors entered the apartment; their company made her anxious. She disliked their Yiddish speech. She poked fun at their dress and mannerisms. "I hate those people. They're so funny. Look at them," she told her older sister. If the physical act of hiding in armoires and closets wounded Anne's identity, at least she never became confused about who she was. But the Catholic culture in which eight-year-old Lila had concealed her Jewishness was not some garment one packed away in a cedar chest at summer's end. The adopted identity stayed with her: "It took me a long time to realize I was Jewish," Lila admits, and to get over the religious prejudices she had picked up along the way. "Everything I had heard about Jews while I was little was bad."

Her anti-Semitism was so noticeable that the community did not request that Lila ask the traditional four questions at the communal Seder held on Passover night in 1946. As the youngest of the four girls, Lila should have posed the questions during the narration of the expulsion from Egypt. The community leaders asked Danusia, the second youngest, instead. "I remember it because it must have been very traumatic, having to stand up," Dr. Kunstadt says. "The Jewish community arranged for the whole community to have this communal Seder. It was the first Passover Seder that anyone had had since the war."[35] There was no way that Lila could have performed that role at the time.

There is no inkling in Ruth's memoir of the distress she and Mark must have felt at seeing their youngest daughter transmuted into a Polish anti-Semite. But they were extremely upset. It took them a while to bring her back, as it did to reacculturate many Jewish children who had been sent to convents and Catholic homes and had trouble after the war breaking with their adopted religion. An untold number never did return to Judaism.[36] In fact, Lila became angry when Mark and Ruth said she was Jewish. She refused to part with her rosary and prayer book, which were a source of comfort. "These were the only possessions that were mine," Lila says of her beaded crucifix and prayer book. "I had them all the time; they were part of me." Mark and Ruth tried prying them loose with chocolate. When bribes failed, they threatened to cut off her candy allowance. Both approaches were ineffectual.

One Sunday afternoon Mark ordered Lila to hand over her religious icons. The whole family was in the living room, including a Polish Catholic with whom Ruth had become friendly. She and Mark tried to convince Lila that the rosary belonged to the visitor. A tug of war developed. "I put up a fuss. I cried. I fought my father," Lila says. Finally, she turned the other way and closed her eyes. Extending her arms behind her back, she handed the beads to the Catholic woman. But the prayer book stayed clutched in her hand. What happened next Ruth omitted from her memoir. Mark yanked the missive from Lila's grip and threw it in the fireplace. He ordered her to look. "I didn't want to see the book burning," Lila says, "but he said I had to. They wanted me to see that it was gone forever, to make me understand that that was not who we were."

"Looking back on it today," Anne says, "it was a harsh way to deal with the situation. But my parents didn't know any better. Do it right now and get it over with—that was their attitude. It was traumatic for my sister."

Although spared the tribulation of reinventing identities, Anne's own trauma remained unvanquished. Troubled memory, when pushed from consciousness, often resurfaces as anxiety. Anne's trauma came as an intruder in the night. Until the mid-1980s she was plagued by persistent nightmares of being chased by Nazi soldiers, a typical survivor dream.

After reuniting with Haka and his other relatives in Tirschenreuth, Wladek Skorecki spent most days hanging around the Bayerischer Hof Hotel. "I remember him well," says Mark Sudkiewicz, who today runs a jewelry import business in Toronto. "He didn't look Jewish. He looked Aryan. I think he survived by pretending he was a Christian. He was already bald, but in my eyes it just added to his aristocratic bearing. He was refined and cultured and maybe a lady's man." Wladek frequently played cards, usually draw poker and a Polish game called Czerwony Król" (Red King). The games went on all day in the hotel dining room. The women played too. The stakes were small: "You couldn't make a living at it," Sudkiewicz says. A year shy of twenty, Sudkiewicz felt grown up whenever Wladek invited him to sit in for a hand. Wladek's special aura projected even around a card table. "He knew how to lose, not just how to win. I looked up to him as a gentleman." Wladek later told Dolek he played cards all the time so as to avoid working for the Germans.[37]

Although anti-German feelings were common among survivors, Wladek's attitude toward work was far from typical. Many adult members of Tirschenreuth's small Jewish community took their minds off the past by finding employment. Good jobs were not easy to come by in the early postwar period, however. This section of eastern Bavaria was famous for its porcelain factories. But all eight of the district's chinaware plants were idle just after the war for lack of coal, and local glass production was hampered by raw material shortages. UNRRA positions paid good money, also providing uniforms and food. "Those were the best jobs around for a DP, and they were honorable," said Rabbi Lipman. But there were scarcely enough positions to go around.[38]

An alluring alternative was the black market. Faced with across-the-board scarcities, occupational authorities imposed rationing and price controls on everything from food to tobacco. For the DP population the scarcities represented opportunity. Not only did they receive more rations than did Germans, but something just as dear: American cigarettes, which were better than hard currency next to the nearly valueless Reichsmark. With a few packs of Camels or Chesterfields, anything seemed possible.[39] The underground economy involved both cash and goods. Survivors usually controlled the luxury end of the market. Familiarity with Yiddish facilitated quick mastery of spoken German, and the camp experience was an unforgettable training ground for the self-discipline of deferred gratification. Never involved personally in the black market, Roman Kriegstein saw firsthand how it developed: "People received cigarettes and sugar with their rations, and the Germans wanted those articles which were in short supply. They were ready to give big for them. In return the DP's either got money, which was not worth much at the time, or they got articles of jewelry and such. And this was how the black market started. The same thing as in the concentration camps. I remember people were giving away bread for a cigarette."[40]

Anne's father avoided large operations on the black market, but he did reconnoiter the surrounding countryside scouting for bargains, often with Anne in tow. They traveled in an old car Mark had purchased with funds brought from Poland. Anne identified with her father. "I was more my father's daughter and Lila was my mother's daughter," she says. Like him, she enjoyed working with her hands. Give her a hammer and she would build anything, Mark would joke. She could drive a truck, her parents often said. Although most of Mark's prewar spontaneity had died in the war, Anne still enjoyed her father's company. They spent countless hours driving from town to town, trading with local farmers for eggs and foodstuffs. "I always loved those trips," she says. "Where we were going, what we could do—it was an endless adventure to me." Once they visited nearby Castle Falkenberg, overlooking a town by the same name, where scars from the Thirty Years' War are still visible. Formerly owned by Count Werner von der Schulenberg, a former ambassador to Moscow who was executed in 1944 for his part in the Hitler assassination plot, the moated fortress was used in the war's waning days as an SS prison for Greek generals. Now it was filled with rugs and old furniture.[41]

One thing Mark discovered from his travels around the Bavarian countryside was the need for public transportation. The nearest train station was at Weiden, twenty miles to the south. The roads were winding and hilly. Yet, there was no bus line. In the meantime, Mark had become friendly with Roman Kriegstein. Though separated in age by almost twenty-five years, they took an instant liking to each other. Before the war Kriegstein had been a dental technician. Now he was looking for something to do and was drawn to Mark's quiet resolution: "He was very decisive. He knew where he was going. But he would never make himself big and important, he would never brag about himself, and he was quiet, very quiet." The two of them also drove around the countryside together. They came across an abandoned German army bus, which they decided to purchase. Overhauling the broken-down bus was a major job. Because gasoline was at a premium, they replaced its internal combustion engine with one of the wood-burning devices widely used just after the war. The vehicle lacked seats, so Mark built wooden benches. He added racks in the back of the bus for storing firewood. The vehicle was too primitive for commercial use. They used it chiefly to transport members of the Jewish community to movie theaters in neighboring towns. Every forty or fifty miles the stove had to be reloaded, and because the engine did not use lubricants, the pistons and rings constantly wore out. "The bus didn't have enough strength to go up the hills," Kriegstein says, "so the people got out to push it up. But everybody was young, and everything was taken in stride."[42]

Shortly afterward, Mark and Kriegstein established a local bus line, a first for the area. The biggest problem was cutting through the red tape. "I remember just to get a driver's permit for a car, it was really like moving mountains," said Henry Wahrman. Local German bureaucrats were the chief obstacle. They complained to officers of the local Office of Military Government, United States (OMGUS), about Jewish DP's who refused to take no for an answer, saying that the DP's were browbeating and intimidating them.[43] Mark and Kriegstein ultimately sought the intercession of UNRRA officials in Munich, who finally cut the Gordian knot. Thanks to a bank loan, the two men bought another old bus, fixed it up, and converted both vehicles back to gasoline engines after receiving petrol allocations. They hired drivers, established a regular schedule between the various towns within the Landkreis, and named their new company EsKa (for Skorecki and Kriegstein). The line was an immediate success. "When they made the conversion from reichsmarks to Deutsch marks and German currency became valuable," Kriegstein says, "we had money before anybody else." Eventually they were able to expand the EsKa fleet to five vehicles. Both shared overall responsibility for running the company, but Kriegstein mainly dealt with civil authorities. Mark pretty much stuck to the mechanical problems. "You know, he liked to do things with his hands," Kriegstein says. "And he always liked to do what he liked to do."[44]

Theirs was a special relationship, avuncular yet comradely. Among themselves they always spoke Polish. "In Polish, it is customary to address strangers with the formal *pan*. It means 'mister,'" Kriegstein says, laughingly. "And it was very strange because we worked together so long, and we addressed each other as mister. I called him Pan Skorecki and he called me Pan Roman. So that's how it worked."[45]

Meanwhile, other survivors began settling into various lines of work. The Kryss family established a small shoemaking business. Alfred Slomnicki, Mark's predecessor as president of the Jewish Committee, took over a grocery store that had belonged to one of Tirschenreuth's prewar Jewish families. Some survivors became tailors. A few women resumed dressmaking trades. With two other men Henry Wahrman set up a business that reprocessed old wool into long staple fiber for resale to textile mills. "Everybody was trying to put themselves back into normal, regular life and pick up the pieces like before," explains Kriegstein. It was one strategy for getting rid of the past, though, again, things were never that simple. "You subconsciously try to erase a lot of the bad memories from your mind," said Wahrman not long before his 1993 death from stomach cancer. "You have to build your own family, and go on on a daily basis. You can't live with this day in and day out. But it comes back to haunt you anyway."[46]

The bus company's surprising success put many material comforts within reach. From the first days of marriage Ruth had aspired to a high standard of living, and she began stockpiling chinaware and porcelain. She bought a lot of bric-a-brac. "My mother always liked nice things," Anne says. Her real passion was clothing. Everyone from those days in Tirschenreuth recalls her grooming. Elegant and charming, she never ventured outdoors except in nice clothing. And she carried herself with class and dignity. "You see," Kriegstein explains, "they came from a very fine family in Poland, and it was showing." Ruth's strengths and flaws, however, were indivisible. The injured dignity she summoned forth to protect her Aryan cover during dangerous encounters in wartime Warsaw could look like excessive pride in different circumstances. She could be prickly about her status, and she let youngsters know that she expected deference. Once Ruth reminded Marek Sudkiewicz that he was still wet behind the ears. "Being eighteen I felt insulted," he says. "And my immediate response was, 'I can still get older but you can never get younger.' It was stupid. She was rebuffed. There was a silence, because among the ladies she was the oldest." A permanent chill descended on their relationship. It even cooled Ruth's attitude toward the young man's future wife. "I think she didn't like me so much," Janiá Sudkiewicz says.[47]

The Skoreckis' unexpected financial success further strained Ruth's relationship with her husband's relatives. Although her watchmaking father in Łódź was much poorer than the Skoreckis, Ruth had always felt superior to Mark's family. The Tempelhofs originally came from Germany, which automatically placed them higher up on the status hierarchy than were Jews from Poland, especially those from Galicia. Ruth's newfound prosperity reinforced her snobbishness. She broke with Haka; the hard feeling between them had worsened after Wladek's disappearance on the way from Poland. Then she broke with Wladek. In the meantime, Pola had arrived in town, after receiving a letter from the family. She had left Kraków with a Brichah convoy, eventually reaching Tirschenreuth by way of Vienna. Mark found her a secretarial job with the local Joint office. Ruth's relationship with Pola quickly deteriorated as well. "Ruth was a difficult person," Pola says. "She was a handsome woman. She took good care of the children. But she was greedy. She liked only money. Money and jewelry." The coldness in their relationship soon became arctic.[48]

It would be a gross oversimplification to say Ruth was materialistic. She could be extremely selfless toward those in need. Some of the altruism doubtless reflected an abiding concern for outward appearances. But much of it was genuine, springing from religious belief. Many survivors during the war came to question the existence of a God who allowed the slaughter of innocent millions. "I think my father lost faith because of what he went through," Anne says. By contrast, because Ruth attributed the family's survival to divine intervention, she felt the need (to quote from her memoir) "to do something to pay back my debt of gratitude to God for letting me come out with no ill effects from the hands of Hitler's terrible regime." Tirschenreuth had a 150-bed hospital named St. Stephen's that serviced the general area. After the war UNRRA doctors from Poland and Argentina, assisted by an American nurse, administered the facility.[49] Most of its patients were DP's, a few were Jewish. The stench of disease permeated the place. "I thought I'm going to die from the smell, from the aroma around," says Janiá Sudkiewicz, who took nursing classes at St. Stephen's. "The situation was like in a military barracks."[50] Ruth started making rounds at the hospital not long after the family arrived in Tirschenreuth.

She was attracted to a young, very sick Jewish boy who had lost his parents in the war. The boy's kidneys had quit functioning because of severe beatings at the hands of camp guards, and his spirits were further depressed because he received no visitors. "I tried to help this boy because he was by himself," Ruth said. His greatest medical need was glucose, which the hospital frequently lacked and the local pharmacist denied having in stock. So, she resorted to the black market, exchanging candy and soap for supplies of glucose—often obtained from the same German druggist who had originally been so emphatic in his denials. Everyday she brought the young boy a fresh dose of glucose, together with a meal she had prepared in conformance with his restricted diet. Yet his medical condition steadily worsened. The hospital gave him transfusions, but the doctors held out little hope for his recovery. "One day when I came to the hospital, I found him not in his room but in the morgue." His death came as a terrible shock. With the help of UNRRA she arranged to have him buried in a nearby cemetery. It was the first survivor funeral to be held in postwar Tirschenreuth.

Ruth's volunteer work at St. Stephen's was not limited to a single patient. Soon she made the care and comfort of the entire hospital her special survivor's mission. The institutional fare was poor, hence she organized a program for distributing cooked meals to the patients. It was a variation on the system she had instituted in her Warsaw Ghetto tenement on Ogrodowa Street, where she had delivered leftovers collected from other tenants to the destitute huddled in the basement. Each afternoon the survivors living at the Bayerischer Hof Hotel gave her extra portions of their main meal, which she then carried to the hospital. She went from bed to bed, usually bringing each patient something special to go with his diet—"dessert, fruit, whatever I could get," she said. And drugs, too, if the hospital's supplies had run low. Around 2:00 P.M. the patients would be glued to the window, waiting for her arrival. Afterward, to make it easier for her fellow survivors to do good, Ruth washed the dishes herself. "I was afraid if I started bothering people with dirty dishes, they wouldn't continue to cook meals for us," she explained. Anne and Lila returned the plates and bowls. Ruth and a few other survivors soon formed an association with the simple name Special Help for Sick People. To raise money the organization held dances and buffets, offering door prizes. With the profits they purchased medicine on the black market. The work gave Ruth's life new purpose and meaning. "Winter, summer, all the time I went to the sick people," she said. "I never tired of this."

Sometime in the summer of 1947, probably August or September, Ruth finally learned Henry's and Vovek's fate. She had never abandoned faith that her brothers had survived, watching and waiting all the while for news of their whereabouts. But that winter a copy of Thaddeus Stabholz's just-published memoir, one of the first survivor stories to appear after the war, came into her possession. Stabholz was a name Ruth remembered from the Warsaw Ghetto. "He was with my brother's wife, the doctor, Mery Mejnster," she said.

Written in Polish and titled *Seven Hells*—for his experiences in the Warsaw Ghetto, Treblinka, Majdanek, Auschwitz-Birkenau, Sachsenhausen, and two of Dachau's satellite camps—Stabholz's book hardly qualifies as bedtime reading. Anne received a copy of the 1990 English translation in 1994: "It was one of the hardest books I've ever read," she says. Stabholz recounted the transport of him and his fiancée to Treblinka and then his miraculous deportation, along with the brothers Tempelhof and Nahum Remba, to Majdanek. He described how Czyste surgeons were machine-gunned while standing over their operating tables during the January 18, 1943, Aktion, and how a close friend was brained with a rifle butt. When the American army liberated Stabholz in April 1945 at Dachau IV (Kaufering), he was, as he wrote in the English edition, "too sick, too numb, too indifferent to comprehend its importance."[51] At the time he weighed less than eighty pounds.

His physical recovery was rapid, but the psychological road back was tortuous. During his convalescence, Stabholz was tormented by nightmares of standing on the ramp between Crematoria II and III in Auschwitz-Birkenau and entering a cavernous gas chamber. He always awoke just as the steel doors slammed shut, soaked in sweat. To take his mind off the past he read voraciously—medical tracts one day, poetry the next. Nothing brought relief. Late one night he switched on the light, found an old notebook and pen, and began writing. "Night and day I wrote, like a man possessed. In two weeks, half of my story was completed," he said later. The entire manuscript was finished after three months. Stabholz recorded his experiences only to get rid of the memories. But friends in the large DP camp at Stuttgart, where he and his new wife moved in early 1946, chanced to read the handwritten notebooks and urged their publication. The broad outlines of his story were familiar to most survivors at the time. What set Stabholz's narrative apart was its specificity, its naming of names, which assured it a ready readership among a DP population desperate for information about missing relatives. Because of rationing controls on paper, it took more than a year to get the manuscript into print. The first edition of *Seven Hells* had a very small run of only four to five hundred paperbound copies. The official publication date was May 15, 1947. Within two days the camp newsstand handling the book's distribution had completely sold out. Only the paper shortage kept Stabholz from bringing out another edition. Carried by hand from camp to camp, *Seven Hells* quickly entered the increasingly interconnected world of Jewish survivors in postwar Germany. Ruth obtained her copy through the DP grapevine.[52]

The first seventy-five pages of *Seven Hells* answered most of Ruth's questions concerning Henry and Vovek. Stabholz recounted their cattle car journey from Treblinka to Majdanek in May 1943, describing the awful smells emitting from Henry's unirrigated colostomy bag, which was literally eating him alive. He recorded their fifty-yard sprint from the Majdanek train platform to the camp gate, to determine who would live and who would die. The Tempelhof brothers made the cut, entering Block Two, where they became clerks. After that Stabholz lost track of Henry and Vovek. Ruth hardly needed further particulars to discern her brothers' fate. By 1947 it was common knowledge that Jews in the Lublin District (including the workers from Schultz's, who had been transferred to Trawniki on Himmler's orders) had been massacred during the Harvest Festival Aktion of November 3–4, 1943.

Ruth went into shock after reading the book. "I was sick for two weeks," she said, "and nobody could make me come out of it." When her health got better she traveled to Munich to locate Stabholz in the central DP registry. She was anxious for more information about not only her brothers but also Mery Mejnster, whom Stabholz never mentioned in his book. She went directly to his apartment in Stuttgart but just missed finding him. "It is a funny story," Stabholz noted, "because the day she was in Stuttgart I was with my wife in Munich visiting a psychiatrist friend who I had known at Czyste Hospital. It had to have been the same day because I never left Stuttgart except on one occasion. And it must have been in the summer of 1947, not long after my book was published, because I remember it was hot." Ruth tried to reach Stabholz by mail several times thereafter, but she never made contact.[53]

Adam was conceived a few months after Ruth learned of her brothers' death, and the inference of a connection is hard to avoid. She and Mark talked constantly about having a son to carry on the family name. "They were looking for a boy," Pola says. Postwar Tirschenreuth made that hope hard to abandon. By their third year in Germany, younger friends were filling the hotel with the scent of talcum powder and freshly laundered diapers. But, judging from the timing of Adam's birth, Ruth must have equivocated about becoming pregnant. A major worry was her age. Almost forty-three when Adam was born, Ruth was as old as her mother-in-law, Natalia, had been when her last child (who lived only seven years) was born. "At her age, having a baby was a brave thing to do," says Kriegstein.[54] Ruth never told friends she was expecting. She avoided wearing maternity clothes. "She was small," Anne says. "She really didn't show her pregnancy until the end. She disguised it." There is a superstition among Orthodox Jews that it is bad luck to prepare for a birth, but Ruth carried the folktale to an extreme.

Adam was born healthy on October 30, 1948—"a 'miracle baby,'" according to Lila. The birth came as a surprise to the community. Mark and Ruth celebrated for an entire month. They threw a large party, inviting city officials. "You would have thought Jesus Christ had just been born," Anne says.

Something more than ordinary sibling rivalry colored Anne's attitude at the time. She was a blossoming teenager, and the last thing she cared to do was baby-sit a kid brother. More than that, she frankly resented sharing with a stranger parental affection she badly needed herself. Lila had the same reaction: "My parents were overjoyed, but I felt like he was intruding in my territory. I guess I was craving attention that I didn't get for a long time and all of a sudden there is a baby and the attention was totally on him. It was jealousy." "Once Adam was born," Anne adds, "Lila and I lost our stature. We went into the background."

Ruth must have anticipated her daughters' hurt and resentment, because even they were kept in the dark about her pregnancy. "I don't remember her preparing us for another sibling," Anne says. In her own fashion Ruth tried to make it up to them. A few months earlier, reichsmarks had been converted to deutsch marks. The currency exchange dramatically improved EsKa's cash flow. With the windfall Ruth was able to buy a baby grand piano for Anne and Lila: "I got it for a gift after Adam was born," she said. Adam, who as the only male would be the bearer of family tradition, remained the center of attention. "With everything they went through, all their hopes and ambitions became focused on him," Anne says. In Ruth's mind there also existed a magical continuity with Henry. For the rest of her life she never ceased admonishing Adam that he was to grow up and become a professional like the uncle he never knew.

One of the worst aspects of the postwar journey from persecution is that it often began in Germany, in part because of fear, which seemed to saturate the very landscape and made even expectant mothers wary of seeking local medical help. Most of the physicians in the Tirschenreuth area, according to military government officials, had been barred from practice owing to Nazi Party membership. "You couldn't believe you could have a baby and survive in a German hospital," says Dora Appel. "Every place you turned, you were still threatened and afraid," notes Erna Rubinstein.[55]

But a deeper discomfort arose from the inner struggle between the survivors' need to forget and their determination not to let the Germans forget. After the war the vanquished, no less than survivors, tried to push the Nazi past from their minds, and the evasion made Jewish DP's in such communities as Tirschenreuth profoundly uneasy. The German motive was to avoid guilt, not ease pain. Absorbed in the day-to-day task of rebuilding shattered communities, they talked themselves into innocence by imagining that they too had been victims of Hitler's oppression, liberated, along with the rest of Europe, by Allied armies. "Man hat uns belogen und betrogen" (We were lied to and betrayed), was a rhyming refrain of weepy rationalization heard often in the immediate postwar period. Even more intently did German civilians focus on their victimization at the hands of the Soviets and their emerging satellites: the loss of the "German East," the mass expulsions of German settlers from Eastern and Central Europe, the 3 million German prisoners of war (POWs) in Soviet prisons—themes of grievance that would resurface anew in the 1980s during the *Historikerstreit* debates over the place of the Third Reich in German historical self-understanding. The Allies tried to make the civilian population own up to their collective responsibility for Nazi war crimes by forcing them to view films depicting camp atrocities, but many in the audience averted their gaze until the projector was turned off. "The unfortunate people to which I belonged," recalls German writer Stephan Hermlin, who sat through one of these showings, "was not interested in being shaken by events, in any 'know thyself.'" Instead of showing remorse, Germans in the immediate postwar period stoutly defended their ignorance concerning the regime's atrocities. The historical amnesia would persist until the student rebellions of 1968, when the generation born after the war began asking fathers and grandfathers, What did you do during Hitler's reign? Until then, as if by instinct, most Germans shied from discussing anti-Semitism's role in Hitler's rise to power.[56]

Downplaying the extent of anti-Semitism came naturally immediately after the war. Certainly, religious anti-Semitism had been around for centuries, while its racist variant had been circulating in German intellectual circles since the nineteenth century. But in a small town such as Tirschenreuth, whose Jewish inhabitants during the 1930s numbered fewer than twenty out of a population of five thousand, arousing mass frenzy over the Jewish menace was not easy to do. And Tirschenreuth was hardly unique. Outside cities and large towns, most Germans had minimal contact with Jews, among Europe's most well-assimilated Jewish communities. Indeed, throughout rural Bavaria, including the Upper Palatinate, where Tirschenreuth was located, the Jewish proportion of the overwhelmingly Catholic population in 1933 was less than 0.5 percent. The paucity of Jews was the reason Hitler modulated his racist extremism once he decided to forsake revolution for electoral politics and forge a broader base of support. During the 1932 Reichstag elections that would catapult Hitler into national power the following year, he refrained from harping on the Jewish Question. Instead, he attacked Bolsheviks and trade unions, playing on middle-class fears of declining status and moral decay. He pledged to restore Germany unity and national greatness. Hitler made deep inroads among the lower middle class, his strongest constituency. But the role of anti-Semitism in his electoral breakthrough is problematic. Nationwide the Nazis received only one-third of the vote. In the Upper Palatinate their support was a mere 18 percent. A classic local study by William Sheridan Allen sums up the attitude: most Germans "were drawn to anti-Semitism because they were drawn to Nazism, not the other way around."[57]

Once in power, Hitler and the Nazis admittedly enjoyed real success molding impressionable German youth in the spirit of Nazism. Otherwise, there is no way to explain the savage fighting on the eastern front.[58] Nonetheless, the active, dynamic hatred infecting the core of the Nazi movement never seeped deeply into public consciousness, and broad segments of the population remained amazingly indifferent to the so-called Jewish Question. Indeed, after the war countless Germans rushed to establish friendly relations with Jews to gain safe distance from the old regime. Tirschenreuth's mayor, a banker by the name of Otto Zahn, even financed and organized Erna Rubinstein's 1946 wedding. "The mayor was very sensitive to the needs of Jewish DP's," she says. There were plenty of others like him. Some of the friendliness was sheer opportunism, a way of gaining political rehabilitation on the cheap. But the philo-Semitism also indicates that the racism found in such pornographic journals as Julius Streicher's *Der Stürmer*, published in nearby Nuremberg, failed to infect the population at large. Nazi genocide is a sobering lesson that mass murder depends less on turning ordinary people into frothing racists than in anesthetizing their civil courage.[59]

If Germans in the early postwar years found sloughing off their anti-

Semitism easy to do, they were even more disingenuous in denying knowledge of the Holocaust. The question of what Germans knew, which the 1945–46 Nuremberg trials brought to the forefront, was hard to evade following the surrender. In such places as Tirschenreuth, the question elicited a stock German response: We didn't know about such things. But how could they not know, survivors wondered? Soldiers home on leave had brought back disquieting rumors of Einsatzgruppen massacres in the east. German social relief agencies had processed boxcar loads of handbags, linen, dolls, pipes, umbrellas, and fountain pens shipped in from Poland. Banks had received deposits of gold fillings, and a Nuremberg felt factory, consignments of women's hair. The sources of information were infinite, and by the end of 1942, according to historian Walter Laqueur, millions of Germans knew that Jews who had been deported to the east were no longer alive. Only the details of their deaths remained unknown. It is hard to fault Primo Levi's conclusion that "most Germans didn't know because they didn't want to know. Because, indeed, they wanted *not* to know."[60] And because—he might have added—they wished to avoid the burden of remembering.

About one thing ordinary Germans could definitely not plead ignorance: the anti-Jewish persecution that ensued after the Nazi seizure of power. The 1933 economic boycott, the 1935 Nuremberg race laws, the Aryanization of Jewish businesses, the barring of Jewish doctors and lawyers from practice— all took place in full public view. Even tiny Tirschenreuth had its Kristallnacht. Never mind that only about three Jewish families still remained in Tirschenreuth in November 1938, all of them shopkeepers who could trace their local roots back to the late 1800s. The family of Max Pick, recently deceased, owned a department store on the Marktplatz. The eighty-four-year-old Eduard Weiss ran a wholesale drygoods business. And Karl Grüner's family operated a grocery store. Though few in number, they possessed the requisite scapegoat visibility to arouse local Brownshirts, who, like their counterparts elsewhere in Germany, were mainly acting on orders from above. Those three families lost everything they owned in two hours or so.

It happened in the early evening of November 9, after the foreman in the local porcelain factory that employed most of Tirschenreuth's storm troopers received orders just before closing time to show up at the Marktplatz after work. The crowd eventually grew to more than a hundred, including young boys, some armed with ax handles. They descended on Pick's department store, hurling rocks at the shop windows, smashing the glass, and emptying out its contents. They climbed the stairs to the living quarters, where they demolished the furniture. Someone then yelled out that they should go to the Jew Weiss's establishment. The crowd destroyed all his belongings, carting off the sugar and flour in the storeroom. Grüner's place was next. the family was away.

A ladder was fetched, and a second-story window shutter was bashed open with an ax. The crowd poured through the window, demolishing and pillaging as they went. Just then the Grüners returned by car. Voices in the crowd started screaming, "Beat them to death, these Jewish swine." Two of the ringleaders eventually pulled the family to safety. The mob then returned to Pick's department store to complete the destruction. Through it all the police stood by silently, except for rescuing the Grüners and Max Pick's daughter-in-law.

Many townspeople witnessed the destruction. A few even accepted invitations from Karl Links, one of the SA (Sturmabteilung) leaders, to help themselves to the contents of Pick's store. Only one woman, a neighbor of the Grüners, openly expressed indignation. Links silenced her with a threat: "Be off with you, else the same will happen to you." In 1939 and 1940, the Picks, Grüners, and other Jews left for Berlin and Munich. Eduard Weiss stayed behind, dying in Tirschenreuth in 1941. A few of the Grüners eventually make it to America. Those who stayed put, according to surviving records, were deported to the east in the spring of 1942. German trustees had meanwhile taken over their Aryanized businesses.[61]

And then there was nearby Flossenbürg. Opened in 1938 as an SS industrial enterprise and quarry to provide paving stone for the fast-spreading autobahn, Flossenbürg started out as a punishment center for political prisoners and German criminals. After the Russian invasion in 1941, it became a warehouse for Soviet POWs and "a significant contingent of Jews." Nearly thirty thousand victims perished in the camp, which was a high mortality rate, given the relatively small number of inmates. Flossenbürg had a single gas chamber and a small crematorium, which functioned twenty-four hours a day. When its capacity was strained, which was often, the SS guards simply tossed the overflow into hillside pits. Later dismissed for drunkenness and "feasts of debauchery," the commandant once erected a huge Christmas tree from which he hung six inmates on Christmas Day.[62]

Staring across a narrow valley at the ruins of a medieval castle, the camp crowned the slope where the small town of Floss reclined. Floss's main street ran past the camp's entrance. As Jewish prisoners in Flossenbürg during the war's last years, arriving in Tirschenreuth shortly after the liberation, Henry Wahrman and his teenage brother had descended the slope almost every day. "They used to march us out from the camp to the Messerschmidt factory in Mitterteich," Wahrman said. "On Sundays, when we used to see people go to church, they saw us horrible creatures walking in those rags and in prison attire. Some of us were shoeless, barely able to walk or march. But after the liberation the local Germans said they never knew such a thing took place. At Flossenbürg they were burning people twenty-four hours a day, yet they denied that they ever heard or knew anything. It was really unbelievable."[63]

In the winter and spring of 1945, Flossenbürg became a switching yard for death march shuttles and evacuations. Beginning in January and running through March, prisoners from Auschwitz, Buchenwald, and lesser camps limped into the quarry-camp. Thousands died or were executed on the way. In early April, as Allied armies bore down from two directions, Flossenbürg itself was evacuated, though not before the ss executed such prominent political prisoners as the anti-Hitler conspirator Admiral Wilhelm Canaris (hung slowly with a piano wire) and Pastor Dietrich Bonhöffer. The largest evacuation, involving nearly thirty thousand prisoners, set off for Dachau in mid-April through incessant rain. It was one of those aimless, meandering marches whose sole purpose seemed to have been the infliction of death and misery for their own sake. Fewer than a quarter of the inmates reached their destination. At least seven thousand were shot by ss guards on the way. The others simply disappeared. Jews were singled out for the most inhumane treatment.[64]

Work squads hastily buried the gunshot victims in shallow graves, and the bodies started turning up shortly after the American army arrived in the region. In the Tirschenreuth area alone, two mass graves were discovered at the end of June 1945; ten days later another grave, containing the bodies of fifty-one camp prisoners, was unearthed.[65] The following August, forty-nine additional victims of the Buchenwald death march surfaced in a field freshly planted with potatoes. The farmer, who was arrested by the U.S. military after admitting knowing bodies were buried on his land, "thought it sufficient to heap additional dirt over the graves before planting over them." Some of the corpses were a mere nine inches below the surface. As they had done in similar cases, American authorities compelled local inhabitants over the age of sixteen to witness the exhumation. Former Nazi party members dug up the bodies and placed them in pine coffins. omgus officers who circulated among the workmen were stunned by the stubborn defiance they overheard: "The Jews are advertising their persecution again"; "What fuss over a lot of rotten bones"; "The Jews cause us trouble even after they are dead."[66]

If the perpetrators remained unrepentant, the bystanders forswore responsibility. They "seem to have no sense of guilt at all," the local military government officer told Stars and Stripes, the U.S. Army newspaper, "and said it is 'all the fault of the ss anyway.'" One Tirschenreuth resident flatly declared, "The war is over, and it would be best to forget the whole business."[67]

Occupational officials decided to rebury the bodies at Flossenbürg. Having witnessed Nazi crimes firsthand, the first American troops were sympathetic toward Jewish survivors. Lyle Robert Mariels, the local military governor at the time, once complained to higher authorities of "the well known German trait of blaming every nation and people except themselves for their troubles and shortcomings." Mariels helped arrange a thirty-truck convoy to carry the coffins to Flossenbürg. Hundreds of Jews from nearby DP camps attended. Representatives from OMGUS, UNRRA, and the German *Landrat* (county government) stood at the gravesite. A rabbi from the American Chaplaincy was brought in to perform the burial ceremony. Wahrman, the group's cantor, chanted the kaddish—the traditional prayer for the dead—over the grave.[68]

Tirschenreuth's small survivor community, however, was determined that local Germans be exposed to the service. Several Jewish DP's, such as Wahrman and his brother, had lived through death marches and witnessed the shooting deaths of numerous fellow prisoners. That they should be forced to grapple with traumatic memories while local Germans wallowed in historical amnesia disturbed them deeply.

Before the drive to Flossenbürg, Tirschenreuth's survivors marched with floral wreaths and banners around the Marktplatz. Although Anne and Lila had already seen more death than children their age typically ever do, they were unaccustomed to funerals. "We never attended them until we became adults," Anne says. This ceremony was different. The survivors were no less intent on shaming the Germans than honoring the Jewish dead. Standing on either side of Ruth, their arms draped with flowers, Anne and Lila were made the procession's centerpieces—reminders to German bystanders that Jewish family life had not been completely extinguished. Then, after circling the Marktplatz, the group filed down the street leading to the trucks parked in the yard adjacent to the public brew house. The 1946 memorial procession was not a one-time event. Every year until their dispersal in 1949, Tirschenreuth's survivor community made a point of marching around the Marktplatz before driving to Flossenbürg, where they placed floral wreathes at a marble obelisk they had arranged to have erected in the shadow of the crematorium, just beneath the watchtower.

But bearing witness against German forgetfulness also meant, for Tirschenreuth's survivors, reliving the original trauma. Laid out in formal gardens, its granite gash shaded by leafy trees, Flossenbürg today can easily be mistaken for an urban park. Even the gas chamber has been overshadowed by a recently constructed chapel. But during the occupation American authorities had ordered that the camp be left undisturbed, and the artifacts of death were everywhere. Ruth remembered the scene vividly: "We saw terrible pictures. We saw the oven where they put the people and the long shovel with which they put the people in. We saw thousands of pairs of shoes. We saw clothes, hills of clothes. We saw a place where the people were hung. We saw the barracks where the Jews were living. Terrible conditions. We saw the tower where the Germans watched. The chimney on the oven was very high, and on the chimney we saw how many were burned—Jews, German, Polish, Greek, Russian, gypsies, French—all the people who didn't comply with the Nazis." Mounds of human ashes were visible, too, but the communal graves evoked the great-est heartbreak. No one could be sure whether some friend or relative was buried in one of the pits. "The view was terrible," Ruth said. "We came home, and everybody was sick." Afterimages of camp scenes lingered for weeks. So did anger at the Germans, which flared up anew, causing survivors to break out with questions compulsively put to the locals about their knowledge of the camp. Always they met with the same protestations of ignorance. They knew nothing about all that. "This was the biggest lie that they could say," Ruth said disgustedly. "It was impossible not to see."[69]

The commemoration ceremonies with their aftermath of Jewish confron-tation and German denial quickly became a wearisome routine, one that Tirschenreuth's tiny survivor community would just as soon have avoided. Why go through the ordeal of witnessing if the locals remained unfazed? It was because silence in the face of German obtuseness evoked shame and survivor guilt. The Jewish DP's in Tirschenreuth really had no choice but to carry on with the depressing ritual.

Several of them, including Ruth, even attended the local denazification hear-ings, which commenced in August 1946, shortly before the first Flossenbürg reinterment ceremony. The tribunals, called *Spruchkammern*, were German-run courts set up by the American occupation authorities to review the status of more than 3 million members of "criminal" Nazi organizations like the ss and the sA. The Spruchkammern overlapped the major war crimes trial then drawing to a close in the Palace of Justice in nearby Nuremberg. All leading Nazis (save those who had committed suicide, such as Hitler, Joseph Goeb-bels, and Heinrich Himmler, or who had escaped, as did Martin Bormann) and much of the German high command were in the docket at Nuremberg—from Governor-General Hans Frank, who found religion after a suicide attempt, to the voluptuary Herman Göring, even down to the pathetic Julius Streicher, who used to talk dirty to children and did his morning ablutions in his jail cell toilet bowl. Nineteen of the twenty-two defendants completing the trial were convicted on October 1, 1946, largely on the strength of voluminous docu-mentation recovered from the Nazis themselves (including forty volumes of Frank's diary); ten of the convicted were hung fifteen days later, cremated, their ashes scattered in a tributary of the Danube.[70] The prosecution of the major war criminals in Nuremberg set the tone for the denazification hearings. In theory, mere membership in the ss, sA, Gestapo, or sD would be ipso facto proof of criminal wrongdoing. That notion of presumptive guilt cut a broad swath through German society, and everyone knew it.

Before the empanelment of the Spruchkammern, U.S. military government officials had done much of the work of denazification themselves. In Tirschen-reuth alone, American forces had by October 1945 registered over four-fifths of the Landkreis's sixty thousand inhabitants, removing hundreds of Nazi officials, two of them leading industrialists. The sheer scope of the denazification purge—which initially envisioned decartelizing the economy, democratizing the polity, and disarming the military (the four "Ds")—soon overwhelmed OMGUS's dwindling staff. The administrative bottleneck was particularly acute in such remote border regions as Tirschenreuth, where Nazis fleeing to anonymity tried to blend in with the thousands of German refugees pouring in from Prussia, Silesia, and the Sudetenland, swelling the population by a third. "This Landkreis is not able to absorb so many Nazis, especially those who did not live here," complained the American military commandant. Complaints even arrived from Palestine stating that Fritz Schultz, the owner of the Warsaw Ghetto slave factory where Mark had once worked, was hiding in the Tirschenreuth area—an allegation that was never verified. Because of denazification's expanding scope and the felt need to force Germans to assume responsibility for the forging of democratic norms, American zonal authorities decided, in March 1946, to turn matters over to native judges and prosecutors, who in turn required everyone over sixteen years of age to fill out questionnaires detailing their political history and wartime experience. Tirschenreuth's Spruchkammer hearings finally commenced in the Rathaus on August 9, 1946, continuing intermittently for nearly two years. By the time it ceased functioning, the local German tribunal had processed several thousand cases.[71]

Tirschenreuth's tiny Jewish community viewed the hearings as an opportunity to watch justice in action. Thus every morning Ruth and her friends traipsed across the Marktplatz "to listen to the terrible things that had happened," to use her language. In the beginning local interest was intense, and the sessions became downright boisterous. "Too often," Tirschenreuth's OMGUS commander wrote, "witnesses and respondents become embroiled in arguments, with some of the ever-present spectators taking sides in the argument." The room rang out with denials. We were just taking orders, went the refrain. We were underlings, was the answering echo. The perpetrators of Kristallnacht in Tirschenreuth were also interrogated and eventually hauled before the Spruchkammer, after the German courts ruled that their crime was still prosecutable.[72] Many of the defendants said they were mere bystanders. Those admitting they had entered Jewish homes and businesses claimed they were prompted only by curiosity. Injured dignity filled the witness stand. "The charge that I destroyed the wall clock and glass panes [at Grüner's] is a slippery lie and I repulse it," ran a typical response.[73]

Several local Nazis were sentenced and punished. "This was the one satisfaction of the people who had lost their families, children, parents, wives," Ruth said later. But daily attendance at the hearings nonetheless exacted a psychic price from Ruth and her friends. "Not one time in a trial like this, when there was a lunch break, did we come home but broken hearted," she said. "Throats closed up and we couldn't swallow anything." But this was the price of trying to begin life anew in postwar Germany. Torn between the wish to forget and the resolve to confront German amnesia, Jewish survivors in communities like Tirschenreuth were continually brought face-to-face with the very troubled memories they were trying to suppress.

By the spring of 1948 American authorities, bowing to cold war pressures to make West Germany into an anticommunist bulwark, set a two-month deadline for completing Spruchkammern proceedings. Denazification throughout the American zone had long since shifted from purging Nazis to removing their stigmas in order that they might resume peacetime professions. The new deadline placed the hearings on the same level as a traffic court. In Tirschenreuth, cold war normalization—which included reindustrializing the shattered Germany economy—was already fairly well advanced. Local elections two years earlier had brought to power the conservative and Catholic-based Christian Social Union Party (CSU), which worked to rehabilitate former members of the Nazi Party. CSU member Mayor Zahn, himself a former Nazi, hired several old party members. Christian Hecht was restored to police chief, the post he had held during Kristallnacht. Intent on bringing wayward souls back into the fold, the Catholic clergy regularly vouched for accused Nazis. Even the SA received a clean bill of health: "They were a parade group and had no importance in this area," averred the city priest. OMGUS officials usually acquiesced in the political normalization. When higher German courts reversed stiff local sentences, as they often did, zonal authorities might complain, but they let the reversals stand.[74] "I saw that the Americans right away were much too good," says Dora Appel. "The denazification thing was really a sham," added Henry Wahrman. Even the original commander of the local military government unit was disgusted: "It is discouraging to see former Nazi party members rolling in wealth they obtained during the Nazi regime."[75]

As the pace of denazification slackened, local German officials grew more recalcitrant. Friction between survivors and petty bureaucrats, often over driver's licenses, became commonplace. Tirschenreuth's Jewish survivors were in no frame of mind to back down. "We were, let's say, drunk with freedom and power and even with wealth, because we had the cigarettes," Marek Sudkiewicz says. In fairness to local German officialdom, it must be admitted that they were antagonistic to refugees in general, especially newcomers from Prussia and the Sudetenland, who were overburdening local housing stock. (So much for ties of "blood and soil," which, according to Nazi propaganda, bonded Germans in mystical union.) Invariably, hostility aimed at more familiar scapegoat targetry, in part because of the stereotyped perceptions that local Jews dominated the black market. Deeply troubling was that the new set of

American officers rotated in to replace the original OMGUS officials had never seen firsthand the evidence of Nazi atrocities and thus lacked the empathy of their predecessors. They were more impressed with the deportment of the conquered. "Their attitude towards the courteous German bourgeoisie who had managed to preserve their culture and fortunes, and towards the pretty, cheerful German girls, as kind and gentle as their sisters, was one of understanding and friendly admiration," wrote one Polish DP who had been imprisoned in Auschwitz. That transfiguration of emotional loyalties was occurring all over western Germany as denazification drew to a close.[76]

In Tirschenreuth, where local bureaucrats often called on OMGUS officials to mediate conflicts with survivors, the new indifference was manifested in the way the Americans began seeing things from the German point of view. "The belief exists in the town that anything from American dollars to a goose can be bought and sold at the Bayerischer Hof Hotel," reported the new American military governor, without comment, in the summer of 1947. The following spring he complained that most of Tirschenreuth's Jewish DP's were living high without any visible means of support, "centered on one activity," to quote his colloquialism—"sorta 'ride the horse till it drops.' "[77] The American officer could not have been talking about Mark Skorecki and Roman Kriegstein or, for that matter, Henry Wahrman.

So far as the Wahrman brothers were concerned, the local atmosphere had long ago grown poisonous. At Mayor Zahn's suggestion they had rented a room from an older woman whose husband had been detained by American authorities. It just so happened that she was the wife of SA leader Karl Links, one of the instigators of Kristallnacht in Tirschenreuth. A pleasant, gentle woman, she helped them with the cooking. But almost immediately she started in with how innocent her husband was. Links himself returned home after a few months' detention. "When he came back, he didn't know what was going to happen to him," Henry said. "So, he was like a pussycat for the first few weeks. And then when he became aware of the fact that he was giving away a room and his wife was actually busying herself with us, he became very annoyed. He wrote a letter to the mayor. It was very abrasive. The mayor showed me a copy. Links said that although he was let go and declared not guilty, he found two Jews living in his house. Then he started acting very unfriendly and his true colors came through. He was a ruffian, a real no-good. I found it unpleasant to see him every morning when I got up and every time I had to come to the house. And so by default he won. I looked around for another place to rent."[78]

But avowed former Nazis were not the only ones winning the psychological tug-of-war with local survivors. Judging by their newfound smugness, most of the German population was purchasing peace of mind at the expense of the

Jewish community. "I could have made some sort of living for myself there," Henry Wahrman said. His wool-reprocessing business was starting to thrive. But it was galling to deal daily with German businesspeople, eavesdropping on their conversations, stomaching their self-righteousness. "I'm not telling you that every German was guilty, but I didn't know who was not guilty. I knew that there were a multitude of Germans, hundreds of thousands, who were absolutely involved in murder, and I didn't know who I was talking to. At times I was wondering, maybe I'm talking to somebody that killed my family. That sort of feeling made me feel unworthy of existence. As soon as I got my papers, there was no question I was leaving. I did not profit by anything. I almost gave it away."

Ruth experienced the same feelings of shame and guilt: "I couldn't look into the faces of most Germans. I had to meet them every day and deal with them for groceries or go to the park. I was next to them. They were all friendly, because after what had happened plenty of them never forgave the ss and the Gestapo. But it was hard for me to live with them after what had happened. And it was hard to send my kids to school with their children."

Or to music classes. Even the self-dramatic Professor Adam Dolzycki, Anne and Lila's Polish piano teacher, had been a Nazi sympathizer who once conducted concerts for the occupiers during his tenure as director of the Warsaw Opera House symphony. "Once we found out that he had had something to do with the Germans, we didn't like him," says Erna Rubinstein's younger sister Rose Rosenberg, who had taken lessons from Dolzycki.[79]

Anne's and Lila's education caused Ruth a great deal of inner turmoil. The UNRRA-run Polish school in which she initially enrolled her daughters eventually shut down for lack of students. The only alternative was to send them to the local German school, but Ruth resisted the idea. Schoolteachers in the old Reich had been among the earliest and most fervent converts to Nazism, and in such places as Tirschenreuth they were removed wholesale after the war. "With the denazification of educational institutions, so many teachers have been removed that our schools are now operated by persons unqualified in intellect and experience," the OMGUS commander observed in his October 1946 report.[80] Ruth's concern, however, was mainly with her daughters' acculturation. They were becoming German children a little too swiftly. The language came easily, as did friendships. Neither Anne nor Lila could understand why their mother was so opposed to their mixing with the local kids. "They wanted to go to a regular school with all the other kids," Ruth said. "Looking back I know it was tough on my mother. But we were just kids and didn't know any different," Anne says.

Ruth relented about school attendance. Her children's education always took top priority. She and other Jewish parents forced the school to grant certain concessions, however, such as allowing the Jewish students to sit in the hall during religious classes. But Ruth never felt comfortable with Anne and Lila being brought up in the national traditions of her oppressors. The irony was depressing beyond words. It steeled her determination to emigrate to America.

By the spring of 1948 many Jewish DP's in Tirschenreuth had begun to leave for other countries. Haka was the first Skorecki to depart. Sometime in late 1946 she made contact through the international tracing service with her Kielce cousins, Dolek and his brother, in Haifa. But entry into Palestine at the time was extremely difficult, and so she emigrated to Malmö, Sweden, instead, where one Działoszyce cousin, Cecylia Skorecka, had landed in June 1945. Sweden attracted a disproportionate number of Jewish survivors just after the surrender, including Haka's cousin.[81] Wladek followed Haka to Malmö a short time later. They eventually married but had no children, both working at the Underwood Olivetti typewriter company until retirement, each dying of cancer within a few years of the other in the 1980s.

The principal exodus from Tirschenreuth and other DP centers, however, occurred following the establishment of the state of Israel in May 1948. But Pola was the only Skorecki in Tirschenreuth who went to Palestine, in March 1949. With Mark's help she had found a secretarial job in Tirschenreuth with the American Joint Distribution Committee, which helped transport nearly two hundred thousand survivors to the new Jewish state. For a brief period she lived in one of the tents where survivors were placed on arriving in Haifa. Then she moved in with Dolek. "She was living a few months with us," Dolek said. "After that she started to work." Until her death in 1998, she had lived in a small apartment on the outskirts of Israel's port city.[82]

Although Mark and Ruth had filed papers to emigrate either to Israel or to America, the United States was always their first choice. Thanks to the help of a Tirschenreuth-based American official vacationing in the states, they established contact with the New York families of Mark's two sisters. Sala, the oldest, had died in childbirth in the early 1920s, but Mark and Ruth were able to reach her husband, a patent medicine distiller on the Lower East Side, and through him Mark's younger sister, Celia, who had married an English émigré and stockbroker named Harry Tenser. Celia knew that her older sister Stefa and family had survived the war by fleeing to Russia. She had received cards from them in Vladivostok. But, after losing touch in 1940 with her family back in Łódź, Celia was sure everyone else had been slaughtered. The news that Mark's family was alive in Germany came as a big surprise. "She was very excited to hear from Mark and Ruth," her son, Arthur, says, and immediately bent her energies toward bringing them to the United States.[83]

Gaining entry to America just after the surrender was easier said than done. Barring the way were stiff immigration quotas imposed in the 1920s to reduce inflows from southern and eastern Europe. Abiding fears of foreign job competition kept the barriers up, as did the same anti-Semitism that had dulled America's response to the Holocaust: according to opinion polls taken just after World War II, over half the American public harbored anti-Jewish attitudes. Under a December 1945 executive order mandating DP exceptions to the quota system, President Harry S. Truman made it possible for some twenty-eight thousand Jewish survivors to enter the United States, which left little hope for the Skoreckis.

Then Mark heard that Canada was recruiting tailors. He traveled to a site where applicants were instructed to sew pockets on a jacket. Mark knew little about tailoring, but he had agile hands and passed the test. "He made the pocket perfectly," Ruth said, "and there were people there who had been tailors all their lives and they flunked." By the time the Canadian government was ready to issue visas to the Skoreckis, Ruth was already eight months pregnant and doctors refused to authorize her emigration. They said she could not travel until her newborn was at least half a year old. Meanwhile, in July 1948, Truman had signed the first Displaced Persons Act into law, opening America to more immigrants. It was bitterly ironic that the legislation showed more partiality toward Volksdeutsche expellees from Communist-dominated Europe than Jewish survivors, but the new law was sufficiently flexible to allow another sixty-eight thousand survivors to enter the country between 1948 and 1952. The Skoreckis came to the United States under its provisions.[84]

Anne was not excited about emigrating to America. She and Lila were doing well in school. They had made close friends for the first time in their lives, although some of them, like the Rubinstein sisters, were also leaving (they emigrated to Australia, another popular destination for survivors).[85] They believed Germany was going to be their home and could not understand why their parents were anxious to leave. But Anne also felt that if she had to pull up roots again, she would rather set them down in Palestine. Zionism had become a civil religion in the DP centers of Germany and Austria, and several of Tirschenreuth's Jewish leaders were enthusiastic converts. "Long live Palestine! Long live our own free Fatherland!" declared the secretary of the local Jewish Committee in a 1946 speech during one of the community's dramatic presentations.[86] Anne remembers standing in the Marktplatz with a crowd of other survivors listening to a live radio broadcast of the United Nations vote approving the partition of Palestine. Her Jewish patriotism was instinctual, not ideological. It stemmed from an inferiority complex inflicted by history. "I felt different," she says. "I still feel different. I wanted to go to Israel because that's where everybody was Jewish and I would be like them and I would never have to worry about being different." But after the 1948 Displaced Persons Act widened the door, her parents ruled out resettling anywhere but North America. At forty-nine, Mark was too tired to begin pioneer life in Israel.

There were a slew of last-minute details to tend to before departing, such as getting Anne's teeth straightened. "My mom was always aware of appearance, of saying and doing the right thing," she says. "We had to arrive in the United States as perfect individuals, and having straight teeth was part of it." It meant wearing a mouth cast for about six weeks, because braces were not yet in wide use.

Shipping the baby grand piano Ruth had bought following Adam's birth was a major production. Ruth hired a German cabinetmaker to build a packing crate almost as large as the wood shed in which they had lived in Praga, then paying to have it transported to New York. The piano remained in a bonded warehouse for months, storage charges mounting all the while.[87] Later, after the Skoreckis settled in New Orleans, the piano had to be shipped to Louisiana. "I have no idea what she thought when she shipped this thing here," Anne says. "It must have cost a fortune. All I know is that the piano was a symbol, but of what I'm not sure."

The most important matter was selling the bus company. "We had put money and time and ideas into this, so we couldn't just let it go," Ruth said. The mayor and other local officials badly wanted Mark and his partner Kriegstein to become permanent residents. "Why don't you stay here?" Mayor Zahn told Kriegstein. "We need people with energy, with ideas. Why do you want to go to America?" There was a hint in all this of traditional stereotypes being stood on their head—Shylock become economic savior. But the mayor seemed genuine in his appeals. "You know, he was trying sincerely to convince me I should stay. I remember this conversation very well," Kriegstein says. From a financial standpoint, remaining in Tirschenreuth had real attractions. EsKa had prospered to the point where both families were living comfortably. They had nurses for the babies, maids, and housekeepers. Kriegstein had his own chauffeur. "We had a very, very fine life," he admits. "But I couldn't see myself living in Germany."[88] Nor could the Skoreckis. There was no question but that they would sell EsKa, and quickly. After a local German and his New York–based sister put in a bid, the Landkreis matched the offer, later incorporating the company as a public enterprise under the EsKa name. Today the company operates a travel agency and owns twenty-one vehicles, some of them huge touring buses costing $1.3 million each.[89] Kriegstein eventually amassed a small fortune manufacturing watchbands and cases for Bulova. His world-famous collection of dockyard ship models has even been featured in *Forbes* magazine.[90] But for Mark and Ruth, the EsKa bus company represented an economic pinnacle. Never again would they have so much success in business.

According to International Tracing Service (ITS) records, the Skoreckis left Tirschenreuth for the port city of Bremerhaven in early August 1949. They missed their ship when Adam contracted measles and was quarantined for a few weeks. They finally sailed on September 26, on the U.S. Army Transport *General Leroy Eltinge*. The 1948 Displaced Persons Act required Jewish immigrants (but not ethnic Germans) to secure American sponsorship and to prove they had jobs and housing. Celia and Harry Tenser readily agreed to act as sponsors. The Tensers naturally assumed Mark's family would settle in the New York area. Its large Jewish population made it the destination of choice among survivor-immigrants to the United States. But Mark and Ruth had been working all along with the Hebrew Immigrant Aid Society (HIAS) to find other American destinations. A proud man, Mark wanted to avoid a situation where he might become dependent on his sister, and so he accepted a West Coast assignment when HIAS found sponsors in San Jose, California.

There was another reason the Skoreckis ruled out living in the New York City area: the undercurrent of tension between Ruth and Mark's relatives. There were no farewells exchanged with Pola when she left for Israel. "With him, yes," Pola says. "He came to the train. But she wanted nothing to do with the family."[91] Mark's sister Stefa had also emigrated to Israel with her husband and children, but Ruth never forgave them for real and imagined wrongs during the Nazi occupation of Łódź. When Anne's oldest daughter Sheryl spent six weeks in Israel in the 1960s, Ruth said nothing about getting in touch with the Mediterranean branch of the Skoreckis. "It was kind of curious," Anne says, "because they lost all this family and there were just these few individuals that survived. I never knew what the strain was all about. We weren't brought up that we could question it, so we never did. I just thought they wanted to make a new life for themselves and they were leaving everything behind."

If the source of the rift was mysterious, Mark and Ruth's capacity for shutting down their emotions was less surprising. For five years survival itself had depended on self-control—on hiding grief, feigning agreement, and telling poker-faced lies. But the stage discipline did not end with the drama. As Anne explains: "My parents had the ability to cut off their feelings and say, 'Okay, that's the end. I'm never going to talk to this person again.' Some people have that capability. They make a decision: 'I'm angry. That's it, I won't deal with this any longer.' Is it strength or is it discipline, to cut yourself off emotionally? I don't know the answer. All I know is that my parents could do that." That capability also meant Mark and Ruth were always able to present two sides: one to the world, another to their children.

Top: Postwar wedding scene in Łódź with Anne and Lila, ca. May 1945. The son of Mark's barber, whom Ruth befriended after the war, stands in uniform with his new bride. Ruth, the proud hostess, is second from the right.

Bottom: "EsKa" bus in Tirschenreuth, one of the early vehicles in the bus company set up by Mark and his young partner Roman Kriegstein in postwar Germany. "EsKa" is the phonic spelling of the initials of their surnames.

Top: Lila, Ruth, and Anne in Tirschenreuth, ca. 1946.

Bottom: Wreath laying at Flossenbürg concentration camp, with Anne.

Facing page: Anne, Helen Rubinstein, Lila, and Danusia Rubinstein, ca. 1947–48. The Rubensteins were Anne and Lila's first childhood friends after the war. The future Dr. Dorothy Kunstadt is the young girl on the right.

Top: Wladek and Haka Skorecki in Malmö, Sweden, ca. 1970s.

Bottom: Ruth, Adam, and Mark on the *General Leroy Eltinge* en route to New Orleans, November 1949.

Top: Josephine Street Passover dinner, New Orleans, 1950, the family's first in the New World. Ruth's close friend Mrs. Goldfarb (Niusia) is on the right.

Bottom: A new American family, ca. 1954–55.

Anne Skorecki and Stan Levy at the Fortier High School prom, 1955.

When the Skoreckis missed the boat to America, it set their lives on an unexpected course. The original itinerary had them sailing for New York from Bremerhaven, in August 1949, and then traveling by rail to their resettlement assignment in San Jose, California. The schedule left time for visiting with Harry and Celia Tenser. There was much family news to catch up on, and the Skoreckis wanted personally to thank Arthur Tenser, Harry and Celia's attorney son, for taking care of storing the piano Ruth had shipped from Tirschenreuth earlier that summer. But slightly before the Skoreckis' scheduled embarkation, ten-month-old Adam contracted measles and had to be quarantined for several weeks. An entire month passed before the Skoreckis could book passage on another U.S. Army transport ship, the *General Leroy Eltinge*, which was bound for New Orleans, not New York. Nosing southward toward the hurricane corridor linking Africa and the Gulf of Mexico, the *General Leroy Eltinge* encountered rough weather three days from land. The choppy seas sent Anne to the ship's infirmary, where she stayed for the rest of the voyage.

Those brief separations from Anne and Adam foreshadowed anxieties that would dominate Ruth's time in America. For the rest of her life she was haunted by fears of losing her children. Many aspects of becoming an American she found immensely appealing: the civic patriotism, the voluntarism and joiner mentality, and especially the bargain-hunting consumerism that cold war prosperity would soon spur to new heights. But the side effects of American mobility were another story. Achieving the American dream often fragmented and dispersed families, undermining traditional authority. It often led to a reversal of roles between immigrant parents and children. Assimilation's unintended consequences confronted Ruth with dilemmas she never was able to resolve. The central struggle was between a Holocaust mother's overpossessiveness and an immigrant parent's desire for her children to fit in. But because assimilation frequently subverted parental control, Ruth, Old World to the core and conditioned by the Holocaust to distrust the external world, had trouble letting go.

As the *General Leroy Eltinge* sailed past the mud spouts guarding the Mississippi River's crowfoot passes, it never crossed Ruth's mind that her own family's version of Americanization might be shaped in south Louisiana. The semiaquatic landscape, built from alluvial ooze deposited by a millennium of spring floods, was a world apart from the Polish plain. Instead of alternating forests and fields dropping away to the horizon, the vista presented a watery expanse of sedge grass flecked by wind-driven foam off the gulf. Occasionally ibis and egrets swept across the sky. In the fall, waterfowl on their way to winter quarters hung high overhead in slow-flight formation. Forty miles upstream the twisting river, now pinched between manmade levees, lifted above the land. Once in a while passengers up on deck caught glimpses of solitary fishing cabins teetering on stilts. On the batture between shore and levee, pioneer swamp willows were colonizing territory where hundred-foot bald cypresses once soared, until lumber syndicates denuded the land. Sugar cane harvesting was just getting under way, the sweet-pungent haze from its fires mingling with refinery odors from the emerging American Ruhr. As the ship neared New Orleans, piers and bulkheads jutted into the olive-drab river. It took the river pilot who had boarded at Pilot Town, near the passes, almost two days to guide the army transport to the Crescent City.

The *General Leroy Eltinge* docked on Monday morning, October 10, at the ironically named Poland Avenue wharf, the official Port of Embarkation, adjacent to the Industrial Canal and across the river from the Algiers drydocks.[1] The day was cloudy. Hundreds of European passengers leaned over the rails, sweltering in clothing much too heavy for the subtropical climate. Down below a military band played martial music. Armbanded representatives from several religious and community-based organizations were waiting at the gangplank to offer assistance: HIAS, the United Service for New Americans (USNA), the Catholic Resettlement Committee (CRC), and the Red Cross. Inside the large warehouse a makeshift constellation of tables and folding metal chairs had been set up to process the newcomers through naturalization and customs. "We came to our new adopted country, and we were taken in with music and care," was Ruth's first impression of America.

Like the nearly 1 million newcomers who had streamed through New Orleans before World War I, most of the *General Leroy Eltinge*'s thousand-plus passengers arrived as sojourners bound for inland destinations. On any given ship the Jewish contingent seldom exceeded 160 individuals, and it was often much less. On the theory that scattershot placement would hasten assimilation to American society, national Jewish organizations made every effort to divert Holocaust survivors away from New York City (which nonetheless received two-thirds of the 140,000 Jewish DP's emigrating to America) and settle them in communities where Jews formed small minorities. After the passage of the 1948 Displaced Persons Act, which required that Jews alone show proof of employment and housing before receiving visas, hundreds of Jewish federations around the country sprang into action. A key cog in this national resettlement was the New Orleans federation, which like its counterparts elsewhere functioned as an umbrella organization for all community-based Jewish groups. Informed ahead of time by the Displaced Persons Commission in Washington that "New Orleans will probably be one of the principal ports of entry," it swiftly assembled local forces to assist Jewish refugees in transit.[2]

A lot of the hands-on work was done by the New Orleans chapter of the National Council of Jewish Women, especially its Service to Foreign Born (SFB) Division. Although the national SFB had been established in 1903 to protect single Jewish immigrant women from the white slave trade, the New Orleans division had come into existence only during World War II. Much of its work was concentrated in the immediate postwar period, when New Orleans served as a transit center for refugee ships arriving from Europe. The Port and Dock Committee established by members of the local council stayed on twenty-four-hour standby, greeting ships at the docks and helping with baggage and customs. A Motor Corps of private automobiles driven by council women shuttled recent arrivals to their air and rail connections. "It was a great movement," says Rosalie Cohen, who was serving at time as president of the local Jewish Family Services organization. The surviving records bear out her self-congratulatory assessment.[3]

The Skoreckis had disembarked the *General Leroy Eltinge* fully expecting to be transferred along with the rest of the passengers to their next travel connection. But after reaching the processing shed, Nathan Bronstein, the executive director of the local federation, pulled them to one side. He had been poring over their papers with a troubled look, conferring with national representatives of HIAS and the recently formed USNA. Through a German interpreter he told the Skoreckis that their relocation documents had gotten fouled up. "I'm sorry Mr. Skorecki," he explained to Mark. "You have a private affidavit from your sister in New York, who has paid plenty of money and gone to great trouble. We can't send you to San Jose. You have to go to New York."

Nearly bald save for a wisp of a widow's peak, Mark grew grave when Bronstein broke the news. His five-foot-seven frame, lean and muscular and unusually fit for a man approaching fifty, became tense and erect. He usually talked with his large, powerful hands, but they now hung stiffly at his sides. Mark looked the federation head directly in the eye, never averting his gaze, and said plainly that the war had frayed his family's nerves. "We want to find a quiet city, not a rushed-up one." There was another reason for Mark's aversion to settling in New York: fear of becoming dependent on his sister Celia and her prosperous husband. "He was anxious to become self-sufficient," wrote a New Orleans official in a report filed a few days after the *General Leroy Eltinge*'s arrival.[4] Like many Holocaust survivors who emerged from the war determined to control their destinies, Mark's habitual resolve had metamorphosed into granite obstinacy. "Mr. Skorecki was a man that had his own mind," says a council volunteer who came regularly to greet the DP boats.[5] Bronstein pleaded with Mark. Rules were rules, he said. Mark would not budge. Defeated, Bronstein finally directed the family to wait with their baggage inside the saunalike warehouse. Coffee, donuts, and soft drinks were available. Outside the temperature climbed into the high eighties.

All day long, woman volunteers from the local council shuttled Jewish refugees to their next travel connection. Displaced persons with long layovers were driven to the Jewish Community Center on stately St. Charles Avenue, in Uptown New Orleans, where they rested and ate before being shuttled to their next travel connections. Those whose trains were scheduled for the next day were put up at nearby hotels. "Our new hosts gave us moral support," attested one survivor who received travel assistance from the New Orleans Jewish community, "and I really felt that I was among friends."[6] Meanwhile, the Skoreckis marked time at the Poland Avenue embarkation shed, growing hot and uncomfortable—and fearful. The unpleasant sensation of feeling different, of being branded and set apart, came rushing back. "Everybody was looking at us," Ruth said. "They thought something was wrong." A few council volunteers approached, asking questions in German. Black luggage handlers looked over in puzzlement. Every so often customs officials came across refugees wearing forearms of expensive wristwatches smuggled in as a hedge against rainy days, but the inspectors usually looked the other way. "After what those poor devils have been through, we don't have to punish them," they said to each other.[7]

After the crowds thinned, Bronstein returned, but only to renew his insistence that the Skoreckis travel by train to New York. Mark offered a compromise. If San Jose was out of the question, he and his family were willing to stay in New Orleans. Bronstein thought about it for a minute. Then he left to consult with local leaders from the Jewish community and HIAS and USNA representatives who had come down from New York. Bronstein had been around long enough to know that twentieth-century New Orleans was not a place where anonymous Jewish immigrants casually set down roots.

It was not because the Crescent City lacked room for one more survivor family. Immediately after the war, the local Jewish community probably numbered fewer than eight thousand individuals, a mere 1 percent of the overall population, which was a tiny proportion for a city of New Orleans's size. Nor did incoming refugee ships alter the demographic balance, because, as the local federation's president put it, the Jewish community had agreed to accept "not more than five family units per month," all of whom had local sponsors, usually relatives.[8]

That self-imposed quota was the product of a deep-rooted assimilationism stemming from the community's unique makeup. In no other major American city was Reform Judaism so dominant as in New Orleans. Composed of old-line families, mainly German and French, who had long since adapted to the city's mores, this outward-looking community cared less for preserving a separate Jewish identity than achieving social acceptance in the wider world. Its religious services—rational, decorous, and bereft of most identifying marks of traditional Judaism, such as chanting in Hebrew and wearing yarmulkes inside the sanctuary—represented a kind of spiritual acculturation to American Protestantism. The emphasis on assimilation produced success, not to mention a high rate of intermarriage (many in the original Sephardic contingent had long ago been absorbed into the Catholic majority). The men who filled the pews at such Reform temples as Sinai, Touro, and Gates of Prayer had reached the summit of the local power structure. They owned large downtown department stores and brokerage businesses. They headed prestigious law firms. They were leaders of the bar and presidents of local and state medical societies. They sat on hospital and university boards. Excluded at the turn of the century from the status rituals of the Mardi Gras debutante season, they poured their energies into funding museums, local theater, and the symphony—although some paid the non-Jewish aristocracy the sincerest form of flattery by mimicking its obsession with genealogy. So well assimilated had they become by mid-century that the city's leading Reform rabbi, Julian Feibelman, could declare in 1941: "One cannot say there is a distinct Jewish community in New Orleans. There is rather a distinct New Orleans culture of which the Jewish community is a part."[9]

The turn-of-the-century immigration from Eastern Europe that vastly changed the face of American Judaism largely bypassed the Crescent City. The customary explanation is immigrant dread of yellow fever and the city's nonindustrial character. But efforts by Reform Jews to filter out Polish and Russian coreligionists also kept the numbers small. "It is not the intention of the Israelites of New Orleans to bring down in great masses these Russian refugees and disturb the labor markets," a Reform rabbi reassured the New Orleans press during the height of the Eastern European influx to East Coast cities.[10] "As selfish as it may seem today," explains Moise Steeg, himself descended from an Alsatian Jewish family and today a leading lawyer and behind-the-scenes power broker, "these old line families didn't want to be routed out of their position by this distinctive influx from Eastern Europe."[11]

The prescreening not only strengthened assimilationist dominance (as late as 1960 the city's three Reform temples had twice the number of congregants as New Orleans's three Orthodox synagogues) but also precluded the emergence of a recognizable Jewish culture based on diet, dress, and ritual observance. Admittedly, several vestiges of the old religion existed within the Orthodox neighborhood that once stretched from Melpomene to Jackson Avenue, on the "wrong side" of the St. Charles streetcar tracks. In those days Dryades Street, the district's commercial artery, supported a kosher butcher, a kosher baker, and a kosher delicatessen—"everything that you can name in the way of making life comfortable and enjoyable," says octogenarian Rosalie Cohen, whose parents settled in the vicinity in the early 1900s after emigrating from Białystok, Poland. For forty years the local Communal Hebrew School was even able to support a well-known scholar of modern Hebrew who had taught the language to future Israeli prime minister Golda Meir when both lived in Milwaukee. But, apart from diet and observance of Jewish festivals, New Orleans was scarcely fazed by the Yiddish revival that had swept urban areas in the East, mainly because the Polish and Russian immigrant community sustaining that tradition was dwarfed by the larger Reform community. Nor were there many social connections between the two groups, separated as they were by acculturation and, for many years, by economic status. One old-line German Jewish family in the city refused to let their daughter attend United Service Organization (USO) dances for fear she might be obliged to dance with servicemen from Eastern Europe.[12] In fact, as late as the mid-1950s, New Orleans was without a Conservative synagogue to bridge the gulf between tradition and assimilation. "There was Reform and there was Orthodoxy," says Sylvia Gerson, of *Cajun Kosher* cookbook fame, "and nobody crossed the line. It was absolute." Gerson, who moved to New Orleans from Pittsburgh after the war and belonged to the Port and Dock Committee that greeted DP ships, recalls being asked by council volunteers whether she knew anyone who spoke Yiddish. Nearly all the women with whom she worked were Reform Jews. "They were stunned that I could speak Yiddish and that I would admit it," she says.[13]

Despite social divisions, the two worlds of New Orleans Jewry could pull together in the face of common peril. "It's an old story with Jews," says Rosalie Cohen. "Immigrants come, and Jews learned long ago to take care of their own, to see that they are cared for, that they have the tools they need to make their way." In the late 1930s and early 1940s the community had united behind a private national effort to rescue victims of Nazi persecution whom the

American government was reluctant to assist for fear of inflaming an anti-Semitic public opinion. "Would the gentleman advocate bringing the hordes of Europeans here when the record shows we have thousands and thousands of poor people in this country who are in want?" demanded Leonard Allen, a congressman from Huey Long's hometown of Winnfield, during hearings on a 1939 bill to allow twenty thousand German Jewish children into the country. The bill was withdrawn by its sponsor.[14] From 1937 to 1942, the local Refugee Service Committee, acting in conjunction with the New York–based committee and composed of leading businessmen from both the Reform and Orthodox communities, worked behind the scenes to resettle German and Austrian Jews fleeing Hitler's grasp. The resettlement project was modest in scope, however—"two refugee units a month" was the self-imposed limit—and very low-key. Concerned about provoking a backlash from the local gentile community, the New Orleans federation banned all publicity regarding wartime Jewish refugees who relocated to the city.[15]

Indeed, nervousness about latent anti-Semitism even hampered the community's response to the Holocaust itself. No accusation made leaders of the Reform community more uneasy than the charge of harboring dual loyalties, a staple of anti-Semitic rhetoric. To counter that libel they staunchly opposed attempts by American Zionists to link rescue efforts to the creation of a Jewish state in Palestine. Hard-core resistance was centered in Temple Sinai, the city's wealthiest congregation, then headed by Rabbi Julian Feibelman, editor of the local *Jewish Ledger* and a cofounder of the anti-Zionist American Council on Judaism. Feibelman, who is justly famed for courageously opening his synagogue in 1949 to an integrated lecture by black UN official Ralph Bunche, during the war editorially chastised Rabbi Stephen S. Wise, America's leading Zionist, for publicizing back-channel intelligence he had received regarding the Final Solution. Feibelman was worried the reports might be discredited as groundless German atrocity stories, as had happened during World War I, and heighten feelings of anti-Semitism. His criticisms drew a stinging rebuke from Wise ("I consider your attitude disgraceful in every sense") and demands by New Orleans Zionists to open up the *Ledger*'s columns to different points of view.[16]

By war's end the acrimony had cooled considerably, as the two communities, Reform and Orthodox, Zionist and non-Zionist, joined hands once again in the more wide-reaching resettlement program of which the Skoreckis were a part. But the prewar quotas, as we have seen, remained in evidence, as did the old concerns. According to a 1948 USNA Report, New Orleans was one of those American cities that was loathe to accept "Sabbath observers"—that is, Jews who refused to work on Saturday.[17] When Nathan Bronstein, the federation head, left to consult with community leaders about Mark's willingness to settle in the Crescent City, he was assuredly mindful of prevailing attitudes in this uniquely assimilated community.

Bronstein spent some time mulling over Mark's offer. Nobody knew anything about the Skoreckis; they were complete strangers to the city. After what must have seemed like an eternity to the family, Bronstein returned with a telling question: "Do you work on Saturdays?" Mark answered honestly and, given the circumstances, wisely. "I work anytime," he said through an interpreter. "I find my bread, and I'm sure I can get a job and support my family. I won't give you any trouble." Apparently that was all Bronstein needed to hear. He said they could stay. It was not until a few years later that the Skoreckis learned they had been swapped for a large, ultra-Orthodox family that was having trouble adjusting to New Orleans.

Late in the day, after everyone was gone, a council volunteer drove the Skoreckis to the Jewish Community Center. All their fellow passengers had already freshened up. But the Skoreckis were feeling, as Ruth put it, "not so fresh." After washing, the family joined other new arrivals, mainly sojourners awaiting evening rail connections, for a sit-down dinner prepared and served by local volunteers. The atmosphere was warm, like one big family. After supper a gentleman from the federation gathered up the Skoreckis and their luggage. He gave them a quick automobile tour of the city, and then drove to Walgreen's Drugstore on Canal Street, across the wide boulevard from the D. H. Holmes Department Store clock under which generations of New Orleanians had rendezvoused. He bought the girls ice cream. Although Christmas was more than eight weeks away, already Yuletide decorations were starting to bedeck the city's major shopping thoroughfare.

The Skoreckis appreciated their guide's kindness, but they were anxious to go to the hotel. Their heavy clothing advertised them as greenhorns from Europe. Anne and Lila's long pigtails looked out of place. "Everybody was looking at us," Ruth said. "I was sure that people knew we were newcomers."

Ruth had always been acutely self-conscious of other people's perceptions. During the Holocaust that sixth sense functioned as a guidance system, steering the family through numerous tight situations. In postwar New Orleans, where 1950s other-directedness reigned supreme, it would also facilitate her quest for an American identity. Ruth exemplified the well-known Russian Jewish impulse swiftly to "green out," to become an "allrightnik," as the Yiddish phrase for assimilation had it. Unlike many peasants from southern Italy who sojourned in America only long enough to accumulate funds to buy land in the Old Country, Russian and Polish Jews came to stay, and for that reason they were extraordinarily anxious to fit in. Ruth was just as determined to acquire an American identity, but she had additional reasons for doing so: wartime persecution made her all the more eager to don the camouflage of conformity.

But into what kind of society was the Skorecki family supposed to blend? New Orleans in 1949 was nearly 40 percent African American, and the racial unrest that would eventually propel the direct-action campaigns of the civil rights era was just beginning to stir. And how far could one let the assimilation process go without sacrificing Jewish identity and diluting Jewish culture? The latter concern aroused Ruth's deepest unease as nothing else could. As for the pervasive reality of racial injustice, her and Mark's attitudes were far from atypical among Jewish refugees who settled in the Crescent City, notwithstanding reports of survivors who left the city because of discomfort with segregation.[18] "They looked at it this way: As long as they [survivors] weren't picked on," explains the American-born son of one survivor couple who settled in New Orleans. Personal survival was always uppermost in their minds.[19] The "second generation," as the children of survivors are called, eventually came to draw a connection between their parents' persecution and the racial discrimination they saw all around them in their new hometown. Acutely sensitive to injustice, Anne was one who did so.

After they finished their ice cream, the man from the federation drove the Skoreckis to the Orleans Hotel, on St. Charles Avenue, a few blocks upriver from Lee Circle. High atop a marble shaft rising from the grassy knoll, his arms crossed, his back turned toward the North, stood the great Confederate captain of war. All day and night clanging streetcars circumnavigated the Civil War monument, carrying passengers to and from the fleshpots of the Vieux Carré.

Postwar New Orleans was Ignatius J. Reilly's kind of town, the haunt of picaresque slobs and libertines straight from the pages of John Kennedy Toole's *A Confederacy of Dunces*. Although a young, dynamic, silk-stocking reformer named DeLesseps S. Morrison was in his first term as mayor, both city and state lived in the shadow of Morrison's chief rival, Earl Long, Huey's younger brother. "Uncle Earl" served one partial and two full terms as governor, the last one climaxed by a drunken breakdown during a speech to the state legislature. A roistering populist and, in an odd, Louisiana sort of way, a defender of black civil rights, Earl frequented the bars and strip joints on Bourbon Street, openly philandering with such showgirls as Blaze Starr. But his major vice was betting on the ponies. Every morning in the governor's mansion, before receiving visitors, he pored over the tout sheets, placing bets with racetracks around the country. The mob, which contributed heavily to his campaigns, tipped him off to fixed races. Under Governor Long's neglectful eye, metropolitan New Orleans was awash in illegal gaming establishments. Upriver, just west of the city, Jefferson Parish alone sported several swank casinos along old River Road, next to the Mississippi levee. In the city's demimonde saloons, slot and pinball machines were as commonplace as oysters and draft beer. Policy and bookie joints were just as ubiquitous. Around the time of the Skoreckis' arrival, the *New Orleans Item* was running a front-page series exposing neighborhood taverns for brazenly violating state antilottery laws.[20] As for "reform" mayor Morrison, whom Earl nicknamed "Delasoups" and chided for pumping perfume under his arms, his involvement with local vice interests soon became a matter of public record.[21]

In their temporary lodgings at the Orleans Hotel, the Skoreckis had a front-row seat onto Crescent City hedonism. This section of St. Charles Avenue was in the early stages of urban blight. Across the street, round-the-clock bars welcomed unescorted women at all hours of the day and night. Their first full morning in New Orleans, the Skoreckis woke to see a drunken woman lying motionless on the sidewalk. "In the beginning I was sure something had happened to her. Maybe she was dying," said Ruth, whose frame of reference was the cadaver-strewn streets of the Warsaw Ghetto. But pedestrians walked around or stepped over her, laughing. The police were mirthful when they took her off in the paddy wagon. Such incidents kept Ruth and Mark from ever feeling completely comfortable in the Big Easy.

The Skoreckis stayed in the Orleans Hotel more than a month. Like many American cities at the time, postwar New Orleans had a significant apartment shortage, and landlords were picky about whom they would accept as tenants. Most vacancy signs announced, "No Dogs and Children Allowed." Federation leaders wanted Mark and Ruth to stay in the Orleans Hotel until a rental turned up in the city's more desirable Uptown section. But Ruth, who had yet to grasp the city's peculiar social geography, had wearied of hotel life and was ready to live anywhere so long as it promised stability. Anne and Lila had yet to enroll in school, which had been under way over eight weeks. The entire family was unaccustomed to New Orleans restaurant food. The first time Mark ordered soup, the waitress brought him a bowl of nonkosher gumbo swimming with beaded eye crab and shrimp shells. He made her take it back, explaining he could not eat anything that stared him in the face. Above all, Ruth was tired of sojourning. "From the time the war stopped in 1945 my life was temporary," she said, "like waiting in a station for a bus or train."

From a survivor couple who preceded them to New Orleans, they learned of a vacancy at 1326 Josephine Street, at the corner of Coliseum, within walking distance of the hotel. It was in an area of town called the lower Garden District. Many New Orleans survivors, drawing comfort from one another's company, initially rented apartments in the area owing to its proximity to the

Orthodox synagogues and business community around Dryades, Baronne, and Carondelet Streets. Located directly behind Trinity Episcopal Church, on Jackson Avenue, where the city's gentility prayed, the apartment was in one of those clapboarded Greek Revival mansions that had been built before the Civil War by American businessmen in flight from downtown Creole majorities. It had a cast-iron gallery shaded by a massive parapeted cornice. Fluted columns crawling with acanthus leaves framed the front door. The vacancy was a two-bedroom apartment on the second floor, with a kitchen, living room, and dining area, all steeped in the gloom of high ceilings and mahogany molding. On summer evenings night-blooming jasmine perfumed the air outside, adding a whiff of decadence. The Skoreckis agreed to the monthly rent of seventy-five dollars, not including gas and electricity. It was home for slightly more than a year.

Ruth had barely unpacked when a *New Orleans Item* photographer and reporter, briefcase in hand, knocked on the apartment door announcing that they wanted to do a Thanksgiving Day story about the Skoreckis and include Lila's picture on the front page. To a family used to regarding privacy and survival as reverse sides of the same coin, the notoriety was disorienting, and the questions, downright silly. Did the Skoreckis know what a chicken was? Of course, Ruth said, using her daughters as translators, "we have all kinds of birds in Europe." Lila was unable to understand the reporter's description of a typical Thanksgiving dinner. "Cran-berry? Anna, what is cran-berry?" she asked her sister, who was also at a loss. Less difficult to grasp was the scene the reporter asked Lila to stage. It was a performance she knew by heart. When the photo appeared Thanksgiving Day on the front page, the mise-en-scène resembled a genre painting by Vermeer: an angelic girl in braided pigtails looking heavenward as she knelt in Catholic prayer beside her bed. Propped against the Chippendale headboard were the dolls Mark had purchased in Tirschenreuth to replace sand-filled surrogates he had improvised during the family's double life on the Aryan side.[22] It was a poignant blending of old and new, of continuity and change, of being agreeable and of being on guard.

"It probably bothered my mother at the time," Anne says, "but she didn't want gentiles to think bad of her. She didn't want to come across as an abrasive Jew. That was kind of inbred. So was her self-control." Adam elaborates: "My mother used to say, 'You have to be nice to people. You have to make them like you.'"[23]

The mixed character of their new surroundings only reinforced Ruth's conformist instincts. Sandwiched between Magazine and Prytania Streets, the Josephine neighborhood had been in sociological transition for generations. Though forming the upriver boundary of a once tony suburb, Josephine Street had been abandoned decades ago by New Orleans patricians fleeing across

Jackson Avenue to the oak-shaded exclusiveness of the Garden District proper, as well as other neighborhoods farther uptown. Between the river and Magazine, for several miles along the river's crescent curvature, stretched a racially mixed, working-class neighborhood of closely packed shotgun houses called the Irish Channel. Long-leafed banana trees rubbed against peeling millwork, giving the area a faintly charming, subtropical seediness. On Magazine Street two cultures clashed and mingled, saloons and body shops coexisting amiably with antique stores and upscale boutiques. Prytania Street, one block removed from St. Charles and parallel to the city's grandest avenue, likewise possessed an endearing out-at-the-elbow ambience. At its intersection with Josephine, less than one hundred yards from the Skoreckis' doorstep, a bookie joint took bets day and night.[24]

Some of the neighborhood's inhabitants were less than neighborly. New Orleans was scarcely exempt from the postwar competition for jobs and housing that bred open resentment toward recent immigrants elsewhere in America. One Polish Jewish survivor who barely preceded the Skoreckis to the Lower Garden District found a note in his mailbox the day after moving into his new apartment, warning, "If Hitler didn't get you, we will."[25] But such threats were rare. Petty harassments, on the other hand, were not. Several of the Skoreckis' new neighbors were, to quote Ruth, "not so nice to us." Shortly after the family had unpacked, a grammar school boy from across the street threw a roll of burning film into Adam's stroller while Anne and Lila were taking him for a walk. It singed their baby brother's hair, burning him in a few places. The sisters were so rattled, they were unable to speak to the police, and Ruth could not make herself understood. First, she was nervous around people in uniform—a typical survivor phobia that neither she nor Lila ever overcame. Second, survivors had a generalized distrust of the outside world, the Holocaust's most enduring legacy. As Ruth admitted, "We were afraid to tell who had done this; maybe they could do something worse to us." Their gentile neighbor downstairs, who had immigrated from Germany four decades earlier, interpreted Anne and Lila's account for the police. The officers said they would talk to the boy's parents.

The incident had the happy outcome of breaking the ice with the downstairs neighbor, Mrs. Irvin. She practically adopted the Skorecki family—checking on Adam's health, translating documents, interpreting the mysteries of an unusual city. She even included the Skoreckis in her 1949 Christmas Eve buffet dinner, buying presents for Mark, Ruth, and the children. Being made a part of Mrs. Irvin's Yule celebration stirred bittersweet memories of their Aryan double life, especially the make-believe Christmas parties they staged under the direction of Natalia Piotrowska in Praga. But it also helped reduce feelings of isolation and aloneness. Mrs. Irvin took a special liking to Anne, who earned spending money tending her garden. Later, Mrs. Irvin helped her find weekend and summer work at a ladies wear department store on Dryades Street, a few blocks on the other side of St. Charles Avenue, where the old Orthodox community serviced the segregated black market.

In the meantime, Anne and Lila had enrolled in the Jackson School, a four-story structure on Camp Street with a grand marble staircase just inside the foyer. The building fronted a grassy triangle of moss-draped live oaks called Coliseum Square. Radiating from the knoll was a grid of streets whimsically named for Greek and Roman muses. Jackson School was only six blocks from the Skoreckis' apartment. Anne and Lila would walk past Mayor Morrison's house on Coliseum Street and then cut through the park. Anne was placed in the eighth grade, Lila in the sixth, and though it was already late in the semester and they were the only Jewish children in the student body, they had no trouble fitting in. With their peers they were instant hits, notwithstanding the fact teachers often held them up as models of deportment. "We were the curiosity kids," Anne says. The faculty were amazed at how well Anne and Lila were prepared for their assigned grade level—testament to Ruth's home schooling—and at how well they played the piano. Mrs. Mary Davis, Lila's teacher, often stayed after school to help her learn English. "I knew a few words when we came to this country," Lila says, "but not enough to hold a conversation. Just the basics, like 'Good Morning,' 'How Are You,' 'Thank You.'" During the Christmas break Mrs. Davis gave Anne and Lila a picture dictionary of English words. "That lady was unbelievable," Lila says.

Ruth beamed with pride at Anne's and Lila's quick adjustment to their new surroundings. Like many immigrant parents, especially Jews from Eastern Europe, she desperately wanted her children to become Americanized. In 1950s America, then drenched in sitcom nostalgia, all roads leading from greenhorn status seemed to converge on idealized television families like the Cleavers and the Ozzie Nelsons. It was hardly surprising that Ruth came to believe the child-centered domesticity glorified by Hollywood and New York offered a yardstick by which the Skoreckis could measure out new American identities—and conquer Holocaust-enhanced insecurities about feeling different. But, as always, acculturation precipitated conflicts between tradition and American norms. For no sooner had Ruth congratulated herself on Anne's swift adjustment to American public schooling than she discovered her daughter was being drawn into a Madison Avenue–molded youth market that increasingly circumvented parental authority.[26]

Teen fashions and the precocious sexualization of America's youth bothered Ruth, as did the sensate temptations of their new city. Ruth's inner conflicts began with little things like wearing blue jeans. Anne and Lila begged for Levi denims, for example, because their classmates all owned pairs. "At first I hated this since this is what the country people wore in Europe," Ruth said, reflecting an extreme European formality that many survivors carried across the Atlantic. But she bought the jeans anyway, sacrificing Old World decorum to New World identity. Then girlfriends at school started putting lipstick on Anne. Ruth tried to draw the line at cosmetics. Before long Anne herself was applying makeup after reaching the street, smudging it off just before returning home. Ruth exploded when she caught her daughter in the apartment stairwell wiping lipstick from her face. "Anne, what happened? You didn't listen to me." Anne said she was afraid of appearing different from the other students. Ruth replied that children should obey their parents, not listen to strangers. "But on the other hand," she admitted to herself, "I was thinking that maybe Anne might feel a little held back." So, the rigid code was relaxed once again.

The teenage social scene continued to trigger all kinds of alarms. Anne's first dance, an eighth grade mixer at Jackson School, remained burned in Ruth's memory long after the fact. Her oldest daughter had always loved to dance, even as a small child in prewar Łódź. Ruth enjoyed recounting how Anne would bob up and down in the theater aisle during showings of subtitled Shirley Temple movies. But the notion of grammar school children attending dances together was far outside Ruth's comfort zone. Ruth tried to laugh it off when Anne's date came by the apartment. "It was funny for me—two little kids going to a dance—but I am in the United States, and I didn't want my kids to be different from the others," she said. But she was dying inside.

Mrs. Irvin, who had paid for Anne to take dancing lessons until the instructor told her she knew enough steps already, was standing on the porch next to Ruth when the little girl who tended her garden left with her date. "Have a good time," Mrs. Irvin said in English. Ruth, speaking in Polish, and betraying an Eastern European discomfort with New World allurements, had different parting words: "Behave and be good," she said.

Of course, that her children were being acculturated to a city famed for its dancing and other libidinal attractions scarcely eased Ruth's concerns. It was a party year-round, it seemed, and in New Orleans they did not stop even for Lent. Shortly before Anne attended that first school mixer, Mark and Ruth dutifully carted their children to Mardi Gras. Or, to be more accurate, they were pulled by the rush of their neighbors toward St. Charles Avenue when the parades started to roll. New Orleans carnival was then in the process of acquiring its modern form. Just several months before the Skoreckis had arrived in the city, Louis Armstrong had returned home to serve as King of Zulu, and several old-line white krewes had reestablished the tradition of hiring black men to carry flambeaux and bob and weave for tips in front of the elite float parades.[27] Now that the depression had ended there were more plastic beads and trinkets to hurl to fawning crowds, and more stepladder seats for positioning young children to catch the dime store benevolence. Ruth and her family were spellbound by the phantasmagoria of color and sound. "It was like a dream or a movie, I can't explain it," Ruth said. "We tried not to miss one night." Her two daughters were not immune to the crowd hysteria, either. "Everybody was screaming, 'Mister. Throw me something!' So, of course," Ruth said, "my girls started doing the same thing."

Shrovetide 1950, Mardi Gras day, drew record crowds. The Duke and Duchess of Windsor had joined the mayor in the reviewing stands outside Gallier Hall. "I've never seen anything like it," gushed the former Mrs. Simpson. "Fabulous and such fun." The Skoreckis had never seen anything like it either, but they were more scandalized than excited. Advised by friends that she should outfit her kids for Fat Tuesday, Ruth had bought costumes for Anne and Lila at a Dryades street store. The streets that day were filled with revelers dressed as tigers and clowns, gypsies and Cossacks. A procession of tractor-drawn dreamy floats passed in review recounting, in papier-mâché, childhood adventures in slumberland. But the other type of costuming on display came as a shock: harem girls jitterbugging suggestively on the sidewalk, cross-dressing men and women, neighborhood marching clubs lurching drunkenly down the avenue behind their jazz band escorts. That evening Mark and Ruth even joined late-night revelers on Canal Street to watch the Comus parade head for its midnight rendezvous with the court of Rex. "We were like little kids excited over a new toy," Ruth said. Yet the novelty faded quickly. The next day's paper reported the usual Mardi Gras fatalities, such as the carnival club president who died of a heart attack while leading his organization on its annual parade or the bystander crushed beneath a truck float while ducking under the trailer to reach the opposite side of the street.[28]

New Orleans would take some getting used to, and Mark and Ruth, possessed of an Eastern European reserve concerning pleasure, never became fully reconciled to its hedonism.[29] "My parents were very serious people who never knew how to enjoy life," Anne says. "And being brought up in that environment, it took me years to learn how to enjoy life too."

Anne returned from her first school mixer slightly dejected. For one, her young date did not know how to dance. For another, she was much too guarded to relax, even as a young girl.

"Have a good time but behave." "Be a good American child but honor your grandparents." The contradictory advice had echoed across generations in countless immigrant households of the recent American past, as parents pushed their children into the outer social world, only to reassert traditional authority once Americanization began to erode parental status. The same dynamic played itself out in the Skorecki household, and not just in value conflicts over the proper balance between work and leisure. Like other immigrant children, Anne and Lila, forced by circumstances to act as the family's eyes and ears, its guides and interpreters, soon found themselves in confusing role reversals with their parents. "My mother and father took us with them wherever they went so we could talk for them," Lila says. "They didn't know what to call things; all they could do was point."

Before long the sisters began thrusting Americanization into everyday life, insisting that English be spoken around the house, to force their parents to learn the language—which Mark and Ruth, like most Jewish immigrants, were eager to do. Later, when preparing to take the citizenship test, the sisters guided their mother and father through American history and civics. Previous waves of immigrant parents never became reconciled to their children assuming the role of cultural caretaker for the family. The experience deepened feelings of powerlessness that immigrants coming to America feel as a matter of course. The way Mark and Ruth compensated for the inversion of traditional authority was to lay down a magical system of rules, so that the more roles between them and their daughters became reversed, the more Mark and Ruth insisted on strict deference to parental authority. In fact, after a while, the "have-a-good-time" side of the contradiction became completely overwhelmed by its "do-the-most-important-thing" antithesis.[30]

Other advice became increasingly insistent as well, such as, "Take it from me. I know." Or, more common still, "You don't know what you're talking about." "That was a favorite saying with them—'You don't know'—and there was no disagreeing, either," says Anne, "because talking back was considered a form of disrespect"—not to mention a violation of the cardinal rule that "children were to be seen, and not heard."

If the intergenerational drama occurring in the Skorecki home followed an old script of assimilation, one of its scenes was never reenacted. The literature of American immigration is replete with stories of how second-generation children rebelled against Old World parents, feeling ashamed of their antique ways.[31] It was a life course Anne and Lila failed to follow. They almost always toed the line. Being daughters, they likely had a stronger sense of fealty toward their parents, staying close to them throughout their lives. But a gendered explanation only scratches the surface. What truly set the two sisters apart from other immigrant children is that they were child survivors—"hidden children," actually—for whom being quiet, obedient, and grown-up before their time had literally been key to survival.

In fact, a playbook approach to life had become central to their character. No doubt Anne and Lila had been obedient children before the war, otherwise there is no accounting for their heroic feats of motionless silence beneath floorboards and inside vegetable bins during the liquidation of the Warsaw

Ghetto. But they seem to have emerged from the war with the trait of obedience enlarged. That was characteristic of the Holocaust. It magnified and amplified everything. The writer Dorothy Rabinowitz has observed how Nazi persecution bred extremity in its victims, making them expanded versions of their prewar selves. "The experience had confirmed, and thus enlarged, certain traits of character," she writes, "so that in some traits the survivors were what they had been before, only now they were more so."[32] Much evidence for this natural selection theory exists in the Skorecki family psychology. The Holocaust made Mark more cunning and resourceful and Ruth more attuned to the social cues in her environment. With Anne and Lila, obedience was the trait confirmed and enlarged.

The intergenerational conflict within the Skorecki home, therefore, was pretty one-sided. Such adolescent rebellions as did occur were skirmishes rather than battles and quickly quelled. From time to time Ruth and Anne argued over small things such as wearing high heels to her eighth grade graduation. "Daughter, I told you before," Ruth said triumphantly when Anne limped home carrying her new shoes. A missed curfew, even by a few minutes, provoked further confrontations. Anne was always more apt than Lila to question parental authority. But even those mutinies were sporadic and held within narrow limits. Long after establishing a family of her own, she still had difficulty going against her parents' wishes. "I was so used to listening to what my parents said that it became a habit, and a hard habit to break," Anne says, "I guess because for so long life itself depended on obedience."

In the spring of 1950 Celia and Harry Tenser drove their new Cadillac to New Orleans. It was one of the first models with electric windows. "They were very wealthy people," Ruth said of the English-born stockbroker and his wife. Ruth had written her sister-in-law bragging how she had fixed up their new apartment, and Celia wrote back saying she was sure the place was just as Ruth described it. The Skoreckis had been reunited with Mark's sister six months earlier. As soon as Celia had heard by phone that Mark's family was staying in New Orleans, she caught a train with a friend to see her Polish relatives. The last time they had been together was the summer of 1935, just after Anne was born, when Celia vacationed in Łódź with her two children. The Skoreckis were still living in the Orleans Hotel when Celia made her first trip to the Crescent City. On that occasion she took her nieces shopping for new dresses and ice cream sodas, their first ever. She brought Anne, who, by self-admission, looked like "an Old Country girl," to a beauty parlor to have her pigtails cut off. "When she came home I saw a different girl," Ruth said.

Anne and Lila always enjoyed having Celia and Harry come for a visit, which did not happen very often. Jealous of playmates who had grandparents, the sisters cherished all the more the only aunt and uncle they believed still survived. Lila became close to the Tensers. But there had always been a competitive edge between Ruth and Celia, and Mark and his younger sister had practically no relationship. Whether or not caused by Mark's habitual silence after the war, the lack of open affection between Mark and Celia was a topic of conversation among the Skorecki clan in New Orleans. "You'd never think that they were sister and brother," says Lila's oldest daughter, Jennifer.[33]

Ruth worked hard to get ready for the Tenser visit. The baby grand piano, which had been sitting in New York storage, was shipped to New Orleans by rail earlier that spring. It took a six-man crew just to maneuver it up the Josephine apartment building's switchback landing. The china she had purchased in the porcelain factories of the Oberpfalz was put on display. "My mother liked fine things," Anne says, "figurines, cut glass." Indeed, for the rest of her life Ruth was constantly scouting stores and shops for elegant bric-a-brac. It was as if material possessions indicated not merely status lost and won but also that she had a past, that she came from somewhere and was somebody. "Plenty of people in the United States thought that we didn't know what nice things like pianos were," Ruth said, "but we were living a normal nice life with a maid when the war broke out. I came from a big city."

If material goods signified she had a past, Ruth learned they were also markers of American identity. Adapting to abundance was not just a matter of improving living standards but a way to adopt an American identity as well. No other immigrant group had grasped that truth more quickly than did Jews from Eastern Europe, who took readily to the American habit of converting luxuries into necessities. And fleeing persecution, they felt all the more anxious to blend in with their surroundings, to look and act like Americans. Learning the language was one way to merge with the host culture, but that took time. The genius of American institutions was that immigrants just off the boats could literally change identities by merely changing clothes—which many Eastern European Jews proceeded to do by buying new suits—or by purchasing pianos for the parlor, ornamenting their apartments with popular mass-market merchandise, and, after gaining a more solid financial footing, taking vacations in the Catskills. The installment plan, along with other instruments of easy credit, made the shopper's road to American identity seem like an effortless journey, even as it undermined European notions of frugality. Ruth took little time adapting to American abundance.[34]

Providing coaching as well as material assistance, the New Orleans Jewish community played a role in speeding the transition to an American identity. The local federation, operating principally through the Reform-dominated National Council of Jewish Women (NCJW), made it a project to Americanize survivor families such as the Skoreckis, bringing to that task the same reform-ist zeal that had fueled turn-of-the-century efforts to remold the lifestyles of Jewish immigrants from Eastern Europe.[35] The council's Social Adjustment Committee not only furnished incoming DP's with clothes and furniture but also showed them, through "friendly visiting," how to shop for groceries, raise children the American way, dress, and fit in. It sponsored English classes, conducted tours of the city, operated a thrift shop ("We begged for everything and got whatever the refugees needed," recalls one volunteer).[36] It ran a "craft corner" that marketed refugee handiwork.[37] The Skoreckis, like other sur-vivors assigned to New Orleans, received a lot of attention. Both the council and the federation helped Mark find employment in a furniture restoration firm not far from Josephine Street. They gave the Skoreckis three hundred dollars to buy furniture and appliances. Two German-speaking council volun-teers regularly dropped by the apartment to check up on how the family was doing. Ruth never learned to drive, so they brought her to the grocery store and the doctor's office. They baby-sat for Adam and remained in the hospital waiting room while Lila's tonsils were removed. "I will remember for the rest of my life the wonderful work that was done by the Council of Jewish Women," Ruth said. However appreciative she may have been of the help, the cultural condescension accompanying the generosity troubled her more than a little. After all, it conveyed the message that European newcomers were un-familiar with "nice things like pianos." Ruth was much too polite to express her feelings publicly, however. Instead, she chose to make actions speak louder than words by preparing for the Tenser visit. It represented the first real op-portunity to show that her family's process of Americanization could be as swift as anyone's.

Harry and Celia parked in front of the converted apartment house on Jo-sephine Street and rang the doorbell. "I saw in her face coming up the steps that she didn't like the place," Ruth said. As soon as she entered, Celia scanned the apartment. The two couples sat and talked for a spell. Ruth and Mark had never before met Celia's husband, Harry. They caught up on family news, little of it pleasant. Celia never raised the subject of the apartment or its tattered environment. She and Harry checked into the swank Roosevelt Hotel (now the Fairmont), where both Huey and Earl Long had maintained suites, the latter because of easy access to a bookie joint across the street. The Tensers stayed a week. They took the family to the best restaurants, cruising the city in their Cadillac. But not until they were about to leave for New York did Celia mention Ruth's new home. The advice was terse: "Start looking for an apart-ment in a better neighborhood and with three bedrooms. The girls need bet-ter associates." Ruth was stung: As soon as the Tensers departed, she began thumbing through the classifieds.

She encountered familiar obstacles: no dogs and children allowed, high rents, neighborhoods in decline. A friend from the Council of Jewish Women suggested the Skoreckis buy a house instead. Young American families in the cold war era were quickly moving to buy homes, thanks to pell-mell suburbanization and government-subsidized, low-interest mortgages.[38] The friend said Ruth and Mark should join the rush. The monthly mortgage would be less than current rental rates, and they would not have to worry about the landlord asking them to vacate the apartment on short notice. Ruth's response was lukewarm. "Listen," she told American friends, "people will think I am crazy. I have just come from Europe. I don't know the language. I don't know where to look for a place. I don't know where a good neighborhood is." Furthermore, the idea of buying a house before the Skoreckis achieved financial security seemed wildly at variance with their Eastern European notions of frugality. Mark let Ruth know that he was against mortgaging the immediate future for a house. His mindset was that of a nineteenth-century artisan who believed the most important thing in life was avoiding debt and controlling productive property. Homeownership could await the attainment of economic independence. Ruth initially shared his outlook.

But then she changed her mind. "I was tired of having to tell my girls to keep quiet for fear of disturbing our neighbors, as I did in Poland, when we were living in cellars and different hiding places," she rationalized. "After six years I think this was enough." But her acute need to keep up with the Jones probably swayed her decision as well. If it is true, as Andrew Heinze has written, that "Jewish women were catalysts for the adaptation of newcomers to the American standard of living," then Ruth Skorecki was quick to play the role history had assigned her.[39] To overcome his reluctance, she reminded Mark that his sister Celia was urging the same advice as members of the local Jewish community. But most of all she brought incessant pressure. Indeed, about domestic consumption she could be as relentless as Mark was stubborn—their arguments over money sometimes escalating into the psychological equivalent of irresistible forces colliding with immovable objects—and she usually got her way by dint of sheer psychological attrition. The strategy that worked for her had been suggested by council volunteers who advised locating property that was cheap and rundown. They told her that Mark would be able to fix things up nice. It was as though a lightbulb had been switched on in her mind. When it came to craftsmanship she knew her husband could be fiercely competitive. Thus she set out to find a home within the Skoreckis' financial means.

Every afternoon a woman realtor recommended by American friends showed them homes they could not afford in neighborhoods they did not want. Once she tried selling them a multiplex apartment building, arguing that rent receipts would cover the large note. Finally, survivor friends told Ruth about a house in the Broadmoor section of town, near midcity: 4201 Eden Street, on the corner of Gayoso, two blocks from Washington Avenue. It had six rooms and a big backyard but needed a lot of work.

The property was indeed run down to the point of blight. Because of soil subsidence, the rear of the house was sagging badly. The current tenants had let the yard go to seed. "I saw a big jungle," Ruth said, when the realtor brought her and Anne to inspect the house. Tall grass choked the berry and pine trees in the backyard, and an untrimmed ligustrum bush sat along the Gayoso property line. Anne's heart sank when she saw the place. Through social functions at the Jewish Community Center, she had been exposed to the New Orleans class system. "I thought no one would come and see me if we moved in," she says, "and if they would I'd be too embarrassed to invite them over." But Ruth sensed possibilities.

After getting off work, Mark went to look over the property. He peered under the house. He studied the yard and went inside. His hands stroked the peeling clapboard. He knocked on the walls to find the joists. "This is not bad," he said. That night he told Ruth that if he bought a house at all, it would be this one. The neighborhood was nice. The building was structurally sound. He could improve it.

Negotiations with the realtor who carried the listing went smoothly. Anne translated, which added to the role confusion. The rule about children being seen and not heard had to be put in abeyance. This was one time that they needed her to speak up. "Momma, before you all the time told me not to ask so many questions, and now look what you are making me do," Anne said. But a better deal depended on Anne's skill as a translator. Though the property was listed at twelve thousand dollars, the Skoreckis offered nine, which was accepted. A lawyer who spoke German did the title search and sat in on the closing. Lewis Regenbogan, Mark's boss at the time, vouched for his employee's creditworthiness at the Whitney Bank.

The act of sale took place on September 16, 1950. The Skoreckis put three thousand dollars down, with the balance payable in sixty-dollar monthly installments, at 6 percent interest, compounded semiannually. The owner agreed to take a private mortgage.

During colonial times, the midcity neighborhood now called Broadmoor lay beneath a twelve-acre lake watered by streams running from Bayou St. John. Heavy rains can still turn the area into a low-lying pond. Because the city sits in a shallow saucer rimmed by river and lake, residential development came late to New Orleans. Many empty lots were not filled until the First World War, after modern drainage technology pumped out the mud. Broadmoor's biggest growth spurt occurred during the 1920s and 1930s. Napoleon Avenue above Claiborne is still lined with Spanish Mission Revival houses made popular in California. Stores and movie houses soon cropped up on Washington Avenue, near its intersection with Napoleon. Built around 1918, St. Matthias Catholic Church lured many new homeowners into the area. Eden Street, to the north, was one of the last areas of Broadmoor to be built up: a pre-Levittown conglomeration of double shotguns and brick stucco cottages. The house at 4201 Eden was a raised three-bedroom bungalow, the oldest and most dilapidated property on the street.

The tenants, whose lease expired at the end of the year, were still occupying the house when Mark launched his home improvements. The first thing he tackled was the backyard, working evenings and weekends through the liquid heat of the late New Orleans summer to hack away the weeds and branches. He picked up the pace in late October after the weather broke. By Thanksgiving he was so exhausted he had to be hospitalized for kidney stones. Determined to have the place ready for occupancy by year's end, he resumed the grueling schedule within days of his discharge. The house was still unheated when the Skoreckis moved in on New Year's Eve. "It was the happiest moment in my life," Ruth said. "My children would no longer live like prisoners." While she and the girls unpacked the cardboard boxes, Mark continued to hammer away at the dilapidated bungalow, echoing the frenetic building activity then transforming the suburbs and the Central Business District—a new city hall, the filling and greening of canals, strip shopping malls.[40] Few of the Skorecki home improvements were contracted out. Mark did practically all the work himself, with Ruth as helper. "We all the time worked hand-in-hand," she said.

He added a vast amount of new soil, landscaped the backyard, and then built a garage qua workshop for storing his machinery. He poured his own concrete, under floodlights that allowed him and Ruth to work until three in the morning, smoothing the foundation. He jacked up the rear of the house, positioning blocks underneath to level it off. Next, he gutted the inside, ripping out walls and the fireplace, removing sliding doors to create better room flow. Down came the chimney. All the while debris piled up along Gayoso Street. Dump trucks had to be hired to haul away the trash.

Mark then remodeled the kitchen, building wooden cabinets from floor to ceiling. He redid the bathroom, leaving in place the claw-footed tub next to the wall gas heater. Ruth wanted a big picture window, hence Mark installed one on the Gayoso side of the house, the first such window on the block. There were few building tricks he did not know. Before hanging wallpaper, Mark sized the walls with newspapers to cover the cracks. "For the longest time Mr.

Skorecki had pages from *The Times-Picayune* on all the walls," says one of Anne's high school friends. "It was like that for the longest time."[41] When he was done the wallpaper was as smooth as marble.

For more than a year renovation on the house continued at a breakneck pace. Drivers stopped to ask directions because the rundown corner house had lost landmark familiarity. Neighbors, accustomed to a slower pace in New Orleans, drifted over to watch Mark saw and plane boards in the floodlit backyard and to solicit home improvement advice. Sometimes they stood around for hours admiring the tireless activity taking place on the corner. "We were all curious to see this energetic family," says Lorena Doerries, who had moved into a house two doors away shortly before the Skoreckis arrived. "I just marveled at the man. He would stay up until midnight, and then rise early the next morning to go to work. You could hear him leave at 7:00 A.M. because his car had to be revved up and it made a lot of noise."[42]

Next to the garage Ruth planted a flower garden. She dug another garden in the front and planted roses. "She liked rose bushes," Adam says. There were a few kitschy additions, such as the plastic ducks she stationed in the backyard— middle-American lawn accessories then coming into vogue. But the home interior, where Mrs. Irvin's housewarming curtains were hung, exemplified American moderne, with a trace of European formality. "If you walked into our Eden Street house, other than a mezuzah on the door frame, you wouldn't have thought it was a Jewish home," Anne says. The sentimentalized Judaica then coming into vogue in some postwar American Jewish homes held lit-tle appeal for Ruth. Obvious cultural markers conflicted with her instinct to blend in, to be unnoticed. "I never could figure out how they got all that beautiful crystal and china over here," says Mrs. Nathan Forman, who later lived next door to the Skoreckis. "She had some magnificent pieces."[43]

When the renovations were complete more than a year later, Ruth held an open house. "It was my first official party in the United States," she said. She planned it for a Sunday and invited the staff and board of both the Jewish Federation and the NCJW. Most of Skoreckis' survivor friends attended, as did several of their gentile acquaintances, such as Mrs. Irvin. Celia Tenser came as well, arriving that Friday with Harry. She offered Ruth all manner of helpful tips about hosting an American-style cocktail party. The open house was a triumph. Strolling from room to room, the guests shook their heads in amaze-ment at the transformation of the Eden Street property. Ruth brimmed with pride that "the ideas were our own; we had no decorator other than ourselves." But what really lifted her spirits was Celia's presence at the party. Her sister-in-law was able to witness the high esteem in which the local community held the Skoreckis. "You have done a wonderful job," Celia told Ruth before departing. "You've done more than some people who have lived here for years." That was exactly what Ruth wanted to hear—comforting reassurance that her family was making unbelievable progress toward Americanization.

According to Mark's handwritten mortgage book, it took slightly more than twelve years to pay off the Eden Street house note. After Adam was old enough to ride a bicycle, Mark gave him $64.03 in cash the middle of every month to hand-carry to the former owner of the house. The man's Jefferson Avenue residence was only a short ride away. The delivery became so punctual and routine, the former owner kept candy in the foyer as a treat for Adam.[44]

Even as the Eden Street renovations were in full swing Mark was working long hours at a furniture repair and upholstery shop near the Garden District. Owned by auctioneer Lewis Regenbogan, the two-story business was located on the corner of Prytania and Terpsichore Streets, a few blocks from the Jackson School. The Council of Jewish Women had made a point to solicit employment from small Jewish businesses for the new arrivals from Europe. "Constitute every member . . . a committee of one to interpret to the men in her family the importance of finding jobs for new arrivals," advised the national office.[45] Within weeks of landing in New Orleans, the council placed Mark at the Regenbogan shop. He was easy to place: the federation staff found him "serious minded. Responsible." "Impresses one better as one becomes acquainted with him," wrote one interviewer three days after Mark's arrival in the city. "It is my impression that he is a very skillful man in his trade."[46] Determined to become economically independent, he always considered the position at Regenbogan's temporary.[47] His ultimate intention was to return to general contracting, the trade he had pursued in Poland before the Nazi invasion. But New Orleans was terra incognita, and his grasp of English was poor. A more serious obstacle was the paucity of Jewish-owned construction firms. "The Jewish population is . . . a mercantile group," concluded a 1941 sociological study of the New Orleans community.[48]

In the meantime, the work at Regenbogan's was challenging enough. Mark knew a lot about wood but little regarding furniture repair, the shop area to which he had been assigned. Getting the tools he needed was often an anthropological exercise in pointing and listening as the foreman carefully pronounced the name of each implement. A fellow Polish survivor, who had apprenticed in the Old World as a cabinetmaker and labored at an adjoining bench, remembers Mark's work at the time as a "little rough."[49] But Mark was a quick study. He had a natural feel for the ergonomic grace of well-crafted furniture and was hungry for knowledge, finding reasons to go upstairs to watch the upholsterers at their work after fellow employees mentioned that furniture covering was a profitable business. And he continued to impress employers ("Tell them you will work for nothing, just to show them what you can do," he used to advise Anne's husband, Stan). Surprised and pleased, Regenbogan and the foreman soon started giving him more important jobs.

Antique restoration work was just beginning to take off in New Orleans when Mark commenced his self-instruction in cabinetmaking. At first he was amused by it all, returning home in the evening chuckling about American tastes. "Sometimes people bring furniture to the shop that I would never have in my house and pay a good deal of money to prepare this junk," he told his wife. Nonetheless, the rising volume of work flowing through Regenbogan's shop gave him pause. "We thought there might be a future for us in cabinet-making," Ruth said. Mark reassessed his plans, buying used machinery advertised in the local paper and putting aside money to start his own antique restoration business. In 1949 only 15 percent of America's workers were self-employed, but discouraging odds had never stymied him in the past. He would bide his time.[50]

Meantime, Mark switched jobs while still in the throes of renovating the Eden Street house. Ruth said it happened by accident, during one of her frequent bargain-hunting forays, but there was a pattern to Mark's career changes, and Ruth was usually part of it. Someone had told Ruth that a local furniture store, Kirschman's, had good deals on rugs. Today the metropolitan area's largest furniture store, with three locations in the suburbs, Kirschman's was then located on Dauphine Street in the Ninth Ward. Taking buses to the distant downriver neighborhood, Ruth initially had trouble making herself understood to the salespeople, who often mistook her for the Spanish and Italian residents of the area. Memories of Poles who ridiculed Jews for their Yiddish accents, even exposing them to the Nazis during the war, made her chary of betraying her broken English. But polyglot New Orleanians were used to strong dialects, and their patience with Ruth's heavy accent made her relax. "It made you lose your fear," Ruth said of the friendly encouragement. At Kirschman's she encountered the same attitude. As soon as the salesman learned her birthplace, he said, "Wait a minute, my boss is from Łódź, Poland, too." And he hastened to get the owner, Morris Kirschman.

Son of a Łódź tailor, Morris Kirschman had emigrated to New York in 1903 when he was sixteen, moving to New Orleans a few years later after losing his savings in a poker game. He started out as a peddler, selling umbrellas, rugs, and vases from his horse-drawn wagon. Then he opened a furniture store beneath his upstairs apartment. Several enterprising eastern European Jews who trickled into New Orleans before World War I, such as the Breners, the Palters, the Mintzes, and the Rosenbergs, followed similar paths into the furniture business.[51] Because the Ninth Ward location was a working-class, immigrant area, merchants had trouble making money there. But Morris, according to his son, Victor, who manages the business today, used location to advantage. "My father promoted the theme that we were out of the high rent district and that you saved the difference. That was our motto for many, many years." The store grew and grew. Morris had a good nose for current trends. But his real genius was getting customers and employees to say what was really on their mind. That sensitivity seems to have deepened after he suffered a nervous breakdown in 1940 and was later diagnosed as manic depressive.[52] "My father was a very unusual friend," Victor Kirschman says. "He was the kind of person that if he was devoted to you today, he's going to be devoted to you until the day he dies, and there is very little that you can do to turn him off." Adds Rosalie Cohen, who knew him very well, "He was a very fine gentleman."[53]

During the 1930s and 1940s Morris Kirschman belonged to the Committee on Planning for German and Austrian Refugees, which worked in concert with national Jewish organizations to rescue Jews from Nazi-controlled territory. In the presence of this group of prominent German Jewish merchants and attorneys, Morris could be withdrawn and introspective, "a little bit shy," recalls Steeg. But during monthly meetings Morris was usually among the first to offer employment to jobless refugees. And when it was suggested that members pledge a sizable sum of money every year toward the rescue effort, he signed up immediately.[54]

Not surprisingly, Morris Kirschman came right away when his salesman told him a survivor from Łódź was in the store. "He was very happy to talk to somebody from his hometown," Ruth said. They chatted for a long time. He asked where she was living. His ears pricked up when she told him where Mark worked. "Listen," he said, "I would like to talk to your husband. I can give him a job in my place paying him what he makes over there or more." Then he drove her home. Later in the week, on a day the store stayed open for evening shoppers, Mark went across town to pay Kirschman a visit. He said he might be interested in changing jobs if he could be guaranteed a chance every so often to make deliveries and pickups around town, in order to become better acquainted with the city. They quickly came to terms. After training a replacement for Regenbogan, who tried to persuade him to stay on, Mark began working for Kirschman's in the spring of 1952.

The connection between Mark and Morris Kirschman was instantaneous. "He and Dad had an unusual relationship," Victor Kirschman says, "due to the fact Mark was just an exceptionally talented person." At Kirschman's Furniture Mark started out as a warehouseman. Then he was given a truck to pick up supplies. Before long Kirschman's put him in charge of the preparation department, where furniture was readied for home delivery. "Mark was doing sometimes the work of three men," Ruth said, and the arrangement soon caused friction between Morris and his son. The elder Kirschman insisted on raising Mark's salary, but Victor feared the favoritism might anger other employees and trigger a union election in the tough working-class neighborhood.[55] Father and son argued about the matter so often that Morris resorted to paying Mark secret bonuses, personally dropping them off at the Eden Street house. He once even gave Mark a 1950 Chevrolet for his private use. "You see, I am coming to you instead of paying attention to my son," Morris told him. "Maybe someday he will open his eyes." Something besides economic calculus obviously drew these two men together. Maybe it was Old World memory and an ineffable sense of Jewish loss, the fact that each was able to speak familiarly about Jewish landmarks they knew had been erased forever from their native city.

Mark worked at Kirschman's almost two years, marking time until he was able to go out on his own. When he could, he did side jobs in his own garage, but not very often because of residential zoning restrictions. As was becoming a pattern, Ruth once again played the broker when Mark decided to leave Kirschman's. She had become acquainted with Morton Goldberg, who was working as a general auctioneer at a store across from Regenbogan's. She and Mark frequently dropped by the auction house to learn, as Ruth put it, "all the secrets of the business." A Philadelphian who had served as a military policeman in the Deep South during the war transferring German POWs between stateside stockades, Goldberg had married a New Orleans girl upon his discharge and settled in the city. He told Ruth about his plan to establish a large auction house called Morton's at Magazine and Julia Streets in the New Orleans warehouse district. Was Mark interested in getting into the antique restoration business? Goldberg said he would lease him shop space and guarantee him customers who needed to have furniture repaired. "Why couldn't Mark go by himself, when he does so well for others?" he asked. "He could be his own boss, rent a place, and not have to depend on anybody." The next day Mark called on Goldberg. They knew each other slightly from Mark's earlier visits to the auction house. "He was a little shy of me at first," Goldberg says. "I still had my crew cut. He thought I looked like a German."[56]

Mark signed the lease in September 1954, moving the machinery he had stored in his garage into his new shop. The address was 516 Magazine Street, in the middle of the block, just upriver from the city's central business district along Canal Street. Unhappy about Mark's departure, Morris Kirschman talked Mark into staying on until after Christmas. He promised him a 1952 Chevrolet, plus help with the rent at Morton's Auction Exchange, as Goldberg's new business came to be known. Kirschman, who three decades earlier had made the same journey into self-employment, knew it was futile to try to change Mark's mind. Mark's individualism ran wide and deep. "He was a very independent person," Goldberg says. "He worked strictly by the piece."[57]

The William B. Reily Company, where Lee Harvey Oswald briefly worked before his assignation with history, was directly across the street from Morton's Auction Exchange. Dark roasted coffee smells from its warehouse used to waft through the windows of Mark's shop, fueling the caffeinated energy that enveloped his work bench. Goldberg kept his word by feeding his new cabinetmaker a steady stream of customers, and Mark fulfilled his promise by turning out speedy, reliable work. "Quickness. That was his secret," says Stan Levy, who in the early 1960s became a salesman at Morton's before going into business for himself. "My father-in-law didn't work cheap. He charged a good price. But he turned it out fast, because he knew exactly what to do and when to do it, and how long the job would take." In the early phases of Mark's arrangement with Goldberg, Morton's dealt mainly in railroad salvage and furniture seconds. Goldberg would send Mark broken pieces bought by the gross at steep discount: fifty tables, say, that were chipped or missing legs or leaves. Mark's challenge was to repair them at prices that allowed both Goldberg and himself to make a profit.[58] It was not much of a challenge. As a foreman in Schultz's Shop in the Warsaw Ghetto, where survival had often depended on keeping wooden soles flowing through the pipeline, Mark had learned all he needed to know about scheduling. Restoring secondhand furniture for postwar American consumers, even on quick turnaround, was not difficult.

Mastering the finer techniques of cabinetmaking, however, was another matter. But like everything else involving wood and artifice, he acquired these skills quickly too. Goldberg was lucky to have found a craftsperson who possessed Mark's short learning curve. It enabled him to shift his business toward the more profitable antique furniture trade then spreading from its French Quarter confines to the small shops that began to line Magazine Street. The antique business involves more than putting fine merchandise on display; to close the deal customers have to be convinced that broken hinges or missing inlays can be mended quickly. Once Goldberg started importing large numbers of English antiques, he increasingly relied on his self-taught cabinetmaker to move the inventory. Says Goldberg, "Something would come in broken, and I'd tell a customer who wanted to buy it to come back tomorrow and you can have it." The next day it was fixed, and the sale was consummated. "We never had anybody like Mr. Skorecki, and I've been in business since 1949. He could do anything you want. He could fix it, refinish it, turn it on a lathe." "He had a tremendous sense of color," adds Morris Kirschman's nephew, Mike Yuspeh, who saw him work. "When it came to mixing varnishes, he could match anything. That was a real sign of an artist."[59]

Mark mastered wood carving. "I was just amazed," marveled one of Anne's high school friends at the way her father transformed a block of wood into an ornate table leg. "He took a piece of four-by-four and within days had shaped it into a beautiful lion's paw."[60]

More remarkable, while Mark upscaled his business, he never lost his time-is-money ability to repair furniture quickly. "He was a one-man operation," Goldberg sums up. "And the best thing about it, he was reasonable. His productivity was good. He'd come in early and knock it out, so he didn't have to get a big price for everything he did, which made it easier for me to sell. Sure, we'd argue about a price once in a while, but we worked it out. These other cabinetmakers could care less. I don't know if it's because they sniff glue or what. They don't produce. Or you have to bring the work back. Or you don't get the work back at all. Mr. Skorecki was the only guy I would have given the key to. In fact, he might have had a key."[61]

Even after establishing his own business and finishing the Eden Street renovations, Mark didn't ease up on his pace of work. Economic survival was no longer a spur to action. Work had become a way of life. Every day at five he would come home, shower and eat, clean his nails, and maybe watch the *Twentieth Century*, the popular *Molly Goldberg*, or the news on television. Then he would head for his workshop in the garage, not turning in until late at night. Relaxation was one skill he never mastered. Once an American Jewish friend tried to talk Mark into joining the B'nai B'rith bowling team. "I remember my dad saying after Mr. Becker left, 'Bowling?! What am I going to do with bowling?' That was his attitude," Adam says. "My father worked, came home, read his paper, and that was it," Anne says. "He was a hard worker," adds another survivor who knew him well at the time. "He was work, work, work."[62]

There was little doubt in anyone's mind who exercised sovereignty in the Skorecki household. "My grandmother was definitely the matriarch," says Robin Levy, Anne's second daughter. "She wore the pants in the family. Everybody knew that," adds New Orleans survivor Shep Zitler.[63] While Ruth was living Mark always seemed to be in the background, the person in old home movies who was sitting impassively off to the side while the party swirled around him. Domestic decisions were his wife's alone. "My father never voiced an opinion," Anne says. "Whatever my mother decided was all right with him. I never knew how he felt. He tuned everything out."

Ruth's household authority certainly fit the temper of the times. Impelled by cold war conventions concerning woman's proper sphere and the economic flood of returning servicemen, postwar American women in massive numbers abandoned the workplace for the home, marrying younger, having more children, shunning divorce, and most of all converting their households into havens sheltered from a world increasingly beset by atomic age anxieties. After years of persecution and deprivation, it was hardly surprising that survivor mothers such as Ruth fell in with the yearning for stability.[64] Yet Ruth's domestic authority reflected gender roles carried over from Eastern Europe as well. She was—to use the classic Yiddish term for the domineering Jewish mother—a *baleboste*. The term harked back to shtetl traditions wherein men held sway in the spiritual realm, burying themselves in the Torah and the Talmud, while women ran the home. Restricted although their sphere might be, Jewish women controlled the cultural inflections that helped define Jewish identity. More than keepers of domestic sacraments, balebostes were arbiters of household consumption as well.[65]

It was a role that traveled well across the Atlantic, encouraging Eastern European Jewish women to guide their families toward the promise of American abundance. Ruth took to the American baleboste's retooled functions with relish, especially the expectation, to take one notable example, that mothers and wives oversee their family's wardrobe.[66] Dressing sharply had been Ruth's trademark, even in prewar Łódź. But the trait was powerfully confirmed—not to mention enlarged—during the Nazi occupation, when stage presence meant everything. When she discovered that, in the States, clothes helped establish American identity, she needed no coaching on what to do next. "Clothes were my mother's weakness," says Lila. But not just her own wardrobe. Ruth wanted the entire family, especially Anne and Lila, to dress the part, fitting them out in matching outfits, like sisters in some television sitcom or child models frozen on the pages of *Life* and *Look* magazines. In her concern for appearances, something more was at work than the baleboste's determination that her family fit in or a desire to recapture dignity and respectability: there was also a survivor's caution about letting an untrustworthy world know how she really felt inside.[67]

Ruth therefore worked hard on her appearance, and people still remember her grooming. "She was neat as a pin, always smiling, always happy," says Grace Zelman, who had gotten to know Ruth through the Council of Jewish Women.[68] Ruth perfected a routine for fine-tuning her image. It began every Saturday morning when Anne, and later Lila or Adam, drove her to the new Carrollton Shopping Center on Palmetto Street, the first shopping mall in New Orleans, to have her hair done at the Venus Beauty Parlor. She always arrived promptly at 8:00 A.M., when the salon opened. After her hair had been set, she walked over to Gus Mayer's, then New Orleans's most exclusive clothing store. Gus Mayer's clothing line was out of Ruth's price range, so she mainly browsed, chatting with the salesclerks, who got to know her well. She was a smart shopper, though, watching for sales, cultivating informants who would tip her off when prices were about to be slashed on some blouse or dress that had caught her eye.

Ruth's early wardrobe was acquired at the Council of Jewish Woman's Thrift Shop on Dryades Street. For shoppers who could spot quality, the store had great deals, usually top-flight hand-me-downs from the German Jewish community. "We used to get designer clothes, as well as people's silver, linen, and crystal. Absolutely gorgeous stuff," noted Zelman, who managed the store at the time. "People would just give it away." Once a year beginning in the 1960s the Council of Jewish Women also sponsored a "Bargains Beautiful" fundraising affair at the Fairmont Hotel. Ruth was a regular customer at both the shop and the annual bazaar, where she also had informants. She must have told the Thrift Shop staff she was looking for a fur coat to replace the one confiscated by the Germans in December 1941, because someone called her about a mink coat that had just arrived in the store. Despite the garment's impracticality in subtropical New Orleans, Ruth sped down to Dryades Street. The coat had a reddish tinge. She bought it on the spot. "She just kept rubbing it and rubbing it," says Zelman. "You know how some things stand out in your mind? That's one thing that always did, because she was so proud of the coat and you remember how good you felt about doing this for her."[69]

However much her attention to appearance and grooming bespoke an immigrant survivor's longing to fit in, they also reflected Ruth's determination to reign supreme over the tiny community of postwar Jewish refugees who settled in New Orleans around the same time as the Skoreckis. It is hard to be precise about exact numbers. Scarcely more than thirty survivor families put down roots in the Crescent City, several of whom later moved to different cities. Polish Jews for the most part, and usually in their late twenties and early thirties, many were considerably younger than Mark and Ruth. They came from the camps, the ghettos, the woods. Ralph Rosenblat survived by fleeing to the Soviet sector, where he had worked in Siberian coal mines. Solomon Radasky and his wife, Frieda, lived through the Warsaw Ghetto; Radasky himself, who grew up in Praga and knew Mr. Smolenski, survived Majdanek, Auschwitz-Birkenau, and a death march to Dachau. Shep Zitler, a Vilna native whose family was massacred at Ponary, was a Lithuanian POW in Germany. Many couples had met and married in German DP camps, arriving in the United States with young children Adam's age, many of whom Anne and Lila ended up baby-sitting. Several came from the same towns—Radom and Łódź were common birthplaces, reflecting the origins of their New Orleans family sponsors—but never in numbers large enough to constitute a *Landsmanschaft* (immigrant society of natives from a particular town in Europe) of the kind immigrants to larger American cities often sought affiliation with. Coming from the same Polish communities, a few had even known each other's murdered spouses before the war. After liberation it was not uncommon for them to marry for companionship rather than love. But they stayed in those relationships for the duration. The urge was strong to reconnect with living symbols of a vanished world.

Most of the survivors who relocated to New Orleans purchased homes in the Broadmoor section where the Skoreckis lived, affiliating with Chevra Thilim, one of the city's oldest Orthodox congregations, or Anshe Sfard, its most observant. After Chevra Thilim relocated in 1948 from its old Dryades Street neighborhood to its present-day location on Claiborne Avenue, many congregants moved with it, and the survivors tailed along.[70] "There must have been twenty survivor families on Louisiana Avenue Parkway alone," one of the Broadmoor section's main streets, says Maureen Kurtz, the American-adopted daughter of Łódź Ghetto survivors Solomon and Niusia Goldfarb. Henry Brum and the Sher brothers, Leo and Joseph, who endured the Częstochowa Ghetto as well as several camps, resided a few houses away. Two other Łódź Ghetto survivors, Max and Felicia Fuksman, lived across the street. The Skoreckis were within walking distance of all of them, as were the Borensteins, the Gallers, the Radaskys, and the Rosenblats. Only the Niedermayers and the Rottersmans lived far away. They were a tight-knit group. It was as if New Orleans Jewish survivors were mimicking the novel communities, based on homeownership, childrearing, and consumer-oriented living standards, that rootless suburban families had begun forming in the 1950s.[71]

But joining a PTA was the least of their motives for coming together. Holocaust survivors in New Orleans coalesced mainly because they were looking for confirmation of their past, they had much in common, and they felt like outsiders even within the American Jewish community. Says Eva Galler, who, along with her husband, Henry, grew up in a Galician hamlet not far from the lumbering village where Skoreckis had cut and milled timber for the Łódź and Warsaw markets: "We associated because of our past. We cooked the same foods. We came from the same country."[72] So it was only natural that they sought one another's company, which, after all, was what immigrants to America had always done, forming in the process compound national identities that had scarcely existed in the Old World. But, as with everything the Holocaust touched, there was in this communal melding a special longing, a unique poignancy of loss, like the unusual bond between Mark and Morris Kirschman. To chat with people who had walked the same streets in Poland, had bought from the same butcher, knew so-and-so, and had been pierced by the same winter winds—this, in an emotional sense, gave back a part of them that was lost and irreplaceable.[73] "Look," says David Radasky, "the reason my parents and the Skoreckis became friends is that they had been in the Warsaw Ghetto and in Praga around the same time and probably knew some of the same people."[74] It was a community built from the shards of memory.

But feelings of marginality also drew New Orleans's survivors together.

They stemmed from a shared awareness that they were less than full-fledged members of the city's larger Jewish community. Certainly New Orleans Jews had eased the refugees's passage to the New World, acting as sponsors, finding them jobs and homes, helping with rent and initial household expenses, running English classes, conducting city tours. They had done everything except, as Toby Kornreich, David Radasky's sister, puts it, "invite them to become part of their lives." "Basically, we were just there," adds Martin Sher, Joseph's son.[75] In the synagogues the survivors sat in the back. They lacked money and prestige. Their English was poor. Nobody knew what to do with them. Around town American Jews called them the *grina*—the greenies—but the nickname, meant to be endearing, carried the hurt of stigma in the eyes of the survivors themselves. It was not an unusual situation. Survivors in other American cities experienced the same feelings of exclusion, as had previous waves of European émigrés. "To me it sounds like history, like what happened within the Orthodox and Reform communities years ago," says Rosalie Cohen, whose own family, fresh from Czarist Poland, had also felt temporarily isolated from more assimilated American Jews earlier in the century. "It's the human element at work. People will show you all the courtesies and offer all the assistance, but whether they are prepared to make you an intimate part of their lives is another story, and I think it's much to expect that it will happen."[76] All the same, New Orleans survivors resented their outsider status and felt terribly frustrated with the larger Jewish community. But only to one another did they ever vocalize their feelings. Mostly, they kept to themselves.

Yet, they did crave acceptance and want admittance to that wider society. "We were new Americans, so we called ourselves New Americans," says Ralph Rosenblat.[77] The term signified new beginnings, a hankering to get on with American lives, even a lust for all things American. "I always admired Mrs. Goldfarb's quest for Americana," says Kornreich of the Łódź Ghetto survivor who became like an aunt to her. "She loved being in the United States. She loved everything from food to cars to clothes. She read the Hollywood gossip magazines and knew all about the love life of the stars and the latest in movies and television. And in my child's mind I used to think, she's like any other American. She's really into this society." A lot of the New Americans shared Mrs. Goldfarb's passion for American culture, especially the women, including Ruth, who was her closest friend. "They were all balebostes," says Martin Sher, in the sense of not only running the home but taking charge of the family's acculturation to American lifestyles. "Like my mother, for example, who was very loving, very caring. She wanted the best for her boys." In this context the best meant fitting in, being accepted.[78]

As much as memory and feelings of rejection initially united the group, it was their American children who primarily held them together. The children represented the Jewish future, cultural survival and continuity, even proud defiance of Hitler's mad blueprint to destroy European Jewry. And, feeling so strongly about perpetuating the next generation, the New Americans understandably became surrogate relatives to one another's children. Toby Kornreich was not the only child of survivors with an honorary aunt or uncle. All the survivors' children had them. "At one point I was calling everybody uncle and auntie," notes Kurtz.[79]

The fictive kinship, overlaid with shared historical experience and common tastes and reinforced by the small size of this unique survivor community, created an unusual dynamic. The New Americans are still prone to violent, sometimes major disagreements. Even today the mutual dislike between several survivors is hard to miss. A few have dropped out of the group over the years because of bitter feuds. But they have remained oddly tolerant of one another's idiosyncrasies, mainly because they are like one big family, tied together by a web of invented family relationships. "Membership in the New Americans Social Club is not waivable," says Shep Zitler's son Justin, a local civil rights lawyer. "It is what it is, and they know they're stuck with each other."[80]

Although many survivors had lost faith, for the children's sake they joined synagogues. In a small Jewish community such as New Orleans, where synagogue affiliation exceeds 80 percent owing to the omnipresent temptations of assimilation, there was no question but that they too would join a congregation. They readily absorbed the remarkably flexible religious style of Orthodox Jewry in New Orleans. In fact, the only truly observant Jew among them is Eva Galler. "When I came to New Orleans and somebody told me she was an Orthodox Jew, I said, 'What kind of Orthodox? An Orthodox Jew doesn't drive a car on Saturday. An Orthodox Jew doesn't eat nonkosher food.'" Eva Galler still walks to synagogue on Saturdays. But the rest of the New Americans do not. None was troubled by the fact that Saturday services mainly drew women and a few old men. Few were bothered by the huge schism that rent Chevra Thilim in the late fifties and produced a lawsuit over the issue of allowing women to sit with the men, a break with Orthodox tradition that proved the opening step in the synagogue's later shift toward Conservatism.[81] They belonged to the congregation on behalf of the children and for the sake of cultural survival, which in their minds came down to the same thing. To facilitate their children's assimilation, the survivors swiftly adapted to the different emphases that American life imparted to the Jewish calendar. If New Orleans Jews downplayed the religious holiday of Sukkoth, building their harvest huts in the synagogue rather than the backyard, the New Americans could live with the change. If American Jews magnified a minor historical holiday like Hanukkah, so as to keep Jewish children from feeling left out during America's consumer-oriented Christmas, that adaptation was fine too.[82]

During the years when the children were young, the New Americans came together quite often. They held joint Hanukkah parties for their youngsters and took them on Sunday picnics, gathering at the Rosenblats' to make sandwiches and drinks before heading for Audubon Park or, when the weather was nice, to the Lakefront. The girls played board games such as checkers and Monopoly. The boys played pitch and catch. The parents talked and ate and argued. "I remember having this feeling," says Kornreich, "that if somebody were to have an extended family picnic, this is what it would be like, when all the aunts and uncles and cousins got together."[83] On a few occasions the New Americans even rented rooms in the Fountainbleau Hotel, at the intersection of Tulane and Carrollton, where the old Pelican Stadium once stood, because it had a swimming pool and a kosher kitchen.

Most summer weekends, especially the Fourth of July and Labor Day, the group drove to Bay St. Louis on the Mississippi gulf coast. On the outskirts of town was a beach called Henderson Point where an American Jewish woman who had befriended the group owned a three-story Victorian beach house, filled with antiques and girdled by a huge wraparound porch. Across the narrow street was a sandy ribbon shaded by a mammoth live oak. A patch of grass bordered the beach. The Sunday afternoon picnic followed a set routine: Set up on the grassy patch under the live oak canopy, rows of folding tables lay heavy with food. "It was a real classic male-female breakdown," remembers Kornreich. The women never went into the water; they rarely even put on a swimsuit because few of them knew how to swim. "They tended to the food and the children, sitting under the shade of this big tree in folding chairs, while the men made a big production of being out on the beach, galloping in the waves—such as these are in Bay St. Louis—which was kind of amusing because they really didn't know how to swim, either. And then the kids would do their own thing. It was incredible quality time."

Once they all trekked across the lake to a farm in Abita Springs, in the Florida parishes, to expose the children to horseback riding. Sam Radasky, father to Toby and David, provided the lessons. Although a furrier by trade, he had learned to handle horses in his youth. Erect in the saddle, in complete control, Radasky made the horse prance; he squeezed its girth with his legs, gently relaxing the reins, coaxing the animal into an athletic transition from halt to walk. To American-born children sensitive to the cultural handicaps their immigrant parents frequently encountered in America, the scene left a vivid impression. "That picture has always stayed in my mind. It was incredible to me," remembers Adam Skorecki. "It was the good years," says Joseph Sher.

"The children was little, we came together every Saturday and Sunday. We met together. We went to the beach with the children. It was the good times."[84]

In the early years much of the group's social life revolved around Eden Street, with Ruth very much at the center of things. Older than others, she was always the most vocal woman in the group, and perhaps even the most self-confident New American, men not excluded. She was outgoing, very active, full of energy, a doer and a problem solver. "If there was an activity, she would have been involved in it," says Kornreich. "She could tackle any problem."[85] Ruth expected the deference that age had always been shown in the Old Country, and everybody accordingly called her Mrs. Skorecki, not Ruth, in a manner faintly evocative of her formal Polish past. But her senior status cut both ways, imbuing her with a self-imposed responsibility for younger survivors, for whose well-being she could be extraordinarily solicitous. "She was everything," Shep Zitler says. "Good organizer. Good cook. She was running the whole show. She was the mother of the New Americans."[86]

It helped immensely that Ruth loved to entertain. "I tried every Saturday evening to invite a few people to my house to come together," she said of her first days on Josephine Street. "I was used to this before the war." Her Eden Street home likewise filled quickly with company. She liked to bake and cook, preparing everything from memory. It was typical Jewish fare, kosher and copious. Boiled chicken and pot roast, chicken soup on Friday nights, latkes. Her pastries were popular among friends who often gathered at Eden Street to play cards. Ruth made a thick potato soup, heavy and brown, that guests found special. For the Jewish holidays she prepared her own gefilte fish, dragging Mark to the fish stalls at the French Market to select the freshest catch. "She would do everything from scratch, boiling the fish in fat, which you don't see done much anymore," says Adam. And all the while, during occasions such as Thanksgiving, she took special pains to include survivors who might feel left out. "If people didn't have nobody, they were invited to her house," says Joseph Sher.[87] It was a special mitzvah—a Jewish good deed—to unite people who were alone.

The same occurred at Ruth's Seder dinner, the traditional Passover meal during which family heirlooms grace the table and young children pose questions to grandfathers in ritualized exercises of collective memory. A popular holiday by virtue of its family reunions, for survivors it was tinged with melancholy. "We felt sort of lonesome on that holiday," says Henry Galler.[88] Ruth tried to lessen the solitude by bringing unattached survivors and childless couples within the orbit of the Skorecki family service. She prepared all the food: the turkey (in place of roasted lamb), the hard-boiled eggs, the herbal salads.

Seder was one of those rare times when tradition forced Ruth to relinquish household authority. As male head of the household Mark was supposed to preside over the ceremony, and he insisted on exercising his prerogatives to the hilt, despite his conspicuous lack of religiosity. (The quintessential Yom Kippur Jew, he attended synagogue services only during the High Holidays.) "The Passover service can be very long or very short, depending on how you want to do it," says Adam, "and we would have people at the table that would want to do the short version. 'Let's get on with the service,' they would say. 'Let's get to the wine and food.' But Daddy wouldn't allow that. Daddy was in control, and we went through the whole hour and a half service as he said the Hebrew prayers in a sort of quiet hum."[89] Except for that occasion, Ruth maintained firm grip on domestic affairs. That control augmented her power over not merely her immediate family but also those New Americans who early on looked to Ruth for social leadership in their new homeland.

And heightening Ruth's social cachet were her gala New Year's Eve parties. Fancy and elaborate occasions for dressing up, they were highlights of the social calendar among New Americans. Mark's early success in business was the principal reason Ruth was able to entertain so lavishly; in the beginning he was financially better off than younger survivors. But Ruth's brimming self-confidence in the presence of American Jews gave her New Year's Eve gatherings their special distinction. As had been the case with her housewarming cocktail party, Ruth's guest list spanned the New Orleans social spectrum. "My mother had the capability of throwing a party, and all these people—German Jews, Polish Jews, American Jews, whoever—would come," Anne says. Among a people who wanted to be accepted as authentic Americans, Ruth's ability to bridge the social gap between American Jews and survivors, between Reform and Orthodox, between Jews and gentiles, carried enormous prestige, making her the doyenne of the small, close-knit world of New Orleans Holocaust survivors. It was an eminence she took extremely seriously.

For all her sociability, Ruth had few intimate friends. The couple with whom she was on closest terms were the Goldfarbs, Solomon and Niusia, who were also from Łódź. They had met at the Army port in Bremerhaven and developed a friendship during the voyage over. In New Orleans Ruth Skorecki and Niusia Goldfarb became inseparable, calling each other at least once, sometimes twice a day. "My mother and Mrs. Skorecki were as close as sisters at one time," says Kurtz.[90]

Ruth became friendly as well with a non-Jewish neighbor, Lorena Doerries, a gentle, soft-spoken woman eleven years her junior who lived two doors away. They were drawn to each other by the closeness in age between Adam and Mrs. Doerries' second child, Charles. "We were real pals as kids," Charles says of his friendship with the new Jewish kid on the block, "so I was in and out of the house all the time, and there weren't many kids that were."[91] Mrs. Doerries' friendship with Ruth graduated from casual to close after returning one evening from walking her husband, Ernest, to the bus stop on Washington Avenue, where he caught the night train for one of his Procter and Gamble sales trips. Mark and Ruth were sitting on their raised front porch behind a cast-iron railing Mark had built. It was in the mid-1950s, before air conditioning had pulled New Orleanians from the stoops where they would enjoy the night air and one another's neighborliness. Mrs. Doerries exchanged pleasantries with the Skoreckis on the way to the bus stop and then joined them on the porch after her walk back. "That was when Mrs. Skorecki kind of opened up and started telling me a little bit about what they had been through." The conversations about the war never went on for long. "Both of us were busy with our children," Mrs. Doerries says. And the relationship between the two neighbors always retained a certain European formality. "She called me Miss Doerries, and I called her Miss Skorecki," Mrs. Doerries says. "We never did call one another by our first names. But we got to be good friends."[92]

The two women often shopped together. When Mrs. Doerries mentioned wanting to buy a new couch, Ruth said, "Let me tell you. You want a sofa? I know a place where I can get sofas and Mark can cover it over. I'll take you downtown." Ruth brought her to a used furniture warehouse where she bought a couch that Mark reupholstered for next to nothing. "It cost me seven dollars, I think. It was ridiculously inexpensive." When Ruth saw Mrs. Doerries struggling with the drawers in her china cabinet, once again she volunteered Mark's services. "Mark can fix that," she said, and he came over the next day and repaired the runners. He even restored an antique dining room table the Doerries had purchased from the owner of a plantation, smoothing out the deep gouges left by young flappers who had danced the Charleston on the tabletop. After Mark had finished, the Civil War–era piece looked like new.

They talked somewhat about Ruth's family in prewar Poland. "I gathered that they had been kind of well-to-do people," Mrs. Doerries says. That had not been the case, of course. But Ruth's autobiographical embellishment was typical of the way that survivors often idealized their prewar past.[93]

Mrs. Doerries grew so close to the Skoreckis that she even caught a rare early glimpse of Mark's playful personality. It happened after a run to the supermarket. She locked herself out of the house while returning to the car for the rest of the groceries. Inside the house with the grocery bags was Charles, still a preschooler. Grinning and eating cookies he discovered in one of the bags, he refused to let her in. Mark came right over and jimmied open the door. "He did it in no time flat," says Mrs. Doerries, "which impressed me, because he could do anything." She was also taken by his quick wit and ability to see things in ironical ways. "He had a sly sense of humor," she says, which came as a complete revelation.[94] People were always thrown off guard by Mark's drollery. It was hard to square with his long silences.

Yet one barrier stood in the way of the two women's friendship: the matter of religion and identity, which goes to the anxiety felt by all Jewish parents who raise children in largely non-Jewish environments. Ruth could be extraordinarily solicitous of gentile opinion, not allowing Adam to cut the grass on Sunday mornings for fear of offending Christian sensibilities. But even her determination to fit in had limits. The past continued to exert a strong pull. When a naturalization official asked, during their citizenship swearing-in ceremony, why they were not Americanizing their surname, Ruth and Mark were plainspoken: "We told him there were not too many Skoreckis left after the tragedy in Europe." As much as Ruth wanted her three children to become all-American kids, she was just as determined that they retain their Old World Jewish identities. And for her the perennial question was, where do you draw the line?

Ruth herself was not very observant, although she did believe in God. Her own Judaism continued to be an intensely private ceremony of lighting candles in the kitchen, haphazardly and inconspicuously, much as she had done while posing as a Christian in the Praga lumberyard. Even so, a minor crisis developed in her friendship with Mrs. Doerries when her gentile neighbor one summer invited Adam to accompany Charles to the half-day vacation Bible camp at their church The two boys were already going to the same elementary school, so it seemed natural that they attend summer camp together too. The camp was located at the Carrollton Presbyterian School, near the Claiborne and St. Charles Avenue intersection, where streetcars reverse direction for the return trip downtown. The morning activities included not merely play and games but Bible instruction as well. Adam was always excused from the religious lessons: "I thought it was great because I got a head start on the milk and cookies that were served right afterward."[95] But when Ruth learned Christian classes formed part of each morning's activities, she yanked him out of the camp and never let him go back.

In Ruth's defensiveness there was, of course, a normal Jewish guardedness around Southern evangelicals, who did view the conversion of the Jews as "a special blessing," a fulfillment of God's Judgment Day plans for bringing Israelites back to the fold.[96] Though hardly a Christian fundamentalist—New Orleans did not encourage the practice—Lorena Doerries did take her religion seriously, and Ruth knew it. She spoke often of her fascination with scriptural prophecies concerning Jewish travails. "It was a privilege to know these people, because of what they went through and what I read in the Bible," Doerries admits. She also fretted about the Skorecki souls. "I know my mother worried about them not being Christian," Charles adds with a soft laugh. But Ruth's instinctual opposition to Adam's attendance at the Bible vacation camp was something more than usual Jewish ambivalence toward southern evangelism. It had been conditioned and magnified by the Holocaust itself. She *had* lost Lila's soul to Christianity, if only temporarily, and it had taken quite a while following the war to bring her back from the adopted Catholicism that had given her terrified daughter so much solace. But Mrs. Doerries never evangelized for her faith, and once that hurdle was cleared the relationship between the two women deepened into genuine friendship. "I think Mrs. Skorecki must have trusted me when I didn't push my beliefs on her children," Mrs. Doerries says.[97]

The two women ended up talking often about religion. During Hanukkah and Christmas, the families exchanged gifts. Before long Ruth was giving Christmas presents to all the kids in the neighborhood. She occasionally invited Charles to join in the Skoreckis' Passover Seder. After Mrs. Doerries asked what matzos were, Ruth sent her a box annually. "It got to be a ritual," Mrs. Doerries says. "The family really got with it in this country," she adds. "They picked up the customs very readily. The girls spoke the language fine."[98]

The family was indeed adapting swiftly to its new surroundings, including the American tradition of joining voluntary associations. The volunteer work meshed well with Ruth's own impulse—and that of many Holocaust survivors—to repay society for help received.[99] American Jews place heavy emphasis on giving something back to the community, and Ruth wasted little time contributing her share. Within weeks of the Skoreckis' arrival she joined the Council of Jewish Women's Port and Dock Committee to help greet DP's disembarking at the Poland Avenue wharf. "I remember my first minutes coming to the United States and being in the same shoes as these people on the boat," she explained. Out of that same desire to give something back—and perhaps also satisfy the need to belong—she began contributing generously to the Jewish welfare fund. The Council of Jewish Women president, incredulous at her wish to make annual donations three times larger than the average gift, told her she was being much too generous. But Ruth insisted. "I told her please accept this," she said. "So I buy one dress less a year. I want to be like everybody else."

Ruth even volunteered Anne and Lila to serve as interpreters at the Poland Avenue Port of Embarkation, since their English was rapidly nearing the fluency of Polish and German. Both girls were released from school whenever a boat was due to dock. Anne would guide newcomers from the Orleans Hotel to the federation's office or to the hospital, if health problems arose, and both she and her sister served meals to sojourners at the Jewish Community Center. Ruth and her daughters never missed a boat.

Anne adjusted quickly to American life, although it was clear to everyone that Ruth still exercised a domineering influence. "Her mother overshadowed her a lot," remembers Honorine Weiss, one of Anne's teenage friends.[100] After graduating from the Jackson School, she transferred to McMain Junior High on Claiborne and State Streets, albeit reluctantly, because friends at Jackson had warned her that rich uptown kids, whose cast-off clothing she still wore, went to McMain and she would not fit in. The following year Anne transferred to Fortier Senior High, on Freret Street, near Tulane. It was the city's premiere public high school during the era of segregation. Due to the insistence of Mrs. Davis, Lila's favorite teacher, Lila remained at the Jackson School through the eighth grade, but after graduating she followed her sister to McMain and Fortier. Both girls were popular with peers. They looked for all the world like 1950s teenagers, in bobby socks and saddle shoes, their hair worn at the ear. Anne, whose smile could move quickly to laughter, played in the high school band—the violin, not the piano, which was finally sold. Like her father, whom she took after, Anne was constantly busy, working on the weekends and during summer vacations. Her senior year she was elected president of her high school sorority. At graduation classmates awarded her a trophy for school spirit. Her grades were respectable: mostly Bs with a C+ in English and an A+ in typing.[101]

She became active in the Junior Red Cross, too, advising the organization about what to put inside gift boxes being sent to European children. The local paper ran a story and picture about the "sparkling-eyed high school senior" and her work for the organization. "Polish Girl Who Received Now Gives," ran the header. John Tucker, the local Red Cross director, took Anne around to other schools to tell student assemblies about her wartime experiences.[102] She never pulled the veil back very far. "Because of her background she kept things in," says high school friend Honorine Weiss.[103] But she revealed enough to arouse the sympathy of students who heard her. Once they even collected gifts that Tucker delivered personally to the Eden Street house, as a token of appreciation.

Anne's reticence to talk about the past was typical of the entire family at the time—indeed, of the survivor community everywhere in America. If she spoke at all, it was only because she was asked to do so and felt too much gratitude toward her new country to say no. The war was an event few survivors in America dwelled on at the time, probably because Americans had so quickly forgotten the past.

WHEN MEMORY RETURNS

Primo Levi has written that Holocaust survivors fall into two groups: those who talk about the past, and those who remain silent. The former category has recently ballooned in response to public receptivity to survivor testimony and the reckonings of old age. All outward indications suggest that Ruth had retreated into assimilationist silence, losing herself in hard work and conspicuous consumption. None of the New Orleans survivors still alive remember Ruth talking about the war, particularly in the 1950s, when public interest was low. Her Eden Street neighbors likewise cannot recall the past creeping often into Ruth's conversations. "Every now and then things would spill out," Lorena Doerries says. "But she didn't dwell on these things with me. She didn't go back a lot. And I hesitated to ask too much."[1]

Once Charles Doerries, Adam's neighborhood chum, tore into the Skorecki house when the kitchen table was piled with family photographs. Ruth had been showing them to Adam. To the two boys she pointed out several relatives who had been murdered by the Nazis. "She was lost in her thoughts," Charles says. "There were a few other occasions I can remember when war memories slipped in. But that veil didn't go back very often."[2]

For as little as Ruth spoke about the Holocaust, though, she had long harbored a desire to recount the Skorecki family's wartime history. But she maintained silence until two events intruded themselves into everyday awareness. Both converged during the spring of 1961: one was the trial of Adolf Eichmann in Jerusalem; the other, the "hate ride" to New Orleans of a small band of storm troopers led by the self-styled American führer George Lincoln Rockwell. The civil rights movement had catalyzed an ultra-rightist backlash, revitalizing not only the Ku Klux Klan but also the American fascist movement, whose noisiest exemplar was Rockwell's American Nazi Party (ANP).

The pretext for the New Orleans "hate ride" was to picket the movie *Exodus*. But the real motive was to attract publicity and inflame a racial tinderbox that already was on the verge of explosion.

The principal impact was on the local Jewish community. "Rockwell's 'hate ride' aroused the community pretty damn good," says Barney Mintz, long-time board member of the New Orleans Anti-Defamation League (ADL). But there was much division as well. The "hate ride" literally arrayed American Jews against local survivors over the conflicting values of free speech and direct action. "We just came from the Nazi camps," says Shep Zitler, the Vilna survivor. "It was too early to see Swastikas and Nazis."[3] They were angry and afraid; more than that, they were torn by that inner conflict between the need to forget and the obligation to remember. This much they knew: they had to protest. What the New Americans of New Orleans failed to anticipate is how the return of troubled memory would prompt a search for ritualizing Holocaust remembrance.

In Ruth's case, on the other hand, the Rockwell episode, coinciding as it did with Eichmann's trial, led to a different kind of witnessing, bringing her to the point that she was finally willing to put down in words the family's searing wartime history. Nothing she had undertaken since the surrender was more psychologically wrenching. "My mother always wanted to tell our story," Anne says. "The memories were with her, and she wanted to share them because she felt that she and my father had achieved something special by saving an entire family. I think the 'hate ride' made her more determined than ever by putting her experiences more into focus—that it can happen again, so we must tell the story. Then, too, the Eichmann trial brought back all those awful memories. She was angry, and writing a book was her way of dealing with it."

Son of "Old Doc" Rockwell, a radio comedian who counted among his friends such Jewish artists and entertainers as Benny Goodman and Groucho Marx, George Lincoln Rockwell was a seminal figure in America's postwar "white power" movement. Indeed, to a generation of American racial extremists he was practically a role model. William Pierce, founder of the neo-Nazi National Alliance and pseudonymous author of *The Turner Diaries*, which inspired both a murderous bank-robbing spree in the early 1980s and, apparently, the 1995 bombing of the federal building in Oklahoma City, got his start in neofascist politics by editing a Rockwell quarterly.[4] David Duke was another disciple. "The greatest American who has ever lived has been shot down and killed," the then high school senior sobbingly told a friend, after learning of Rockwell's 1967 assassination by a disgruntled former follower.[5]

Yet Rockwell's enormous influence within the neofascist movement had little to do with organizational prowess. In 1959 he founded and then served as commander of the ANP, but the party never built a mass following similar to that of the anti-Semitic radio priest Father Charles Coughlin in the 1930s. At its height the ANP probably claimed fewer than three thousand members. And his hard core followers—mostly young men from broken homes and lower-middle-class backgrounds, many with criminal records—could hardly have exceeded thirty. These he formed into storm trooper units, replete with khaki uniforms and swastika armbands. He and his men lived together in a ramshackle, two-story frame house in Arlington, Virginia, on a rise Rockwell called "Hatemongers Hill," just across the Potomac River from Washington, D.C. One visitor to Rockwell's headquarters was struck by unpaid bills piled high on the table.[6]

There is no question that Rockwell was a troubled man. He failed at nearly everything he tried—from commercial art to magazine publishing. Personal relationships were a challenge, including marriage (he was divorced twice). His autobiography, *This Time the World*, reads like a Rorschach test of conflicted sexuality. He brims with anger at his mother for programming his wedding night with store-bought gadgets. He rages at "masculinized" women. He swoons with admiration for the naked male body over that of nude women. Dread of black male sexual potency ("Negroes can beat white men any day in speed of sex maturity and accomplishment") literally haunts the book.[7]

For all his quirks and organizational shortcomings, the commander did possess a rare tactical genius. It was Rockwell who devised the shock tactics favored by neo-Nazis before they began experimenting with electioneering in the 1980s. The tactics were mostly publicity stunts calculated to provoke a reaction from such Jewish defense groups as the American Jewish Committee and the ADL. With the sharp ebbing of anti-Semitism from its wartime high, organized American Judaism sought to capitalize on the improved climate by giving professional Jew haters the silent treatment, denying them the headlines that counterdemonstrations by angry Jews might produce. The strategy had a name: the "quarantine policy." Some called it "the cold-shoulder treatment." Whatever the nomenclature, the policy meshed well with the American Jewish community's traditional commitment to defending civil liberties, even those of the enemy, a stance that had virtually become a cultural value.[8] Rockwell reasoned that he could lift the news blackout by ceasing to be "a sneaky Nazi," like his "sissy" comrades on the extreme right, and becoming an "OPEN, ARROGANT, ALL-OUT NAZI." The aim was to "aggravate them so bad . . . that they will have to notice us."[9]

There was nothing halfway about the commander's provocations. Bathed in floodlights, a huge swastika nailed to its front gable, his house in Arlington, Virginia, became a veritable Nazi shrine. The "Horst Wessel" hymn blared from its wire-mesh windows. Two guard dogs—a Doberman named Gas Ovens, and a German shepherd called Auschwitz—patrolled the premises. "When I was in the advertising game, we used to use nude women. Now I use the *Hakenkreuz* and stormtroopers. You use what brings them in," he said. Students from local universities came to gawk and returned with Nazi flags to fly from their fraternity houses. In the summer of 1960 Rockwell vaulted to national attention when he staged a series of open-air meetings in full Nazi regalia on the Washington Mall next to the Smithsonian Institute. Angry Jews mobbed him. On July 4 he tried to hold a rally in New York City's Union Square. The New York mayor's office denied him a permit, an action later reversed by state courts. At the turn of the year, Rockwell mounted a picketing campaign in selected American cities against the newly released film *Exodus*, a box office hit recounting the founding of the state of Israel. Carefully pre-announced, often by flyers declaring "He Is Coming" or "We Are Back," Rockwell's appearance, together with a handful of armbanded storm troopers, triggered major riots in Chicago, Boston, and Philadelphia, reaping the ANP a publicity bonanza.[10]

Meanwhile, Rockwell hit on another headline-grabbing stunt: a "hate ride" to New Orleans. On Saturday, May 20, 1961, he wired the New Orleans Police Department (NOPD) that he intended to picket the Wednesday evening premiere of *Exodus*, as well as the local headquarters of the National Association for the Advancement of Colored People (NAACP). A few days earlier the New Orleans theater where the film was scheduled to open had received anonymous letters daubed with red paint and stamped with swastikas. Flyers announcing that "the commander is coming" also appeared in the mailboxes of selected New Orleans Jews.[11]

The commander's latest project sought to exploit recent headlines. On the same day that Rockwell wired the NOPD, Alabama Klansmen had assaulted an integrated group of Freedom Riders in the Greyhound bus terminal in Montgomery. A week earlier, white racists had firebombed the first bus of Freedom Riders on a highway outside Anniston, Alabama, savagely beating its occupants. Both civil rights contingents were on their way to New Orleans. The brutal attacks made front-page news around the world. For the next several days public opinion was riveted on the furious negotiations taking place between the Kennedy Justice Department and Alabama state officials to arrange safe passage for fresh reserves of civil rights protesters. To make sure his "hate ride" arrived in town in tandem with the Freedom Ride (the civil rights bus never made it, incidentally), Rockwell waited until Monday, May 22, to dispatch his "hate bus" from Arlington.[12] Not really a bus, the vehicle was a blue and white Volkswagen van carrying five storm troopers. Painted beneath the rear window were the words, "LINCOLN ROCKWELL'S HATE BUS. Emblazoned on the top and sides were the statements: "WE DO HATE RACE MIXING" and "WE HATE JEW-COMMUNISM." The driver was one of Rockwell's most zealous supporters, an action-loving, former Marine and Greek American from New York who had Americanized his name to John Patler. Blessed with dark good looks, he had been drummed out of the Corps for moonlighting as a storm trooper while stationed at Quantico, Virginia. Shadowing the "hate bus" southward was a 1961 green Chevrolet carrying three more troopers. Rockwell himself did not enplane for New Orleans until the following day.[13]

A United Press International (UPI) reporter quoted the commander describing New Orleans as "a real hot spot."[14] Rockwell had obviously been following the local news. For seven months white housewives had been picketing nonstop two recently desegregated public elementary schools in a poorer section of town. In November 1960, hundreds of white teenagers had run amok through the central business district, assailing blacks and tearing through public buildings. Five special sessions of the state legislature in Baton Rouge managed to keep the pot boiling by seizing control of the Orleans Parish School Board, only to have their obstructionist enactments quickly annulled by a federal district judge.[15] By May 1961, the city was rife with racial unrest.

To national Jewish leaders, the "hate ride" was a calamity waiting to happen. Rockwell's recent escapades in northern cities had proven that American Jews were far from complete agreement concerning the "quarantine policy." Not only teenagers but also Holocaust survivors mobbed Rockwell's picketers at theaters where *Exodus* was showing. "It is emotional satisfaction that the counter-demonstrators seek and obtain," wrote an official of the American Jewish Committee. These New Americans had to be taught that in a democracy the only thing they need be afraid of was fear itself, he said.[16]

But national leaders were themselves afraid. Their greatest concern was that Rockwell's southern forays might cement a union between American Nazis and the resurgent Ku Klux Klan. Between 1954 and 1959, there had been a rash of bomb attacks against southern synagogues: almost 10 percent of all bomb targets in the region had been Jewish. Just as worrisome was the potential that such headline-grabbing stunts like the "hate ride" might deflect racial backlash into anti-Semitic channels.[17] It was an anxiety that the organized Jewish community in New Orleans knew all too well.

The city's Jewish leadership never doubted for a moment where it stood on the "quarantine policy." The cold-shoulder strategy formulated by national Jewish organizations harmonized perfectly with their assimilationist desire to avoid controversy—indeed, to keep the word "Jew" or "Jewish" off the front page. The community's upper echelon was well represented on the board of the local ADL. "We had top quality not only in terms of contacts but actual ability, men and women who had direct access to the mayor and the police. We had everything in place here," says the slight, goateed Irwin Schulman, who headed the branch office at the time. The executive committee included such local influentials as board president Moise Steeg, the corporate lawyer, and Barney Mintz, a furniture store owner and legendary football halfback at Tulane in the 1930s. Alerted by the national office months in advance that the ANP would likely demonstrate in their city, the local ADL called an emergency meeting of the executive committee as soon as news broke that Rockwell's "hate bus" was journeying toward New Orleans, with the commander soon to follow. The committee met on Monday evening (May 22, 1961). There was scant debate over tactics and philosophy. Everyone agreed that Rockwell's civil liberties must be respected. Quickly attention focused on the real task at hand: devising a plan for choking off Rockwell's publicity. With little prompting, committee members volunteered to contact the city's three television stations, ten radio stations, and three major dailies. Others promised to use their good offices with the mayor, the governor, the governor's secretary, the Tulane dean of students, the American Legion, the Veterans of Foreign Wars, and the Civil Defense director in Washington. "We didn't have to start de novo," Schulman explains. "We just started pressing buttons and making calls."[18] The contacts were all completed by noon the following day.

If the ADL leadership acted with more than usual dispatch, it was probably because the city's mounting racial tensions were fast eroding the middle ground of political moderation. Since the 1930s numbers of New Orleans Jews had been trying to occupy the center. A common history of persecution forged a feeling of shared minority status between blacks and Jews. A sense of justice, embedded in the Jewish prophetic tradition, led scores of southern Jews into ameliorative, moderate civil rights activities. They included Edith Stern, Julius Rosenwald's daughter, who would shortly underwrite a major voter registration drive in the Deep South, and Rabbi Julian Feibelman, who had thrown open the doors of Temple Sinai in 1949 for the address by Ralph Bunche to the first integrated audience in the city's modern history. Yet in a region where difference was penalized, the pressure to conform, to fit in, was implacable, and in the South that meant toeing the color line. Jews quickly realized that race, not religion, was the great fault line in the American South and that the very sharpness of this division served to heighten equality among whites—indeed, subsuming all other differences, even creating a privilege that Jews could acquire merely by embracing white supremacy. That southern Jews and blacks were separated by class differences—as merchants and croppers, landlords and tenants, employer and domestic—made assimilation to white supremacy all the easier. And clear psychic advantages were to be had as well:

in the American South, blacks, not Jews, were the lightning rod for prejudice. "By and large southern Jews felt comfortable about blacks being a buffer," admits the cigar-smoking Schulman.[19]

As the center started to collapse in the 1950s and 1960s—enfeebled by picketing white housewives, by black students sitting in at downtown lunch counters, by ongoing battles between federal courts and state officials—southern Jews felt added pressure to stand up and be counted in favor of white supremacy. Certainly, the segregationist coercion fell with particular severity on southern Jews in isolated rural communities. But their coreligionists in such cities as New Orleans were not immune from the coercive pressure. A major source of discomfort was that northern Jews were prominent participants in the Freedom Rides. " 'Oh, they're just Yankees. They think different,' I remember southern Jews saying to take the heat off themselves," notes Anne. But the heat rose steadily all the same, and it began to take disturbing forms. Virulent anti-Semitism even began appearing on bumper stickers around town. One read, "I Like Eich"—a reference to the Adolf Eichmann trial then under way in Jerusalem. Social discrimination was nothing new to Crescent City Jews, having long barred their entrance to the city's elite Mardi Gras carnival krewes. But tongue-in-cheek endorsements of genocide bespoke a conspiratorial anti-Semitism that was somewhat new to the Crescent City, raising the troubling specter of the 1915 lynching of Leo Frank, an Atlanta plant owner wrongly convicted of murdering one of his white female employees. The mob was led by some of Georgia's "best citizens." Occurring in an evangelical culture where Jews were constantly reminded of their minority status and where violence lay just below the surface, the "American Dreyfus Case" was a searing reminder of the precariousness of Jewish life in the Diaspora. New Orleans Jews had good reason to feel edgy about the worsening racial climate. The ADL's Schulman was worried: "We lived with the fact that many segregationists had a kernel or more of anti-Semitism."[20]

The segregationist who troubled Schulman and his associates more than anyone, however, was no run-of-the-mill anti-Semite. Judge Leander Perez, the absolute boss of mineral-rich Plaquemines Parish, carried racial extremism so far as to cause his excommunication from the Catholic Church. Perez dominated the White Citizens Council of Greater New Orleans, the vehicle of massive resistance in southern Louisiana; he even stage-managed the Louisiana legislature's massive resistance to desegregation from behind the scenes. The nonstop picketing against two integrated public elementary schools in the lower Ninth Ward was largely instigated by the silver-haired judge. In November 1960 he even incited teenage rowdies to riot in downtown New Orleans. During a speech to a massive rally at Municipal Auditorium the night before the melee, he thundered: "Don't wait for your daughter to be raped by these

Congolese. Don't wait until the burr-heads are forced into your schools. Do something about it now." And then he lashed out against "Zionist Jews," whom he regarded as "the most dangerous people in the country today." The warning reflected his worldview that both the Communist conspiracy and "forced integration" were Jewish plots to destroy "our white Christian civilization" by manipulating "emotional Negroes."[21]

Perez's anti-Semitism and growing political strength powerfully concentrated the Jewish community's attention on its own vulnerability, which doubtless explains the leadership's resolve to separate Jewish concerns from those of Rockwell's other major target, African Americans. The commander was open about his intent to picket both the *Exodus* premiere and a meeting of the New Orleans branch of the NAACP. But the ADL board never considered forging a cross-racial alliance of tolerance against the forces of bigotry. "As I recall," says Schulman of the Monday evening strategy session, "there was no mention of desegregation, no concern about civil rights and anti-Semitism, except that Rockwell was linking the two." The ADL leaders were determined to keep those concerns apart. "This was '*Tokkes an der Tisch*' time," says Schulman, employing the Yiddish phrase for "important business"—the old reflex of placing self-preservation ahead of sympathy for the oppressed, of blending in. During the Rockwell crisis, anti-Semitism was not just the primary concern, it was the *only* concern.[22]

Thus it should come as no surprise that New Orleans's Jewish elite tacitly fell in behind the white establishment's consensus regarding "outside agitators." The consensus was premised on a specious argument of immoral equivalence: "The 'Nazi Storm Troopers' and the 'Freedom Riders' . . . mean nothing but trouble and are not welcome here," Mayor Chep Morrison declared in a press release, denouncing with misguided impartiality "publicity stunts continuously put on by agitators representing extreme and radical view points." *The Times-Picayune* echoed the argument, as did the Young Men's Business Club, which passed resolutions chastising Nazis and civil rights activists alike for provoking federal interference with states' rights. The city council passed a resolution urging the police "to escort 'freedom riders' and other agitators through the city nonstop."[23]

Through it all, the paramount concern of the city's Jewish leadership remained what it had always been: to keep a damper on their own community and thereby deny Rockwell an incident that could win his party fresh recruits from the kind of people then swelling Perez's racist movement. But there were early signs that micromanaging this crisis might not be easy. A few younger men in the community were angry enough to provoke a confrontation. Bernard Bennett, a six-foot-four, athletically built Jewish contractor and his cousin Sam Katz, both members of one of the oldest Reform synagogues, declared flat out that they planned to challenge Rockwell and his men. "I was determined those guys weren't going to march," Bennett says. A cousin who worked for the mayor called to try to talk him out of it. "Will you go to jail?" she asked. "Well, I'm prepared to do that," was his reply.[24]

The biggest worry of ADL leaders was the reaction of the city's New Americans, as local Holocaust survivors were now known. Members of the executive committee were all too familiar with refugee involvement in anti-Rockwell demonstrations in Boston, Chicago, New York, and Philadelphia. Would survivors who had settled in New Orleans also take to the streets? The answer was not long in coming. During the ADL's Monday evening strategy meeting, the head of the NOPD's Counterintelligence Unit called Schulman with information that a group of "local refugees" was planning a counterdemonstration at the opening of *Exodus*. Shortly after, Schulman received a call from one of the New Americans. A large group of survivors had been meeting in Ralph Rosenblat's butcher shop on Carondelet Street, in the heart of the old black-Jewish shopping district, at the very moment the ADL board was formulating its hush-hush strategy. Schulman and the survivor talked and argued for nearly two hours. They hung up agreeing that a delegation of survivors would meet the next day at noon with the full ADL board, which included the presidents of the Jewish federation, the Jewish Welfare Fund, and B'nai B'rith.[25]

More than twenty men had responded to the call for an emergency meeting at Ralph's Butcher Shop, and they took about as little time to reach consensus as had their ADL counterparts. But they were coming from the other side of the spectrum. The New Americans decided to confront the commander rather than give him the cold shoulder. It was not outrage over Rockwell's explicit antiblack racism that moved them to action. Like southern Jews generally, New Orleans's survivors also readily acquiesced in the dominant racial order, steering clear even of moderate civil rights activism, leaving all that to the next generation. No matter how uncomfortable they may have felt in the presence of racial segregation—the movable screen on buses and streetcars, the incivilities and brutalities of quotidian Jim Crow—the New Americans were prepared to go along if that was the price of getting along. One reason is that several of them had become landlords and employers to African Americans. Moreover, as Anne's husband, Stan, put it, "they weren't philosophically stretched by their experience with persecution." It was too soon after freedom for them to universalize the Holocaust and seek out parallels to other persecuted groups. To the New Americans the Final Solution was quintessentially a Jewish tragedy, and for some it would always be seen in this particularist light.[26] So they gave highest priority to the matter of Jewish survival and, more than that, to their own survival.

Thus the decision to confront Rockwell's storm troopers derived from a different kind of fury, one deeper and more profound than any fear survivors may have felt about the reappearance of Nazism in their midst. "The anger gave us courage to fight," says Felicia Fuksman, a Łódź Ghetto survivor. "And this time we were in a position to fight back."[27] But Rockwell was not the only object of their anger. They were also upset with their adopted country for allowing Nazism to make a comeback. They tended to view American politics through the lens of recent European history and were baffled by the paradox of defending the speech rights of individuals dedicated to abolishing free speech. The bewilderment widened the rift between them and American Jews, who looked on civil liberties as both a cultural value and a political strategy. Let Reform Jews exercise their quiet power behind the scene, New Americans told themselves. As far as they were concerned, they were going to protest Rockwell's visit no matter what the consequences. After all, were they not witnesses to an epochal catastrophe? And for that reason, did they not have a message for the future—the warning, as Primo Levi has succinctly put it, "It happened, therefore it can happen again"?[28]

This felt imperative to bear witness sprang from the deepest wells of survivor guilt. Like survivor communities elsewhere in America, the refugees who had settled in New Orleans after 1948 as displaced persons had experienced the Holocaust in all of its dimensions. But however they had experienced Nazi persecution, each was oppressed by a sense of having usurped earthly places belonging by right to murdered loved ones or close friends. That unwarranted guilt stemmed from the belief that "the worst survived, that is, the fittest; the best all died."[29] So why were they spared while saintly sisters perished? "I felt disappointed when I survived," says Gita Rosenblat, Ralph Rosenblat's wife and the only surviving member of a Jewish family that had once made up a large proportion of her Polish village.[30] The murder of those innocent victims seemed so senseless. How could their deaths be rendered meaningful? There was only one way: by never forgetting and never letting the world forget the memory of perished martyrs. An obligation, remembrance was also a means of assuaging guilt. Or, as Ralph Rosenblat bluntly puts it, "I owe a debt to remember those losses."[31]

Nonetheless, until Rockwell came to town, New Orleans's New Americans had put more energy into forgetting than remembering. Dredging up the painful past only made things worse, causing the guilt and fear to return with the immediacy of direct experience. Why relive the trauma if cold war America seemed so little interested in what they had undergone? After the revelations of the liberated camps sent shudders of revulsion through the public mind, Americans quickly shrank from the smell of quicklime and ash. In the 1950s it was tempting to sublimate horrific scenes of corpse-strewn pits in vague anxiety about nuclear war and meaningless mass death. The times were unreceptive to survivor testimony. "Nobody was listening to us back then," says Shep Zitler. Indeed, the very subject of the Holocaust, with its imagery of victims tramping off to death like sheep to slaughter, raised troubling issues concerning Jewish honor and self-worth. How did survivors manage to survive? Why didn't they put up more of a fight? American Jews were reluctant to ask, and survivors, fearful that the audience they sought to reach might be repelled by the story they tried to tell, found it easier to keep their memories private.[32] "They were afraid of being judged," remembers Anne. "Nonsurvivors didn't understand," adds Zitler. "How could they? It was beyond belief."[33]

Given the climate of the 1950s, one can understand why New Orleans survivors lost themselves in the present and fled from the past. They had enough to do building new lives. "We didn't have much time to think about the past," says Ralph Rosenblat. In those early years, every effort went toward making it in America. When there was time for leisure activities, survivors came together for picnics and parties, taking pains to bar the past. "We were trying to have a little good time," Rosenblat says, "we were trying to forget."[34] But it was not always easy to keep the past at bay. Merely slicing bread could trigger memories of the camps and how good it would have felt then to possess the entire loaf. Or someone might say, "Look what our family is missing. I wish our family would be here." The reminiscing often happened over coffee and dessert, during games of gin rummy, or while on Sunday afternoon outings to the Lakefront or the beach, when breezes off the water rustled blankets heaped with food and the children played Parcheesi or pitch and catch under ancient live oaks bearded with Spanish moss. Then survivors might release themselves in Yiddish and start comparing notes about who was in which camp when, and what they each saw and knew. "I was there then." "My brother went to that Lager." "My grandmother used to live in such-and-such town." In the fifties these moments happened rarely and never lasted long.[35]

But the trial in Jerusalem of Adolf Eichmann and Rockwell's "hate ride" abruptly wrenched survivors back to the past. The former head of the ss "Jewish desk," Eichmann had been abducted by Israeli agents in front of his home in Buenos Aires, Argentina, for his role in organizing the death camp transports. Commencing in April 1961 and lasting through August, the trial featured testimony from a parade of Holocaust survivors living in Israel. Along with a multitude of other witnesses, Zivia Lubetkin and Yitzhak Zuckerman testified about the Warsaw Ghetto uprising. Now married to Zuckerman and living on a kibbutz in Israel, the beautiful Lubetkin, according to Hannah Arendt, on assignment from the *New Yorker*, delivered some of the trial's most striking testimony—"completely free of sentimentality or self-indulgence, her facts well-organized, and always quite sure of the point she wished to make."[36] The New Orleans's media gave the proceedings extensive coverage.

Rockwell's "hate ride" happened to coincide with the Eichmann trial's climactic moment, the riveting testimony by Joel Brand and others concerning the 1944 extermination of five hundred thousand Hungarian Jews.[37] By itself the Eichmann drama was enough to awaken long-dormant memories; all across America, the publicity surrounding the trial bestirred Holocaust survivors into breaking their silence.[38] But survivors in New Orleans confronted the added provocation of neo-Nazi exhibitionism on their hometown streets. The effect of Eichmann and Rockwell barging simultaneously into consciousness was cathartic. A tidal wave of returning memory engulfed the city's New Americans, bringing with it that debt of remembrance which, to many survivors, was the only reason they survived.

Thus, when twenty or so survivors gathered that Monday evening in Ralph's Butcher Shop, the air was charged with electricity and filled with anger. Solomon Radasky, a Warsaw furrier who had survived the ghetto uprising and subsequent imprisonment in Majdanek and Auschwitz-Birkenau, said: "I come from a family of seventy-eight people. Aunts and uncles, nieces and nephews, cousins. A large family, and not one is alive now." He was determined to stand tall. "I survived to speak in the name of my family."[39] Everyone else present that evening spoke with equal vehemence and the same sense of loss. They were simply in no mood to listen patiently to reasoned appeals from American Jews about the political wisdom of keeping the peace and avoiding controversy.

Because it was a workday, only five participants from Monday night's gathering at Ralph's Butcher Shop met with the full ADL board the following day. The delegation included Sam Radasky and Ralph Rosenblat, Max Fuksman, David Meisel, and Leo Scher—all activists in the survivor community. Some were known for quicksilver tempers. Given the conflicting agendas, the meeting would have been turbulent in the best of circumstances. But the ADL executive committee made the New Americans wait nearly two hours in the anteroom while sifting through unfinished business, which only heightened the survivors' resentment. "The ADL didn't take us seriously, like we didn't know nothing," says Solomon Radasky.[40]

The meeting was tense throughout. For ADL executive director Schulman, it was "one of the most difficult sessions I have sat through in my five years with the league," as he wrote in his official report.[41] Leo Scher recited his travails in the Częstochowa Ghetto and several labor camps. Another survivor gave testimony. Their English was broken, their words thick in sibilants. One American said he didn't understand what they were trying to say. Solomon Radasky raised his hand: "Can I say something?" Sure, he was told. Radasky's speech often begins softly, with faint traces of Jewish singsong. He is raw boned, with a shock of wavy hair. "Look, I am from Poland. I am from Warsaw." Radasky proceeded to tell his history: "Where I was, about the ghetto uprising, which concentration camp I was in, everything. And I showed him the number on my arm." The man said he now understood but quickly added that the ADL was powerless to keep Rockwell from picketing. The survivors lived in a democracy now, he told Radasky and his companions; they had the police on their side. Things were done differently in America; here there was a constitution. It was important to avoid violence and confrontation. They should deny Rockwell publicity. This was the way to handle the situation. This was sound politics. Everybody needed to follow the plan that community leaders had already painstakingly devised. The lecture did not sit well with the New Americans. "I started talking rough," Radasky says, who flushes when he becomes angry. " 'Well, if you and the ADL cannot do nothing, we gonna do it, because it's not 1939 or '40 or '44. We gonna do it.' " "We batted heads on this at length," Schulman's report stated.[42]

Several ADL leaders in the room that day were World War II veterans who wore their self-possession easily. But the New Americans, seething with frustration over their status as poor relatives, spoke from experiences possessed by few others. "You *gentlemen*," they said, "you *gentlemen*, what do you know about this stuff? You don't know anything about how to survive. You don't understand the Nazis. We know. Let us handle it." The message could not have been clearer: you might be good Reform American Jews, but your knowledge of the world is not as deep as you think. "It was like an épée, just slicing them to pieces, like Zorro with a Z," Schulman remembers. "And they did it so finely, I'm not sure the guys knew exactly what was happening. They tried to respond with quiet, sophisticated frustration."[43]

Says ADL board member Barney Mintz, "There was no way of discussing anything with them. They were going to beat the hell out of Rockwell and his men with baseball bats. They didn't care what the law said. In my opinion, they didn't have the sophistication and the understanding of what our constitutional rights were." Mintz, whose department store was firebombed during his stint as president of the local ADL, is an uncompromising defender of civil liberties. "We've got to be purer than Caesar's wife on free speech, because as a minority Jews are the first people to feel a backlash." Still, even he admits that constitutional arguments seemed abstract at the time. "They were adamant. 'Did you see it? Do you know what it's like?' It's pretty damn hard to answer that."[44]

It is unclear how the meeting ended. The record indicates that the ADL board persuaded the New Americans to go along with its strategy on a trial basis. But it must have lacked confidence in the agreement, because it called a larger meeting for 5:00 P.M. the same day in the International House downtown. All day Monday and Tuesday the phones in the ADL office had been ringing off the hook. Rumors were flying right and left. One indicated that survivors intended to bring bags of unopened razor blades to the theater to avoid charges of carrying concealed weapons. "If these people [the storm troopers] gave them any trouble they were going to slice them up with single-edge razor blades," says Moise Steeg, the ADL board president at the time.[45] It is one of those details that American Jews recall vividly but local survivors cannot remember at all.

"They got a little bit scared," notes Zitler of the city's Jewish leadership. "Maybe they were thinking, 'These Goddamn refugees, maybe they're going to start killing. That's all we need in the city of New Orleans. These crazy people just might do it. What can we do?' "[46]

The late-afternoon meeting was heavily attended. All the city's rabbis were present, as were the heads of the Jewish federation, the Jewish Welfare Fund, the National Council of Jewish Women, and Hadassah. Many survivors showed up as well. For good measure, Steeg had invited police superintendent Joe Giarrusso to address the crowd. Steeg calmly set forth the steps taken so far to deal with the crisis and "implored the dissidents to refrain from using violence."[47] Then Superintendent Giarrusso reassured the audience that the police department had matters well in hand. "I just told them we would be right on top of the situation," he says.[48]

The New Americans were still angry from the ADL meeting earlier in the day. Radasky raised his hand and proceeded to give a minilecture about Hitler's rise to power and his double game of professing respect for the rights of Jews and gypsies while actually hating both groups—"like people here are hating the blacks." Then he issued the same ultimatum he had put to the ADL board. "You're the chief of police. If you want to help us, you can help us. If not, we gonna take Rockwell off the street."[49]

Giarrusso vowed to arrest anyone who broke the law. But now other survivors were piping up. "I recall a guy sitting in the front row," Giarrusso says. "He got up and got beside himself with what he might do."[50] It was probably Ralph Rosenblat. "Chief, I don't care what you gonna do or how you gonna do it. I cannot be responsible for my blood. I cannot say at that moment how I am going to react if I'm walking on the sidewalk and see Rockwell with his people wearing ss uniforms with the Hakenkreuz." Giarrusso reiterated his threat to arrest lawbreakers. "Chief, you will have to do your duty, but I cannot endure. You do your part; I will do my part," Rosenblat replied.[51]

The meeting broke up with another vague pledge by the survivor group to abide by the communal consensus to let the ADL and the police handle the situation. But the ADL still lacked confidence that the agreement would stick. So Schulman and one of his board members showed up at Ralph's Butcher Shop later that night to implore the New Americans to stay calm.

They clustered around the deli case near the walk-in cooler where Rosenblat stored kosher meat, close to the chopping block and grinding machine. "People were talking. We were shouting," says Shep Zitler. "I will kill him! I will shoot him!" screamed one survivor, referring to Rockwell.[52] "Trust us," Schulman pleaded. "I pledged my reputation, which is pretty good," he says. "They trusted me 70 or 80 percent, maybe. But they trusted only themselves, and probably not each other." The meeting concluded with further promises to abide by agreements reached earlier in the day. But the situation remained tense. "It was a bitch," Schulman admits.[53]

Superintendent Giarrusso was not the sort of man who worried easily. A World War II Navy veteran, he had a well-deserved reputation for crisis management. Upon taking office, he wasted little time cleaning up a police corruption scandal. He dealt peremptorily with lunch counter sit-ins at downtown department stores, arresting civil rights activists for "criminal mischief." With fine impartiality, he moved vigorously against the thousands of prosegregation rowdies who had stormed the school board offices in November 1960 following Judge Perez's inflammatory speech in Municipal Auditorium. Giarrusso ordered the fire department to spray blue dye at the rioters' feet or arc it high above their heads, to make it easier to identify participants. Sympathetic toward the crowd, the firemen instead turned on a garden hose at low pressure. Giarrusso was known for speaking plainly: "I can piss a harder stream than you're putting out there," he barked.[54]

But the superintendent knew a dangerous situation when he saw one, and he had seen enough of the local survivors' volcanic emotions to sense the potential, as a subsequent police report put it, for "a full-scale riot."[55] Something of the kind had taken place earlier inside the New York County Courthouse at Foley Square during a hearing on the American Nazi Party's legal battle with Gotham authorities to obtain a speaking permit. Rockwell stepped up to the television microphones planted in the rotunda and shouted, "Eighty percent of the American Jews are traitors and should be exterminated."[56] The crowd exploded in a flurry of punches, as umbrellas sliced the air. Giarrusso was worried enough to employ personal diplomacy. He telephoned contractor Bernard Bennett with a plea to avoid violence, and he had his oldest brother, Rudy, intercede with Solomon Radasky, who lived a block away. Rudy, like the other Giarrusso boys, also served on the police force, and his son was good friends with Radasky's son David. Rudy came over one night to talk Radasky out of confronting Rockwell. "Do you really want to do this?" he asked.[57]

Toby Radasky Kornreich was listening in the next room: "I remember my father saying, 'Yeah, we want to do this. It's really important. You have to understand it.' And then there was this discussion about World War II and Hitler." Rudy Giarrusso left, shaking his head. "Yeah, yeah, you're right," he said. "I'll talk to my brother. We'll take care of it. You don't have to come with your bats and whatever."[58]

The superintendent went all out to prevent trouble. "We watched them the whole time they were here," he says of Rockwell and his men. He was hardly exaggerating. According to the police report, as soon as Rockwell and his traveling companion, Roy James, landed at Moisant Airport on the afternoon of Tuesday, May 23, 1961, the two men came under continuous surveillance. Just as the Volkswagen "hate bus" crossed the straits separating the lakes from the gulf and reached city limits, NOPD squad cars picked up the tail from state police units. It was ten in the evening. Fifty minutes later the graffiti-covered vehicle turned into a restaurant and trailer court on Chef Menteur Highway. Several police cruisers pulled up alongside. The head of police intelligence approached John Patler, the driver, and told him to remove the lettering from his bus, quoting Revised Statutes of 1950, title 14, paragraph 7. "We cautioned them in strong words. We told them to take that swastika off that Volkswagen," says Giarrusso, who was also at the scene. Patler and his companions immediately complied.[59]

Thereafter police surveillance grew even more suffocating. Because the picketing at the Civic Theater and the NAACP meeting was not scheduled to take place until the next evening, the Rockwell group drove across Lake Pontchartrain the morning of May 23 to stage a rally at the Fontainebleu State Park in Mandeville, but state authorities had padlocked the entrance, forcing the commander and his men to turn around immediately on arrival. Such police attention was starting to make the storm troopers jumpy. One Bernard David Jr. was behind the wheel of the "hate bus" on the drive back, and he tried to elude the police tail by speeding down one of the causeway's ramps. The vehicle caromed off the concrete railing while trying to avoid hitting a state police car, and David was taken into custody for "reckless driving." The police released the bus, however.[60]

Even Rockwell himself was becoming unnerved by the scrutiny, for later that morning he called police headquarters from the Canal Street hotel room where he was huddling with his remaining nine followers. How many pickets would he be allowed to put on the streets that night? he asked. Were there any restrictions as to lettering? Would he be permitted to make a speech in a public park? The police advised that no more than two pickets would be allowed at both the Civic Theater and the NAACP meeting at Corpus Christi Church. As for his signs, he should use his own discretion, but under no circumstances would he be "permitted to make a speech here in New Orleans due to the present situation." All the while, a police detective was monitoring the Rockwell group's conversations from an adjoining hotel room. The superintendent was leaving nothing to chance.[61]

Yet one factor in the equation seemed beyond Giarrusso's control: what were local survivors planning to do? The fury he had witnessed at the International House meeting the previous day had him worried. Late in the afternoon, a few hours before the movie was due to start, he sent a patrol car to Ralph's Butcher Shop to reiterate his threat to arrest anyone caught disturbing the peace.[62]

Despite the official warnings, the gentle admonitions, the pleas and moral arm-twisting, the New Americans remained determined. As the 8:00 P.M. screening time for *Exodus* approached, twenty survivors piled into five cars and drove to the Civic Theater on Baronne Street, in the heart of the central business district. They were armed, but not with razor blades. "Just baseball bats and pieces of iron pipe, half inch, three-quarters of an inch pipe," says Solomon Radasky. "We was ready to fight."[63]

Giarrusso also arrived prepared for trouble. Thirty-five to forty patrolmen had been detailed to the vicinity of the theater alone. "We had them all over the place," he says.[64] The ADL likewise appeared in force—"eight or ten of our friends who were fairly physically inclined," as Steeg describes them. Even the local Federal Bureau of Investigation (FBI) office had set up a surveillance post on the second floor of Barney Mintz's furniture store, across the street from the theater.[65]

Because New Orleans sits on the hinge of two weather systems that are often in collision, downpours here can be biblical. At about 7:00 P.M. a thunderstorm blew in from the gulf, dumping several inches of rain on the downtown area. In a matter of minutes two feet of water was streaming down Baronne Street in front of the Civic Theater. Groups of moviegoers took shelter inside covered doorways up and down the street. A sodden crowd stood shivering in the theater arcade. Having trouble parking, the New Americans waded to the phone company's arched entranceway just down the block from the theater. "It was a pouring day," remembers Ralph Rosenblat. "We was swimming."[66] The rain pelted the downtown area for forty-five minutes. Then, almost as suddenly as it started, the storm slackened to a drizzle and the waters parted, as the city's elaborate hydraulic system pumped the runoff into Lake Pontchartrain. A few minutes later a 1961 green Chevrolet carrying six storm troopers pulled up in front of the theater. Rockwell and Roy James climbed out, wearing khaki uniforms and red armbands emblazoned with swastikas. The square-jawed commander, his trademark dark cowlick drooping over his forehead, was carrying a sign that read: "EXODUS . . . Written by a Communistic Jew." On the other side were the words, "AMERICAN [*sic*] FOR WHITES—AFRICA FOR BLACKS—GAS CHAMBERS FOR TRAITORS."[67]

Events unfolded quickly. Rockwell and James made a few passes in front of the theater, forty feet in each direction. Then the New Americans emerged from the phone company entranceway and started walking in formation toward the two picketers. The crowd packed under the theater marquee pressed forward. The atmosphere was electric, as if the fast-moving weather front had deposited a charge outside the theater. Bernard Bennett, who had been waiting in the arcade with his cousin Sam Katz, had to restrain a male survivor standing near him, because, as Bennett later testified, "the sight of the swastika armbands caused an emotional reaction almost uncontrollable." As soon as the New Americans got within twenty feet of the sign-carrying picketers, Giarrusso ordered Rockwell and James arrested, charging them with violating the same "criminal mischief" statute under which civil rights lunch counter demonstrators had been arrested the year before.[68]

The police then moved quickly against the four storm troopers parked nearby in the green Chevrolet, taking them into custody and confiscating a toy gun and a "stiletto-type knife" found under the front seat of the car. Just then the blue and white "hate bus" drove up in front of the theater. Police had chased it from the NAACP meeting at Corpus Christi Church for "obstructing traffic." Giarrusso had its four passengers placed under arrest as well. The entire operation was over by half past eight.[69] ADL director Schulman, in his official postmortem, characterized Giarrusso's crisis management as "one of the swiftest and most effectively carried out bits of police action I have ever seen." But the arrests also happened to be unconstitutional.[70]

As for the New Americans, they bought tickets for the evening's performance and went inside and watched the movie. Their role in the controversy was a deeply satisfying experience, one they still talk about with great animation. They had confronted a specter that had destroyed their families in the Old World. And, perhaps just as important, they had forced the local community, Jewish and non-Jewish alike, to take them and their experiences seriously.

It was the first time since their reception as refugees that they had been re-garded with anything except benign indifference.

Like most real-life crises, Commander Rockwell's 1961 "hate ride" to New Orleans lacked neat resolution. Because the Freedom Riders never made it to New Orleans, the ANP was deprived of the publicity bonanza that Rockwell had been counting on. Refusing bail, Rockwell demanded that the FBI investi-gate the NOPD's violation of his "civil rights." Then, mimicking Freedom Rid-ers who were fasting at the time in a Mississippi prison, the commander and his men staged a hunger strike in the Orleans Parish Jail. Rockwell stayed in jail until only June 1, when he posted bond and, according to some reports, made a beeline for a local steak restaurant, wiring the troopers still behind bars to end their fast. "Your will and dedication is inspiring white men everywhere to stand up and fight," it read. "Start eating and God Bless you. Sieg Heil."[71]

Beginning on June 13, the trial lasted two days. The local chapter of the American Civil Liberties Union (ACLU) assumed the defense of everyone ex-cept Rockwell, who acted as his own attorney. All ten Nazi defendants were convicted, fined, and sentenced to jail terms ranging from thirty to sixty days. A three-judge panel overturned the verdict in 1962, however. A year later the U.S. Supreme Court struck down the "criminal mischief" statute used by New Orleans authorities to stifle civil rights activists and neo-Nazis alike. Rockwell was now in his glory. "The 'HATE BUS' tour of the South has ended, at last, with total victory for the White Man and the American Nazi Party!" he crowed in the pages of the *Stormtrooper*.[72]

After his jailing in New Orleans, Rockwell remained in the national lime-light off and on for the next several years. In 1962 he attended a Nation of Islam convention in Chicago, heaping praise on black separatist Elijah Mu-hammed as "the Adolf Hitler of the Black Man." He toured the college and university lecture circuit, producing tumult and news coverage wherever he went. When street protests against the Vietnam War erupted, Rockwell and his storm troopers pelted "peace creeps" with eggs, paint, and fists.[73]

His face scarred from numerous street battles, his finances shakier than ever (most of his income derived from a mail-order business in "hatenany" records and "White Power" T-shirts), Rockwell grew morose toward the end of his life. He was depressed at losing control of youthful storm troopers who had been drawn to the ANP by the romance of street-fighting action. They soon grew frustrated with the commander's legalistic strategy of notifying the police of his next move so as to maximize publicity. One of the malcontents was swarthy John Patler, the "hate bus" driver. Rockwell had expelled him from the ANP in April 1967 for fomenting discord between dark-skinned and fair-skinned party members, whom Patler habitually referred to as "blue-eyed devils." Four months later, as the commander was backing his car out of a parking space, Patler fired several shots from a Mauser semiautomatic pistol through Rockwell's windshield, killing Rockwell. Patler was convicted in December 1967 of first-degree murder and sentenced to twenty years in prison.[74]

Rockwell's "hate ride" seared the consciousness of nearly every member of New Orleans's tiny survivor community, no matter what their level of participation may have been in the actual confrontation. Awakening unbidden memories, the episode taught the lesson of collective action. It even became something of a template for later confrontations with Louisiana's future exemplar of Rockwellian grandstanding, David Duke. But it is hard to gauge Mark Skorecki's reaction to the uproar. He never joined in the stormy meetings at Ralph's Butcher Shop, and it is doubtful he ever would have under any circumstances. Nearly sixty-one at the time, much older than the other men, he was something of a loner, and he lacked their angry temperament. "He wasn't that fervent," Anne explains. "He had his opinions, but I never saw him be demonstrative." Stan agrees: "Once he was away from Europe and in New Orleans he wanted to get on with the rest of his life. He wanted to put the past behind him. His attitude was, 'That was then and this is now and I don't want to have anything to do with it.' "[75]

Conflicted feelings about the past doubtless had something to do with Mark's disinclination to engage in public witnessing. Three days after disembarking from Germany, a staff member of the Jewish federation apparently asked how he avoided being sent to a concentration camp. "He advised that the reason he was not in a concentration camp was because of his skill in running a wood making factory." This was not a memory he cared to revisit. How could his American hosts possibly be made to comprehend the moral complexities of his wartime experiences? His arrangement with Stelmaszek? The lengths to which he was forced to go to protect his wife and daughters? No, let others get steamed over the past. He would lose himself in his work. That seemed to be the stance he adopted toward Holocaust memory for most of his years in America.[76]

On the other hand, Ruth was much less reticent about expressing her feelings over Nazism's sudden reappearance in America, even if domestic events kept her temporarily on the sidelines. The "hate ride" occurred just weeks before Lila's June 11 wedding to Norman Millen, a mild-mannered, bespectacled army veteran from Knoxville, Tennessee, who had been lured to New Orleans by a steel factory job. The wedding preparations absorbed all Ruth's energies and kept Mark working overtime to pay the bills. "She put pressure on my father to make sure they had the money," Anne says. "And I'm sure my mother would have been scared for him to participate in a political confrontation."

But once the wedding was over, Ruth jumped into the business of institutionalizing a survivor response to future threats to memory by helping reorganize the New Americans Social Club. It was not without some misgivings on her part over tactics. As much as Ruth supported the end of defending historical truth from its enemies, she was of two minds about the means fellow survivors favored: changing the group's legal identity. The club had been a loose and informal grouping of friends, but the younger survivors in the forefront of the anti-Rockwell protest decided to incorporate shortly after the "hate bus" incident, to guard against forgetting a newly learned lesson. "When we went through the Rockwell experience," Shep Zitler says, "we figured out that one individual cannot do anything, but as a group we can do something."[77] The local survivors held their organizational meeting in the Jewish Community Center (JCC), replete with campaign speeches and an election of officers. Shep Zitler was elected president; Leo Scher, Ralph Rosenblat, and Sam Radasky became vice presidents. But Ruth looked on the enterprise with a wary eye. "Mr. Zitler, you are making a mistake," she told Shep, as the group prepared to file its incorporation papers with the secretary of state in Baton Rouge. "I know our people better than you because you're a newcomer to them."[78] She was probably recalling the fallout from an ill-fated 1952 Holocaust Memorial service staged by the group. Mark had even built a wooden tombstone bearing the number 6 million in both English and Hebrew for the ceremony. But jealous squabbling discouraged the New Americans from following up with similar events for another decade.

The young organizers were not about to be deterred, however. The first order of business taken up by the "new" New Americans was the organization of an annual Holocaust remembrance ceremony on or near the April 19 anniversary of the Warsaw Ghetto uprising, now one of the oldest such ongoing ceremonies in the country. Like other Jewish communities that use the uprising to memorialize the Holocaust, the city's New Americans liked the linkage to an event that belied the sheep-to-slaughter imagery. But the ceremony sprang from impulses deeper than the urge to refurbish Jewish heroism: it was a mourning ritual, an opportunity at long last to grieve and say good-bye to murdered loved ones. In its public truth telling, it was an expression of social action—group therapy in the service of politics and vice versa.[79] It was an assertion of Jewish communal identity based on the collective memory of World War II. And, finally, it was an attempt by the New Americans to become a social force within the wider Jewish community.

Thus, for that first ceremony in April 1962, the fledgling club pulled out all the stops. They raised five thousand dollars for a wood-carved sculpture to be placed in the lobby of the Jewish Community Center, where the annual event continues to be held. And they invited every Jewish organization in the city to send representatives. But that first audience, like many subsequent ones, consisted mainly of New American family members. Few members of the city's Reform community were in attendance, and only the National Council of Jewish Women bothered to send a representative, and she brought her knitting. "We were disappointed," complains Shep Zitler of that first service. "We were treated like poor cousins."[80] The disappointment would last until the mid-1980s, when the Holocaust started to become a new civil religion and substantial numbers of American Jews, their numbers augmented by a heavy influx of transplants from the North, began attending the annual Holocaust Remembrance Ceremony.

Meanwhile, Ruth was correct that organizers of the club were inviting problems by incorporating. The city's survivors paid a high price for this new foray into public life. Almost immediately the New Americans were torn asunder by schisms and secessions. The small contingent of German survivors, always standoffish toward their Polish counterparts, were the first to leave. Then several Polish survivors dropped out. Club meetings became stormy, at times nearly pugilistic. Language difficulties lay at the root of some of the fights. "There was always misunderstanding because we were having the meeting in English and our people are thinking in Yiddish and to translate from Yiddish to English isn't easy," notes Zitler. Thus, as a member of the second generation explains, someone might blurt out, "Your daughter is a dog, when they really meant to say she was in puppy love."[81] Electioneering added new friction. Strong-willed individualists clashed over who was going to be in charge, who was going to be the *macher*, to use the Yiddish term for "big shot." "You have a room full of bosses," explains David Radasky, Solomon's son, now a lawyer in Kansas City. "When it comes to New Americans Club politics, there are a lot of people who say it's not worth it, and I'm one of them."[82]

But most of all there were shouting matches over the primacy of suffering and the ownership of memory. "We were competitive people with strong ideas," says Zitler with considerable understatement. Quarrels broke out over what should be included in the ceremony, who should read the kaddish, who should sing the song of remembrance. Increasingly the issue of leadership became mixed up in the contentious issue of memory. Should the president be the most acculturated member of the group, so as to let American Jews know that they, the survivors, had long ago sloughed off their greenhorn roughness? Or should the club's leader be the individual possessing the most authentic Holocaust experience? Solomon Radasky, the Majdanek and Auschwitz-

Birkenau survivor, believes that "a person [who] was not in a concentration camp cannot assume the feeling of speaking about the Holocaust."[83] He eventually withdrew from the club.

If Ruth was prescient concerning New American factionalism, it was probably because she was often in the thick of the fray. Older than the rest and sure of her opinions, Ruth waded into the early organizational debates, the only woman to have done so. But there was no give and take with her. Things had to be done her way or not at all. "She was a very bossy woman," one New American says. "She bossed her husband. She bossed her children." "She wore the pants," says another local survivor. "She knows what is." "She was a *starke Frau*," adds a third. "My mother was a strong woman," Anne admits.[84]

Within a year Ruth resigned from the club, bringing a few close friends and allies with her. By that time the New Americans were bickering over everything, as the community fissured into rival factions and cliques. Business quarrels were dragged into club meetings. The competition over who would give the next party became intense, a snub of one couple causing ripples of social realignment. "How come so-and-so wasn't invited? I'm not coming. I'm not talking to you." Gossip, the time-honored method that tightly bonded groups use to enforce conformity, became more sharp tongued. "All you heard was this one insulted that one, that one insulted this one. He said this, she said that," says Isak Borenstein, the survivor-carpenter from Radom.[85] It was as if membership in the same extended family made private feuds everybody's business, and nobody could refuse to choose sides.[86] The ensuing ruptures could be permanent. "They hold grudges forever," says Maureen Kurtz of her New American aunts and uncles. Ruth herself eventually broke with Niusia Goldfarb, Maureen's mother. "They were as close as sisters at one time, and then—I don't know why—they just weren't as close anymore."[87].

The underlying problem was growing prosperity, which caused the small group to stratify. Status competition mounted. The New Americans had assaulted New World barriers with the same focused energy that helped them brush aside other obstacles in their path. They pored over English grammar books at night. They challenged employers to give them a chance. As quickly as possible they established small businesses, where husband and wife alike worked long hours. And once they amassed a little capital, a few, such as Shep Zitler, Ralph Rosenblat, and Max Fuksman, pooled their savings to buy rental property. "I still remember when my dad and Mr. Rosenblat and Fuksman bought that first piece of property together," says Justin Zitler. "They were proud that they were making it in America."[88] The mobility was geographic as well as economic. Shep abandoned the Broadmoor neighborhood for a ranchstyle home in the upscale Lakefront area, where the streets are named for precious gems. Before long other New Americans were doing the same. It was a social mobility drama that had been reenacted countless times in American immigration history, except the New Americans achieved their success in the span of a single generation.[89]

Financial success disrupted the camaraderie of the early days, supplanting it with assimilation's unavoidable concomitant: social one-upsmanship. "Everybody came with empty pockets," says Toby Lederman. "Some came up a little earlier to make a good living. Some people had to work harder and couldn't make a good living right away. People were a little bit jealous of one another."[90]

Much of the rivalry came to focus on the new American children, with bragging over whose kids were earning straight As and making the honor roll, attending the best colleges, pledging this sorority or that fraternity, winning acceptance to law school or medical school. "It was as if they were trying to outdo one another through their children," observes Kurtz. Ruth's competitiveness centered less on Anne and Lila than on Adam, the postwar miracle baby and perpetuator of the family name. To Ruth, he became a magical replacement for her engineer-brother, Henry Tempelhof, who perished at Majdanek. "In her mind, she wanted me to be like him," Adam says, whose resemblance to his uncle is striking, down to the famous half-smile tinged with melancholy that Henry's associates in the ghetto hospital still recall more than fifty years later.[91] Beginning in grade school, Ruth and Adam would sit in the front-porch swing on Eden Street mapping out his future. "You're not going to come home with dirt under your fingernails like your father," she told him over and over again. He would go to law school instead, make lots of money, and buy her a new house and other luxuries beyond imagining. "In other words, to pay them back for everything they had done, everything they had gone through, everything they had been deprived of. We used to have lots of these grand talks sitting and laughing on the porch," Adam says. He is wistful about his own obvious achievements. "I always wanted to be more than I was. But I don't know whether it was because I really wanted it or because I wanted to make her happy."[92]

Adam's successes, however, were one of the few arenas in which Ruth held her own in the status race, for otherwise her social cachet had eroded. It was mainly because Mark failed to achieve the financial success of younger survivors. He never got involved in their joint real estate ventures, never came close to recapturing the prosperity he enjoyed as a bus company owner in postwar Germany. In New Orleans, he was always off to the side, overshadowed by his more gregarious wife. Anne and Lila believe that by the time he reached America, a history of multiple new beginnings had exhausted him. "There was no way in the world he could have kept up with people twenty years younger than himself," Anne says. "He lost two decades." But he was also indifferent to power and wealth and did not care about the status rivalries. "I don't think he thought the social competitiveness was important," Stan says.[93]

But unlike her husband, Ruth approached status rivalries in deadly earnest. "There were many arguments with my dad," Adam remembers. "A lot of loud fights. Often it was my mother's frustration at seeing other people doing things, going places, living in nice houses, driving nice cars, dressing nicely, and my father's lack of interest in those things. He lived for his family and his work. He didn't want money, and he didn't want power. But she would start in with him about wanting more, and they would end up in a fight. Daddy didn't want to hear all this. 'Just leave me alone,' he'd tell her. 'That's their business.' But she couldn't leave it alone. It was killing my mother, because it went to being part of the group, to being accepted."[94]

They argued heatedly over his refusal to apply for German reparations, which Ruth, Anne, and Lila began receiving after Bonn amended its indemnification law in 1965 to allow compensation for psychological distress inflicted by the Holocaust.[95] "He would have no part of it," Adam explains. He was too proud to accept anything from West Germany, and he was not about to subject himself to psychological scrutiny. "My father was willing to say, 'I'll give up x number of dollars a year for the rest of my life because I don't want to do these things.' And trust me, we could have used the money."[96]

Thus Mark and Ruth squabbled over buying a new sectional sofa. She wanted the latest in mass merchandising so as to keep up with the Jones, but he objected and she could not budge him. Ruth ended up buying one anyway, and without his approval—a three-piece, brownish-tweed sofa that curved beneath the bayed picture windows overlooking the ligustrum bush. During all the years it remained in the house, Mark never sat on it. "That was the nature of their relationship. She pushed and pushed until he gave in, while he tried to fight for equality," Stan says.[97]

Ruth's competitiveness with other New Americans even colored her relationship with her son-in-law. When Stan bought a new car, she became instantly unhappy with the one Mark owned. When Stan and Anne bought a new color TV, she purchased a model just like it a few days later. Shortly after Stan and Anne moved to the Lakeview area, buying a tiled-roof, Spanish mission–style house, Ruth pressured Mark into selling their Eden Street home and moving to a pleasantly shaded suburban neighborhood less than a mile from her daughter's new residence. More and more, she let her daughter know that she disapproved of the way in which Anne and Stan were raising their daughters.

Things came to a head during one of those Sunday afternoon dinners at

Eden Street which Ruth insisted both daughters' families attend and which Stan had come to dread. Ruth and her son-in-law quickly fell into one of their running arguments. This spat was over whether he should buy a car radio, and she let him know that the fifty dollars it would cost to have one installed was a waste of money.

"Stay out of my business!" he exploded. "I don't want to hear from you at all." Then he turned to Anne. "I'm leaving. You can come with me or you can stay here. But if you stay here, you're going to stay for good because I'm tired of this bullshit. Make up your mind." Anne and the kids followed him to the car. He never returned to Eden Street. Anne continued visiting her parents alone, still trying to patch things up, still attempting to play the diplomat, but she was emotionally pulled asunder because of the irreconcilable differences between the warring parties.[98]

For all her inner turmoil, Ruth remained outwardly pleasant. She never let her appearance go, never let people see how she felt inside. Her smile still flashed when she ran into acquaintances on the street. Her eyes sparkled when she laughed. But inside, the worm of unhappiness gnawed away at her soul. "My grandmother was a very pleasant person, socially liked, but very serious at the same time," says Robin of her grandmother's personality. "But I always felt she was profoundly broken."[99]

Rockwell's "hate ride" stirred Ruth deeply. "Coming to the United States, we were sure we never would see or hear more of Hitler's business, like Swastikas and Nazi speeches," Ruth said almost two years after the event. She was equally aroused by the Eichmann trial. She closely monitored the court proceedings on television and in the paper. Eichmann's appearance took her completely aback. He seemed so ordinary, hardly the monster Holocaust survivors often require to make sense of their memories. "He was sitting in a booth dressed like a human being," Ruth said, "with a suit on, like everybody else, and a clean white shirt, a tie, and a beautiful white handkerchief." Yet, this was the same man who "broke up families, killed children who had never done any harm in their lives. And now he had the nerve to say he was just a tool. This was a big lie." Ruth was not a philosophical person, so she never throught through the implications of her own insight (originally enunciated by Hannah Arendt in her controversial book on the Eichmann trial, revealingly subtitled "A Report on the Banality of Evil") that the Nazi evil was best understood less in terms of its savage bestiality than its capacity for corrupting the moral fiber of ordinary people.[100] Ruth was sure that, deep down, Eichmann felt guilty, for why would he conceal his real identity from his own children by telling them he was their uncle? "When a father cannot tell his own children that he is their father, he has plenty on his conscience," Ruth reasoned. "Listening to him and watching him, we went through again the tragedy which happened to millions of people."

And then, while still wrestling with painful memories resurrected by the Eichmann trial, she was jolted anew by Rockwell's visit. "When I hear today that people, like Hitler, start following the same program, it makes me sick just to think of it," she said. She was still churning inside over the trial and Rockwell's publicity stunt two years later, so much so that she finally decided to set the Skorecki family saga down on paper. Hers was a special story, she fervently believed, whose message to the future was even more urgent now that the present was starting to forget the past.

Conveying the message was not an easy task. Ruth lacked the language and literary skills to write the story herself. She would have to tell it to someone else. Typically, she worried whether nonsurvivors would understand the horrors she had witnessed, and she feared being judged for the moral compromises that survival exacted. "What other people thought was very important to my mother," Anne says. There was a young man in the neighborhood named Harry Hull whom Ruth knew slightly. His family had moved to Eden Street in the late 1950s. The Hulls' only tie to the Skoreckis was young Adam, who was the same age as their daughter and thus often in and out of their house. Harry himself, tall and athletic, remembered by neighbors as courteous and quiet, was hardly ever at home, boarding during high school and much of college at a Benedictine Abbey across the lake until he left the seminary in 1960 to attend Loyola Law School in New Orleans. He eventually became a prosecutor in District Attorney Jim Garrison's office, doing minor work on the controversial attempt to prosecute local businessman Clay Shaw for conspiring to assassinate President John F. Kennedy. Today he teaches math and serves as athletic director at a Catholic girl's school on the Mississippi gulf coast. In February 1963, just after finishing law school and passing the bar, while waiting to report to the Marine Corps in early March, he sat down with Ruth to record her story. "I had the time," Hull says in slow, deliberate speech, "and I had an interest in the Second World War. I must have just read William Shirer's *The Rise and Fall of the Third Reich*. And I remember following the Eichmann trial with some interest. Mrs. Skorecki and I used to run into each other on the street, and we talked. We became good friends. Somehow or other Mrs. Skorecki broached the subject of writing a book, and I offered to help her."[101]

Why Ruth turned to Harry Hull, a comparative stranger, is a minor mystery. Adam believes it had something to do with young Hull's having attended law school. In her mind it indicated he possessed the skills she lacked. But Hull's seminary background may have been the more decisive influence. "To become a priest, you have to be sympathetic and people oriented and willing to listen," Anne says. "My mother needed someone who would not give her secrets away, because she was baring her soul to this young man, and she wasn't used to speaking openly. All her life she was afraid to let somebody know too much. She was always on guard. You just don't say too much, was her philosophy, and the mind-set probably goes back to our experiences in the Holocaust."

Theirs was an unusual collaboration. Every day Hull would bring over the upright Underwood typewriter he had learned to use while taking a typing course at a local business college. They would sit at the dining room table. The sessions usually ran two hours, occasionally twice a day, lasting about a month, give or take a few days. Hull was basically a scribe, the classic *sofer* of Jewish tradition: "She talked and I typed."[102] After several weeks the two of them produced a 128-page manuscript, single-spaced, squeezed between cramped margins and smudged by numerous deletions. But it was packed with precise names, dates, and addresses—a veritable road map back into that time and place.

Oral testimony by Holocaust survivors possesses a distinctive quality. The narration seldom unfolds in a linear manner, being fragmentary and disconnected and jumping around in time. It focuses on traumatic incidents and returns to them insistently. It is haunted by a divided self: a narrator in the here and now trying to impose some pattern on arbitrary cruelties that are bereft of meaning, and a victim who remains chained to horrific episodes that are not so much remembered as relived. Survivors during interviews frequently become lost in those indelibly etched moments, unable to connect senseless atrocities to the chronology of their pre- and postwar lives. And they seem forever stymied by attempts to resolve inner moral conflicts. They know that self-preservation robbed them of moral choice, yet because modern conventions dictate that events and actors be judged and evaluated, they reflexively blame themselves for not having behaved differently. Their encounter with the world of "choiceless choice," as the literary historian Lawrence Langer has characterized the moral terrain of the Holocaust, is at the heart of the deep ambivalence that runs through Holocaust testimony: " 'You won't understand' and 'you must understand' are regular contenders in the multiple voices of these testimonies," Langer writes.[103]

But Ruth, though recounting her story orally, was not talking into a tape recorder, comfortable in the knowledge that the confused threads of her story could be untangled later. She was dictating to a typist and thus she had to compose the story in her head, abiding all the while by literary conventions concerning chronology, characterization, and narrator voice, not to mention a unifying sense of purpose. Her memoir is therefore something of a hybrid: an oral interview refashioned on the spot into a constructed narrative. There are telltale signs of the manuscript's one-step removal from an interview. Ruth repeats herself frequently. She mistakenly has the Warsaw Ghetto liquidation beginning in July 1941 instead of July 1942. She becomes lost in her thoughts, frozen in time. "There were moments when her eyes watered up," Hull recalls. "These were hard times she was recounting. Some of the memories were painful."[104]

"There was a lot of crying," Adam remembers, who sometimes helped interpret his mother's imperfect English to Hull, occasionally pecking out with two fingers some of the typed story himself. "Harry would come over, and they'd sit down and might go for an hour or, at best, a couple of hours. That was it for that session."[105]

Ruth was clearly uncertain how Hull and future readers would react to her wartime conduct. There is no mention, for instance, of the fact that their benefactor in Schultz's, Stelmaszek, had a reputation for treating Jews brutally, which would have been hard for them not to know. Ruth glosses over the agonizing discussions that she and Mark must have carried on during the fall of 1942, after the liquidation of the ghetto, when they were among the handful of couples in Schultz's Shop—indeed, the entire ghetto—who still had young children.[106]

And then there is the cockamamy story about the Jewish woman posing as a Polish peasant whom she encountered at a friend's house in Aryan Warsaw and who told Ruth about her college-age daughters, one dark-complected and forced to remain hidden, the other blond and allowed to pass as a Catholic Pole. The two daughters were only thinly veiled stand-ins for Anne and Lila. Even though two decades had passed, Ruth was still unable to face long-buried guilt about having had to hide Anne more than Lila. "It's strange," Anne says today, "because she talked about it otherwise, like taking Lila to church on Easter. But I don't know where I was during those times. She never voiced where I was." On the Aryan side Ruth had no choice but to treat her daughters differently. But she was never able to resolve the moral quandary in her own mind, and her fictional narrative is another instance of how everyday norms intrude themselves into wartime memories of situations where "normal" morality did not and could not apply.

Ruth's memoir was a story in progress, nowhere more evident than in her determination to give the Skorecki tale a redemptive ending capable of making sense of the war's tribulations. So, unlike most Holocaust memoirs, which end with liberation, Ruth's narrative extended through 1963, metamorphosing along the way into a classic American immigrant success story. The Skorecki version largely centered on how her two daughters succeeded in school and in marriage and then blessed her with all-American grandchildren. For this was why the family survived, to save those children and give them not merely a normal life but also the American dream—a singular accomplishment in which Ruth took enormous and justifiable pride. But the emphasis in her narrative on her daughters, particularly Anne, the big sister who leapfrogged childhood and of whom more was always expected, obscured the real situation. In the United States it was Adam, not Anne or Lila, who became the center of attention. "All you heard from my grandmother was 'Adam, Adam, Adam,' " says Lila's oldest daughter, Jennifer.[107] Toward Anne, Ruth was stingy with her praise. "If I heard compliments, it was when my mother was talking to one of her survivor friends," Anne says. In fact, it was only in the 1990s that she encountered Ruth's praise directly, after Harry Hull found the concluding third of the the memoir among his possessions. "I was stunned to read her compliments on paper," Anne says. "It was the closest thing to her telling me this in person."

There is an interesting footnote to Ruth's story. Several times before approaching Harry Hull, Ruth had tried to persuade Anne and Lila "to write a book about what happened to us in the days after 1939," as she put it. But the two girls were uninterested. "They never wanted to recall their terrible childhood. They said just forget it, and of course I never pushed them to this." Nonetheless, both the Rockwell incident and the Eichmann trial "stirred up in Anne the terrible memories she and Lila had had as kids." A day or two after Rockwell's arrest, her oldest daughter called. She was crying. "Momma, I have to do it." At first Ruth had no idea what she was talking about, then it became clear that Anne was upset by Rockwell's statement to the press denying the Holocaust had ever happened. It moved the characteristically reticent Anne to fire off a letter to the *New Orleans States-Item*, which ran on May 30, 1961, under the heading "Afraid Suffering of World War II in Vain," just beneath a letter from a right-wing zealot accusing the scriptwriter for the *Exodus* of being one of "the pro-Red Hollywood 'ten.' "

Editor, States-Item:

It is unbelievable that there are men (who call themselves American) in this wonderful land who have the nerve to show their faces wearing Nazi swastikas. I know what it means to see a German Gestapo. A survivor of the last war, when I see such men, it kills all my hope for the betterment of the human race.

I could hardly believe my ears when I heard George Lincoln Rockwell say that the United States should have joined Hitler in World War II. If that statement wasn't enough, when a reporter asked if Hitler was right in murdering six million Jews, Mr. Rockwell had the audacity to say that it was a fabrication, that he (Mr. Rockwell) didn't believe that Hitler was responsible for mass murder. . . .

Sure, I am one of the lucky ones who wasn't in a concentration camp, but I do know what it means to live in the Warsaw ghetto. Although I was only a child, I saw more suffering and dead people than some grownups will see in a lifetime.

In the past month we have heard enough proof during the Eichmann trial to disprove Mr. Rockwell's beliefs. . . .

Since I am the mother of two children now, I would have hoped that my suffering could spare the children of the new generation the agony of hatred, but as long as we have people like the Nazi, I am afraid that all the suffering of World War II was in vain.

"I don't remember writing that letter," Anne says. After mailing it off to the *States-Item*, her wartime memories went back into hibernation, not to reemerge for another quarter century. The later triggering mechanism resembled the circumstances that had brought Ruth face-to-face with the painful past: a neo-Nazi assault on truth and memory. "I guess my mother felt the same way I did when Duke was running for office. I take after her in that respect," notes Anne. But, unlike her mother, Anne would make her witnessing the basis of political action.

Moreover, Anne was always more troubled than her parents by the segregation in which she came of age in America. "I never could get used to the outward signs of segregation," she says. "I never could make myself move the 'colored only' signs that were attached to the seat backs in buses and streetcars and that white passengers moved backward or forward whenever they wanted the seat of some black rider. That was one of the most awful sensations I ever experienced growing up in New Orleans, seeing those signs."

Ruth was diagnosed with breast cancer in September 1968. Two months earlier she had discovered a lump in one of her breasts but put off seeing a doctor until after Adam's August wedding to his first wife. The specialists performed a radical mastectomy. Chemotherapy was then in its infancy, thus Ruth received heavy radiation treatment, which continued off and on for several years. "It was absolutely horrible," Anne says. "Her skin turned brown. They burned her body to a crisp." Though never again as outgoing and gregarious as before her cancer, Ruth did resume her social schedule once she began feeling a little better, going to the beauty parlor, making the rounds of her favorite department stores. But then she developed sharp back and leg pains and splitting headaches. The doctor told her she had a pinched nerve, though it seems likely in hindsight that the cancer had spread to her spinal cord.

She was angry about her illness. Why me? she used to ask. "She was a fighter," Anne says. "She was fighting it as much as she could." To the outside world Ruth continued to show a brave face. Forced to use a cane, she bought umbrellas by the gross instead, and in every conceivable color, to match her wardrobe. (Anne and Lila found an unopened box of umbrellas under her bed after she died.) Her competitiveness remained hardy. When Stan opened an antique shop on Magazine Street in 1969, putting Anne in charge until the business began generating enough income to justify quitting his job at Morton's, Ruth opened a rival antique business across the street and had Mark move his shop to the new store.

Toward the end, when she was confined to home, she asked Lila to call Mrs. Doerries, who had since moved across the lake. Ask her to come for visit, she said. It was a farewell visit. "Evidently she was in the last stages and she knew it," Mrs. Doerries says. "I went to see her. She was really yellow at the time. But I didn't face up to death very well. It was hard for me talk to her, and I acted like she was going to get well."[108]

In July 1973 Ruth came down with a bad case of flu. Everyone thought she would recover soon, but she continued to worsen. An ambulance took her to the hospital on Friday, July 20. She could barely do more than talk in a whisper. Anne and Stan were in Rome at the time, on a brief vacation during one of his increasingly frequent European buying trips. Anne tried calling her mother but received no answer. She also failed to reach Lila. "Stan, something's wrong. I want to go home." They arrived back in New Orleans on Sunday, July 22. "I went to see her at the hospital. She recognized me. It was as though she was waiting for me." Ruth died the next day, before daybreak.

Adam, who had been extremely close to his mother, was devastated by her death. Lila took her mother's passing extremely hard. She had just miscarried the week before and was about to move into a new house she and Norman had bought so as to be closer to her parents. "I didn't think anything could hurt me any more than when my mother died," Lila says.

Anne was also deeply affected by her mother's death. "She felt sorrow like anybody would who lost a mother," Stan says. "But from my observation, probably deep, deep down where nobody sees, there was a little relief, because the pressure was off."[109]

fourteen

AWAKENING

David Duke's meteoric rise in Louisiana politics was not the only reason Anne Levy began beckoning memories from her wartime past. Filial obligation was already pulling her backward in time. But with Anne the obligation to remember surged from such a troubling and profound experience, its awakening came on her like an implacable instinct. The personal dimension was the physical deterioration of her father, who died in 1991; Mark Skorecki's decline affected Anne deeply, but when her personal loss became intermingled with political events both unbidden and unwanted, the fusion transformed grieving into a survivor's mission. It was as though the challenge represented by David Duke's political ascendancy at long last allowed Anne to find meaning in the trauma of a stolen childhood and to unify, across the caesura of war, fragments of life that seemed forever disjointed by the Holocaust itself.

Anne was extremely close to her father, temperamental affinities that dated back to prewar strolls for ice cream in downtown Łódź and postwar car trips through the rolling Bavarian countryside searching for eggs and fresh flowers. Most of all, the close bonding was anchored in survival itself. "He was the reason my sister and I are here today," Anne says. Thus, when her father's health started deteriorating rapidly, practically in tandem with Duke's astonishing political advance, Anne reacted with a fury almost uncontrollable. It was as though her father was being defamed as he lay dying, as though a world historical tragedy responsible for ruining Mark's life was being derided and discounted. This was more than political. It was personal, and she took it that way. Says Robin, Anne's second daughter, "I think my mother's political activism was a kind of payback to my grandfather for saving the family."[1]

Mark outlived Ruth by more than two decades, and there were some happy moments during that period. Most of them occurred at work, however. Soon after closing the antique store Ruth had opened to compete with Stan, Mark moved his business back to Morton's Auction Exchange in the warehouse district. Then, several years later, following an unsuccessful attempt at retirement, he moved his shop to Stan's new store on Louisiana Avenue. He never lost his perfectionism, refusing to allow salespersons into his shop before repairs were completed on some customer's order. "You can't see this yet. You have to come back," says Bevy Kearney, who sold antiques at Stan's store during Mark's stay there. His independent streak was as strong as ever. Rather than seek help when gluing pieces together, he would rig up a contraption to hang furniture from the ceiling so as to get the perfect fit. He continued to lose himself in his work. Often Anne had to remind him it was time for lunch. Then he would come up front with his brown bag and whole wheat bread, meticulously slice two hard-boiled eggs, neatly placing them on top of the cream cheese spread, and then quietly—gratefully—eat his sandwich. In the work setting he became "quite the character," notes Kearney.[2]

By that point everybody was calling him Tata—the Polish diminutive for *Tataschu*, or "father"—and they often dropped in at Morton's or Stan's store to see him or just to be entertained. Short and wiry, his nose now blurring across his face, Mark had the stage presence of a thick-spectacled George Burns, even down to the cheap cigar. "For anyone who really knew my grandfather there was always an opportunity to chuckle because he had this quirky, fun sense of humor," says Robin, "and he was a flirt and a tease, especially with older women." "I'm glad you're here. The day would not be complete without you," he used tell the attractive Bevy Kearney every morning, revealing some of the charm he had doubtless displayed during his courtship of Ruth. "Women just loved him because he was a tender, funny, innocent old man," Robin says.[3]

Mark enjoyed playing with English words, using his accent to set up a joke or mask ridicule. "So you're a radiologist? What kind of radios you work on?" he once asked a young medical resident. He ridiculed the city's new domed stadium. "Superdumb," he scoffed, and people were never quite sure where the accent left off and the sarcasm began. "Visiting Tata in his shop, there was always a joke," says Bevy Kearney. "But you'd have to sit and look at him and think about it for a few minutes, and then you'd say, 'Oh, my goodness.'"[4]

Mark and his granddaughter Robin grew especially close because she shared his fascination with wood and artifice. A graduate of the Rhode Island School of Design, she would seek Tata's assistance with some of her projects. He seldom understood her artwork, which tended toward the abstract. "Why do you want this? This is no good." He poked fun at her Bohemian dress. "Are you going to a circus today?" "What is that thing you have on? Your skirt. There's only half of it. Only half a skirt."[5] But he took pride in his granddaughter's sense of artisanry. "What separated me from my siblings and cousins was that I really shared Tata's intrigue with this tactile experience," she says. "And there was an element of warmth that I pulled out of my grandfather because I knew that I could. I didn't sense I could pull that out of my grandmother."[6]

But outside the workplace, Mark was taciturn, emotionally withdrawn, and unhappy—just the opposite of what he was in public. "He didn't relate to his family," says Stan, with the exception of Robin.[7]

Simply, Mark Skorecki never rebounded from the death of his wife. Despite their bickering, the two had been extremely close, as only couples could be who had experienced what they had gone through together. "Though people never saw it, because my parents weren't demonstrative people," Anne says, "there had to have been a strong bond between my mother and father for him to have come back to the ghetto to rescue the family." After Ruth's death, Mark refused to let anyone disturb her belongings, except the jewelry, which Anne and Lila divided. He slept in the same bedroom. Everything had to stay the way she had left them just before being rushed to the hospital. The wardrobe Ruth had pinched pennies to accumulate still hung in the closet. Dress boxes, some never opened, filled the cedar chest in the bedroom. Umbrellas of every hue gathered dust under the bed. Even Ruth's breast prosthesis, purchased after her radical mastectomy, was tucked away inside a dresser drawer. "The house was like a mausoleum," Anne says.

"My mother should not have died so young, and he should not have died so old," says Adam, who has prospered as an attorney in Atlanta. The famous Tempelhof grin tightens into a narrow slit as he gazes on the postmodernist sprawl just outside his twenty-eighth-floor office window. "If there is a God, and he ordains a destiny, it was wrong to make them suffer through the war together, have a life like they did, and then separate their deaths by such a long period of time. It was hell on my sisters. They were the ones who felt the burden of his unhappiness."[8]

Anne caught most of the brunt, torn by the same conflicting loyalties that had pulled at her while her mother was still alive. Things became even more difficult after she and Stan separated for a six-month period in the mid-1970s. It was partly a delayed reaction to Ruth's death. "I had a lot of resentment in my system, and it festered," Stan admits.[9] Still mourning her mother, Anne was devastated. "I blame it on his forties. I guess he had had enough. It was one of the hardest times I have ever gone through." Worst was Mark's insistence that his daughter have all the Levy property placed in her own name. He complained about Stan's social drinking. He let his anger splash over onto her children. "My grandfather would say very nasty things to me about my father," says Sheryl, Anne's oldest. "He'd say that my father was a drunk and that he was going to lose everything and that the business was going down the tubes."

Sheryl, who could be as outspoken as her mother was reticent, would shoot back, "You're just a bitter old man, and I don't know why you're doing this to me." It took only a few of these exchanges for the rupture to become permanent. Mark nursed grudges, like survivors often do, and he never grew accustomed to American children sassing their elders. It was not the way European children behaved. Thereafter he refused even to acknowledge Sheryl's presence when she entered the room. "It made me a little nuts because he and Robin were very close, and I was like my father, whom he didn't like," Sheryl says. Anne tried to mend fences between the estranged members of her family. "You should never say anything like that," she told her father. "My relationship with my husband has nothing to do with you." Mark's coolness toward her thawed over the years, "but it was just degrees of ice," Sheryl says.[10]

With Anne's youngest daughter, Carol, Tata's relationship was equally strained. Under five feet in height and slight in stature, Carol had the quickest temper of all Anne's daughters and a sharp tongue to match. She never thought twice about talking back to her grandfather. After Carol moved in with her Irish Catholic boyfriend (they later married and divorced), Anne was desperate to conceal the affair from her father. It was not so much the living together that she wanted to keep secret as the young man's Catholicism. Tata was not religious; the Holocaust had extinguished his faith in God. But his views on Jewish cultural continuity and connectedness with other Jews were annealed in the fires of the Shoah. "Marrying outside the group was his cutoff point," says Robin. At one point she too was seeing an older, non-Jewish man. Mark warned her she would end up isolating herself from family and friends if they married. "It was clear to me his bottom line was: you don't have to keep kosher, you don't have to observe the Sabbath, you don't have to go to synagogue once a week. But you gotta marry a Jew. You gotta be with your own people. He didn't know any differently."[11]

When he discovered that Carol was living with her non-Jewish boyfriend, he thus demanded that Anne disown her daughter. Anne, displeased about the relationship but reluctant to intervene, tried to reason with her father. But he was adamant. There was no other side, no other alternative but to do as he ordered. "You know, I'm in my middle forties," Anne told Sheryl at the time, "and my father is still giving me crap because my kids are doing stuff that I have no control over." This time she stood up to him. "Daddy, believe what you want," she said, her voice cracking and going soft, as it normally does when moroseness sets in, "but this is my life."[12]

"My mom was put in the middle of having to choose between her father and her child," notes Carol. It was an old pattern, set early in the marriage by Ruth's ceaseless demands and expectations, and now Mark was keeping the inner turmoil churning. In 1983 doctors found a tumor on Mark's lung and intimated to the family that he had less than six months to live; he had just turned eighty-three. Carol, seeking to make amends, visited him in the hospital. She asked if he would give her a hug. "No, you're too old for that," he snapped.[13] He lived for seven more years. They had to have been the most emotionally tumultuous yet strangely transformative years of Anne's life to that point in America.

As stormy as Anne's family life could be, the Levy and Skorecki households seem Edenic by comparison with the dysfunctional family dynamics that molded David Duke. Born in 1950, the year after the Skoreckis disembarked in the Crescent City, Duke spent his teenage years in the same Lakefront neighborhood where several New Americans had relocated after achieving prosperity. Unhappiness stalked the Duke residence. His father, a petroleum engineer with Shell Oil who was often away on business for long stretches of time, was a disciplinarian around the home. Duke nonetheless revered him. His mother, on the other hand, an accomplished golfer who became addicted to alcohol and prescription pills, growing reclusive during her son's early adolescence, was the target of Duke's anger. He once threatened to set her on fire if she refused to stop drinking. "A lot of David's anger is against my mom," Duke's older sister and only sibling, Dotti, told the writer Jason Berry. "To this day he'll say it wasn't that bad, but it was worse for him than me. He never came to terms with it." Dotti eloped when she was seventeen to escape the domestic turmoil.[14]

Tall, gangling, and bookishly fascinated with insects and chemistry sets, the nonathletic Duke was the butt of schoolyard jokes. "Puke Duke" or "Duke Puke," classmates jeered in his face. His friends were few, and those who did befriend him were put off by his know-it-all pushiness. When he was fourteen Duke visited the White Citizens Council offices in downtown New Orleans to gather material for a paper on integration. The council was a sort of Klan without sheets, a Rotary Club of hard-line segregationists. The New Orleans office gave him a copy of *Race and Reason* (1961) by Carleton Putnam, a northern-born Ivy League graduate who, in his vigorous defense of scientific racism following the 1954 *Brown* decision, resembled a "latter-day Madison Grant." Arch-segregationists lionized Putnam, Mississippi even proclaiming a "Race and Reason Day." In Louisiana the State Board of Education made the book mandatory reading for all college faculty and deans and for all students enrolled in anthropology, sociology, and psychology courses.[15] Duke thought the book was the best thing he had ever read.

The year he plunged into Putnam's white supremacist tract, the racial crisis in Louisiana was coming to a head. The Congress of Racial Equality (CORE) and the Student Non-Violent Coordinating Committee (SNCC) were dispatching student activists into rural parishes, the Louisiana Ku Klux Klan exploded in racial violence, and Congress enacted the 1964 Public Accommodations Act. Duke claims he was liberal up to that point, but his father, a staunch segregationist, was "conservative to the max," as sister Dotti puts it, and the private Christian school he was then attending was a segregationist academy. And the year before, in 1963, Duke had shocked his Sunday school class by openly endorsing Hitler's views on the Jews. Before long he was sporting swastika rings, brandishing a copy of *Mein Kampf*, and draping his bedroom with Nazi flags. Soon he would go on a "racial odyssey" to India, the original heartland of Aryanism, returning home with a Hitlerian mustache and a Führer-like forelock drooped over his brow.[16] Where his obsession with Jews originated is not easy to discern. Putnam's book, like that of other so-called racial scientists, blamed the "equalitarian dogma" of the times on "minority" Jewish social scientists. But it is just as likely that Duke acquired his anti-Semitism from a Catholic priest who became a sort of father figure to the lonely teenager during the elder Duke's long absences from home. Clearly, unlike most other white supremacists in the American South, Duke came to racism by way of National Socialism, and not the other way around. He was a Nazi before he was an antiblack racist.[17]

In any event, by age nineteen, during his sophomore year at Louisiana State University in Baton Rouge, Duke was a self-proclaimed professional Nazi, heading a succession of student groups—the National Socialist Liberation Front, the White Student Alliance, the White Youth Alliance—that had links to William Pierce's National Alliance and to the National Socialist White People's Party, the successor organization to Lincoln Rockwell's American Nazi Party. From a makeshift forum in front of the Student Union called Free Speech Alley, Duke regularly harangued students about Jews, communism, and the black menace. Student antiwar sentiment was just starting to take hold on the Baton Rouge campus, leading Duke to receive catcalls and heckling. But he had become inured to such treatment in grade school, and he threw the taunts back in the crowd's face: "I'm a National Socialist. You can call me a Nazi if you want to." Sixteen years later, he said the same thing in a taped interview with Evelyn Rich, a Ph.D. student from Boston researching Ku Klux Klan ideology. "My basic ideology, as far as what I believe about race, about the Jewish question, is the same. My difference is in tactics and organization." This was recorded in 1985, a scant four years before Duke stunned the nation with his election as a "mainstream conservative" Republican to the lower house of the Louisiana legislature.[18]

Duke's core beliefs derive from Nazi race theory—basically, an amalgam of conspiratorial anti-Semitism and biological determinism. The former blames Jews for modernity's woes, from rampant materialism to soulless communism. Jews are "cultural distorters," purveyors of pornography (the Talmud, he once said, is steeped in pedophilia). The latter, the biological tenets of Duke's thought, embodies a utopian faith in what he is pleased to call, after Hitler, "racial idealism." It is the notion that culture resides in the genes, "that the real answer to the world's problems was not in better tools of men, but in better men," to quote from his 1985 interview with Rich. Blacks are almost incidental in Duke's scheme. He has long regarded them as an inferior species, not major threats. Jews, on the other hand, fill him with obsessional dread. The civil rights movement was not a grassroots struggle for black liberation but a plot by Jewish financial and media moguls to undermine "white Christian civilization" through forced busing and miscegenous pollution of the gene pool. Applied biology—eugenics and sterilization—is the best way of fighting back. But before that defense could be mounted, Jewish power had to be smashed. Duke's belief that the American "melting pot" was a prescription for "race suicide" went far beyond traditional antialien nativism. He was an unabashed revolutionary. He even envisioned the demographic restructuring of America, confining Jews to Long Island, sequestering African Americans within a Madagascar-like ribbon of land along the gulf coast, a plan harking back to efforts by Nazi race theorists during the World War II to Germanize the "east" by shunting millions across national frontiers.[19]

Throughout the 1970s and 1980s the American far right engaged in lively intramural debates over strategy and tactics. Violence has always possessed a seductive appeal to the kind of people aroused by the rhetoric of hate. But among neo-Nazi leaders and theoreticians in America, from George Lincoln Rockwell through Willis Carto of the Liberty Lobby, the appeal of electoral politics has had a constant allure. Indeed, for Rockwell, rabble-rousing was merely the first phase in a multifaceted campaign to build a majority political party around an inner core of race-conscious movement activists. The model was suggested by Hitler, who captured national power only after shelving the tactics of the putsch in favor of running for office. There were also theoretical reasons for resorting to mass politics—namely, the biologistic assumption that racial consciousness was genetically imprinted in every individual and merely required proper nourishment to blossom into "spiritual unity" among genetically like-minded individuals.[20]

Early on, Duke gravitated toward the movement-building and electioneering strategy, not least because of a delusional belief that he alone was the charismatic "great white hope."[21] In his new guise he had an American role model to draw on: Rockwell himself. Duke consciously patterned his speaking style after that of the commander, reciting some of his speeches word for word. His early media antics mimicked Rockwell's theatricality. The most famous publicity stunt was his 1970 picketing in full Nazi regalia outside a Tulane University auditorium where William Kunstler, the radical activist lawyer, was delivering a speech. Duke paraded back and forth with a placard reading "Kunstler is a Communist Jew" and "Gas the Chicago Seven." At the height of the 1974 Boston school bus crisis, Duke tried to reprise Rockwell's 1961 "hate ride" by threatening to dispatch a caravan of "Freedom Rides North."[22]

Duke—and other neo-Nazis, for that matter—ultimately broke with the commander's teachings over the wisdom of using an explicitly Nazi organization to build a popular movement. It quickly became apparent that even staunch Klansmen, particularly veterans of World War II, were repelled by associations with the Third Reich. James K. Warner, who joined the American Nazi Party after being thrown out of the U.S. Air Force for Nazi sympathies and lived in wooded seclusion with Rockwell during a period when the commander was in suicidal despair over the breakup of his second marriage, broke with the commander largely for this reason, accusing Rockwell of "trying to discredit and smear all those who are the top fighters against Communism by labeling them as Nazis or worse!" Warner eventually threw in with the neo-Nazi National States Rights Party led by J. B. Stoner and Dr. Ed Fields.[23]

Duke followed a similar path in 1973 when he formed his own sheeted organization, the Knights of the Ku Klux Klan, naming himself Grand Wizard and confecting a mythical Tennessee lineage for the organization to forestall criticism that his was an "upstart Klan." The Klan's long tradition and native roots furnished ideal cover for propagating Nazism. "It's very difficult to label us neo-Nazi because we are a completely American organization," explained Don Black, one of Duke's early lieutenants, who is currently married to Duke's first wife.[24] Duke was never committed to the Klan as an institution; it was merely a means to an end. At the outset the *Crusader*, the organization's newspaper, announced that the Knights were a different kind of Klan. Of central importance was the task of smashing "Jewish power." In addition, the Knights favored political activism instead of "nigger bashing." An editorial in the *Crusader*'s first issue called for constructing a "White political machine" to combat the "minoritization" of America. The project would have to be grass roots in nature, owing to the nature of Jewish control. "Jewish power comes from a national level downward with only its weakest tentacles reaching down to the local community. Local politics, working upward, is the soft underbelly of their empire, one that can be pierced." The idea was vintage Rockwell.[25]

At the same time, Duke set about to bring his Klan into the modern age, opening membership to women, preaching nonviolence, and constantly striving to give the Klan a patina of respectability. "For Duke image was everything."[26]

The new emphasis on decorum led him to refine Rockwell's media strategy. Instead of shock, Duke would employ the element of surprise, confounding conventional stereotypes of Klansmen as rural know-nothings and slack-jawed droolers. The strategy was tailor-made for the dawning era of tabloid television journalism, with its call-waiting interest in the "newest" this or "zaniest" that. Duke noticed that the NBC talk show host Tom Snyder was building ratings by inviting devil worshipers and sideshow curiosities on his program, and he was willing to come on the show as a guest Grand Wizard. Snyder jumped at the offer. Duke, appearing in three-piece suit, his lines well rehearsed, soon had Snyder gushing. "I'd always thought of the Klan as being a bunch of old fogies who were concerned with yesterday," he told Duke. "But you're intelligent, articulate, charming."[27] More radio and television appearances quickly followed. Duke started making the rounds on the college lecture circuit, taping most of his appearances, which he later sold through his mail-order catalog. The *Crusader* ran several puff pieces extolling the Grand Wizard's charisma and brilliance, most of them penned by Duke himself.[28]

Meanwhile, as foretold in the *Crusader*'s maiden issue, he campaigned for office as well, running for seats in the state senate from Baton Rouge and Metairie, in 1975 and 1979, respectively. He did surprisingly well, garnering as much as a third of the vote in one primary race, but it is far from certain that he ran to win. The paramount motivation seems to have been the lure of media attention. "Through a political campaign we can get thousands of dollars worth of free publicity," he argued in one of his newspapers.[29]

Duke's new media strategy and Klan makeover paid quick dividends. The Knights's roster began to grow. The ADL said Duke was chiefly responsible for reversing a decade-long decline in Klan membership. A four-part series in the *Los Angeles Herald Examiner* marveled, "Duke—an articulate, media-hip Louisianian who prefers a finely tailored business suit to a loose-fitting robe—has taken a dying hate group and tried to turn it into a mainstream 'movement of love' every bit as respectable as the Elks, Masons or Rotarians."[30]

More significant was the sort of follower Duke was beginning to attract, men such as James K. Warner, Tom Metzger, Don Black, Karl Hand, William Grimstead, and Louis Beam. What they generally had in common, besides a college education, was prior involvement in the neo-Nazi movement and a shared interest in finding an appropriate vehicle for mainstreaming their beliefs.[31] Duke seemed to have solved the extreme right's image problem. He was ideologically attuned. He was mediagenic. He appealed to youth. He came across as "the thinking man's racist." Warner, Metzger, and the others all became officers in Duke's Knights of the Ku Klux Klan. Warner relocated to the New Orleans area, moving his Identity Church ministry to Metairie (it is now in St. Bernard Parish).[32]

Their accession to Duke's organization accelerated the Nazification of the Klan, a trend for which Duke can claim major responsibility. Older, more traditionalist Klan leaders were displeased about this development. It was not just the adulation of Hitler they found disturbing but also the overweening emphasis on anti-Semitism. True, they themselves were anti-Semitic. They frequently railed against Communist Jewish outside agitators in their publications and during their cross-burning rallies. But they never embraced conspiratorial anti-Semitism, nor did they agree that hatred of Jews should receive greater priority than antiblack racism. Duke and his lieutenants tried to camouflage their project by minimizing overt Nazi associations. But it was obvious what was taking place. Within the Klan movement the *Crusader* had swiftly become the central clearinghouse for disseminating ideas from the neofascist right. Its mail-order columns peddled the movement's canonical works—such publications as Hitler's *Mein Kampf*, Rockwell's *White Power*, Francis Yockey's *Imperium*, Wilmot Robertson's *The Dispossessed*, and pamphlets and books by former physics professor and Rockwell ideologist William Pierce, founder of the National Alliance. It was through Duke's *Crusader* that the doctrines of Christian identity—which hold that Jews are the children of Satan and blacks are "mud people"—seeped into Klan discourse. Holocaust revisionism was introduced to hooded Americans through the paper. William Grimstead, author of *The Six Million Reconsidered*, one of the earliest statements of Holocaust denial, was an early Duke recruit whose columns appeared regularly in the *Crusader*. The stress on Holocaust revisionism underscored the new anti-Semitic agenda gaining ground within the Klan movement. Holocaust denial refurbished conspiratorial anti-Semitism. Who else but Jews had the media power to hoodwink unsuspecting masses with one of the greatest hoaxes in history? And for what motive? To promote the claims of the illegitimate state of Israel by making non-Jews feel guilty, of course. Writes Evelyn Rich, "An ideological osmosis was occurring at a rapid pace, accompanied by a physical osmosis, to the extent it was becoming more and more difficult to know where the Klan ended and the neo-Nazi movement began."[33]

But if Duke succeeded brilliantly in Nazifying the Klan and training a new generation of white activists, he fell far short of galvanizing a mass following. At its height the Knights numbered about three thousand members, and there is reason to believe that even these numbers are inflated. The seventies were unpropitious times for building a right-wing populist movement. Granted, the fall of Vietnam, followed by stagflation and the oil crisis, undermined a national sense of mastery. The Watergate scandal and the Iran hostage crisis then shook public confidence in the integrity and efficacy of governmental institutions. These developments would have long-range implications for national politics. But in the meantime, white attitudes on race were softening, receding from old-fashioned notions of black biological inferiority, and the trend was evident even in the former Confederacy. After passage of the 1965 Voting

Rights Act, a new generation of moderate Democrats, such as Bill Clinton in Arkansas, William Winter in Mississippi, and Edwin Edwards in Louisiana, pieced together low-status coalitions of blacks and whites by muting racial issues. In the 1980s these biracial alliances would fall apart owing to white fear and resentment, but in the 1960s they stymied efforts by far-right agitators to gain backlash support.[34]

By the time Reagan became president, most neo-Nazi leaders had given up on using electoral politics to win power. Terrorism began to loom as a popular alternative. Duke's Nazified Knights attracted its share of what he later called "weirdos, or nuts looking for publicity and violence." They showed up at his headquarters wanting his organization to carry out the moral vigilantism long practiced by the traditional Klan, like disciplining errant husbands, bashing local drunks, and intimidating "uppity" blacks. James K. Warner abandoned Duke's Knights because it appealed mainly to society's failures. "You couldn't educate them except for niggers. . . . They couldn't get into the Masons and they couldn't get into the Moose, so they joined the Klan. They could show their card at the bar. . . . It was a temporary fix for their lives." They weren't "good material." They had no grasp of the Jewish question.[35]

By the late 1970s Duke had already begun to lose members and subscribers to a rival Klan headed by Bill Wilkinson (who later proved to be an FBI informant). Wilkinson's organization, also based in Louisiana, was folksier and more traditional than the Knights, but its chief advantage was its incitement to violence. The racial strife that occurred in Alabama and Mississippi in 1978 and 1979, as well as the Klansmen massacre in 1979 in Greensboro, North Carolina, of five radical leftist activists participating in a civil rights rally, is widely attributed to Wilkinson's action-oriented tactics. Around the same time, several Klan organizations set up secret paramilitary training camps.[36]

Propelled by political frustration and conspiratorial anti-Semitism, the escalation of rightist violence prefigured a revolutionary shift within the neo-Nazi and Klan movement in general. For all the emphasis on mass conversions of white racialists, the previous decade's movement-building labors—mugging for the camera, running for office, staging rallies and cross burnings—were largely barren of results. Theoreticians on the ultra-right attributed the dismal recruiting harvest to white false consciousness, which they blamed in turn on the "Jewish-run" media and the Zionist Occupied Government (ZOG) in Washington, D.C. Given the ubiquity of Jewish domination, there was only one avenue of escape: vanguard politics and guerrilla terrorism, culminating in a full-scale violent revolution. This was a new departure for hooded Americanism, the first time in American history that the Klan movement became truly revolutionary, as opposed to merely reactionary, a change that "could not have occurred," according to Evelyn Rich, "without the elevation of antisemitism to the position of cornerstone of Klan ideology." A few older Klan stalwarts, such as Robert Shelton, refused to go along with the new policy, but the revolutionary tide soon swamped the Nazified redoubts of the American Klan.[37]

A sense of history also helped propel the strategic shift, articulated by Robert Miles, a former insurance executive who had headed Michigan's 1968 George Wallace for President campaign and later served time in prison for plotting to bomb school buses used in Detroit's school busing program. In 1983 he authored a sweeping historical overview of the Ku Klux Klan, dividing the organization's history into five eras and arguing that the "Fourth Era"—the "Television Era" of the late 1960s and 1970s—was "dying and passing into history." Although the leading personalities of the "Fourth Era" were sincere, Miles wrote, in pointed allusion to Duke, they were actors, not leaders. The eighties would usher in the "Fifth Era," a period of revolutionary violence waged by underground cells. While Miles's widely influential manifesto was circulating in Klan circles, William Pierce published *The Turner Diaries*, a futuristic fantasy that glorified bank robberies, bombings of government installations, and public lynchings of race traitors. Before long the neo-Nazi movement was conducting Boer-like "outtreks" to Aryan compounds in the Pacific Northwest, mountain fastnesses in the Ozarks, and backwood hideaways in the Blue Ridge Mountains.[38]

The Midwest faced a raft of shootouts. In 1983 and 1984, a neo-Nazi terrorist group called the Order, drawing inspiration from *The Turner Diaries* and led by a disaffected construction worker named Robert Mathews, unleashed a multistate crime spree of bank robberies and armored car heists that ended in the assassination of Alan Berg, a Jewish talk show host in Phoenix, followed soon after by Mathews's death in a shootout in Washington state. The militia-related bombing activity in the 1990s derived from the shift toward revolutionary violence that had occurred in the preceding decade.[39]

This sharp turn toward vanguard politics within the racist right threw Duke into a quandary. One lieutenant after another joined the revolutionary trend. In 1981 Tom Metzger left the Knights to form a Nazi skinhead organization called the White Aryan Resistance (WAR). Louis Beam, leader of the Texas Knights, dismissed Duke's vision of "numberless masses marching behind the banner of the Ku Klux Klan" as an "unobtainable illusion." Instead of the ballot box he preferred "knives, guns, and courage," the Klan tactics of southern Reconstruction, the "First Era." He went underground.[40]

All the while, Duke's personal stature within the Klan movement was badly eroding, leaving him isolated. *The Truth about David Duke*, a 1976 pamphlet penned by a disaffected follower, characterized the Grand Wizard as a "money-hungry egomaniac." Duke's narcissism added to his growing list of internal enemies. For the finale of a 1979 Klan National Leadership Meeting in Metairie, the Grand Wizard came on stage bare-chested and clad in shorts and started lifting weights to show off his new physique. "It was all some people could do to avoid laughing," said Metzger. A few years earlier, under the pseudonyms James Konrad and Dorothy Vanderbilt, Duke authored a "sexual self-help book" for women called *Finders Keepers*, crammed with helpful advice about vaginal contraction exercises, oral and anal sex, and adultery. Steeped in traditional puritanism, the Klan movement was scandalized. Duke's womanizing bordered on the compulsive.[41] One breakaway member of Duke's Knights accused him of "conduct unbecoming a racist." "Don't leave your wife, your girlfriend or your daughter alone with this guy," he warned.[42] By the end of the seventies, Duke's marriage was dissolving, along with his ties to the Klan movement. The final rupture occurred in 1979 after Duke was secretly videotaped trying to sell his Knights's mailing list to Klan rival Bill Wilkinson—an egregious breach of the absolute rule of Klan confidentiality.[43]

That same year, after leaving the Klan, which for him had always been an instrumentality rather than an end in itself, Duke formed the National Association for the Advancement of White People, a name he appears to have borrowed, without attribution, from a racist organization that had operated in Baltimore in the 1950s. He described his new organization as a "white rights" association, but it was the Klan without sheets. The classified section of the NAAWP News advertised Duke's backlist of mail-order Nazism: books by Hitler, Rockwell, and Alfred Rosenberg; publications downplaying and denying the Holocaust; audio- and videotapes of Duke and Rockwell expatiating on the Jewish question. Throughout the 1980s contributors to its columns extolled Aryan supremacy, advocating separate racial homelands for hyphenated nationalities—ethnic cleansing American-style. They proposed low-interest loans to cum laude college graduates who agreed to have more children—a knockoff of the Nazi *Lebensborn* program. Another suggestion was colonization of the heavens with a super race of Aryanauts. And Duke changed his face, as well as his masthead. He had his nose fixed, his chin lifted. Chemicals burned away the crowsfeet around his eyes. The drooping Hitler forelock was recoifed into news anchor perfection. His polyester wardrobe became more modish, to showcase the body. But the surgical changes were consistent with his lifelong quest to find the right vehicle for recruiting Americans to Nazism. For as Lance Hill, a close student of Duke's political makeovers, has put it, "Ironically, the less Duke appears to be a Nazi, the more he fits the historical uniform."[44]

Yet, Duke seemed adrift in the go-go eighties, "a prophet without an audience," according to biographer Tyler Bridges. Flirting with the new revolutionary activism, he played labor broker to a 1980 right-wing filibuster expedition—dubbed the Bayou of Pigs by local wags—seeking to overthrow the government of Dominica. (Arrested before debarking, the mercenaries were later convicted and imprisoned, though Duke himself was not indicted.) He popped up in such racial trouble spots as Howard's Beach in Queens, New York, and Forsyth County, Georgia, where he raised legal defense funds under false pretenses. He attended annual conferences of the California-based Institute for Historical Review, for refresher courses in Holocaust denial. He studied German in Austria, cultivating ties with the neofascist movement on the Continent. Once, he gave his girlfriend a "revisionist" tour of the Mauthausen concentration camp. And for his close friends he continued throwing a yearly Adolf Hitler birthday party in his Metairie residence.[45] Careerwise, however, he seemed stalled.

There were significant money problems as well. At one point he was reduced to hustling money for meals in local restaurants by table-hopping for handouts. "I'm David Duke, and I'm the head of the NAAWP. Can you make a donation?" he would ask startled diners. Later in the decade, following a good run playing the stock market, his finances improved enough to finance gambling junkets to Las Vegas.[46]

By now a more rational person would have thrown in the towel or joined the revolutionary underground. But Duke never wearied of running for office. His delusional self-image as the white messiah no doubt buoyed his spirits in the face of repeated setbacks. It also helped that Willis Carto, the Liberty Lobby head and founder of the Institute for Historical Review who was steadfastly committed to electoral politics, remained in Duke's corner. As publisher of the country's foremost anti-Semitic newspaper, the *Spotlight*, Carto possessed the financial wherewithal to fund far-rightist campaigns. After campaigning in the 1988 Democratic presidential primaries on a "send them a message" platform, Duke became the standard-bearer of Carto's Populist Party, an aggregation of skinheads, white supremacists, and neo-Nazis. Duke garnered a minuscule percentage of the vote, but he had not entered the race expecting to win. He was after headlines.[47]

It was therefore ironic when the NAAWP leader erupted into mainstream politics in 1989. The breakthrough caught everyone off guard, including local pollsters who underestimated Duke's hidden vote. It happened when an incumbent state legislator from the 81st House District in Metairie suddenly resigned his seat to become a state judge. Duke swiftly changed his registration to Republican, moved to an apartment inside the district, and ran first in the primary. Then he eked out a runoff victory against a long-time Republican stalwart. The Jefferson Parish sheriff, a heavyset, Chinese American good old boy named Harry Lee, famously characterized the choice as one between "a bigot and an asshole." The bigot won partly because of a sudden infusion of money from Carto's organization—nearly $140,000, or six times the amount spent by Duke's opponents. Carto even dispatched a staff member to work on Duke's campaign, keeping her on after the election to manage Duke's legislative office.[48]

Notwithstanding Carto's timely support, Duke's narrow victory was hardly a fluke. The racial and economic polarization that defined politics in the late 1980s got a headstart in Louisiana. Throughout the preceding decade, the Republican Party's "southern strategy" of race-tinged attacks on welfare and "big government" steadily shunted substantial numbers of the state's blue-collar Democrats into the Reagan-Bush column, disrupting the biracial coalition that the heirs of Huey and Earl Long had carefully assembled following the civil rights movement. The realignment was happening nationally, of course, with Wallace Democrats mutating steadily into Reagan Democrats. What made Louisiana unusual, however, was the early arrival of economic downsizing brought on by the collapse of the state's oil economy in the early 1980s. Hard times further undermined white, middle-class faith in established institutions just as soaring crime rates, exacerbated by the Reagan administration's deep cuts in urban expenditures, raised anxiety levels about the moral order. Immediately bordering primarily black New Orleans, Duke's overwhelmingly white suburban district was on the front lines of the emerging racial conflict. Duke's message had resonance, and not merely because of what he said (which differed little from what he had been saying since 1975). Who he was formed part of the message too. By 1989, politically alienated white voters in District 81 wanted a stronger voice for "white people," and Duke's Klan past heralded him as somebody capable of delivering on his threats for a change. "We need him now," a Duke supporter said during the runoff. "We have to send a message to the blacks."[49]

Yet, for all of his past extremism, Duke worked to keep up the appearance of centrist moderation, even after the center began shifting to the right. He took pains to renounce the Klan. He apologized for "youthful indiscretions." He cast aside explicit racism. He now spoke in the language of racial "differences," not racial inferiority. Blacks he criticized for cultural rather than genetic failings, which meshed with the national mood of blaming inner city poverty on a deficiency of family values. Admittedly, another layer of codespeak encrusted Duke's rhetoric—Nazi euphemisms such as "founding white majority" in lieu of Aryan supremacy, or simply "majority"—but it would take time for the untrained ear to catch on.[50]

Meanwhile, national Republicans were thrown into confusion by Duke's use of party credentials to achieve his breakthrough. The last thing they expected was a challenge from the white supremacist right. Outflanking Duke on race was out of the question, if only because it risked pulling a symbolic hood over the head of every Republican in the country. As events would show, many state Republican leaders were scarcely bothered by these concerns. But such Washington insiders as Presidents George Bush and Ronald Reagan, as well as Lee Atwater, then head of the Republican National Committee, were sufficiently alarmed to issue personal pleas to support Duke's runoff opponent. Their unprecedented intervention in an obscure local election may have backfired, fueling populist "outsider" resentments.[51]

Rather than an aberration, Duke's legislative victory represented a fortuitous union of symbol and mood, a classic instance of the wrong man being in the right place at the wrong time. His breakthrough unleashed a far-right insurgency that kept Louisiana's electoral waters roiling for two more election cycles, even moving national politics further to the right. One day Louisianians were debating fiscal reform. The next they were talking about race. And Duke was largely the reason why.

Anne Levy was as stunned as anyone by the political developments in neighboring Jefferson Parish. They impelled her confrontation with the freshman lawmaker at the Simon Wiesenthal exhibit just after his election. They prompted her obsessive scanning of the radio dial to keep up with Duke's ever increasing talk show appearances. Anne's political engagement seemed to move in lockstep with Duke's increasing prominence. "With his progression came her progression," says Elinor Cohen, one of Anne's closest friends. "The bigger he loomed in the eyes of the public, the bolder she became. It was like he was breathing down her back."[52]

Anne's upsurging memories did not spring de novo from the swamp of Louisiana politics. Long before her open clashes with Duke, she was alternately approaching her traumatic past and then pulling back. At first there was mainly avoidance. If survivors divide into those who talk about the Holocaust and those who will not, for many years Anne marched in the ranks of the silent. Try as she might, Ruth could never persuade her daughters to record their wartime memories or even help reconstruct the Skorecki family narrative. Anne was either too busy trying to become an American teenager or too preoccupied raising a New Orleans family, and Lila was too fragile. Wartime memories continued to exert an influence on Anne's life, in the realm of habit and compulsion: the fretting over appearances; the what-will-the-neighbors-think anxiety; the obsessional need to keep the freezer stocked with bread; and, most of all, a sheer inability to do anything on the spur of the moment. Then there were Anne's heavy moods, those shadows of melancholy that beclouded her temperament. "I remember one time when I climbed into bed with my mom," says Anne's daughter Robin. "We were living in our split-level house in Lakeview. My parents' bedroom was at the top. It was late at night, really dark, and the room was flickering with that strange incandescence that emanates from the TV when the lights are off. A documentary about World War II came on. There wasn't a lot of emotion, but I remember difficulty."[53]

Like many survivors, by the 1980s Anne had begun edging closer to her memories, sampling them in measured doses. At those times Stan and her daughters were at a loss over how to show their support, which is not unusual among close relatives of survivors who did not share the same experience. All they knew is that return trips to the past made Anne inconsolable. Stan felt powerless in the face of his wife's engulfing emotions. "Why do you want to watch this? Why do you want to make yourself upset?" he would ask, and then he and Sheryl would leave the room. There came a point, during the televised broadcast of the 1979 NBC miniseries on the Holocaust, when Anne finally said, "Well, because I think it needs to be done."

"I guess that was the first time I said that, because it was the beginning of where I felt that my pain didn't matter so long as other people were exposed to the subject." Four years later she traveled to the American Gathering of Holocaust Survivors in Washington, D.C., and became immersed in its collective remembrance. And in June 1988, the year before Duke's legislative election, she and Lila sat down in the privacy of Anne's upstairs apartment above the Levy store—a room of vaulted ceilings and furniture pieces large enough to hide a family—and shared their wartime memories with the New Orleans public radio journalist and freelance writer Plater Robinson. Yet each of these early encounters with the past was fleeting and tentative. Sustained engagement would not begin until Duke burst into Anne's consciousness.

Through it all, however, was Mark's declining health, drawing Anne back to memories of a lost childhood. Her father had had a long history of health problems—kidney stones, heart problems, high blood pressure, and, finally, a life-threatening but indeterminate carcinoma. "We always thought my dad would die before my mother," Anne says. Though he outlived his wife by nearly two decades, his last seven years were a period of dread for the family, and Anne felt it most keenly. "Maybe you see your own mortality when you're the oldest and your last parent dies," she says. "But Tata's decline and passing was like putting an end to the story, like completing this other life."

Despite failing health, Mark was fine so long as he stayed busy. "Being needed and productive kept him going," Anne says. He actually remained on the job beyond all actuarial expectations. From time to time the family had to force lifestyle changes on Mark, usually against his wishes. By 1985, when it was clear he could no longer live alone or drive a car, Anne and Lila moved him into an assisted care unit called the Orleanian, on St. Charles Avenue, near the old Orleans Hotel where the Skoreckis had sojourned in 1949 after debarking the troopship that had brought them to America. Mark's continued employment at Stan's store nearby somewhat smoothed the transition to institutional living. And it also helped that old acquaintances still dropped by his workshop to see how he was doing. He enjoyed holding court.

The bad feeling between Stan and his father-in-law never went away, although Stan eventually learned to bite his tongue. "I improved the relationship at the end," Stan says. "I mean, the guy's old and he's Anne's father. But emotionally he was hard to know."[54] For his part, Mark came to respect his son-in-law's business acumen. The antiques now arriving regularly from England and Argentina impressed him. "We've had some really fine pieces come through here," Anne says, "Georgian lowboys and chests-on-chests, Regency tables, Victorian rockers. You could tell Tata couldn't wait to get his hands on them." But he never expressed his approval to Stan or Anne directly.

Mark's famous wit remained strong to the end. Once, after returning to the Orleanian from a brief hospital stay for a minor stroke, one of the other residents exclaimed in relief: "Oh, Mr. Skorecki! You're back! You're okay after all! What was the problem?" Mark replied that he'd had a stroke. The man grew grave. "What kind of stroke?" Mark smiled: "Oh, just a small stroke. A five-thousand-dollar stroke. Not a bad one that would cost ten or twenty thousand."[55]

In the spring of 1986 Adam brought his father to Atlanta to live in the newly constructed Jewish Home Tower where Adam served as board chair. Anne and Lila flew with their father to Atlanta. Says Adam, "He was very popular in the building. The women liked him. He was going to dinner here and there."[56] But six weeks after moving to Atlanta, Tata called Anne at five in the morning. He was on the verge of hysteria. "You better come up here because I'm not going to make it. This is the end. I can't take it. I want to come home. I want to die at home." Lila called him back immediately after hearing the news from Anne. "Daddy was crying like a baby," she says. This was the first time the two sisters had seen their father cry inconsolably. They flew to Atlanta on the next available flight to bring him home.

Mark next tried moving in with Norman and Lila, at least until his furniture could be crated and shipped back to New Orleans. They put him up in the guest bedroom. Toward the end of his stay, wartime recollections began to flood back. He had begun reminiscing a few years earlier, in his early eighties, talking about his experiences in Białystok during the two-year Soviet occupation before Operation Barbarossa, even describing how the Nazis torched the great circular shul in the center of the city. Occasionally he would reminisce about his time at Big Schultz's in the Warsaw Ghetto and the September 1942 selection when the girls were secreted in the abandoned leather factory in the subbasement while he and Ruth spent four anxious days in the "cauldron." "It was very touching," says Dolek, his cousin from Israel, who was present for one of Mark's storytelling sessions.[57] Mark's wartime reminiscences were seldom morbid. Mostly they were adventure stories, some dating to his service in the Polish army during the First World War. But, as Mark's life began ebbing away, more and more the unbidden flashbacks were of terror-filled moments deeply engraved in cortical memory. Waking suddenly from a nightmare about hiding in the Polish woods from Nazi patrols, Mark grabbed the twenty-one-inch television set Lila had placed in the guest bedroom and hurled it through the window, damaging the entire bedroom in his attempt to escape. Her nerves completely shot, Lila had no choice but to send her father back to the Orleanian care center on St. Charles Avenue.

By now, Mark's physical and mental decline was significant. Heavily medicated, he had drugs for every conceivable ailment—angina, hypertension, diabetes—plus a varied assortment of laxatives, sleeping pills, and painkillers. They filled an entire shoebox. Stubbornly he insisted on controlling the dosage himself, changing his medication on whim. Soon he became disoriented, showering at three in the morning, losing track not only of time but of reality as well. Paramedics had to rush him to the hospital when he went into a hallucinatory rage.

Although all three siblings were wrenched by Mark's worsening condition, Anne was devastated. "Tata was more codependent with Anne," says Bevy Kearney, who saw her everyday in the store. "If Adam did something, he did appreciate it. And if Lila did it, well, that was okay, that was nice. But Anne was the person he depended on."[58] It was a deeply set disposition, this late-in-life reliance on his firstborn, indeed, an expectation originally shaped by the wartime roles Anne had been scripted to play as the daughter who reached adulthood before her time. Mark took Anne's caretaker role for granted, not once expressing his gratitude. Anne's custodianship was simply downpayment on the debt owed for survival. She displayed no resentment. She never questioned the moral calculus by which her father had reckoned the sum total of filial indebtedness. "He was the reason why we were here," Anne says dolefully. "I always said that. And Lila and I really tried to show that we appreciated it. We were there. We were *always* there." "They told us at the Orleanian they had never had anybody living there whose family visited as much as we did," Lila adds. "There was always one of us over there, because we felt obligated to do that." "I think deep down he knew we were grateful," Anne says, growing distraught as she relives her father's final years. "But in the end there was no closure."

In the meantime, Mark's deteriorating condition frayed her nerves to the breaking point. He began phoning in the middle of the night in tears, saying he was about to die and insisting she come over right away. He started calling the store while she was in the middle of preparing that week's payroll, demanding that she bring him to such and such a place immediately. "Tata, I cannot go right now. We have to wait a half an hour," she would say. Whereupon he would threaten to call a cab, and she would have to drop her work to go fetch him. "That was when his mean streak came out," observes Kearney.[59] Increasingly, Adam had to fly to New Orleans to force his father to heed his sister's instructions. There came a point when Mark had to be moved to the Jewish nursing home across the river, first to a private room and then to the wing where residents incapable of caring for themselves were housed. It fell to Anne to make the decision to have Tata institutionalized. By now—1990–1991—her father had become totally disoriented, wandering the halls half-clad, sometimes without any clothes on at all. "That was the saddest time in my life, watching this man to whom I had been so close completely deteriorate," Anne says.

During her father's slow descent, Anne's thoughts kept reverting to the Holocaust and those fragments of the prewar past still accessible to memory. She began letting casual acquaintances catch glimpses of her hidden history. "I remember the first time she told me the story of their experience in the war," says Kearney. "Tata was getting older then. She cried in telling it. She became more upset the sicker he got."[60] And as Mark's dependence on Anne deepened, almost in tune with his querulous demands and none-too-subtle reminders that he was responsible for not just fathering but also saving her, Anne's returns to the past grew more and more frequent, causing her feeling of filial debt to compound with every surge of memory.

Throughout the period of Anne's grieving, Duke's political popularity continued to spread beyond the boundaries of his Metairie district. His statewide name recognition increased significantly when he opposed Governor Buddy Roemer's Fiscal Reform program, an ambitious plan to shift the tax burden from business to homeowners. A Harvard graduate and an original "boll weevil" Democratic congressman whom House Speaker Tip O'Neil once described as "often wrong, never in doubt," Roemer packaged his tax restructuring program into a ballot referendum and took off for the hustings. Duke dogged the governor's tracks with rallies of his own. The essence of right-wing populism, Duke's message—that liberal federal policies were taxing white workers for the benefit of "unqualified minorities" and the "undeserving poor"—was a sort of "Huey in reverse." The voters loved it. By the time he and Roemer reached Shreveport, Duke was outdrawing the governor by four to one. Roemer's reform initiative was defeated handily, and Duke claimed much of the credit. "That campaign against the amendment showed me for the first time that I had statewide appeal," he told the Louisiana political columnist John Maginnis. "That's what started my campaign for the [United States] Senate."[61]

After his setback at the polls, Roemer retreated into self-absorbed remoteness, lost in books. He canceled meetings, failed to return phone calls, avoided parties and receptions. His wife and nine-year-old son moved out of the mansion. He plunged into a crash program of personal growth, forcing his staff to attend New Age seminars where participants snapped rubber bands on their wrists to banish negative thoughts. He opened the next legislative session by urging legislators to "meet me at the campfire, so that we can build a future for our children." The lawmakers harrumphed, deposed his legislative leadership, and proceeded to treat the national press to a political horselaugh, passing bills that winked at assaults on flag burners and mandated jail time for selling obscene record albums to minors. They also criminalized abortions after a Christian Coalition lawmaker handed out plastic fetuses to the packed galleries. Although he vetoed every measure, Roemer had lost control of state government.[62]

The out-of-control legislative session, following the defeat of fiscal reform, provided an ideal time for Duke to spread his brand of politics. During his two-year term in the lower house, he introduced a raft of race-tinged bills: to abolish affirmative action and set-asides; to drug-test public-housing tenants; to implant Norplant birth-control devices in the arms of welfare mothers. Only one of his proposals ever passed so much as one house of the legislature—a measure outlawing affirmative action—and it never became law. Duke knew little about the parliamentary process and cared less. To him the legislature was a vehicle not for enacting law but for galvanizing a mass following. He was frank about wanting to use race to disrupt the biracial, blue-collar coalition cobbled together by such economic populists as John McKeithen and Edwin Edwards. "For years and years, all these legislators . . . always voted with the minority-liberal programs because they're afraid of this 25 or 30 percent black constituency going against them," he told a Populist Party convention in Chicago shortly after his election to the legislature. Duke promised to make lawmakers start "worrying about the 70 percent."[63] Lest his legislative colleagues overlook the frenzy of racial resentment he had unleashed, the freshman legislator made a practice of opening stacks of letters stuffed with campaign contributions as he sat at his desk in the rear of the house chamber. Much of the mail came from archconservative mailing lists that Duke was now mining with considerable success.[64]

If there was ever any doubt about Duke's racial politics having statewide appeal, it was dispelled during his 1990 race for the U.S. Senate against three-term incumbent Democrat J. Bennett Johnston. Astonishingly, the challenger began the campaign with greater statewide name recognition than the incumbent. Crisscrossing the state at breakneck speed as state troopers waved him on, the novice lawmaker unveiled a style of retail politics not seen in Louisiana since the days of Earl Long. With "The Ballad of David Duke" blaring from the sound system, angry white voters packed country and western bars and Howard Johnson meeting rooms. They thronged prearranged "Dukefests" in public parks. They tossed five- and ten-dollar bills into the oyster buckets that served as collection plates at his campaign stops. Jobless oil workers told Duke about the latest affirmative action outrage. Mothers asked him to kiss their babies. His face had become nicely bronzed by tanning creams daubed on during car trips to the next campaign stop. Back in Baton Rouge Duke often made eugenic come-ons to attractive legislative aides, telling them that God had enjoined Nordic people to preserve their genetic heritage and that his date du jour should seriously consider mating with him.[65]

The crowd frenzy crested in the campaign's closing days. Excited followers, wearing blue-and-white T-shirts and baseball caps emblazoned with Duke's name, swelled into doo-wop renditions of "Duke, Duke, Duke, Duke." It wasn't in appreciation of his oratorical gifts, which were surprisingly slight.[66] There was something Pavlovian about the furious responses Duke's campaign elicited from audiences. The Duke bandwagon was less an election campaign rally than a rock-and-roll tour grafted onto a prayer meeting. "He's a celebrity, he's like a messiah," exclaimed one rural lawmaker.[67] Republican candidate Ben Bagert, a former New Orleans state senator, withdrew from the race to prevent a runoff between Duke and the incumbent. Although Johnston won reelection outright in the October 6, 1990, primary, garnering 56 percent of the vote, everyone conceded that Duke was the real victor. He had captured nearly three-fifths of the white vote, established credentials as a mainstream conservative, built the state's largest volunteer base, and acquired a fifty-thousand-name mailing list. His campaign treasury was bulging.

Duke's skyrocketing popularity fired the imagination of the far right, which viewed his electoral breakthrough as "a significant bellwether of the hardening of Majority race-consciousness." A few purists grumbled that the NAAWP head was prostituting racialist principles by downplaying his past and mouthing egalitarian rhetoric. Tribunes for the "majority" should campaign to be believed, not elected. The sprightly written *Instauration*—whose racial apartheid map assigning America's ethnic minorities to separate homelands was later republished in the NAAWP *News*—approved Duke's opportunism, however: "Duke's campaigns can be viewed as laboratory experiments, lessons to be learned. In this sense they transcend any moralistic interpretations of the candidate's character. *Politics* will always transcend such concerns."[68] That editorial assessment did not come from left field. "Republican" racialists in Tennessee, Georgia, and Arkansas paid Duke the sincerest form of flattery by running copycat stealth campaigns.[69]

If Duke's breaching of the electoral ramparts lifted neo-Nazi spirits, it caused considerable consternation within the opposition camp. The immediate defense was to embrace conventional wisdom. The strategy seemed to have common sense in its favor, the reasoning being that since attacks on Duke only stoked the antielite resentments fueling his rise, his extremist past should be ignored to ward off a sympathy backlash. Early in Duke's insurgency, B. I. Botnick, the local ADL head, counseled the usual "quarantine" strategy. Even negative publicity helped Duke, he told a Jewish paper in New York. "The reality is that [the media] generate more publicity for [Duke] and they give him a stage and spotlight."[70] Upset with a Jewish Defense League (JDL) official who flew in from New York during the legislative contest vowing to "meet force with force," the Jewish Federation of Greater New Orleans likewise adopted the "cold-shoulder" policy of according anti-Semitic agitators the silent treatment. "I strongly disapprove his tactics," said the federation's executive director, Jane Buchsbaum, who told the JDL head by phone not to come.[71] An influential segment of the city's small Jewish community still viewed Duke as a Rockwell redux who would wither away if denied the lifeblood of publicity. The major flaw in their logic was that picketing movie theaters and winning statehouse seats were hardly equivalent political facts; Duke's sudden acquisition of political respectability might warrant a strategic reassessment, a realization that soon dawned on Buchsbaum herself.

But all the city's major institutions, including *The Times-Picayune*, the city's only daily and therefore the newspaper of record, initially fell back on conventional wisdom when confronted with the politics of racial hatred, and they stayed in that mode for a long time. To the editors the Duke phenomenon admittedly posed an unusual challenge. Clearly he was no ordinary politician, but did that fact alone dictate according him special coverage? The conundrum bedeviled the paper for nearly three years. The initial editorial decision was to treat Duke as merely another conservative candidate. After he won a seat in the legislature, it was then decided to invest more resources in the Duke beat. The paper assigned Tyler Bridges to cover him almost full-time. "We need to take a look at this guy and find out exactly who he is," then editor Charles Ferguson told Bridges. Bridges, who had been with the paper only a few months, uncovered several fresh revelations: that Duke lived off his NAAWP mailing list through a dummy corporation; that he failed to pay taxes; that he had a gambling habit; that he had had plastic surgery; that he threw a yearly Adolf Hitler birthday party in his home. But, at the same time, in the eyes of its critics, *The Times-Picayune* had a tendency of burying stories belying

Duke's self-serving claims that he had long ago put on a new face. When offered an exclusive concerning Duke's continued peddling of Nazi books from his Metairie legislative office, the editors ran the story in the Metro section, not the front page. When anti-Duke activists hand-delivered the ethnic cleansing map that Duke had approvingly republished in the mid-1980s, only the paper's local columnist James Gill covered the topic at any length—in Section B of the paper. Meanwhile, the *Louisiana Weekly*, a black paper published in New Orleans, and the small-circulation *Shreveport Journal*, now defunct, were scooping *The Times-Picayune* right and left. "It was clear that Charlie Ferguson was very uncomfortable with Duke," Bridges says, "very much in the mode of thinking that we not give this guy too much coverage. I think he underplayed him deliberately." Several of Mike Luckovich's political cartoons on Duke (Luckovich was working for the paper at the time) were turned down by the editors.[72]

The paper shifted emphasis after James Amoss took over as editor in the summer of 1990. The Nazi connection started receiving more attention. The number of articles on Duke increased. "If you total up the column inches we devoted to David Duke in 1989 through the fall of 1991," says Amoss, a Yale-educated Rhodes Scholar, "I dare say they came close to outweighing the space we devoted to [former governor] Edwin Edwards. And I'm not talking about 'Duke said today' kind of stories, but investigative journalism."[73] Amoss was painting an accurate picture; still, the continuities in the paper's coverage of Duke were obvious. In a long biographical profile Bridges wrote in August 1990, during the United States Senate campaign, *The Times-Picayune* for the first time set forth Duke's conspiratorial anti-Semitism as revealed in audiotapes compiled by Evelyn Rich in the mid-1980s during her Ph.D. research on Klan ideology. But the incriminating material was placed on page seven.[74]

The fact is, *The Times-Picayune*, like most daily newspapers in America, was handcuffed by the conventions of balanced coverage. "We treated Duke more aggressively in the 1990 Senate race," Bridges says, "but the paper was also trying very hard to be fair to him, trying very hard not to step outside of the bounds of traditional daily journalism. It was a real dilemma."[75] For its even-handedness *The Times-Picayune* drew fire from both camps. The writer Jason Berry blasted the paper's low-key coverage in a *New York Times* op-ed piece, later saying it was "absolutely one of the worst journalistic blunders that I think this city has ever seen." A contributor to the *Columbia Journalism Review* faulted *The Times-Picayune* for its "minimalist coverage," prompting a sharp rebuttal from editor Amoss.[76] From the Duke camp came numerous pieces of mail and phone calls complaining that their man was being treated unfairly. Bombarded on both flanks, the editors hunkered down on the middle ground. "That's what daily journalism does," says Bridges, "because you have people on both sides pushing and pulling you. So, newspapers try to treat everybody the same and not get accused of being partisan and attacking somebody."[77] Biographical profiles of candidates were therefore allocated the same amount of column inches; photographs were cropped to the same dimensions. And if more dirt turned up on Duke than on his opponent, as happened with the Evelyn Rich tapes during the Senate race, for balance's sake it was placed in a sidebar on the inside. "Whatever coverage we run is criticized by someone," Amoss told a British scholar in August 1991. "Therefore I have had to be especially vigilant to ensure he is treated fairly." Or, as he explained to a journalistic ethics seminar the following year, the paper was "caught between our own convictions and the imperative that we be trustworthy chroniclers."[78]

Louisiana's broadcast media, which traditionally took their cues from print journalists, likewise worked within established conventions. They played the Duke story as a personality contest, focusing on the visuals, and attuning their coverage to McLuhanesque notions of hot and cool. Duke had a field day with them—"barraging interviewers or debating opponents with streams of distortions, interrupting to throw people off guard, hogging air time, insulting interviewers, blasting 'the liberal media'—in short violating the unwritten rules of television decorum and cowering his questioners," to quote Berry. That most deadline-driven reporters lacked the time or inclination to do their homework gave Duke's browbeating tactics an immense advantage.[79]

If the local media had trouble covering Duke, the political class was flummoxed by the Metairie lawmaker's rising popularity. Almost in unison the professionals argued that Duke was impervious to attacks on his extremist past. "Basically, we found that the guy was bulletproof," said Raymond Strother, a national political consultant originally from Louisiana.[80] The received wisdom followed two predictable paths. Democratic handlers advised assailing Duke on economic issues. Republicans said find a challenger who could run on his conservative platform but without the political baggage. And both groups searched for such issues as tax evasion, gambling, or questionable sexuality to bring him down.

But industry professionals were examining the problem from the wrong end of the microscope. The challenge was never to pull votes off Duke by arousing economic fears or co-opting his platform. It was not even to keep his electoral base from crossing the high school diploma line and spreading into the educated middle class. The real goal was always to create a countermovement based on moral concern. The big problem with issue-oriented attacks, whether from right or left, is that they legitimated Duke by taking seriously his reinvented persona as a mainstream conservative politician. Ironically, the traditional mudslinging approach did the same thing by implying a rough sort of immoral equivalence between Duke's antidemocratic extremism and the conventional peccadilloes of traditional politicians, as though accepting illegal campaign contributions and palliating genocide were commensurable misdeeds. In short, by leaving unchallenged the big lie that Duke's Nazi and Klan phase reflected the fleeting rebelliousness of a callow youth, the pundits missed the point entirely: that Duke's latest mask reflected ongoing neo-Nazi efforts to find the best vehicle for galvanizing a white consciousness movement capable of seizing power. The chameleon strategy dated back at least to the early 1970s, when he formed the Knights of the Ku Klux Klan. It received a new look in the 1980s when he founded the NAAWP. Now it was appareled in the pin-striped uniform of Republican conservatism, and the major institutions responsible for shaping public opinion seemed incapable of blowing the cover.

If any political party had reason to strip away the mask, it would seem to have been the Republicans. Duke was giving their codespeak southern strategy a bad name. The national GOP saw the danger immediately after Duke's election to the legislature. The reemergence of the racist right, combined with the Los Angeles race riots following the first Rodney King trial, induced President George Bush to sign the Civil Rights Act of 1990—doubtless the last piece of civil rights legislation that will be enacted in this century. Meanwhile, the Republican National Committee (RNC), having earlier censured Duke, renewed its pressure on Louisiana Republicans to oust him from the party. "We would hope the state party would follow our lead," said a spokesperson for RNC chief Lee Atwater.[81] But the chain-smoking, gravel-voiced state party chairman Billy Nungesser rebuffed national leaders. Ostracizing Duke would give him "undue publicity," Nungesser said.[82] But the real explanation for his reluctance is that Duke had captured the state party's rank and file, including the religious right, which had recently won control of a substantial voting bloc on the state central committee. The Reverend Billy McCormack, state director of the Christian Coalition and leader of the committee's evangelical delegation, told a reporter for the *Los Angeles Times* that Duke represented less of a threat to Christianity than the Jewish lawyers in the ACLU.[83] One of the party's fund raisers said she had never seen a grassroots groundswell like the one for Duke. "We get so many letters telling us he's converted, that we should leave him alone," she told a national reporter. "They even say, 'Didn't you ever hear of St. Paul?'"[84]

In the meantime, while state party leaders sought to downplay Duke, a powerful coterie of Republican legislators tried to exploit his political popularity. "When your party has only 25 legislators out of 144, you don't take a member lightly," admitted an eighteen-year House veteran. "Republicans don't come easy around here." Emile "Peppi" Bruneau, the bantamweight, blunt-talking, and shrewd chairman of the Republican legislative caucus, even took Duke under his wing, helping him craft bills and resolutions. Simply put, the freshman lawmaker was proving to be a useful point man for controversial race-wedge issues long pushed by Republican legislators but "to little effect and much criticism." "He helps them," said a lawmaker from Cajun country. "He's kind of taken the heat." "See him?" said Bruneau, gesturing toward a black Democrat sitting at his desk on the house floor. "He was named as an unindicted co-conspirator in a recent financial scandal. . . . And now I'm looking at a guy [another black member] who ought to be in prison on cocaine charges. But I work with both of *them*." In Bruneau's eyes there was seemingly little difference between a proven record of neo-Nazi activism and allegations of substance abuse or financial impropriety.[85]

Indeed, within the 140-member state central committee, only two individuals voiced strong dissent from the prevailing opportunism, and one of them was practically read out of the party because of her principled stand. Dark-haired, with a gift for mimicry, Beth Rickey had been a poster child for Louisiana's first post-Reconstruction Republican governor, David Treen; Ronald Reagan had been her personal hero. Rickey, however, was shaken by the discovery made while researching his past during the legislative race that Duke was a dyed-in-the-wool Nazi and a Holocaust denier. After the election she traveled to Chicago and secretly taped Duke crowing to the Populist Party convention, "We did it!" A short while later she bought Holocaust "revisionist" and Nazi literature from the bookstore that he continued to operate in the basement of his home. This was in the spring of 1989.

She then called a press conference immediately after Anne Levy's confrontation with Duke at the state capitol, arguing that the Nazi books purchased from Duke the previous week mocked his claim to have turned over a new leaf. Duke's efforts to blur the line between racism and conservatism affronted Rickey. Her great-grandfather, while serving as sheriff in one of the Florida parishes, had rescued a black man from a lynch mob. Her deceased father had served in George Patton's Third Army when it liberated concentration camps in eastern Bavaria. To Rickey it was morally imperative that Duke be cast from the party. She and another member of the Republican State Central Committee, Neil Curran, a born-again Christian, announced they would introduce a censure motion at the September 1989 statewide meeting. "We have a moral responsibility to speak out," she said. "We have a Nazi in our midst." But party leaders, meeting secretly beforehand, arranged to have the motion killed when it reached the floor.[86] The intransigence of Louisiana Republican leaders caused RNC head Atwater to do a complete about-face. Their refusal to expel Duke was understandable "from a tactical point of view," he now believed. "People down there understand he's trying to get into a fight. Anyone generating publicity for Duke is in concert with him. Without publicity, he just flattens out."[87]

As for Rickey, the only reward she got for her censure efforts was four months of unwanted courtship from Duke himself. More convinced than ever of his charismatic power to arouse the latent racial consciousness of white people, especially white women, Duke showered Rickey with attention. He took her to lunch and dinner. They went on Sunday afternoon drives together with his two daughters. He called her late at night, droning on for hours about the Indian caste system and "genius" sperm banks, as she faded in and out of sleep with the phone receiver propped on her pillow.

While lunching at a Metairie Chinese restaurant, Duke tossed on the table the denial book written in the mid-1970s by his erstwhile Klan lieutenant, William Grimstead. Duke ran through the standard revisionist litany. Rudolf Hess should have received the Nobel Peace Prize. Josef Mengele, the "Auschwitz Angel of Death," was a great medical researcher. Adolf Eichmann had been done a great injustice. The gas chambers were delousing units. The extermination story was a Hollywood myth. Duke was animated, his eyes flashing. "This is too bizarre," Rickey thought to herself. "I've got to get out of here." Cutting lunch short, she permanently severed her relationship with Duke.[88] The luncheon gave Rickey a new insight into her temporary suitor. "He still sees himself as a skinny kid who is not very popular."[89]

For all of his personal insecurities, Duke nonetheless represented a political cancer that would continue metastasizing until a moral countermovement drove him into remission. But such a movement was unlikely to emerge until the antidemocratic agenda at the core of his movement was unmasked. Because both the mainstream media and the two major parties were reluctant to accept the challenge, the responsibility fell by default to a third political force—a bipartisan political action committee (PAC) called the Louisiana Coalition against Racism and Nazism. It was formed in the fall of 1989 once it became obvious that Duke intended to stand for Bennett Johnston's United States Senate seat. Beth Rickey was a cofounder, along with the PAC's chairperson, James L. Stovall, a Methodist minister from Baton Rouge, and Lance Hill, an erstwhile civil rights activist from Lawrence, Kansas, then a graduate student in history at Tulane University. Although drawing heavily on black and Jewish support, including federation head Jane Buchsbaum, who served on the executive committee, white non-Jews dominated the leadership. "The coalition was an odd arrangement," says Hill, "in that it was primarily a coalition of blacks and Jews publicly led by white Christians. And that structure was by design, because we believed it was important that Duke's opposition come from the same kind of people to whom he was appealing. It was part of our strategy to break the illusion of a white Christian consensus, in which we all secretly and 'genetically' were predisposed to favoring Duke and his politics."[90]

A huge man of comedic genius, in his Yippie days in Lawrence, Hill had engineered his older brother's election as justice of the peace. It was a classic stealth campaign. "Secrecy was the secret of my success," his brother Philip told the media. "I had the unswerving support of the Democrats without their knowing it." Kansas authorities vowed Hill's brother would serve the briefest office term in history, which was a cheap prophecy, since the state legislature had already abolished the office before the election.[91] Hill became not only the coalition's executive director but also its chief strategist and tactician. In the 1970s he made a personal project out of studying European and American fascism, past and present. To keep tabs on Duke's activities, he clandestinely subscribed to the NAAWP News, and although he had tossed most of his files just before Duke's legislative election, enough clippings survived to splice together the media resource kit that ultimately became the principal source of information about Duke's neo-Nazi extremism. It was Hill who suggested to Rickey that she buy Nazi books from Duke's NAAWP residential headquarters and who had prepped a Tulane undergraduate for a postlegislative election interview that caught Duke in several damaging admissions about Hitler and eugenics.

The coalition prepared and revised thousands of media resource packets for distribution to the press; sent out direct mailings throughout Louisiana; and ran statewide television and radio commercials. It took out full-page newspaper ads. During the senate campaign, while Republican and Democratic partisans played up Duke's tax evasion and plastic surgery, for fear of offending his supporters' racist sensibilities, the coalition beamed the spotlight on the germ of hate infecting Duke's public issues agenda. "Duke must be defeated because of his political beliefs, not in spite of them," Hill wrote in an early strategy paper. Granted, the political professionals were correct to argue that harping on Duke's hidden extremism would probably make his voters defensive, only causing them to become more entrenched in their support. "Yet," Hill countered, "to ignore Duke's bigotry—to attune a strategy exclusively to the Duke supporters—can lead to a failure to mobilize the anti-Duke vote as well as the undecided. A central task of the stop-Duke movement is to consolidate and mobilize the opposition as well." There was striking indirect evidence for that analysis in the stay-at-home apathy of both the black vote and the upscale Republican electorate during the United States Senate contest. Had those two groups turned out at comparable rates to Duke's voters, Bennett Johnston would have won by a commanding 22 percent margin.[92]

There were many bumps in the roads. The coalition's strategy of emphasizing Duke's covert Nazism conflicted sharply with *The Times-Picayune*'s commitment to balanced coverage. In the summer of 1991, incensed at the paper's failure to make use of a coalition report delineating the eugenicism embedded in a Duke bill offering cash incentives to welfare mothers who volunteered to receive Norplant contraceptive implants, Hill arranged a meeting with the paper's editors and publisher, Ashton Phelps. "It got heated," Hill says. "Ashton Phelps turned red. They were convinced that they were doing a good job of covering him, and they weren't going to single him out for any special attention at that point. It was just kind of a natural part of their traditional journalistic boosterism that they would either dismiss Duke or assign his popularity to something other than a racist insurgency. That's why the Coalition made it a deliberate strategy to provide as many stories as we could to the national media, on the assumption that out-of-state reporters, who were not under the same social pressures to downplay Duke, would eventually shame the local media into doing what they were supposed to do."[93]

"There's no way to justify that stance," says Amoss of the argument that the paper should have run a full-court press against Duke during the legislative and senate races. "It would have been journalistically intolerable. It would have backfired. I don't think any sane citizen or journalist would have been able to justify it or stomach it." But there would come a time when the paper did shift its coverage dramatically—in 1991 when Duke seemed poised to win the governorship—and Amoss would be the first to defend the change of course.[94]

If the Louisiana Coalition was right that mass movements are aroused by moral passion, Louisiana's experience with the Duke insurgency would shortly illustrate how even ethical behavior can come in strange guises. Morality is not always manifested in what people say, but in what they do or in the intensity that they bring to what they say and do.

Meanwhile, Mark Skorecki's condition was fast deteriorating. In the fall of 1990, not long after the conclusion of the United States Senate race, the nursing home moved him to its wing for the terminally ill. For the last six months of his life, he was mostly bedridden, confined to a wheelchair when he did rise. He would often become lost in memories hazed over by time. There were moments when he lay in bed crying over and over again, "Stefa, Stefa, Stefa"—the name of the older sister with whom Mark had been very close as a boy growing up in Łódź. After the war a wedge had come between them because of Ruth's long-simmering rancor at Stefa and her family for failing to offer her greater help during the Nazi occupation of Łódź. If Mark remembered the quarrel, it must have struck him as senseless now.

Once during his stay in the nursing home there was a moment of recognition when Robin showed him pictures she had taken in Łódź during a Jewish federation tour of Poland and Israel. She had carried a copy of her grandmother's memoir on the trip, visiting the addresses it mentioned, snapping photos of Legionów 8, the massive Second Empire apartment building on Kościuszko Avenue where the Skoreckis were living at the time of the German invasion. She photographed the Poznański textile factory and palace at the end of Gdańsk Street, not far from her maternal grandmother's childhood home. Tata came to life at the picture of the Poznański mansion. He had once worked and lived there as a caretaker. He broke down when she showed him a picture of the Jewish cemetery. "It was very painful for him to see that," Robin says. "But he was touched, he was grateful."[95]

Shortly before his death, Carol and her grandfather reached closure. By now he had practically ceased eating, and Anne, Lila, and Adam had decided against prolonging his life with oxygen and intravenous fluids. When Carol entered his room, Mark was having difficulty. "I held his hand and he just looked so sad and tired. And I said, 'Tata, would you like a hug?' "

"Who me?"

"Yeah, you."

"From who?"

"From me!"

"Okay."

"I leaned down and we hugged. He was hugging me back and kissing me all over my head and neck, which he had never done before. He knew he was about to die and had prepared himself."[96]

The nursing home called Anne and Lila at seven in the morning on May 14, 1991, saying that their father would not live out the day and that they should come right over. Anne arrived first. Tata was in a coma. All his senses except hearing had gone. "Are you cold," Lila asked her father. He shook his head. Then his heart stopped. For a while his diaphragm alone seemed to force air into his lungs. The doctors pronounced him dead at one o'clock in the afternoon. "It was eerie, it was sad," says Anne. "All the emotions of innocence, of life, of pain, were in the room at the time. For me it was like the closing of a chapter in my life, and now I was truly on my own."

SOME CHANGE IS ONLY SKIN DEEP

BEFORE   AFTER

He changed his face. He changed his political image. But he can't change the truth.

David Duke is skillfully exploiting our racial resentments and fears. He's using race to elevate himself to power.

Duke has forewarned us of his secret agenda. In 1986 Duke chillingly discussed his ominous plans in a taped interview with Evelyn Rich. Duke was a mature 35 years old. He had long since left the klan and declared himself a born-again Christian.

Duke told the interviewer that he thought that "the Jewish people have been a blight . . . And they probably deserve to go into the ashbin of history . . . " Reminiscent of Hitler's anti-Semitic plans, Duke calmly suggested that Jews should be removed from America. "I think the best thing is to resettle them some place where they can't exploit others."

There's more. The topic of Hitler arose in the interview. Joe Fields, an avowed Nazi, reminded Duke that "Hitler started with seven men." Duke promptly responded:

"Right! And don't you think it can happen here, right now, if we put the right package together? . . . I might have to do it because nobody else might come along to do it."

This was David Duke's dream only five years ago.

Your vote on November 16th will decide something far greater than the governorship. It will signal to the world not only our choice of candidates, but also our choice of values. It will determine in coming years how Americans will confront the problems of poverty, crime, drugs, and unemployment.

Will we turn to one another, or against one another? Will we extend a hand of friendship, or point the finger of hate?

Many argue that we are confronted with two bad choices. But there is considerable difference between good-ole-boy politics and genocide.

Someday we will all have to account for how we chose between the two.

Imagine the future. Imagine explaining to your grandchildren the actions you took when the merchant of hate begged your support. Rogues come and go. But a Duke victory threatens more than our state treasury or environment. A Duke victory threatens to irreparably injure our state's reputation, our human dignity, and our nation's principles.

Some argue that Duke would be ineffective as Governor — thus harmless. Perhaps he would be. But think for a moment about the meaning of a Duke victory. What moral lesson would our children learn? That hatred toward minorities is acceptable — a mere blot on an otherwise fine resume.

The Governorship is not the only office at stake. The Governor's mansion will provide Duke with a springboard to develop a national movement. He is an ambitious man with no commitment to Louisiana. He has been frank about his designs on the White House. Imagine the daunting power. The Armed Forces. The Nuclear arsenal. This in the hands of a man who only five years ago embraced Hitler. Will history record that David Duke was Louisiana's contribution to humanity? A sad legacy for future generations.

The events of the past weeks have turned friend against friend, neighbor against neighbor. We have been pilloried by the world press. We are portrayed as a state of mean-spirited, half-witted bigots.

We know another Louisiana. We know the kindness of the Bayou fisherman. The hospitality of the upcountry farmer. The generous spirit of the urban dweller.

We've seen hard times in Louisiana. And we are angry. But we are not blind. We will not allow our passions and fears to deliver our State to the demagogues.

The Louisiana Coalition Against Racism and Nazism.
The Louisiana Coalition Against Racism and Nazism is a statewide organization committed to racial and religious understanding.
Yes, I want to help build a better future for Louisiana. Enclosed is my contribution for:

$100 $50 $25 $10
☐   ☐   ☐   ☐

Mail To:
Louisiana Coalition Against Racism and Nazism.
234 Loyola Suite 915, New Orleans, LA 70112

IT IS NOT HIS PAST THAT WE FEAR. IT IS HIS FUTURE.

Sources: Evelyn Rich Interview with Joe Fields and David Duke, 1986. Culver City, California. A copy of this audio-taped interview is held in the Evelyn Rich Collection, Rare Books and Manuscripts, Howard-Tilton Memorial Library, Tulane University, New Orleans. The complete transcript is available through the Coalition.

Paid for by the Louisiana Coalition Against Racism and Nazism, a political action committee, James L. Stovall, Chairman. Not authorized by any candidate or candidate's committee. Contributions for this state campaign are not deductible for federal income tax purposes.

Louisiana Coalition campaign advertisement, "Some Change Is Only Skin Deep." (Courtesy of Lance Hill)

Above: David Duke reading morning-after headlines. (AP/World Wide Photos)

Facing page, top: Mark ("Tata") Skorecki in his late eighties.

Facing page, bottom: Lila, Adam, and Anne.

Top: Anne speaking with teachers at Edward Douglas White High School, Thibodaux, Louisiana. (Courtesy of Plater Robinson)

Bottom: Lila and Anne, fourth and sixth from right, at the Southern Institute for Education and Research (SIER) summer institute, 1998. (Courtesy of Plater Robinson)

fifteen

REDEMPTION

On October 19, 1991, while Anne was still mourning her father's death, David Duke shocked the state and nation by placing second in Louisiana's open primary election for governor. He had bumped the incumbent governor Buddy Roemer from the November 16 runoff. Now the only person standing between him and the governor's mansion was the sole candidate Duke had a realistic chance of defeating—the colorful and controversial three-time former governor, Edwin Edwards.[1] "The election from hell," groaned local pundits. Louisiana had gotten itself into unpleasant situations in the past but this one took the cake. The issue of who was going to run Louisiana's public business for the next four years had come down to a choice between a rogue and a Nazi, and for several suspenseful weeks the outcome was far from certain. The nation looked on in stunned amazement. Because of the state's odd off-year election cycle, the political news from Louisiana commanded the front pages of papers across the country, filling America's television screens each evening. This was the last major state election before the 1992 presidential primary season kicked off, and out-of-state observers were puzzled and more than a little worried. Was this insurgency contagious?

No one was more astonished and terrified at the results of the October primary than Anne Levy. For more than four decades she had been assimilating the values of pluralism and democracy. In her mind they embodied the very essence of American nationalism, so vastly different from the völkisch variety that had brought her family in Poland to ruin. In America citizenship was universal, open to all, not restricted to Jews or gentiles, to this race or that religion; it was not even the exclusive property of the native born. Here, one simply had to subscribe to a common creed. But now those values were under assault by a political candidate whom Anne knew deep down, because of his evasions on the Holocaust, harbored a secret desire to refurbish Nazism itself. She hardly needed a history class to realize where the impulse for cultural and biological purity can lead when carried to logical conclusions. The lesson was scarred deeply in memory.

So, she was terrified, confused, bewildered, still grieving her father's death. How could this be, this affront to his memory so soon after his passing? But greater than fear and bewilderment was her anger. She was angry enough to do something about it.

Anne was hardly alone in her astonishment. Most of the state's political class were numbed by the outcome. Although preelection polls indicated Duke was gaining ground, much of his support remained hidden, and most pundits predicted an Edwards-Roemer runoff. That was the mood at Ruth's Chris Steak House, in midcity New Orleans. The mother restaurant of the national chain, Ruth's Chris has long been a popular watering hole for the city's political service industry as well as the people they service. They crowd in on Friday afternoons, especially preceding election eve (Louisiana elections usually occur on Saturday). Sometimes things get rowdy, but generally good cheer and smooth whiskey prevail. The day before the October 19, 1991, open primary the mood was jocular as usual, if a little tense. For the past decade, a dozen of the city's leading political reporters, consultants, and pollsters had been reserving a table in the restaurant's main dining area to swap last-minute gossip and organize a betting pool, a luncheon ritual they called FEEDBAG. "That's the 'Friday Evening Ensemble to Develop FeedBack and Gossip,'" explains pollster Joe Walker. The betting pool resembles a political trifecta, everyone wagering five dollars for a chance to pick the top three finishers and the winner claiming the entire kitty. The FEEDBAG regulars have been following state politics so long that most election trifectas end in a twelve-person tie, in which case the pool goes to whoever comes closest to guessing the final percentages. At the Friday luncheon preceding the October primary, only two old-timers picked Duke to make the runoff.[2]

Roemer, who had switched to the Republican Party only months earlier in a feckless positioning for a run at the White House (the first sitting governor ever to change parties), was the election's biggest surprise and his supporters' worst disappointment. The Republican Party had invested substantial resources in Roemer's campaign, to defeat Duke and take control of another Deep South state on the eve of a presidential election. But the governor fell short of expectations. "I mean, here's a guy who had the money, the press, the power of the incumbency, and he still did not get as many votes as he had when he ran four years before," says long-time political consultant James Carvin.

"Furthermore, he didn't bother to have any significant field organization for getting out postcards and bumper stickers that would allow supporters to extend their partisanship to friends and neighbors." Lured into false confidence by the massive shift toward the GOP in the rest of the South, Roemer thought he could waltz to reelection by means of airwave appeals alone. But Duke's low-tech campaign walked off with the governor's rural base in the northern parishes. Meanwhile, dithering like Hamlet, Roemer alienated his business supporters by failing to keep his promises and by not returning phone calls. Some of governor's critical upscale vote in the metropolitan areas seems to have "gone fishing" on election day.[3]

Roemer supporters now found themselves in a quandary. For years Edwin Edwards, the silver-haired, Cajun Pentecostal, had in their eyes symbolized everything that was wrong with Longite politics: too much government, too much graft, too much cronyism. Plus Edwards was a rapscallion. The target of more than a dozen grand jury hearings during his long political career, the former governor had barely avoided conviction on federal racketeering charges in the mid-1980s. His only saving grace was an impish sense of humor, especially where his sex life was concerned. Set to marry a twenty-six-year-old nearly four decades his junior, Edwards cracked to a group of campaign supporters, "A man is as old as the woman he feels." He joked that he and Duke had a lot in common: "We're both wizards under the sheets." Due to the collapse of oil prices, however, the state treasury had been depleted, and Edwards's raffish style was fast losing its entertainment value. Roemer's core constituency was up in arms about the former governor's plan to solve the state's fiscal problems by legalizing casino gambling. Edwards was a heavy bettor in Las Vegas, on at least one occasion paying off his $2 million gambling debt with suitcases stuffed with cash. The state's reformers shuddered at visions of Edwin Edwards fueling his campaigns with contributions from an industry famously connected to organized crime.[4]

The first instinct of most Roemer supporters was to sit this one out. But there were a surprising number of Republican lawmakers who signaled willingness to vote for Duke as the lesser evil, rationalizing that he would last only a single term, while the wily Cajun would be around for two. "Nine out of ten of the people who voted for Roemer are going to vote for Duke," predicted one Republican legislator.[5] That might have been true of the state's Republican delegation in Baton Rouge, but early polling indicated most Roemer supporters, overwhelmingly upscale and Republican in registration, were paralyzed by indecision and reeling from shock. "I guess you could say I'm caught between a rock and a hard place," confessed a New Orleans restaurant owner during the runoff campaign's first week.[6] Ten days after the primary election, a Mason-Dixon Opinion Research poll had Edwards leading Duke by only a four-point margin, with 12 percent undecided. And truly frightening was that the undecided voters seemed likely to break for Duke by virtue of Edwards's higher negative numbers.[7]

Indeed, from the tipoff of the primary to the runoff's final week, the Duke phenomenon seemed like a runaway train. Duke's blue-and-white signs hung high on the pines fringing country roads. Supporters whooped it up in bars and festivals across the state, hoisting beer cans aloft as they waved their Duke-emblazoned baseball hats. Duke made a triumphant return to Free Speech Alley on the Louisiana State University campus. A generation earlier he had been comic relief for students heading to lunch in the university cafeteria. Now hundreds jammed the oak-shaded driveway, erupting into choruses of "Duke, Duke, Duke" when their idol lashed out at affirmative action. At Northeastern State University in Monroe, a packed auditorium, primed beforehand by slide-show images of bayou rusticity and strains of Randy Newman's "Louisiana," gave way to religious rapture. "I touched him," squealed a young woman as Duke squeezed through the crowd. Down in the southwest corner of the state, at the annual Rice Festival parade in Crowley, Edwards's hometown, Duke received a hero's welcome. At an American Association of Retired Persons (AARP) convention in Baton Rouge, where he stumbled into a verbal brawl with the former governor over welfare, Duke won over the compassion-weary senior citizens, who showered Edwards with boos and catcalls. It was widely conceded that Duke had bested his opponent in the runoff campaign's first statewide television debate, held in Baton Rouge; Edwards emerged confused and off his stride. Meanwhile, Duke was airing thirty-minute television info-mercials staged in a book-lined study seeded with potted plants. Relaxing in a wingback chair beside his two adolescent daughters, he reassured Roemer voters that he shared the governor's belief in leaner government and cleaner air.[8]

From the outset it was obvious that galvanizing Roemer's benumbed supporters held the key to halting the Duke juggernaut. But it was a surprisingly daunting a task in the beginning. Only a month separated the primary and the election. "Good-government" voters would have to be convinced not only to vote but also to vote for their bête noire, Edwin Edwards. The New Orleans business community needed little convincing. Straightaway following the primary many of the state's major players marched down to Edwards's Monteleone Hotel headquarters in the Vieux Carré to hand over five-thousand-dollar checks, the legal limit. Within a week of the primary the Edwards campaign had its get-out-the-vote resources fully in place. "The money began coming early, but I don't think the vote was there until the last two weeks," said lawyer Donald Mintz, a civic activist and two-time mayoralty candidate, of the Roemer undecideds.[9]

Most everyone agreed that the message would have to be single-mindedly economic: the incalculable damage a Duke victory would inflict on the Louisiana economy. The Chamber of Commerce circulated a position paper by a local university economist proving that very point. The Business Council of New Orleans, made up of the city's top executives, declared its wholehearted agreement with the argument. Jim Bob Moffett, chief executive officer of Freeport McMoran, then New Orleans's only Fortune 500 corporation, used the pulpit of his business-oriented political action committee to sound the alarm. "If Duke is elected, . . . Louisiana wouldn't just be redlined by business around the world; we'd be X-rated," he told an October 25 press conference. A hastily formed business and professional group called the Louisiana Council for Economic Development (LCED) broadcast the same message and began raising money for an independent statewide get-out-the-vote campaign. Former Republican governor David Treen established "Louisianians for Truth," to persuade the state's registered Republicans of the economic importance of voting for Edwards. Although stopping short of endorsing Edwards outright, Roemer did say he would vote for him reluctantly, because Duke would be "death to the state."[10]

The LCED hired Jim Carvin and his associate Ron Faucheux to create an umbrella organization to coordinate the mushrooming stop-Duke movement. But coordination was easier said than done, for this campaign was no ordinary one. It defied top-down management. To the veteran handler Carvin, the task was like riding a saddleless bronco. "Did I have a plan? Yeah, but it disintegrated in the first week," he says. "Endless meetings. One law office to the next, or one corporate office to the next, and everybody maneuvering to get the credit, to be the five-star general, and there was room for only one five-star general. A lot of the conversations were basically the same: 'We want to do this but we don't want to do that. And we want to do this.' In the end, it came down to every group doing their own thing."[11]

Or every individual doing his and her own thing. There was a time when it seemed as though every third Roemer supporter had set himself or herself up as a one-person PAC. Employers wrote employees making known their opposition to Duke. Doctors and dentists sent foreboding messages to their patients. From the old-line Jones, Walker law firm in downtown New Orleans issued a letter cosigned by Uptown establishmentarians to thirty-six hundred "good-government types." "We were trying to legitimize the candidacy of somebody like Edwards," explains George Denegre, one of the signatories and a senior partner in the firm.[12] "In my brief political career I've never seen anything like it," says the attorney Donald Mintz of the do-your-own-thing activism. "It was absolutely unprecedented."[13]

One New Orleans business leader even reached deep into his own pocket to televise private commercials. Owner of a large antique store in the French Quarter and a manufacturer of prefinished plywood before that, David Dixon had been the driving force behind the construction of the Superdome and the campaign to bring a National Football League franchise to the city. Three days following the primary, he began running testimonials on statewide television. With the city's domed stadium as backdrop, the tall and bespectacled Dixon pointedly warned viewers that "David Duke says his election won't hurt the convention industry. He's right. He won't hurt it. He'll eliminate it." Dixon says he seized the initiative because he feared the stop-Duke forces would take too long to get moving. "I felt it was time to put everything in perspective in a hurry." The ads cost him nearly fifty thousand dollars.[14]

But the curious thing about the save-our-economy theme was less the content of the message than the moral fervor with which the message was communicated. You cannot talk to the major principals without gaining the impression that economic self-interest was merely a smoke screen for masking moral concern. "Frankly, I was outraged by the immorality of Duke's candidacy," says Dixon, "but I felt it probably wouldn't do a whole lot of good to express my outrage."

Denegre has said pretty much the same thing. Descending, on one side, from French exiles from the great Saint Domingue slave revolution of the 1790s and, on the other, from the Charles Colcock Joneses of *Children of Pride* fame, the Denegre family has been a fixture of the local aristocracy since the early antebellum period. "Huey Long always said the state was run by New York banks and New Orleans lawyers, and I think that's still pretty true," says Denegre. "The lawyers in our kind of firm represent the vested interests." Surveying the port from a corner office high above the river, Denegre, a past president of the New Orleans Chamber, grows wistful about his native city. "This is a truly noble city," he says, paraphrasing Gabriel García Márquez's *A Hundred Years of Solitude*. "We've been trying to kill it for three hundred years, and we haven't succeeded yet." During the runoff, however, Denegre's paramount concern was not solely the economic peril stalking his hometown but also the menace of racial division. "I had never seen an election where you could say, 'This is a moral question. You have to do this. You don't have a choice.' Fortunately, it was also an economic issue."[15]

In short, if the message was economic, the impulse was moral. And frequently the moral passion spoke more loudly than the message itself.

Passion even permeated the press release of Jim Bob Moffett. "People who support reform and good government can't sit this one out. This is beyond politics-as-usual. Dante wrote that the hottest places in hell are reserved for those who, in times of crisis, remain neutral. We can't be neutral. We have to take a stand, and voting for Edwards is our only choice."[16] This is hardly the language of lost jobs and vanishing conventions. It is the idiom of moral principle and civic duty.

A sense of moral urgency seemed to sweep across the top echelons of Louisiana society. Ansel M. Stroud, the commanding general of the fourteen-thousand-member state National Guard, took everyone by surprise when he appeared in television ads wearing his major general's uniform and saying, with hangdog seriousness, that he did not believe a former Nazi and Klansman should serve as governor of the state. Little in this Republican appointee's past foreshadowed his assuming a public stance. Born and raised in Dixie, Louisiana, just north of Shreveport, up to now Stroud had studiously steered clear of partisan politics. His racial views had evolved in tandem with the South's, and it affected his moral outlook. "In 1948, by today's standards, I was an extreme racist. I didn't think I was. Today, by 1948 standards, I'm an ultra-liberal. But things have changed, and I've changed with them."[17]

Although headquartered in Jackson Barracks, just downriver from New Orleans, his duties kept him constantly on the road traveling around the state, inspecting local units, delivering luncheon speeches. As the Duke movement ignited grassroots enthusiasm in the hinterland, Stroud grew alarmed. Racial polarization was spreading. What if Duke was elected? He pulled from his personal library books on Huey Long and Adolf Hitler. He even reread the Kingfish's *My First Hundred Days in the White House*. The ghost of Huey haunts Jackson Barracks where Stroud makes his home. "We have twelve Thompson submachine guns that Huey bought back in our museum." "Hell, [a fascist takeover] could happen here," he said to himself while reading T. Harry Williams's magisterial biography.[18]

Stroud probably would have kept his concerns to himself had one of his senior staff officers not approached him about climbing on the Duke band-wagon. It was the Sunday morning following the primary election. Stroud was in his Jackson Barracks office taking care of last-minute business before departing that afternoon for an air commander's conference in Washington. The officer entered Stroud's office.

"I have supported Duke," he told his commander, "and if you want to stay as the adjutant general I could get it worked out."

Stroud laughed. "You've got to be kidding!"

"No. He's going to be the next governor, and you can be the AG."

"You're really serious?" Stroud asked, incredulously.

"Yeah, and I'm supposed to ask you this question."

The general leveled his gaze. "Well, you tell whoever told you to ask me that, that I wouldn't work for David Duke one fucking minute."

"That kind of ended the conversation," Stroud admits. But his anger was undiminished. The general shoved his trip preparations off to one side of his desk and immediately drafted a personal letter to every member of the Louisiana Guard, paying for the postage, copying, and stationery costs out of his own pocket. "I didn't tell anybody who to vote for. I just said that in my opinion it would be unwise to have a Klansman and a neo-Nazi as the commander-in-chief of the Louisiana National Guard." When asked a short while later to repeat the same message in a television commercial, he did not hesitate one second. "I did the shoot two ways. One in uniform, one not. I wasn't very effective not in uniform." He decided to go with the uniform version after the Pentagon gave him legal clearance. (The loophole is that he had just reached the legal retirement age from the military.)[19]

His office was soon deluged with letters and abusive phone calls; a few were threatening, and most came from Duke phone banks. "Basically they were all saying the same thing." Two members of his staff were tied up for days just logging all the calls. The Duke camp even contacted the Pentagon and the Justice Department to have Stroud fired or indicted. "This was my first active involvement in an election, and probably my last," Stroud says. "But I'd do it again. There are certain issues [about which] there's no room for compromise. . . . David Duke stands for everything that I fought against in World War II. This was a moral issue."[20]

If Louisiana's "race from hell" was a postmodernist carnival of multiple meanings and concealed motives, its most famous bumper sticker embodied many of the paradoxes: "Vote for the Crook: It's Important." David Brinkley held up the blue-and-white sticker at the conclusion of his *Sunday Morning with David Brinkley* show. A reporter from the *Philadelphia Inquirer* wrote an article entitled "In La., a Crook Is Lookin' Good," exclaiming, "And you thought Pennsylvania was the state of champions."[21] To many outsiders the slogan exemplified all that was wrong with Louisiana politics. But the bumper sticker was conceived out of moral urgency and probably played a critical role in helping Roemer voters over the moral hump of voting for Edwin Edwards.

The brainstorm of a young stockbroker by the name of Kirby Newburger, the idea for the bumper sticker came to him suddenly on the Sunday morning following the primary. For more than a week before the primary election, he had the troubling premonition that the state was headed for a runoff between Duke and Edwards, both of whom enjoyed avid support. "I detected very little enthusiasm for Buddy Roemer, although I voted for him," Newburger says. He began asking his friends what they planned to do in the event Roemer was knocked out of the general election by Duke and Edwards. Many replied there was no way they would ever vote for Edwards.

"Then you're going to vote for Duke?"

"No, I'm not going to vote for Duke, either."

"Then you're not going to vote?"

"For some reason they didn't understand that not voting would effect the outcome of the election. But to me it was just so black and white. It was a moral issue. I told my wife that we would have moved *immediately* had Duke been elected. In fact, I had given her a map of where my company has offices and asked her to pick where she would like to live." Newburger was so upset about the campaign, he left a blistering message on his sister's answering machine for leaving town to visit her husband the day before the election. "I was so mad that she had chosen not to vote in such an important election. If everybody who had supported Roemer had chosen not to vote, David Duke would have been elected governor of the state of Louisiana."[22]

"Also, I was convinced that David Duke had not changed. I knew him personally. We had attended a seminar together. He never opened his mouth; he just sat there on the edge of his seat, very interested. So when friends kept telling me that there was no way they would ever vote for Edwards, I thought let's be cute about it. We have a bad guy on one side, and we have a guy who is nearly as bad on the other. He's a crook. So, vote for the crook. That's what we're going to go with. I thought it just might work."

"That morning I called my printer at home and said, 'Dart, would you print me up 250 bumper stickers that read "Vote for the Crook: It's Important"?' And he said yes. He didn't need to talk about color, size, or any of that stuff. He understood immediately what I wanted and what I was trying to do."

"It really struck a chord with people. They would stop me on the street and say, Where can I get one of those bumper stickers? and I'd say, hold on, I'll get one for you out of my trunk. People called me from Lafayette wanting bumper stickers. I ran through them pretty quickly."

Soon people were calling the printer directly to have extra copies made up. "We must have printed five thousand of them altogether," notes Dart Fee, who did the initial run for Newburger. Rhoda Faust, owner and cofounder of the local Maple Leaf bookstore chain, personally ordered several batches. She explains her motives thus: "The utter cynicism and yet the utter truth of what the bumper sticker said is what caused it to catch on. It was Louisiana outrageous, another example of the fix we've gotten ourselves into without the possibility of graceful exit. I also think it was just fun for people to be able to say out loud that they were going to have to vote for a crook, and maybe it also helped some of the Roemer voters to come out of denial. We still get asked for the bumper stickers now and then."[23]

Even Edwin Edwards got into the act. "He called me personally asking for twelve bumper stickers and sent over an aide to pick them up," Newburger says. "I asked the aide what the governor intended to do with them. He said put them on his car. And Edwards did. Now, I guess it is sickening to have a governor drive around with a bumper sticker that says 'Vote for the Crook.' But it's also funny."[24]

So, the bumper sticker had a double meaning all along. "Vote for the Crook" got the laughs. But "It's Important" was the subliminal spur to action. As for the humor, which has always been the saving grace of Louisiana politics, it was mere sugarcoating for the bitter pill of civic duty. And Roemer supporters seemed to swallow it gladly.

"Vote for the Crook" was one of the campaign's few light moments; otherwise, the public mood was serious. It was hard to stand in a supermarket checkout line without being soaked in suspicion: Was he a hidden Duke voter? Did she sympathize with Nazis? Who do I talk to every day that I really don't know? The grim feeling robbed the campaign of all enjoyment. "Louisiana elections to me are fun, and most people who service the political industry have fun at it," says the pollster Joe Walker. "It's part of the reason we do it. But there was no fun in it. It was too damn serious. Everybody was uptight and tense and calling you to meetings to do this and do that, and everybody you ran into was depressed."[25]

The grave earnestness gripped all strata of the incipient anti-Duke movement. At the grassroots level the moral intensity was even more implacable and difficult to control. In his long career as a political consultant, Jim Carvin had never seen its like: "I've lived through various intense campaigns. But with this one, there was no comparison." Joe Walker agrees: "This was the first time that everyone was involved."[26]

While rank-and-file Roemer supporters took two weeks to stir, African American voters catapulted into action immediately after the primary election. The mass mobilization reflected a dramatic change in attitude in the black community. "Believe it or not, people were not excited about the primary," says Cleo Fields, who was a state senator at the time.[27] (Fields won a black majority congressional district in north Louisiana in a subsequent election, only to lose it later after federal courts ordered that his district be redrawn.) Distressed by the deepening racial polarization, black Louisianians had begun to lose faith in the efficacy of the ballot. But despair vanished instantly when confronted with stark electoral choices. Nor was there any agonizing over whether to support Edwards. Louisiana's African Americans had backed the Cajun governor in the past, and he had rewarded their loyalty with jobs, contracts, and generous appropriations. Duke represented a clear and present danger, and the old civil rights leadership wasted no time countering it. The NAACP, which still maintained a statewide network of local branches reaching into nearly every significant black community across the state, concentrated immediately on ratcheting up voter registration and voter turnout. But following the primary they faced an unaccustomed challenge. It was not how to drum up interest but how to channel the excitement suddenly engulfing the African American electorate.

In Louisiana voter registration books are customarily reopened for two working days following a primary election, usually to a desultory business. This time things were different. By 8:00 A.M. on Monday morning, registrars across the state were fighting off huge crowds. Black church congregations arrived by the busload. In New Orleans the lines ran for blocks. "It looks like judgement day out here," said an off-duty security guard waiting in a lengthening registration queue in the city's Carrollton section.[28] In Baton Rouge, outside the government building where the registrar's office was housed, the column fell away to infinity.

The mood was festive considering the circumstances. Southern University's famous marching band showed up to serenade the would-be registrants. Vans and cars jammed with students shuttled back and forth nonstop from the nearby black campus. Automobiles pulled up with trunkloads of soft drinks for distribution to the crowd. Someone even set up a barbecue grill in the parking lot to roast hotdogs. Late in the afternoon a tornado-spawning thunderstorm swept in from the west. As Edwards's north Louisiana coordinator, Fields was on hand to oversee the voter registration drive. He blared from the megaphone that people needed to move inside the underground parking garage and re-form the line there. But the line's tail end was still pelted by the driving rain. A middle-aged black man near the front immediately marched to the rear. "I don't want anybody here to have an excuse to go home and not bother to register to vote," he said. It was five o'clock in the afternoon, and moving to the back of the line meant the man would have to wait another six to seven hours to register.

And then the crowd was taken aback by a ninety-two-year-old, first-time registrant who stood for hours outside the registrar's office and refused to sit down for fear of losing his place in line. He said he intended to cast an absentee ballot as well. There were no pressing travel plans in his future. He merely wanted to ensure his vote was cast in case he died before the election.

"Among these older people the motives were simple," Fields explains. "They saw a vision of the past flash before their eyes, and they saw pain and hurt, and they said 'when that first happened I didn't have the right to vote. But now I do.' " But the motive impelling younger voters was not fear but civic patriotism. They were insulted by the thought the contest might be close. "Let's send a message to the rest of the country that we're not asleep. Let's take it upon ourselves to be the champions or saviors of this state. That was their attitude," Fields says. "In my opinion the fear factor played less of a role than these other factors."[29]

The two-day registration set an all-time record. "We have never seen anything like this before," said state elections commissioner Jerry Fowler. Over sixty-eight thousand new voters were added to the rolls, and half of them were black.[30]

The excitement pervading the black community intensified rather than lessened after the closing of the registration books. During the primary Fields had needed to scramble to build an audience for Edwards's rallies. But once the runoff campaign shifted into gear, the state senator was overwhelmed by voters who wanted to get involved. His office in Baton Rouge was flooded with phone calls when word leaked out that he or another Edwards staffer was scheduled to appear in some remote town. "I heard that Senator Fields is going to be in town tonight," a caller would say. "I want to talk to him *personally* about what I can do to help the governor's campaign." No one was ready to take no for an answer. Fields spent significant time mediating organizational rivalries. "Whenever you deal with local politics every group feels that they should be in charge of that particular parish," he says. "But in this campaign everybody wanted to play a major role, everybody was excited, and everybody wanted to wear the chief's hat. That caused some problems."[31] It was a headache with which Carvin and his associates were familiar. They too were having trouble controlling this growing moral movement.

If the Roemer electorate was slow to become involved, it moved quickly once it did start. Says Cherie Gauthier, Edwards's coordinator in suburban Jefferson Parish, "It was BOOM. One week we had one hundred volunteers, the next we had seven hundred. The volunteer base grew so rapidly, we were scrambling to figure out how to fit these people into the campaign." They were caught short in the way of signage and campaign literature and lacked enough trucks to handle the proliferating sign crews. Average citizens streamed through the door waving their checkbooks, insisting on making a campaign contribution then and there. Gauthier, the daughter of a hugely successful personal injury lawyer who organized the class action suit against the major tobacco companies that succeeded, made it a point not to ask whether the recent converts had supported Roemer. "At least that was my rule: 'Ye shalt not harbor a grudge.'"[32]

For Roemer supporters unable to bring themselves to work in the Edwards organization, there were plenty of campaign alternatives from which to choose. Ten days after the primary election, ad hoc phone banks had been established in several downtown law firms. They operated five days a week and never wanted for volunteers. The Louisiana Coalition alone ran two for several nights, but there were many others.

It was inevitable that the New Americans Social Club would get involved in the burgeoning crusade. Not since Rockwell's 1961 "hate ride" had the city's small survivor community been so riled up. They were considerably older now. Several were infirm; many had died. A few had cut their ties with the club long ago because of feuds and petty squabbles. But the opinionated vim for which members were justly famous was as strong as ever, and their intensely felt obligation to honor the memory of the Holocaust's slaughtered millions had deepened over the years.

Like Anne Levy, as the 1980s drew to a close the city's New Americans were starting to disinter buried memories. By then a wider public had rediscovered the Jewish tragedy and actually seemed willing to bear witness to the stories survivors had to tell. Their status as survivors had undergone a remarkable metamorphosis: from poor cousins to saints and relics in a new Jewish civic religion. The transformation took place in New Orleans, too, as the New Americans's "Warsaw Ghetto Uprising Memorial Service" became a focal point of the Jewish community's rituals of collective memory.[33] Grandparenthood was kind to the city's survivors, even if they did grouse about how American mobility had scattered their children to the four winds. People were now listening to them, taking them seriously. Their sons and daughters had scaled the ladder of success with astonishing speed. After the trauma and guilt of survival, the New Americans had finally achieved a measure of inner peace. But the Duke-Edwards runoff shattered the surface calm. The possibility of David Duke winning political power posed an actual, rather than a symbolic, threat. There was no question they had to act. After talking it over with club president Felicia Fuksman, Shep Zitler called an emergency meeting.[34]

It took place a few days after the primary election in one of the meeting rooms in the Jewish Community Center on the corner of Jefferson and St. Charles Avenue. As these events go, it was well attended: virtually all forty surviving members showed up. Survivor meetings are invariably stormy, and this one also had its inclement moments. Everyone's question was, What are we going to do? Clouding the answer was the ingrained instinct of New Orleans's organized Jewish community to stay in the background. "Jewish institutions should maintain a low profile," declared a letter sent by the city's Jewish federation to its affiliated groups immediately after the primary election. "Jews should get involved as citizens but not as Jewish organizations" to avoid a backlash that might contribute votes to David Duke.

Henry Galler, a Galician Jew who survived by escaping to Russia, later becoming an officer in the Polish army that formed in Soviet territory following the German invasion, was the first to express an opinion. A successful tailor, he speaks with forceful gestures and a steady gaze. He said the club needed to take the federation's directive into consideration when crafting its strategy. But there was little sentiment just then for sitting on one's hands, nor did Galler himself feel that way. He had raised the issue to start discussion.[35] Not surprisingly, several New Americans, still recalling the intracommunal conflicts thirty years earlier over how to respond to Rockwell's "hate ride," interpreted the directive as another effort by Reform leaders to muzzle hot-headed survivors. "They took the letter as though it had been written to them, which it wasn't," says Jane Buchsbaum, the federation's executive director and secretary of the Louisiana Coalition. "It was written to all forty-two affiliated groups. We felt it was a time for well-thought-out action, and not for everybody to go off and do crazy things, like Mordechai Levy [of the Jewish Defense League] had done during Duke's legislative race. The New Americans got very exercised, however."[36]

The person who captured the mood of activism spreading through the room was not a survivor but a member of the second generation—Shep Zitler's son, Justin. Short like his father and compactly built, Justin had been a professional dancer in San Francisco before a career-ending injury led him into the practice of civil rights law. Early in the discussion Shep asked his son to state his opinion. Justin was overwrought. "This particular group of Holocaust survivors was required morally and ethically to make a statement, notwithstanding the federation's directive," he declared. How often do you have the opportunity to proclaim to the world that you have a message that needs to be heard, "which is that we've seen it before?" What banner will you leave us, the second generation, if you fail to thunder in unison, "Never again?"[37]

The meeting suddenly became charged with emotion. "People made some impassioned speeches," Justin says. Anne, who had renewed the Skorecki connection to the New Americans Social Club in the early 1980s, also spoke in favor of acting as a group. A consensus quickly crystallized that the survivors would make some sort of a public statement. No vote was taken. The club had never operated that way in the past, and the members were not about to now. There was talk of writing separate letters as individuals, but that option was discarded because some members objected to affixing their signatures to public documents. "It was a holdover fear of retribution that has always been there and probably always will be on the part of Holocaust survivors," Justin says. The group ultimately decided to issue the letter not in the name of the New Americans Social Club but simply as "Holocaust Survivors."[38]

They deputed Justin Zitler to draft the letter. Legal work around his law office came to a two-day standstill while he, his partner, and an attorney friend ran through multiple drafts. Because the statement had to pass muster with every member of the club, Justin went without sleep to ensure that every phrase was just right. "I had no desire to get involved in the internal dynamics of the New Americans Social Club by having one word or one sentence that people did not agree with, and that meant recirculating the letter and getting notes backs," he says. There were the additional expectations that Justin—the surrogate son of the New American family—would naturally produce a statement that would reflect credit on the entire community. The phrasing finally agreed on was pitched to Roemer supporters " 'who can't bring themselves' to vote for Edwin Edwards and are considering sitting out the governor's election." The survivors offered themselves as messengers to the future. "We speak out now so that never again should anyone have to endure what we have survived." Before Hitler ruined their lives, the letter said, they had belonged to the middle class just as the Roemer supporters do today. But the Führer fooled everyone, concealing his true agenda, as Duke himself was trying to do now, and then swiftly amassing dictatorial powers after becoming Reich's Chancellor. Louisiana was not immune from history. Its experience with political bosses and powerful governors was proof of that. A Nazi-like tragedy could happen here, the group warned, concluding with the adjuration to vote against David Duke on November 16. "There is no other choice." The letter was signed by Shep Zitler, "Chairman of the Board, Holocaust Survivors."[39]

Club members wanted to hand-deliver their letter personally to *The Times-Picayune*, and on the day designated for doing so, about a dozen of them gathered at Henry Galler's shop. Shep Zitler and Felicia Fuksman were on hand, as were Anne Levy and Jeannine Burke, a Belgian Jewish child survivor who was starting to become active in the club. As a matter of courtesy, the group had decided to show the letter to Jane Buchsbaum at the federation before releasing it to the press. But the local CBS affiliate had already been tipped off that a group of local survivors was planning to issue a statement about the election, so a film crew showed up at Galler's shop insisting on shooting the letter and conducting interviews. Galler said, "No, no, no, we can't show it to the media people. Bring it to Jane Buchsbaum first." Thus the crew tagged along as the New Americans trooped from Galler's tailor shop to the federation offices two blocks away. And there the familiar conflict between a Reform community's instinct to blend in and the memory-burdened survivor obligation to cry "never again" surfaced once more.[40]

Jane Buchsbaum was angry and alarmed when she saw the television crew outside the federation's offices, together with the delegation of New Americans. A day or two earlier, when the CBS reporter had asked for names of survivors available to be interviewed, Buchsbaum had said the federation had to clear the matter with local survivors first. She made the crew wait outside while the New Americans filed into her office.

"Jane, do you like the letter?" Justin Zitler asked, who was with the group.

"I just don't think we should do this," Buchsbaum replied, and then called her media relations staffer into the room. He looked the letter over and then said, "What if it succeeds?"

"What do you mean?"

"Well, what if you get calls for a lot of interviews from this? Let's say a lot of people read this and are very interested in it and then, all of a sudden, the Jewish community comes into the forefront. This is exactly what we are worried about."[41]

But public interest was precisely the response Shep Zitler and the others were hoping for, and Buchsbaum, sensing the club's strong feelings on the matter, gave the letter her blessing and allowed them to use the federation's conference room for the television shoot.

That evening Shep Zitler and other survivors appeared on camera complaining that the federation had tried to stop them from speaking out against Duke, and they were not about to be silenced. "I can't tell you the betrayal I felt," Jane says when she saw broadcast. She had always been close to the club, and she felt hurt, calling several survivors for an explanation.[42] Anne was mortified. She herself had already called Buchsbaum to apologize. "It was like a ball that was rolling and we couldn't stop it," Anne explains.

But the bad feeling was probably unavoidable given the long history of intracommunity tension between assimilation and memory. The only surprising thing about the episode was not the recurrence of conflict but the belatedness of its return.

After the meeting at the federation office, Shep Zitler, Henry Galler, and Felicia Fuksman went directly to *The Times-Picayune*, marching into the office of Malcolm Forsyth, the editorial page editor. By now the paper had gone on full-scale alert to defeat Duke, dispatching forty reporters a day to gather election news, each day publishing prize-winning editorials and investigative stories that did not blur as much as erase the line between news coverage and editorials. "There was certainly a quantum leap in the way we covered Duke between the primary and the runoff," admits Jim Amoss, the editor, "but it was journalistically and morally fully justified."[43] The no-holds-barred strategy, though, stirred controversy on the newsroom floor. "There was poison in the air," said Keith Woods, the former African American city editor. "Reporters crying, depression, constant bickering."[44]

One manifestation of the abrupt change was the suspension of the paper's long-standing policy of not printing letters for or against a political candidate. During the runoff campaign, every few days the paper now ran a full-page "Readers Respond" collection of letters on Duke and Edwards. "The response was extraordinary," states Forsyth. "We received letters by the basketful. We even had a call-in line for people and transcribed their messages and ran them too. We did some different kinds of things than we would for just an ordinary run."[45] Zitler, Galler, and Fuksman told Forsyth they had a letter for publication. Forsyth pointed to a stack three feet high sitting on his desk and said, in his soft southern drawl, "yes, and I have these letters for publication." The three survivors were in no mood to be put off, however. "Basically, my dad, Henry Galler, and Felicia cornered this guy and forced him to read the letter," says Justin Zitler. The recognition on Forsyth's part was instantaneous. "This is just the message we've been looking for," he said. "We're going to put it right at the top of the next bunch of letters that we publish." And that is where it appeared in the November 5 issue of "Readers Respond," under the title, "History Lesson: Tyranny Comes Step by Step."[46]

The letter elicited the wide response desired by the New Americans and dreaded by some federation staffers. Newspaper editors in Lafayette and Alexandria called asking permission to reprint the letter. Ordinary citizens around the state telephoned Shep and Justin Zitler to express approval. The statement touched some kind of nerve. "Everbody in the New Americans club was so proud and happy about that letter," Justin says. "We all felt really proud that we had done what we wanted to do," says Felicia Fuksman. "We felt like we accomplished something. And we were very proud of Justin."[47]

It was as if the New Americans had finally received unfettered freedom to broadcast to the future the message that both guilt and memory dictated that they proclaim. Could any survivor mission have been more therapeutic?

All the while, Anne Levy was struggling to make public her own testimony concerning history's lessons. She was still grieving her father's death six months earlier, yet her grief seems only to have heightened the fear and anger she felt in common with other New Americans toward David Duke's terrifying proximity to actual power. Anne concluded the best medicine for what ailed her was becoming more politically involved. She participated in one of the Louisiana Coalition's phone banks. "It was a good experience," she says. "I was afraid of getting a real Duke supporter. But I was lucky. It was just the opposite. I got mostly people who were voting with us."

But the atmosphere of menace hanging over the election left her deeply unsettled, and itching to do something more. "It was strange," Anne said, not long after the runoff election. "All of a sudden you really had to be cautious who you spoke with, even here at the store. As a matter of fact, a repairman was in right before the election. We're kind of talking, and I was upset about the campaign. He returned to the store the other day and said, 'You see, I told you he wouldn't win.' But I wasn't too sure about this man, how he felt. And there were a couple of young people, just draymen, who would come in here. You knew they were for David Duke. I tried to explain to them why he was bad news for all of us. I tried to convince them it was important that he be defeated. But I just knew deep down that they were going to vote for him. It was a bad time for me and for a lot of other people."

Since the 1990 Senate race, Anne's close friend Elinor Cohen had been goading her to be more vocal in public. After Anne backed out of speaking at the Rock against Racism concert at the University of New Orleans (UNO), her friend stepped up the needling. Anne's youngest daughter, Carol, had spoken in her mother's place at the concert. Elinor was in attendance. "I said to Anne, 'You would have been so proud of your child.' What I was thinking was, 'Your kid said what you needed to say. Your kid told the story to these students that you needed to say, and now you've got to go tell it.' "[48]

But Anne was afraid to address large groups, especially ones whose sympathies she held in doubt. Victims of trauma need safe spaces in which to express their feelings of loss and violation, requiring audiences who are willing to bear witness to those sufferings. It is the way survivors reconnect with the larger world, the way they reestablish the basic trust shattered by the original offense.[49] But Duke had poisoned the environment, spreading unreason and hate, especially among young people, the very audience she felt it so important to reach. She had tried to reach them once before, during a Free Speech Forum at the UNO campus in late November 1989 while Duke was positioning himself for a run at Bennett Johnston's senate seat, and the result was emotionally devastating. In 1959 UNO had opened its doors as the Deep South's first desegregated public university. But most of its undergraduates, a large percentage of whom worked part-time, were commuter students from surrounding white suburbs, and they were deeply alienated from the political status quo. They blamed corrupt politicians for gorging themselves on Louisiana's mineral riches instead of using the windfall oil and gas revenues of the 1970s and early 1980s to diversify the economy. All that survived of their patrimony were fouled bayous and streams, an underwater junkyard of rusted pipelines, and the highest cancer rate in the country. Any outsider candidate with the sex appeal of youth and a coherent explanation for why society had suddenly become unfair stood an excellent chance of winning their allegiance. And on the eve of his run for the United States Senate, it was clear that Duke was doing just that. By the summer of 1990, according to a poll conducted for the Louisiana Coalition, nearly 80 percent of the state's young white men between the ages of eighteen and twenty-four who had graduated from high school or were still in college were favoring Duke in the senate election.[50]

Staged in an open-air amphitheater called the Student Park, UNO's Free Speech Forums were usually widely advertised and poorly attended. The forum at which Duke was slated to speak was deliberately played down to keep the audience small. "We did not want to have any publicity in advance, because certain groups who support Duke could have created a serious disturbance," the president of the Student Government Association told the school newspaper. Many Duke well-wishers showed up for the noontime event anyway, along with the simply curious and clusters of protesters. The crowd surpassed a hundred. The campus police turned out in force to assure Duke's safety.[51] Learning of the forum by word of mouth, Carol Levy asked her mother to attend. Anne said she would. "At that particular time I felt an urge to challenge this man wherever he went, especially when it came to the young people. He had a following with some of them. I had to speak up. And maybe Tata's illness had something to do with it, too. Who knows why you do certain things at any given moment in your life? It was like I was on automatic pilot."

Duke, wearing a turtleneck, pacing across the stage, described himself to the audience as "a writer and an environmentalist," calling his opponents "Zionists," especially *The Times-Picayune*, a Newhouse chain paper. An attractive young girlfriend was in tow. He was full of animation. Self-confidence exuded from every pore. "He looked kind of hip," remembers Tyler Bridges, then covering the event for *The Times-Picayune*. The high point came during the question-and-answer period, when Anne, lost in her own drama, finally got her turn at the mike. "Mr. Duke, you say that you are a writer and a bookseller. But why don't you tell them that you sell anti-Semitic books?" Anne's voice cracked, and her small frame shook. Duke gave his stock answer: the major book chains sold those books, so what was the big deal? Then Carol reached the microphone: "Mr. Duke, the reason why this lady is so upset is because in the past you denied that the Holocaust ever happened. If it never happened, then I'd like you to tell me where my family is. A very simple question. My family was wiped out by the Nazis, and if you say it never happened, then please tell me where my family is." Duke looked Anne straight in the eye, coolly answering, "Well, actually, I realize the Holocaust may have happened, but it wasn't as bad as they made it out to be." Anne jumped to her feet. "You weren't even there!" she screamed. "Do you want to hear my side of the story? I was there!" She was unrelenting. Duke accused her of paranoia, quickly segueing to his position on welfare illegitimacy. At that point a segment of the crowd began to chant, "Let her speak." They said it over and over again. But the student moderator denied her another turn at the microphone, and save for a vocal minority, the audience endorsed the decision.[52]

Anne wanted to leave as quickly as possible. The mood of the crowd scared her. "For me to see the younger generation following and believing him was devastating," she says. "It was as though what had happened fifty years ago was in vain, and whatever I had to say was useless." Carol tried to reassure her mother. "No, this is your place," she said. "He doesn't belong. Listen to the crowd. The crowd is behind you 100 percent."[53] People did come up to her afterward, showing the support she desperately needed in a moment of extremely vulnerability.

Nonetheless, the audience was with the day's featured speaker, not with Anne. "Duke had generally won over that crowd," says Bridges. "A lot of the students liked him, and here was this woman raising something that seemed out of left field. She didn't seem to fit in. Duke did a good job of silencing her."[54] Anne came away from the forum with powerful feelings of futility and estrangement.

It therefore took her quite a while to recover from the UNO encounter. When campus organizers of the Rock against Racism rally asked her to speak the following summer, during the height of the U.S. Senate campaign, Anne declined. Sharing painful memories with strangers was difficult enough even under ideal circumstances. But testifying before large, potentially hostile audiences made her panic stricken.

But her friend Elinor kept egging her on, growing relentless during the governor's race. If guilt is what it took to arouse Anne, Elinor would not flinch. "Anne, you have no family. They perished. So that their deaths should not be in vain, get up and talk about Duke. Go tell your story to avenge every cousin, every aunt, every uncle that you lost. For them, go tell your story!" And then Anne would shrug and say, "Yeah, you're right! That's what I really ought to do." But then she would do nothing. "I guess deep down I knew I really should do it," Anne admits, "but I never had the gumption. I was not a public speaker. I was shy about it. I was also a little uncomfortable about how the audience would react." Elinor kept up the moral pressure. "I used to stir Anne up to no end," she confesses. "I used to needle her unmercifully."[55] "She was persistent, that's for sure," Anne says.

Then a speaking opportunity arose at UNO at the height of the Duke-Edwards runoff campaign. A European history professor named Jerry Bodet told Cohen how upset he was at the political support Duke was enjoying among Bodet's students. A native New Orleanian, Bodet has a smiling affability that belies his cast-iron principles. Campus skinheads had keyed a swastika onto the front fender of his car and smashed the windshield. Bodet was angry and more than a little apprehensive. Elinor Cohen was a former student. "I have a friend who lived through the Holocaust," she told him. "How would you feel about her coming in here and telling these kids some firsthand stories about how it really was?" Bodet replied, "Oh, I would love nothing better. Who is it?" "Anne Levy."[56]

Elinor drove directly to the Levy store to tell her friend about a UNO professor interested in having a Holocaust survivor speak to his students, asking if she would like to be that guest speaker. This time Elinor had no need to use cajolery: "I could see Anne go off like a firecracker." "I would like that," Anne said. "I think it's time I told my story."

About fifty to sixty students were enrolled in Bodet's European history course, and most showed up for that morning's class. Anne felt as though her stomach had been invaded by butterflies. She was going to face not warmly disposed friends but avid Duke supporters, and there was no way of gauging ahead of time how they might respond to her remarks. Were they going to display the same callow indifference that many students had exhibited at the Free Speech Forum two years earlier? "I knew she was deathly scared going in, but she was also angry," Elinor says. "She had gotten to that point where she had to come out in public and say, 'You've heard the David Duke story. Now let me tell you mine.'"

Anne began tentatively, in a soft voice crinkling with emotion. The modulations of tone betrayed faint traces of Jewish singsong. She was immaculately dressed as always—"like somebody's sharp-looking mother, not somebody's grandmother," remembers Cohen. Early in the talk doors kept slamming as the commuter students trickled in late. There was nervous rustling of paper. Then the room became absolutely silent.

As straightforwardly as she could, Anne narrated the key points of the Skorecki saga—the escape from Łódź in a milk wagon, the family's near starvation in the Warsaw Ghetto, Tata's miraculous return from Białystok, the days of silence in the vegetable bin, the escape to Praga in a smelly garbage truck and more hiding and more silence, the outtrek to the American zone of occupied Germany—it was all there, in a technicolor detail that even her close friend Elinor was hearing for the first time. Anne sobbed audibly at many points but held tightly to the narrative thread. Then she did a soft landing, gently bringing the class from that place and time to the menacing Louisiana present:

> You can't imagine the cruelty performed on innocent people. And why? [Cries] What did they do? What in the world did four-year-olds or six-year-olds or even ten-year-olds do? Nothing, except we were Jews. We look the same. We eat the same. We breathe the same [air]. We believe in God. But because we didn't believe in the right God, we weren't good enough.
>
> People say it couldn't happen again. I hate to tell you, it can. The hatred, the bigotry . . . you always have to blame it on someone, whether it's the Jews, the blacks, the reds, the Catholics. But everybody suffered.

Look how divided we are right now. And how do we pull ourselves together? How can we have one person talking to one group and ignoring the other? I know you are not going to want to hear this, but if you read your history about what happened in Germany in 1930, you're right at the brink of it. And if you don't speak out—and that's why I am here—don't be surprised. It can happen.

The class was speechless. Students stared in slack-jawed amazement. "They were numb," Elinor says. "They were too stunned to ask questions." And then the classroom erupted in loud applause. Bodet went over to hug Anne. Several other students did likewise. "I thought to myself, 'you've come a long way, baby.' And she had. It was a real turning point for her. She's not afraid anymore."

That much was true. But Anne was still seething about the politics of unreason enveloping her community, and she was poised to pounce on the first chance that presented itself for striking back.

Another opportunity did arise as the gubernatorial race entered the home stretch. It followed in the wake of the second televised debate between Duke and Edwards at a public television station in Baton Rouge, on November 6, 1991, less than two weeks from election day. In a campaign famous for its defining moments, the debate was one of the election's more riveting events. Overconfident, Duke had given himself little time to prepare. Earlier that afternoon, during an appearance at an American Legion Hall in Uptown New Orleans, boisterous protesters rattled him as he entered and left the building. Then on the way to the interstate his driver got stuck in rush hour traffic. The debate was slated for six in the evening, it was after four o'clock already, and Baton Rouge was eighty miles away. After his vehicle crawled free of traffic, the car hurtled northwest at Grand Prix speed.

Duke arrived at the station one minute before six, barely enough time to get miked. He was still agitated about the run-in at the American Legion Hall and the last-minute rush to make the debate. Meanwhile, Edwin Edwards, already wired and made up, was going over the notes he had carefully prepared earlier that afternoon.

For Duke the debate could not have gotten off on a worse foot. He flubbed his opening statement. When asked to itemize his legislative accomplishments, he launched into an antitax diatribe. When invited to specify how he would scrub the budget, he waxed vague. When queried about his employment history, he fired back, "This is a job. This is work." The reporters on the panel were clearly gunning for him. They pressed him to answer the question. They interrupted him, demanding that he be more specific. They chided him for the self-incriminating admission that his job résumé consisted of little more than running for office. The barrage threw Duke off balance.

The coup de grâce was delivered by the panel's only African American journalist, Norman Robinson, the news anchor of the New Orleans NBC affiliate. Tall, with a round face and full mustache, Robinson had left a coveted network position as CBS White House correspondent to return to New Orleans. Born in St. Louis but raised in rural Mississippi and Mobile, Alabama, he had risen rapidly through the ranks of broadcast journalism. The rudiments of his craft he had acquired from a California correspondence school while serving in the Marine Corps band. There followed a brief stint at an alternative rock station in Los Angeles; a job with a five-thousand-watt radio station in Mobile; television news reporting in Mobile and New Orleans; and, then, in rapid-fire order, a Nieman Fellowship at Harvard, the White House job, and finally the position at Channel 6 in New Orleans. Robinson is fond of New Orleans and considers it home. "I'm not here looking to catapult to some place higher. To me this is higher. At some point you've got to stay at home and water your own grass. This is what community is all about."[57]

The deepening racial polarization of the governor's election caused him anguish, though, reminding him of the ethnic warfare tearing at the fabric of Africa and Eastern Europe. He had not the slightest doubt who was to blame. "Duke was beginning to make it acceptable for people to hate one another and to point the finger of blame," he says. As an African American, he felt a sense of personal vulnerability. There was no way he could ignore the increasing racial rancor, even were he of a mind to do so. "You can escape crime by putting bars on the windows, but you can't all of a sudden not be black," he says.

For Robinson, one incident during the runoff race threw everything into sharp perspective. He and his cameraman were doing a stand-up shoot by the side of the highway when a school bus carrying young white kids drove by. "They shouted 'nigger' out of the window of the bus. I didn't know whether to laugh or be outraged. And I thought, 'this kind of thing is really awful.' Everywhere I turned I felt this hatred. I'd see little black kids with the same kind of malice and hatred, and I wondered, 'what for?'"

When Louisiana Public Broadcasting (LPB) asked Robinson to be one of the questioners on the second TV debate, he decided then and there to raise the issue of race at some point during the broadcast. He discussed his intentions with his own management and with officials at LPB. They never said not to raise the subject: "What they said was, 'Be nice.' But it was a matter of conviction for me." Robinson was not sure how he would broach the subject until the debate got under way and he witnessed Duke bobbing and weaving and ducking every question the panelists tossed his way. "Duke is very television savvy, very debate savvy in the way he takes control of the rules and operates according to his own interpretation."[58]

That was the moment Robinson decided to make the issue personal, to force the former Klansman to deal with Norman Robinson as an African American, not as an abstraction to be sliced into sound-bite morsels for mass consumption. "He had to deal with me," Robinson says. "I could speak from experience." It was the same fundamental impulse that had impelled Anne Levy at the Wiesenthal exhibit at the State Capitol two years earlier to confront David Duke with the raw experience of her own tragic history. It was the personal made political, which is the moral essence of politics itself.

"Mr. Duke," Robinson began, "I have to tell you that I am a very concerned citizen. I am a journalist, but first and foremost I am a concerned citizen. And as a minority who has heard you say some very excoriating and diabolical things about minorities, about blacks, about Jews, about Hispanics, I am scared, sir."

There was a pause, as though Robinson was mentally flipping through the Media Resource Kit disseminated by the Louisiana Coalition looking for choice Duke quotations. "I have heard you say Jews deserve to be in the ashbin of history. I've heard you say that horses have contributed more to the building of America than blacks did. Given that kind of past, sir, given that kind of diabolical, evil, vile mentality, convince me, sir, and other minorities like me to entrust their lives and the lives of their children to you."

Duke launched into one of his pat answers about everybody at one time or another having been guilty of intolerance. Didn't Jesse Jackson once confess to having spit in white people's food as a young man?

But the alibi of amoral equivalency only deepened Robinson's anger. "Sir," Robinson barked, "we are talking about political, economic genocide. We're not talking about intolerance. We are not talking about spitting on people, sir. As a newfound Christian, a born-again, are you here willing now to apologize to the people, the minorities of this state, whom you have so dastardly insulted, sir?"

The former Klansman and the former Marine sparred for a few more rounds. "Look, Mr. Robinson, I don't think you are really being fair with me," Duke said in exasperation. "I don't think you are really being honest, sir," Robinson replied.

The closing statements by Edwards and Duke placed an exclamation mark at the end of the sharp exchange. Duke was flat and defensive. Edwards was anything but vintage Edwards: serious, moving, even high-minded. The former governor had used the whole afternoon to rest and prepare for the evening's debate. He was angry that tracking polls showed him pulling only 52.7 percent of the vote. It was enough to win, but not enough to enable Louisianians to redeem their image in the eyes of the nation. Edwards did not want to defeat Duke—he wanted, as Huey used to say, to stomp him. His closest advisers decided that the governor had to become more aggressive. He had to change focus, painting the election as a moral choice. Edwards agreed. The spin, if not the language itself, seems to have been drawn from a strategy paper that Lance Hill at the Louisiana Coalition had mailed to the Edwards camp a week or so earlier. The day of the debate, one of the governor's staffers called to talk it over. The coalition strategy paper urged Edwards to contrast his "record" with Duke's, but to do so over the span of twenty years, not eighteen months. Such an approach would make an issue of Duke's character. It would prevent Duke from running away from his extremist past, as many of his mainstream opposition had been allowing him to do up until now. Edwards's summation followed the outline of Hill's suggested strategy: "While David Duke was burning crosses and scaring people, I was building hospitals to heal them. When he was parading around in a Nazi uniform to intimidate our citizens, I was in a National Guard uniform bringing relief to flood and hurricane victims. When he was selling Nazi hate literature as late as 1989 in his legislative office, I was providing free textbooks for the children of this state. When he was writing porno books, I was signing anti-pornographic legislation."

There was a brief pause. "I have been in this business for a long time. I have a record, and he has a record. I suggest to you he has given us twenty years of hate and hurt, and I don't think he has earned the right to ask you to be governor. . . . Don't let him separate us from the rest of the nation. Don't let him make a mockery of Louisiana. We're too important, we're too good for that. The people of this state need a governor as good as the people of this state, not someone whose reputation, deserved or not, around the nation is one of hate and division. I don't want my Louisiana to fall into that morass. We went down that road one time a long time ago, and we suffered for it for many decades. We'll not let David Duke take us down that same road again. Not ever."

There was in Edward's concluding remarks echoes of Huey Long's 1928 Evangeline Oak speech, even resonances of Abraham Lincoln's appeal to the country's better angels on the eve of the Civil War. But there was scant evidence of the Edwards of yore—no wisecracks about the women he had bedded or the honest graft he had received. Not even so much as a raffish wink and sly-fox smile at his chuckling supporters. There was only righteous indignation, and it seemingly came straight from the heart. Even the wily Cajun had come to the realization that the triumphalist victory he desired required tapping a moral current that was now running as wide and deep as the river beyond the levee.

As soon as the debate in Baton Rouge had ended, the switchboards at LPB and Channel 6 in New Orleans lit up. "I would imagine my station received at least a thousand calls, if not several thousand," says Robinson. "At first his people called. It was an organized phone bank. Then, after word got out that Duke's people were calling, people supportive of me began to call." The inflow of letters, many of them accusing Robinson of "reverse discrimination," was just as heavy. A few contained death threats. For the next two weeks Robinson was given round-the-clock police protection. The station changed his parking assignment in the French Quarter. Some Duke supporters even phoned the CBS affiliate swearing they would never watch its programming again. "We told them he works for Channel 6 now," said the local news director, "but they don't believe us."[59]

Channel 6 decided to respond to the uproar by scheduling a television call-in show on November 10, with Duke as the guest and Norman Robinson acting as host. This time Robinson played things strictly according to journalistic Hoyle. "I used a different approach, because he was a guest on my set, a guest in my home. Debates are different. They are like political forums."[60] Robinson gave the candidate untrammeled freedom to deliver pat campaign speeches about how he would reduce crime, end welfare abuse, clean up Lake Pontchartrain. Viewers lined up at remote sites in the new Riverside Marketplace complex in Uptown New Orleans and at Lakeside Shopping Center in Metairie.

Anne went to the Riverside Marketplace, only three blocks from the Levy apartment. People already queued up when she arrived recognized Anne immediately and pushed her to the front of the line. When it was her turn to ask a question, she ignored the specifics of his agenda. By now everything had become strictly personal. "How is it you ignored me?" she screamed. "Why wouldn't you talk to me when I approached you?" Duke was at a loss for a response. In fairness, no one living would have known what to say to her at that moment. She was seething with anger, she was inconsolable, and she was emotionally spent.[61]

Her daughter Carol went to the Lakeside remote in Metairie. She had intended to join her mother, but because classes had run late at UNO and she lived in Metairie and had her three-month-old baby in tow, she decided to go to the Jefferson Parish location instead. The Lakeside crowd was on the other end of the ideological spectrum from the group at the Uptown remote. "It was like standing in the middle of a KKK meeting," Carol says. "I had my baby in a sack next to me, and I was upset. I kept rocking him just to control myself, and it put him fast asleep." About twenty-five Duke supporters were standing in the line grousing about black welfare cheats and rehearsing the questions they planned to ask when their turn at the mike arrived. "I started arguing with them because what they said was so stupid. I said, 'Instead of blaming everything on welfare, give them a way out, some kind of job opportunity.' We went back and forth. The voices got louder, but I wasn't going to let them intimidate me." Then somebody asked what she planned to say to the candidate. She said she intended to ask Duke to clarify his statement that the Holocaust was not as bad as people made it out to be. A sixty-year-old man standing next to her then piped up: "Do you believe it happened?"

"I know it happened because my family perished there!"

"No, it's mathematically impossible."

"What do you mean 'mathematically impossible'?" Carol's voice was rising now.

The man coolly answered, "If six million Jews died, there wouldn't be any Jews left on the earth."

"I lost my cool at that and yelled, 'Where in the fuck is my family?' That's all I want to know. A simple question.'"

The entire Duke crowd erupted. They started piling on, twenty-five against a solitary individual who was maybe four-foot-ten if she stood on tiptoe, carrying an infant in a sack. "Officer, officer, she's cursing right in front of my kid," one Duke supporter screamed. Meanwhile, the "kid" was cursing back at Carol. A Jefferson Parish sheriff's deputy escorted Carol and the baby to the parking lot, threatening to arrest her if she kept it up. The crowd applauded loudly as she left, whooping and hollering. But Carol's back was up. From the trunk of her car she fetched a homemade stop-Duke sign. It was plastered with "No Dukes" bumper stickers, a swastika circled in red with a diagonal slash slanting across the middle, and the bold slogan, "Never Again!" Then she marched back inside the shopping mall. Her adversaries started buzzing. "What is she doing back? I can't believe she's back." She shoved the sign in their face. There was an eruption of yelps and screams. "Ah, no, she's got a sign! She can't hold up a sign!" Then she put it down, did an interview with *The Times-Picayune* reporter covering the event, and went home.

"That was a bad experience for me," says Carol. But she did manage to change one voter's mind. During the newspaper interview, a young white man waiting in line to question Duke came up to her. He had been leaning toward voting for Duke. Her confrontation with the crowd had unsettled his views. "You know, I never realized what Duke's supporters were like until I saw this go down," he said. "Now, I can see what's going on."[62]

But Carol's shopping center face-off was just one example of the stop-Duke movement at large, as neighbors and relatives across the state made known their moral outrage in ways fence-sitters could neither dismiss nor ignore. The gist of it all was simply this: a Duke victory would do more than hurt the economy. It would rend the moral fabric binding family and community. It would make democratic governance difficult. There was no way you could sit this one out. And few people did. In this moment of moral decision, by-standers were few and far between.

She was indisputably her mother's daughter. Like Anne's ongoing confron-tations with the neo-Nazi, Carol's shopping mall encounter helped rip away the mask of hate veiling the face of the Duke movement.

When the polls closed at 8:00 P.M. five days later, it took the experts all of thirty minutes to call the election. It was Edwards by a landslide—61 to 39 percent—the exact percentage the Louisiana Coalition's Lance Hill had predicted would be the case once the stop-Duke forces were morally aroused. The turnout was enormous. Four-fifths of the electorate went to the polls—a percentage al-most unheralded in contemporary American politics. The van and bus drivers hired by the Edwards campaign and assorted business PACs to carry black voters to the polls drove up to the polling places half full, if they had that many passengers. By midmorning, most black registrants had already trooped to the voting booths on their own.

A *New York Times* exit poll registered the political tremor, but there is some-thing curious about how it was interpreted. When Edwards's voters were asked to name the most important issue in the election, 69 percent said the "Louisiana economy," a fact that pundits and reporters alike made the focus of their postmortems. Yet those same voters gave an even higher response—81 per-cent—to the question concerning the "candidates' racial views," a fact strangely shunted aside by conventional wisdom. Indeed, fully three-fifths of the voters (the proportion of the electorate captured by Edwards) said Duke's views remained unchanged from his days in the Ku Klux Klan, and 91 percent of them voted against Duke. The message had finally gotten through that Duke was a moral fraud and a political faker. And it was that realization, as much as economic fear, that finally brought the Duke juggernaut to a grinding halt.[63]

Anne was overjoyed when the television flashed the news that Duke had been soundly defeated. "I thought she was going to dance naked with a beer in her hand on Magazine Street," Elinor Cohen says.[64]

But the closure was more profound than momentary elation. It went to the very core of who she was, to her rulebook approach to life itself. She started relaxing more. She became more adventurous. She laughed and giggled spontaneously, as though the child she never was had finally begun to get out. And she carried her survivor mission into the classroom, speaking with increasing frequency to elementary and high school students throughout the greater metropolitan area.

Invariably, the students are engrossed at hearing a grandmother explain how a childhood much like their own was stolen before it had begun. Just as invariably she is flooded afterward with moving letters from those same students. The mission gives her an ongoing and deepening sense of accomplishment. She feels continuity with her past, not estrangement. She feels whole, complete. And for the first time since she can remember, she is at peace with herself and truly happy.

"We can't be anything but proud of mom," Carol says. "If there's an award to give her, we'd give it to her without question. The metamorphosis she's gone through has been amazing to watch, like from a cocoon to a butterfly. And it's still continuing. It's never ending."[65]

"I guess we have Duke to thank for my mother's transformation," Robin says. "It was very timely that Duke's presence reached a peak at a point when she had recently lost a man whose life was ruined because of something that Duke discounted. The two experiences blew her out of the water. Before she was drowning. Now she is swimming. And the Duke hoopla and the positive feedback strangers gave her along the way made her realize that she could make her way from here on out as an independent woman. 'My father is not here to take care of me any more,' she said to herself. 'I have to take care of me. And, hey, I'm not going to drown.'"[66]

The obligation to remember that Anne Levy embraced for reasons entirely personal turns out to have political meanings after all. For the burden of preserving memory against those who would erase the past was not hers alone. It is a collective responsibility, a civic duty. Erecting monuments and museums is one way to prevent forgetfulness. But in the final analysis only a morally concerned citizenry has the full power to transmit the lessons of the past to a present increasingly anxious to get on with the future. For one brief, shining moment, in a state not generally known for political ethics, a moral movement of people from across the spectrum said the past could not be brushed aside so easily.

"I guess that's why I like living here," Anne says. "Even in Louisiana politics there is hope for redemption."

Unless otherwise noted, all translations are the author's.

CHAPTER ONE

1. Duke, interview by Rich.

2. Bridges, *Rise of David Duke*, 1–20.

3. Lipstadt, *Denying the Holocaust*, xii.

4. Bill McMahon, "Poll Finds Few Know about Hitler, Nazis," *Baton Rouge Morning-Advocate*, January 18, 1992. The editor kindly allowed me to inspect the cross-tab results of the poll, which are available at the newspaper's offices.

5. Interview with Noles (quotation). Also interviews with Coward; Sartisky; and Barad and Weitzman.

6. *New Orleans Jewish Ledger*, June 2, July 21, 1961; interviews with Justin Zitler, March 11, 1992; Shep Zitler, February 26, 1992; and Buchsbaum, February 13, 1992.

7. Steven Watsky, "David Duke Confronted by Holocaust Victim," *LSU Daily Reveille*, June 8, 1989; Ronni Patriquin, "Duke Acknowledges Holocaust Did Occur," *Shreveport Journal*, June 7, 1989; and interviews with Buchsbaum, February 13, 1992, and with Sartisky.

8. Seidel, *Holocaust Denial*, 66–92; Lipstadt, *Denying the Holocaust*, 1–29.

9. Duke, interview by Rich.

10. Watsky, "Duke Confronted by Holocaust Victim"; Patriquin, "Duke Acknowledges Holocaust Did Occur."

11. Herman, *Trauma and Recovery*, 86.

12. Powell, "Read My Liposuction," *New Republic*, October 15, 1990, 18–22; Jason Berry, "Duke's Disguise," *New York Times*, October 16, 1991.

13. Duke, interview by Rich (quotation); *NAAWP News*, 31, 1984, p. 10; Hill and Wise, *Media Resource Packet*; Hill, "Nazi Race Doctrine," 94–111.

14. Zeskind, "Ballot-Box Bigotry"; Ridgeway, *Blood in the Face*, 63–66; Mintz, *Liberty Lobby and the American Right*, 104. See also Dionne, *Why Americans Hate Politics*, 158–59, and Judis, *William F. Buckley, Jr.*, 113–41.

15. "End of File," *Instauration*, February 1989, 36.

16. Allen Johnson, "Duke Tape: Blacks Argued for Racial Discrimination in B.R.," *(New Orleans) Louisiana Weekly*, March 18, 1989, 1.

17. Powell, "Slouching toward Baton Rouge," 12–40. For a brilliantly rendered study of the life and times of George Wallace, see Carter, *Politics of Rage*, esp. 294–370.

18. Wayne King, "Bad Times on the Bayou," *New York Times Magazine*, June 11,

1989, 120. On Metairie and the house race, see my "Slouching toward Baton Rouge, 12–40.

19. Allen, *Nazi Seizure of Power*, 84.

20. On Jewish foreboding about potential anti-Semitism, see Lipset and Raab, *Jews and the New American Scene*, 88–89, 105–8.

21. Lucian K. Truscott IV, "Hate Gets a Haircut," *Esquire*, November 1989, 184.

22. Ibid.

23. "David Duke Digest," *Instauration*, March 1990, 37.

24. Eli N. Evans, *Provincials*, 239–46; Reissman, "New Orleans Jewish Community," 300–303; Lipset and Raab, *Jews and the New American Scene*, 82–86.

25. Judith Miller, "Holocaust Survivors, in U.S. Reunion, Ask World to Remember," *New York Times*, April 12, 1983, A1; Caryle Murphy, "Survivors Give Thanks, Honor Dead," *Washington Post*, April 12, 1983; *Newsweek*, April 25, 1983, 30–35; *Time*, April 25, 1983, 19.

26. Anne Levy, "A Survivor Shares," *New Orleans Times-Picayune*, April 28, 1983, A10.

27. Ibid.

28. For the story of the successful, if somewhat contentious, effort to build the United States Holocaust Memorial Museum on the mall in Washington, see Linenthal, *Preserving Memory*.

29. *Holocaust: The Obligation to Remember*, 22.

30. Levi, *Reawakening*, 2.

31. Interview with Shep Zitler, February 26, 1992.

32. "Forty Years after Warsaw," *Time*, April 25, 1983, 19.

33. Lipstadt, *Denying the Holocaust*, 2.

34. See, for example, *Journal of Historical Review* 1 (Spring 1980), and Lipstadt, *Denying the Holocaust*, 137–208. On the connection between Holocaust revisionism and German neoconservatism, see Richard J. Evans, *In Hitler's Shadow*, esp. 166 n, and Maier, *Unmasterable Past*.

35. Apfelbaum, "Forgetting the Past," 612.

36. Butz's argument, as well as that of other "revisionists," is conveniently delineated in Lipstadt, *Denying the Holocaust*, 123–36, and in Seidel, *Holocaust Denial*, 74–82. See also Stern, *Holocaust Denial*, 10, 11, 70–71. For the *NAAWP News* quotation, see "Suppressed Books," *NAAWP News*, 24, 1983, p. 14.

37. Levy, "A Survivor Shares."

38. Levi, *Survival in Auschwitz*, 5–6.

39. Interview with Tritt.

40. Interview with Robin Levy, February 25, 1992.

41. Ibid.

42. Interview with Rickey; Rickey, "The Nazi and the Republicans," 65–71.

43. Ibid.

44. Herman, *Trauma and Recovery*, 133.

45. Interview with Robin Levy, February 25, 1992.

46. In her treatment of survivors, the psychiatrist Yael Danieli encourages patients to reconstruct their family trees, recording the death of each relative, to re-create continuity between past and present. See her "Treating Survivors and Children of Survivors of the Nazi Holocaust," 23–42.

1. Interview with Dolek Skorecki, Haifa, Israel, October, 5, 1993.

2. Death Certificate of Szmil-Zawel Skorecki, Łódź Birth, Marriage, and Death Records Office; interview with Bresler.

3. Epstein, "Uncovering Moravia," 95.

4. I bought eleven unbound synagogue journals, dating from the 1820s, 1830s, and 1840s, from a young Pole who stumbled out of a tavern as I was leaving Działoszyce during a brief 1993 car trip to the town. They are currently housed in the Jewish Historical Institute in Warsaw.

5. Quoted in "Fifty Years of the Voluntary Fire Brigade of Działoszyce," in *Yizkor Book*, 7.

6. The Hebrew word for Germany, Ashkenazi is the term for Jews from Central and Eastern Europe.

7. In fact, by 1880, the eve of the great migration to the United States, four-fifths of world Jewry lived within the boundaries of the former Polish Commonwealth.

8. Marcus, *Social and Political History of the Jews in Poland*, 3–8.

9. Rosman, *The Lord's Jews*, 2–17, 36–40, 71, 75–87, 104, 112–13; Levine, *Economic Origins of Anti-Semitism*, 9, 57–74; Barbara Kirshenblatt-Gimblett, introduction to Zborowski and Herzog, *Life Is with People*, xv, xix–xxii; Schama, *Landscape and Memory*, 42–43; Epstein, "Uncovering Moravia," 98–102; Davies, *God's Playground*, 1:256–72; Ascherson, *Struggles for Poland*, 18–19. See also Weinryb, *Jews of Poland*.

10. Rosman, *The Lord's Jews*, 106–7, 112–13, 115; Schama, *Landscape and Memory*, 27; Davies, *God's Playground*, 1:265–82; Opatoshu, *In Polish Woods*, 27–33; Schama, "Stopping by Woods," 31–37.

11. *Słownik Geograficzny Królestwa Polskiego*, 263; *Wielka Encyklopedya Powszchna*, 558; *Yizkor Book*, 8–10, 21 (quotation).

12. Richmond, *Konin*, 29; Zborowski and Herzog, *Life Is with People*, 63–66.

13. Interview with Riba.

14. Interview with Bejski.

15. Schama, *Landscape and Memory*, 64–67; Marcus, *Social and Political History of the Jews in Poland*, 87; Baron et al., *Economic History of the Jews*, 88.

16. Interview with Eva Galler, July 7, 1995.

17. Interview with Dolek Skorecki, New Orleans, April 4, 1992.

18. Schama, *Landscape and Memory*, 47–48, 64.

19. Interview with Dolek Skorecki, New Orleans, April 4, 1992; interview with Arthur Tenser, May 26, 1993 (quotation). Most Jews never bothered using surnames until after the Third Partition of 1795, when all Polish subjects were ordered to register as citizens of the state. Some Jews were forced to accept whatever name the local registry official felt like bestowing. The author of *Tales of Hoffmann*, for example, who ran the registry office during the time Warsaw was a Prussian appendage, out of whimsy one day began naming Jewish clients after assorted fish because his wife had served him pike with parsley for dinner. Davies, *Heart of Europe*, 245–46. On the adoption of Jewish surnames and the prevalence of nicknames in the shtetl, see also Zborowski and Herzog, *Life Is with People*, 150.

20. *Yizkor Book*, 10 and 12. See also Mokotoff and Sack, *Where Once We Walked*, xx.

21. Kirshenblatt-Gimblett, introduction, ix–xii; Dawidowicz, *Golden Tradition*, 5.

22. Interview with Skoretsky, October 2, 1993.

23. Zborowski and Herzog, *Life Is with People*, 46–53; Howe, *World of Our Fathers*, 13; Heller, *On the Edge of Destruction*, 47–76; Nordon, *Education of a Polish Jew*, 27–28.

24. *Yizkor Book*, 10–16.

25. Ozick, "Sholem Aleichem's Revolution," 99; Heller, *On the Edge of Destruction*, 65–68.

26. Epstein, "Uncovering Moravia," 105–6; see also Zborowski and Herzog, *Life Is with People*, 129–31.

27. His children were, in order of birth, Morris, Wladek, Henry, Esther, Sala, Stefa, Julius, Mark, Celia, Frances, Anna, and Rose.

28. Interview with Dolek Skorecki, New Orleans, April 4, 1992.

29. Material here and in the following two paragraphs is from my interview with Zuckerman.

30. Howe, *World of Our Fathers*, 15–23.

31. He had a lot of company. In 1880 a majority of Łódź's population were "temporary residents." Janczak, "National Structure of the Population in Łódź," 22.

32. Marcus, *Social and Political History of the Jews in Poland*, 88–89; Pus, "Development of the City of Łódź," 3–19; Janczak, "National Structure of the Population in Łódź," 20–26; Jack Taylor, *Economic Development of Poland*, 84–87. For more information on one of the German textile pioneers in Łódź, see *Nordrhein-Westfalen und der Deutsche Osten*, 30–39. I would like to thank Herman Freudenberger for calling this study to my attention.

33. Rubinstein, *My Young Years*, 3–4.

34. Marcus, *Social and Political History of the Jews in Poland*, 88–89.

35. Ibid., 13, 49, 55–57.

36. *Lodz Ghetto*, 35–36.

37. Asch, *Three Cities*, 474–75.

38. Interview with Silberberg.

39. Interview with Gerver, May 29, 1993.

40. Interview with Silberberg. On the tradition of learned arbiters in the shtetl, see Zborowski and Herzog, *Life Is with People*, 80–81.

41. Interview with Gerver, May 29, 1993; Death Certificate of Szmil-Zawel Skorecki, Łódź Birth, Marriage, and Death Records Office.

42. Interview with Dolek Skorecki, New Orleans, February 11, 1992. According to the 1939 phone book for Łódź, located in the Łódź State Archives, the lumberyard was at Łagiewnicka 126.

43. Interview with Silberberg; interview with Dolek Skorecki, Haifa, Israel, February 11, 12, 1994.

44. Marcus, *Social and Political History of the Jews in Poland*, 99–101, 110–12, 119.

45. "Marek Skorecki," Jewish Federation, Committee for New Americans, Job Applicant, October 13, 1948, on file at the Jewish Federation, New Orleans.

46. Interview with Skorecka; interview with Silberberg; interview with Dolek Skorecki, Haifa, Israel, February 12, 1994.

47. Interview with Lorena Doerries, June 3, 1944. On survivor tendency to idealize the prewar past, see Hass, *In the Shadow of the Holocaust*, 16, 21.

48. Certificate, City Administration of Łódź; Department of Community Care, Outpatient Division, Łódź, October 8, 1935, signed by the interim president of the city: Tadeusz Wislawski, Dept. Head, in Hersz Tempelhof Student Record File, War-

saw Polytechnic University. On Abram Tempelhof's "bourgeois origins," see *Księga Ludności Stałej miasta Łódźi*, Łódź State Archives. In 1939, five zlotys were equivalent to one dollar, so 1,600 zlotys equaled $320 (*Stroop Report*, n. 32).

49. Interview with Lorena Doerries, June 3, 1994.

50. Interview with Kriegstein, New York, July 6, 1992.

51. Interview with Lorena Doerries, June 3, 1994. Doerries is quoting Ruth from memory.

52. Heller, *On the Edge of Destruction*, 211–47.

53. Interview with Silberberg.

54. Interview with Fuksman, August 1, 1993.

55. Interview with Gerver, May 29, 1993.

56. Mark Skorecki, taped reminiscence (ca. 1983).

57. Interview with Baranowski.

58. Ibid. See also Rejestr Mieszkancow Miasta Łódźi z Lat, 1931–32, Łódź State Archives. According to the 1910 Łódź City Directory, also in the Łódź State Archives, Pinkus had operated a yarn and spinning factory at Legionów 8.

59. Interview with Adam Skorecki, New Orleans, April 4, 1992.

60. For example, Stabholz, *Seven Hells*; Stanislaw Waller testimony, Yad Vashem, Jerusalem; and Fenigstein, "The Holocaust and I." I thank Dr. Charles G. Roland of McMaster University in Hamilton, Ontario, Canada, for letting me borrow his copy of the late Dr. Fenigstein's manuscript.

61. Interviews with Thaddeus Stabholz, September 8, 13, 14, 1993; Roland, *Courage under Siege*, 76.

62. Marcus, *Social and Political History of the Jews in Poland*, 66–67; Heller, *On the Edge of Destruction*, 119–25; Rudnicki, " 'Numerus Clausus,' " 246–68; Nordon, *Education of a Polish Jew*, 77–79, 82–83.

63. Richmond, *Konin*, 168.

64. Rosman, *Lord's Jews*, 4, 38, 206. "Blood libel" refers to the accusation that Jews kidnapped Christian children to use their blood in making matzos. For a provocative interpretation of how the Polish gentry, during a period of declining grain prices, used the Jewish tavern as a mechanism to squeeze more surplus out of an increasingly alcohol-dependent peasantry, see Levine, *Economic Origins of Anti-Semitism*, 140–52.

65. Richmond, *Konin*, 168 (first quotation); Zborowski and Herzog, *Life Is with People*, 67 (second quotation).

66. Heller, *On the Edge of Destruction*, 47–76; the quotations are on 62 and 76. See also Marcus, *Social and Political History of the Jews in Poland*, 97–98, and Hertz, "Jewish Caste Status in Poland," 1153–64.

67. Anti-Semitism became a more structured belief system as the old agrarian order collapsed under the strain of industrialism and overpopulation. The dislocations of the late nineteenth century begat both anticapitalist *and* anticommunist ideologies, and Jewish scapegoats figured prominently in each. Polish aristocrats and their romantic defenders blamed the erosion of bucolic virtues on exploitative Jews, the country's most urban population. The emerging Polish middle class, alarmed by a socialist movement in which Jewish radicals and trade union activists played visible roles, decried communism as a "Jewish menace." Though mutually contradictory, both images were ultimately fused to form the myth of a secret Jewish plot to take over the world, with Jewish bankers working one side of the conspiratorial street as Jewish Bolshevists worked the other. That irrational conception was the thrust of the 1905

Russian-inspired hoax "The Protocols of the Elders of Zion," which profoundly influenced the thinking of Adolf Hitler and Henry Ford alike. On interwar Polish anti-Semitism, see Heller, *On the Edge of Destruction*, 47–139; Marcus, *Social and Political History of the Jews in Poland*, 11, 66–69, 97–98; Mendelsohn, "Relations between Jews and Non-Jews in Eastern Europe," 71–83; Mendelsohn, "Interwar Poland," 130–39; and Ascherson, *Struggles for Poland*, 34–86.

68. Interview with Dolek Skorecki, Haifa, Israel, February 11, 1994.

69. Pulzer, *Rise of Political Anti-Semitism in Germany and Austria*, 299; Marcus, *Social and Political History of the Jews in Poland*, 356.

70. Marcus, *Social and Political History of the Jews in Poland*, 96.

71. Hersz Tempelhof to Head of the Mechanical Department at Warsaw Polytechnic, October 10, 1934, and September 30, 1935, and Public Patient Card signed by Dr. M. Stefanowski, Student Clinic Physician, December 11, 1935, both in Hersz Tempelhof Student Record File, Warsaw Polytechnic University. The student record file also includes transcripts of his course and exam work.

72. Rankin and Graham, *Cancer of the Colon and Rectum*, 146–47, 206, and 212; Harry E. Bacon, *Cancer of the Colon, Rectum, and Anal Canal*, 207, 210.

73. Certificate of Dr. J. Rutkowski II, Surgical Clinic of Josef Piłsudski University in Warsaw, Electoralna 12, September 30, 1935; H. Tempelhof to the Dept. Council, March 11, 1936, both in Hersz Tempelhof Student Record File, Warsaw Polytechnic University.

74. Hersz Tempelhof to His Magnificent, Mr. Rector of Warsaw Polytechnic, April 24, 1936, ibid.

75. Interview with Thaddeus Stabholz, September 14, 1993. See also her Certificate of Maturity, Łódź, May 24, 1939, as well as her medical school transcript, both in Mery Mejnster Student Record File , Warsaw University.

76. Rudnicki, " 'Numerus Clausus,' " 253; interview with Thaddeus Stabholz, Canton, Ohio, September 14, 1993; Mery Mejnster Grade Transcript, Mery Mejnster Student Record File, Warsaw University.

77. Fenigstein, "The Holocaust and I," 69–70.

78. Mery Mejnster to the Board of the Medical School, September 23, 1932, and to His Magnificent, Rector of the University, March 8, 1934, both in Mery Mejnster Student Record File, Warsaw University.

79. Interview with Thaddeus Stabholz, September 14, 1993.

80. Fenigstein, "The Holocaust and I," 59 (quotations); Rudnicki, " 'Numerus Clausus,' " 253–57; Marcus, *Social and Political History of the Jews in Poland*, 344; Richmond, *Konin*, 112; Heller, *On the Edge of Destruction*, 119–25; Kac, *Enigmas of Change*, 34–35.

81. Interview with Thaddeus Stabholz, September 14, 1993.

82. Ibid.; Rudnicki, " 'Numerus Clausus,' " 257–60; Wynot, " 'A Necessary Cruelty,' " 1035–58.

83. Quoted in Rudnicki, " 'Numerus Clausus,' " 258, 264. See also Goldstein, *Stars Bear Witness*, 11–12.

84. The historiography on this subject is surveyed in Mendelsohn, "Interwar Poland," 130–39.

85. Marcus, *Social and Political History of the Jews in Poland*, 68–69; Nordon, *Education of a Polish Jew*, 77–79.

86. Mery Mejnster to His Magnificent, Rector of Józef Piłsudski University, De-

cember 10, 1937, and Józef Piłsudski University, Answer to Application of December 10, 1937, both in Mery Mejnster Student Record File, Warsaw University. See also her "Fragebogen" (questionnaire) file, created by the Nazi regime, in the archives of the Main Medical Library, Warsaw University.

87. Interview with Dr. Ernie Cohen, New Orleans, October 26, 1993; interview with Thaddeus Stabholz, September 8, 1993, October 27, 1993.

88. Broyard, *Intoxicated by My Illness*, 25; Cousins, *Anatomy of an Illness*, 27. See also Lerner, *Wrestling with the Angel*, 33.

89. Interview with Thaddeus Stabholz, September 8, 1993.

90. Interview with Balin; Stanislaw Waller testimony, Yad Vashem, Jerusalem.

91. Interview with Balin; interview with Bresler.

92. Nordon, *Education of a Polish Jew*, 180–81.

93. Rich, *Hitler's War Aims*, 121–23; Dwork and Pelt, *Auschwitz*, 78–91; Koehl, *RKFDV*, 2–7.

94. *Diary of Dawid Sierakowiak*, 27.

95. Ibid., 27–29.

96. Davies, *God's Playground*, 2:435.

CHAPTER THREE

1. Davies, *God's Playground*, 2:438; *Diary of Dawid Sierakowiak*, 34.

2. Gutman, *Jews of Warsaw*, 120–22.

3. Ibid., 36. See also Richmond, *Konin*, 68–69.

4. Davies, *God's Playground*, 2:438–40. Hitler's speech appears in *Documents on British Foreign Policy*, 257. On the execution of Poles, see Lukas, *Forgotten Holocaust*, 3; Gutman, *Jews of Warsaw*, 158–59; Breitman, *Architect of Genocide*, 66–72; and Höhne, *Order of the Death's Head*, 335–39.

5. *Diary of Dawid Sierakowiak*, 39.

6. Schleunes, "Retracing the Twisted Road," 54–70 (the quotation is on 70).

7. *Chronicle of the Lodz Ghetto*, xxxiii; *Diary of Dawid Sierakowiak*, 43. On the creation of the Judenräte, see Hilberg, *Destruction of the European Jews*, 145–46 (all references will be to the Quadrangle edition unless otherwise noted), and Trunk, *Judenrat*, 1–42.

8. Berg, *Warsaw Ghetto*, 20; *Lodz Ghetto*, 21–23.

9. *Diary of Dawid Sierakowiak*, 47.

10. Tec, *When Light Pierced the Darkness*, 40; Marrus, *Holocaust in History*, 96–99.

11. Höhne, *Order of the Death's Head*, 340; Broszat, *Nationalsozialistische Polenpolitik*, 47; *Diary of Dawid Sierakowiak*, 36.

12. *Diary of Dawid Sierakowiak*, 63.

13. Ibid., 73; *Chronicle of the Lodz Ghetto*, xxiv; *Nordrhein-Westfalen und der Deutsche Osten*, 30–39.

14. The order, issued on November 11, 1939, gave Jews until November 15 to turn in their radios. *Diary of Dawid Sierakowiak*, 61.

15. Ibid., 63, 70.

16. *Chronicle of the Lodz Ghetto*, xxxiii.

17. *Diary of Dawid Sierakowiak*, 69.

18. *Lodz Ghetto*, 70.

19. Ibid., 69–71. A picture of the burning Kościuszko Temple appears on page 68.

20. Levy and Millen, interview by Robinson.

21. *Lodz Ghetto*, 71; *Diary of Dawid Sierakowiak*, 63; *Chronicle of the Lodz Ghetto*, xxxiv.

22. *Diary of Dawid Sierakowiak*, 69.

23. "The First Mass Deportation from Lodz," from "Oskar Rosenfeld's Notebooks," in *Lodz Ghetto*, 27. See also *Chronicle of the Lodz Ghetto*, xxxiv–v; *Diary of Dawid Sierakowiak*, 70; Christopher R. Browning, "Nazi Resettlement Policy and the Search for a Solution to the Jewish Question, 1939–41," in his *Path to Genocide*, 12; and Breitman, *Architect of Genocide*, 80–81.

24. Although several Skoreckis appear in the Łódź Ghetto files housed in the Łódź branch of the state archives, Frania and Hanna's names are not among them.

25. Interview with Silberberg.

26. *Chronicle of the Lodz Ghetto*, xxxiv.

27. Her name is misspelled Skurecka in the records; see "Nacha Einhorn Skureck," Łódź Birth, Marriage, and Death Records Office.

28. *Diary of Dawid Sierakowiak*, 74; Nordon, *Education of a Polish Jew*, 210.

29. Höhne, *Order of the Death's Head*, 360.

30. Koehl, *RKFDV*, 53–54; Broszat, *Nationalsozialistiche Polenpolitik*, 20–21; Hilberg, *Destruction of the European Jews*, 127–28; Browning, "Nazi Resettlement Policy," 6–11; *Chronicle of the Lodz Ghetto*, xxiii–xxiv. For a somewhat different interpretation, see Friedman, "The Jewish Ghettos of the Nazi Era," in his *Roads to Extinction*, 59–61.

31. Quoted in Dwork and Pelt, *Auschwitz*, 11. On völkisch nationalism, see Mosse, *Crisis of German Ideology*, esp. 3–66.

32. Rich, *Hitler's War Aims*, 3–10; Jäckel, *Hitler's World View*, 90–98.

33. This may seem like a problematic assertion, but the weight of the historical scholarship seems to support it. See Browning, "Nazi Resettlement Policy," 3–27, who does a masterful job of synthesizing the evidence and weighing the conflicting interpretations.

34. Dwork and Pelt, *Auschwitz*, 19–21, 47–49; Koehl, *RKFDV*, 3–6. A hundred years later, the Prussian Settlement Commission (1886–1916) transplanted an additional 130,000 Germans to the east.

35. Hitler, *Hitler's Secret Book*, 46–48, 100–108 (the quotation is on 106); Hitler, *Mein Kampf*, 286, 400–403, 654–55. See also Rich, *Hitler's War Aims*, 3–10, and Dwork and Pelt, *Auschwitz*, 69–70.

36. Höhne, *Order of the Death's Head*, 33–34; Crankshaw, *Gestapo*, 20–27 (quotation); Koehl, *RKFDV*, 21–23; Segev, *Soldiers of Evil*, 62–63, 72–81; Breitman, *Architect of Genocide*, 34–35, 108–10.

37. Koehl, *Black Corps*, 157–222. For an insightful analysis of the SS, see Krausnick et al., *Anatomy of the SS State*, which contains the depositions of four leading German historians who testified for the prosecution in the Frankfurt Auschwitz trials in 1963. For an equally astute reading of the Waffen-SS, see Sydnor, *Soldiers of Destruction*.

38. Browning, "Nazi Resettlement Policy," 8–11, 16; Dwork and Pelt, *Auschwitz*, 119–20, 136–38; Koehl, *RKFDV*, 78–79; Gross, *Polish Society under German Occupation*, 45–48, 76; Moser, "Nisko," 1–21; Korzec and Szurek, "Jews and Poles under Soviet Occupation," 210–11; Breitman, *Architect of Genocide*, 125.

39. Koehl, *RKFDV*, viii (quotation), 78–79, 101.

40. Ibid., 53–54; Gross, *Polish Society under German Occupation*, 71–73. The figures are conveniently summarized in Yahil, *Holocaust*, 136–40, 150; see also Höhne, *Order of the Death's Head*, 354.

41. Koehl, *RKFDV*, 74, 78, 86, 102–9, 114–15. See also Browning, "Nazi Resettlement Policy," 3–25. To preclude local German residents and officials from engrossing all the property that had been confiscated from Poles and Jews alike, Nazi officials distributed the booty "in trust" only, deferring until after the war the final disposition of the property. On the Selbstschutz, see Christian Jansen and Arno Weckbecker, *Der "Volksdeutsche Selbstschutz" in Polen*, 73–77.

42. On the polycratic nature of the Nazi regime, see Rich, *Hitler's War Aims*, 12–13; Marrus, *Holocaust in History*, 33–34; Mason, "Intention and Explanation," 24–25 (first quotation); Crankshaw, *Gestapo*, 63 (second quotation); and Höhne, *Order of the Death's Head*, 353 (third quotation). There is a striking portrait of Hitler's moodiness in Fest, *Hitler*. Unfortunately, Ian Kershaw's masterful new biography of Hitler appeared too late to be incorporated in my text.

43. Höhne, *Order of the Death's Head*, 360–61; Browning, "Nazi Resettlement Policy," 13–15; Dwork and Pelt, *Auschwitz*, 143; Gross, *Polish Society under German Occupation*, 72–73; Koehl, *RKFDV*, 76–77; *Chronicle of the Lodz Ghetto*, xxxv–xxxvi.

44. Appearing in the Nuremberg Trial documents, Heydrich's *Schnellbrief* is conveniently reprinted in *Documents on the Holocaust*, 173–78.

45. Christopher R. Browning, "Nazi Ghettoization Policy in Poland," in his *Path to Genocide*, 31–32 (the Greiser quotation appears on 32); *Chronicle of the Lodz Ghetto*, xxxvi–xxxvii. In mid-December a secret SS police memorandum referred to the creation of a "closed ghetto." The memo concluded with the assertion that "the final aim must be to burn out entirely this pestilent abscess." For the entire text, see *Lodz Ghetto*, 23–26.

46. *Diary of Dawid Sierakowiak*, 64.

47. Interview with Silberberg.

48. Jakub Poznanski, "Lodz Ghetto Diary," in *Lodz Ghetto*, 34.

49. Hilberg, *Destruction of the European Jews*, 149.

50. *Chronicle of the Lodz Ghetto*, xxxvi. See also *Lodz Ghetto*, 33–36; and Hilberg, *Destruction of the European Jews*, 149–50.

51. *Anmeldung*, Wolf Skorecki, "Der Aelteste der Juden in Litzmannstadt-Getto," Nr. K 099531, and *Anmeldung*, Gisla Skorecka, "Der Aelteste der Juden in Litzmannstadt-Getto," Nr. K 99532, both in the Łódź State Archives. The *Anmeldungen* for Abram and Sara Tempelhof, on the other hand, are dated April 15, 1940. But these dates may reflect the times that they were assigned permanent housing.

52. *Lodz Ghetto*, 33–36, particularly Irena Lieberman's vivid description of the move to the ghetto on page 35.

53. *Chronicle of the Lodz Ghetto*, xxvi–xxviii, xliii–li; Hilberg, *Destruction of the European Jews*, 145–46, for discussion of "automatic compliance." See also Fein, *Accounting for Genocide*, 121–42; Steinlauf, *Bondage to the Dead*, 28.

54. The standard treatment of the Jewish councils is Trunk, *Judenrat*. See pages 400–413 for a discussion of the "rescue-through-work" strategy.

55. Korzec and Szurek, "Jews and Poles under Soviet Occupation," 219; Gross, *Revolution from Abroad*, 187–224; Pinchuk, *Shtetl Jews under Soviet Occupation*, 114–16; Levin, *Lesser of Two Evils*, 191–97; Davies, *God's Playground*, 2:447–49; Szwajger, *I Remember Nothing More*, 9; Gutman, *Jews of Warsaw*, 16–17.

56. Davies, *God's Playground*, 2:451–53. See also Nordon, *Education of a Polish Jew*, 212–14.

57. Levin, *Lesser of Two Evils*, 188.

58. Ringelblum, *Notes from the Warsaw Ghetto*, 43.

59. Szwajger, *I Remember Nothing More*, 10–11 (quotation); Zuckerman, *Surplus of Memory*, 39.

CHAPTER FOUR

1. Gutman, *Jews of Warsaw*, 34.

2. Berg, *Warsaw Ghetto*, 31; Kaplan, *Scroll of Agony*, 173, 187, 200; Yahil, *Holocaust*, 153.

3. Zuckerman, *Surplus of Memory*, 211.

4. Kaplan, *Scroll of Agony*, 200; Gutman, *Jews of Warsaw*, 18–36.

5. Kaplan, *Scroll of Agony*, 134–35 (quotation), 144–45; Goldstein, *Stars Bear Witness*, 51–53.

6. This district was about 40 to 60 percent Jewish, according to sources at the Jewish Historical Institute in Warsaw. Interview with Jagieliski.

7. Warsaw telephone directory, 1938–39, Jewish Historical Institute, Warsaw; Mery Mejnster "Fragebogen," Warsaw University, Warsaw.

8. History of the Czyste Hospital (Polish), Jewish Historical Institute, Warsaw. I thank Tadeusz Kaźmierak for translating this document.

9. Interview with Balin. Another physician from that period also remembers Henry Tempelhof: "He was a very handsome man and worked together with my father, the engineer Ignacy Stabholz," writes Dr. Ludwig Stabholz from Tel Aviv. Letter to the author, September 30, 1993.

10. Kaplan, *Scroll of Agony*, 200.

11. "Schön Report," *Faschismus-Getto-Massenmord*, 110 (quotation); Browning, "Nazi Resettlement Policy," 18–19; Browning, "Nazi Ghettoization Policy," 33; Gutman, *Jews of Warsaw*, 48–52; Friedman, "Jewish Ghettos of the Nazi Era," in his *Roads to Extinction*, 70–77.

12. Hilberg, *Destruction of the European Jews*, 150–51; Browning, "Nazi Resettlement Policy," 19–21.

13. Kaplan, *Scroll of Agony*, 206.

14. Ringelblum, *Notes from the Warsaw Ghetto*, 55.

15. Hilberg, *Destruction of the European Jews*, 149–51; Friedman, "Jewish Ghettos of the Nazi Era," 71.

16. Kaplan, *Scroll of Agony*, 353; Gutman, *Jews of Warsaw*, 61; Ringelblum, *Notes from the Warsaw Ghetto*, 59.

17. "Schön Report," 110.

18. Donat, *Holocaust Kingdom*, 25–27; Gilbert, *Holocaust*, 129–30; Kaplan, *Scroll of Agony*, 212; Ringelblum, *Notes from the Warsaw Ghetto*, 62, 73–74; Goldstein, *Stars Bear Witness*, 61–66.

19. Gutman, *Jews of Warsaw*, 60; Kaplan, *Scroll of Agony*, 217; Ringelblum, *Notes from the Warsaw Ghetto*, 87 and 91.

20. Ringelblum, *Notes from the Warsaw Ghetto*, 61–62, 75–78 (the quotation is on 77); Kaplan, *Scroll of Agony*, 211–12; Donat, *Holocaust Kingdom*, 26; Gutman, *Jews of Warsaw*, 55–61.

21. Ringelblum, *Notes from the Warsaw Ghetto*, 86–88 (quotations), and 167. The

"Siegfried Line Extension" was a reference to the German underground defense network opposite the more well-known French Maginot Line.

22. Ibid., 86–87, 91, 107; Goldstein, *Stars Bear Witness*, 62–66, 81; Berg, *Warsaw Ghetto*, 93.

23. At its peak, 445,000 Jews occupied one hundred square blocks.

24. According to Gunnar S. Paulsson, formerly at the University of Leicester, the faulty estimate derives from a computational error by a Nazi bureaucrat. See his January 31, 1997, posting to the H-Holocaust Listserv.

25. Kaplan, *Scroll of Agony*, 246; Gutman, *Jews of Warsaw*, 77; Helen Fein, "Genocide by Attrition, 1939–1993: The Warsaw Ghetto, Cambodia, and Sudan: Links between Human Rights, Health, and Mass Death," *Health and Human Rights* 2, no. 2 [no date]: 16; Trunk, "Epidemics and Mortality," 87–89.

26. Berg, *Warsaw Ghetto*, 69.

27. See the mortality estimates in Roland, *Courage under Siege*, 221–25.

28. Zinsser, *Rats, Lice, and History*, 153 (quotation), 216–17.

29. Ibid., 241–301.

30. Browning, "Genocide and Public Health: German Doctors and Polish Jews, 1939–41," in his *Path to Genocide*, 145–61 (the quotation is on 152); Roland, *Courage under Siege*, 123–28; and Kaplan, *Scroll of Agony*, 160. The argument that Nazi ghettoization was a species of germ warfare is put forward by Trunk in "Epidemics and Mortality," 82–83.

31. Roland, *Courage under Siege*, 132–37; Trunk, "Epidemics and Mortality," 121.

32. Ringelblum, *Notes from the Warsaw Ghetto*, 86–87, 195; Berg, *Warsaw Ghetto*, 74; Kaplan, *Scroll of Agony*, 220; Szwajger, *I Remember Nothing More*, 35.

33. Interview with Dr. Thaddeus Stabholz, June 1, 1997.

34. Roland, *Courage under Siege*, 136–37; Trunk, "Epidemics and Mortality," 96–97; Henry Fenigstein, "History of Czyste Hospital" (Munich, 1948), reprinted in Fenigstein's unpublished memoir "The Holocaust and I," xviii.

35. Goldstein, *Stars Bear Witness*, 73; Kaplan, *Scroll of Agony*, 133.

36. Roland, *Courage under Siege*, 137–47; Trunk, "Epidemics and Mortality," 106–13; Gutman, *Jews of Warsaw*, 26–27; Ringelblum, *Notes from the Warsaw Ghetto*, 169, 195.

37. Quoted in Trunk, "Epidemics and Mortality," 101.

38. Ringelblum, *Notes from the Warsaw Ghetto*, 194.

39. Interview with Thaddeus Stabholz, September 8, 1993.

40. Roland, *Courage under Siege*, 81–84; Ringelblum, *Notes from the Warsaw Ghetto*, 113.

41. Fenigstein, "History of Czyste Hospital," xv–xvi (quotation); Kaplan, *Scroll of Agony*, 240–41; interview with Dr. Thaddeus Stabholz, September 8, 1993.

42. Roland, *Courage under Siege*, 84–86 (the quotation is on 85); Ringelblum, *Notes from the Warsaw Ghetto*, 121; Trunk, "Epidemics and Mortality," 101–3.

43. Interview with Thaddeus Stabholz, September 8, 1993; Adler, *In the Warsaw Ghetto*, 229.

44. Interview with Thaddeus Stabholz, September 8, October, 11, 1993.

45. "Scenes from a Children's Hospital," in *To Live with Honor*, 403–4 (quotation); Szwajger, *I Remember Nothing More*, 34–42, 62; Roland, *Courage under Siege*, 84.

46. Roland, *Courage under Siege*, 135.

47. Interview with Thaddeus Stabholz, June 1, 1997.

48. Ringelblum, *Notes from the Warsaw Ghetto*, 194.

49. Browning, "Nazi Ghettoization Policy," 36–37 (the quotation is on 36); Gutman, *Jews of Warsaw*, 66–67 (for the 1941 Polish source).

50. See Jack Eisner's lively account of his days as a teenage smuggler in the Warsaw Ghetto, in *Survivor of the Holocaust*, 18–85.

51. Gutman, *Jews of Warsaw*, 67–72, 90–94; Goldstein, *Stars Bear Witness*, 76–79; Trunk, "Epidemics and Mortality," 91–94; Ringelblum, *Notes from the Warsaw Ghetto*, 99–100, 113, 133–34, 136–40, 146, 216; Roland, *Courage under Siege*, 50.

52. Kaplan, *Scroll of Agony*, 233.

53. Berg, *Warsaw Ghetto*, 53, 130–31; Roland, *Courage under Siege*, 99, 112.

54. Kaplan, *Scroll of Agony*, 188, 230–31; Gutman, *Jews of Warsaw*, 72; Goldstein, *Stars Bear Witness*, 90; Trunk, "Epidemics and Mortality," 89–90, 95; Ringelblum, *Notes from the Warsaw Ghetto*, 139, 172, 227.

55. Ringelblum, *Notes from the Warsaw Ghetto*, 98, 112, 182 (quotation); Gutman, *Jews of Warsaw*, 24–25; Berg, *Warsaw Ghetto*, 53, 59–60, 130–31; Roland, *Courage under Siege*, 40, 99, 112.

56. Trunk, "Epidemics and Mortality," 95–96.

57. Gutman, *Jews of Warsaw*, 40–47 (the quotation is on 45); "Answers to a Questionnaire by Dr. Milejkowski," in *To Live with Honor*, 743. See also Trunk, *Judenrat*, 342–45.

58. Goldstein, *Stars Bear Witness*, 71–72 (quotation), 85; Berg, *Warsaw Ghetto*, 34.

59. Berg, *Warsaw Ghetto*, 55; Kaplan, *Scroll of Agony*, 169, 227–29, 259 (quotation); Ringelblum, *Notes from the Warsaw Ghetto*, 99, 101–2, 144; Roland, *Courage under Siege*, 56–59.

60. Ruth said the nursery was operated by the TOZ, an acronym for the public health branch of ZTOS.

61. Gutman, *Jews of Warsaw*, 109; Berg, *Warsaw Ghetto*, 73; Roland, *Courage under Siege*, 99; Kaplan, *Scroll of Agony*, 220–21 (the quotation is on 220); Ringelblum, *Notes from the Warsaw Ghetto*, 133, 140–41, 143, 153, 202; Szwajger, *I Remember Nothing More*, 36.

62. Ringelblum, *Notes from the Warsaw Ghetto*, 141.

63. History of Czyste Hospital (English), Yad Vashem, Jerusalem.

64. From Stanislaw Rozycki's Warsaw Ghetto diary, in *The Warsaw Ghetto in Photographs*, 130. See also Ringelblum, *Notes from the Warsaw Ghetto*, 189–90, 204, and Berg, *Warsaw Ghetto*, 115–16.

65. History of Czyste Hospital (English), Yad Vashem, Jerusalem.

66. Interview with Dr. Thaddeus Stabholz, June 1, 1997.

67. *Hunger Disease*, 4. (This document was originally published in 1946 under the auspices of the American Joint Distribution Committee, a cosponsor of the study.) See also Roland, *Courage under Siege*, 86–88, 114–19, 187–97, and Tushnet, *Uses of Adversity*.

68. Ringelblum, *Notes from the Warsaw Ghetto*, 130, 165, 177; Berg, *Warsaw Ghetto*, 86–89, 115–16; Goldstein, *Stars Bear Witness*, 79–82; History of Czyste Hospital, as told to Stefania Beylin by Dr. Emil Apfelbaum.

69. Roland, *Courage under Siege*, 98, 223–25; Gutman, *Jews of Warsaw*, 64–65.

70. Ringelblum, *Notes from the Warsaw Ghetto*, 138 (quotation), 156, 197.

71. Kaplan, *Scroll of Agony*, 255, 267.

72. Ringelblum, *Notes from the Warsaw Ghetto*, 194, 225. See also Berg, *Warsaw Ghetto*, 73.

73. Kaplan, *Scroll of Agony*, 262, 266; Ringelblum, *Notes from the Warsaw Ghetto*, 140.

74. Kaplan, *Scroll of Agony*, 230, 243 (quotation); Ringelblum, *Notes from the Warsaw Ghetto*, 106, 125, 140; Gutman, *Jews of Warsaw*, 111–12.

75. Gutman, *Jews of Warsaw*, 112.

76. Kaplan, *Scroll of Agony*, 272. For a brief summary of the opening phases of "Operation Barbarossa," see Yahil, *Holocaust*, 243–47. For a fuller treatment see Weinberg, *World at Arms*, 187–205, 264–94, and Bartov, *Hitler's Army*, 12–28, 45.

77. Lewin, *Cup of Tears*, 122; Ringelblum, *Notes from the Warsaw Ghetto*, 249.

78. Browning, "Genocide and Public Health," 155–56; Gutman, *Jews of Warsaw*, 71.

79. Kaplan, *Scroll of Agony*, 277; Gutman, *Jews of Warsaw*, 106.

80. Ringelblum, *Notes from the Warsaw Ghetto*, 215, as well as 146 and 150–51. See also Berg, *Warsaw Ghetto*, 60–61.

81. Levi, *Survival in Auschwitz*, 36.

82. Browning, "Genocide and Public Health," 156; Gutman, *Jews of Warsaw*, 99; Ringelblum, *Notes from the Warsaw Ghetto*, 221; Kaplan, *Scroll of Agony*, 272–75, 282.

83. Czerniakow, *Warsaw Diary* (hereinafter cited as *Czerniakow Diary*), 270, 274, 279–80, 283–86, 288, 291–92, 294, 296, 298–300, 302, 306.

84. Szwajger, *I Remember Nothing More*, 42.

85. Interview with Silberberg.

86. Interview with Adam Skorecki, New Orleans, April 4, 1992.

87. Hilberg, *Destruction of the European Jews*, 190.

88. Mark Skorecki taped at a Thanksgiving Dinner, 1983. On the initial *Einsatzkommando* activities in Białystok, see Browning, *Ordinary Men*, 11–12; Gilbert, *Holocaust*, 160–61, and Yahil, *Holocaust*, 261.

89. The debates are surveyed in Marrus, *Holocaust in History*, 31–54; Mason, "Intention and Explanation"; and Christopher R. Browning, "The Decision concerning the Final Solution," in his *Fateful Months*, 8–38. See also the insightful essays in Browning's *Path to Genocide*, which come at the question from other intriguing angles.

90. Browning, "Nazi Resettlement Policy," 23–25.

91. Quoted in Dawidowicz, *War against the Jews*, 158.

92. Marrus, *Holocaust in History*, 46. For an interesting argument concerning Himmler's role in designing the Final Solution, see Breitman, *Architect of Genocide*, 145–228.

93. Quoted in Browning, "Genocide and Public Health," 158.

94. Hilberg, *Destruction of the European Jews*, 177–256; Yahil, *Holocaust*, 255–87; *Einsatzgruppen Reports*. On "execution tourism," see *"Good Old Days,"* 126–29, and Bartov, *Hitler's Army*, 104–5. On the psychological makeup and motivations of the killers, see the starkly opposing views in Browning, *Ordinary Men*, and Goldhagen, *Hitler's Willing Executioners*. Stressing situational factors over the culturally embedded "eliminationist anti-Semitism" emphasized by Goldhagen, Browning's interpretation is more plausible and persuasive, not least because it comports better with the known facts.

95. Yahil, *Holocaust*, 261–64.

96. Ibid., 264.

97. Gutman, *Jews of Warsaw*, 163–64; Donat, *Holocaust Kingdom*, 48.

CHAPTER FIVE

1. Kaplan, *Scroll of Agony*, 232 (first quotation), and Berg, *Warsaw Ghetto*, 82 (second quotation). See also Ringelblum, *Notes from the Warsaw Ghetto*, 283.

2. Gutman, *Jews of Warsaw*, 21–24; Ringelblum, *Notes from the Warsaw Ghetto*, 150–54 (the quotation is on 154); Kaplan, *Scroll of Agony*, 171, 180, 190. On the Jewish police,

see Berg, *Warsaw Ghetto*, 41–42, and Goldstein, *Stars Bear Witness*, 66–68. See also Donat, *Holocaust Kingdom*, 16–19, and Gilbert, *Holocaust*, 111–15.

3. For discussions of the temporary shift in the ghetto's economic direction, see Browning, "Nazi Ghettoization Policy in Poland," in his *Path to Genocide*, 34–42; Gutman, *Jews of Warsaw*, 74–77, 199, 437 n; Aly and Heim, "Economics of the Final Solution," 3–48, esp. 29–35; and the excellent introduction by Raul Hilberg and Stanisław Staron to *Czerniakow Diary*, esp. 45–53.

4. These were the so-called *Handelshausen*, which later established their own *Handelgesellschaft* (trade association) for German merchants in the General Government. Grabitz and Scheffler, *Letzte Spuren*, 297. I thank Ingrid Richards for helping with the translation.

5. Schwarberg, *Das Getto*, 7–15.

6. For a prewar description of Nowolipie Street, see Hen, *Nowolipie*, 9, 24, 28–29, 37–39, 41, 53, 88, 92; I thank Tadeusz Kaźmierak for translating these passages. See also Adler, *In the Warsaw Ghetto*, 254.

7. Grabitz and Scheffler, *Letzte Spuren*, 23–25, 207, 297.

8. Goldstein, *Stars Bear Witness*, 39–40.

9. This estimate assumes that the percentage of wooden sole workers relative to total payroll was the same in December 1941 as it was in July 1942. See Grabitz and Scheffler, *Letzte Spuren*, 162–63, 207.

10. See the photo album section in ibid.

11. Gutman, *Jews of Warsaw*, 74–75, 436 n (for a secret nutritional survey indicating that "shop" employees received 1,229 calories per day). Hilberg and Staron, introduction to *Czerniakow Diary*, 55–60; Ainsztein, *Jewish Resistance*, 615; Grabitz and Scheffler, *Letzte Spuren*, 303; Browning, "Nazi Ghettoization Policy in Poland," 44–49.

12. According to the one deponent, the daily rations consisted of a bowl of soup, 250 grams of bread (about nine slices), and a small portion of marmalade. Grabitz and Scheffler, *Letzte Spuren*. 303.

13. The original deadline, according to Adam Czerniakow, president of the Judenrat, was December 15–21, 1941. *Czerniakow Diary*, 306.

14. Kaplan, *Scroll of Agony*, 288. See also Berg, *Warsaw Ghetto*, 122, 127, and Gutman, *Jews of Warsaw*, 113–14.

15. *Czerniakow Diary*, 309–14.

16. See the list of addresses controlled by Schultz's given in Grabitz and Scheffler, *Letzte Spuren*, 302.

17. Ringelblum, *Notes from the Warsaw Ghetto*, 240–41. For the boundary changes, see the map in the frontispiece of the *Czerniakow Diary*.

18. On the fluctuations in Schultz's payroll, see Grabitz and Scheffler, *Letzte Spuren*, 207.

19. Quoted in Browning, "Nazi Resettlement Policy," in his *Path to Genocide*, 11.

20. MacDonald, *Killing of Heydrich*, 3–44; Höhne, *Order of the Death's Head*, 182–292.

21. Breitman, *Architect of Genocide*, 229–30; Hilberg, *Destruction of the European Jews*, 262–63.

22. In the fall of 1941, transports of German Jews were shot when they arrived in Kovno and Riga.

23. Breitman, *Architect of Genocide*, 194–204; Hilberg, *Destruction of the European Jews*, 563–67; Friedlander, *Origins of Nazi Genocide*, 284–87.

24. Hilberg, *Destruction of the European Jews*, 263.

25. Ibid., 263–66.

26. Ibid., 263–66 (the quotation is on 266). A copy of the Wannsee Protocols can be found in Wolfe, *Wannsee Protocol*. Also, a translation done by Dan Rogers at the University of South Alabama is available in the H-Holocaust Archives, March 4, 1995, *http://www.h-net.msu/logs/*.

27. Quoted in Burleigh and Wippermann, *Racial State*, 103.

28. Hilberg, *Destruction of the European Jews*, 267–84. The details were not finalized during two subsequent "Final Solution" conferences. Hannah Arendt, in her coverage of the Eichmann trial, treats the whole discussion as a species of Nazi cynicism, which it doubtless was to a degree: "Needless to say, the Nazis themselves never took these distinctions seriously, for them a Jew was a Jew, but the categories played a certain role up to the very end, since they helped put to rest a certain uneasiness among the German population: only Polish Jews were deported, only people who had shirked military service, and so on." See her *Eichmann in Jerusalem*, 132.

29. Hilberg, *Destruction of the European Jews*, 285–89, 333–34; Grabitz and Scheffler, *Letzte Spuren*, 159; MacDonald, *Killing*, 130.

30. Interview with Stan Levy, April 10, 1992.

31. Ringelblum, *Notes from the Warsaw Ghetto*, 263; Kaplan, *Scroll of Agony*, 375.

32. Quoted in Hilberg, *Destruction of the European Jews*, 308–9; see also Gutman, *Jews of Warsaw*, 198.

33. "Eichmann Tells His Own Damning Story," 14. See also Gideon Hausner, *Justice in Jerusalem*, 96, and Levin, *Holocaust*, 294–95.

34. MacDonald, *Killing of Heydrich*, 103–29, 169–82.

35. Ibid., 3 (quotation), 183–97.

36. Hilberg, *Destruction of European Jews*, 309; Scheffler, "Forgotten Part of the 'Final Solution,'" 36.

37. Kaplan, *Scroll of Agony*, 312 (quotation); Meed, *On Both Sides of the Wall*, 14.

38. Kaplan, *Scroll of Agony*, 312. See also Höhne, *Order of the Death's Head*, 357–60; Arad, *Belzec, Sobibor, Treblinka*, 14–15; Koehl, *RKFDV*, 130–34; Breitman, *Architect of Genocide*, 184–86, 190; Dwork and Pelt, *Auschwitz*, 290.

39. Wdowinski, *And We Are Not Saved*, 55. See also Gutman, *Jews of Warsaw*, 165–68, and Trunk, *Judenrat*, 420–36.

40. Kaplan, *Scroll of Agony*, 162, 248, and 287 (quotation).

41. Ibid., 288, 296–97, 304, 351, 352 (first quotation); Lewin, *Cup of Tears*, 115 (second quotation).

42. Ringelblum, *Notes from the Warsaw Ghetto*, 269.

43. Gutman, *Jews of Warsaw*, 130–32, 144–54, 1767–68; Edelman, *Ghetto Fights*, 51; Goldstein, *Stars Bear Witness*, 100–104; Fein, *Accounting for Genocide*, 238; Donat, *Holocaust Kingdom*, 48.

44. Interviews with Dr. Thaddeus Stabholz, September 8, 13, 1993.

45. Kaplan, *Scroll of Agony*, 344.

46. This was Ringelblum's interpretation (*Notes from the Warsaw Ghetto*, 266), which is shared by Gutman (*Jews of Warsaw*, 179).

47. All the extant ghetto diaries for this period record intensifying violence, but Lewin's *Cup of Tears* has several specific references to Nowolipie Street. See pages 107, 114, 123, and 129.

48. Ringelblum, *Notes from the Warsaw Ghetto*, 298–301; Kaplan, *Scroll of Agony*, 361–62.

49. Lewin, *Cup of Tears*, 73.

50. Ringelblum, *Notes from the Warsaw Ghetto*, 263; Grabitz and Scheffler, *Letzte Spuren*, 207. See also Trunk, *Judenrat*, 400–413.

51. Grabitz and Scheffler, *Letzte Spuren*, 162.

52. Ringelblum, *Notes from the Warsaw Ghetto*, 265–66, 277–78; Kaplan, *Scroll of Agony*, 331–32; Goldstein, *Stars Bear Witness*, 91–92; Berg, *Warsaw Ghetto*, 148–49; Lewin, *Cup of Tears*, 71, 75, 80, 256 n; Grabitz and Scheffler, *Letzte Spuren*, 32–33.

53. Adler, *In the Warsaw Ghetto*, 272, especially the map inside the back cover; Roland, *Courage under Siege*, 89–90. See also Fenigstein, "History of 'Czyste,'" xxvii. Originally published in Munich in 1948, it was translated and included in his unpublished memoir, "The Holocaust and I."

54. *Czerniakow Diary*, 348.

55. Ibid., 382–85; Gutman, *Jews of Warsaw*, 201–3.

56. Gutman, *Jews of Warsaw*, 203.

57. Arad, *Belzec, Sobibor, Treblinka*, 46–47.

58. Gutman, *Jews of Warsaw*, 197–200; Breitman, *Architect of Genocide*, 235–38; Höhne, *Order of the Death's Head*, 362–66.

59. Edelman, *Ghetto Fights*, 54.

60. Gilbert, *Holocaust*, 387–89; Gutman, *Jews of Warsaw*, 203; Höhne, *Order of the Death's Head*, 45.

61. *Czerniakow Diary*, 384.

62. Gilbert, *Holocaust*, 389.

63. This is Gutman's estimation, based on German statistics (*Jews of Warsaw*, 212).

64. Quoted in Josef Kermisz's introduction to *Czerniakow Diary*, 23. See also Adolf Berman, "The Fate of the Children in the Warsaw Ghetto," 409, and Gutman, "Adam Czerniakow—the Man and His Diary," 485, both in *The Catastrophe of European Jewry*.

65. Ringelblum, *Notes from the Warsaw Ghetto*, 316; Edelman, *Ghetto Fights*, 56. See also Dawidowicz, *War against the Jews*, 300–301; and Donat, *Holocaust Kingdom*, 60–61.

66. Gutman, *Jews of Warsaw*, 206–7; Gutman, "Adam Czerniakow," 485–86.

67. Meed, *On Both Sides of the Wall*, 13; Arad, *Belzec, Sobibor, Treblinka*, 60–61.

68. An English translation of the order is reprinted in Donat, *Holocaust Kingdom*, 55–56. See also Gutman, *Jews of Warsaw*, 204.

69. Gutman, *Jews of Warsaw*, 214–15; Ringelblum, *Notes from the Warsaw Ghetto*, 327.

70. Gutman, *Jews of Warsaw*, 199–200; Ainsztein, *Jewish Resistance*, 604–5.

71. There is a particularly graphic description of the frenzied search for employment in Meed, *On Both Sides of the Wall*, 15–20. See also Adler, *In the Warsaw Ghetto*, 252 (quotation), 272; Edelman, *Ghetto Fights*, 54; Donat, *Holocaust Kingdom*, 58–59; Gutman, *Jews of Warsaw*, 205–6; Grabitz and Scheffler, *Letzte Spuren*, 163, 207; Kaplan, *Scroll of Agony*, 390, 394; Goldstein, *Stars Bear Witness*, 110; and Lewin, *Cup of Tears*, 140.

72. See, for example, Grabitz and Scheffler, *Letzte Spuren*, 27–28.

73. Testimony of Leon Barnes, no. 4179 (quotation), and Adam Bojmowicz, no. 4178, in "Relacja" (Reports) on the Warsaw Ghetto, Jewish Historical Institute, Warsaw, Poland. I thank Tadeusz Kaźmierak for translating these documents.

74. Arad, *Belzec, Sobibor, Treblinka*, 54; Gutman, *Jews of Warsaw*, 207–10.

75. Zuckerman, *Surplus of Memory*, 207; Adler, *In the Warsaw Ghetto*, 143–44; Ringelblum, *Notes from the Warsaw Ghetto*, 329–31; Hilberg, *Perpetrators, Victims, Bystanders*, 161–62.

76. Donat, *Holocaust Kingdom*, 62–63 (the quotation is on 63); Edelman, *Ghetto Fights*, 58–59.

77. Meed, *On Both Sides of the Wall*, 29.

78. Kaplan, *Scroll of Agony*, 386; Lewin, *Cup of Tears*, 141.

79. Kaplan, *Scroll of Agony*, 395; Edelman, *Ghetto Fights*, 58–59; Goldstein, *Stars Bear Witness*, 117; Arad, *Belzec, Sobibor, Treblinka*, 54–61; Zylberberg, *Warsaw Diary*, 68.

80. Lewin, *Cup of Tears*, 135–47 (the quotations are on 136 and 140).

81. Ibid., 141, 146.

82. Ringelblum, *Notes from the Warsaw Ghetto*, 315; Lewin, *Cup of Tears*, 144–45, 149 (the quotation is on 145); and Kaplan, *Scroll of Agony*, 395–96.

83. Gutman, *Jews of Warsaw*, 208; Adler, *In the Warsaw Ghetto*, 273; Ringelblum, *Notes from the Warsaw Ghetto*, 333–34.

84. Lewin, *Cup of Tears*, 159; Kaplan, *Scroll of Agony*, 391–94.

85. Levy and Millen, interview by Robinson.

86. Meed, *On Both Sides of the Wall*, 48–49.

87. Adler, *In the Warsaw Ghetto*, 273. On August 5, Lewin recorded in his diary: "The 'action' continues unabated. We have no more strength to suffer. There are many murders. They kill the sick who don't go down to the courtyards" (*Cup of Tears*, 147).

88. Arad, *Belzec, Sobibor, Treblinka*, 56; Hilberg, *Perpetrators, Victims, Bystanders*, 96–97; Browning, *Ordinary Men*, 52, 76–77. These Ukrainian auxiliaries, called "Hiwis," after *Hilfswillige* (volunteers), served as well in various Selbstschutz units, which were also used in ghetto-emptying operations. See Black, "Rehearsal for 'Reinhard'?" 204–26.

89. Szwajger, *I Remember Nothing More*, 48.

90. Adler, *In the Warsaw Ghetto*, 272; Ringelblum, *Notes from the Warsaw Ghetto*, 312. For Calel Perechodnik's story, see his remarkable memoir *Am I a Murderer*.

91. Lewin, *Cup of Tears*, 282 n.

92. Dawidowicz, *War against the Jews*, 304–6; Lewin, *Cup of Tears*, 148; Meed, *On Both Sides of the Wall*, 43; Goldstein, *Stars Bear Witness*, 111–12; Kaplan, *Scroll of Agony*, 391.

93. Kaplan, *Scroll of Agony*, 11 and 390 (quotation).

94. Gutman, *Jews of Warsaw*, 207–8, table on 212; Gilbert, *Holocaust*, 396–97.

95. Szwajger, *I Remember Nothing More*, 48. See also Kaplan, *Scroll of Agony*, 391.

CHAPTER SIX

1. Ringelblum, *Notes from the Warsaw Ghetto*, 315. See also Kaplan, *Scroll of Agony*, 396, and Lewin, *Cup of Tears*, 154–55, 162, and 282 n.

2. Levy and Millen, interview by Robinson. See also Lewin, *Cup of Tears*, 145.

3. Lewin, *Cup of Tears*, 160, 282 n; Ringelblum, *Notes from the Warsaw Ghetto*, 310, 329.

4. Lewin, *Cup of Tears*, 153. The incident is alluded to in Sophia Leviathan's 1945 testimony "Der Krieg von Innen," Yad Vashem, Jerusalem. On page 42 of her testimony, she describes what happened: "Die Jagd geht letztens auf Kinder. Bei Többen haben die arbeitenden Frauen ihre Kinder in dem Kinderhort der Fabrik gelassen, um sie abends wieder abzuholen. In der Zwischenzeit kamen die Deutschen. Sie haben die vierzig heulenden, schreienden Kinder mitgenommen, weg von ihren Müttern." (The hunt goes after the children last. Working mothers at Többen have left their

children at the factory day care center, and then pick them up in the evening. In the meantime, the Germans came. They took forty bawling, screaming children with them, away from their mothers.) See also Gutman, *Jews of Warsaw*, 216–17, and Berg, *Warsaw Ghetto*, 173–74.

5. Leviathan, "Der Krieg von Innen," 46. (Dieses eine Wort, rechts oder links, entscheidet über Tod oder Leben. Links bedeutet, dass du weiter leben darfst, rechts, dass du zum Tode bestimmt bist.)

6. Lewin, *Cup of Tears*, 173–74.

7. Leviathan, "Der Krieg von Innen," 42, 48.

8. Lewin, *Cup of Tears*, 173–75.

9. Ibid., 153–54.

10. Ibid., 163. See also Edelman, *Ghetto Fights*, 64–65. There is a harrowing description of the Otwock deportations in Perechodnik, *Am I a Murderer*, 25–51.

11. Ringelblum, *Notes from the Warsaw Ghetto*, 317; Lewin, *Cup of Tears*, 162, 282 n.

12. Lewin, *Cup of Tears*, 168, 174 (quotation), and 285 n. See also Leviathan, "Der Krieg von Innen," 46–54; Meed, *On Both Sides of the Wall*, 60; Gutman, *Jews of Warsaw*, 209; and Hilberg, *Destruction of the European Jews*, 320 n. According to Hilberg, the agreement set the overall ghetto workforce at twenty-one thousand; a proclamation posted in the ghetto at the time placed the number at slightly less than twenty-five thousand. Both figures are puzzling shortfalls from the thirty-five thousand that Himmler is known to have established.

13. Levi, *Survival in Auschwitz*, 145. "Lager" is German for "camp."

14. Lewin, *Cup of Tears*, 149; Meed, *On Both Sides of the Wall*, 24–25, 49; Gutman, *Jews of Warsaw*, 205.

15. Ringelblum, *Notes from the Warsaw Ghetto*, 311; Trunk, *Judenrat*, 432; Edelman, *Ghetto Fights*, 69.

16. Leviathan, "Der Krieg von Innen," 46, 48, 53.

17. Interview with Dolek Skorecki, New Orleans, April 4, 1992.

18. Quoted in Sereny, *Into That Darkness*, 213.

19. Levi, *Survival in Auschwitz*, 84.

20. Interview with Adam Skorecki, New Orleans, April 4, 1992.

21. Interview with Prekerowa, June 16, 1993. The Prekerowa quotations here and in the following paragraphs are from this interview.

22. Levy and Millen, interview by Robinson.

23. The quotation from Lila is from ibid.

24. Peretz testimony at Eichmann Trial, from *Witnesses to the Holocaust: The Trial of Adolf Eichmann*, 1987; Szwajger, *I Remember Nothing More*, 30, 44. See also Hilberg, *Perpetrators, Victims, Bystanders*, 146.

25. Dwork, *Children with a Star*, 275 n.

26. Lewin, *Cup of Tears*, 163.

27. Rymkiewicz, *Final Station*, 46–59.

28. Kaplan, *Scroll of Agony*, 384; Edelman, *Ghetto Fights*, 60–61; Arad, *Belzec, Sobibor, Treblinka*, 61.

29. Edelman, *Ghetto Fights*, 61.

30. Meed, *On Both Sides of the Wall*, 40–41.

31. Ringelblum, *Notes from the Warsaw Ghetto*, 285, 291.

32. Krall, *Shielding the Flame*, 43. See also Edelman, *Ghetto Fights*, 61–62, and Ringelblum, *Notes from the Warsaw Ghetto*, 311.

33. Quoted in Edelman, *Ghetto Fights*, 54.

34. Gutman, *Jews of Warsaw*, 209; Adler, *In the Warsaw Ghetto*, 229.

35. Korczak's famous last march is movingly recounted in Lifton, *King of Children*, 338–45; the quotation appears on 345. See also Meed, *On Both Sides of the Wall*, 51.

36. Interview with Dr. Thaddeus Stabholz, September 8, 1993.

37. Edelman, *Ghetto Fights*, 65.

38. Interviews with Dr. Thaddeus Stabholz, September 8, 13, 1993.

39. Gutman, *Jews of Warsaw*, 224.

40. Quoted in Roland, *Courage under Siege*, 212.

41. Ibid., 210–11.

42. Interview with Balin.

43. Edelman, *Ghetto Fights*, 63; Arad, *Belzec, Sobibor, Treblinka*, 61–66 (the quotation in on 63); Sereny, *Into That Darkness*, 151–52.

44. Friedlander, *Origins of Nazi Genocide*, 287. In the student edition of his massive work, Hilberg estimates that 750,000 died at Treblinka; see *Destruction of the European Jews*, student ed., 239.

45. Arad, *Belzec, Sobibor, Treblinka*, 40–42; Sereny, *Into That Darkness*, 236.

46. Henry Friedlander's important work is far and away the most exhaustive and satisfying of the histories of the euthanasia program; see *Origins of Nazi Genocide*, 61, 109–10, 151.

47. Ibid., 284–87; Arad, *Belzec, Sobibor, Treblinka*, 42; *Shoah*, 46 (quotation).

48. *Shoah*, 52.

49. Arad, *Belzec, Sobibor, Treblinka*, 27 (first quotation), 86 (second quotation), 109.

50. Ibid., 49. On carbon monoxide poisoning, see Nuland, *How We Die*, 159.

51. Arad, *Belzec, Sobibor, Treblinka*, 121–22; *Shoah*, 110.

52. The quotation appears in Friedlander, *Origins of Nazi Genocide*, 299. See also Arad, *Belzec, Sobibor, Treblinka*, 87, and Sereny, *Into That Darkness*, 170.

53. The transportation bottlenecks occasioned another Final Solution Conference on September 26 and 28, 1942, with Adolf Eichmann again in attendance. Arad, *Belzec, Sobibor, Treblinka*, 51.

54. Ibid., 46, 66–67.

55. Quoted in ibid., 84.

56. Ibid., 84–95, 119–20; *Shoah*, 46.

57. Sereny, *Into That Darkness*, 157.

58. Arad, *Belzec, Sobibor, Treblinka*, 96–99, 107–13, 119, 122–23, 158–61. See also Steiner, *Treblinka*, 153–54.

59. Arad, *Belzec, Sobibor, Treblinka*, 120; Sereny, *Into That Darkness*, 219; Steiner, *Treblinka*, 246–47.

60. Sereny, *Into That Darkness*, 200–201.

61. Quoted in Arad, *Belzec, Sobibor, Treblinka*, 157.

62. Willenberg, *Surviving Treblinka*, 79–80.

63. Dawidowicz, *War against the Jews*, 309; Gutman, *Jews of Warsaw*, 210–13; Hilberg, *Destruction of the European Jews*, 320; Donat, *Holocaust Kingdom*, 86.

64. Meed, *On Both Sides of the Wall*, 62; Ringelblum, *Notes from the Warsaw Ghetto*, 314; interview with Solomon and Frieda Radasky. The order is reprinted in Grabitz and Scheffler, *Letzte Spuren*, 170. The shoot-on-sight clause reads: "Wer diese Anordnung nicht befolgt und ab Sonntag, den 6.9.1942, 10 Uhr vormittags im Ghetto . . . anget-

roffen wird—wird erschossen" (Whoever fails to follow this order and is found in the ghetto after 10:00 A.M. on Sunday, September 6, 1942, will be shot dead).

65. Leviathan, "Der Krieg von Innen," 49; Goldstein, *Stars Bear Witness*, 136–37; Edelman, *Ghetto Fights*, 65–66; Grabitz and Scheffler, *Letzte Spuren*, 24.

66. Mark Skorecki, taped reminiscence (ca. 1983); see also Lewin, *Cup of Tears*, 175–76.

67. Leviathan, "Der Krieg von Innen," 49.

68. Ibid.; Lewin, *Cup of Tears*, 177; Meed, *On Both Sides of the Wall*, 64–65.

69. Lewin, *Cup of Tears*, 178.

70. Interview with Solomon and Frieda Radasky.

71. Lewin, *Cup of Tears*, 177–78.

72. Meed, *On Both Sides of the Wall*, 65; Szwajger, *I Remember Nothing More*, 52.

73. Edelman, *Ghetto Fights*, 66.

74. Meed, *On Both Sides of the Wall*, 65.

75. Bartoszewski, *Warsaw Death Ring*, 132.

76. Goldstein, *Stars Bear Witness*, 137.

77. Leviathan, "Der Krieg von Innen," 49. The German version reads thus: Ein jüdischer Angestellter der Firma sizt unten in der Portierswohnung. Er ist von Schulz [*sic*] angewiesen, achthundert Nummern auszustellen und achthundert auf einer Liste engetragenen Arbeitern zu übergeben. Kinder bekommen prinzipiell keine Nummern. Er schreibt und schreibt. Heute entscheidet der Besitz einer Nummer über Tod und Leben. Und wieder ist die Sorge um die Kinder da? Was macht man nur mit den Kindern? Der Morgen kommt. Wir müssen uns auf der Strasse in alphabetischer Ordnung aufstellen. Wer keine Nummern bekommen hat, bleibt zurück. See also Meed, *On Both Sides of the Wall*, 63–64.

78. Goldstein, *Stars Bear Witness*, 137.

79. Szwajger, *I Remember Nothing More*, 55.

80. See Meed, *On Both Sides of the Wall*, 62–64, and Lewin, *Cup of Tears*, 178–79.

81. Leviathan, "Der Krieg von Innen," 49.

82. Of the extant accounts in English of the selection in the "kesl," Lewin's *Cup of Tears*, 175–79, is written closest to the time of the actual events. For this reason I have adopted it as a guide. The quotations are on 179.

83. Donat, *Holocaust Kingdom*, 91.

84. Lewin, *Cup of Tears*, 177; Meed, *On Both Sides of the Wall*, 66; Bartoszewski, *Warsaw Death Ring*, 132; Grabitz and Scheffler, *Letzte Spuren*, 24.

85. Mark Skorecki, taped reminiscence (ca. 1983).

86. Ibid. The term "elusive entity" is Nechama Tec's; see *When Light Pierced the Darkness*, 51.

87. Donat, *Holocaust Kingdom*, 93; Lewin, *Cup of Tears*, 179.

88. Kaplan, *Scroll of Agony*, 389.

89. Anne Levy (and Lila Millen), interview by Robinson; Mark Skorecki, taped reminiscence (ca. 1983).

90. Edelman, *Ghetto Fights*, 66; Szwajger, *I Remember Nothing More*, 54.

91. Szwajger, *I Remember Nothing More*, 55–58.

92. Gutman, *Jews of Warsaw*, 212–13.

93. Ibid., 270–71, esp. the table on 271.

94. Donat, *Holocaust Kingdom*, 99; Lewin, *Cup of Tears*, 179.

95. Zuckerman, *Surplus of Memory*, 245; Willenberg, *Surviving Treblinka*, 131; Gutman, *Jews of Warsaw*, 211; Dawidowicz, *War against the Jews*, 309.

CHAPTER SEVEN

1. My calculation derives from figures compiled for Belżec, Sobibór, and Treblinka by Yitzhak Arad, who estimates that over 1.5 million died in those camps during their seventeen months of operation. See charts and tables in Arad, *Belzec, Sobibor, Treblinka*, 383–98. The Browning quotation is from his *Ordinary Men*, xv.

2. Moshe Rozenek, "The Outbreak of World War Two," 23–25; Dov Bejski, "My Own Experience in the Holocaust," 27; and Dr. Moshe Bejski, "Działoszyce during the Holocaust," 32–39, all in *Yizkor Book*.

3. Moshe Bejski, "Działoszyce during the Holocaust," 40. See also Hausner, *Justice in Jerusalem*, 162–63, 176–77, 329–30.

4. Moshe Bejski, "Działoszyce during the Holocaust," 39–41; Rozenek, "Outbreak of World War Two," 25; Dov Bejski, "My Own Experience," 26.

5. The firsthand accounts disagree as to whether the work Jews were carried on the same train that transported the condemned Jews to Belżec. I therefore follow Moshe Bejski's account of events, because his is the longest and most detailed ("Działoszyce during the Holocaust," 41–42).

6. Arad, *Belzec, Sobibor, Treblinka*, 388. The record, which is conveniently tallied in the appendix, gives only the date of deportation and the estimated number of deportees: ten thousand, which is probably on the conservative side.

7. Dov Bejski, "My Own Experience," 27 (quotation); Moshe Bejski, "Działoszyce during the Holocaust," 42–44. See also the testimony of Marian Zonnenfeld, May 20, 1959 (Polish), Yad Vashem, 03/1281. Thanks to Dolek Skorecki and Mickey Tuttnauer for help with the translation.

8. Moshe Bejski, "Działoszyce during the Holocaust," 44; Dov Bejski, "My Own Experience," 26–31. Presumably, several hundred had died before this transfer to Brinnlitz.

9. Marrus, *Holocaust in History*, 133–48; Bauer, *Jewish Emergence from Powerlessness*, 26–40.

10. Krakowski, *War of the Doomed*, 104–5, 231; Gutman and Krakowski, *Unequal Victims*, 220; Ainsztein, *Jewish Resistance*, 427.

11. Zuckerman, *Surplus of Memory*, 197. See also Gutman, *Jews of Warsaw*, 236.

12. Shlomi, "A Jewish Island in a Gentile Sea," 10–11, and Leibel Yutchenka, "The Agudat Israel," 17–19, both in *Yizkor Book*.

13. Hoffman, *Shtetl*, 175–85.

14. Ringelblum, "'Comrade Mordecai,'" 90.

15. Zuckerman, *Surplus of Memory*, 192–97; the first quotation is on 192, the second quotation is on 197. See also Gutman, *Jews of Warsaw*, 228–36, and Lubetkin, *Days of Destruction*, 106–7.

16. Gutman, *Jews of Warsaw*, 243–45.

17. Zuckerman, *Surplus of Memory*, 207.

18. Lubetkin, *Days of Destruction*, 121. Ringelblum captured the mood in his famous notebook just following the Great Deportations: "Now we are ashamed of ourselves,

disgraced in our own eyes, and in the eyes of the world, where our docility earned us nothing. This must not be repeated now. We must put up a resistance" (*Notes from the Warsaw Ghetto*, 326).

19. Gutman, *Jews of Warsaw*, 256–61; Szwajger, *I Remember Nothing More*, 49. When the news of the Final Solution was confirmed in November 1942, the *New York Times*, the newspaper of record, buried the story on page 10. Other major dailies did likewise. See Lipstadt, *Beyond Belief*, 180–88.

20. Zuckerman, *Surplus of Memory*, 214–16; Lubetkin, *Days of Destruction*, 121–23.

21. Right-wing Zionists affiliated with the Jabotinsky faction, the forerunner of Menachem Begin's Likud coalition in Israel, preferred to go it alone, forming their own combat unit, the Jewish Military Union. See Gutman, *Jews of Warsaw*, 287–97.

22. Ringelblum, " 'Comrade Mordecai,' " 85.

23. Zuckerman, *Surplus of Memory*, 253–54; Gutman, *Jews of Warsaw*, 257, 300; Edelman, *Ghetto Fights*, 73; Bauer, *American Jewry and the Holocaust*, 327.

24. Zuckerman, *Surplus of Memory*, 254–55; Rotem, *Memoirs of a Warsaw Ghetto Fighter*, 22.

25. Zuckerman, *Surplus of Memory*, 245–47; Gutman, *Jews of Warsaw*, 301.

26. Zuckerman, *Surplus of Memory*, 184.

27. Rotem, *Memoirs of a Warsaw Ghetto Fighter*, 22 (quotation), 26–28; Krall, *Shielding the Flame*, 48.

28. Zuckerman, *Surplus of Memory*, 230.

29. Meed, *On Both Sides of the Wall*, 73; Lubetkin, *Days of Destruction*, 123. See also Goldstein, *Stars Bear Witness*, 153.

30. Krall, *Shielding the Flame*, 10.

31. Zuckerman, *Surplus of Memory*, 201 (quotation), 219–20; Lubetkin, *Days of Destruction*, 99.

32. Ringelblum, " 'Comrade Mordecai,' " 90.

33. Krall, *Shielding the Flame*, 64.

34. Ibid., 45, 86 (first quotation); "The Second Report from the Jewish Workers' Underground Movement, 15 November 1943," in Edelman, *Ghetto Fights*, 100.

35. My discussion of Edelman, the revolutionary romanticism of the ZOB, and the distinction between "heroic virtues" and "ordinary virtues" is heavily indebted to Todorov, *Facing the Extreme*, 3–30, 71–90.

36. Gutman, *Jews of Warsaw*, 283–84; Ringelblum, *Notes from the Warsaw Ghetto*, 321, 324–25.

37. Ringelblum, *Notes from the Warsaw Ghetto*, 321, 338–44 (the quotation is on 344); Donat, *Holocaust Kingdom*, 111–12; Gutman, *Jews of Warsaw*, 284–85.

38. Dawidowicz, *War against the Jews*, 332–33. See also Donat, *Holocaust Kingdom*, 111–12, and Ringelblum, *Notes from the Warsaw Ghetto*, 338–44.

39. Zuckerman, *Surplus of Memory*, 221 (quotation), 227; Edelman, *Ghetto Fights*, 67.

40. Lewin, *Cup of Tears*, 188–89, 194; Gutman, *Jews of Warsaw*, 277; Ringelblum, *Notes from the Warsaw Ghetto*, 320; Zuckerman, *Surplus of Memory*, 224–25.

41. Ringelblum, *Notes from the Warsaw Ghetto*, 323–24.

42. Goldstein, *Stars Bear Witness*, 154.

43. The rental rate was five zlotys per day per worker. Gutman, *Jews of Warsaw*, 274, 326–28 (the quotes are on 327 and 274, respectively). See also *Documents on the Holocaust*, 289–90, and the original in *Faschismus—Getto—Massenmord*, 355.

44. Lewin, *Cup of Tears*, 194; Ringelblum, *Notes from the Warsaw Ghetto*, 321.

45. Ringelblum, *Notes from the Warsaw Ghetto*, 316–19 (the quotation is on 318); Lewin, *Cup of Tears*, 193–94.

46. Ringelblum, *Notes from the Warsaw Ghetto*, 318–19.

47. Lewin, *Cup of Tears*, 181, 204–7; Gutman, *Jews of Warsaw*, 327–28; Zuckerman, *Surplus of Memory*, 227.

48. Lewin, *Cup of Tears*, 204–7 (first quotation is on 205); *Documents on the Holocaust*, 135 (second quotation).

49. Jäckel, *Hitler's World View*, 62–64 (the quotation is on 64).

50. Lewin, *Cup of Tears*, 210.

51. Zuckerman, *Surplus of Memory*, 227–28; Gutman, *Jews of Warsaw*, 243–46.

52. Gutman, *Jews of Warsaw*, 302 (quotation); Zuckerman, *Surplus of Memory*, 245 n; Edelman, *Ghetto Fights*, 69.

53. There was one cell inside Schultz's proper, commanded by Avron Feiner of the Bund, presumably containing only five members, in keeping with the philosophy of the "fives." Most ZOB fighters were concentrated in Landau's Shop, a carpentry shop owned and managed by two Jewish brothers. Meed, *On Both Sides of the Wall*, 73; Edelman, *Ghetto Fights*, 68; Gutman, *Jews of Warsaw*, 304.

54. Gutman, *Jews of Warsaw*, 354.

55. Ringelblum, *Notes from the Warsaw Ghetto*, 340.

56. Ibid.

57. Ringelblum, *Polish-Jewish Relations*, 143–44.

58. Ringelblum, *Notes from the Warsaw Ghetto*, 324–25; Lewin, *Cup of Tears*, 204.

59. Two Polish historians argue that 42,000 escaped. Ringelblum (in *Polish-Jewish Relations*, 247) indicated that "probably no more than 15,000 Jews are hiding in the capital"; Gutman (in *Jews of Warsaw*, 265) says 15,000–20,000. The best estimates are the extrapolations performed by Gunnar S. Paulsson on Żegota lists collected by Adolf Berman. Paulsson posits 15,000–24,000 Jews in hiding. See his "Demographic Characteristics."

60. Ringelblum, *Polish-Jewish Relations*, 95–96, esp. 95 n; Meed, *On Both Sides of the Wall*, 182.

61. Ringelblum, *Polish-Jewish Relations*, 96.

62. Ibid., 235, 95.

63. For similar concerns, see Meed, *On Both Sides of the Wall*, 104.

64. Polonsky, "Polish-Jewish Relations," 226–42 (the quote is on 227). The thaw, if not warming, trend set in with the January 1987 publication by one of Poland's leading literary critics of a controversial mea culpa titled "A Poor Christian Looks at the Ghetto," in Steinlauf, *Bondage to the Dead*, 113–17.

65. It used to be argued that 3 million Poles perished by Nazi hands, a figure that has been revised downward to 2 million victims—still a significant number. Steinlauf, *Bondage to the Dead*, 23–42 (the quotation is on 31); Polonsky, "Polish-Jewish Relations," 226–27.

66. The actual cryptonym was Konrad Żegota, a totally fictitious person.

67. Tomaszewski and Werbowski, *ZEGOTA*, 39–79; Kermish, "Activities of the Council for Aid to Jews," 367–98; Bartoszewski, "On Both Sides of the Wall," xliv–l; Paulsson, "Demographic Characteristics"; Gutman, *Jews of Warsaw*, 264; Tec, *When Light Pierced the Darkness*, 121–22; Lukas, *Forgotten Holocaust*, 147–51.

68. A more realistic estimate is that Żegota probably supported between five and six thousand Jews on the "Aryan side," with another three or four thousand receiving

financial support from such Jewish organizations as the Bund. "Generally each political party or group took care of its own members and periphery," wrote Bernard Goldstein of the Bund; see his *Stars Bear Witness*, 218. For the best estimates of the number of Jews assisted by Żegota and the level of funding, based on actual Żegota records, see Paulsson, "Demographic Characteristics." For Polish assessments, see Bartoszewksi, "On Both Sides of the Wall," xlviii, and Lukas, *Forgotten Holocaust*, 150. For a sampling of Jewish criticisms, see Ringelblum, *Polish-Jewish Relations*, 212–16 (esp. 213 for the quotation); Kermish, "Activities of the Council for Aid to Jews," 367–69; and Gutman and Krakowski, *Unequal Victims*, 252–71.

69. Meed, *On Both Sides of the Wall*, 114–15.

70. Tec, *When Light Pierced the Darkness*, 140. See also Ringelblum, *Polish-Jewish Relations*, 140–43.

71. Ringelblum, *Notes from the Warsaw Ghetto*, 336–38 (the quotations are on 337); Ringelblum, *Polish-Jewish Relations*, 151. See also Kurek-Lesik, *Your Life Is Worth Mine*, 55–56, 229 n; Kurek-Lesik, "Conditions of Admittance," 244–75; and Kloczowski, "Religious Orders and the Jews," 238–43.

72. Ringelblum, *Polish-Jewish Relations*, 150–51.

73. For examples of Polish military veterans involved in rescue activity, see Paldiel, *Path of the Righteous*, 199–200.

74. Ringelblum, *Polish-Jewish Relations*, 140.

75. Bettelheim, "Ignored Lessons of Anne Frank," in his *"Surviving" and Other Essays*, 248. See also Dwork, *Children with a Star*, 31–34; Donat, *Holocaust Kingdom*, 124–25; Meed, *On Both Sides of the Wall*, 83, 110–11; and Todorov, *Facing the Extreme*, 81–82.

76. Meed, *On Both Sides of the Wall*, 76–78 (the quotation is on 76); Ringelblum, *Polish-Jewish Relations*, 96–98; Rotem, *Memoirs of a Warsaw Ghetto Fighter*, 50.

77. Ringelblum, *Polish-Jewish Relations*, 99.

78. Meed, *On Both Sides of the Wall*, 110–11; Goldstein, *Stars Bear Witness*, 157; Ringelblum, *Polish-Jewish Relations*, 140–43.

79. Meed, *On Both Sides of the Wall*, 111.

80. Krall, *Shielding the Flame*, 42–43.

81. Delbo, *Auschwitz and After*, 192.

82. Des Pres, *Survivor*, 160.

83. Interview with Gorecka; interview with Gneidziejko.

84. Lewin, *Cup of Tears*, 229.

85. Szwajger, *I Remember Nothing More*, 22.

86. Quoted in Gutman, *Jews of Warsaw*, 272. A copy of the original order appears in *Faschismus—Getto—Massenmord*, 342–44, esp. 343. See also Bartoszewski, "On Both Sides of the Wall," xxviii–xxix, and Lewin, *Cup of Tears*, 210–11.

87. Lewin, *Cup of Tears*, 233.

88. Ibid., 237. See also Ainsztein, *Jewish Resistance*, 605–6.

89. Gutman, *Jews of Warsaw*, 307–8, 328–29 (the quotation is on 329). For the text of Himmler's angry letter following his surprise visit to Warsaw, see Grabitz and Scheffler, *Letzte Spuren*, 180–81. See also Speer, *Infiltration*, 266–67. Ainsztein, *Jewish Resistance*, 606–7; and Hilberg, *Destruction of the European Jews*, 322–23.

90. Lifton, *King of Children*, 293; Edelman, *Ghetto Fights*, 67.

91. Ringelblum, *Polish-Jewish Relations*, 123–28 (the quotation is on 125); Goldstein, *Stars Bear Witness*, 208–10; Meed, *On Both Sides of the Wall*, 90; Szwajger, *I Remember Nothing More*, 76.

92. Ringelblum made this cryptic though interesting observation at the end of October 1942: "Polish streetcar peoples' attitude to the Jews very good." See his *Notes from the Warsaw Ghetto*, 322.

93. Interview with Gorecka.

94. She was born March 28, 1916, according to church records. Interview with Gneidziejko.

95. Ringelblum, *Polish-Jewish Relations*, 89–90; Meed, *On Both Sides of the Wall*, 96.

96. Gutman, *Jews of Warsaw*, 307–10. Lewin captured the prevailing mood of distrust in his reaction to a December 1942 proclamation from the SS commandant decrying baseless rumors of resettlement: "Of course proclamations of this kind cannot reassure us. On the contrary, they increase our fear and agitation." See his *Cup of Tears*, 220.

97. Zuckerman, *Surplus of Memory*, 281–85 (the quotations are on 283 and 285, respectively). See also Lubetkin, *Days of Destruction*, 152–53.

98. Zuckerman, *Surplus of Memory*, 251.

99. Ainsztein, *Jewish Resistance*, 608; Borzykowski, *Between Tumbling Walls*, 29; Meed, *On Both Sides of the Wall*, 120–21.

100. Grabitz and Scheffler, *Letzte Spuren*, 182–83.

101. Goldstein, *Stars Bear Witness*, 156; Meed, *On Both Sides of the Wall*, 101.

102. Fenigstein, "Holocaust and I," 165; Roland, *Courage under Siege*, 92–94; Szwajger, *I Remember Nothing More*, 62–65.

103. Falstein, *Martyrdom of Jewish Physicians*, 418.

104. Interview with Dr. Thaddeus Stabholz, September 8, 1993.

105. Fenigstein, "Holocaust and I," 164.

106. Interview with Dr. Thaddeus Stabholz, September 8, 1993.

CHAPTER EIGHT

1. Precise figures are lacking. Emmanuel Ringelblum says a majority remained "under the surface" (*Polish-Jewish Relations*, 116). A sample of hidden Jews compiled by Nechama Tec indicates that only around 25 percent did, which makes sense. Chances are that mainly secular Jews considered the escape option, those with superior prospects for "passing." See Tec, *When Light Pierced the Darkness*, esp. the table on 213 n.

2. Gutman and Krakowski, *Unequal Victims*, 271–75; Meed, *On Both Sides of the Wall*, 82; Tomaszewski and Werbowski, *Zegota*, 57–60; Goldstein, *Stars Bear Witness*, 218, 223; "Stanisław Karsov-Szymaniewska," in *Righteous among Nations*, 159–66; Ringelblum, *Polish-Jewish Relations*, 102–3.

3. Ringelblum, *Polish-Jewish Relations*, 144–45.

4. The Lvov Ghetto was liquidated in May 1943, driving some survivors into the sewer system where they lived for over a year in filth and darkness, besieged constantly by rats. See Marshall, *In the Sewers of Lvov*.

5. Nir, *Lost Childhood*, 42–43.

6. Ringelblum, *Notes from the Warsaw Ghetto*, 167; Donat, *Holocaust Kingdom*, 113–14; Oliner and Oliner, *Altruistic Personality*, 110.

7. Browning, *Ordinary Men*, 71. Hannah Arendt made the same point nearly forty years ago in her classic essay on the Eichmann trial, subsequently reprinted in book form: "That the ideal of 'toughness,' except, perhaps, for a few half-demented brutes,

was nothing but a myth of self-deception, concealing a ruthless desire for conformity at any price, was clearly revealed at the Nuremberg Trials, where the defendants accused and betrayed each other and assured the world that they 'had always been against it' or claimed, as Eichmann was to do, that their best qualities had been 'abused' by their superiors." *Eichmann in Jerusalem*, 175. For a sharply conflicting interpretation of the same phenomenon which stresses the "eliminationist anti-Semitism" of German perpetrators, see Goldhagen, *Hitler's Willing Executioners*. For an insightful discussion of perpetrator psychology, see Sabini and Silver, "Destroying the Innocent," 329–58.

8. Quoted in Marrus, *Holocaust in History*, 25–26.

9. Rotem, *Memoirs of a Warsaw Ghetto Fighter*, 97.

10. Interview with a Gorecka, June 18, 1993.

11. "Stanisław Karsov-Szymaniewska," 165–66 (quotation is on 166); Ringelblum, *Polish-Jewish Relations*, 118.

12. See, for example, Oliner and Oliner, *Altruistic Personality*, 68–69.

13. Ringelblum, *Polish-Jewish Relations*, 126.

14. Ibid., 100–104, 120–22; Rotem, *Memoirs of a Warsaw Ghetto Fighter*, 62–63; Meed, *On Both Sides of the Wall*, 89, 194; Tec, *When Light Pierced the Darkness*, 37–39, 47; Goldstein, *Stars Bear Witness*, 176; Szwajger, *I Remember Nothing More*, 76, 111.

15. Meed, *On Both Sides of the Wall*, 194; Rotem, *Memoirs of a Warsaw Ghetto Fighter*, 10.

16. Rotem, *Memoirs of a Warsaw Ghetto Fighter*, 62–63 (quotation), 90–91; Meed *On Both Sides of the Wall*, 105, 199; Ringelblum *Polish-Jewish Relations*, 120, 127; Goldstein, *Stars Bear Witness*, 176.

17. Szwajger, *I Remember Nothing More*, 133–35 (the quotation is on 133). See also Oliner and Oliner, *Altruistic Personality*, 67.

18. Meed, *On Both Sides of the Wall*, 175–80; Ringelblum, *Polish-Jewish Relations*, 155. The major treatment of the Hotel Polski episode is Shulman, *Case of Hotel Polski*. See also Steve Paulsson, posting, *http://www.h-net.msu.edu/logs*, December 19, 1995.

19. Meed, *On Both Sides of the Wall*, 198; Ringelblum, *Polish-Jewish Relations*, 101–2; Rotem, *Memoirs of a Warsaw Ghetto Fighter*, 76–77, 101.

20. Interview with Gorecka; city planning maps of Ząbkowska Street and Lochowska Street, Polish State Archives, Warsaw (copies in the author's possession).

21. Sydnor, *Soldiers of Destruction*, 334; Ainsztein, *Jewish Resistance*, 619–20.

22. Höhne, *Order of the Death's Head*, 440–43, 458–61 (the quotation is on 442); Hilberg, *Destruction of the European Jews*, 556–61, 340–42; Gutman, *Jews of Warsaw*, 325, 330–33.

23. Borzykowski, *Between Tumbling Walls*, 29.

24. Zuckerman, *Surplus of Memory*, 288.

25. Ibid., 296–97, 303. Gutman, *Jews of Warsaw*, 291–93, 339, and especially 348, where he says that the ZOB had about 350 fully mobilized fighters and a total strength of 400–450; Marek Edelman, on the other hand, told the Polish journalist Hanna Krall that there were only 220 fighters (Krall, *Shielding the Flame*, 10). In addition, the revisionist Żydowski Związek Wojskowy (Jewish Fighting Union, or ZZW) units are estimated to have fielded a combined force of 250.

26. Zuckerman, *Surplus of Memory*, 305, 315–16, 330–35 (the quotation is on 333); Borzykowski, *Between Tumbling Walls*, 35–37, 43–44.

27. "Things hitherto held sacred were desecrated, all authority was undermined,"

complained one ZOB fighter, adding that "each day deepened the corruption." Borzykowski, *Between Tumbling Walls*, 18–19, 42–43; Lubetkin, *Days of Destruction*, 167.

28. Lubetkin, *Days of Destruction*, 277–78.

29. "We didn't get many rifles," Zuckerman wrote. "I was happy when I could distribute two rifles to every unit" (*Surplus of Memory*, 304).

30. Lubetkin, *Days of Destruction*, 165; Zuckerman, *Surplus of Memory*, 300, 312; Gutman, *Jews of Warsaw*, 300.

31. Borzykowski, *Between Tumbling Walls*, 54; Zuckerman, *Surplus of Memory*, 307–8; Gutman, *Jews of Warsaw*, 316.

32. Zuckerman, *Surplus of Memory*, 307; Borzykowski, *Between Tumbling Walls*, 33; Gutman, *Jews of Warsaw*, 350–51.

33. The evidence is surprisingly less than clear-cut regarding the ZOB's moral authority in the ghetto. For example, Gutman argues that the uprising on January 18 "forged a bond of courage between the fighters and the rest of the ghetto's population, and a consciousness that rather than bring ruin down on the ghetto, resistance might be the only solution to the existing situation" (Gutman, *Jews of Warsaw*, 320). On the other hand, one of the fighters, Simha Rotem (Kazik), writes that as late as February or March 1943, "Our environment wasn't very encouraging. The relatively few Jews left in the Ghetto were generally not enthusiastic about our operations. Thus the ZOB was in a double underground, hiding from the Germans and from most of the Jews as well. We got sympathy and good will only from a small group who were close to us" (Rotem, *Memoirs of a Warsaw Ghetto Fighter*, 26).

34. Gutman, *Jews of Warsaw*, 345.

35. Borzykowski, *Between Tumbling Walls*, 31, 41. Judging from the propaganda drawings disseminated by management which showed the communal luxuries awaiting Jewish workers at Trawniki, Fritz Schultz made the same misleading claims. See Grabitz and Scheffler, *Letzte Spuren*, 214–17. See also Zuckerman, *Surplus of Memory*, 314–15; Edelman, *Ghetto Fights*, 71–72; Lubetkin, *Days of Destruction*, 169–71; and Gutman, *Jews of Warsaw*, 333–35.

36. Grabitz and Scheffler, *Letzte Spuren*, 210.

37. Gutman, *Jews of Warsaw*, 354–55.

38. Donat, *Holocaust Kingdom*, 132.

39. Borzykowski, *Between Tumbling Walls*, 45, 47 (quotation).

40. Ibid., 48.

41. Lubetkin, *Days of Destruction*, 178–79; Borzykowski, *Between Tumbling Walls*, 48–49; Gutman, *Resistance*, 204. There is minor disagreement about when the Germans surrounded the wall. Gutman says it occurred at 1:00 A.M. (Gutman, *Jews of Warsaw*, 367); Edelman says it was at 2:00 A.M., as does Goldstein (Edelman, *Ghetto Fights*, 75; Goldstein, *Stars Bear Witness*, 189–90). Jürgen Stroop's report says the encirclement took place at 3:00 A.M. ("Daily Report, 20 April 1943," in *Stroop Report*).

42. Again accounts differ about the time of day when the Germans entered the ghetto, ranging between four and seven in the morning. Stroop's report says 6:00 A.M. ("Daily Report, 20 April 1943").

43. Borzykowski, *Between Tumbling Walls*, 50–55; Gutman, *Jews of Warsaw*, 372, 374; Ainsztein, *Jewish Resistance*, 625 and 628.

44. Quoted in Gutman, *Jews of Warsaw*, 375.

45. Quoted in Gutman, *Resistance*, 207.

46. Borzykowski, *Between Tumbling Walls*, 60.

47. Gutman, *Jews of Warsaw*, 372–74; Gutman, *Resistance*, 206–10; Ainsztein, *Jewish Resistance*, 625; Lubetkin, *Days of Destruction*, 180; Edelman, *Ghetto Fights*, 76.

48. Gutman, *Jews of Warsaw*, 375.

49. Gutman, *Resistance*, 208–9 (the quotation is on 209); Gutman, *Jews of Warsaw*, 394; Ainsztein, *Jewish Resistance*, 627.

50. Rotem, *Memoirs of a Warsaw Ghetto Fighter*, 34.

51. "Daily Report, 20 April 1943."

52. Gutman, *Resistance*, 213–14; Gutman, *Jews of Warsaw*, 376–79; Ainsztein, *Jewish Resistance*, 630–31, 635–36; Rotem, *Memoirs of a Warsaw Ghetto Fighter*, 38; Lubetkin, *Days of Destruction*, 186–87; Edelman, *Ghetto Fights*, 77–79.

53. Interview with Thaddeus Stabholz, June 23, 1998.

54. The tunnel mine excavated by the ZOB in this area failed to detonate owing to a power outage in Schultz's Shop.

55. The explanation for shopworker compliance is twofold: first, bunkers in which to take shelter were much scarcer in the Többens-Schultz compound; and second, ZOB influence never percolated as deeply in these shops as in the workplaces in the central ghetto and the Brushmakers area. At Többens-Schultz, many Jewish foremen, whose moral sway among the workers was substantial, continued clinging to the illusion that the shop owners could protect them when all was said and done. One trusted Jewish supervisor at Schultz's may have even suppressed the attack order he received from the Aryan side by telephone on April 19, instead of relaying it to the ZOB unit stationed in his shop. He chose to place his trust in the promises of his German bosses "that nothing would happen to the 'productive Jews.'" *Stroop Report*, 24 (first quotation), and Zuckerman, *Surplus of Memory*, 354–55 (second quotation). See also Gutman, *Jews of Warsaw*, 376–79; Gutman, *Resistance*, 217; and Ainsztein, *Jewish Resistance*, 633, 636. The progress of the evacuation in the central shop area is recorded in Fritz Schultz's diary, reprinted in Grabitz and Scheffler, *Letzte Spuren*, 195–205. There is some disagreement over the degree of compliance with the April 20 transfer order. Ainsztein, who writes in the heroic mold, says that few Jewish workers inside Többens-Schultz volunteered and that the SS had to storm the area to seize workers (Ainsztein, *Jewish Resistance*, 636). Stroop says much the same thing in his face-saving daily reports. Gutman (*Resistance*, 222), on the other hand, gives a more balanced—and more believable—account. See also Berg, *Warsaw Ghetto*, 232, for a firsthand account of the evacuation in Többens.

56. Gutman, *Jews of Warsaw*, 383. In his postwar trial, Többens contrasted the cooperative attitude of Globocnik with the burn-them-out recklessness of Stroop. Tusk-Scheinwechslerowa, "Fabryka Waltera C. Többensa w Getci Warszawskim," 62–70.

57. Edelman, *Ghetto Fights*, 81–82; Wdowinski, *And We Are Not Saved*, 93–94; Ainsztein, *Jewish Resistance*, 636, 638–39, 643, 644, 647–49; Gutman, *Resistance*, 636; Zuckerman, *Surplus of Memory*, 354–55.

58. Grabitz and Scheffler, *Letzte Spuren*, 205 (Alles ist in Rauch und Staub gehüllt von den um uns herum brennendedn Häusern).

59. Ibid., 204–5, and especially the *Betriebschema* (organization chart) on 238–41.

60. Borzykowski, *Between Tumbling Walls*, 60; Zuckerman, *Surplus of Memory*, 372–73; Ainsztein, *Jewish Resistance*, 637–47 (quotation on 646).

61. Lubetkin, *Days of Destruction*, 202; Zuckerman, *Surplus of Memory*, 310.

62. Borzykowski, *Between Tumbling Walls*, 61–63 (the quotation is on 63).

63. "Summary Report, 24 May 1943," in *Stroop Report*.

64. Gutman, *Resistance*, 225 (quotation); Borzykowski, *Between Tumbling Walls*, 64–65; Stabholz, *Seven Hells*, 4.

65. Borzykowski, *Between Tumbling Walls*, 68, 70; Ainsztein, *Jewish Resistance*, 638.

66. Rotem, *Memoirs of a Warsaw Ghetto Fighter*, 39 (quotation); Borzykowski, *Between Tumbling Walls*, 63; Lubetkin, *Days of Destruction*, 218.

67. Borzykowski, *Between Tumbling Walls*, 66.

68. Lubetkin, *Days of Destruction*, 203, 205.

69. They escaped through the underground tunnel that the revisionist fighters had excavated in the Muranowska Square area.

70. This is a contentious story. When the uprising broke out, the Communist underground army (Armia Ludowa [AL], or Polish People's Army) offered to turn over its entire stock of twenty-eight weapons to the ZOB but lacked the military wherewithal to deliver the weapons personally. A few AK commanders, operating on their own, did make diversionary strikes against German and Polish police detachments next to the wall. So did the AL. But they were all without effect. Rotem, *Memoirs of a Warsaw Ghetto Fighter*, 40–42; Zuckerman, *Surplus of Memory*, 338–44, 348–49, 363–64 (quotation), 375; Ainsztein, *Jewish Resistance*, 634–35, 638, 640–42.

71. Borzykowski, *Between Tumbling Walls*, 75–79; Lubetkin, *Days of Destruction*, 218.

72. Quoted in Zuckerman, *Surplus of Memory*, 356–57.

73. Lubetkin, *Days of Destruction*, 220; Borzykowski, *Between Tumbling Walls*, 81.

74. Borzykowski, *Between Tumbling Walls*, 90–94; Lubetkin, *Days of Destruction*, 222–23.

75. Lubetkin, *Days of Destruction*, 229–33; Borzykowski, *Between Tumbling Walls*, 96–99; Zuckerman, *Surplus of Memory*, 370.

76. Rotem, *Memoirs of a Warsaw Ghetto Fighter*, 52; Borzykowski, *Between Tumbling Walls*, 101–3; Lubetkin, *Days of Destruction*, 240–42. One of Zuckerman and Kazik's graver disappointments was the Home Army's failure to share its Warsaw sewage system maps, without which a journey into those muck-filled channels was invariably doomed to failure. Those two sewer workers were Zuckerman and Kazik's ad hoc response to a desperate situation. Zuckerman, *Surplus of Memory*, 380.

77. Interview with Thaddeus Stabholz, June 23, 1998.

78. Lubetkin, *Days of Destruction*, 243–44. In his interview with Krall, Marek Edelman tells the story of Pola Lifszyc, who ran after her mother when Pola discovered she had been taken to the Umschlagplatz. "Pola ran after this column alone, she ran after this column from Leszno Street to Stawki—her fiancé gave her a lift in his riksa so that she could catch up—and she made it. At the last minute she managed to merge into the crowd so as to be able to get on the train with her mother. Everybody knows about [Janusz] Korczak, right? Korczak was a hero because he went to death with his children of his own free will. But Pola Lifszyc, who went with her mother—who knows about Pola Lifszyc?" (*Shielding the Flame*, 45).

79. Lubetkin, *Days of Destruction*, 245–50 (the quotation is on 245); Borzykowski, *Between Tumbling Walls*, 104–5.

80. Borzykowski, *Between Tumbling Walls*, 107; Krall, *Shielding the Flame*, 73.

81. Lubetkin, *Days of Destruction*, 251–55 (the quotation is on 255); Borzykowski, *Between Tumbling Walls*, 108.

82. Borzykowski, *Between Tumbling Walls*, 107–8; Rotem, *Memoirs of a Warsaw Ghetto Fighter*, 54–58; Lubetkin, *Days of Destruction*, 256–57; Meed, *On Both Sides of the Wall*, 159–60.

83. *Stroop Report*, 11.

84. Lubetkin, *Days of Destruction*, 235–36.

85. Goldstein, *Stars Bear Witness*, 205 (quotation); Gutman, *Jews of Warsaw*, 400.

86. Quotations from Edelman here and in the following two paragraphs are found in Krall, *Shielding the Flame*, 81–82.

87. Lubetkin, *Days of Destruction*, 244; interview with Thaddeus Stabholz, June 23, 1998 (quotations); Stabholz, *Seven Hells*, 1–8. The capture of the German garrison at Tunis and Bizerta occurred on May 7, 1943.

88. Interview with Thaddeus Stabholz, June 23, 1998; Stabholz, *Seven Hells*, 10.

89. His book was originally published in 1947. Stabholz, *Seven Hells*, 10–18 (the quotation is on 17).

90. Ibid., 24–27 (the quotation is on 27).

91. Interview with Thaddeus Stabholz, June 23, 1998.

92. "Excremental Assault" is the name of chapter 3 in Des Pres, *Survivor*, 57–80; Stabholz, *Seven Hells*, 32.

93. Stabholz, *Seven Hells*, 32–35, 70; Wdowkinski, *And We Are Not Saved*, 66 n. On the physical layout of Majdanek, see *Historical Atlas of the Holocaust*, 100–102. On *Blockälteste* and *Stubendiensts*, see Yisrael Gutman, "Auschwitz—an Overview," in *Anatomy of the Auschwitz Death Camp*, 22.

94. Zuckerman, *Surplus of Memory*, 374; Ringelblum, *Polish-Jewish Relations*, 172, 178.

95. Rotem, *Memoirs of a Warsaw Ghetto Fighter*, 62.

96. Ringelblum, *Polish-Jewish Relations*, 182–85.

97. Meed, *On Both Sides of the Wall*, 88.

98. Krall, *Shielding the Flame*, 7; Lubetkin *Days of Destruction*, 200. The carousel has been immortalized in Czeslaw Milosz poem "Campo Dei Fiori," penned in Warsaw in 1943 and movingly reprinted in Szwajger, *I Remember Nothing More*, 98–100.

99. Quoted in Ainsztein, *Jewish Resistance*, 629. Passover fell on April 20, Easter on April 25, in 1943.

100. See also Ringelblum, *Polish-Jewish Relations*, 77–78.

CHAPTER NINE

1. Vladka Meed tells a similar story of Aryanized Jews who sent letters to themselves. See *On Both Sides of the Wall*, 196.

2. Fogelman, *Conscience and Courage*, 139; Ringelblum, *Polish-Jewish Relations*, 226.

3. Interview with Gorecka, June 18, 1993.

4. Nir, *Lost Childhood*, 54.

5. "Eliasz Pietruszka," in *Righteous Among Nations*, 139–40.

6. Ringelblum relates the prisonlike experiences of one twelve-year-old boy confined to a one-room flat: "If somebody came, he had to hide in a cupboard, behind a sofa, in the toilet, etc., and stay there for hours without moving until the guests departed." See his *Polish-Jewish Relations*, 141. See also Meed, *On Both Sides of the Wall*, 204–5.

7. Quotations from Höfle here and from Hilberg in the following paragraph are in Hilberg, *Destruction of the European Jews*, 332.

8. Interview with Gorecka, June 18, 1993.

9. Meed, *On Both Sides of the Wall*, 91–92; Ringelblum, *Polish-Jewish Relations*, 109; Rotem, *Memoirs of a Warsaw Ghetto Fighter*, 85. See also Goldstein, *Stars Bear Witness*, 222.

10. It calls to mind the sudden metamorphosis from stoop-shouldered older woman to sharply dressed bourgeois matron undergone by the protagonist in Louis Begley's classic novel of passing in Nazi-occupied Poland, when the aunt qua mother pulled her young nephew aside from a mob of deportees waiting on a Warsaw train platform for shipment to Auschwitz and demanded that a *Wehrmacht* officer standing nearby perform his gentlemanly duty and extricate her from this riffraff and direct her and her son to the right train. See *Wartime Lies*, 133–37.

11. Ringelblum, *Polish-Jewish Relations*, 133, 227; Tec, *When Light Pierced the Darkness*, 80; Oliner and Oliner, *Altruistic Personality*, 73; Fogelman, *Conscience and Courage*, 30, 168.

12. Interview with Prekerowa, June 16, 1993.

13. Ringelblum, *Polish-Jewish Relations*, 230; Oliner and Oliner, *Altruistic Personality*, 72, 77, 83; Tec, *When Light Pierced the Darkness*, 78–79; Fogelman, *Conscience and Courage*, 68; Rotem, *Memoirs of a Warsaw Ghetto Fighter*, 77.

14. Fogelman, *Conscience and Courage*, 136.

15. Hilberg, *Destruction of the European Jews*, 342–43.

16. Browning, *Ordinary Men*, 135–37 (the quotation is on 135); Arad, *Belzec, Sobibor, Treblinka*, 171, 175–77, 271–341, 365; Sereny, *Into That Darkness*, 236–50.

17. Browning, Ordinary Men, 137–42 (the quotation is on 142); Arad, *Belzec, Sobibor, Treblinka*, 366–69; Grabitz and Scheffler, *Letzte Spuren*, 262–72, 328–34.

18. Quoted in Gilbert, *Holocaust*, 629–32.

19. Interview with Thaddeus Stabholz, September 8, 1993.

20. Browning, *Ordinary Men*, 141–42.

21. This was told to my interpreter during a tour of the courtyard on June 18, 1993.

22. Interview with Solomon and Frieda Radasky.

23. Ruth does not identify him by name, but subsequent events strongly suggest it was Smolenski that Mark approached.

24. Compare the moral agonizing of Protestant rescuers in Le Chambon-sur-Lignon. Hallie, *Lest Innocent Blood Be Shed*, 125–26.

25. Interview with Solomon and Frieda Radasky. It was probably the Rozycki Bazaar, which was not as large as Radasky remembers.

26. Ringelblum, *Polish-Jewish Relations*, 119–21 (the quotation is on 119), 154–55. For an account of the betrayal of Ringelblum's hiding place and his and his family's execution, see the Josef Kermish introduction, xxvi. For more on the intensifying Nazi reign of terror, see Meed, *On Both Sides of the Wall*, 163, 226, and Goldstein, *Stars Bear Witness*, 228.

27. Meed, *On Both Sides of the Wall*, 184.

28. Interview with Gorecka, June 18, 1993, and interview with Gniedziejko.

29. Interview with Gorecka, June 18, 1993.

30. Interview with Gniedziejko.

31. Meed, *On Both Sides of the Wall*, 177.

32. The classic study of religious faith among Holocaust survivors is Brenner, *Faith and Doubt of Holocaust Survivors*; see also Helmreich, *Against All Odds*, 237–47.

33. Actually, the rule is that the Torah is supposed to be taken from the Ark for public readings on the Sabbath, holidays, fast days, and Mondays and Thursdays.

34. For a balanced assessment see Philip Friedman, "Ukrainian-Jewish Relations during the Nazi Occupation," in his *Roads to Extinction*, 176–208.

35. Szwajger, *I Remember Nothing More*, 120; Helmreich, *Against All Odds*, 240.

36. Quoted in Tec, *When Light Pierced the Darkness*, 51.

37. Fein, *Accounting for Genocide*, 33; see also Mason, "Testing Human Bonds Within Nations," 315–43.

38. Fein, *Accounting for Genocide*, 115–16, 120; Steinlauf, *Bondage to the Dead*, 21; Ringelblum, *Polish-Jewish Relations*, 193.

39. Fogelman explains the origin of the "righteous gentile" terminology thus: "They are spiritual heirs to the *Lamed Vav*—the thirty-six people of Jewish tradition whose sole task it is, in every generation, unknown to themselves or others, to do good for their fellow men. In Hebrew these non-Jews are called *Hasidei U'Mot Ha'Olam*—'righteous among nations of the world.' They are the rescuers." See her *Conscience and Courage*, 3.

40. Fogelman, *Conscience and Courage*, 12–13; Oliner and Oliner, *Altruistic Personality*, 2.

41. The exact figures are 4,613 out of 13,223. See Steve Paulsson, "Posting on righteous gentiles."

42. Marrus and Paxton, "The Nazis and the Jews in Occupied Western Europe," 713.

43. Interview with Gorecka, June 18 and 19, 1993.

44. Quoted in Steinlauf, *Bondage to the Dead*, 129; see also Fogelman, *Conscience and Courage*, xvi, 274–76.

45. Fogelman, *Conscience and Courage*, 73–74, 226.

46. Oliner and Oliner, *Altruistic Personality*, 109 (quotation), 124–25.

47. Interview with Gorecka, June 18, 1993.

48. Interview with Prekerowa, June 16, 1993; Gushee, "Many Paths to Righteousness," 385; Ringelblum, *Polish-Jewish Relations*, 235 (quotation); Fogelman, *Conscience and Courage*, 80, 150, 158; Oliner and Oliner, *Altruistic Personality*, 7, 49–50, 93–103, 131, 136 ("foot in the door"), 216; Hallie, *Lest Innocent Blood Be Shed*.

49. Oliner and Oliner, *Altruistic Personality*, 80–81; Fogelman, *Conscience and Courage*, 73–74.

50. Interview with Gorecka, June 18, 1993.

51. Aszkenazy-Engelhard, *Pragnelam Zyc*, 81–98 (the quotations are on 83–84); these facts are confirmed by the rectory cook at the time, Sabina Swidzinska (interview with Swidzinska). Thanks to Tadeusz Kaźmierak for doing the translation.

52. Interview with Prekerowa, June 16, 1993.

53. The ZOB remnant from the ghetto uprising used to mislead Polish landlords into believing they were actually working for the Polish underground. It enhanced the safety of the Jews whom the landlords were being paid to hide. "In general, when a Polish Christian who gave protection to a Jew learned that a Polish underground group was also interested in the fate of those hiding, and even came to visit them, the Jew's stock rose in their eyes. The Pole was also filled with the sense that his activity

was important and necessary and that, somewhere, he was registered in the 'annals of the underground.'" Rotem, *Memoirs of a Warsaw Ghetto Fighter*, 96.

54. The term is Fogelman's. See her *Conscience and Courage*, 68.

55. The classic sociological study of Polish rescuers is Tec's splendid *When Light Pierced the Darkness*. See also Oliner and Oliner, *Altruistic Personality*, 128–29, 156–59; Gushee, "Many Paths to Righteousness," 377–80; and Baron, "The Holocaust and Human Decency," 237–51.

56. The keynote study on rescuers and social marginals is London, "Rescuers," 241–51. Although Tec offers cautious endorsement of London's findings, most students of rescue register sharp dissent. See Tec, *When Light Pierced the Darkness*, 152–54; Gushee, "Many Paths to Righteousness," 382–83; and Fogelman, *Conscience and Courage*, 68.

57. Gender interpretations begin with Carol Gilligan's widely influential *In a Different Voice*. See also Ringelheim, "Women and the Holocaust," 741–61; Anderson, "Gender Differences in Altruism," 43–58; Eagly and Crowley, "Gender and Helping Behavior," 283–308; and Fogelman, *Conscience and Courage*, 237–51.

58. Pierre Sauvage interview with Bill Moyers at the end of Sauvage's film documentary *Weapons of the Spirit* (1989). Another rescuer put it thus: "The hand of compassion was faster than the calculus of reason" (quoted in Fogelman, *Conscience and Courage*, 57).

59. Murdoch, *Sovereignty of Good*, 37; Oliner and Oliner, *Altruistic Personality*, 168–69, 222 (for the Murdoch quotation); Fogelman, *Conscience and Courage*, 57–61, 157; Tec, *When Light Pierced the Darkness*, 163–83; Hallie, *Lest Innocent Blood Be Shed*, 20–21, 127; Paldiel, "Altruism of the Righteous Gentiles," 187–96.

60. Interview with Prekerowa, June 16, 1993.

61. Rotem, *Memoirs of a Warsaw Ghetto Fighter*, 72.

62. Much of the social psychological literature on the origins of altruism trace it to core values inculcated by specific styles of parenting, family nurture, and moral reasoning. See, for example, Fogelman, *Conscience and Courage*, 255–63, and Oliner and Oliner, *Altruistic Personality*, 179–83, 249–51.

63. Interview with Gorecka, June 18, 1993; Fogelman, *Conscience and Courage*, 152.

64. Zawodny, *Nothing but Honour*, 139.

65. Nir, *Lost Childhood*, 97–98.

66. Interview with Gorecka, June 18, 1993.

67. Interview with Dolek Skorecki, New Orleans, April 4, 1992.

68. Ibid.

CHAPTER TEN

1. Bartoszewski, *Warsaw Death Ring*, 195–292. For an eyewitness account of one of these street raids, see Nir, *Lost Childhood*, 137–38.

2. Werth, *Russia at War*, 861. For a concise and readable overview, see Keegan, *Second World War*, 458–73. The standard account is John Erickson's magisterial but densely complex *Road to Berlin*, 87–330.

3. Helpful overviews of the Byelorussian offensive of the summer of 1944 are Ziemke, *Stalingrad to Berlin*, 313–45; Dupuy and Martell, *Great Battles on the Eastern*

Front, 150–66; Keegan, *Second World War*, 182, 479–81; and Werth, *Russia at War*, 858–66. See also Rokossovsky, *Soldier's Duty*.

4. Meed, *On Both Sides of the Wall*, 226. See also Ciechanowski, *Warsaw Rising*, 229–30; Goldstein, *Stars Bear Witness*, 237–38; Bartoszewski, *Warsaw Death Ring*, 324–30; Lukas, *Forgotten Holocaust*, 186.

5. Goldstein, *Stars Bear Witness*, 239. See also Meed, *On Both Sides of the Wall*, 251–52, for a description of the bombing raids, and Ciechanowski, *Warsaw Rising*, 235.

6. Meed, *On Both Sides of the Wall*, 252; Rotem, *Memoirs of a Warsaw Ghetto Fighter*, 118; Lukas, *Forgotten Holocaust*, 184–87.

7. Zawodny, *Nothing but Honour*, 30.

8. Meed, *On Both Sides of the Wall*, 252.

9. Lukas, *Forgotten Holocaust*, 72–73.

10. Roos, *History of Modern Poland*, 201 (first quotation); Korbonski, *Polish Underground State*, 152–54, 169, 171 (second quotation). See also Ciechanowski, *Warsaw Rising*, 149–71, 212–42, and Lukas, *Forgotten Holocaust*, 182–84.

11. Lukas, *Forgotten Holocaust*, 193. See also Keegan, *Second World War*, 482–83.

12. Lukas, *Forgotten Holocaust*, 187–211 (the quotation is on 209); Erickson, *Road to Berlin*, 272–90; Meed, *On Both Sides of the Wall*, 255; Zawodny, *Nothing but Honour*, 137–49; Ziemke, *Stalingrad to Berlin*, 344 n. There is a particularly gripping account of an AK expedition through the sewers in Nir, *Lost Childhood*, 179–84. Likewise compelling is Białoszewski, *Memoir of the Warsaw Uprising*.

13. Quoted in Werth, *Russia at War*, 872, 877–88.

14. Zawodny, *Nothing but Honour*, 172–75 (the quotation is on 175); Ziemke, *Stalingrad to Berlin*, 344–45.

15. Meed, *On Both Sides of the Wall*, 253–57 (the quotation is on 257); Rotem, *Memoirs of a Warsaw Ghetto Fighter*, 123–34; Lubetkin, *Days of Destruction*, 266–70; Zuckerman, *Surplus of Memory*, 520–63; Gilbert, *Holocaust*, 716–17.

16. Orpen, *Airlift to Warsaw*, 156.

17. Mark Skorecki, taped reminiscence (ca. 1983).

18. Ibid.

19. Ibid.

20. Ibid.

21. Ibid.

22. Erickson, *Road to Berlin*, 288–99.

23. Davies, *God's Playground*, 2:476–77 (first quotation); Hirschmann, *Embers Still Burn*, 185–86 (second quotation). See also Erickson, *Road to Berlin*, 290; Zawodny, *Nothing but Honour*, 180–81; Korbonski, *Polish Underground State*, 188, 200–204; Lukas, *Forgotten Holocaust*, 215–18; Meed, *On Both Sides of the Wall*, 258–59.

24. Mark Skorecki, taped reminiscence (ca. 1983).

25. Stone, *Underground to Palestine*, 58; Bauer, *Jewish Emergence from Powerlessness*, 64.

26. Dobroszycki, *Survivors of the Holocaust in Poland*, 25.

27. Mark Skorecki, taped reminiscence (ca. 1983).

28. Dobroszycki, *Survivors of the Holocaust in Poland*, 5–13, esp. table 1.2. See also Rotem, *Memoirs of a Warsaw Ghetto Fighter*, 147, and Zuckerman, *Surplus of Memory*, 564–95.

29. Everyone's name but Ruth's appears in the published list released in 1945 by the Jewish Agency for Palestine: Search Bureau for Missing Relatives. See the entries for "Anna Skorecka," "Leokadia Skorecka," and "Mordka Skorecki," in *Register of Jewish*

Survivors, vol. 2, *List of Jews in Poland (58,000 Names)* (Jerusalem, 1945), 239. This rare publication can be found in "Register of Jewish Survivors . . . ," MSS Col. 361, folder D55/6, World Jewish Congress Collection, American Jewish Archives, Hebrew Union College, Cincinnati, Ohio.

30. Mark Skorecki, taped reminiscence (ca. 1983).

31. *Abmeldung*, Abram Tempelhof, and *Abmeldung*, Sara Tempelhof, both in the Łódź State Archives.

32. Quoted in Dinnerstein, *America and the Survivors of the Holocaust*, 28.

33. Mark Skorecki, taped reminiscence (ca. 1983).

34. Ibid.

35. *Abmeldung*, Wolf Skorecki, and *Abmeldung*, Gitla Skorecka, both in the Łódź State Archives. Interview with Baranowski.

36. Interview with Skorecka. "Pola Skorecka," T/D 276 702, ITS Microfilm Project, roll T29, Yad Vashem, Jerusalem.

37. Interview with Silberberg.

38. Meed, *On Both Sides of the Wall*, 262–63.

39. Hirschmann, *Embers Still Burn*, 201–2; Zuckerman, *Surplus of Memory*, 627.

40. Wyman, *DP*, 141–44 (the quotation is on 143).

41. Hirschmann, *Embers Still Burn*, 188–89; Dinnerstein, *America and the Survivors of the Holocaust*, 108–9.

42. *Yizkor Book*, 44 (quotation); Bejski, "The 'Righteous among the Nations' and Their Part in the Rescue of Jews," in *Catastrophe of European Jewry*, edited by Gutman and Rothkirchen, 587.

43. Wyman, *DP*, 143–44; Dinnerstein, *America and the Survivors of the Holocaust*, 107–8; Hirschmann, *Embers Still Burn*, 188 (quotation); Bauer, *Jewish Emergence*, 65.

44. Steinlauf, *Bondage to the Dead*, 57.

45. Mark Skorecki, taped reminiscence (ca. 1983).

46. For a similar experience, see Rotem, *Memoirs of a Warsaw Ghetto Fighter*, 146.

47. Kersten, *Establishment of Communist Rule*, 239–40.

48. Interview with Skorecka.

CHAPTER ELEVEN

1. Interview with Skorecka; Zuckerman, *Surplus of Memory*, 587, 614 (quotation); Stone, *Underground to Palestine*, 17, 47–50 (the quotation is on 47). See also Bauer, *Flight and Rescue*, 116.

2. It is possible to trace the postwar movements of many displaced persons (DP's), Jewish survivors included, through the master index of the ITS Microfilm Project of Yad Vashem. These are microfilms of the card index file of the International Tracing Service, whose files are presently housed in Arolsen, Germany. They are arranged alphabetically. The Skoreckis appear on roll T29 (S287).

3. Interviews with Lipman, June 25, 1992, and Morton R. Levy. The Brichah story is recounted in Bauer, *Flight and Rescue*, and Zuckerman, *Surplus of Memory*. See also Barish, *Rabbis in Uniform*, 21–25, 42–52; Grob, *Rekindling the Flame*, 112–20; and Luza, "Liberation of Prague," 41–57.

4. Marrus, *Unwanted*, 324–31.

5. Dinnerstein, *America and the Survivors of the Holocaust*, 9, 17–18; Ziemke, *U.S. Army*

in the Occupation of Germany, 52–53, 167, 200–201, 239–40, 284–87, 355–56; Wyman, *DP*, 17–46; Bischof and Ambrose, *Eisenhower and the German POWs*, 2–4.

6. Interview with Kriegstein, Boca Raton, Fla., January 16, 1993.

7. "Monthly Historical Report for December, 1945," December 29, 1945, Historical Report—1947 folder; "Historical Report, 28 April 1945 to 30 June 1946," pp. 28–29, 176 folder; and "Historical Report for Month of March," April 4, 1946, Historical Report—1947 folder, all in box 898. See also Second Lieutenant James H. Boyd to Dr. Nmemic, City Commissioner of Marienbad, [ca. November–December 1945], Refugees folder, box 897, and "Weekly Summary, No. 12," September 28, 1945, Historical Reports, box 898. All of the above are in OMGUS, RG 260, National Archives, Suitland, Md. (hereinafter cited as OMGUS).

8. Dinnerstein, *America and the Survivors of the Holocaust*, 16–17; Bauer, *Flight and Rescue*, 80–89, 111.

9. Interview with Rubinstein, June, 28, 1992.

10. Douglas Deane to A. C. Dunn, May 24 and June 6, 1946, Team 168, UNRRA, United Nations Archives, New York (hereinafter UNA); Broszat, "Concentration Camps," 456, 459; Siegert, "Das Konzentrationslager Flossenbürg," 482–90.

11. Dinnerstein, *America and the Survivors of the Holocaust*, 29–47, and Bauer, *Flight and Rescue*, 80–89, 111.

12. Interview with Ferber.

13. "Report of Inspection of Displaced Persons Camp," December 4, 1945, Team 168, UNRRA, UNA.

14. "The core experiences of psychological trauma are disempowerment and disconnection from others," explains psychiatrist Judith L. Herman, in her study of victims of domestic abuse and political terror, *Trauma and Recovery*, 35–53, 133 (quotation). See also Eitinger, "Concentration Camp Syndrome," 131–45, and Krystal, "Trauma," 11–28.

15. Quoted in Levi, *The Drowned and the Saved*, 79.

16. Interview with Rubinstein, June 28, 1992, and interview with Appel. Rubinstein provides a fictionalized account of her Holocaust experiences in *Survivor in Us All*. Her subsequent memoir, *After the Holocaust*, delineates her experiences in postwar Germany.

17. Interview with Rubinstein, June, 28, 1992. For the debates within the Jewish resistance movement over postwar revenge, see Zuckerman, *Surplus of Memory*, 628–35.

18. Levi, *The Drowned and the Saved*, 24.

19. Quoted in Epstein, *Children of the Holocaust*, 99; see also Herman, *Trauma and Recovery*, 70, 155–183.

20. Interviews with Kriegstein, New York, July 6, 1992, and Boca Raton, Fla., January 16, 1993.

21. Interview with Henry Wahrman.

22. Mark Wyman, *DP*, 132–37; Peck, "Liberated but Not Free," 222–35; interview with Rubinstein, June 28, 1992.

23. Besides the testimony of living survivors, the collective life of the Tirschenreuth community can be followed in the microfilm collection of the Central Committee of Liberated Jews in the American Zone, in YIVO, New York. See especially Alfred Slomnicki to Central Committee of Liberated Jews in the American Zone, April 12, 1946. See also "Monthly Historical Report for December, 1945," December 29, 1945,

box 898, OMGUS. Flyer for production of *Shulamit*, by Abraham Goldfaden, Yad Vashem Archives, Jerusalem (hereinafter YVA).

24. Interview with Marek Sudkiewicz, March 10, 12, 1994.

25. Interview with Appel; interview with Strauch; and interview with Kriegstein, New York, July 6, 1992. See also Wyman, *DP*, 151; Report of H. W. O. Matthews, February 27 and 28, 1946, Team 168, UNRRA, UNA.

26. "Polish Refugees in Sweden, List No. 3" (ca. 1945–1946), D56/5, ser. D, Relief and Rescue Departments, World Jewish Congress Collection, American Jewish Archives, Cincinnati, Ohio.

27. Interview with Dolek Skorecki, Haifa, Israel, October 5, 1993.

28. "Historical Report for Month of August, 1946," August 31, 1946, Historical Report—1947 folder, box 898, OMGUS; Peck, "Liberated but Not Free," 231. A brief but excellent psychological study of the Holocaust's impact on family formation and dynamic is Klein, "Children of the Holocaust, 2:393–410. Because of its personal nature, I have chosen not to divulge the name of the Tirschenreuth survivor who did not feel love.

29. Interview with Appel; interview with Jania Sudkiewicz.

30. Interview with Kunstadt, July 7, 1994.

31. Interview with Rosenberg.

32. Interview with Kunstadt, July 7, 1994.

33. Report of H. W. O. Matthews.

34. Interview with Rubinstein, June, 28, 1992.

35. Interview with Kunstadt, July 7, 1994.

36. Tec, *When Light Pierced the Darkness*, 142–44; Marks, *Hidden Children*, 35–40.

37. Interview with Sudkiewicz; interview with Dolek Skorecki, Haifa, Israel, February 11, 1994.

38. Interview with Lipman, June 25, 1992.

39. Kimche and Kimche, *Secret Roads*, 80; "Historical Report, 28 April 1945 to 30 June 1946," pp. 28–29.

40. Interview with Kriegstein, New York, January 16, 1993.

41. "Historical Report, 28 April 1945 to 30 June 1946," pp. 28–29; interview with von Schulenberg.

42. Interview with Kriegstein, Boca Raton, Fla., July 6, 1992.

43. Interview with Henry Wahrman; "Historical Report, 1 July 1946–30 June 1947," p. 6, Historical Reports—1947 folder, box 898, OMGUS.

44. Interview with Kriegstein, New York, July 6, 1992.

45. Ibid.

46. Ibid.; interview with Henry Wahrman.

47. Interview with Marek Sudkiewicz, March 12, 1994, and interview with Janiá Sudkiewicz.

48. Interview with Skorecka.

49. Report of Visit of Health Division to Camp Tirschenreuth, August 12, 1946, Team 168, UNRRA, UNA.

50. Interview with Janiá Sudkiewicz.

51. Stabholz, *Seven Hells*, xi.

52. Interview with Thaddeus Stabholz, February 3, 1994.

53. Ibid.

54. Interview with Kriegstein, July 6, 1992.

55. "Historical Report for Month of October 1946," October 31, 1946, p. 1, Historical Report—1947 folder, box 898, OMGUS; interview with Appel and interview with Rubinstein, June 28, 1992.

56. The best brief summary of postwar German attitudes was penned by an American officer involved with displaced persons after the war; see Moskowitz, "The Germans and the Jews," 7–14. See also Persico, *Nuremberg*, 86 (first quotation); Stern, *Whitewashing of the Yellow Badge*, 1–158 (the second quotation is on xvi); and Moeller, "War Stories," 1008–48.

57. Allen, *Nazi Seizure of Power*, 84; Kershaw, *Popular Opinion*, 23–29. As usual, Michael R. Marrus offers an exceptionally lucid and succinct summary of the literature on German anti-Semitism and Hitler's rise to power; see *Holocaust in History*, 85–94.

58. Bartov, *Hitler's Army*, esp. 106–78. Also, according to OMGUS opinion surveys conducted early in the occupation, six of ten Germans were "deeply imbued with racist feeling." See Stern, *Whitewashing of the Yellow Badge*, 122–23.

59. Interview with Rubinstein, June 28, 1992; Kershaw, *Popular Opinion*, 224–77, 370–72.

60. Laqueur, *Terrible Secret*, 17–40; Levi, *Reawakening*, 201; Bankier, *Germans and the Final Solution*, 101–15.

61. The story of Kristallnacht in Tirschenreuth is contained in ten affidavits, all in German, collected in 1946 and deposited at Yad Vashem, Jerusalem. The quotation comes from the affidavit of the police chief at the time, Christian Hecht. For a succinct analysis of Kristallnacht throughout Germany and Austria, see Yahil, *Holocaust*, 109–14. For the reaction of the German public, see Bankier, *Germans and the Final Solution*, 85–88.

62. Feig, *Hitler's Death Camps*, 129–32; Horwitz, *In the Shadow of Death*, 9.

63. Interview with Wahrman.

64. Goldhagen, *Hitler's Willing Executioners*, esp. 364–67; Krakowski, "Death Marches," 482–86; Bauer, "Death-Marches," 491–511; Siegert, "Das Konzentrationslager Flossenbürg," 482–90; Gilbert, *Macmillan Atlas of the Holocaust*, 214, 218, 224; Abzug, *Inside the Vicious Heart*, 80; Horwitz, *In the Shadow of Death*, 144–63, 214–16.

65. "Historical Report, 28 April 1945 to 30 June 1946," p. 26. For a survivor account of the Buchenwald-to-Flossenbürg evacuation, see Franz Freihut, "Todesmarsch durch den Bayerischen Wald" (undated), YVA E-1452, YVA.

66. "Historical Report for Month of August 1946," August 31, 1946, p. 4, box 898, OMGUS.

67. *Stars and Stripes*, August 21, 1946, European edition, 4.

68. "Historical Report for Month of August 1946," p. 7, and "Historical Report for Month of September 1946," September 30, 1946, p. 6 (quotation), both in box 898, OMGUS. See also interview with Mariels, and undated [ca. 1977] obituary of L. R. Mariels from the *Portland Oregonian*.

69. For a comparable instance of German denial, see Horwitz, *In the Shadow of Death*, esp. 144–63.

70. Two additional death sentences were handed down: one for Bormann (in absentia), and the other for Göring, who cheated the hangman by swallowing a cyanide capsule hours before he was slated for the gallows. For a gripping account of the

Nuremberg trial, see Persico, *Nuremberg*. See also Tusa and Tusa, *Nuremberg Trial*, and Taylor, *Anatomy of the Nuremberg Trials*.

71. Gimbel, *American Occupation of Germany*, 101–10; Gimbel, *German Community under American Occupation*, 139–64; and Taylor, *Anatomy of the Nuremberg Trials*, 278–80. See also "War Diary," August 8, 1945; "Weekly Summary #11," September 21, 1945; "Historical Report for October, 1946," October 31, 1946; and "Historical Report for November, 1946," November 30, 1946, all in box 898; and S. Glickson and W. Baruch to American Military Government, September 20, 1946, General Records, box 897, Refugees—1946 file, OMGUS.

72. "Historical Report, 1 July 1946 to 30 June 1947," p. 8; "Historical Report for July 1946," August 1, 1946, p. 7, box 898, OMGUS.

73. The Jewish Committee recorded the Kristallnacht defendants's affidavits, which they later deposited in Yad Vashem in Jerusalem. See, in particular, the affidavit by Karl Schmidt, "Kristallnacht in Tirschenreuth," April 14, 1946, YVA M-1/31, YVA.

74. "Political Survey [1946?]," in Political Activity Reports, 1946–1947, folder. The shift in political mood and its affect on denazification can be followed in the various historical surveys, all in box 898, OMGUS. See also Gimbel, *American Occupation of Germany*, 48–51, 106–7, 158–62; Stern, *Whitewashing* of *the Yellow Badge*, 131–32; and Wyman, *DP*, 171–76.

75. Interview with Appel, and interview with Wahrman. See also "Historical Report for September, 1946," September 30, 1946, p. 10, box 898, OMGUS.

76. Borowski, *This Way for the Gas*, 165.

77. "Historical Report, July 1–September 30, 1947," p. 19, and "Historical Report, 1 January 1948 to 31 March 1948," both in box 898, OMGUS.

78. The quotations in this and the following paragraph come from interview with Wahrman.

79. Interview with Rosenberg.

80. "Historical Report for October 1946," p. 4.

81. For reference to Cecilia Skorecka, see *Liberated Jews*, 117, YVA.

82. Interview with Skorecka; ITS Microfilm Project, roll T29 (S287), YVA.

83. Interviews with Arthur Tenser and Harry Tenser, New York, May 26, 1993; interview with Gerver, May 29, 1993.

84. The story of postwar survivor emigration to the United States is ably recounted in Dinnerstein, *America and the Survivors of the Holocaust*, esp. 114–16, 167, 174–75, and 251. See also Bauer, *Out of the Ashes*, 261–99. On American anti-Semitism and anti-immigrant sentiment before and during the war, see David Wyman's two books: *Paper Walls* and *Abandonment of the Jews*.

85. Interview with Kunstadt, July 7, 1994.

86. A. Slomnicki to Central Committee of Liberated Jews in the American Zone, April 12, 1946, in the microfilm collection of the Central Committee of Liberated Jews in the American Zone, YIVO, New York.

87. Interview with Arthur Tenser, May 26, 1993.

88. Interview with Kriegstein, New York, July 6, 1992; Stern, *Whitewashing of the Yellow Badge*, xviii.

89. Interview with EsKa manager Hans Prücker.

90. Brown, "Down to the Sea in Ship Models," 336–40.

91. Interview with Skorecka.

CHAPTER TWELVE

1. See "Port and Shipping" news, *New Orleans Times-Picayune*, October 11, 1949, 4.

2. Beatrice Behrman to Dr. David Fichman, August 31, 1948, National Quota Correspondence, New Orleans Section, National Council of Jewish Women Papers, Howard-Tilton Library, Tulane University (hereinafter NCJW, TU). And [Dr. David Fichman] to Dr. Isidore Cohen, November 11, 1948, General Files, Refugee Service Committee (hereinafter RSC), Jewish Federation of Greater New Orleans Records, TU. For a national overview of the postwar machinery assisting DP immigration into the United States, see Helmreich, *Against All Odds*, 14–53.

3. Interview with Rosalie Cohen. See, for example, Annual Report of the President, May 9, 1949; Board of Directors Minutes, May 2, 1950; and Herman Hyman to Mrs. Simon Marx, October 28, 1948, all in NCJW, TU. For a comparative look at another American community's reception of Holocaust survivors, see Burstin, *After the Holocaust*.

4. "Marek Skorecki," Committee for New Americans, Job Applicant, October 13, 1948, federation files, Jewish Federation, New Orleans.

5. Interview with Gerson; Helmreich, *Against All Odds*, 102.

6. Korn, *Abe's Story*, 176.

7. Interview with Rosalie Cohen.

8. [Fichman] to Cohen. Of the *General Leroy Eltinge*'s 169 Jewish passengers, for example, only nine remained in New Orleans. Minutes of the Board Meeting, November 8, 1949, NCJW, TU.

9. Feibelman, *New Orleans Jewish Community*, 133; Eli N. Evans, *Provincials*, 227–46; Reissman, "New Orleans Jewish Community," 288–304; Trillin, "U.S. Journal," 138–44.

10. Quoted in Malone, *Rabbi Max Heller*, 62. As an alternative to urban settlement, leading New Orleans Jews instead sponsored agricultural colonies in the Louisiana hinterland and supported the efforts of German Jews in New York to divert their Russian counterparts to Galveston, Texas. Some of that population stream, however, trickled into the Crescent City anyway, via Texas. Feibelman, *New Orleans Jewish Community*, 66, 87–88.

11. Interview with Steeg.

12. Interview with Rosalie Cohen. See also Stern, "Origins of Reform Judaism in New Orleans," and Parsons, "New Orleans Jewish Federation," 2. The USO dance story comes from Yaffe, *American Jews*, 23.

13. Interview with Gerson; Reissman, "New Orleans Jewish Community," 289.

14. Interview with Rosalie Cohen. The Allen quotation is in Morse, *While Six Million Died*, 265. See also David S. Wyman, *Paper Walls*, and Saul S. Friedman, *No Haven for the Oppressed*, 92–103.

15. Minutes, Committee on Planning for German and Austrian Refugees, September 7, 1938, May 18, 1939, January 8, 1941, June 25, 1942, General Files, RSC, Jewish Federation of New Orleans Papers, TU. For an excellent account of the Refugee Service Committee's work in New Orleans, see Parsons, "New Orleans Jewish Federation."

16. The controversy is recounted in Feibelman's autobiography, *The Making of a Rabbi*, 384–95 (the quotation is on 392); see also the editorials he wrote for the *New Orleans Jewish Ledger* from the summer of 1942 through the spring of 1943. The most balanced treatment of the anguished debates over American Jewry's response to the

Holocaust is the work of Feingold, particularly "Who Shall Bear Guilt for the Holocaust," 261–82, and *Did American Jewry Do Enough during the Holocaust?*.

17. Helmreich, *Against All Odds*, 68.

18. See, for example, Rabinowitz, *New Lives*, 106–7.

19. Interview with Martin Sher, August 26, 1995.

20. Haas, *DeLesseps S. Morrison*, 18–25, 98–139; Kurtz and Peoples, *Earl K. Long*, 86–89; *New Orleans Item*, November 24, 1949, 1. In many ways, Liebling's delightful *Earl of Louisiana* remains the best introduction to both Earl Long and the roguish culture of New Orleans.

21. Haas, *DeLesseps S. Morrison*, 104–8.

22. *New Orleans Item*, November 24, 1949, 1.

23. Interview with Adam Skorecki, November 8–9, 1994.

24. Haas, *DeLesseps S. Morrison*, 108.

25. Interview with Martin Sher, August 26, 1995. See also Helmreich, *Against All Odds*, 72–73.

26. Coontz, *The Way We Never Were*, 23–38.

27. Mitchell, *All on a Mardi Gras Day*, 147–64, 175–76.

28. *New Orleans Times-Picayune*, February 22, 1950, 1–6, Huber, *Mardi Gras*, 58–59.

29. Howe, *World of Our Fathers*, 182.

30. For comparable examples, see Epstein, *Children of the Holocaust*, 39–49, 168, and Hass, *In the Shadow of the Holocaust*, 33.

31. Howe, *World of Our Fathers*, 180–88; Helmreich, *Against All Odds*, 132; Guttmann, *The Jewish Writer in America*.

32. Rabinowitz, *New Lives*, 87. On the psychology of hidden children, see Marks, *Hidden Children*, especially the essays by Nechama Tec, "A Historical Perspective: Tracing the History of the Hidden-Child Experience," 273–91, and Eva Fogelman, "The Psychology behind Being a Hidden Child," 292–307. Fogelman observes that "one had always to be a 'good child,' which meant not being seen or heard or making any trouble. Such strategies became second nature" (295).

33. Interview with Brown and Fertel.

34. Heinze, *Adapting to American Abundance*, 1–18, 33–48.

35. Feibelman, *New Orleans Jewish Community*, 99–100; Joselit, *Wonders of America*, 137–42.

36. Interview with Zelman.

37. The various activities of the NCJW's Service to Foreign Born Department are detailed in the Service to Foreign Born (SFB) folder and the council's minutes and annual reports, all in TU. See also "The Volunteer in Social Work," *New Orleans Jewish Ledger*, October 7, 1949, 5.

38. Polenberg, *One Nation Indivisible*, 127–32; Katz, *Home Fires*, 53.

39. Heinze, *Adapting to American Abundance*, 105.

40. Widmer, *New Orleans in the Fifties*, 23–31.

41. Interview with Honorine and Al Weiss.

42. Interview with Adam Skorecki, Atlanta, November 8–9, 1994; interview with Lorena Doerries, June 3, 1994.

43. Interview with Mrs. Nathan Forman.

44. Mark Skorecki mortgage book.

45. "Employment Stimulation Suggestions," July 13, 1950, in SFB, NCJW, TU.

46. "Marek Skorecki."

47. Helmreich, *Against All Odds*, 112–13.

48. Feibelman, *New Orleans Jewish Community*, 42–50.

49. Interview with Borenstein.

50. Katz, *Home Fires*, 43.

51. Interview with Rosalie Cohen.

52. "Caring for the People," *New Orleans Times-Picayune*, August 9, 1992, F1.

53. Interviews with Victor Kirschman and Rosalie Cohen.

54. Interview with Steeg. Minutes, Committee on Planning for German and Austrian Refugees, August 10, 1938, March 1, 1939, February 14, 1940, General Files, RSC, Jewish Federation of Greater New Orleans Records, IV-Box 45, Howard-Tilton Library, TU.

55. Interview with Kirschman.

56. Interview with Goldberg.

57. Ibid. See also Greg Thomas, "Going, Going, Gone," *New Orleans Times-Picayune*, October 20, 1996, F1.

58. Interview with Stan Levy, June 27, 1994.

59. Interviews with Goldberg and with Yuspeh.

60. Interview with Faye and Stanley Parnes.

61. Interview with Goldberg.

62. Interview with Adam Skorecki, Atlanta, November 8–9, 1994; interview with Joseph Sher.

63. Interview with Robin Levy, February 25, 1992; interview with Shep Zitler, August 14, 1995.

64. May, *Homeward Bound*, 3–36; Coontz, *Way We Never Were*, 23–45; Joselit, *Wonders of America*, 4–6, 58–71.

65. Heinze, *Adapting to American Abundance*, 106–7; Myerhoff, *Number Our Days*, 242–46, 256–57.

66. Ibid., 89–104.

67. Hass, *In the Shadow of the Holocaust*, 37–38.

68. Interview with Zelman.

69. Ibid.

70. "Broadmoor Neighborhood Profile," edited by Darlene M. Walk, New Orleans Office of Policy Planning, (December 1980), Louisiana Collection, Howard-Tilton Library, TU. See also "Work Commences on New Synagogue," *New Orleans Times-Picayune*, June 21, 1948, 15.

71. Interview with Kurtz; May, *Homeward Bound*, 25.

72. Interview with Eva Galler, July 7, 1995.

73. See also Rabinowitz, *New Lives*, 107.

74. Interview with David Radasky.

75. Interview with Toby Kornreich, and interview with Martin Sher, August 26, 1995.

76. Interview with Rosalie Cohen.

77. Interview with Ralph Rosenblat, February 1, 1995.

78. Interview with Toby Kornreich, and interview with Martin Sher, August 26, 1995.

79. Interview with Kurtz.

80. Interview with Justin Zitler, March 11, 1992.

81. Interview with Eva Galler; Sarna, "Mixed Seating in the American Synagogue," 363–94, esp. 386–87.

82. Joselit, *Wonders of America*, 229–59.

83. Quotations here and in next paragraph from interview with Kornreich.

84. Interview with Adam Skorecki, Atlanta, November 8–9, 1994; interview with Joseph Sher.

85. Interview with Kornreich.

86. Interview with Shep Zitler, October 23, 1992.

87. Interview with Adam Skorecki, Atlanta, November 8–9, 1994; interview with Joseph Sher.

88. Interview with Henry Galler, July 7, 1995.

89. Interview with Adam Skorecki, Atlanta, November 8–9, 1994.

90. Interview with Kurtz.

91. Interview with Charles Doerries.

92. Interview with Lorena Doerries, June 3, 1994.

93. Ibid. See also Haas, *In the Shadow of the Holocaust*, 16; Myerhoff, *Number Our Days*, 34.

94. Interview with Lorena Doerries, June 3, 1994.

95. Interview with Adam Skorecki, Atlanta, November 8–9, 1994.

96. Eli N. Evans, *Provincials*, 124.

97. Interview with Charles Doerries, and interview with Lorena Doerries, June 3, 1994.

98. Interview with Lorena Doerries, June 3, 1994.

99. Helmreich, *Against All Odds*, 204–5.

100. Interview with Honorine and Al Weiss.

101. Anne Skorecki Report Card, Alcee Fortier High School, June 9, 1954, in Skorecki Family File, Jewish Federation, New Orleans.

102. Interview with Tucker; *New Orleans Times-Picayune*, September 27, 1953.

103. Interview with Honorine and Al Weiss.

CHAPTER THIRTEEN

1. Levi, *The Drowned and the Saved*, and Levi, *Reawakening*, 207; interview with Lorena Doerries, June 3, 1944.

2. Interview with Charles Doerries, August 10, 1994.

3. Interview with Barney Mintz, and interview with Shep Zitler, January 10, 1996.

4. Anti-Defamation League, *Extremism on the Right*; Ridgeway, *Blood in the Face*, 66.

5. Bridges, *Rise of David Duke*, 13 (quotation), 40; Zatarain, *David Duke*, 116–17.

6. Bell, *In Hitler's Shadow*, 112–13; Ridgeway, *Blood in the Face*, 66; Simonelli, "American Nazi Party," 559–61; Ulasewicz, *President's Private Eye*, 134–39; "Death of a Storm Trooper," *New York Times*, August 27, 1967, sec. 4, 1.

7. Rockwell, *This Time the World*, 95, 98, 128, 173, 45. At Brown University, where he contributed cartoons to the school magazine before dropping out to become a naval pilot during World War II, Rockwell's artwork betrayed a "consistent preoccupation with violence" and "themes of death, cannibalism." See ADL, *Facts: Rockwell* 13, 10 (September 1960): 161–62, George Lincoln Rockwell file, General Files II, IV, B45,

Jewish Federation of Greater New Orleans Records, Howard-Tilton Library, Tulane University, (hereinafter GLR, JFGNO, TU).

8. Dinnerstein, *Anti-Semitism in America*, 151–52; Cohen, *Not Free to Desist*, 375–76.

9. Rockwell, *This Time the World*, 245–46, 253–54; American Jewish Committee (AJC), "Rockwell Scores in His Campaign to Stir Up Trouble," *For Your Information* 6, 2 (February 1961): 4, GLR, JFGNO, TU.

10. "Rockwell Scores," 1–4; "Bigot Seeking Buildup: The 'News' Techniques of George Lincoln Rockwell," a fact sheet from the AJC [March 1962]; "Rockwell and 'Exodus,'" confidential AJC memorandum, March 6, 1961; ADL, *Facts: Rockwell*, 163 (quotation); all in GLR, JFGNO, TU. See also Bell, *In Hitler's Shadow*, 112, and Ulasewicz, *President's Private Eye*, 139–42.

11. "Supplemental Report relative to the Arrest of GEORGE LINCOLN ROCKWELL, ET ALS," from Presly J. Trosclair to Joseph A. Guillot, May 30, 1961, Offense Reports, Item E-11897-61, NOPD Records, City Archives, New Orleans Public Library (NOPL), (hereinafter "Rockwell Police Report"). A copy of one of the flyers can be found in "American Nazi Party, 1961," delesseps S. Morrison Papers, NOPL.

12. Branch, *Parting the Waters*, 412–70.

13. "Rockwell Police Report." See also ADL, "Facts: Rockwell," 164.

14. "Rockwell Police Report."

15. Fairclough, *Race and Democracy*, 234–64.

16. "The Time to Educate about Quarantine Is Now," memorandum from Dr. S. Andhil Fineberg, AJC Institute of Human Relations, New York, February 6, 1961, GLR, JFGNO, TU.

17. Ulasewicz, *President's Private Eye*, 131, 136; Greene, *Temple Bombing*, 6.

18. Interview with Schulman; Schulman to Moise Steeg, June 15, 1961, ADL files, ADL, New Orleans. Thanks to Jerry Himmelstein, current ADL director, for sending me a copy of this detailed report on the Rockwell incident. See also the memorandum of Isaiah Terman to Harry Baron, "Picketing of 'Exodus,'" February 6, 1961, AJC, in GLR, JFGNO, TU.

19. Interview with Schulman. See also Dinnerstein, *Anti-Semitism in America*, 175–96; Eli N. Evans, *Provincials*, 211–13; and Forman, "Unbearable Whiteness of Being Jewish," 121–42.

20. Interview with Schulman. See also Reissman, "New Orleans Jewish Community," 303–4; Evans, *Provincials*, 310–15; and Dinnerstein, *Anti-Semitism in America*, 188–91.

21. Fairclough, *Race and Democracy*, 244; Jeansonne, *Leander Perez*, 225–26.

22. Interview with Schulman. See Eli Evans's sensitive and insightful observations about southern Jewish dilemmas during the civil rights movement in *Provincials*, 311–12, a theme that Greene likewise develops brilliantly in her *Temple Bombing*. See also Forman, "Unbearable Whiteness of Being Jewish," 121–42.

23. "Statement by Mayor Chep Morrison," May 24, 1961, deLesseps S. Morrison Papers, NOPL. See also the editorial "Same Purpose," *New Orleans Times-Picayune*, May 25, 1961, 19, as well as "Club Condemns 'Riders,' 'Nazis,'" ibid., 10, and "Agitators Face Non-Stop Order," ibid., May 26, 1961, 22.

24. Interview with Bennett.

25. Schulman to Steeg.

26. Interview with Stan Levy, June 27, 1994. There is a striking discussion of the

intramural Jewish debate over universalist versus particularist interpretations of the Shoah in Roiphe, *Season for Healing*, 15–28.

27. Interview with Fuksman, February 3, 1996.

28. Levi, *The Drowned and the Saved*, 199.

29. Of all the voluminous writing about survivor guilt and testifying, Primo Levi's insights remain the most penetrating. See his *Survival in Auschwitz*, 5–6, 36; *Reawakening*, 207; and esp. *The Drowned and the Saved*, 12, 76–84, 149–51 (the quotation is on 82). There is also deep insight in Robert Jay Lifton's essay "On Survivors," in his *History and Human Survival*, esp. 169–70. Langer, *Holocaust Testimonies*, esp. 39–76, is indispensable.

30. Interview with Gita Rosenblat, February 17, 1996.

31. Interview with Ralph Rosenblat, February 14, 1996.

32. Interview with Shep Zitler, January 10, 1996. It is worth noting that the term "Holocaust" did not come into general circulation until the 1960s. On the conspiracy of silence in the 1950s and 1960s, see Rabinowitz, *New Lives*, 93, 120, 193–94; Lipstadt, "Holocaust," 73–88; Helmreich, *Against All Odds*, 39–42, 69–70; Epstein, *Children of the Holocaust*, 26, 97–98; Linenthal, *Preserving Memory*, 1–15; and Marrus, *Holocaust in History*, 3–5, 108–12. See also Langer, *Holocaust Testimonies*, iv–xv. Lawrence Graver's *Obsession with Anne Frank* is a moving study of the struggle between assimilationist Jews and Jewish novelist Meyer Levin for ownership of Anne Frank's memory.

33. Interview with Shep Zitler, January 10, 1996.

34. Interview with Ralph Rosenblat, February 17, 1996.

35. Interview with Fuksman, February 3, 1996.

36. Arendt, *Eichmann in Jerusalem*, 121.

37. Segev, *Seventh Million*, 323–66; *New York Times*, May 25, 1961, A12.

38. Segev, *Seventh Million*, 327, 350–51, 361; Rabinowitz, *New Lives*, 193.

39. Interview with Solomon Radasky, February 3, 1996.

40. Ibid., September 10, 1995.

41. Schulman to Steeg.

42. Ibid. (for the Schulman quotation); interview with Solomon Radasky, September 10, 1995 (for the Radasky quotations), and February 3, 1996.

43. Interview with Schulman.

44. Interview with Barney Mintz.

45. Interview with Steeg.

46. Interview with Shep Zitler, January 10, 1996.

47. Schulman to Steeg.

48. Interview with Giarrusso.

49. Ibid.; interview with Solomon Radasky, September 10, 1995.

50. Interview with Giarrusso.

51. Interviews with Ralph Rosenblat, February 1, 1995, February 14, 1996, and interview with Giarrusso.

52. Interview with Ralph Rosenblat, February 14, 1996; interview with Shep Zitler, January 10, 1996.

53. Interview with Schulman.

54. Interview with Giarrusso; Haas, *DeLesseps S. Morrison*, 217, 261, 269–71.

55. "Rockwell Police Report."

56. Ulasewicz, *President's Private Eye*, 135.

57. Interview with Bennett; interview with Kornreich (quotation).

58. Interview with Kornreich.

59. "Rockwell Police Report"; interview with Giarrusso.

60. *New Orleans States-Item*, May 24, 1961, 1; *New Orleans Times-Picayune*, May 25, 1961, 1.

61. "Rockwell Police Report." According to the police report, the detective overheard snippets of conversation about the use of a shotgun or "about a BB gun in place of a shotgun."

62. Interview with Giarrusso.

63. Interview with Solomon Radasky, September 10, 1995.

64. Interview with Giarrusso.

65. Interview with Steeg, and interview with Barney Mintz.

66. Interviews with Giarrusso and with Ralph Rosenblat, February 1, 1995.

67. "Rockwell Police Report."

68. Ibid.; *New Orleans States-Item*, May 25, 1961, 1; interview with Bennett.

69. "Rockwell Police Report."

70. Schulman to Steeg.

71. AJC, "Neo-Nazi Hate Bus Tours South," *For Your Information* 6, 6 (June 1961): 2 (quotations), GLR, JFGNO, TU; *New Orleans States-Item*, May 27, 29, 1961; *New Orleans Times-Picayune*, May 31, June 1, 2, 7, 1961.

72. *Stormtrooper*, August 1962, 14; *State of Louisiana v. Seth David Ryan* "ETALS," (June 12–14, 1961), 170–951, sec. C, Clerk of Court Records, Orleans Parish Criminal Courthouse. See also *New Orleans Times-Picayune*, June 13, 14, 1961, May 29, 1962, and *Lombard v. Louisiana*, 373 U.S.

73. Bell, *In Hitler's Shadow*, 118–19.

74. "Rockwell, U.S. Nazi, Slain: Ex-Aide Is Held as Sniper," *New York Times*, August 26, 1967, A1; "Rockwell Burial Causes a Dispute," August 27, 1967, ibid., A28; "Ex-Nazi Aide Guilty in Rockwell Death; Gets 20-Year Term," December 16, 1967, ibid., A33. See also Bell, *In Hitler's Shadow*, 115–23, and Ulasewicz, *President's Private Eye*, 141, 144. After Rockwell's murder the Nazi and Klan movements achieved a fusion during the 1970s and 1980s. See Rich, "Ku Klux Klan Ideology," and Ridgeway, *Blood in the Face*, 79–91.

75. Interview with Stan Levy, February 16, 1996.

76. "Marek Skorecki," Jewish Federation, Committee for New Americans, Job Applicant, October 13, 1948, Federation file, Jewish Federation, New Orleans.

77. Interview with Shep Zitler, January 10, 1996; *New Orleans Jewish Ledger*, July 21, 1961, 2.

78. Interview with Shep Zitler, August 14, 1995.

79. Herman, *Trauma and Recovery*, 69–70, 133–35, 181–83, 207–9.

80. Interview with Shep Zitler, January 10, 1996.

81. Ibid., August 14, 1995, and interview with Martin Sher, August 26, 1995.

82. Interview with David Radasky.

83. Interview with Shep Zitler, August 14, 1995, and interview with Solomon Radasky, February 3, 1996.

84. Interviews with Gita Rosenblat, February 17, 1996 (first quotation); Shep Zitler, August 14, 1995 (second quotation); and Martin Sher, August 26, 1995 (third quotation).

85. Interviews with Martin Sher, New Orleans, August 26, 1995, and with Borenstein.

86. See, for example, Myerhoff, *Number Our Days*, 161–73.

87. Interview with Kurtz.

88. Interview with Justin Zitler, August 14, 1995.

89. Rapid mobility was the norm for Jewish immigrants, who often achieved in one generation what other immigrant groups took three to accomplish. See, for example, Kessner, *Golden Door*, and Myerhoff, *Number Our Days*, 17.

90. Interview with Lederman.

91. On tendency of survivors to regard their children as magical replacements, see Klein, "Children of the Holocaust," 394, and Bergmann and Jucovy, *Generations of the Holocaust*, 19, 22.

92. Interview with Adam Skorecki, Atlanta, November 8–9, 1994. Obedient overachievers are common among the second generation. See Hass, *In the Shadow of the Holocaust*, 28–29, and Bergmann and Jucovy, *Generations of the Holocaust*, 19.

93. Interview with Stan Levy, June 27, 1994.

94. Interview with Adam Skorecki, Atlanta, November 8–9, 1994.

95. The change in the law spawned a new legal and psychiatric cottage industry, eventually impelling the latter profession to acknowledge the clinical legitimacy of the post-traumatic stress disorder known as "survivor syndrome." To qualify for indemnification, applicants had to undergo psychiatric examination, often at the hands of psychiatrists who erected a harsh facade so as to shield themselves from the engulfing emotions of their survivor patients. Kestenberg, "Discriminatory Aspects of the German Indemnification Policy," 65–68; Epstein, *Children of the Holocaust*, 99–104.

96. Interview with Adam Skorecki, Atlanta, November 8–9, 1994.

97. Interview with Stan Levy, April 10, 1992.

98. Ibid., June 27, 1994.

99. Interview with Robin Levy, February 25, 1992.

100. Segev, *Seventh Million*, 359; Arendt, *Eichmann in Jerusalem*.

101. Interviews with Hull, April 1, 1992, and March 31, 1996, and with Lorena Doerries, April 4, 1996.

102. Interview with Hull, April 1, 1992; interview with Adam Skorecki, New Orleans, April 4, 1992.

103. This discussion owes much to the penetrating insights in Langer's *Holocaust Testimonies*, esp. chaps. 1 and 2; the quotations are on 26 and xiv. See also Herman, *Trauma and Recovery*, 1–4, 177–79.

104. Interview with Hull, April 1, 1992.

105. Interview with Adam Skorecki, New Orleans, April 4, 1992.

106. Keeping the family together was the ignored lesson of the Anne Frank case, wrote Bruno Bettelheim, the child psychologist and Buchenwald survivor, in a controversial 1960 article. He viewed attempts to maintain a semblance of family life as emblematic of a larger Jewish failure to comprehend the nature of the Nazi threat and to plan accordingly—"the final step of surrender to the death instinct," he suggested, "which might also be called the principle of inertia." The article, which originally appeared in *Harper's* magazine, was serialized later in the year in the *New Orleans Jewish Ledger*. Whether Ruth ever read the article is impossible to ascertain. But she doubtless knew about it, which helps explain why she said very little concerning the option she and Mark were once offered to send their daughters to a Catholic orphanage. In any event, a slightly expanded and enlarged version of "The Ignored Lesson of Anne Frank" was republished in Bettelheim's *Surviving and Other Essays*, 246–57. See the *New*

Orleans Jewish Ledger for November through December 1960 for Bettelheim's critique of the Anne Frank story. See also Dwork, *Children with a Star*, 31–33.

107. Interview with Brown and Fertel.

108. Interview with Lorena Doerries, June 3, 1994.

109. Interview with Stan Levy, June 27, 1994.

CHAPTER FOURTEEN

1. Interview with Robin Levy, June 10, 1994.

2. Interview with Kearney.

3. Interview with Robin Levy, June 10, 1994.

4. Interview with Brown and Fertel (first quotation); interview with Kearney.

5. Interview with Kearney.

6. Interview with Robin Levy, June 10, 1994.

7. Interview with Stan Levy, April 10, 1992.

8. Interview with Adam Skorecki, Atlanta, November 8–9, 1994.

9. Interview with Stan Levy, June 27, 1994.

10. Interview with Udin.

11. Interview with Robin Levy, June 10, 1994.

12. Interview with Udin.

13. Interview with Carol Levy.

14. Jason Berry, "Duke Caucus: Will the Republicans Censure David Duke?" *New Orleans Gambit*, September 19, 1989, 11. See also Bridges, *Rise of David Duke*, 3–7.

15. Bridges, *Rise of David Duke*, 7 (first quotation); Tucker, *Science and Politics of Racial Research*, 157–61 (the second quotation is on 157).

16. Bridges, *Rise of David Duke*, 5 (quotation), 29–30.

17. Berry, "Duke Caucus," 11; Bridges, *Rise of David Duke*, 7–12, 17–18; Zatarain, *David Duke*, 109. See also Fairclough, *Race and Democracy*, 297–343.

18. Bridges, *Rise of David Duke*, 14–16, 91 (quotation).

19. On Duke's Nazi ideology, see ibid., 21–26, 116–17 (for his comments about the Talmud); Hill, "Nazi Race Doctrine," 94–111 (the comments on race suicide are on 108); and Rich, "Ku Klux Klan Ideology," 157–223.

20. Rich, "Ku Klux Klan Ideology," 203–4; Hill, "Nazi Race Doctrine," 107–8; Bell, *In Hitler's Shadow*, 121.

21. The theme of Duke's megalomania runs like a leitmotiv through Tyler Bridges's biography (*Rise of David Duke*) and even the "as told to" treatment by Zatarain (*David Duke*). See also Berry, "Duke Caucus," 11.

22. Bridges, *Rise of David Duke*, 13, 39–40 (quotation); Rich, "Ku Klux Klan Ideology," 228; Bell, *In Hitler's Shadow*, 116.

23. Rockwell, *This Time the World*, 342; Warner, "Swastika Smearbund." This March 1961 pamphlet has been mislaid. The quotation comes from the ADL files. Gerald Baumgarten to author, April 9, 1997, ADL, New York. There is a good discussion of the National States Rights Party in Greene, *Temple Bombing*.

24. Quoted in Rich, "Ku Klux Klan Ideology," 170.

25. Quoted in Bridges, *Rise of David Duke*, 39; see also Rich, "Ku Klux Klan Ideology," 180–81.

26. Rich, "Ku Klux Klan Ideology," 175.

27. Bridges, *Rise of David Duke*, 45–46.

28. Ibid., 75–76; and Rich, "Ku Klux Klan Ideology," 206. See also the scathing denunciation of Duke by his former lieutenant Karl Hand: "Why Not David Duke?" [ca. 1979], in the Karl Hand folder, Louisiana Coalition against Racism and Nazism Collection (hereinafter LCARN), Amistad Research Center (hereinafter ARC), TU. Wrote Hand: "As Grand Wizard of the Ku Klux Klan, he later instituted an oath that included a pledge of loyalty to himself. Publishing biographical information that was self-laudatory and written by himself under various names, he made himself out to be the second coming of Christ."

29. Quoted in the *NAAWP News*, 34, 1985, p. 10. See also Bridges, *Rise of David Duke*, 55–57, 80–81.

30. Quoted in Bridges, *Rise of David Duke*, 74.

31. Beam and Metzger are the exceptions, in that their careers as Nazis postdated their Klan involvement.

32. Rich, "Ku Klux Klan Ideology," 196–97.

33. Ibid., 196–200, 304 (quotation).

34. Black and Black, *Politics and Society in the South*, 66–72; Lamis, *Two Party South*.

35. Rich, "Ku Klux Klan Ideology," 239, 271–73, 281. The quotations are on 273.

36. Ibid., 240–57.

37. Ibid., 321–26, 334–35. The quotation is on 334.

38. Ibid., 321–26, 366; Ridgeway, *Blood in the Face*, 79–91.

39. The best overview is Ridgeway, *Blood in the Face*, 91–129.

40. Rich, "Ku Klux Klan Ideology," 323–24 (quotations); Ridgeway, *Blood in the Face*, 87–89.

41. Bridges, *Rise of David Duke*, 75–80 (the quotations are on 75 and 76).

42. Quoted in Ridgeway, *Blood in the Face*, 146.

43. Bridges, *Rise of David Duke*, 80, 86–87.

44. Hill, "Nazi Race Doctrine," 104–8 (the quotation is on 108).

45. Bridges, *Rise of David Duke*, 84–138 (quotation is on 84).

46. Ibid., 106–10 (quotation is on 106).

47. Zeskind, "Ballot Box Bigotry"; *NAAWP News*, 34, 1985, p. 10.

48. Powell, "Slouching toward Baton Rouge," 13, 27 (quotation); Duke Campaign Financial Reports, January 12, 1989, February 31, 1989, and March 30, 1989, LCARN, ARC, TU. See also "Media Resource Packet: The Politics and Background of David Duke" (January 1992), prepared by the Louisiana Coalition against Racism and Nazism, LCARN.

49. For the quotation, see Iris Kelso, "Message Senders," *New Orleans Times-Picayune*, January 29, 1989. For analysis of class and race politics in the 1980s and 1990s, see Powell, "Slouching toward Baton Rouge," 12–34, and Edsall and Edsall, *Chain Reaction*, 3–31, 172–255.

50. Hill, "Nazi Race Doctrine," 102–4.

51. Bridges, *Rise of David Duke*, 152; Powell, "Slouching toward Baton Rouge," 12–34.

52. Interview with Elinor Cohen.

53. Interview with Robin Levy, February 25, 1992.

54. Interview with Stan Levy, April 10, 1992.

55. Interview with Robin Levy, June 10, 1994.

56. Interview with Adam Skorecki, Atlanta, November 8–9, 1994.

57. Interview with Dolek Skorecki, Haifa, February 11, 1994.

58. Interview with Kearney.

59. Ibid.

60. Ibid.

61. "Boll weevil" is the nickname given to conservative southern Democrats, many of whom later jumped to the Republican Party during Ronald Reagan's presidency. Bridges, *Rise of David Duke*, 156–57, 196 (first quotation); Maginnis, *Cross to Bear*, 38–39, 50 (second quotation), 91 (third quotation); Powell, "Slouching toward Baton Rouge," 30–33.

62. Maginnis, *Cross to Bear*, 50–53, 134–37; William B. McMahon, "David Duke and the Legislature: 'A Mouth That's Different,'" in Rose, *Emergence of David Duke*, 126–27.

63. Quoted in Powell, "Slouching toward Baton Rouge," 34.

64. McMahon, "David Duke and the Legislature," 112–35.

65. Maginnis, *Cross to Bear*, 73–81; "Latest Scoop on Duke," *Instauration*, August 1990, 34.

66. Powell, "Read My Liposuction," 18–22; Bethell, "Hazards of David Duke," 20–21.

67. Bridges, *Rise of David Duke*, 181.

68. "A Spoilsport Sounds Off against Duke," *Instauration*, April 1990, 33; "Duke and His Critics," ibid., July 1991, 6. The paper is published by Wilmot Robertson, the pseudonymous author of *The Dispossessed Majority*, a sweeping reinterpretation of American history and politics from a nativist and white supremacist perspective.

69. A few were grizzled veterans like Ralph Forbes, who had served as a Rockwell subcommander and later managed Duke's 1988 Populist presidential campaign; in 1990 Forbes ran for lieutenant governor of Arkansas, reaching the runoff. Even Bernard David Jr., one of Rockwell's old "hate riders," did a pilgrimage to Duke's Metairie campaign headquarters. Still lean and sandy-haired, David was the storm trooper who had crashed Rockwell's "hate bus" into the causeway's concrete stanchions in 1961 while trying to elude state police. "You're with the Mossad," he screamed at *Times-Picayune* reporter Tyler Bridges when, late in the senate race, Bridges confronted him in a crowded Lion's Club Hall about his American Nazi Party background. Interview with Bridges, June 18, 1996; Bridges, *Rise of David Duke*, xv, 175; Larry Cohler, "Ex-Klan Wizard Duke Forges Links with Dixie Republicans," *Washington Jewish Week*, August 10, 1989, 27.

70. "Will David Duke Go Away If No One Pays Attention?" *Jewish World*, September 8–14, 1989. See also Nossiter, *Of Long Memory*, 139–40.

71. Robert Rhoden and Barri Marsh, "Jewish Group Vows to Disrupt Duke," *New Orleans Times-Picayune*, January 26, 1989, B1.

72. Interview with Bridges, August 29, 1996; Marsh, "David Duke," 4–18.

73. Interview with Amoss.

74. Interview with Bridges, August 29, 1996; Bridges, *Rise of David Duke*, xi–xii. See *The New Orleans Times-Picayune*, August 26, 1990. Amoss offers this explanation for the sidebar: "The anti-Semitism material was judged to merit a separate story with its own headline, to run as a sidebar on the page facing the jump of the profile, so as to catch

the attention of readers immersed in the Duke package." Letter from Amoss to author, January 5, 1999.

75. Interview with Bridges, August 29, 1996.

76. Jason Berry, "Duke's Disguise," *New York Times*, October 16, 1991, A17; Amend, "*Picayune* Catches Up," 35; "David Duke: A Rerun," exchange of letters between Amoss and Amend, in *Columbia Journalism Review* (March/April 1992): 4–6. See also Weill, "Classic Case," 16.

77. Interview with Bridges, August 29, 1996.

78. Quoted in Marsh, "David Duke," 24, and in Woods, "David Duke and the *Times-Picayune*," 63.

79. Berry, "David Duke," 15–21 (the quotation is on 21); Gary Esolen, "More Than a Pretty Face: David Duke's Use of Television as a Political Tool," in Rose, *Emergence of David Duke*, 136–55; Marsh, "David Duke," 14–17, 21–22. Once, after being cornered by television reporters about a fictitious fifty-five-thousand-dollar contribution that had turned up in his campaign finance records, Duke appeared before the cameras brandishing a check for the same amount. "Who knows where that check came from or if it was real," said one of Duke's leading critics. "Just by having a prop on hand he got away with it. Plus the clip ended with Duke saying he was getting more and more in debt when the whole point of the report is that Duke is profiting personally from his campaigns" (quoted in Marsh, "David Duke," 1). It was all too reminiscent of how Wisconsin senator Joseph McCarthy, at his routine press conferences in the 1950s, would hoist aloft handfuls of documents purporting to prove Communist infiltration of the State Department and how the media would "take the symbol of the fact as proof of the fact" (Rovere, *Senator Joe McCarthy*, 169).

80. Quoted in Maginnis, *Cross to Bear*, 194.

81. Quoted in Cohler, "Ex–Klan Wizard Duke Forges Links," 8.

82. Quoted in Bridges, *Rise of David Duke*, 162.

83. *Religious Right*, 45–46. For more on McCormack, see Rickey, "Nazis and the Republicans," 75–78.

84. Quoted in Cohler, "Ex–Klan Wizard Duke Forges Links," 8.

85. All quotes come from Larry Cohler, "Duke's Smooth Entry into Mainstream Politics," *Jewish World*, August 11–17, 1989, 3, 10.

86. Bridges, *Rise of David Duke*, 162–63 (quotation is on 163); Rickey, "Nazis and the Republicans," 59–79.

87. Larry Cohler, "Atwater Defends Louisiana GOP's Silence on Duke," *Washington Jewish Week*, August 24, 1989.

88. Bridges, *Rise of David Duke*, 162–66 (quotation is on 165); Rickey, "Nazis and the Republicans," 59–79.

89. Quoted in Maginnis, *Cross to Bear*, 61.

90. Interview with Hill. Full disclosure: The author was also cofounder, as well as vice-chairman, of the group.

91. "Hippies in Kansas Rejoice as Brother Is Elected Justice," *New York Times*, November 7, 1970, A23.

92. Lance Hill memorandum to Board members, "Strategy Paper," January 29, 1991, LCARN, ARC, TU.

93. Interview with Hill; Bridges, *Rise of David Duke*, 206; Larson, *Sex, Race, and Science*, 165–66.

94. Interview with Amoss.

95. Interview with Robin Levy, February 25, 1992.

96. Interview with Carol Levy, April 18, 1992.

CHAPTER FIFTEEN

1. The top three finishers in the primary were Edwards, 523,195 (33.8 percent); Duke, 491,342 (31.7 percent); and Roemer 410,690 (26.5 percent). Bridges, *Rise of David Duke*, 216.

2. Interview with Walker, 1992.

3. Interview with Carvin; interview with Donnie Mintz; Bridges, *Rise of David Duke*, 211–16. See also Maginnis, *Cross to Bear*, 264–66, and Rose, with Esolen, "DuKKKe for Governor," 217–19.

4. Bridges, *Rise of David Duke*, 198–201 the quotations are on 201).

5. Iris Kelso, "Two Legislators on Duke Problem," *New Orleans Times-Picayune*, October 24, 1991, B9.

6. Peter Nichols, "Roemer Fans Bitter about Leftovers," *New Orleans Times-Picayune*, October 24, 1991, A1.

7. Rose and Esolen, "DuKKKe for Governor," 221–22.

8. Maginnis, *Cross to Bear*, 182–83, 192–93, 220–21, 283, 294–98 (quotation is on 297); Bridges, *Rise of David Duke*, 207–9, 223–25. See also *New Orleans Times-Picayune*, October 31, 1996, A1.

9. Interview with Donald Mintz. See also Rose, "DuKKKe for Governor," 221; Maginnis, *Cross to Bear*, 287–88, 304; and Bridges, *Rise of David Duke*, 230–31. Edwards's campaign raised so much money in the first three weeks ($3 million) that much of it went unspent.

10. Charley Blaine, "Duke Victory Would Cost State, Execs Say," *New Orleans Times-Picayune*, October 26, 1991, A1; Ed Anderson and Jack Wardlaw, "Roemer: I'll Vote for Edwards," ibid., November 1, 1991, A1. Interview with Denegre, and interview with Steeg, February 12, 1992. See also Rose, "DuKKKe for Governor," 221, and Bridges, *Rise of David Duke*, 220–21.

11. Interview with Walker, and interview with Carvin.

12. Interview with Denegre. See also Elizabeth Mullener, "Businesses Take Stand against Duke," *New Orleans Times-Picayune*, November 14, 1991, A1.

13. Interview with Donald Mintz.

14. The quotations in this and the succeeding paragraph come from interview with Dixon.

15. Denegre repeated the same message in a memo to the managing partner of Jones, Walker: "As a matter of self-preservation, as well as conscience, I think the firm should make a contribution to Edwin Edwards. I would personally like to see us give the maximum of $5,000." Denegre to Charles W. Lane III, October 25, 1991, in George Denegre's personal files.

16. Press Release of the Business Council of New Orleans and the River Region, October 24, 1991. I thank George Denegre for allowing me to make a copy of this document from his personal files.

17. Interview with Stroud.

18. Ibid.

19. Ibid.

20. Ibid. See also interview with Kirby.

21. Steve Lopez, "In La., a Crook Is Lookin' Good," *Philadelphia Inquirer*, B1.

22. Quotations here and in the following paragraphs from interview with Newburger.

23. Interview with Fee, and interview with Faust.

24. Interview with Newburger.

25. Interview with Walker.

26. Interview with Carvin; interview with Walker.

27. Interview with Fields.

28. James Hodge, "Thousands Claim Right to Vote," *New Orleans Times-Picayune*, October 23, 1991, A1.

29. Interview with Fields.

30. Hodge, "Thousands Claim Right to Vote"; Bridges, *Rise of David Duke*, 218.

31. Interview with Fields.

32. Interview with Gauthier.

33. See Leon Wieseltier's insightful observations in Miller, *One by One*, 231–32.

34. Interview with Justin Zitler, March 11, 1992.

35. Ibid.

36. Interview with Buchsbaum.

37. Interview with Justin Zitler, March 11, 1992.

38. Ibid.; interview with Buchsbaum.

39. Interview with Justin Zitler, March 11, 1992.

40. Ibid.

41. The quotations are all in ibid. See also interview with Buchsbaum.

42. Interview with Buchsbaum.

43. Interview with Amoss.

44. Woods, "David Duke and the *Times-Picayune*," 62.

45. Interview with Forsyth.

46. *New Orleans Times-Picayune*, November 5, 1991; Bridges, *Rise of David Duke*, 221–22; interview with Justin Zitler, March 11, 1992.

47. Interview with Justin Zitler, March 11, 1992; interview with Fuksman, September 10, 1996.

48. Interview with Elinor Cohen.

49. Herman, *Trauma and Recovery*, 9.

50. These are from cross tabs provided by the consulting firm Penn-Schoen, as part of the July 1990 statewide poll commissioned by the Louisiana Coalition. The poll is available in LCARN, ARC, TU.

51. Kazzem Kashan, "Duke Denies Holocaust, Calls Opponents Zionists," *UNO Driftwood*, January 8, 1990, 1; interview with Carol Levy.

52. Interview with Bridges, June 18, 1996; interview with Carol Levy.

53. Kashan, "Duke Denies Holocaust"; interview with Carol Levy.

54. Interview with Bridges, June 18, 1996.

55. Interview with Elinor Cohen.

56. Ibid. I thank Jerry Bodet for allowing me to copy the audiotape of Anne's address to his class. This and material that follows are from interview with Elinor Cohen and the audiotape.

57. Interview with Robinson. All the material in this and the following two paragraphs come from this interview.

58. For the second television debate in this and the next nine paragraphs, I've drawn heavily on Tyler Bridges's superb account in *Rise of David Duke*, 225–30. Lance Hill's memo to the Edwards campaign can be found in box 5, LCARN, ARC, TU.

59. Interview with Robinson; Mark Lorando, "WDSU Reporter Flooded with Calls for Grilling Duke," *New Orleans Times-Picayune*, November 8, 1991, A8.

60. Interview with Robinson.

61. Interview with Robin Levy, February 25, 1992; Tyler Bridges and Christie Harrison, "Benson Endorses Edwards," *New Orleans Times-Picayune*, November 12, 1991, A1.

62. The account above derives from interview with Carol Levy, and Bridges and Harrison, "Benson Endorses Edwards."

63. "A Portrait of Louisiana's Voters," *New York Times*, November 18, 1991, A8; see also Rose and Esolen, "DuKKKe for Governor," 228–30.

64. Interview with Elinor Cohen.

65. Interview with Carol Levy.

66. Interview with Robin Levy, June 10, 1994.

BIBLIOGRAPHY

Most of the family narrative that forms the backbone of this book comes from Ruth Skorecki's unpublished memoir and extensive interviews with Anne Levy and Lila Millen. I have chosen not to reference any of this material in the text for fear of making the pages overly busy.

To call Ruth's manuscript a memoir is a bit of a stretch. It is actually more akin to a transcribed oral interview, but one originally recorded on a typewriter instead of a tape machine. Understandably, the manuscript abounds in typos and misspellings. I therefore took the liberty of making silent corrections when quoting from the memoir, which struck me as a better solution than cluttering the text with [*sic*]. On occasion, for clarity's sake I have also silently altered some of the interviews without changing the meaning.

Almost all the interviews have been tape-recorded and transcribed and will be deposited, along with Ruth Skorecki's memoir, in the Special Collections division of the Howard-Tilton Library at Tulane University.

MANUSCRIPTS AND ARCHIVES

Europe / Asia

Jerusalem, Israel

Yad Vashem Archives

Flyer for production of *Shulamit*, by Abraham Goldfaden

Freihut, Franz, "Todesmarsch durch den Bayerischen Wald" (Death march through the Bavarian woods), undated, YVA E-1452, Jerusalem (German)

Hecht, Christian, "Kristallnacht in Tirschenreuth," YVA M-1/31 (181–192)

History of Czyste Hospital, as told to Stefania Beylin [Bejlin] by Dr. Emil Apfelbaum, translated from the Polish by Martha Osnos and Dr. Robert Osnos, summer 1945, YVA E/104-4-7, 0-33/1558 (English)

International Tracing Service (ITS) Microfilm Project

Leviathan, Sophia, "Der Krieg von Innen" (The war within), E/1280

Liberated Jews Arrived in Sweden in 1945 List no. 1 (Malmö, Sweden, 1946)

Schmidt, Karl, "Kristallnacht in Tirschenreuth," April 14, 1946, YVA M-1/31

Stanislaw Waller testimony, YVA/03-2358

Marian Zonnenfeld testimony (Polish), May 20, 1959, YVA 03/1281

Łódź, Poland

Łódź Birth, Marriage, and Death Records Office

Death Certificate of Szmil-Zawel Skorecki, October 25, 1934, Nr. IV-1787/

45/34, Urząd Stanu Cywilnego Łódź Sródmiescie (Downtown Łódź Marriage Office)

"Nacha Einhorn Skureck," *Rejestr Zgonów, 1939* (Register of death certificates), vol. 98, in Urząd Stanu Cywilnego Łódź Sródmiescie

Łódź State Archives

Abmeldung, Gitla Skorecka, "Der Aelteste der Juden in Litzmannstadt-Getto," Nr. 99532

Abmeldung, Wolf Skorecki, "Der Aelteste der Juden in Litzmannstadt-Getto," Nr. 099531

Abmeldung, Abram Tempelhof, "Der Aelteste der Juden in Litzmannstadt-Getto," Nr. 10306

Abmeldung, Sara Tempelhof, "Der Aelteste der Juden in Litzmannstadt-Getto," Nr. 12042/42

Anmeldung, Wolf Skorecki, "Der Aelteste der Juden in Litzmannstadt-Getto," Nr. K 099531

Anmeldung, Gisla Skorecka, "Der Aelteste der Juden in Litzmannstadt-Getto," Nr. K 99532

City Directory, 1910

Księga Ludności Stałej miasta Łódźi, Nr. 1152 k. 392 (Book of permanent inhabitants in Łódź, vol. no. 1152, pp. 391–92)

Rejestr Mieszkancow Miasta Łódźi z Lat, 1931–32 (Register of permanent inhabitants, 1931–32)

Warsaw, Poland

Jewish Historical Institute

History of the Czyste Hospital, as told to Stefania Bejlin by Dr. Emil Apfelbaum, 1945 (Polish)

"Relacja" (Reports) on the Warsaw Ghetto

Warsaw telephone directory, 1938–39

Polish State Archives

City Planning Maps of Ząbkowska Street and Lochowska Street

Warsaw Polytechnic University

Hersz Tempelhof Student Record File, Mechanical Division, file 11213

Warsaw University

Mery Mejnster "Fragebogen," registered as Akta Izby Lekarskiej Warszawsko— Białostockiej (files of the Warsaw Białstock Medical Clinic), Mery Mejnster, in the archives of the Main Medical Library (Główna Biblioteka Lekarska)

Mery Mejnster Student Record File 30404

United States

Cincinnati, Ohio

American Jewish Archives, Hebrew Union College

World Jewish Congress Collection

New Orleans, Louisiana

Amistad Research Center, Tulane University

Louisiana Coalition against Racism and Nazism Collection (LCARN)

Anti-Defamation League (ADL), New Orleans Office

ADL files

Howard-Tilton Library, Tulane University
    Jewish Federation of Greater New Orleans Records
    National Council of Jewish Women Records
    Ruth Skorecka unpublished memoir
    Mark Skorecki mortgage book
Jewish Federation of Greater New Orleans
    Skorecki Family Files
New Orleans Public Library
    deLesseps S. Morrison Papers
    New Orleans Police Department Records, City Archives
Orleans Parish Criminal Courthouse
    Clerk of Court Records
New York, N.Y.
Anti-Defamation League
    Archives
United Nations Archives
    Team 168, United Nations Relief and Rehabilitation Administration (UNRRA)
YIVO (Institute for Jewish Research)
    Central Committee of Liberated Jews in the American Zone (microfilm)
Washington, D.C.
National Archives
    OMGUS (Office of Military Government, U.S.) Records, Bavaria, District 2,
    Tirschenreuth, RG 260

INTERVIEWS

Interviews by the Author

Jim Amoss, September 12, 1996, New Orleans
Charles Anish, September, 19, 1995, New Orleans
Dora Appel, January 20, 1993, New York
Dr. Mark Balin, September, 20, 1993, Mentor, Ohio
Rhonda Barad and Mark Weitzman, February 25, 1992, New York
Julian Baranowski, June 22–23, 1993, Łódź, Poland
Judge Moshe Bejski, March 26, 1998, Tel Aviv, Israel
Bernard Bennett, December 19, 1995, New Orleans
Isak Borenstein, November 7, 1994, New Orleans
Malgorzata Bresler, June 23, 1993, Łódź, Poland
Tyler Bridges, June 18, August 29, 1996, Tallahassee, Fla.
Natalie Brown and Jennifer Fertel, July 20, 1994, Metairie, La.
Jane Buchsbaum, February 13, 1992, April 10, 1992, New Orleans
James Carvin, January 20, 1992, New Orleans
Elinor Cohen, May 17, 1992, New Orleans
Dr. Ernie Cohen, October 26, 1993, New Orleans
Rosalie Cohen, October 26, 1995, New Orleans
Jeff Coward, February 12, 1992, Baton Rouge
George Denegre, February 7, 1992, New Orleans

David Dixon, February 10, 1992, New Orleans

Charles Doerries, August 10, 1994, Hammond, La.

Lorena Doerries, April 2, 1992, June 3, 1994, April 4, 1996, Covington, La.

Rhoda Faust, July 24, 1996, New Orleans

Dart Fee, July 23, 1996, New Orleans

Mary Ferber, January 19, 1994, Detroit

Cleo Fields, February 18, 1992, Baton Rouge

Mrs. Nathan Forman, December 9, 1994, New Orleans

Ron Forman, August 4, 1994, New Orleans

Malcolm Forsyth, September 10, 1996, New Orleans

John Fowler, June 23, 1992, New Orleans

Felicia Fuksman, August 1, 1993, July 7, 1995, August 15, 1995, February 3, 1996,
    February 22, 1996, September 10, 1996, New Orleans

Eva Galler, August 27, 1993, July 7, 1995, New Orleans

Henry Galler, August, 11, 1993, July 7, 1995, New Orleans

Cherie Gauthier, February 9, 1992, Metairie, La.

Sylvia Gerson, December 6, 1994, New Orleans

Ruth Gerver, May 29, 1993, August 28, 1993, December 9, 1993, New York

Joe Giarrusso, September 12, 1995, New Orleans

Father Jan Gneidziejko, June 19, 1993, Praga, Poland

Morton Goldberg, June 8, 1994, New Orleans

Natalia (Piotrowska) Gorecka, June 18, 1993, June 19, 1993, Praga, Poland

Nat Halpern, June 15, 1995, New Orleans

Lance Hill, September 2, 1996, New Orleans

Harry Hull, April 1, 1992, March 31, 1996, Bay St. Louis, Miss.

Jan Jagielski, June 16, 1993, Warsaw, Poland

Mrs. Sam (Jean) Katz, July 7, 1994, New Orleans

Bevy Kearney, July 16, 1994, New Orleans

Vicki Kirby, February 27, 1992, New Orleans

Victor Kirschman, October 25, 1993, New Orleans

Toby Kornreich, September 2, 1995, Tucson, Ariz.

Roman Kriegstein, July 6, 1992, January 16, 1993, December 28, 1993, July 7, 1994,
    Boca Raton, Fla., and New York

Dr. Dorothy Kunstadt, July 7, 1994, New York

Maureen Kurtz, February 4, 1995, New Orleans

Toby Lederman, September 19, 1995, New Orleans

Rene Lehmann, December 12, 1992, New Orleans

Anne Levy, January 29, 1992, March 9, 1992, March 25, 1992, April 20, 1992, June 23,
    1992, June 24, 1992, August 11, 1992, January 13, 1993, February 2, 1993, April 7,
    1993, April 14, 1993, September 23, 1993, September 29, 1993, October 1, 1993,
    October 5, 1993, November 6, 1993, November 18, 1993, January 17, 1994,
    March 10, 1994, May 24–25, 1994, July 9, 1994, July 18, 1994, November 8, 1994,
    December 5, 1994, June 23, 1995, July 1, 1995, August 23, 1995, October 18, 1995,
    February 5, 1996, February 16, 1996, April 2, 1996, April 4, 1996, April 5, 1996,
    July 2, 1996, July 19, 1996, May 12, 1998, New Orleans

Carol Levy, April 18, 1992, New Orleans

Morton R. Levy, June 28, 1992, Allentown, Pa.

Robin Levy, February 25, 1992, June 10, 1994, September 19, 1995, New Orleans

Stan Levy, April 10, 1992, June 27, 1994, February 16, 1996, New Orleans
Eugene Lipman, June 25, 1992, Bethesda, Md.
Raymond Mariels, December 20, 1993, Portland, Oreg.
Lila Millen, April 4, 1992, February 14, 1993, April 7, 1993, July 13, 1994, August 5,
    1994, November 18, 1994, August 23, 1995, October 7, 1995, February 5, 1996,
    April 4, 1996, May 24–25, 1996, September 19, 1996, Metairie, La.
Norman Millen, August 7, 1994, Metairie, La.
Barney Mintz, October 5, 1995, New Orleans
Donald Mintz, February 4, 1992, New Orleans
Kirby Newburger, June 21, 1996, New Orleans
Dora Niederman, August, 23, 1995, New Orleans
Karyn Noles, February 13, 1992, New Orleans
Faye and Stanley Parnes, June 27, 1994, New Orleans
Lane Plauche, March 29, 1992, Lake Charles, La.
Teresa Prekerowa, June 16, 1993, Warsaw, Poland
Hans Prücker, June 30, 1993, Tirschenreuth, Germany
David Radasky, August 26, 1995, Kansas City, Mo.
Solomon Radasky, September 10, 1995, February 3, 1996, February 16–17, 1996,
    Metairie, La.
Solomon and Frieda Radasky, February 24, 1993, Metairie, La.
Mendel Riba, December 15, 1996, Tampa, Fla.
Beth Rickey, November 11, 1992, New Orleans
Norman Robinson, March 25, 1992, New Orleans
Rose Rosenberg, January 18, 1994, Boca Raton, Fla.
Gita Rosenblat, February 3, 1996, February 17, 1996, New Orleans
Ralph Rosenblat, February 1, 1995, February 14, 1996, February 17, 1996, New
    Orleans
Erna Rubinstein, June 28, 1992, January 17, 1993, January 17, 1994, Boca Raton, Fla.
Michael Sartisky, February 12, 1992, New Orleans
Irwin Schulman, October 2, 1995, New Orleans
Joseph Sher, January 31, 1995, New Orleans
Martin Sher, August 26, 1995, September 2, 1995, Dallas, Tex.
Moshe Silberberg, February 16–17, 1994, Tel Hashomer, Israel
Pola Skorecka, February 12, 1994, Haifa, Israel
Adam Skorecki, April 4, 1992, November 7, 1992, November 8–9, 1994, August 26,
    1995, September 3, 1995, September 19, 1995, October 18, 1995, April 2, 1996,
    New Orleans and Atlanta
Dolek Skorecki, February 11, 1992, April 4, 1992, May 23, 1993, October 5, 1993,
    December 31, 1993, February 11–12, 1994, February 17, 1994, New Orleans and
    Haifa, Israel
Mark Skorecki, taped reminiscence (ca. 1983)
Ervin Skoretsky, May 24, 1993, October 2, 1993, San Francisco
Ludwig and Maria Stabholz, February 14, 1994, Tel Aviv, Israel
Dr. Thaddeus Stabholz, September 8, 1993, September 13–14, 1993, October 11,
    1993, October 27, 1993, November 7, 1993, November 9–10, 1993, November 14,
    1993, December 7–8, 1993, December 11, 1993, February 3, 1994, May 25, 1994,
    June 1, 1997, September 1, 1997, May 10, 1998, June 23, 1998, Canton, Ohio
Moise Steeg, February 2, 1995, New Orleans

Lucille Strauch, June 25, 1992, Boca Raton, Fla.
Ansel Stroud, February 27, 1992, New Orleans
Janiá Sudkiewicz, March 13, 1994, Toronto
Marek Sudkiewicz, March 10, 1994, March 12, 1994, March 17, 1994, May 25, 1994, Toronto
Sabina Swidzinska, June 19, 1993, Praga, Poland
Arthur Tenser, May 26, 1993, December 9, 1993, New York
Harry Tenser, May 26, 1993, New York
Claire Tritt, October 31, 1992, New Orleans
John Tucker, December 6, 1994, New Orleans
Sheryl Udin, June 9, 1994, New Orleans
Ludwig Völke, June 30, 1993, Tirschenreuth, Germany
Countess von Schulenberg, July 1, 1993, Castle Falkenberg, Germany
Henry Wahrman, January 9, 1993, Delray Beach, Fla.
Joe Walker, February 3, 1992, New Orleans
Honorine and Al Weiss, July 5, 1994, New Orleans
Mrs. Herbert Yellin, December 17, 1995, New Orleans
Mike Yuspeh, September 4, 1995, New Orleans
Grace Zelman, October 7, 1993, New Orleans
Leonard Zeskind, July 8, 1992, August 30, 1996, Kansas City, Mo.
Justin Zitler, March 11, 1992, August 14, 1995, New Orleans
Shep Zitler, February 26, 1992, October 23, 1992, July 8, 1995, August 14–15, 1995, January 10, 1996, February 19, 1996, March 20, 1996, New Orleans
Ilana Zukerman, February 17, 1994, Jerusalem, Israel

Other Interviews

David Duke. Interview by Evelyn Rich, 1985, Howard-Tilton Library, Tulane University
Anne Levy, talk at New Orleans Jewish Community Center, April 26, 1992
Anne Levy, talk at University of New Orleans (UNO), November 1991
Anne Levy and Lila Millen, interview by Plater Robinson, New Orleans, June 17, 1988
Mark Skorecki, taped at a Thanksgiving Dinner, 1983

NEWSPAPERS AND MAGAZINES

Baton Rouge Morning-Advocate
Esquire
Harper's
Instauration
Jewish World
Louisiana Weekly (New Orleans)
LSU Daily Reveille, June 8, 1989
NAAWP News
New Orleans Gambit
New Orleans Item
New Orleans Jewish Ledger

New Orleans States-Item
The New Orleans Times-Picayune
New Republic
Newsweek
New York Times
The New Yorker
Philadelphia Inquirer
Shreveport Journal
Stars and Stripes (European edition)
Stormtrooper
Time
UNO Driftwood
Washington Jewish Week
Washington Post

BOOKS, ARTICLES, AND THESES

Abzug, Robert H. *Inside the Vicious Heart: Americans and the Liberation of the Nazi Concentration Camps*. New York: Oxford University Press, 1985.

Adler, Stanislaw. *In the Warsaw Ghetto, 1940–1943: An Account of a Witness: The Memoirs of Stanislaw Adler*. Translated from the Polish by Sara Philip. Jerusalem: Yad Vashem, 1982.

Anti-Defamation League. *Extremism on the Right: A Handbook*. Rev. ed. New York: Anti-Defamation League, 1988.

———. *The Religious Right: The Assault on Tolerance and Pluralism in America*. New York: Anti-Defamation League, 1994.

Ainsztein, Reuben. *Jewish Resistance in Nazi-Occupied Eastern Europe*. New York: Barnes and Noble, 1974.

Allen, William Sheridan. *The Nazi Seizure of Power: The Experience of a Single Town, 1922–1945*. Rev. ed. New York: Franklin Watts, 1984.

Aly, Götz, and Susanne Heim. "The Economics of the Final Solution: A Case Study from the General Government." *Simon Wiesenthal Center Annual* 5 (1988): 3–48.

Amend, Jeanne W. "The *Picayune* Catches Up with David Duke." *Columbia Journalism Review* (January/February 1992): 35.

The American Synagogue: A Sanctuary Transformed. Edited by Jack Wertheimer. Cambridge: Cambridge University Press, 1987.

Anatomy of the Auschwitz Death Camp. Edited by Yisrael Gutman and Michael Berenbaum. Bloomington: Indiana University Press, 1994.

Anderson, Vicky L. "Gender Differences in Altruism among Holocaust Rescuers." *Journal of Social Behavior and Personality* 8 (1993): 43–58.

Apfelbaum, Erika. "Forgetting the Past." *Partisan Review* 48 (1981): 608–17.

Arad, Yitzhak. *Belzec, Sobibor, Treblinka: The Operation Reinhard Camps*. Bloomington: Indiana University Press, 1987.

Arendt, Hannah. *Eichmann in Jerusalem: A Report on the Banality of Evil*. Rev. and enl. New York: Penguin, 1965.

Asch, Sholom. *Three Cities: A Trilogy*. Translated by Willa Muir and Edwin Muir. New York: G. P. Putnam, 1933.

Ascherson, Neil. *The Struggles for Poland*. New York: Random House, 1987.

Aszkenazy-Engelhard, Halina. *Pragnelam Zyc: Pamietnik* (Pragnelam Zyc: Diary). Warsaw: Wadawnictwo Salezjanskie, 1991.

Bacon, Harry E. *Cancer of the Colon, Rectum, and Anal Canal*. Philadelphia: Lippincott, 1964.

Bankier, David. *The Germans and the Final Solution: Public Opinion under Nazism*. Oxford: Blackwell, 1992.

Barish, Louis, ed. *Rabbis in Uniform: The Story of the American Jewish Military Chaplain*. New York: J. David, 1962.

Baron, Lawrence. "The Holocaust and Human Decency: A Review of Research on the Rescue of Jews in Nazi Occupied Europe." *Humboldt Journal of Social Relations* 13 (1985/86): 237–51.

Baron, Salo W., et al. *Economic History of the Jews*. Edited by Nachum Gross. New York: Schocken, 1975.

Bartoszewski, Wladyslaw. *"On Both Sides of the Wall."* In *Righteous among Nations: How Poles Helped the Jews, 1939–1945*, edited by Wladyslaw Bartoszewski and Zofia Lewin, xvi–lxxxvii. London: Earlscourt Publications, 1969.

———. *Warsaw Death Ring, 1939–1944*. Warsaw: Interpress Publisher, 1968.

Bartov, Omer. *Hitler's Army: Soldiers, Nazis, and War in the Third Reich*. New York: Oxford University Press, 1992.

Bauer, Yehuda. *American Jewry and the Holocaust: The American Joint Distribution Committee, 1939–1945*. Detroit: Wayne State University Press, 1981.

———. "The Death-Marches in the Period of the Evacuation of the Camps." In *The End of the Holocaust*. Vol. 9 of *The Nazi Holocaust*, edited by Michael R. Marrus, 491–511. Westport: Meckler, 1989.

———. *Flight and Rescue: Brichah*. New York: Random House, 1970.

———. *The Jewish Emergence from Powerlessness*. Toronto: University of Toronto Press, 1979.

———. *Out of the Ashes: The Impact of American Jews on Post-Holocaust European Jewry*. Oxford: Pergamon, 1989.

Begley, Louis. *Wartime Lies*. New York: Ivy Books, 1991.

Bell, Leland V. *In Hitler's Shadow: The Anatomy of American Nazism*. Port Washington, N.Y.: Kennikat, 1973.

Berg, Mary. *Warsaw Ghetto: A Diary by Mary Berg*. Edited by S. L. Shneiderman. New York: L. B. Fischer, 1945.

Bergmann, Martin S., and Milton E. Jucovy, eds. *Generations of the Holocaust*. New York: Basic, 1982.

Berry, Jason. "David Duke: Triumph of the Image." *Television Quarterly*, March 1992, 15–21.

Bethell, Tom. "Hazards of David Duke." *National Review*, August 20, 1990, 20–21.

Bettelheim, Bruno. *Surviving and Other Essays*. New York: Alfred A. Knopf, 1979.

Białoszewski, Miron. *A Memoir of the Warsaw Uprising*. Edited and translated by Madeline Levine. Evanston, Ill.: Northwestern University Press, 1991 [1977].

Bischof, Gunter, and Stephen E. Ambrose, eds. *Eisenhower and the German POWs: Facts against Falsehood*. Baton Rouge: Louisiana State University Press, 1992.

Black, Earl, and Merle Black. *Politics and Society in the South*. Cambridge: Harvard University Press, 1987.

Black, Peter R. "Rehearsal for 'Reinhard'?: Odilo Globocnik and the Lublin *Selbst-schutz*." *Central European History* 25 (1992): 204–26.

Borowski, Tadeusz. *This Way for the Gas, Ladies and Gentlemen*. Selected and translated by Barbara Vedder. New York: Penguin, 1959.

Borzykowski, Tuvia. *Between Tumbling Walls*. Translated by Mendel Kohansky. Tel Aviv: Hakibbutz Hameuchad Publishing House, 1964.

Branch, Taylor. *Parting the Waters: America in the King Years, 1954–63*. New York: Simon and Schuster, 1988.

Breitman, Richard. *The Architect of Genocide: Himmler and the Final Solution*. New York: Alfred A. Knopf, 1991.

Brenner, Reeve Robert. *Faith and Doubt of Holocaust Survivors*. New York: Free Press, 1980.

Bridges, Tyler. *The Rise of David Duke*. Jackson: University Press of Mississippi, 1994.

Broszat, Martin. "The Concentration Camps, 1933–45." In *Anatomy of the SS State*, edited by Helmut Krausnick et al., translated from the German by Richard Barry, Marian Jackson, and Dorothy Long, introduction by Elizabeth Wiskemann, 397–504. New York: Walker, 1965.

——. *Nationalsozialistische Polenpolitik, 1939–1945*. Frankfurt: Fischer Bucherei, 1961.

Brown, Christie. "Down to the Sea in Ship Models." *Forbes*, November 13, 1989, 336–40.

Browning, Christopher R. *Fateful Months: Essays on the Emergence of the Final Solution*. New York: Holmes and Meier, 1985.

——. *Ordinary Men: Reserve Police Battalion 101 and the Final Solution in Poland*. New York: HarperCollins, 1992.

——. *The Path to Genocide: Essays on Launching the Final Solution*. Cambridge: Cambridge University Press, 1992.

Broyard, Anatole. *Intoxicated by My Illness*. Foreword by Oliver Sacks. New York: Fawcett Columbine, 1992.

Burleigh, Michael, and Wolfgang Wippermann. *The Racial State: German, 1933–1945*. Cambridge: Cambridge University Press, 1991.

Burstin, Barbara Stern. *After the Holocaust: The Migration of Polish Jews and Christians to Pittsburgh*. Pittsburgh: University of Pittsburgh Press, 1989.

Carter, Dan T. *The Politics of Rage: George Wallace, the Origins of the New Conservatism, and the Transformation of American Politics*. New York: Simon and Schuster, 1995.

The Catastrophe of European Jewry: Antecedents, History, Reflections. Edited by Yisrael Gutman and Livia Rothkirchen. Jerusalem: Yad Vashem, 1976.

Chronicle of the Lodz Ghetto, 1941–1944. Edited and with an introduction by Lucjan Dobroczycki. New Haven: Yale University Press, 1984.

Ciechanowski, Jan M. *The Warsaw Rising of 1944*. Cambridge: Cambridge University Press, 1974.

Cohen, Naomi W. *Not Free to Desist: The American Jewish Committee, 1906–1966*. Introduction by Salo W. Baron. Philadelphia: Jewish Publication Society of America, 1972.

Coontz, Stephanie. *The Way We Never Were: American Families and the Nostalgia Trip*. New York: Basic, 1992.

Cousins, Norman. *Anatomy of an Illness as Perceived by the Patient*. New York: Bantam, 1979.

Crankshaw, Edward. *Gestapo: Instrument of Tyranny*. New York: Da Capo, 1994 [1956].

Czerniakow, Adam. *The Warsaw Diary of Adam Czerniakow: Prelude to Doom*. Translated by Stanislaw Staron and the staff of Yad Vashem. Edited by Raul Hilberg, Stanislaw Staron, and Josef Kermisz. New York: Stein and Day, 1979.

Danieli, Yael. "Treating Survivors and Children of Survivors of the Nazi Holocaust." *Psychoanalytic Psychology* 1 (1984): 23–42.

Davies, Norman. *God's Playground: A History of Poland*. 2 vols. New York: Columbia University Press, 1982.

——. *Heart of Europe: A Short History of Poland*. Oxford: Oxford University Press, 1984.

Dawidowicz, Lucy. *The War against the Jews, 1933–1945*. New York: Holt, Rinehart and Winston, 1975.

——, ed. *The Golden Tradition: Jewish Life and Thought in Eastern Europe*. New York: Schocken, 1989.

Delbo, Charlotte. *Auschwitz and After*. Translated by Rosette C. Lamont, with an introduction by Lawrence Langer. New Haven: Yale University Press, 1995.

Des Pres, Terence. *The Survivor: An Anatomy of Life in the Death Camps*. New York: Oxford University Press, 1976.

Dinnerstein, Leonard. *America and the Survivors of the Holocaust*. New York: Columbia University Press, 1982.

——. *Anti-Semitism in America*. New York: Oxford University Press, 1994.

Dinnerstein, Leonard, and Mary Dale Palsson, eds. *Jews in the South*. Baton Rouge: Louisiana State University Press, 1973.

Dionne, E. J. *Why Americans Hate Politics*. New York: Simon and Schuster, 1991.

Dobroszycki, Lucjan. *Survivors of the Holocaust in Poland: A Portrait Based on Jewish Community Records, 1944–1947*. Armonk, N.Y.: M. E. Sharpe, 1994.

Documents on British Foreign Policy, 1918–1939: 1939. London: H.M. Stationery Office, 1946.

Documents on the Holocaust: Selected Sources on the Destruction of the Jews of Germany and Austria, Poland, and the Soviet Union. Edited by Yitzhak Arad, Yisrael Gutman, and Abraham Margaliot. Jerusalem: Yad Vashem, 1981.

Donat, Alexander. *The Holocaust Kingdom*. New York: Holt, Rinehart and Winston, 1965.

Dupuy, T. N., and Paul Martell. *Great Battles on the Eastern Front*. Indianapolis: Bobbs-Merrill, 1982.

Dwork, Debórah. *Children with a Star: Jewish Youth in Nazi Europe*. New Haven: Yale University Press, 1991.

Dwork, Debórah, and Robert Jan van Pelt. *Auschwitz: 1270 to the Present*. New York: W. W. Norton, 1996.

Eagly, Alice H., and Maureen Crowley. "Gender and Helping Behavior: A Meta-Analytic Review of the Social Psychological Literature." *American Psychological Bulletin* 3 (1986): 283–308.

Edelman, Marek. *The Ghetto Fights: Warsaw, 1941–43*. Introduction by John Rose. London: Bookmarks, 1990 [1945].

Edsall, Thomas Byrne, and Mary D. Edsall. *Chain Reaction: The Impact of Race, Rights, and Taxes on American Politics*. New York: W. W. Norton, 1991.

"Eichmann Tells His Own Damning Story." *Life*, January 9, 1961, 9–19.

The Einsatzgruppen Reports: Selections from the Dispatches of the Nazi Death Squads' Cam-

paign against the Jews, July 1941–January 1943. Edited by Yitzhak Arad, Shmuel Krakowski, and Shmuel Spector. New York: Holocaust Library, 1989.

Eisner, Jack. *The Survivor of the Holocaust*. New York: Kensington, 1980.

Eitinger, Leo. "The Concentration Camp Syndrome and Its Late Sequelae." In *Survivors, Victims, and Perpetrators: Essays on the Nazi Holocaust*, edited by Joel E. Dimsdale, 131–45. Washington: Hemisphere Publishing, 1980.

Epstein, Helen. *Children of the Holocaust: Conversations with Sons and Daughters of Survivors*. New York: Penguin, 1979.

———. "Uncovering Moravia." *Cross Currents* 11 (1992): 93–116.

Erickson, John. *The Road to Berlin*. Boulder, Colo.: Westview, 1983.

Evans, Eli N. *The Provincials: A Personal History of Jews in the South*. New York: Atheneum, 1973.

Evans, Richard J. *In Hitler's Shadow: West German Historians and the Attempt to Escape from the Nazi Past*. New York: Pantheon, 1989.

Fairclough, Adam. *Race and Democracy: The Civil Rights Struggle in Louisiana, 1915–1972*. Athens: University of Georgia Press, 1995.

Falstein, Louis, ed. *The Martyrdom of Jewish Physicians in Poland*. New York: Exposition Press, 1963.

Faschismus—Getto—Massenmord. Berlin [East]: Rütten and Loening, 1960.

Feibelman, Julian B. *The Making of a Rabbi*. New York: Vantage, 1980.

———. *A Social and Economic Study of the New Orleans Jewish Community*. Philadelphia: University of Pennsylvania Press, 1941.

Feig, Konnilyn G. *Hitler's Death Camps: The Sanity of Madness*. New York: Holmes and Meier, 1979.

Fein, Helen. *Accounting for Genocide: National Responses and Jewish Victimization during the Holocaust*. Chicago: University of Chicago Press, 1979.

Feingold, Henry L. *Did American Jewry Do Enough during the Holocaust?* Syracuse: Syracuse University Press, 1985.

———. "Who Shall Bear Guilt for the Holocaust: The Human Dilemma." *American Jewish History* 68 (March 1979): 261–82.

Fenigstein, Henry, as told to Saundra Collis. "The Holocaust and I: Memoirs of a Survivor." Unpublished manuscript. Toronto, 1990. In author's possession.

Fest, Joachim C. *Hitler*. New York: Random House, 1975.

Fogelman, Eva. *Conscience and Courage: Rescuers of Jews during the Holocaust*. New York: Doubleday, 1994.

Forman, Seth. "The Unbearable Whiteness of Being Jewish: Desegregation in the South and the Crisis of Jewish Liberalism." *American Jewish History* 85 (June 1997): 121–42.

Friedlander, Henry. *The Origins of Nazi Genocide: From Euthanasia to the Final Solution*. Chapel Hill: University of North Carolina Press, 1995.

Friedman, Philip. *Roads to Extinction: Essays on the Holocaust*. Edited by Ada June Friedman, with an introduction by Salo Baron. New York: Jewish Publication Society of America, 1980.

Friedman, Saul S. *No Haven for the Oppressed: United States Policy toward Jewish Refugees, 1938–1945*. Detroit: Wayne State University Press, 1973.

Gilbert, Martin. *The Holocaust: A History of the Jews of Europe during the Second World War*. New York: Henry Holt and Company, 1985.

———. *The Macmillan Atlas of the Holocaust*. New York: Macmillan, 1982.

Gilligan, Carol. *In a Different Voice: Psychological Theory and Women's Development*. Cambridge: Harvard University Press, 1982.

Gimbel, John. *The American Occupation of Germany: Politics and the Military, 1945–1949*. Stanford: Stanford University Press, 1968.

———. *A German Community under American Occupation: Marburg, 1945–52*. Stanford: Stanford University Press, 1961.

Goldhagen, Daniel Jonah. *Hitler's Willing Executioners: Ordinary Germans and the Holocaust*. New York: Alfred A. Knopf, 1996.

Goldstein, Bernard. *The Stars Bear Witness*. Translated and edited by Leonard Shatzkin. New York: Viking, 1949.

"The Good Old Days": The Holocaust as Seen by Its Perpetrators and Bystanders. Edited by Ernst Klee, Willi Dressen, and Volker Riess, with a foreword by Hugh Trevor-Roper. New York: Free Press, 1991.

Grabitz, Helge, and Wolfgang Scheffler. *Letzte Spuren: Ghetto Warschau, SS-Arbeitslager Trawniki, Aktion Erntefest*. Berlin: Edition Hentrich, 1988.

Graver, Lawrence. *An Obsession with Anne Frank: Meyer Levin and "The Diary."* Berkeley: University of California Press, 1995.

Greene, Melissa Fay. *The Temple Bombing*. Reading, Mass.: Addison Wesley, 1996.

Grob, Alex. *Rekindling the Flame: American Jewish Chaplains and the Survivors of European Jewry, 1944–1948*. Detroit: Wayne State University Press, 1993.

Gross, Jan T. *Polish Society under German Occupation: The Generalgouvernement, 1939–1944*. Princeton: Princeton University Press, 1979.

———. *Revolution from Abroad: The Soviet Conquest of Poland's Western Ukraine and Western Belorussia*. Princeton: Princeton University Press, 1988.

Gushee, David P. "Many Paths to Righteousness: An Assessment of Research on Why Righteous Gentiles Helped Jews." *Holocaust and Genocide Studies* 7 (Winter 1993): 372–401.

Gutman, Yisrael. *The Jews of Warsaw, 1939–1943: Ghetto, Underground, Revolt*. Translated by Ina Friedman. Bloomington: Indiana University Press, 1982.

———. *Resistance: The Warsaw Ghetto Uprising*. Translated by Ethel Broido. Boston: Houghton Mifflin, 1994.

Gutman, Yisrael, and Shmuel Krakowski. *Unequal Victims: Poles and Jews during World War II*. Translated by Ted Gorelick and Witold Jedlicki. New York: Holocaust Library, 1986.

Guttmann, Allen. *The Jewish Writer in America: Assimilation and the Crisis of Identity*. New York: Oxford University Press, 1971.

Haas, Edward F. *DeLesseps S. Morrison and the Image of Reform*. Baton Rouge: Louisiana State University Press, 1974.

Hallie, Philip. *Lest Innocent Blood Be Shed*. New York: Harper and Row, 1979.

Hass, Aaron. *In the Shadow of the Holocaust: The Second Generation*. Ithaca: Cornell University Press, 1990.

Hausner, Gideon. *Justice in Jerusalem*. New York: Schocken, 1968.

Heinze, Andrew R. *Adapting to American Abundance: Jewish Immigrants, Mass Consumption, and the Search for American Identity*. New York: Columbia University Press, 1990.

Heller, Celia. *On the Edge of Destruction: Jews of Poland between the Two Wars*. New York: Columbia University Press, 1977.

Helmreich, William B. *Against All Odds: Holocaust Survivors and the Successful Lives They Made in America*. New York: Simon and Schuster, 1992.

Hen, Jósef. *Nowolipie*. Łódź: Prospero, 1991.

Herman, Judith Lewis. *Trauma and Recovery: The Aftermath of Violence—from Domestic Abuse to Political Terror*. New York: Basic, 1992.

Hertz, Aleksander. "Jewish Caste Status in Poland." In *Austria, Hungary, Poland, Russia*. Vol. 3/2 of *Hostages of Modernization: Studies on Modern Antisemitism, 1870–1933/39*, edited by Herbert A. Strauss, 1153–64. Berlin: Walter de Gruyter, 1993.

Hilberg, Raul. *The Destruction of the European Jews*. Chicago: Quadrangle, 1961.

———. *The Destruction of the European Jews*. Student ed. New York: Holmes and Meier, 1985.

———. *Perpetrators, Victims, Bystanders: The Jewish Catastrophe, 1933–1945*. New York: HarperCollins, 1992.

Hill, Lance. "Nazi Race Doctrine in the Political Thought of David Duke." In *The Emergence of David Duke and the Politics of Race*, edited by Douglas Rose, 94–111. Chapel Hill: University of North Carolina Press, 1992.

Hill, Lance, and Tim Wise. *Media Resource Packet: The Politics and Background of David Duke*. New Orleans: Louisiana Coalition against Racism and Nazism, 1992.

Hirschmann, Ira A. *The Embers Still Burn*. New York: Simon and Schuster, 1949.

Historical Atlas of the Holocaust, by the United States Holocaust Memorial Museum. London: Macmillan, 1996.

Hitler, Adolf. *Hitler's Secret Book*. Introduction by Telford Taylor. New York: Grove, 1961.

———. *Mein Kampf*. Translated by Ralph Mannheim. Boston: Houghton Mifflin, 1943.

Hoffman, Eva. *Shtetl: The Life and Death of a Small Town and the World of Polish Jews*. Boston: Houghton Mifflin, 1997.

Höhne, Heinz. *The Order of the Death's Head: The Story of Hitler's SS*. Translated by Richard Barry. New York: Ballantine, 1971 [1966].

Holocaust: The Obligation to Remember. Washington, D.C.: Washington Post, 1983.

Horwitz, Gordon J. *In the Shadow of Death: Living Outside the Gates of Mauthausen*. New York: Free Press, 1990.

Howe, Irving, with the assistance of Kenneth Libo. *World of Our Fathers*. New York: Harcourt Brace Jovanovich, 1976.

Huber, Leonard V. *Mardi Gras: A Pictorial History of Carnival in New Orleans*. Gretna, La.: Pelican Publishing, 1989.

Hunger Disease: Studies by the Jewish Physicians in the Warsaw Ghetto. Edited by Myron Winick, M.D. New York: John Wiley and Sons, 1979.

Jäckel, Eberhard. *Hitler's World View: A Blueprint for Power*. Translated by Herbert Arnold. Cambridge: Harvard University Press, 1981 [1969].

Janczak, Julian K. "The National Structure of the Population in Łódź in the Years 1820–1939." *Polin* 6 (1991): 20–26.

Jansen, Christian, and Arno Weckbecker. *Der "Volksdeutsche Selbstschutz" in Polen, 1939/40*. Munich: R. Oldenbourg Verlag, 1992.

Jeansonne, Glen. *Leander Perez: Boss of the Delta*. Baton Rouge: Louisiana State University Press, 1977.

Joselit, Jenna Weissman. *The Wonders of America: Reinventing Jewish Culture, 1880–1950*. New York: Hill and Wang, 1995.

Judis, John P. *William F. Buckley, Jr.: Patron Saint of the American Conservatives.* New York: Simon and Schuster, 1988.

Kac, Marc. *Enigmas of Change: An Autobiography.* New York: Harper and Row, 1985.

Kaplan, Chaim. *Scroll of Agony: The Warsaw Diary of Chaim A. Kaplan.* Rev. ed. Translated and edited by Abraham I. Katsh. New York: Collier, 1973.

Katz, Donald. *Home Fires: An Intimate Portrait of One Middle-Class Family in Postwar America.* New York: HarperCollins, 1992.

Keegan, John. *The Second World War.* New York: Penguin, 1989.

Kermish, Joseph. "The Activities of the Council for Aid to Jews ('ZEGOTA') in Occupied Poland." In *Rescue Attempts during the Holocaust: Proceedings of the Second Yad Vashem International Historical Conference*, edited by Yisrael Gutman and Efraim Zuroff, 367–98. Jerusalem: Yad Vashem, 1977.

Kershaw, Ian. *Hitler, 1889–1936: Hubris.* New York: W. W. Norton, 1999.

———. *Popular Opinion and Political Dissent in the Third Reich.* Oxford: Oxford University Press, 1983.

Kersten, Krystyna. *The Establishment of Communist Rule in Poland, 1943–1948.* Translated and annotated by John Micgiel and Michael H. Bernard, foreword by Jan T. Gross. Berkeley: University of California Press, 1991 [1984].

Kessner, Thomas. *The Golden Door: Italian and Jewish Immigrant Mobility in New York City, 1880–1915.* New York: Oxford University Press, 1977.

Kestenberg, Milton. "Discriminatory Aspects of the German Indemnification Policy: A Continuation of Persecution." In *Generations of the Holocaust*, edited by Martin S. Bergmann and Milton E. Jucovy, 62–82. New York: Basic, 1982.

Kimche, Jon, and David Kimche. *Secret Roads: The "Illegal" Migration of a People, 1938–1948.* New York: Farrar, Straus, and Cudahy, 1955.

Klein, Hilel. "Children of the Holocaust: Mourning and Bereavement." In *The Child in His Family*, edited by E. James Anthony and Cyrille Koupernick, 2:393–410. New York: Wiley, 1973.

Kloczowski, Jerzy. "The Religious Orders and the Jews in Nazi-Occupied Poland." *Polin* 3 (1988): 238–43.

Koehl, Robert L. *The Black Corps: The Structure and Power Struggles of the Nazi SS.* Madison: University of Wisconsin Press, 1983.

———. *RKFDV: German Resettlement and Population Policy, 1939–1945.* Cambridge: Harvard University Press, 1957.

Korbonski, Stefan. *The Polish Underground State: A Guide to the Underground, 1939–1945.* New York: Columbia University Press, 1978.

Korn, Abram. *Abe's Story: A Holocaust Memoir.* Edited by Joseph Korn, annotated by Richard Voyles. Atlanta: Longstreet, 1995.

Korzec, Pawel, and Jean-Charles Szurek. "Jews and Poles under Soviet Occupation (1939–1941): Conflicting Interests." *Polin* 4 (1989): 205–25.

Krakowski, Shmuel. "The Death Marches in the Period of the Evacuation of the Camps." In *The Nazi Concentration Camps: Proceedings of the Fourth Yad Vashem International Historical Conference*, 482–86. Jerusalem: Yad Vashem, 1984.

———. *The War of the Doomed: Jewish Armed Resistance in Poland, 1942–44.* Foreword by Yehuda Bauer. New York: Holmes and Meier, 1984.

Krall, Hanna. *Shielding the Flame: An Intimate Conversation with Dr. Marek Edelman, the Last Surviving Leader of the Warsaw Ghetto Uprising.* Translated by Joanna Stasinska and Lawrence Weschler. New York: Henry Holt, 1986 [1977].

Krausnick, Helmut, and others. *Anatomy of the SS State*. Translated from the German by Richard Barry, Marian Jackson, and Dorothy Long. Introduction by Elizabeth Wiskemann. New York: Walker, 1963.

Krystal, Henry. "Trauma: Considerations of Its Intensity and Chronicity." In *Psychic Traumatization: Aftereffects in Individuals and Communities*, edited by Henry Krystal and William G. Niederland, 11–28. Boston: International Psychiatry Clinics, 1971.

Kurek-Lesik, Ewa. "The Conditions of Admittance and the Social Background of Jewish Children Saved by Women's Religious Orders in Poland from 1939–1945." *Polin* 3 (1988): 244–75.

———. *Your Life Is Worth Mine: How Polish Nuns Saved Hundreds of Jewish Children in German-Occupied Poland, 1939–1945*. Introduction by Jan Karski. New York: Hippocrene Books, 1997.

Kurtz, Michael L., and Morgan D. Peoples. *Earl K. Long: The Saga of Uncle Ear and Louisiana Politics*. Baton Rouge: Louisiana State University Press, 1990.

Lamis, Alexander P. *The Two-Party South*. New York: Oxford University Press, 1984.

Langer, Lawrence. *Holocaust Testimonies: The Ruins of Memory*. New Haven: Yale University Press, 1991.

Laqueur, Walter. *The Terrible Secret: Suppression of the Truth about Hitler's "Final Solution."* Boston: Little, Brown, 1980.

Larson, Edward J. *Sex, Race, and Science: Eugenics in the Deep South*. Baltimore: Johns Hopkins University Press, 1995.

Lerner, Max. *Wrestling with the Angel: A Memoir of My Triumph over Illness*. New York: W. W. Norton, 1990.

Levi, Primo. *The Drowned and the Saved*. Translated from the Italian by Raymond Rosenthal. New York: Vintage, 1988.

———. *The Reawakening*. Translated from the Italian by Stuart Woolf. New York: Collier, 1965.

———. *Survival in Auschwitz*. Translated from the Italian by Stuart Woolf. New York: Collier, 1961.

Levin, Dov. *The Lesser of Two Evils: Eastern European Jewry under Soviet Rule, 1939–1941*. Translated by Naftali Greenwood, with a foreword by Mordechai Altschuler. Philadelphia: Jewish Publication Society, 1995.

Levin, Nora. *The Holocaust: The Destruction of European Jewry, 1933–1945*. New York: T. Y. Crowell, 1968.

Levine, Hillel. *Economic Origins of Anti-Semitism: Poland and Its Jews in the Early Modern Period*. New Haven: Yale University Press, 1991.

Lewin, Abraham. *A Cup of Tears: A Diary of the Warsaw Ghetto by Abraham Lewin*. Edited by Antony Polonsky, translated by Christopher Hutton. Oxford: Basil Blackwell, 1988.

Liebling, A. J. *Earl of Louisiana*. Baton Rouge: Louisiana State University Press, 1961.

Lifton, Betty Jean. *The King of Children: A Biography of Janusz Korczak*. New York: Farrar, Straus and Giroux, 1988.

Lifton, Robert Jay. *History and Human Survival*. New York: Vintage, 1971.

Linenthal, Edward T. *Preserving Memory: The Struggle to Create America's Holocaust Museum*. New York: Viking, 1995.

Lipset, Seymour Martin, and Earl Raab. *Jews and the New American Scene*. Cambridge: Harvard University Press, 1995.

Lipstadt, Deborah. *Beyond Belief: The American Press and the Coming of the Holocaust, 1933–1945*. New York: Free Press, 1986.

——. *Denying the Holocaust: The Growing Assault on Truth and Memory*. New York: Plume, 1993.

——. "The Holocaust: Symbol and Myth in American Life." *Forum on the Jewish People, Zionism, and Israel* 40 (1980–81): 73–88.

Lodz Ghetto: Inside a Community under Siege. Compiled and edited by Alan Adelson and Robert Lapides. New York: Viking, 1989.

London, Perry. "The Rescuers: Motivational Hypotheses about Christians Who Saved Jews from the Nazis." In *Altruism and Helping Behavior: Social Psychological Studies of Some Antecedents and Consequences*, edited by J. Macaulay and L. Berkowitz, 241–51. New York: Academic Press, 1970.

Lubetkin, Zivia. *In the Days of Destruction and Revolt*. Translated by Ishai Tubbin and Yehiel Yanay. Beit Lohamei Haghettaot, Israel: Hakibbutz Hameuchad Publishing House, 1981 [1946].

Lukas, Richard C. *The Forgotten Holocaust: The Poles under German Occupation, 1939–1944*. Lexington: University Press of Kentucky, 1986.

Luza, Radomir. "The Liberation of Prague: An American Blunder?" *KOSMAS* 3 (Summer 1984): 41–57.

MacDonald, Callum. *The Killing of SS Obergruppen-Führer Reinhard Heydrich*. New York: Macmillan, 1989.

Maginnis, John. *Cross to Bear*. Baton Rouge, La.: Darkhorse Press, 1992.

Maier, Charles. *The Unmasterable Past: History, Holocaust, and German National Identity*. Cambridge: Harvard University Press, 1988.

Malone, Bobbie. *Rabbi Max Heller: Reformer, Zionist, Southerner, 1860–1929*. Tuscaloosa: University of Alabama Press, 1997.

Marcus, Joseph. *Social and Political History of the Jews in Poland, 1919–1939*. Berlin: Montow Publishing, 1983.

Marks, Jane. *The Hidden Children: The Secret Survivors of the Holocaust*. New York: Fawcett Columbine, 1993.

Marrus, Michael R. *The Holocaust in History*. New York: Meridian, 1989.

——. *The Unwanted: European Refugees in the Twentieth Century*. New York: Oxford University Press, 1985.

Marrus, Michael R., and Robert O. Paxton. "The Nazis and the Jews in Occupied Western Europe." *Journal of Modern History* 54 (December 1982): 687–714.

Marsh, Virginia. "David Duke: A Foray into the Mainstream?" Master's thesis, City University, London, England, 1991.

Marshall, Robert. *In the Sewers of Lvov: A Heroic Story of Survival from the Holocaust*. New York: Charles Scribner's Sons, 1990.

Mason, Henry L. "Testing Human Bonds within Nations: Jews in the Occupied Netherlands." *Political Science Quarterly* 99 (Summer 1984): 315–43.

Mason, Tim. "Intention and Explanation: A Current Controversy about the Interpretation of National Socialism." In *The "Führer State": Myth and Reality*, edited by Gerhard Hirshfeld and Lothar Kettenacker, 23–40. Stuttgart: Klett-Cotta, 1981.

May, Elaine Tyler. *Homeward Bound: American Families in the Cold War Era*. New York: Basic, 1988.

Meed, Vladka. *On Both Sides of the Wall: Memoirs from the Warsaw Ghetto*. Introduction by Elie Wiesel, translated by Steven Meed. New York: Holocaust Library, 1993 [1948].

Mendelsohn, Ezra. "Interwar Poland: Good for the Jews or Bad for the Jews?" In *The Jews in Poland*, edited by Chimen Abramsky, Maciej Jachimczyk, and Antony Polonsky, 130–39. Oxford: Basil Blackwell, 1986.

———. "Relations between Jews and Non-Jews in Eastern Europe between the Two World Wars." In *Unanswered Questions: Nazi Germany and the Genocide of the Jews*, edited by Francis Furet, 71–83. New York: Schocken, 1989.

Miller, Judith. *One by One, by One*. New York: Simon and Schuster, 1990.

Mintz, Frank P. *Liberty Lobby and the American Right: Race, Conspiracy, and Culture*. Westport, Conn.: Greenwood, 1985.

Mitchell, Reid. *All on a Mardi Gras Day: Episodes in the History of New Orleans Carnival*. Cambridge: Harvard University Press, 1995.

Moeller, Robert. "War Stories: The Search for a Usable Past in the Federal Republic of Germany." *American Historical Review* 101 (October 1996): 1008–48.

Mokotoff, Gary, and Sallyann Amdur Sack. *Where Once We Walked: A Guide to the Jewish Communities Destroyed in the Holocaust*. Teaneck, N.J.: Avotaynu, 1991.

Morse, Arthur D. *While Six Million Died: A Chronicle of American Apathy*. New York: Hart Publishing, 1967.

Moser, Jonny. "Nisko: The First Experiment in Deportation." *Simon Wiesenthal Center Annual* 2 (1985): 1–21.

Moskowitz, Moses. "The Germans and the Jews: Postwar Report." *Commentary* 2 (July–December 1946): 7–14.

Mosse, George L. *The Crisis of German Ideology: Intellectual Origins of the Third Reich*. New York: Grosset and Dunlap, 1964.

Murdoch, Iris. *The Sovereignty of Good*. New York: Schocken, 1971.

Myerhoff, Barbara. *Number Our Days*. New York: E. P. Dutton, 1978.

Nir, Yehuda. *The Lost Childhood: A Memoir*. New York: Berkeley, 1989.

Nordon, Haskell. *Education of a Polish Jew: A Physician's War Memories*. New York: Grossman, 1982.

Nordrhein-Westfalen und der Deutsche Osten (Northern Rhein-Westphalia and the German east). Dortmund, Germany: Dietz, 1962.

Nossiter, Adam. *Of Long Memory: Mississippi and the Murder of Medgar Evers*. Reading, Mass.: Addison-Wesley, 1994.

Nuland, Sherwin B. *How We Die: Reflections on Life's Final Chapter*. New York: Alfred A. Knopf, 1994.

Oliner, Samuel P., and Pearl M. Oliner. *The Altruistic Personality: Rescuers of Jews in Nazi Europe*. Foreword by Rabbi Harold M. Schulweis. New York: Free Press, 1988.

Opatoshu, Joseph. *In Polish Woods*. Translated from the Yiddish by Isaac Goldberg. Philadelphia: Jewish Publication Society of America, 1938.

Orpen, Neil. *Airlift to Warsaw: The Rising of 1944*. Norman: University of Oklahoma Press, 1984.

Ozick, Cynthia. "Sholem Aleichem's Revolution." *The New Yorker*, March 28, 1988, 99–108.

Paldiel, Mordecai. "The Altruism of the Righteous Gentiles." *Holocaust and Genocide Studies* 3 (1988): 187–96.

———. *The Path of the Righteous: Gentile Rescuers of Jews during the Holocaust*. New York: KTAV Publishing House, 1993.

Parsons, Kahne. "The New Orleans Jewish Federation and the Refugee Question, 1937–1942." Master's thesis, University of New Orleans, 1990.

Paulsson, Gunnar S. "Demographic Characteristics and Mortality Rates of Jews in Hiding in Warsaw, 1943–1945," at *http://www.le.ac.uk/history/papers.html*.

———. "Posting on Hotel Polski," December 19, 1995, at *http://www.h=net.msu.edu/logs*.

———. "Posting on righteous gentiles," February 23, 1998, at *http://www.h=net.msu.edu/logs*.

Peck, Abraham J. "Liberated but Not Free: Jewish Displaced Persons in Germany after 1945." In *November 1938: From "Reichskristallnacht" to Genocide*, edited by Walter H. Pehle, 222–35. New York: Berg, 1991.

Perechodnik, Calel. *Am I a Murderer: Testament of a Jewish Ghetto Policeman*. Edited by Pawel Szapiro and Frank Fox, translated by Frank Fox. New York: Westview, 1996.

Persico, Joseph E. *Nuremberg: Infamy on Trial*. New York: Penguin, 1994.

Pinchuk, Ben-Cion. *Shtetl Jews under Soviet Occupation: Eastern Poland on the Eve of the Holocaust*. Oxford: Basil Blackwell, 1990.

Polenberg, Richard. *One Nation Indivisible: Class, Race, and Ethnicity in the United States since 1938*. New York: Penguin, 1980.

Polonsky, Antony. "Polish-Jewish Relations and the Holocaust." *Polin* 4 (1993): 226–42.

Powell, Lawrence N. "Read My Liposuction: The Makeover of David Duke." *New Republic*, October 15, 1990, 18–22.

———. "Slouching toward Baton Rouge: The 1989 Legislative Election of David Duke." In *The Emergence of David Duke and the Politics of Race*, edited by Douglas Rose, 12–40. Chapel Hill: University of North Carolina Press, 1992.

Pulzer, Peter. *The Rise of Political Anti-Semitism in Germany and Austria*. Rev. ed. Cambridge: Harvard University Press, 1988 [1964].

Pus, Wieslaw. "The Development of the City of Łódź (1820–1939)." *Polin* 6 (1991): 3–19.

Rabinowitz, Dorothy. *New Lives: Survivors of the Holocaust Living in America*. New York: Alfred A. Knopf, 1976.

Rankin, Fred W., and A. Stephens Graham. *Cancer of the Colon and Rectum*. 2d ed. Springfield, Ill.: Thomas, 1939.

Reissman, Leonard. "The New Orleans Jewish Community." In *Jews in the South*, edited by Leonard Dinnerstein and Mary Dale Palsson, 288–304. Baton Rouge: Louisiana State University Press, 1973.

Rich, Evelyn. "Ku Klux Klan Ideology, 1954–1988." Ph.D. diss., Boston University, 1988.

Rich, Norman. *Hitler's War Aims: Ideology, the Nazi State, and the Course of Expansion*. New York: W. W. Norton, 1973.

Richmond, Theo. *Konin: A Quest*. New York: Pantheon, 1995.

Rickey, Elizabeth A. "The Nazi and the Republicans: An Insider View of the Response of the Louisiana Republican Party to David Duke." In *The Emergence of David Duke and the Politics of Race*, edited by Douglas Rose, 59–79. Chapel Hill: University of North Carolina Press, 1992.

Ridgeway, James. *Blood in the Face: The Ku Klux Klan, Aryan Nations, Nazi Skinheads, and the Rise of a New White Culture*. New York: Thunder's Mouth Press, 1990.

Righteous among Nations: How Poles Helped the Jews, 1939–1945. Edited by Wladyslaw Bartoszewski and Zofia Lewin. London: Earlscourt Publications, 1969.

Ringelblum, Emmanuel. " 'Comrade Mordecai': Mordecai Anielewicz—Commander of the Warsaw Ghetto Uprising." In *They Fought Back: The Story of the Jewish Resistance in Nazi Europe*, edited and translated by Yuri Suhl, 85–91. New York: Schocken, 1975 [1967].

———. *Notes from the Warsaw Ghetto: The Journal of Emmanuel Ringelblum*. Edited and translated by Jacob Sloan. New York: Schocken, 1958.

———. *Polish-Jewish Relations during the Second World War*. Edited by Joseph Kermish and Shmuel Krakowski, with an introduction by Joseph Kermish. Jerusalem: Yad Vashem, 1974.

Ringelheim, Joan. "Women and the Holocaust: A Reconsideration of Research." *Signs* 10 (1985): 741–61.

[Robertson, Wilmot]. *The Dispossessed Majority*. Cape Canaveral, Fla.: Howard Allen, 1972.

Rockwell, George Lincoln. *This Time the World*. 2d ed. [Arlington?], 1963.

Roiphe, Anne. *A Season for Healing: Reflections of the Holocaust*. New York: Summit Books, 1988.

Rokossovsky, Konstantin K. *A Soldier's Duty*. Translated and edited by Robert Daglish. Moscow: Progress Publishers, 1985.

Roland, Charles G. *Courage under Siege: Starvation, Disease, and Death in the Warsaw Ghetto*. New York: Oxford University Press, 1992.

Roos, Hans. *A History of Modern Poland*. New York, 1966.

Rose, Douglas, with Gary Esolen. "DuKKKe for Governor: 'Vote for the Crook, It's Important.'" In *The Emergence of David Duke and the Politics of Race*, ed. Rose. Chapel Hill: University of North Carolina Press, 1992.

Rose, Douglas, ed. *The Emergence of David Duke and the Politics of Race*. Chapel Hill: University of North Carolina Press, 1992.

Rosman, M. J. *The Lord's Jews: Magnate-Jewish Relations in the Polish-Lithuanian Commonwealth during the Eighteenth Century*. Cambridge: Harvard University Press, 1990.

Rotem, Simha. *Memoirs of a Warsaw Ghetto Fighter: The Past within Me*. Edited and translated by Barbara Harshav. New Haven: Yale University Press, 1994.

Rovere, Richard H. *Senator Joe McCarthy*. New York: Harcourt Brace Jovanovich, 1959.

Rubinstein, Artur. *My Young Years*. New York: Alfred A. Knopf, 1973.

Rubinstein, Erna. *After the Holocaust: The Long Road to Freedom*. Hamden, Conn.: Archon, 1995.

———. *Survivor in Us All: Four Young Sisters in the Holocaust*. Hamden, Conn.: Archon, 1983.

Rudnicki, Szymon. "From 'Numerus Clausus' to 'Numerus Nullus.'" *Polin* 2 (1987): 246–68.

Rymkiewicz, Jaroslaw M. *The Final Station: Umschlagplatz*. Translated by Nina Taylor. New York: Farrar, Straus and Giroux, 1994 [1988].

Sabini, John P., and Maury Silver. "Destroying the Innocent with a Clear Conscience: A Sociopathology of the Holocaust." In *Survivors, Victims, and Perpetrators: Essays on the Nazi Holocaust*, edited by Joel E. Dimsdale, 329–58. Washington, D.C.: Hemisphere Publishing, 1980.

Sarna, Jonathan D. "Mixed Seating in the American Synagogue." In *The American Synagogue: A Sanctuary Transformed*, edited by Jack Wertheimer, 363–94. Cambridge: Cambridge University Press, 1987.

Schama, Simon. *Landscape and Memory*. New York: A. A. Knopf, 1995.

———. "Stopping by Woods." *New Republic*, October 26, 1992, 31–37.

Scheffler, Wolfgang. "The Forgotten Part of the 'Final Solution': The Liquidation of the Ghettos." *Simon Wiesenthal Center Annual* 2 (1985): 31–51.

Schleunes, Karl. "Retracing the Twisted Road." In *Unanswered Questions: Nazi Germany and the Genocide of the Jews*, edited by Francis Furet, 54–70. New York: Schocken, 1989.

Schwarberg, Günther. *Das Getto*. Göttingen: Steidl Verlag, 1993.

Segev, Tom. *The Seventh Million: The Israelis and the Holocaust*. New York: Hill and Wang, 1991.

———. *Soldiers of Evil: The Commandants of the Nazi Concentration Camps*. Translated by Haim Watzman. New York: McGraw-Hill, 1987.

Seidel, Gill. *The Holocaust Denial: Antisemitism, Racism, and the New Right*. Leeds, England: Beyond the Pale Collective, 1986.

Sereny, Gitta. *Into That Darkness: An Examination of Conscience*. New York: Random House, 1974.

Shoah: The Complete Text of the Acclaimed Holocaust Film. By Claude Lanzmann, with a preface by Simone de Beauvoir. New York: Da Capo, 1995.

Shulman, Abraham. *The Case of Hotel Polski*. New York: The Holocaust Library, 1982.

Siegert, Toni. "Das Konzentrationslager Flossenbürg (Concentration Camp Flossenbürg)." In *Bayern in der NS-Zeit, II* (Bavaria in the Time of National-Socialism), edited by Martin Broszat and Elke Fröhlich, 482–90. Munich: Oldenbourg, 1979.

Sierakowiak, Dawid. *Diary of Dawid Sierakowiak: Five Notebooks from the Lodz Ghetto*. Edited and with an introduction by Alan Adelson, translated from the Polish by Kamil Turowski. New York: Oxford University Press, 1996.

Simonelli, Frederick J. "The American Nazi Party: 1958–1967." *Historian* 57 (Spring 1995): 553–66.

Słownik Geograficzny Królestwa Polskiego (Geographical dictionary of the Polish kingdom). Vol. 2. Warsaw, 1881.

Speer, Albert. *Infiltration: How Heinrich Himmler Schemed to Build an SS Industrial Empire*. New York: Macmillan, 1981.

Stabholz, Thaddeus. *Seven Hells*. Translated by Dr. Jacques Grunblatt and Hilda R. Grunblatt. New York: Holocaust Library, 1990 [1947].

Steiner, Jean-François. *Treblinka*. Introduction by Terrence Des Pres, preface by Simone de Beauvoir, translated by Helen Weaver. New York: New American Library, 1979.

Steinlauf, Michael C. *Bondage to the Dead: Poland and the Memory of the Holocaust*. Syracuse: Syracuse University Press, 1997.

Stern, Frank. *The Whitewashing of the Yellow Badge: Antisemitism and Philosemitism in Postwar Germany*. Translated by William Templer. Oxford: Published for the Vidal Sassoon International Center for the Study of Antisemitism (SICSA), the Hebrew University of Jerusalem by Pergamon, 1992.

Stern, Harriet K. "Origins of Reform Judaism in New Orleans." Master's thesis, University of New Orleans, 1977.

Stern, Kenneth S. *Holocaust Denial*. New York: American Jewish Committee, 1993.

Stone, I. F. *Underground to Palestine*. New York: Boni and Gaer, 1946.

Stroop, Jürgen. *The Stroop Report*. Translated from the German and annotated by Sybil Milton, with an introduction by Andrzej Wirth. New York: Pantheon, 1979.

Sydnor, Charles W., Jr. *Soldiers of Destruction: The SS Death's Head Division, 1933–1945*. Princeton: Princeton University Press, 1977.

Szwajger, Adina Blady. *I Remember Nothing More: The Warsaw Children's Hospital and the Jewish Resistance*. Translated by Tasja Darowska and Danusia Stok. New York: Simon and Schuster, 1988.

Taylor, Jack. *The Economic Development of Poland, 1919–1950*. Ithaca, N.Y.: Cornell University Press, 1952.

Taylor, Telford. *The Anatomy of the Nuremberg Trials: A Personal Memoir*. New York: Alfred A. Knopf, 1992.

Tec, Nechama. *When Light Pierced the Darkness: Christian Rescue of Jews in Nazi-Occupied Poland*. New York: Oxford University Press, 1986.

Todorov, Tzvetan. *Facing the Extreme: Moral Life in the Concentration Camps*. Translated by Arthur Denner and Abigail Pollak. New York: Henry Holt, 1996.

To Live with Honor and Die with Honor: Selected Documents from the Warsaw Ghetto Underground Archives "O.S." ["Oneg Shabbath"]. Edited and annotated by Joseph Kermish. Jerusalem: Yad Vashem, 1986.

Tomaszewski, Irena, and Tecia Werbowski. *Zegota: The Rescue of Jews in Wartime Poland*. Montreal: Price-Patterson, 1994.

Trillin, Calvin. "U.S. Journal: New Orleans Mardi Gras." *The New Yorker*, March 9, 1968, 138–44.

Trunk, Isaiah. "Epidemics and Mortality in the Warsaw Ghetto, 1939–1942." *YIVO Annual of Jewish Social Science* 8 (1953): 82–122.

———. *Judenrat: The Jewish Councils in Eastern Europe under Nazi Occupation*. New York: Stein and Day, 1977 [1972].

Truscott, Lucian K., IV. "Hate Gets a Haircut." *Esquire*, November 1989, 183–84.

Tucker, William H. *The Science and Politics of Racial Research*. Urbana: University of Illinois Press, 1994.

Tusa, Ann, and John Tusa. *The Nuremberg Trial*. New York: Atheneum, 1986.

Tushnet, Leonard. *The Uses of Adversity*. New York: Thomas Yoseloff, 1966.

Tusk-Scheinwechslerowa, F. "Fabryka Waltera C. Többensa w Gettcie Warszawskim" (Factory of Walter C. Többens in the Warsaw Ghetto). *Biuletyn Zydowskiego Instytutu Historycznego* (Bulletin of the Jewish Historical Institute) 22 (1957): 62–70.

Ulasewicz, Tony, with Stuart A. McKeever. *The President's Private Eye: The Journey of Detective Tony U. from N.Y.P.D. to the Nixon White House*. Westport, Conn.: MACSAM, 1990.

The Warsaw Ghetto in Photographs. Edited by Ulrich Keller. New York: Dover Publications, 1984.

Wdowinski, David. *And We Are Not Saved*. Introduction by Morris Chariton. New York: Philosophical Library, 1985.

Weill, Jeanne. "Classic Case: Coverage of David Duke." *St. Louis Journalism Review* (May 1991): 16.

Weinberg, Gerhard. *A World at Arms: A Global History of World War II*. Cambridge: Cambridge University Press, 1994.

Weinryb, Bernard Dov. *The Jews of Poland: A Social and Economic History of the Jewish Community in Poland from 1100–1800*. Philadelphia: Jewish Publication Society of America, 1973.

Werth, Alexander. *Russia at War: 1941–1945*. New York: E. P. Dutton, 1964.

Widmer, Mary Lou. *New Orleans in the Fifties*. Foreword by Phil Johnson. Gretna, La.: Pelican Publishing, 1991.

Wielka Encyklopedya Powszchna (Great universal encyclopedia). Vol. 17. Warsaw, 1896.

Willenberg, Samuel. *Surviving Treblinka*. Edited by Wladyslaw T. Bartoszewski. Oxford: Basil Blackwell, 1989.

Wolfe, Robert. *The Wannsee Protocol and a 1944 Report on Auschwitz by the Office of Strategic Services*. New York: Garland, 1982.

Woods, Keith. "David Duke and the *Times-Picayune*." In *Doing Ethics: Accuracy and Fairness*. St. Petersburg: Poynter Institute, ca. 1992.

Wyman, David. *The Abandonment of the Jews: America and the Holocaust, 1941–1945*. New York: Pantheon, 1984.

——. *Paper Walls: America and the Refugee Crisis, 1938–1941*. New York: Pantheon, 1968.

Wyman, Mark. *DP: Europe's Displaced Persons, 1945–1951*. Philadelphia: Balch Institute Press; London: Associated University Press, 1988.

Wynot, Edward D., Jr. "'A Necessary Cruelty': The Emergence of Official Anti-Semitism in Poland, 1936–39." *American Historical Review* 76 (October 1971): 1035–58.

Yaffe, James. *The American Jews: Portrait of a Split Personality*. New York: Random House, 1968.

Yahil, Leni. *The Holocaust: The Fate of European Jewry*. New York: Oxford University Press, 1990.

Yizkor Book of the Jewish Community in Dzialoszyce and Surroundings. Tel Aviv: "Hamenora" Publishing House, 1973.

Zatarain, Michael. *David Duke: Evolution of a Klansman*. Gretna, La.: Pelican, 1990.

Zawodny, J. K. *Nothing but Honour: The Story of the Warsaw Uprising, 1944*. Stanford: Stanford University Press, 1978.

Zborowski, Mark, and Elizabeth Herzog. *Life Is with People: The Culture of the Shtetl*. New York: Schocken, 1995 [1952].

Zeskind, Leonard. "Ballot Box Bigotry: David Duke and the Populist Party." Atlanta: Center for Democratic Renewal, 1989.

Ziemke, Earl F. *Stalingrad to Berlin: The Great German Defeat in the East*. U.S. Army Historical Series. Washington, D.C.: Office of the Chief of Military History, U.S. Army, 1968.

——. *The U.S. Army in the Occupation of Germany, 1944–1946*. U.S. Army Historical Series. Washington, D.C.: Center of Military History, U.S. Army, 1975.

Zinsser, Hans. *Rats, Lice, and History: A Chronicle of Pestilence and Plagues*. Boston: Little, Brown, 1935.

Zuckerman, Yitzhak. *A Surplus of Memory: Chronicle of the Warsaw Ghetto Uprising*. Translated and edited by Barbara Harshav. Berkeley: University of California Press, 1993.

Zylberberg, Michael. *A Warsaw Diary: 1939–1945*. London: Valentine, Mitchell, 1969.

ACKNOWLEDGMENTS

I've accumulated a legion of debts. The largest is to Anne Levy, Lila Millen, Adam Skorecki, and their families. Not only did they allow me into their lives, but they let me rummage freely through their memories, not all of them pleasant. This book would not have been possible without their cooperation.

Dolek Skorecki, Anne Levy's distant cousin, and his family—Mickey and Tutu Tuttnauer and Ilana Zuckerman—were gracious hosts during my stay in Israel, as well as inexhaustible sources of insight and hard-to-obtain information.

Tadeusz Kaźmierak, my guide, interpreter, translator, and research assistant in Poland, unlocked bureaucratic doors that I feared might never be opened and kept me supplied with a steady stream of documents long after I returned to the States. Professor Slawik Kwasik of Tulane extended numerous kindnesses to me over the years, including translating several documents. Thanks are also due Jerzy Halberstadt for guiding me to invaluable files of university student records in Warsaw.

I interviewed nearly a hundred people for this book, way too numerous to mention by name. But two deserve special thanks for their willingness to respond to my myriad questions about the most minute details. Roman Kriegstein, Mark Skorecki's former business partner in Tirschenreuth, was unfailingly helpful in supplying me with fresh information and in leading me to new interview subjects. Responsiveness is hardly the word to describe Dr. Thaddeus Stabholz's long-distance collaboration in this project. If I called him once, I called him a dozen times to double-check this fact or explore that lead, and every query was received with good cheer. It would have been impossible to reconstruct the wartime travails of Henry Tempelhof and his wife, Mery Mejnster, without his vivid memory.

It might sound odd to thank an Internet discussion group, most of whose members I've never met in person, but I would be derelict if I failed to single out H-Holocaust, one of the livelier listservs on the net. For six years I've been a lurker in its midst, gleaning bibliographical leads here, discovering new subjects to interview there, and all the while receiving a crash course in the historiography of the Holocaust. I felt at times as though I were enrolled in a graduate-level correspondence course in a new research field, and in a sense I was.

Then there are the large number of friends who read this manuscript in whole or in part, providing helpful feedback and encouragement: Stephen Ambrose, Gunter Bischof, Marie Caskey, Brewster Chamberlain, Herman Freudenberger, Steven Hahn, Lance Hill, Arnold Hirsch, Susan Larson, Dick Latner, Radomir Luza, Bobbie Malone, Rebecca Mark, Henry Mason, John Menszer, Clarence Mohr, Adam Nossiter, Naomi Paiss, Steve Paulsson, Diana Pinckley, Rebecca Scott, Charlie and Louise Skirven, Christina Vella, Michael Wayne, and Anne Yeoman.

An old and dear friend, Steve Goodell, currently head of the permanent exhibit at the United States Holocaust Memorial Museum, has been both a helpful critic and an indispensable mentor. I owe him a lot.

Both Joseph Roach and the late Joseph Logsdon read most of this manuscript in various iterations, offering helpful stylistic and organizational suggestions, most of which I followed because invariably they were right on target. Henry Mason also gave this manuscript a close reading, saving me from several historical errors. Plater Robinson, whose knowledge of the Holocaust is extraordinary, extended this project more help than he realizes, and I am eternally grateful.

An old Tulane colleague now at the University of South Carolina, Patrick Maney, listened to me drone on for more hours than either of us probably cares to remember. But that is the way I write—with the ear—and he has been an exceptional listener. I cannot imagine what this book might look like without his input.

I also thank the Council of Research at Tulane University and the Louisiana Endowment of the Humanities for travel grants that enabled me to do research in Poland and Germany.

My two readers at the University of North Carolina Press, Charles W. Sydnor Jr. and Dan Carter, have been helpful beyond words. Charles Sydnor saved me from numerous linguistic and historical errors, and Dan Carter warned me off political and partisan excess. Their own scholarship sets high standards that I have tried to emulate.

I have been blessed with exceptional editors, Lewis Bateman foremost among them. He expects much from his authors and knows the value of friendship. Pamela Upton, the assistant managing editor, brings great common sense and unerring judgment to her task. Finally, Nancy Raynor, my copyeditor, has done a marvelous job wrestling a bulky manuscript into the semblance of a book. Authors like to scribble "stet" next to editorial changes made by their editors. But I did so hardly at all. More often than not, she was right and I was wrong.

There is another group of friends to whom I owe special thanks: my colleagues on the Louisiana Coalition against Racism and Nazism. They were steadfast about principle at a time when it was easier to lay low. I've learned from them in more ways than I can count, and I want to make my gratitude explicit here: Lance Hill, Beth Rickey, Reverend James Stovall, Jane Buchsbaum, Fletcher Thorne-Thomsen, Emmett Bashful, Dawn Laguens, June Cahn, Tim Wise, Linda Allen, Pat Aupied, Sylvia Goodman, Sandi Kallenberg, and Jean Mintz.

Last is my wife, Diana, to whom this book is dedicated. Our companionship has deepened over the years. She is truly my best friend and most perceptive critic. It is a relationship I would not have missed for a lifetime.

Lawrence N. Powell
New Orleans, Louisiana

INDEX

Semitic speeches of, 125–26, 187–88; decrees destruction of Warsaw, 298

Hoax of the Twentieth Century (Butz), 16

Höfle, Hermann, 134–35, 139, 143; orders Adam Czerniakow to begin deportations, 130–31; on death of baby twins, 258

Holocaust denial, and colleges, 15. *See also* Carto, Willis; Duke, David; Institute for Historical Review

Home Army. *See* AK

Horyniec, Poland, 25, 31, 72, 220

Hotel Polski incident, 227–28

Hull, Harry: transcribes Ruth Skorecki's memoir, 430–33

Immigrants, Americanization of, 363–64, 370–71, 380

Imperium (Yockey), 445

Instauration, 11, 457

Institute for Historical Review, 4, 15, 449

International Red Cross, tracing service of, 330

Irvin, Mrs., 374–75, 385

James, Roy, 419, 420

Jewish Councils. *See* Judenrat

Jewish Defense League, 458

Jewish Federation of Greater New Orleans, 365, 380, 385, 412, 417, 483–87; and "quarantine policy," 458

Jewish Fighting Organization. *See* ZOB

Jewish Police (Jüdische Ordnungsdienst), 113, 154; during Great Deportation, 134, 163, 146, 154; deported to Treblinka, 174

Jews
—in New Orleans: cultural divisions among, 366–70; "quarantine policy" of toward anti-Semitic agitators, 408–12; and civil rights, 409–10; and conflict with survivors, 415–18. *See also* Immigrants, Americanization of; New Americans
—in Poland: economic history of, 22–24; live in shtetls, 22, 25–26; between tradition and modernity,

26–28; economic discrimination against, 42–43; and Nazi restrictions on, 54–55, 57, 77–79; Nazi colonization plans for, 60, 62, 65; "rescue-through-work" strategies of, 70, 109; armed resistance by during Holocaust, 177–78, 263; political parties of, 179. *See also* Judenrat; Łódź, Poland: ghetto in; Warsaw Ghetto; Warsaw Ghetto revolt

Johnston, J. Bennett, 456–57, 463

"Joint." *See* American Joint Distribution Committee

Journal of Historical Review, 16

Judenrat: in Łódź, 70; in Warsaw, 78–79, 92, 104, 154; in Białystok, 109; and "rescue-through-work," 127; supplanted by ZOB in Warsaw Ghetto, 234

Kaplan, Chaim, 79, 82, 84, 86, 92, 95, 99–100, 125–27, 135–36, 154; disappears during Great Deportation, 140

Katyn Forest massacre, 297

Katz, Sam, 411, 420

"Kazik." *See* Rotem, Simha

Kearney, Bevy, 437, 454–55

Kielce, Poland, 28, 38; postwar pogrom in, 317

Kirschman, Morris: befriends Mark Skorecki, 387–90, 394

Kirschman, Victor, 388–89

Korczak, Janusz, 155, 202

Kornreich, Toby Radasky, 395–98, 419

Kosciuszko Temple (Łódź, Poland), 34; destruction of by Nazis, 58–59

Kraków Ghetto, 176

Krall, Hanna, 183–84, 197, 247, 253, 279

Kresy (Poland), 24–25, 38

Kriegstein, Celia, 330

Kriegstein, Roman, 323, 329–30, 335, 341, 351; on PTSD (Post-Traumatic Stress Disorder), 328–29; and EsKa Bus Company, 335–38, 355; American success story of, 355; on Mark Skorecki's personality, 355–56

Krüger, Friedrich, 237

Kryss family, 336

Stabholz, Thaddeus, 36, 40–42, 44, 86–88, 90, 98, 126, 155–56, 209, 239, 249, 252; on SS savagery at Umschlagplatz, 250; on Henry Tempelhof's medical condition in boxcar, 251; saved by Henry Tempelhof at Majdanek, 265; writes *Seven Hells*, 339–41

Stalin, Joseph, 101, 297–98

Stangl, Franz: reorganizes Treblinka, 161–62

Starr, Blaze, 371

Steeg, Moise, 367, 388, 409, 417, 420

Steinlauf, Michael, 317

Stelmaszek, Stanislaw, 116, 121, 423, 432; accused of mistreating Jewish workers, 133–34; helps Skorecki family, 133–34, 137, 143, 149; possible role in selections, 148–49; concerned for Skoreckis' safety, 188–92; helps Skoreckis escape from Warsaw Ghetto, 191–92, 196, 201–2, 206; disappears after Warsaw Ghetto revolt, 240

Stern, Edith, 409

Stone, I. F., 321

Stoner, J. B., 443

Stop-Duke movement: debates over strategy and tactics, 18–19, 458, 460

Stovall, James L., 463

Streicher, Julius, 343; at Nuremberg trial, 348

Stroop, Jürgen, 230, 237, 255; assumes command of German forces during Warsaw Ghetto revolt, 238; scorched-earth tactics during Warsaw Ghetto revolt, 240–41; dynamites Tłomackie Synagogue, 247

Strother, Raymond, 460

Stroud, Ansel M., 477–78

Stürmer, Der (Streicher), 343

Sudkiewicz, Jania, 331, 337–38

Sudkiewicz, Marek, 334, 337, 350

Survivors: return from captivity, 312–13; flee to Allied zone of occupied Germany, 322–23; and PTSD, 327–29, 337, 347–48; postwar searches for families, 330; involvement in postwar black market, 335; oral testimonies, 431–32

—as DPs in Tirschenreuth, 327; build postwar community, 329–31, economic activities, 334–38, and Holocaust memory, 342, 347; depart for new homes, 353–54

Synagogues, in New Orleans, 367, 369, 394–95

Szapiro, George, 41

Szlachta (Polish nobility), 22–23

Szmalcowniks (blackmailers), 203–4, 226–27, 259

Szwajger, Adina Blady, 139, 141, 152, 167, 228; during "big selection," 172–73; flees to Aryan side, 209

T4 Program, and origins of Final Solution, 158–59

Tec, Nechama, 56, 194

Tenser, Arthur, 353, 363

Tenser, Celia Skorecki (Mark's sister), 353, 356, 363, 382; visits Skoreckis in New Orleans, 379–81, 385

Tenser, Harry, 353–56, 363, 379–81

Tempelhof, Abram (Ruth's father), 32–33, 312, 315

Tempelhof, Henry (Ruth's brother), 21, 33, 58, 67, 74, 110, 131, 164, 180, 184, 199, 287, 314, 330, 339, 340, 342, 427; prewar background and education, 35–36, 39; develops colon cancer, 39–40, 43–44; as Czyste Hospital office manager, 79; supervises Czyste's relocation to Warsaw Ghetto, 87–88; reaction to Nazi atrocities, 126–27; does rescue work at Umschlagplatz, 155–56; moroseness after wife's death, 209; in bunker during Warsaw Ghetto revolt, 239, 245–46; deported to Treblinka and Majdanek after Warsaw Ghetto revolt, 249–52; killed at Majdanek, 265

Tempelhof, Sara (Ruth's mother), 32–33, 312, 315

Tempelhof, Vovek (Wladek—Ruth's brother), 33, 52–53, 67, 79, 131, 314,